McGraw-Hill Connect®
Learn Without Limits

Connect is a teaching and learning platform that is proven to deliver better results for students and instructors.

Connect empowers students by continually adapting to deliver precisely what they need, when they need it, and how they need it, so your class time is more engaging and effective.

73% of instructors who use **Connect** require it; instructor satisfaction **increases** by 28% when **Connect** is required.

Connect's Impact on Retention Rates, Pass Rates, and Average Exam Scores

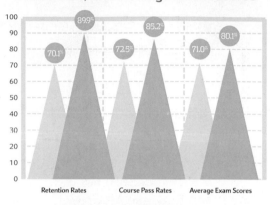

without Connect   with Connect

Using **Connect** improves retention rates by **19.8%**, passing rates by **12.7%**, and exam scores by **9.1%**.

Analytics

Connect Insight®

Connect Insight is Connect's new one-of-a-kind visual analytics dashboard—now available for both instructors and students—that provides at-a-glance information regarding student performance, which is immediately actionable. By presenting assignment, assessment, and topical performance results together with a time metric that is easily visible for aggregate or individual results, Connect Insight gives the user the ability to take a just-in-time approach to teaching and learning, which was never before available. Connect Insight presents data that empowers students and helps instructors improve class performance in a way that is efficient and effective.

Impact on Final Course Grade Distribution

without Connect		with Connect
22.9%	A	31.0%
27.4%	B	34.3%
22.9%	C	18.7%
11.5%	D	6.1%
15.4%	F	9.9%

Students can view their results for any **Connect** course.

Mobile

Connect's new, intuitive mobile interface gives students and instructors flexible and convenient, anytime–anywhere access to all components of the Connect platform.

Adaptive

THE **ADAPTIVE** **READING EXPERIENCE**
DESIGNED TO TRANSFORM THE WAY STUDENTS READ

> More students earn **A's** and **B's** when they use McGraw-Hill Education **Adaptive** products.

SmartBook®

Proven to help students improve grades and study more efficiently, SmartBook contains the same content within the print book, but actively tailors that content to the needs of the individual. SmartBook's adaptive technology provides precise, personalized instruction on what the student should do next, guiding the student to master and remember key concepts, targeting gaps in knowledge and offering customized feedback, and driving the student toward comprehension and retention of the subject matter. Available on tablets, SmartBook puts learning at the student's fingertips—anywhere, anytime.

> Over **8 billion questions** have been answered, making McGraw-Hill Education products more intelligent, reliable, and precise.

www.mheducation.com

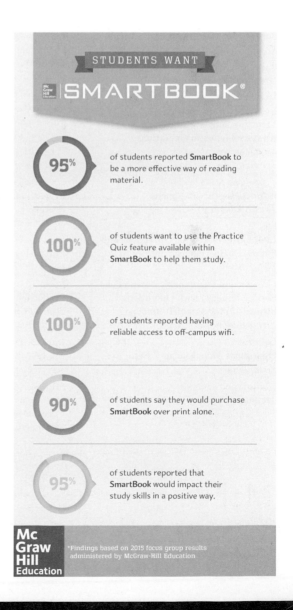

STUDENTS WANT

SMARTBOOK®

95% of students reported **SmartBook** to be a more effective way of reading material.

100% of students want to use the Practice Quiz feature available within **SmartBook** to help them study.

100% of students reported having reliable access to off-campus wifi.

90% of students say they would purchase **SmartBook** over print alone.

95% of students reported that **SmartBook** would impact their study skills in a positive way.

McGraw Hill Education

*Findings based on 2015 focus group results administered by McGraw-Hill Education

The McGraw-Hill Series Operations and Decision Sciences

Project Management:

The Managerial Process

Seventh Edition

Erik W. Larson

Clifford F. Gray
Oregon State University

Mc
Graw
Hill
Education

PROJECT MANAGEMENT: THE MANAGERIAL PROCESS, SEVENTH EDITION

Published by McGraw-Hill Education, 2 Penn Plaza, New York, NY 10121. Copyright © 2018 by McGraw-Hill Education. All rights reserved. Printed in the United States of America. Previous editions © 2014 and 2011. No part of this publication may be reproduced or distributed in any form or by any means, or stored in a database or retrieval system, without the prior written consent of McGraw-Hill Education, including, but not limited to, in any network or other electronic storage or transmission, or broadcast for distance learning.

Some ancillaries, including electronic and print components, may not be available to customers outside the United States.

This book is printed on acid-free paper.

1 2 3 4 5 6 7 8 9 LWI 21 20 19 18 17

ISBN   978-1-259-25387-4
MHID   1-259-25387-2

mheducation.com/highered

About the Authors

Erik W. Larson

ERIK W. LARSON is professor of project management at the College of Business, Oregon State University. He teaches executive, graduate, and undergraduate courses on project management and leadership. His research and consulting activities focus on project management. He has published numerous articles on matrix management, product development, and project partnering. He has been honored with teaching awards from both the Oregon State University MBA program and the University of Oregon Executive MBA program. He has been a member of the Portland, Oregon, chapter of the Project Management Institute since 1984. In 1995 he worked as a Fulbright scholar with faculty at the Krakow Academy of Economics on modernizing Polish business education. He was a visiting professor at Chulalongkorn University in Bangkok, Thailand, and at Baden-Wuerttemberg Cooperative State University in Bad Mergentheim, Germany. He received a B.A. in psychology from Claremont McKenna College and a Ph.D. in management from State University of New York at Buffalo. He is a certified project management professional (PMP) and Scrum Master.

Clifford F. Gray

CLIFFORD F. GRAY is professor emeritus of management at the College of Business, Oregon State University. He has personally taught more than 100 executive development seminars and workshops. Cliff has been a member of the Project Management Institute since 1976 and was one of the founders of the Portland, Oregon, chapter. He was a visiting professor at Kasetsart University in Bangkok, Thailand, in 2005. He was the president of Project Management International, Inc. (a training and consulting firm specializing in project management) 1977–2005. He received his B.A. in economics and management from Millikin University, M.B.A. from Indiana University, and doctorate in operations management from the College of Business, University of Oregon. He is certified Scrum Master.

"Man's mind, once stretched by a new idea, never regains its original dimensions."

Oliver Wendell Holmes, Jr.

To my family, who have always encircled me with love and encouragement—my parents (Samuel and Charlotte), my wife (Mary), my sons and their wives (Kevin and Dawn, Robert and Sally) and their children (Ryan, Carly, Connor and Lauren).

C.F.G.

"We must not cease from exploration and the end of all exploring will be to arrive where we began and to know the place for the first time."

T. S. Eliot

To Ann, whose love and support have brought out the best in me. To our girls Mary, Rachel, and Tor-Tor for the joy and pride they give me. And to our grandkids, Mr. B, Livvy, and Xmo, whose future depends upon effective project management. Finally, to my muse, Neil—Walk on!

E.W.L

Preface

Our motivation in writing this text continues to be to provide a realistic, socio-technical view of project management. In the past, textbooks on project management focused almost exclusively on the tools and processes used to manage projects and not the human dimension. This baffled us since people not tools complete projects! While we firmly believe that mastering tools and processes is essential to successful project management, we also believe that the effectiveness of these tools and methods is shaped and determined by the prevailing culture of the organization and interpersonal dynamics of the people involved. Thus, we try to provide a holistic view that focuses on both of these dimensions and how they interact to determine the fate of projects.

The role of projects in organizations is receiving increasing attention. Projects are the major tool for implementing and achieving the strategic goals of the organization. In the face of intense, worldwide competition, many organizations have reorganized around a philosophy of innovation, renewal, and organizational learning to survive. This philosophy suggests an organization that is flexible and project driven. Project management has developed to the point where it is a professional discipline having its own body of knowledge and skills. Today it is nearly impossible to imagine anyone at any level in the organization who would not benefit from some degree of expertise in the process of managing projects.

Audience

This text is written for a wide audience. It covers concepts and skills that are used by managers to propose, plan, secure resources, budget, and lead project teams to successful completions of their projects. The text should prove useful to students and prospective project managers in helping them understand why organizations have developed a formal project management process to gain a competitive advantage. Readers will find the concepts and techniques discussed in enough detail to be immediately useful in new-project situations. Practicing project managers will find the text to be a valuable guide and reference when dealing with typical problems that arise in the course of a project. Managers will also find the text useful in understanding the role of projects in the missions of their organizations. Analysts will find the text useful in helping to explain the data needed for project implementation as well as the operations of inherited or purchased software. Members of the Project Management Institute will find the text is well structured to meet the needs of those wishing to prepare for PMP (Project Management Professional) or CAPM (Certified Associate in Project Management) certification exams. The text has in-depth coverage of the most critical topics found in PMI's *Project Management Body of Knowledge* (PMBOK). People at all levels in the organization assigned to work on projects will find the text useful not only in providing them with a rationale for the use of project management processes but also because of the insights they will gain on how to enhance their contributions to project success.

Our emphasis is not only on how the management process works, but more importantly, on *why* it works. The concepts, principles, and techniques are universally applicable. That is, the text does not specialize by industry type or project scope. Instead, the text is written for the individual who will be required to manage a variety of projects in a variety of different organizational settings. In the case of some small projects, a few of the steps of the techniques can be omitted, but the conceptual framework applies to all organizations in which projects are important to survival. The approach can be used in pure project organizations such as construction, research organizations, and engineering consultancy firms. At the same time, this approach will benefit organizations that carry out many small projects while the daily effort of delivering products or services continues.

Content

In this and other editions we continue to try to resist the forces that engender scope creep and focus only on essential tools and concepts that are being used in the real world. We have been guided by feedback from practitioners, teachers, and students. Some changes are minor and incremental, designed to clarify and reduce confusion. Other changes are significant. They represent new developments in the field or better ways of teaching project management principles. Below are major changes to the seventh edition.

- Learning objectives have been established for each chapter and the corresponding segment has been marked in the text.
- Chapter 16 Oversight has been eliminated and critical information on project maturity models is now part of Chapter 14.
- Chapter 18 Project Management Career Paths has been eliminated and essential information from this chapter is now in Chapter 1.
- A new set of network exercises have been developed for Chapter 6.
- A new set of crashing exercises have been developed for Chapter 9 which introduce crashing concepts in a developmental way.
- The Chapter 2 Appendix on Request for Proposal is now part of Chapter 12.
- Terms and concepts have been updated to be consistent with the sixth edition of the *Project Management Body of Knowledge* (2015).
- New student exercises and cases have been added to chapters.
- The Snapshot from Practice boxes feature a number of new examples of project management in action as well as new Research Highlights that continue to promote practical application of project management.
- The Instructor's Manual contains a listing of current YouTube videos that correspond to key concepts and Snapshots from Practice.

Overall the text addresses the major questions and challenges the authors have encountered over their 60 combined years of teaching project management and consulting with practicing project managers in domestic and foreign environments. These questions include: What is the strategic role of projects in contemporary organizations? How are projects prioritized? What organizational and managerial styles will improve chances of project success? How do project managers orchestrate the complex network of relationships involving vendors, subcontractors, project team members, senior management, functional managers, and customers that affect project success? What factors contribute to the development of a high-performance project team? What project management system can be set up to gain some measure of control? How do managers prepare for a new international project in a foreign culture?

Project managers must deal with all these concerns to be effective. All of these issues and problems represent linkages to an integrative project management view. The chapter content of the text has been placed within an overall framework that integrates these topics in a holistic manner. Cases and snapshots are included from the experiences of practicing managers. The future for project managers appears to be promising. Careers will be determined by success in managing projects.

Student Learning Aids

Student resources include study outlines, online quizzes, PowerPoint slides, videos, Microsoft Project Video Tutorials and web links. These can be found in Connect.

Acknowledgments

We would like to thank Scott Bailey for building the end-of-chapter exercises for Connect and Tracie Lee for reviewing them; Pinyarat Sirisomboonsuk for revising the PowerPoint slides; Oliver F. Lehmann for providing access to PMBOK study questions; Ronny Richardson for updating the Instructor's Manual; Angelo Serra for updating the Test Bank; and Pinyarat Sirisomboonsuk for providing new Snapshot from Practice questions.

Next, it is important to note that the text includes contributions from numerous students, colleagues, friends, and managers gleaned from professional conversations. We want them to know we sincerely appreciate their counsel and suggestions. Almost every exercise, case, and example in the text is drawn from a real-world project. Special thanks to managers who graciously shared their current project as ideas for exercises, subjects for cases, and examples for the text. Shlomo Cohen, John A. Drexler, Jim Moran, John Sloan, Pat Taylor, and John Wold, whose work is printed, are gratefully acknowledged. Special gratitude is due Robert Breitbarth of Interact Management, who shared invaluable insights on prioritizing projects. University students and managers deserve special accolades for identifying problems with earlier drafts of the text and exercises.

We are indebted to the reviewers of past editions who shared our commitment to elevating the instruction of project management. The reviewers include Paul S. Allen, Rice University; Denis F. Cioffi, George Washington University; Joseph D. DeVoss, DeVry University; Edward J. Glantz, Pennsylvania State University; Michael Godfrey, University of Wisconsin–Oshkosh; Robert Key, University of Phoenix; Dennis Krumwiede, Idaho State University; Nicholas C. Petruzzi, University of Illinois–Urbana/Champaign; William R. Sherrard, San Diego State University; S. Narayan Bodapati, Southern Illinois University at Edwardsville; Warren J. Boe, University of Iowa; Burton Dean, San Jose State University; Kwasi Amoako-Gyampah, University of North Carolina–Greensboro; Owen P. Hall, Pepperdine University; Bruce C. Hartman, University of Arizona; Richard Irving, York University; Robert T. Jones, DePaul University; Richard L. Luebbe, Miami University of Ohio; William Moylan, Lawrence Technological College of Business; Edward Pascal, University of Ottawa; James H. Patterson, Indiana University; Art Rogers, City University; Christy Strbiak, U.S. Air Force Academy; David A. Vaughan, City University; and Ronald W. Witzel, Keller Graduate School of Management. Nabil Bedewi, Georgetown University; Scott Bailey, Troy University; Michael Ensby, Clarkson University; Eldon Larsen, Marshall University; Steve Machon, DeVry University–Tinley Park; William Matthews, William Patterson

University; Erin Sims, DeVry University–Pomona; Kenneth Solheim, DeVry University–Federal Way; and Oya Tukel, Cleveland State University. Gregory Anderson, Weber State University; Dana Bachman, Colorado Christian University; Alan Cannon, University of Texas, Arlington; Susan Cholette, San Francisco State; Michael Ensby, Clarkson University; Charles Franz, University of Missouri, Columbia; Raouf Ghattas, DeVry University; Robert Groff, Westwood College; Raffael Guidone, New York City College of Technology; George Kenyon, Lamar University; Elias Konwufine, Keiser University; Rafael Landaeta, Old Dominion University; Muhammad Obeidat, Southern Polytechnic State University; Linda Rose, Westwood College; Oya Tukel, Cleveland State University; and Mahmoud Watad, William Paterson University.

Victor Allen, Lawrence Technological University; Mark Angolia, East Carolina University; Alan Cannon, University of Texas at Arlington; Robert Cope, Southeastern Louisiana University; Kenneth DaRin, Clarkson University; Ron Darnell, Amberton University; Jay Goldberg, Marquette University; Mark Huber, University of Georgia; Marshall Issen, Clarkson University; Charles Lesko, East Carolina University; Lacey McNeely, Oregon State University; Donald Smith, Texas A&M University; Peter Sutanto, Prairie View A&M University; Jon Tomlinson, University of Northwestern Ohio. We thank you for your many thoughtful suggestions and for making our book better. Of course we accept responsibility for the final version of the text.

In addition, we would like to thank our colleagues in the College of Business at Oregon State University for their support and help in completing this project. In particular, we recognize Lacey McNeely, Prem Mathew, Keith Leavitt and Pauline Schlipzand for their helpful advice and suggestions. We also wish to thank the many students who helped us at different stages of this project, most notably Neil Young, Saajan Patel, Katherine Knox, Dat Nguyen, and David Dempsey. Mary Gray deserves special credit for editing and working under tight deadlines on earlier editions. Special thanks go to Pinyarat ("Minkster") Sirisomboonsuk for her help in preparing the last four editions.

Finally, we want to extend our thanks to all the people at McGraw-Hill Education for their efforts and support. First, we would like to thank Dolly Womack, and Christina Holt, for providing editorial direction, guidance, and management of the book's development for the seventh edition. And we would also like to thank Melissa Leick, Jennifer Pickel, Egzon Shaqiri, Bruce Gin, and Karen Jozefowicz for managing the final production, design, supplement, and media phases of the seventh edition.

Erik W. Larson

Clifford F. Gray

Guided Tour

Established Learning Objectives

Learning objectives have been added to this edition to help students target key areas of learning. Learning objectives are listed both at the beginning of each chapter and are called out as marginal elements throughout the narrative in each chapter.

2 Organization Strategy and Project Selection

LEARNING OBJECTIVES

After reading this chapter you should be able to:

2-1 Explain why it is important for project managers to understand their organization's strategy.

2-2 Identify the significant role projects contribute to the strategic direction of the organization.

2-3 Understand the need for a project priority system.

2-4 Apply financial and nonfinancial criteria to assess the value of projects.

2-5 Understand how multi-criteria models can be used to select projects.

2-6 Apply an objective priority system to project selection.

2-7 Understand the need to manage the project portfolio.

OUTLINE

2.1 The Strategic Management Process: An Overview

2.2 The Need for a Project Priority System

2.3 A Portfolio Management System

2.4 Selection Criteria

2.5 Applying a Selection Model

2.6 Managing the Portfolio System

Summary

Why Project Managers Need to Understand Strategy

 LO 2-1

Explain why it is important for project managers to understand their organization's strategy.

Project management historically has been preoccupied solely with the planning and execution of projects. Strategy was considered to be under the purview of senior management. This is old-school thinking. New-school thinking recognizes that project management is at the apex of strategy and operations. Aaron Shenhar speaks to this issue when he states, ". . . it is time to expand the traditional role of the project manager from an operational to a more strategic perspective. In the modern evolving organization, project managers will be focused on business aspects, and their role will expand from getting the job done to achieving the business results and winning in the marketplace."[1]

There are two main reasons why project managers need to understand their organization's mission and strategy. The first reason is so they can make appropriate decisions and adjustments. For example, how a project manager would respond to a suggestion to modify the design of a product to enhance performance will vary depending upon whether his company strives to be a product leader through innovation or to achieve operational excellence through low cost solutions. Similarly, how a project manager would respond to delays may vary depending upon strategic concerns. A project manager will authorize overtime if her firm places a premium on getting to the market first.

End-of-Chapter Content

Both static and algorithmic end-of-chapter content, including Review Questions and Exercises, are now assignable in Connect.

SmartBook

The SmartBook has been updated with new highlights and probes for optimal student learning.

Snapshots

The Snapshot from Practice boxes have been updated to include a number of new examples of project management in action. New questions based on the Snapshots are also now assignable in Connect.

New and Updated Cases

Included at the end of each chapter are between one and five cases which demonstrate key ideas from the text and help students understand how Project Management comes into play in the real world. New cases have been added across several chapters in the 7th edition.

SNAPSHOT FROM PRACTICE 3.4 Google-y*

In 2016 Google Inc. topped *Fortune* magazine's list of best companies to work at for the seventh time in the past ten years. When one enters the 24-hour Googleplex located in Mountain View, California, you feel that you are walking through a new-age college campus rather than the corporate office of a billion-dollar business. The collection of interconnected low-rise buildings with colorful, glass-encased offices feature upscale trappings—free gourmet meals three times a day, free use of an outdoor wave pool, indoor gym and large child care facility, private shuttle bus service to and from San Francisco and other residential areas—that are the envy of workers across the Bay area. These perks and others reflect Google's culture of keeping people happy and thinking in unconventional ways.

The importance of corporate culture is no more evident than in the fact that the head of Human Resources,

© Caiaimage/Glow Images

teams typically have daily "stand-up" meetings seven minutes after the hour. Why seven minutes after the hour? Because Google cofounder Sergey Brin once estimated that it took seven minutes to walk across the Google campus. Everybody stands to make sure no one gets too comfortable and no time is wasted during the rapid-fire update. As one manager noted, "The whole concept of

Note to Student

You will find the content of this text highly practical, relevant, and current. The concepts discussed are relatively simple and intuitive. As you study each chapter we suggest you try to grasp not only how things work, but why things work. You are encouraged to use the text as a handbook as you move through the three levels of competency:

I know.

I can do.

I can adapt to new situations.

Project management is both people and technical oriented. Project management involves understanding the cause-effect relationships and interactions among the sociotechnical dimensions of projects. Improved competency in these dimensions will greatly enhance your competitive edge as a project manager.

The field of project management is growing in importance and at an exponential rate. It is nearly impossible to imagine a future management career that does not include management of projects. Résumés of managers will soon be primarily a description of the individual's participation in and contributions to projects.

Good luck on your journey through the text and on your future projects.

Chapter-by-Chapter Revisions for the Seventh Edition

Chapter 1: Modern Project Management

- New Snapshot: *Project Management in Action 2016*.
- Information updated.
- New Snapshot: *Ron Parker* replaced Research Highlight: *Works well with others*.
- New case: *The Hokie Lunch Group*.

Chapter 2: Organization Strategy and Project Selection

- New Snapshot: *Project Code Names* replaced *HP's Strategy Revision*.

Chapter 3: Organization: Structure and Culture

- Learning objectives established.
- Snapshot: *Google-y* updated.
- Snapshot: *Skunk Works at Lockheed Martin* updated.

Chapter 4: Defining the Project

- Learning objectives established.
- New case: *Home Improvement Project*.

Chapter 5: Estimating Project Times and Costs

- Learning objectives established.
- New Snapshot: *London 2012 Olympics: Avoiding White Elephant curse.*
- Expanded discussion of Mega Projects including the emergence of *white elephants.*

Chapter 6: Developing a Project Schedule

- Learning objectives established.
- New Exercises 2-15 and Lag Exercises 18-21.
- *Shoreline Stadium* case replaces *Greendale Stadium* case.

Chapter 7: Managing Risk

- Learning objectives established.

Chapter 8 Appendix 1: The Critical-Chain Approach

- Learning objectives established.

Chapter 9: Reducing Project Duration

- Learning objectives established.
- Snapshot: *Smartphone Wars* updated.
- New exercises 1-7.

Chapter 10: Leadership: Being an Effective Project Manager

- Learning objectives established.
- New Research Highlight: *Give and Take.*
- Ethics discussion expanded.

Chapter 11: Managing Project Teams

- Learning objectives established.
- Expanded discussion on project vision.

Chapter 12: Outsourcing: Managing Interorganizational Relations

- Learning objectives established.
- Discussion of RFP process.
- New Snapshot: *U.S. Department of Defense's Value Engineering Awards 2015.*

Chapter 13 Progress and Performance Measurement and Evaluation

- Learning Objectives established.
- Discussion of milestone schedules.
- New Snapshot: *Guidelines for Setting Milestones.*
- Discussion of Management Reserve Index.
- New case: *Shoreline Stadium Status Report.*

Chapter 14: Project Closure

- Major Revision of chapter with more attention to project audit and closing activities.
- New Snapshot: *The Wake*.
- New Snapshot: *2015 PMO of the Year*.
- New Snapshot: *Operation Eagle Claw*.
- Project Management Maturity model introduced.

Chapter 15: International Projects

- Learning Objectives established.

Chapter 16: An Introduction to Agile Project Management

- Learning Objectives established.
- New Snapshot: *Kanban*.

Brief Contents

Contents

Project
Management:

The Managerial Process

CHAPTER ONE

Modern Project Management

LEARNING OBJECTIVES

After reading this chapter you should be able to:

1-1 Understand why project management is crucial in today's world.

1-2 Distinguish a project from routine operations.

1-3 Identify the different stages of project life cycle.

1-4 Understand the importance of projects in implementing organization strategy.

1-5 Understand that managing projects involves balancing the technical and sociocultural dimensions of the project.

OUTLINE

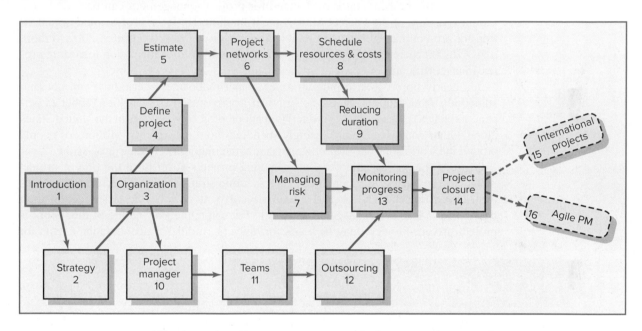

All of mankind's greatest accomplishments—from building the great pyramids to discovering a cure for polio to putting a man on the moon—began as a project.

LO 1-1

Understand why project management is crucial in today's world.

This is a good time to be reading a book about project management. Business leaders and experts have proclaimed that project management is critical to sustainable economic growth. New jobs and competitive advantage are achieved by constant innovation, developing new products and services, and improving both productivity and quality of work. This is the world of project management. Project management provides people with a powerful set of tools that improves their ability to plan, implement, and manage activities to accomplish specific objectives. But project management is more than just a set of tools; it is a results-oriented management style that places a premium on building collaborative relationships among a diverse cast of characters. Exciting opportunities await people skilled in project management.

The project approach has long been the style of doing business in the construction industry, U.S. Department of Defense contracts, and Hollywood, as well as big consulting firms. Now project management has spread to all avenues of work. Today, project teams carry out everything from port expansions to hospital restructuring to upgrading information systems. They are creating next-generation fuel-efficient vehicles, developing sustainable sources of energy, and exploring the farthest reaches of outer space. The impact of project management is most profound in the electronics industry, where the new folk heroes are young professionals whose Herculean efforts lead to the constant flow of new hardware and software products.

Project management is not limited to the private sector. Project management is also a vehicle for doing good deeds and solving social problems. Endeavors such as providing emergency aid to areas hit by natural disasters, devising a strategy for reducing crime and drug abuse within a city, or organizing a community effort to renovate a public playground would and do benefit from the application of modern project management skills and techniques.

Perhaps the best indicator of demand for project management can be seen in the rapid expansion of the Project Management Institute (PMI), a professional organization for project managers. PMI membership has grown from 93,000 in 2002 to more than 478,000 currently. See Snapshot from Practice 1.1 for information regarding professional certification in project management.

It's nearly impossible to pick up a newspaper or business periodical and not find something about projects. This is no surprise! Approximately $2.5 trillion (about 25 percent of the U.S. gross national product) is spent on projects each year in the United States alone. Other countries are increasingly spending more on projects. Millions of people around the world consider project management the major task in their profession.

Most of the people who excel at managing projects never have the title of project manager. They include accountants, lawyers, administrators, scientists, contractors, public health officials, teachers, and community advocates whose success depends upon being able to lead and manage project work. For some, the very nature of their work is project driven. Projects may be cases for lawyers, audits for accountants, events for

SNAPSHOT FROM PRACTICE 1.1   The Project Management Institute*

The Project Management Institute (PMI) was founded in 1969 as an international society for project managers. Today PMI has members from more than 180 countries and more than 478,500 members. PMI professionals come from virtually every major industry, including aerospace, automotive, business management, construction, engineering, financial services, information technology, pharmaceuticals, health care, and telecommunications.

PMI provides certification as a ***Project Management Professional (PMP)***—someone who has documented sufficient project experience, agreed to follow the PMI code of professional conduct, and demonstrated mastery of the field of project management by passing a comprehensive examination. The number of people earning PMP status has grown dramatically in recent years. In 1996 there were fewer than 3,000 certified project management professionals. By 2016 there were more than 695,000 Professional credential holders.

Just as the CPA exam is a standard for accountants, passing the PMP exam may become the standard for project managers. Some companies are requiring that all their project managers be PMP certified. Moreover, many job postings are restricted to PMPs. Job seekers, in general, are finding that being PMP certified is an advantage in the marketplace.

PMI added a certification as a *Certified Associate in Project Management (CAPM)*. CAPM is designed for project team members and entry-level project managers, as well as qualified undergraduate and graduate students who want a credential to recognize their mastery of the project management body of knowledge. CAPM does not require the extensive project management experience associated with the PMP. For more details on PMP and CAPM, google PMI to find the current website for the Project Management Institute.

*PMI Today, March 2016, p. 4.

artists, and renovations for contractors. For others, projects may be a small, but critical part of their work. For example, a high school teacher who teaches four classes a day is responsible for coaching a group of students to compete in a national debate competition. A store manager who oversees daily operations is charged with developing an employee retention program. A sales account executive is given the additional assignment of team lead to launch daily deals into a new city. A public health official who manages a clinic is also responsible for organizing a Homeless Youth Connect event. For these and others, project management is not a title, but a critical job requirement. It is hard to think of a profession or a career path that would not benefit from being good at managing projects.

Not only is project management critical to most careers, the skill set is transferable across most businesses and professions. At its core, project management fundamentals are universal. The same project management methodology that is used to develop a new product can be adapted to create new services, organize events, refurbish aging operations, and so forth. In a world where it is estimated that each person is likely to experience three to four career changes, managing projects is a talent worthy of development.

The significance of project management can also be seen in the classroom. Twenty years ago major universities offered one or two classes in project management, primarily for engineers. Today, most universities offer multiple sections of project management classes, with the core group of engineers being supplemented by business students majoring in marketing, management information systems (MIS), and finance, as well as students from other disciplines such as oceanography, health sciences, computer sciences, and liberal arts. These students are finding that their exposure to project management is providing them with distinct advantages when it comes time to look for jobs. More and more employers are looking for graduates with project management skills.

SNAPSHOT FROM PRACTICE 1.2

A Dozen Examples of Projects Given to Recent College Graduates

1. Business information: Join a project team charged with installing new data security system.

2. Physical education: Design and develop a new fitness program for senior citizens that combines principles of yoga and aerobics.

3. Marketing: Execute a sales program for new home air purifier.

4. Industrial engineering: Manage a team to create a value chain report for every aspect of key product from design to customer delivery.

5. Chemistry: Develop a quality control program for organization's drug production facilities.

6. Management: Implement a new store layout design.

7. Pre-med neurology student: Join project team linking mind mapping to an imbedded prosthetic that will allow blind people to function near normally.

8. Sports communication: Join Olympic project team that will promote women's sports products for the 2016 Games in Rio de Janeiro, Brazil.

9. Systems engineer: Become a project team member of a project to develop data mining of medical papers and studies related to drug efficacy.

10. Accounting: Work on an audit of a major client.

11. Public health: Research and design a medical marijuana educational program.

12. English: Create a web-based user manual for new electronics product.

© John Fedele/Blend Images LLC, RF

See the nearby Snapshot from Practice 1.2 for examples of projects given to recent college graduates. The logical starting point for developing these skills is understanding the uniqueness of a project and of project managers.

1.1 What Is a Project?

Distinguish a project from routine operations.

What do the following headlines have in common?

Millions watch Olympic Opening Ceremony
Citywide WiFi System Set to Go Live
Hospitals Respond to New Healthcare Reforms
Apple's New iPhone Hits the Market
City Receives Stimulus Funds to Expand Light Rail System

All of these events represent projects.

© McGraw-Hill Education

The Project Management Institute provides the following definition of a project:

A **project** is a temporary endeavor undertaken to create a unique product, service, or result.

Like most organizational efforts, the major goal of a project is to satisfy a customer's need. Beyond this fundamental similarity, the characteristics of a project help differentiate it from other endeavors of the organization. The major characteristics of a project are as follows:

1. An established objective.
2. A defined life span with a beginning and an end.
3. Usually, the involvement of several departments and professionals.
4. Typically, doing something that has never been done before.
5. Specific time, cost, and performance requirements.

First, projects have a defined objective—whether it is constructing a 12-story apartment complex by January 1 or releasing version 2.0 of a specific software package as quickly as possible. This singular purpose is often lacking in daily organizational life in which workers perform repetitive operations each day.

Second, because there is a specified objective, projects have a defined endpoint, which is contrary to the ongoing duties and responsibilities of traditional jobs. In many cases, individuals move from one project to the next as opposed to staying in one job. After helping to install a security system, an IT engineer may be assigned to develop a database for a different client.

Third, unlike much organizational work that is segmented according to functional specialty, projects typically require the combined efforts of a variety of specialists. Instead of working in separate offices under separate managers, project participants, whether they be engineers, financial analysts, marketing professionals, or quality control specialists, work closely together under the guidance of a project manager to complete a project.

The fourth characteristic of a project is that it is nonroutine and has some unique elements. This is not an either/or issue but a matter of degree. Obviously, accomplishing something that has never been done before, such as building an electric automobile or landing two mechanical rovers on Mars, requires solving previously unsolved problems and using breakthrough technology. On the other hand, even basic construction projects that involve established sets of routines and procedures require some degree of customization that makes them unique.

Finally, specific time, cost, and performance requirements bind projects. Projects are evaluated according to accomplishment, cost, and time spent. These triple constraints impose a higher degree of accountability than you typically find in most jobs. These three also highlight one of the primary functions of project management, which is balancing the trade-offs among time, cost, and performance while ultimately satisfying the customer.

What a Project Is Not

Projects should not be confused with everyday work. A project is not routine, repetitive work! Ordinary daily work typically requires doing the same or similar work over and over, while a project is done only once; a new product or service exists when the project is completed. Examine the list in Table 1.1 that compares routine, repetitive work and projects. Recognizing the difference is important because too often resources can be used up on daily operations which may not contribute to longer range organization strategies that require innovative new products.

Program versus Project

In practice the terms *project* and *program* cause confusion. They are often used synonymously. A **program** *is a group of related projects designed to accomplish a*

TABLE 1.1 Comparison of Routine Work with Projects

Routine, Repetitive Work	Projects
Taking class notes	Writing a term paper
Daily entering sales receipts into the accounting ledger	Setting up a sales kiosk for a professional accounting meeting
Responding to a supply-chain request	Developing a supply-chain information system
Practicing scales on the piano	Writing a new piano piece
Routine manufacture of an Apple iPod	Designing an iPod that is approximately 2 × 4 inches, interfaces with PC, and stores 10,000 songs
Attaching tags on a manufactured product	Wire-tag projects for GE and Walmart

common goal over an extended period of time. Each project within a program has a project manager. The major differences lie in scale and time span.

Program management is the process of *managing* a group of ongoing, interdependent, related *projects* in a coordinated way to achieve strategic objectives. For example, a pharmaceutical organization could have a program for curing cancer. The cancer program includes and coordinates *all* cancer projects that continue over an extended time horizon (Gray, 2011). Coordinating all cancer projects under the oversight of a cancer team provides benefits not available from managing them individually. This cancer team also oversees the selection and prioritizing of cancer projects that are included in their special "Cancer" portfolio. Although each project retains its own goals and scope, the project manager and team are also motivated by the higher program goal. Program goals are closely related to broad strategic organization goals.

The Project Life Cycle

LO 1-3

Identify the different stages of project life cycle.

Another way of illustrating the unique nature of project work is in terms of the **project life cycle.** Some project managers find it useful to use the project life cycle as the cornerstone for managing projects. The life cycle recognizes that projects have a limited life span and that there are predictable changes in level of effort and focus over the life of the project. There are a number of different life-cycle models in project management literature. Many are unique to a specific industry or type of project. For example, a new software development project may consist of five phases: definition, design, code, integration/test, and maintenance. A generic cycle is depicted in Figure 1.1.

The project life cycle typically passes sequentially through four stages: defining, planning, executing, and delivering. The starting point begins the moment the project is given the go-ahead. Project effort starts slowly, builds to a peak, and then declines to delivery of the project to the customer.

1. **Defining stage:** Specifications of the project are defined; project objectives are established; teams are formed; major responsibilities are assigned.
2. **Planning stage:** The level of effort increases, and plans are developed to determine what the project will entail, when it will be scheduled, whom it will benefit, what quality level should be maintained, and what the budget will be.
3. **Executing stage:** A major portion of the project work takes place—both physical and mental. The physical product is produced (a bridge, a report, a software program). Time, cost, and specification measures are used for control. Is the project on schedule, on budget, and meeting specifications? What are the forecasts of each of these measures? What revisions/changes are necessary?
4. **Closing stage:** Closing includes three activities: delivering the project product to the customer, redeploying project resources, and post-project review. Delivery of

FIGURE 1.1
Project Life Cycle

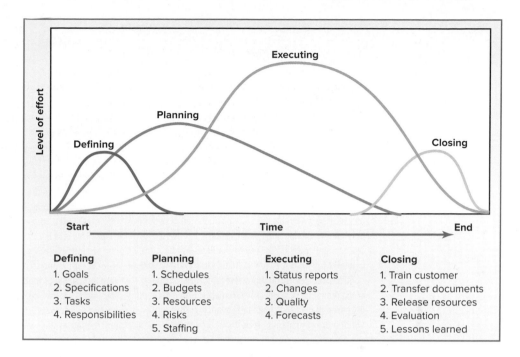

the project might include customer training and transferring documents. Redeployment usually involves releasing project equipment/materials to other projects and finding new assignments for team members. Post-project reviews include not only assessing performance but also capturing lessons learned.

In practice, the project life cycle is used by some project groups to depict the timing of major tasks over the life of the project. For example, the design team might plan a major commitment of resources in the defining stage, while the quality team would expect their major effort to increase in the latter stages of the project life cycle. Because most organizations have a portfolio of projects going on concurrently, each at a different stage of each project's life cycle, careful planning and management at the organization and project levels are imperative.

The Project Manager

At first glance project managers perform the same functions as other managers. That is, they plan, schedule, motivate, and control. However, what makes them unique is that they manage temporary, nonrepetitive activities, to complete a fixed life project. Unlike functional managers, who take over existing operations, project managers create a project team and organization where none existed before. They must decide what and how things should be done instead of simply managing set processes. They must meet the challenges of each phase of the project life cycle, and even oversee the dissolution of their operation when the project is completed.

Project managers must work with a diverse troupe of characters to complete projects. They are typically the direct link to the customer and must manage the tension between customer expectations and what is feasible and reasonable. Project managers provide direction, coordination, and integration to the project team, which is often made up of part-time participants loyal to their functional departments. They often must work with a cadre of outsiders—vendors, suppliers, subcontractors—who do not necessarily share their project allegience.

SNAPSHOT FROM PRACTICE 1.3 Ron Parker

1986	B.S. Business Administration–Oregon State University
1986–1990	Food Products Manufacturing
1990–1994	Wood Products Manufacturing
1994–Current	Glass Products Manufacturing

Upon completion of my business degree at OSU, I was recruited by a Fortune 100 food products company for a first line production supervisor position. In that role, an opportunity came up for me to manage a project that involved rolling out a new statistical package-weight-control program throughout the factory. Successfully completing that project was instrumental in accelerating my career within the company, advancing from supervisor to product manager in less than three years.

After four years in food products I accepted an offer to join a wood products manufacturing company. Initially my role in this company was Human Resources Manager. My HR responsibilities included managing several projects to improve safety and employee retention. Successful completion of these projects led to a promotion to Plant Manager. In the Plant Manager role, I was tasked with building and managing a new wood door manufacturing factory. After successfully taking that factory to full production, I was promoted again to Corporate Manager of Continuous Improvement. This "culture change" project involved

implementing Total Quality Management throughout 13 different manufacturing factories as well as all the indirect and support functions within the corporation. Shortly after we successfully ingrained this new culture in the company, the owner passed away, leading me to look for other employment.

I was able to leverage my previous experience and success to convince the owner of a struggling glass fabrication company to hire me. In this new role as General Manager, I was tasked with turning the company around. This was my largest project yet. Turning a company around involves a myriad of smaller improvement projects spanning from facilities and equipment improvements to product line additions and deletions to sales and marketing strategy and everything in between. In four years, we successfully turned the company around to the extent that the owner was able to sell the company and comfortably retire.

Successfully turning that glass company around got the attention of a much larger competitor of ours, resulting in an offer of employment. This new offer involved the start-up of a $30M high-tech glass manufacturing facility in another state. We were able to take that facility from a dirt field to the highest volume manufacturing facility of its kind in the world in just three years. After building and operating this factory at a world-class benchmark level for eight years, I came across a new and exciting opportunity to help expand a strong glass fabrication company in

Project managers are ultimately responsible for performance (frequently with too little authority). They must ensure that appropriate trade-offs are made among the time, cost, and performance requirements of the project. At the same time, unlike their functional counterparts, project managers generally possess only rudimentary technical knowledge to make such decisions. Instead, they must orchestrate the completion of the project by inducing the right people, at the right time, to address the right issues and make the right decisions.

While project management is not for the timid, working on projects can be an extremely rewarding experience. Life on projects is rarely boring; each day is different from the last. Since most projects are directed at solving some tangible problem or pursuing some useful opportunity, project managers find their work personally meaningful and satisfying. They enjoy the act of creating something new and innovative. Project managers and team members can feel immense pride in their accomplishment, whether it is a new bridge, a new product, or needed service. Project managers are often stars in their organization and well compensated.

Good project managers are always in demand. Every industry is looking for effective people who can get the right things done on time. See Snapshot from Practice 1.3: Ron Parker for an example of a former student who leveraged his ability to manage

Canada. I spent four years successfully transitioning this Canadian company from a medium-size glass fabrication facility to one of the largest and most successful of its kind in North America.

After tiring of the "Great White North," I found an opportunity to tackle the largest and most impactful project of my career. I'm currently VP of Operations in a venture-funded high-tech start-up company. In this role, I'm overseeing the construction and start-up of the first full-scale, high-volume electrochromic glass fabrication factory in the world. This new project involves building a company from the ground up and taking an exciting new technology from the lab to full-scale commercialization. Success in this role, although still far from being certain, will eventually revolutionize the glass industry through the introduction of a product that dramatically improves the energy efficiency and occupant comfort of buildings around the world.

Looking back on my career, it is apparent that my degree of success has largely been the result of taking on and successfully completing successively larger and increasingly impactful projects.

There's a saying that's always resonated with me: "If your only tool is a hammer, all your problems look like nails." Good tools are hard to come by and heavy to carry around. I like my tool bag filled with generalist tools; things like communication skills, leadership, common sense, judgment, reasoning, logic and a strong sense of urgency. I often wonder how much more I could have accomplished had I actually studied project management and had more of that toolset in my bag. With a bag full of strong generalist tools, you can tackle any problem in any business. Project management is clearly one of those skills where the better you are at it, the higher your chances of success in any business environment. Having the tools is only part of the equation though. To be successful, you must also be willing to run at problems/opportunities when everyone else is running away from them.

Courtesy of Ron Parker

projects to build a successful career in the glass products industry. Clearly, project management is a challenging and exciting profession. This text is intended to provide the necessary knowledge, perspective, and tools to enable students to accept the challenge.

Being Part of a Project Team

Most people's first exposure to project management occurs while working as part of a team assigned to complete a specific project. Sometimes this work is full-time, but in most cases, people work part-time on one or more projects. They must learn how to juggle their day-to-day commitments with additional project responsibilities. They may join a team with a long history of working together, in which case roles and norms are firmly established. Alternatively, their team may consist of strangers from different departments and organizations. As such, they endure the growing pains of a group evolving into a team. They need to be a positive force in helping the team coalesce into an effective project team.

Not only are there people issues, but project members are also expected to use project management tools and concepts. They develop or are given a project charter or scope statement that defines the objectives and parameters of the project. They work with others to create a project schedule and budget that will guide project execution. They need to understand project priorities so they can make independent decisions.

They must know how to monitor and report project progress. Although much of this book is written from the perspective of a project manager, the tools, concepts, and methods are critical to everyone working on a project. Project members need to know how to avoid the dangers of scope creep, manage the critical path, engage in timely risk management, negotiate, and utilize virtual tools to communicate.

1.2 Current Drivers of Project Management

LO 1-4

Understand the importance of projects in implementing organization strategy.

Project management is no longer a special-need management. It is rapidly becoming a standard way of doing business. See Snapshot from Practice 1.4: Project Management in Action: 2016. An increasing percentage of the typical firm's effort is being devoted to projects. The future promises an increase in the importance and the role of projects in contributing to the strategic direction of organizations. Several reasons why this is the case are briefly discussed below.

Compression of the Product Life Cycle

One of the most significant driving forces behind the demand for project management is the shortening of the product life cycle. For example, today in high-tech industries the product life cycle is averaging six months to three years. Only 30 years ago, life cycles of 10 to 15 years were not uncommon. *Time to market* for new products with short life cycles has become increasingly important. A common rule of thumb in the world of high-tech product development is that a six-month project delay can result in a 33 percent loss in product revenue share. Speed, therefore, becomes a competitive advantage; more and more organizations are relying on cross-functional project teams to get new products and services to the market as quickly as possible.

Knowledge Explosion

The growth in new knowledge has increased the complexity of projects because projects encompass the latest advances. For example, building a road 30 years ago was a somewhat simple process. Today, each area has increased in complexity, including materials, specifications, codes, aesthetics, equipment, and required specialists. Similarly, in today's digital, electronic age it is becoming hard to find a new product that does not contain at least one microchip. Product complexity has increased the need to integrate divergent technologies. Project management has emerged as an important discipline for achieving this task.

Triple Bottom Line (Planet, People, Profit)

The threat of global warming has brought sustainable business practices to the forefront. Businesses can no longer simply focus on maximizing profit to the detriment of the environment and society. Efforts to reduce carbon imprint and utilize renewable resources are realized through effective project management. The impact of this movement toward sustainability can be seen in changes in the objectives and techniques used to complete projects. See Snapshot from Practice 1.5: Dell Children's Becomes World's First "Green" Hospital.

Increased Customer Focus

Increased competition has placed a premium on customer satisfaction. Customers no longer simply settle for generic products and services. They want customized products

SNAPSHOT FROM PRACTICE 1.4

Project Management in Action: 2016

Businesses thrive and survive based on their ability to manage projects that produce products and services that meet market needs. Below is a small sample of projects that are important to their company's future.

Panama: The Third Set of Locks Project

The expansion of the Panama Canal is scheduled to be operational in 2016. The project doubles the capacity of the Panama Canal by creating a

© Asif Islam/Shutterstock

new lane of traffic and allowing more and larger ships, the new Panamax size, which are about one and a half times bigger than the current size and can carry over twice as much cargo. With the third sets of locks, the canal will be able to manage traffic demand beyond 2025 with a predicted inflationary adjusted revenue of over $6.2 billion per year.

Molinski, D., "Panama Canal, Consortium Reach Deal to Complete Work," *The Wall Street Journal*, February 28, 2014.

Google: Autonomous-Vehicle Project

Google has contracted Roush Enterprises of Detroit, Michigan, to build 150 self-driving car prototypes. With more than 90 percent of U.S. road collisions caused by human error, self-driving cars could prevent over $190 billion in annual damages and health costs as well as greatly reduce fuel consumption.

Parsi, N., "No Driver Necessary," *PM Network,* August 2015, pp. 7–9.

Studio Roosegaarde: Smog Free Tower

The Smog Free tower, which stands 23 feet tall, sucks and cleans 1 million cubic feet of polluted air an hour. Innovator Daan Roosegaarde began working on outdoor air purification after a particularly smoggy 2013 trip to China.

Karif, O., "Innovation: Smog Eater," *Bloomberg Business-Week*, October 15, 2015, p. 22.

Facebook: Oculus Rift Virtual Reality Project

Facebook paid over $2 billion for virtual-reality start-up Oculus, which will release its Rift virtual reality headset

in 2016. Video games will spur early sales of Rift, but mass adoption is likely to depend upon Hollywood. Lions Gate Entertainment and 21st Century Fox have agreed to sell movies via Oculus's online store and Netflix will make its streaming service available on VR headsets.

Shaw, L., "Virtual Reality Goes to the Movies," *Bloomberg BusinessWeek*, Special Issue: Year Ahead 2016, p. 74.

CogniToys: Dino Project

Rather than repeating catchphrases, as "talking" toys have done in the past, this dinosaur taps IBM's Watson technology to engage kids ages 5 to 9 in a more meaningful way. The wi-fi-enabled figurine talks back and learns from kids' responses, helping them hone their math skills by asking harder questions. The trick, according to CogniToys CEO Donald Coolidge, is to make education seem like a "cool, fun experience."

"The Toy That Talks Back," *Time*, November 30/December 7, 2015, p. 81.

Coca-Cola Co.: Replenish Africa Initiative (RAIN)

The global beverage company aims to provide at least 2 million people with safe water by the end of 2020. The firm is investing over $30 million in community-based water projects across Africa. Greg Koch, senior director of global water stewardship says, "We know that to do business we need water. And when communities have access to safe water, you have the foundation of a thriving community, which is a better place for everyone to do business."

"Water Works," *PMNetwork*, September, 2015, p. 53.

SNAPSHOT FROM PRACTICE 1.5

Dell Children's Becomes World's First "Green" Hospital*

Dateline 1/7/2009, Austin Texas: Dell Children's Medical Center becomes the first hospital in the world to receive platinum LEED (Leadership in Energy & Environmental Design) certification. Platinum certification is the highest award granted by the U.S. Green Building Council.

Dell Children's occupies nearly one-half-million square feet on 32 acres that were once part of Austin's old Mueller Airport. Its environmentally sensitive design not only conserves water and electricity, but positively impacts the hospital's clinical environment by improving air quality, making natural sunlight readily available, and reducing a wide range of pollutants.

In order to receive LEED certification, buildings are rated in five key areas: sustainable site development, water savings, energy efficiency, materials selection, and environmental quality. Listed below are some of the accomplishments in each LEED category:

Sustainable Site

- 47,000 tons of Mueller Airport runway material was reused on site.
- About 40 percent fly ash instead of Portland cement in concrete yields a drop in carbon dioxide emissions equivalent to taking 450 cars off the road.
- 925 tons of construction waste was recycled on site.

Water Efficiency and Water Conservation

- Reclaimed water is used for irrigation; xeriscaped landscaping uses native plants, which require less water.
- Low-flow plumbing fixtures.

Energy Efficiency and Energy Conservation

- An on-site natural gas turbine supplies all electricity, which is 75 percent more efficient than coal-fired plants.
- Converted steam energy from a heating/cooling plant supplies all chilled water needs.

Indoor Environment Quality and Lighting

- Most interior spaces are within 32 feet of a window.
- Motion and natural light sensors shut off unneeded lights.

Conservation of Materials and Resources

- Use of local and regional materials saves fuel for shipping.
- Special paints and flooring emit low levels of volatile organic compounds (VOCs).

"Even before the first plans were drawn up, we set our sight on creating a world-class children's hospital, and becoming the first LEED Platinum hospital in the world was definitely part of that," said Robert Bonar, president and CEO, Dell Children's Medical Center of Central Texas. "Our motivation to pursue LEED Platinum was not just environmental. Being a 'green' hospital has a profound, measurable effect on healing. What's good for the environment and good for our neighbors is also good for our patients."

*Austin Business Journal, January 11, 2009, www.dellchildrens.net/about_us/news/2009/01/08.

and services that cater to their specific needs. This mandate requires a much closer working relationship between the provider and the receiver. Account executives and sales representatives are assuming more of a project manager's role as they work with their organization to satisfy the unique needs and requests of clients.

Increased customer attention has also prompted the development of customized products and services. For example, 15 years ago buying a set of golf clubs was a relatively simple process: You picked out a set based on price and feel. Today, there are golf clubs for tall players and short players, clubs for players who tend to slice the ball and clubs for those who hook the ball, high-tech clubs with the latest metallurgic discovery guaranteed to add distance, and so forth. Project management is critical both to development of customized products and services and to sustaining lucrative relationships with customers.

Small Projects Represent Big Problems

The velocity of change required to remain competitive or simply keep up has created an organizational climate in which hundreds of projects are implemented concurrently. This climate has created a multiproject environment and a plethora of new problems. Sharing and prioritizing resources across a portfolio of projects is a major challenge for senior management. Many firms have no idea of the problems involved with inefficient management of small projects. Small projects typically carry the same or more risk as do large projects. Small projects are perceived as having little impact on the bottom line because they do not demand large amounts of scarce resources and/or money. Because so many small projects are going on concurrently and because the perception of the inefficiency impact is small, measuring inefficiency is usually nonexistent. Unfortunately, many small projects soon add up to large sums of money. Many customers and millions of dollars are lost each year on small projects in product and service organizations. Small projects can represent hidden costs not measured in the accounting system.

Organizations with many small projects going on concurrently face the most difficult project management problems. A key question becomes one of how to create an organizational environment that supports multiproject management. A process is needed to prioritize and develop a portfolio of small projects that supports the mission of the organization.

In summary, there are a variety of environmental forces interacting in today's business world that contribute to the increased demand for good project management across all industries and sectors. Project management appears to be ideally suited for a business environment requiring accountability, flexibility, innovation, speed, and continuous improvement. These environmental and other factors have created the necessity for major oversight of all organization projects.

1.3 Project Governance

Competing in a global market influenced by rapid change, innovation, and time to market means organizations manage more and more projects. Some means for coordinating and managing projects in this changing environment is needed. Centralization of project management processes and practices has been the practical outcome. For example, Google, Apple, General Electric, and Sony all have over 1,000 projects being implemented concurrently every day of the year across borders and differing cultures. *Questions: How do these organizations oversee the management of all these projects? How were these projects selected? How do they ensure performance measurement and accountability? How can project management continually improve?* Centralization entails governance of all project processes and practices to improve project management.

Governance is designed to improve project management in the whole organization over the long haul. The rationale for integration of project management was to provide senior management with:

- An overview of all project management activities;
- A big picture of how organizational resources are being used;
- An assessment of the risk their portfolio of projects represents;
- A rough metric for measuring the improvement of managing projects relative to others in the industry;
- Linkages of senior management with actual project execution management.

FIGURE 1.2
Integrated
Management of
Projects

Full insight of all components of the organization is crucial for aligning internal business resources with the requirements of the changing environment. Governance enables management to have greater flexibility and better control of all project management activities.

Operationally, what does project management integration mean? It necessitates combining all of the major dimensions of project management under one umbrella. Each dimension is connected in one seamless, integrated domain. Governance means applying a set of knowledge, skills, tools, and techniques to a collection of projects in order to move the organization toward its strategic goals. This integrative movement represents a major thrust of project-driven organizations across all industries. See Figure 1.2, Integrated Management of Projects.

Alignment of Projects with Organizational Strategy

Today, projects are the *modus operandi* for implementing strategy. Yet in some organizations, selection and management of projects often fail to support the strategic plan of the organization. Strategic plans are written by one group of managers, projects selected by another group, and projects implemented by another. These independent decisions by different groups of managers create a set of conditions leading to conflict, confusion, and frequently an unsatisfied customer. Under these conditions, resources of the organization are wasted in non-value-added activities/projects.

Since projects are the modus operandi, strategic alignment of projects is of major importance to conserving and effective use of organization resources. Selection criteria need to ensure each project is prioritized and contributes to strategic goals. Anything less is a waste of scarce organizational resources—people, capital, and equipment. Ensuring alignment requires a selection process that is systematic, open, consistent, and balanced. All of the projects selected become part of a project portfolio that balances the total risk for the organization. Management of the project portfolio ensures that only the most valuable projects are approved and managed across the entire organization.

1.4 Project Management Today: A Socio-Technical Approach

LO 1-5

Understand that managing projects involves balancing the technical and sociocultural dimensions of the project.

Senior management is often involved in selecting projects but seldom involved in implementing them. Implementing the project is the challenge.

Managing a project is a multidimensional process (see Figure 1.3, A Socio-Technical Approach to Project Management). The first dimension is the technical side of the management process, which consists of the formal, disciplined, purely logical parts of the process. This technical dimension includes planning, scheduling, and controlling projects. Clear project scope statements are written to link the project and customer and to facilitate planning and control. Creation of the deliverables and work breakdown structures facilitates planning and monitoring the progress of the project. The work breakdown structure serves as a database that links all levels in the organization, major deliverables, and all work—right down to the tasks in a work package. Effects of project changes are documented and traceable. Thus, any change in one part of the project is traceable to the source by the integrated linkages of the system. This integrated information approach can provide all project managers and the customer with decision information appropriate to their level and needs. A successful project manager will be well trained in the technical side of managing projects.

The second and opposing dimension is the sociocultural side of project management. In contrast to the orderly world of project planning, this dimension involves the much messier, often contradictory and paradoxical world of implementation. It centers on creating a temporary social system within a larger organizational environment that combines the talents of a divergent set of professionals working to complete the project. Project managers must shape a project culture that stimulates teamwork and high levels of personal motivation as well as a capacity to quickly identify and resolve problems that threaten project work. Things rarely go as planned and project managers must be able to steer the project back on track or alter directions when necessary.

The sociocultural dimension also involves managing the interface between the project and external environment. Project managers have to assuage and shape

FIGURE 1.3
A Socio-Technical Approach to Project Management

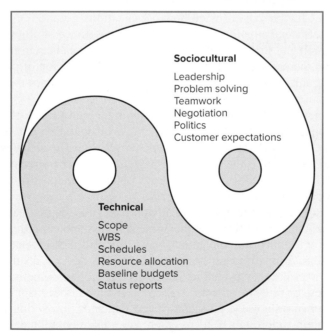

Sociocultural

Leadership
Problem solving
Teamwork
Negotiation
Politics
Customer expectations

Technical

Scope
WBS
Schedules
Resource allocation
Baseline budgets
Status reports

expectations of customers, sustain the political support of top management, negotiate with their functional counterparts, monitor subcontractors, and so on. Overall, the manager must build a cooperative social network among a divergent set of allies with different standards, commitments, and perspectives.

Some suggest that the technical dimension represents the "science" of project management while the sociocultural dimension represents the "art" of managing a project. To be successful, a manager must be a master of both. Unfortunately, some project managers become preoccupied with the planning and technical dimension of project management. Often their first real exposure to project management is through project management software, and they become infatuated with network charts, Gantt diagrams, and performance variances; they attempt to manage a project from a distance. Conversely, there are other managers who manage projects by the "seat of their pants," relying heavily on team dynamics and organizational politics to complete a project. Good project managers balance their attention to both the technical and sociocultural aspects of project management.

Summary

Project management is a critical skill set in today's world. A project is defined as a nonroutine, one-time effort limited by time, resources, and performance specifications designed to meet customer needs. One of the distinguishing characteristics of project management is that it has both a beginning and an end and typically consists of four phases: defining, planning, executing, and closing. Effective project management begins with selecting and prioritizing projects that support the firm's mission and strategy. Successful implementation requires both technical and social skills. Project managers have to plan and budget projects as well as orchestrate the contributions of others.

Text Overview

This text is written to provide the reader with a comprehensive, integrative understanding of the project management process. The text focuses both on the science of project management and the art of managing projects. Following this introductory chapter, Chapter 2 focuses on how organizations go about evaluating and selecting projects. Special attention is devoted to the importance of aligning project selection to the mission and strategy of the firm. The organizational environment in which projects are implemented is the focus of Chapter 3. The discussion of matrix management and other organizational forms is augmented by a discussion of the role the culture of an organization plays in the implementation of projects.

The next six chapters focus on developing a plan for the project; after all, project success begins with a good plan. Chapter 4 deals with defining the scope of the project and developing a work breakdown structure (WBS). The challenge of formulating cost and time estimates is the subject of Chapter 5. Chapter 6 focuses on utilizing the information from the WBS to create a project plan in the form of a timed and sequenced network of activities.

Risks are a potential threat to every project, and Chapter 7 examines how organizations and managers identify and manage risks associated with project work. Resource allocation is added to the plan in Chapter 8 with special attention devoted to how resource limitations impact the project schedule. After a resource schedule is established, a project time-phased budget is developed. Finally, Chapter 9 examines strategies for reducing ("crashing") project time either prior to the initiation of the project or in response to problems or new demands placed on the project.

Chapters 10 through 12 focus on project implementation and the sociocultural side of project management, beginning with Chapter 10, which focuses on the role of the project manager as a leader and stresses the importance of managing project stakeholders within the organization. Chapter 11 focuses on the core project team; it combines the latest information on team dynamics with leadership skills/techniques for developing a high-performance project team. Chapter 12 continues the theme of managing project stakeholders by discussing how to outsource project work and negotiate with contractors, customers, and suppliers.

Chapter 13 focuses on the kinds of information managers use to monitor project progress, with special attention devoted to the key concept of earned value. The project life cycle is completed with Chapter 14, which covers closing out a project and the important assessment of performance and lessons learned. Two "supplemental" chapters are included to augment the project management core. Working on international projects across cultures is the focus of Chapter 15. Agile project management, a more flexible approach to managing projects where requirements cannot be clearly defined, is the subject of Chapter 16.

Throughout this text you will be exposed to the major aspects of the project management system. However, a true understanding of project management comes not from knowing what a scope statement is, or the critical path, or partnering with contractors, but from comprehending how the different elements of the project management system interact to determine the fate of a project. If, by the end of this text, you come to appreciate and begin to master both the technical and sociocultural dimensions of project management, you should have a distinct competitive advantage over others aspiring to work in the field of project management.

Key Terms

Program, *7*
Project, *6*
Project life cycle, *8*

Project Management
Professional (PMP), *4*

Review Questions

1. Define a project. What are five characteristics that help differentiate projects from other functions carried out in the daily operations of the organization?
2. What are some of the key environmental forces that have changed the way projects are managed? What has been the effect of these forces on the management of projects?
3. Why is the implementation of projects important to strategic planning and the project manager?
4. The technical and sociocultural dimensions of project management are two sides to the same coin. Explain.
5. What is the impact of governance on managing an individual project? Why is this approach important in today's environment?

Exercises

1. Review the front page of your local newspaper, and try to identify all the projects contained in the articles. How many were you able to find?
2. Individually, identify what you consider to be the greatest achievements of mankind in the last five decades. Now share your list with three to five other students in the class, and come up with an expanded list. Review these great achievements in terms of the definition of a project. What does your review suggest about the importance of project management?
3. Individually, identify projects assigned in previous terms. Were both sociocultural and technical elements factors in the success or difficulties in the projects?

4. Check out the Project Management Institute's home page at *www.pmi.org*.
   a. Review general information about PMI as well as membership information.
   b. See if there is a PMI chapter in your state. If not, where is the closest one?
   c. Use the search function at the PMI home page to find information on Project Management Body of Knowledge (PMBOK). What are the major knowledge areas of PMBOK?
   d. Explore other links that PMI provides. What do these links tell you about the nature and future of project management?

Note: If you have any difficulty accessing any of the Web addresses listed here or elsewhere in the text, you can find up-to-date addresses on the home page of Dr. Erik Larson, coauthor of this text: http://business.oregonstate.edu/faculty-and-staff-bios/erik-larson

References

Benko, C., and F. W. McFarlan, *Connecting the Dots* (Boston: HBS Press, 2003).

Cohen, D. J., and R. J. Graham, *The Project Manager's MBA* (San Francisco: Jossey-Bass, 2001).

Darnell, R., "The Emerging Role of the Project Manager," *PM Network,* vol. 11, no. 7 (1997).

Derby, Charles, and Ofer Zwikael, "The Secret of (Defining) Success," *PM Network*, vol. 26, no. 8 (August 2012), pp. 20–22.

Gray, Clifford, "Program Management, A Primer," *PM World Today*, vol. 13, no. 8 (August 2011), pp. 1–7.

Jonas, D., "Empowering Project Portfolio Managers: How Management Involvement Impacts Project Management Performance," *International Journal of Project Management,* vol. 28, no. 8 (2010), pp. 818–831.

Koh, Aileen, and Lynn Crawford, "Portfolio Management: The Australian Experience," *Project Management Journal,* vol. 43, no. 6 (2012), pp. 33–41.

Peters, T., *PM Network,* January 2004, vol. 18, no. 1, p. 19.

Project Management Institute, *Leadership in Project Management Annual* (Newton Square, PA: PMI Publishing, 2006).

Project Management Institute, *A Guide to the Project Management Body of Knowledge (PMBOK),* (Newton Square, PA: PMI Publishing, 2013).

Project Management Institute, *PMI Today,* July 2011, p. 11.

The Standish Group, *CHAOS Summary 2009*, pp. 1–4.

Stewart, T. A., "The Corporate Jungle Spawns a New Species: The Project Manager," *Fortune,* September 1996, pp. 14–15.

Case 1.1

A Day in the Life

Rachel, the project manager of a large information systems project, arrives at her office early to get caught up with work before her co-workers and project team arrive. However, as she enters the office she meets Neil, one of her fellow project managers, who also wants to get an early start on the day. Neil has just completed a project overseas. They spend 10 minutes socializing and catching up on personal news.

It takes Rachel 10 minutes to get to her office and settle in. She then checks her voice mail and turns on her computer. She was at her client's site the day before until 7:30 p.m. and has not checked her e-mail or voice mail since 3:30 p.m. the previous day. There are 7 phone messages, 16 e-mails, and 4 notes left on her desk. She spends 15 minutes reviewing her schedule and "to do" lists for the day before responding to messages that require immediate attention.

Rachel spends the next 25 minutes going over project reports and preparing for the weekly status meeting. Her boss, who just arrived at the office, interrupts her. They spend 20 minutes discussing the project. He shares a rumor that a team member is using stimulants on the job. She tells him that she has not seen anything suspicious but will keep an eye on the team member.

The 9:00 a.m. project status meeting starts 15 minutes late because two of the team members have to finish a job for a client. Several people go to the cafeteria to get coffee and doughnuts while others discuss last night's baseball game. The team members arrive, and the remaining 45 minutes of the progress review meeting surface project issues that have to be addressed and assigned for action.

After the meeting Rachel goes down the hallway to meet with Victoria, another IS project manager. They spend 30 minutes reviewing project assignments since the two of them share personnel. Victoria's project is behind schedule and in need of help. They broker a deal that should get Victoria's project back on track.

She returns to her office and makes several phone calls and returns several e-mails before walking downstairs to visit with members of her project team. Her intent is to follow up on an issue that had surfaced in the status report meeting. However, her simple, "Hi guys, how are things going?" elicits a stream of disgruntled responses from the "troops." After listening patiently for over 20 minutes, she realizes that among other things several of the client's managers are beginning to request features that were not in the original project scope statement. She tells her people that she will get on this right away.

Returning to her office she tries to call her counterpart John at the client firm but is told that he is not expected back from lunch for another hour. At this time, Eddie drops by and says, "How about lunch?" Eddie works in the finance office and they spend the next half hour in the company cafeteria gossiping about internal politics. She is surprised to hear that Jonah Johnson, the director of systems projects, may join another firm. Jonah has always been a powerful ally.

She returns to her office, answers a few more e-mails, and finally gets through to John. They spend 30 minutes going over the problem. The conversation ends with John promising to do some investigating and to get back to her as soon as possible.

Rachel puts a "Do not disturb" sign on her door, and lies down in her office. She listens to the third and fourth movement of Ravel's string quartet in F on headphones.

Rachel then takes the elevator down to the third floor and talks to the purchasing agent assigned to her project. They spend the next 30 minutes exploring ways of getting necessary equipment to the project site earlier than planned. She finally authorizes express delivery.

When she returns to her office, her calendar reminds her that she is scheduled to participate in a conference call at 2:30. It takes 15 minutes for everyone to get online. During this time, Rachel catches up on some e-mail. The next hour is spent exchanging information about the technical requirements associated with a new version of a software package they are using on systems projects like hers.

Rachel decides to stretch her legs and goes on a walk down the hallway where she engages in brief conversations with various co-workers. She goes out of her way to thank

Chandra for his thoughtful analysis at the status report meeting. She returns to find that John has left a message for her to call him back ASAP. She contacts John, who informs her that, according to his people, her firm's marketing rep had made certain promises about specific features her system would provide. He doesn't know how this communication breakdown occurred, but his people are pretty upset over the situation. Rachel thanks John for the information and immediately takes the stairs to where the marketing group resides.

She asks to see Mary, a senior marketing manager. She waits 10 minutes before being invited into her office. After a heated discussion, she leaves 40 minutes later with Mary agreeing to talk to her people about what was promised and what was not promised.

She goes downstairs to her people to give them an update on what is happening. They spend 30 minutes reviewing the impact the client's requests could have on the project schedule. She also shares with them the schedule changes she and Victoria had agreed to. After she says good night to her team, she heads upstairs to her boss's office and spends 20 minutes updating him on key events of the day. She returns to her office and spends 30 minutes reviewing e-mails and project documents. She logs on to the MS project schedule of her project and spends the next 30 minutes working with "what-if" scenarios. She reviews tomorrow's schedule and writes some personal reminders before starting off on her 30-minute commute home.

1. How effectively do you think Rachel spent her day?
2. What does the case tell you about what it is like to be a project manager?

Case 1.2

The Hokies Lunch Group[1]

PART A

Fatma settled down for lunch at the Yank Sing Chinese restaurant. She was early and took the time to catch up on her e-mail. Soon she would be joined by Jasper and Viktoria, two fellow 2014 grads from Virginia Tech in Blacksburg, Virginia.

Jasper worked as a software engineer for a start-up company that wanted to expand the boundaries of sharing economy. Viktoria was an electrical engineer who worked for a German healthcare company in San Francisco. They had met each other at a Silicon Valley alumni reception hosted by Virginia Tech. Each of them felt a bit like a fish out of water on the West Coast, so they decided to have lunch together each month. The lunch evolved into a professional support group. A major part of each of their jobs was managing projects, and they found it useful to share issues and seek advice from each other.

Fatma worked for a very successful Internet company whose founders believed that everyone in the firm should devote three days a year to community service projects. The company was partnering with several companies in the construction industry to renovate abandoned buildings for low income families. The next project was the renovation of an empty warehouse into eight two-bedroom apartments. Fatma was part of the core team in charge of scheduling and managing work assignments.

Viktoria and Jasper entered the restaurant together. Viktoria was the first to move to the Bay area. She was currently working on the next-generation neural

---

[1] Hokies is the name associated with Virginia Tech athletic teams.

stimulator ("PAX 2"). Neural stimulators are electronic devices that doctors implant in patients with wires connected to sources of pain in the patient's spine. In the past, patients would have to have an operation to replace the stimulator battery every 10 years. PAX 2 was being designed to take advantage of new battery technologies and use a rechargeable battery. In concept, this battery system would eliminate the need for replacement surgeries and allow the implanted battery to be recharged externally. Viktoria's team had just completed the second prototype and was entering a critical testing phase. It had been tricky trying to predict the life span of the new rechargeable battery without testing it in real time. She was anxious to begin seeing the test results.

Jasper was working for a start-up company after doing contract work for his first nine months in San Francisco. He was sworn to secrecy about the project and all Fatma and Viktoria knew was that the project had something to do with sharing economy. He was working with a small development team that included colleagues from Bangalore, India, and Malmo, Sweden.

After ordering and chit-chatting a bit, Fatma started the discussion. "I will be glad when this week is over," she said. "We've been struggling defining the scope of the project. At first glance our project seems relatively simple, build eight two-bedroom apartments in an old warehouse. But there are a lot of unanswered questions. What kind of community space do we want to have? How efficient should the energy system be? What kind of furniture? Everybody wants to do a good job, but when does low income housing morph into middle income housing?"

Viktoria offered, "Scope defining is one of the things my company does very well. Before a project is authorized, a detailed scope statement is developed that clearly defines the project objectives, priorities, budget, requirements, limits, and exclusions. All of the key stakeholders sign off on it. It is really important to identify priorities up front. I know on the PAX 2 project that scope is the number one priority. I know no matter how long it takes it is imperative that my work is done right."

Fatma responded, "That's exactly what my Project manager is preparing for Friday's meeting. I guess that is one of the things you have to do as a project manager is end discussions. He is going to make the tough calls and finalize the project scope so we can begin planning."

Jasper interjected, "You guys are so lucky, for the most part your scope remains the same. In my work the scope is constantly changing. You show the founders a feature they wanted, and they say well if you can do that, can you do this? You know it's going to happen, but you really can't plan for it."

Jasper went on to say, "We do know what our number one priority is: *time.* There are a lot of players trying to move in to the 'space' we are working on. We have to demonstrate we are ahead of the pack if we are going to continue to get VC funding."[2]

Jasper said that despite the pressure, his project had been a lot of fun. He especially liked working with his Swedish and Indian counterparts, Axel and Raja. They worked like a global tag team on their part of the project. Jasper would code and then pass his work onto Raja who would work on it and pass it on to Axel, who would eventually hand it off to Jasper. Given the time zones, they were able to have at least one person working on the code around the clock.

Jasper said it was hard at first working with someone you never met personally other than on a video screen. Trust was an issue. Everyone was trying to prove themselves. Eventually a friendly competition arose across the team. The programmers

[2] New Venture Capital funding.

exchanged funny cartoons and YouTube videos. He showed Fatma and Viktoria a You-Tube video about scope creep that got a chuckle from everyone.

They made plans to meet next at the New Peruvian restaurant on SE 8th Street.

PART B

The Peruvian cilantro/lime ceviche was a big hit at the next lunch. Viktoria began their discussion by reporting, "I have good and bad news. The bad news is that our first prototype failed its tests miserably. The good news is that I have a smart project manager. She knew this could happen, so she mitigated the risk by having us working on two alternative battery technologies. The alternative technology is passing all of the tests. Instead of falling behind months we are only days behind schedule."

This precipitated a discussion of risk management. Fatma reported that there had been a two-day session on risk management for the renovation project. They spent the first day brainstorming what could go wrong, and the second day coming up with strategies for dealing with risks. A big help was the risk report that was generated after the last project. The report detailed all of the problems that had occurred on the last renovation project as well as recommendations. Fatma said, "I couldn't believe how much time and attention was devoted to safety, but as my project manager said, 'all it takes is one bad accident to shut down a project for weeks, even months.'"

Jasper reported that on his project they spent very little time on risk management. His project was driven by a build-test mentality. "Everybody assumes that daily testing eliminates problems, but when it's time to integrate different features, that's when the real bugs will emerge," Jasper said.

Jasper went on to say that things were not going well at work. They had missed their second straight milestone, and everyone was feeling the pressure to show results. "I even slept by my cubicle three nights ago," Jasper confessed. Fatma asked, "How many hours are you working?" "I don't know, at least 70, maybe 80 hours," Jasper answered. He went on to say, "This is a high stakes project, with a BIG upside if successful. I am doing some of my best programming and we'll just have to see what happens."

Jasper showed them a cartoon that was being circulated across his team. The caption read: "When did you want it done? Yesterday."

Fatma turned to her friends and said, "I need some advice. As you know I'm responsible for scheduling work assignments. Well, some of my colleagues have been pretty aggressive lobbying for choice assignments. Everyone wants to work alongside Bruno or Ryan. Suddenly I am everyone's friends, and certain people are going way out of their way to do favors for me. I am sure they think it will influence my decisions. It's getting awkward and I am not sure what to do."

"Quid pro quo," answered Jasper, "that's how the business world works. You scratch my back and I'll scratch yours. Within reason, I don't have a problem with someone taking advantage of their position to garner favors and build relationships."

Viktoria said, "I disagree. You don't want to be seen as someone whose influence can be bought. You need to think what's best for the company. You need to ask yourself what would Bruno and Ryan want you to do? And if you don't know, ask them."

After much discussion, Fatma left the restaurant leaning towards Viktoria's advice, but she wasn't sure what the guidelines should be.

PART C

It took two months for the Hokie lunch group to get together again. Jasper had canceled the last meeting because of work, so Viktoria and Fatma saw a movie together instead.

Jasper was the last person to arrive and it was clear from the look on his face that things were not going well. He sat down, avoided eye contact, before blurting, "I'm out of work." "What do you mean?" Fatma and Viktoria cried. Jasper explained after months and months of work they had been unable to demonstrate a functional product.

Jasper went on to say, "Despite our best efforts we couldn't deliver. The founders couldn't get an ounce of second round venture funding, so they decided to cut their losses and kill the project. I just spent the best six months of my programming life for nothing."

Fatma and Viktoria tried to comfort their friend. Fatma asked Jasper how the others were taking the news. Jasper said the Swedish programmer, Axel, took the news very hard. He went on to say, "I think he was burning a lot of bridges at home with the long work hours and now he has nothing to show for it. He started blaming us for mistakes we never made." Raja, his Indian counterpart, was a different story. "Raja seemed to shrug his shoulders." Jasper added, "He said, I know I am a good programmer. There are lots of opportunities here in Bangalore."

Fatma broke the silence that followed by saying to Jasper, "Send me your resume. My company is always looking for top notch programmers and it is a really great company. Can you believe it, the two founders, Bruno and Ryan, are working side by side with everyone on renovating the warehouse? In fact, people were amazed at how good Bruno was with sheet rock. A big part of my job now is scheduling their time so they can work with as many different people as possible. They really want to use the project to get to know their employees. This hasn't been easy. I have had to juggle their calendars, their abilities, and work opportunities."

Viktoria interjected, "You're using Microsoft Project to do this?" "Not really," responded Fatma. "At first I tried scheduling their work in Project, but it was too cumbersome and time consuming. Now I just use the Project master schedule and each of their calendars to schedule their work. This seems to work best."

Viktoria added, "Yeah, Microsoft Project is a great program, but you can get lost trying to get it to do everything. Sometimes all you need is an Excel sheet and common sense."

Viktoria felt awkward, given what had happened to Jasper. She was just wrapping up the successful PAX 2 project. She was also getting ready for a well-deserved holiday in Vietnam paid for by her project bonus. "I hate closing out a project," Viktoria said. "It's so boring. Document, document, document! I keep kicking myself for not tracking things when they happened. I am spending most of my time scouring my computer for files. I can't wait to take off to Vietnam."

Viktoria went on to say, "The only thing I liked doing was the project retrospective."

Jasper asked, "What's a project retrospective?" Viktoria answered, "It's when the project team gets together and reviews what went well, what didn't, and identifies lessons learned that we can apply to future projects. For example, one of the things we learned was that we needed to bring the manufacturing people on board a lot sooner in the design process. We focused on designing the very best product possible, regardless of cost. We found out later that there were ways for reducing production costs without compromising quality."

Fatma added, "We do that too at the end of our projects, but we call it an audit."

Fatma asked Viktoria, "Do you know what your next assignment will be?" "No," she replied, "I will probably go back to my department and do some testing. I'm not worried. I did good work. I am sure someone will want me for their project."

Jasper chimed in, "I sure hope someone wants me for their next project." Fatma and Viktoria immediately went into action trying to lift their friend's spirits.

A little while later, they walked out of the Tapa restaurant and gave each other hugs. Fatma reminded Jasper to send her his latest resume.

1. For each part (A, B, C), what phase of the project life cycle is each project in? Explain.

2. What are two important things you learned about working on projects from the case? Why are they important?

2 Organization Strategy and Project Selection

LEARNING OBJECTIVES

After reading this chapter you should be able to:

2-1 Explain why it is important for project managers to understand their organization's strategy.

2-2 Identify the significant role projects contribute to the strategic direction of the organization.

2-3 Understand the need for a project priority system.

2-4 Apply financial and nonfinancial criteria to assess the value of projects.

2-5 Understand how multi-criteria models can be used to select projects.

2-6 Apply an objective priority system to project selection.

2-7 Understand the need to manage the project portfolio.

OUTLINE

2.1 The Strategic Management Process: An Overview

2.2 The Need for a Project Priority System

2.3 A Portfolio Management System

2.4 Selection Criteria

2.5 Applying a Selection Model

2.6 Managing the Portfolio System

Summary

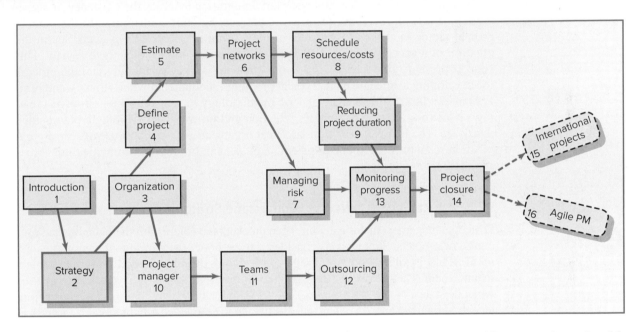

Strategy is implemented through projects. Every significant project should have a clear link to the organization's strategy.

Strategy is fundamentally deciding how the organization will compete. Organizations use projects to convert strategy into new products, services, and processes needed for success. For example, Intel's major strategy is one of differentiation. Its projects target innovation and time to market. Currently, Intel is directing its strategy toward specialty chips for products other than computers, such as autos, security, cell phones, and air controls. Another goal is to reduce project cycle times. Procter and Gamble, NEC, General Electric, and AT&T have reduced their cycle times by 20–50 percent. For example, Toyota and other auto manufacturers are now able to design and develop new cars in two to three years instead of five to seven. Projects and project management play the key role in supporting strategic goals. It is vital for project managers to think and act strategically.

Aligning projects with the strategic goals of the organization is crucial for business success. Today's economic climate is unprecedented by rapid changes in technology, global competition, and financial uncertainty. These conditions make strategy/project alignment even more essential for success. Ensuring a strong link between the strategic plan and projects is a difficult task that demands constant attention from top and middle management.

The larger and more diverse an organization, the more difficult it is to create and maintain this strong link. Companies today are under enormous pressure to manage a process that clearly aligns projects to organization strategy. Ample evidence still suggests that many organizations have not developed a process that clearly aligns project selection to the strategic plan. The result is poor utilization of the organization's resources—people, money, equipment, and core competencies. Conversely, organizations that have a coherent link of projects to strategy have more cooperation across the organization, perform better on projects, and have fewer projects.

How can an organization ensure this link and alignment? The answer requires integration of projects with the strategic plan. Integration assumes the existence of a strategic plan and a process for prioritizing projects by their contribution to the plan. A crucial factor to ensure the success of integrating the plan with projects lies in the creation of a process that is open and transparent for all participants to review. This chapter presents an overview of the importance of strategic planning and the process for developing a strategic plan. Typical problems encountered when strategy and projects are not linked are noted. A generic methodology that ensures integration by creating very strong linkages of project selection and priority to the strategic plan is then discussed. The intended outcomes are clear organization focus, best use of scarce organization resources (people, equipment, capital), and improved communication across projects and departments.

Why Project Managers Need to Understand Strategy

LO 2-1

Explain why it is important for project managers to understand their organization's strategy.

Project management historically has been preoccupied solely with the planning and execution of projects. Strategy was considered to be under the purview of senior management. This is old-school thinking. New-school thinking recognizes that project management is at the apex of strategy and operations. Aaron Shenhar speaks to this issue when he states, ". . . it is time to expand the traditional role of the project manager from an operational to a more strategic perspective. In the modern evolving organization, project managers will be focused on business aspects, and their role will expand from getting the job done to achieving the business results and winning in the marketplace."[1]

There are two main reasons why project managers need to understand their organization's mission and strategy. The first reason is so they can make appropriate decisions and adjustments. For example, how a project manager would respond to a suggestion to modify the design of a product to enhance performance will vary depending upon whether his company strives to be a product leader through innovation or to achieve operational excellence through low cost solutions. Similarly, how a project manager would respond to delays may vary depending upon strategic concerns. A project manager will authorize overtime if her firm places a premium on getting to the market first. Another project manager will accept the delay if speed is not essential.

The second reason project managers need to understand their organization's strategy is so they can be effective project advocates. Project managers have to be able to demonstrate to senior management how their project contributes to their firm's mission. Protection and continued support come from being aligned with corporate objectives. Project managers also need to be able to explain to team members and other

---

[1] Shenhar, A., and Dov Dvie, *Reinventing Project Management* (Harvard Business School, 2007), p. 5.

stakeholders why certain project objectives and priorities are critical. This is essential for getting buy-in on contentious trade-off decisions.

For these reasons project managers will find it valuable to have a keen understanding of strategic management and project selection processes, which are discussed next.

2.1 The Strategic Management Process: An Overview

LO 2-2

Identify the significant role projects contribute to the strategic direction of the organization.

Strategic management is the process of assessing "what we are" and deciding and implementing "what we intend to be and how we are going to get there." Strategy describes how an organization intends to compete with the resources available in the existing and perceived future environment.

Two major dimensions of strategic management are responding to changes in the external environment and allocating scarce resources of the firm to improve its competitive position. Constant scanning of the external environment for changes is a major requirement for survival in a dynamic competitive environment. The second dimension is the internal responses to new action programs aimed at enhancing the competitive position of the firm. The nature of the responses depends on the type of business, environment volatility, competition, and the organizational culture.

Strategic management provides the theme and focus of the future direction of the organization. It supports consistency of action at every level of the organization. It encourages integration because effort and resources are committed to common goals and strategies. See Snapshot from Practice 2.1: Does IBM's Watson's Jeopardy Project Represent a Change in Strategy? It is a continuous, iterative process aimed at developing an integrated and coordinated long-term plan of action. Strategic management positions the organization to meet the needs and requirements of its customers for the long term. With the long-term position identified, objectives are set, and strategies are developed to achieve objectives and then translated into actions by implementing projects. Strategy can decide the survival of an organization. Most organizations are successful in *formulating* strategies for what course(s) they should pursue. However, the problem in many organizations is *implementing* strategies—that is, making them happen. Integration of strategy formulation and implementation often does not exist.

The components of strategic management are closely linked, and all are directed toward the future success of the organization. Strategic management requires strong links among mission, goals, objectives, strategy, and implementation. The mission gives the general purpose of the organization. Goals give global targets within the mission. Objectives give specific targets to goals. Objectives give rise to formulation of strategies to reach objectives. Finally, strategies require actions and tasks to be implemented. In most cases the actions to be taken represent projects. Figure 2.1 shows a schematic of the strategic management process and major activities required.

Four Activities of the Strategic Management Process

The typical sequence of activities of the strategic management process is outlined here; a description of each activity then follows:

1. Review and define the organizational mission.
2. Analyze and formulate strategies.
3. Set objectives to achieve strategy.
4. Implement strategies through projects.

SNAPSHOT FROM PRACTICE 2.1

Does IBM's Watson's Jeopardy Project Represent a Change in Strategy?*

IBM's investment in artificial intelligence paid off. In February 2010, millions of people were glued to their television sets to watch IBM's Watson outclass two former champion contestants on the Jeopardy quiz show. Watson performed at human expert levels in terms of precision, confidence, and speed during the Jeopardy quiz show.

Does Watson represent a new strategic direction for IBM? Not really. The Watson project is simply a manifestation of the move from computer hardware to a service strategy over a decade ago.

© Sean Gallup/Getty

WATSON PROJECT DESCRIPTION

Artificial intelligence has advanced significantly in recent years. Watson goes beyond IBM's chess-playing supercomputer of the late 1990s. Chess is finite, logical, and reduced easily to mathematics. Watson's space is ill-defined and involves dealing with abstraction and the circumstantial nature of language. Since Watson's system can understand natural language, it can extend the way people interact with computers.

The IBM Watson project took three intense years of research and development by a core team of about 20. Eight university teams working on specific challenge areas augmented these researchers.

Watson depends on over 200 million pages of structured and unstructured data and a program capable of running trillions of operations per second. With this information backup, it attacks a Jeopardy question by parsing the question into small pieces. With the question parsed, the program then searches for relevant data. Using hundreds of decision rules, the program generates possible answers. These answers are assigned a confidence score to decide if Watson should risk offering an answer and how much to bet.

WHAT'S NEXT?

Now that the hype is over, IBM is pursuing their service strategy and applying the knowledge gained from the Watson project to real business applications. Watson's artificial intelligence design is flexible and suggests a wide variety of opportunities in industries such as finance, medicine, law enforcement, and defense. Further extensions to handheld mobile applications that tap into Watson's servers also hold great potential. IBM identified the obvious lowest hanging apples on the tree as providing healthcare solutions and has begun design of such a program.

To create a "doctor's consultant" program would likely follow a design platform similar to Watson's. For example, it would be able to:

- Data mine current medical documents to build a knowledge base.
- Integrate individual patient information.
- Use system's complex analytics to select relevant data.
- Use decision rules to provide physicians with diagnostic options.
- Rank options with confidence levels for each option.

Creating a doctor's consultant solution will not replace doctors. Although the system holds tremendous potential, it is man-made and depends on the database, data analytics, and decision rules to select options. Given the doctor's consultant input, a trained doctor makes the final patient diagnosis to supplement physical examination and experience.

The Watson project provides IBM with a flexible component to continue their decade-old strategy, moving IBM from computer hardware to service products.

*Ferrucci et al., "Building Watson," *AI Magazine,* vol. 31, no. 3 (Fall 2010).

FIGURE 2.1   Strategic Management Process

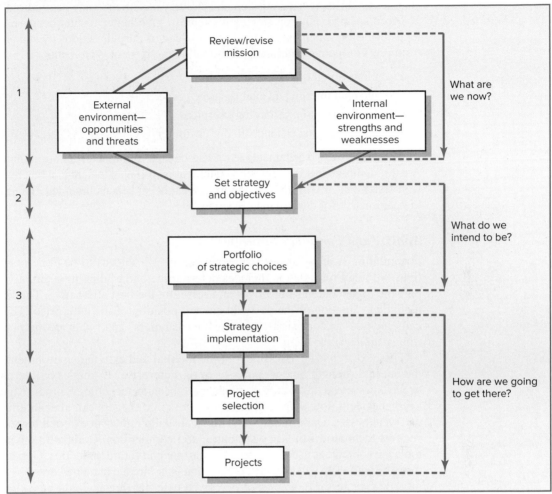

Review and Define the Organizational Mission

The mission identifies "what we want to become," or the raison d'être. Mission statements identify the scope of the organization in terms of its product or service. A written mission statement provides focus for decision making when shared by organizational managers and employees. Everyone in the organization should be keenly aware of the organization's mission. For example, at one large consulting firm, partners who fail to recite the mission statement on demand are required to buy lunch. The mission statement communicates and identifies the purpose of the organization to all stakeholders. Mission statements can be used for evaluating organization performance.

Traditional components found in mission statements are major products and services, target customers and markets, and geographical domain. In addition, statements frequently include organizational philosophy, key technologies, public image, and contribution to society. Including such factors in mission statements relates directly to business success.

Mission statements change infrequently. However, when the nature of the business changes or shifts, revised mission and strategy statements may be required.

More specific mission statements tend to give better results because of a tighter focus. Mission statements decrease the chance of false directions by stakeholders. For example, compare the phrasing of the following mission statements:

Provide hospital design services.

Provide data mining and analysis services.

Provide information technology services.

Provide high-value products to our customer.

Clearly, the first two statements leave less chance for misinterpretation than the others. A rule-of-thumb test for a mission statement is, if the statement can be anybody's mission statement, it will not provide the guidance and focus intended. The mission sets the parameters for developing objectives.

Analyze and Formulate Strategies

Formulating strategy answers the question of *what* needs to be done to reach objectives. Strategy formulation includes determining and evaluating alternatives that support the organization's objectives and selecting the best alternative. The first step is a realistic evaluation of the past and current position of the enterprise. This step typically includes an analysis of "who are the customers" and "what are their needs as they (the *customers*) see them."

The next step is an assessment of the internal and external environments. What are the internal strengths and weaknesses of the enterprise? Examples of internal strengths or weaknesses could be core competencies, such as technology, product quality, management talent, low debt, and dealer networks. Managers can alter internal strengths and weaknesses. Opportunities and threats usually represent external forces for change such as technology, industry structure, and competition. Competitive benchmarking tools are sometimes used here to assess current and future directions. Opportunities and threats are the flip sides of each other. That is, a threat can be perceived as an opportunity, or vice versa. Examples of perceived external threats could be a slowing of the economy, a maturing life cycle, exchange rates, or government regulation. Typical opportunities are increasing demand, emerging markets, and demographics. Managers or individual firms have limited opportunities to influence such external environmental factors; however, in recent years notable exceptions have been new technologies such as Apple using the iPod to create a market to sell music. The keys are to attempt to forecast fundamental industry changes and stay in a proactive mode rather than a reactive one. This assessment of the external and internal environments is known as the SWOT analysis (strengths, weaknesses, opportunities, and threats).

From this analysis, critical issues and strategic alternatives are identified. Critical analysis of the strategies includes asking questions: Does the strategy take advantage of our core competencies? Does the strategy exploit our competitive advantage? Does the strategy maximize meeting customers' needs? Does the strategy fit within our acceptable risk range? These strategic alternatives are winnowed down to a critical few that support the basic mission.

Strategy formulation ends with cascading objectives or projects assigned to lower divisions, departments, or individuals. Formulating strategy might range around 20 percent of management's effort, while determining *how* strategy will be implemented might consume 80 percent.

EXHIBIT 2.1
Characteristics of
Objectives

S	Specific	Be specific in targeting an objective
M	Measurable	Establish a measurable indicator(s) of progress
A	Assignable	Make the objective assignable to one person for completion
R	Realistic	State what can realistically be done with available resources
T	Time related	State when the objective can be achieved, that is, duration

Set Objectives to Achieve Strategies

Objectives translate the organization strategy into specific, concrete, measurable terms. Organizational objectives set targets for all levels of the organization. Objectives pinpoint the direction managers believe the organization should move toward. Objectives answer in detail *where* a firm is headed and *when* it is going to get there. Typically, objectives for the organization cover markets, products, innovation, productivity, quality, finance, profitability, employees, and consumers. In every case, objectives should be as operational as possible. That is, objectives should include a time frame, be measurable, be an identifiable state, and be realistic. Doran created the memory device shown in Exhibit 2.1, which is useful when writing objectives.[2]

Each level below the organizational objectives should support the higher-level objectives in more detail; this is frequently called cascading of objectives. For example, if a firm making leather luggage sets an objective of achieving a 40 percent increase in sales through a research and development strategy, this charge is passed to the marketing, production, and R&D departments. The R&D department accepts the firm's strategy as their objective, and their strategy becomes the design and development of a new "pull-type luggage with hidden retractable wheels." At this point the objective becomes a project to be implemented—to develop the retractable wheel luggage for market within six months within a budget of $200,000. In summary, organizational objectives drive your projects.

Implement Strategies through Projects

Implementation answers the question of *how* strategies will be realized, given available resources. The conceptual framework for strategy implementation lacks the structure and discipline found in strategy formulation. Implementation requires action and completing tasks; the latter frequently means mission-critical projects. Therefore, implementation must include attention to several key areas.

First, completing tasks requires allocation of resources. Resources typically represent funds, people, management talents, technological skills, and equipment. Frequently, implementation of projects is treated as an "addendum" rather than an integral part of the strategic management process. However, multiple objectives place conflicting demands on organizational resources. Second, implementation requires a formal and informal organization that complements and supports strategy and projects. Authority, responsibility, and performance all depend on organization structure and culture. Third, planning and control systems must be in place to be certain project activities necessary to ensure strategies are effectively performed. Fourth, motivating project contributors will be a major factor for achieving project success. Finally, areas receiving more attention in recent years are portfolio management and prioritizing

---

[2] Doran, G. T., "There's a Smart Way to Write Management Goals and Objectives," *Management Review,* November 1981, pp. 35–36.

projects. Although the strategy implementation process is not as clear as strategy formulation, all managers realize that, without implementation, success is impossible. Although the four major steps of the strategic management process have not been altered significantly over the years, the view of the time horizon in the strategy formulation process has been altered radically in the last two decades. Global competition and rapid innovation require being highly adaptive to short-run changes while being consistent in the longer run.

2.2 The Need for a Project Priority System

 LO 2-3

Understand the need for a project priority system.

Implementation of projects without a strong **priority system** linked to strategy creates problems. Three of the most obvious problems are discussed below. A priority driven **project portfolio** system can go a long way to reduce, or even eliminate, the impact of these problems.

Problem 1: The Implementation Gap

In organizations with short product life cycles, it is interesting to note that frequently participation in strategic planning and implementation includes participants from all levels within the organization. However, in perhaps 80 percent of the remaining product and service organizations, top management pretty much formulates strategy and leaves strategy implementation to functional managers. Within these broad constraints, more detailed strategies and objectives are developed by the functional managers. The fact that these objectives and strategies are made *independently* at different levels by functional groups within the organization hierarchy causes manifold problems.

Some symptoms of organizations struggling with strategy disconnect and unclear priorities are presented here.

- Conflicts frequently occur among functional managers and cause lack of trust.
- Frequent meetings are called to establish or renegotiate priorities.
- People frequently shift from one project to another, depending on current priority. Employees are confused about which projects are important.
- People are working on multiple projects and feel inefficient.
- Resources are not adequate.

Because clear linkages do not exist, the organizational environment becomes dysfunctional, confused, and ripe for ineffective implementation of organization strategy and, thus, of projects. The **implementation gap** refers to the lack of understanding and consensus of organization strategy among top and middle-level managers.

A scenario the authors have seen repeated several times follows. Top management picks their top 20 projects for the next planning period, without priorities. Each functional department—marketing, finance, operations, engineering, information technology, and human resources—selects projects from the list. Unfortunately, independent department priorities across projects are not homogenous. A project that rates first in the IT department can rate 10th in the finance department. Implementation of the projects represents conflicts of interest with animosities developing over organization resources.

If this condition exists, how is it possible to effectively implement strategy? The problem is serious. One study found that only about 25 percent of *Fortune 500* executives believe there is a strong linkage, consistency, and/or agreement between the strategies they formulate and implementation. In another study of Deloitte Consulting, Jeff MacIntyre reports, "Only 23 percent of nearly 150 global executives considered their project portfolios aligned with the core business."[3]

Middle managers considered organizational strategy to be under the purview of others or not in their realm of influence. It is the responsibility of senior management to set policies that show a distinct link between organizational strategy and objectives and projects that implement those strategies. The research of Fusco suggests the implementation gap and prioritizing projects are still overlooked by many organizations. He surveyed 280 project managers and found that 24 percent of their organizations did not even publish or circulate their objectives; in addition, 40 percent of the respondents reported that priorities among competing projects were not clear, while only 17 percent reported clear priorities.[4]

Problem 2: Organization Politics

Politics exist in every organization and can have a significant influence on which projects receive funding and high priority. This is especially true when the criteria and process for selecting projects are ill-defined and not aligned with the mission of the firm. Project selection may be based not so much on facts and sound reasoning as on the persuasiveness and power of people advocating projects.

The term **"sacred cow"** is often used to denote a project that a powerful, high-ranking official is advocating. Case in point, a marketing consultant confided that he was once hired by the marketing director of a large firm to conduct an independent, external market analysis for a new product the firm was interested in developing. His extensive research indicated that there was insufficient demand to warrant the financing of this new product. The marketing director chose to bury the report and made the consultant promise never to share this information with anyone. The director explained that this new product was the "pet idea" of the new CEO, who saw it as his legacy to the firm. He went on to describe the CEO's irrational obsession with the project and how he referred to it as his "new baby." Like a parent fiercely protecting his child, the marketing director believed that he would lose his job if such critical information ever became known.

Project sponsors play a significant role in the selection and successful implementation of product innovation projects. Project sponsors are typically high-ranking managers who endorse and lend political support for the completion of a specific project. They are instrumental in winning approval of the project and in protecting the project during the critical development stage. The importance of project sponsors should not be taken lightly. For example, a PMI global survey of over 1,000 project practitioners and leaders over a variety of industries found those organizations having active sponsors on at least 80 percent of their projects/programs have a success rate of 75 percent, 11 percentage points above the survey average of 64 percent. Many promising projects have failed to succeed due to lack of strong sponsorship.[5]

The significance of corporate politics can be seen in the ill-fated ALTO computer project at Xerox during the mid-1970s.[6] The project was a tremendous technological

[3] MacIntyre, J., *PM Network,* vol. 20, no. 11 (November 2006), pp. 32–35.

[4] Fusco, J. C., "Better Policies Provide the Key to Implementing Project Management," *Project Management Journal,* vol. 28, no. 3 (1997), pp. 38–41.

[5] PMI, "PMI's Pulse of the Profession," Project Management Institute, March 2012, p. 7.

[6] Smith, D. K., and R. C. Alexander, *Fumbling the Future: How Xerox Invented, Then Ignored the First Personal Computer* (New York: Macmillan, 1988).

success; it developed the first workable mouse, the first laser printer, the first user-friendly software, and the first local area network. All of these developments were five years ahead of their nearest competitor. Over the next five years this opportunity to dominate the nascent personal computer market was squandered because of internal in-fighting at Xerox and the absence of a strong project sponsor. (Apple's MacIntosh computer was inspired by many of these developments.)

Politics can play a role not only in project selection but also in the aspirations behind projects. Individuals can enhance their power within an organization by managing extraordinary and critical projects. Power and status naturally accrue to successful innovators and risk takers rather than to steady producers. Many ambitious managers pursue high-profile projects as a means for moving quickly up the corporate ladder.

Many would argue that politics and project management should not mix. A more proactive response is that projects and politics invariably mix and that effective project managers recognize that any significant project has political ramifications. Likewise, top management needs to develop a system for identifying and selecting projects that reduces the impact of internal politics and fosters the selection of the best projects for achieving the mission and strategy of the firm.

Problem 3: Resource Conflicts and Multitasking

Most project organizations exist in a multiproject environment. This environment creates the problems of project interdependency and the need to share resources. For example, what would be the impact on the labor resource pool of a construction company if it should win a contract it would like to bid on? Will existing labor be adequate to deal with the new project—given the completion date? Will current projects be delayed? Will subcontracting help? Which projects will have priority? Competition among project managers can be contentious. All project managers seek to have the best people for their projects. The problems of sharing resources and scheduling resources across projects grow exponentially as the number of projects rises. In multiproject environments the stakes are higher and the benefits or penalties for good or bad resource scheduling become even more significant than in most single projects.

Resource sharing also leads to multitasking. Multitasking involves starting and stopping work on one task to go and work on another project, and then returning to the work on the original task. People working on several tasks concurrently are far less efficient, especially where conceptual or physical shutdown and start-up are significant. Multitasking adds to delays and costs. Changing priorities exacerbate the multitasking problems even more. Likewise, multitasking is more evident in organizations that have too many projects for the resources they command.

The number of small and large projects in a portfolio almost always exceeds the available resources (typically by a factor of three to four times the available resources). This capacity overload inevitably leads to confusion and inefficient use of scarce organizational resources. The presence of an implementation gap, of power politics, and of multitasking adds to the problem of which projects are allocated resources first. Employee morale and confidence suffer because it is difficult to make sense of an ambiguous system. A multiproject organization environment faces major problems without a priority system that is clearly linked to the strategic plan.

In essence, to this point we have suggested that many organizations have no meaningful process for addressing the problems we have described. The first and most important change that will go a long way in addressing these and other problems is the development and use of a meaningful project priority process for project selection.

EXHIBIT 2.2
Benefits of Project Portfolio Management

- Builds discipline into project selection process.
- Links project selection to strategic metrics.
- Prioritizes project proposals across a common set of criteria, rather than on politics or emotion.
- Allocates resources to projects that align with strategic direction.
- Balances risk across all projects.
- Justifies killing projects that do not support organization strategy.
- Improves communication and supports agreement on project goals.

How can the implementation gap be narrowed so that understanding and consensus of organizational strategies run through all levels of management? How can power politics be minimized? Can a process be developed in which projects are consistently prioritized to support organizational strategies? Can the prioritized projects be used to allocate scarce organizational resources—for example, people, equipment? Can the process encourage bottom-up initiation of projects that support clear organizational targets?

What is needed is a set of integrative criteria and a process for evaluating and selecting projects that support higher-level strategies and objectives. A single-project priority system that ranks projects by their contribution to the strategic plan would make life easier. Easily said, but difficult to accomplish in practice. Organizations that managed independent projects and allocated resources ad hoc have shifted focus to selecting the right portfolio of projects to achieve their strategic objectives. This is a quickening trend. The advantages of successful project portfolio systems are becoming well recognized in project-driven organizations. See Exhibit 2.2, which lists a few key benefits; the list could easily be extended.

A project portfolio system is discussed next with emphasis on selection criteria, which is where the power of the portfolio system is established.

2.3 A Portfolio Management System

Succinctly put, the aim of portfolio management is to ensure that projects are aligned with strategic goals and prioritized appropriately. As Foti points out, portfolio management asks "What is strategic to our organization?" (2002). Portfolio management provides information that allows people to make better business decisions. Since projects clamoring for funding and people usually outnumber available resources, it is important to follow a logical and defined process for selecting the projects to implement.

Design of a project portfolio system should include classification of a project, selection criteria depending upon classification, sources of proposals, evaluating proposals, and managing the portfolio of projects.

Classification of the Project

Many organizations find they have three basic kinds of projects in their portfolio: *compliance* (emergency—must do), *operational,* and *strategic* projects. (See Figure 2.2.) Compliance projects are typically those needed to meet regulatory conditions required to operate in a region; hence, they are called "must do" projects. Emergency projects, such as building an auto parts factory destroyed by tsunami, or recovering a crashed network, are examples of must do projects. Compliance and emergency projects usually have penalties if they are not implemented. Operational projects are those that are needed to support current operations. These projects are designed to improve

FIGURE 2.2
Portfolio of Projects by Type

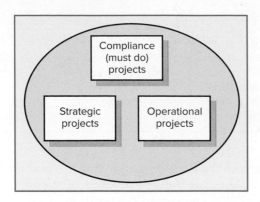

efficiency of delivery systems, reduce product costs, and improve performance. Some of these projects, given their limited scope and cost, require only immediate manager approval, while bigger, more expensive projects need extensive review. Choosing to install a new piece of equipment would be an example of the latter while modifying a production process would be an example of the former. Total quality management (TQM) projects are examples of operational projects. Finally, strategic projects are those that directly support the organization's long-run mission. They frequently are directed toward increasing revenue or market share. Examples of strategic projects are new products, research, and development. For a good, complete discussion on classification schemes found in practice, see Crawford, Hobbs, and Turne (2006).

Frequently, these three classifications are further decomposed by product type, organization divisions, and functions that will require different criteria for project selection. For example, the same criteria for the finance or legal division would not apply to the IT (information technology) department. This often requires different project selection criteria within the basic three classifications of strategic, operational, and compliance projects.

2.4 Selection Criteria

Although there are many criteria for selecting projects, selection criteria are typically identified as *financial* and *nonfinancial*. A short description of each is given next, followed by a discussion of their use in practice.

Financial Criteria

Financial Models

LO 2-4

Apply financial and nonfinancial criteria to assess the value of projects.

For most managers financial criteria are the preferred method to evaluate projects. These models are appropriate when there is a high level of confidence associated with estimates of future cash flows. Two models and examples are demonstrated here—**payback** and **net present value (NPV)**.

Project A has an initial investment of $700,000 and projected cash inflows of $225,000 for 5 years.

Project B has an initial investment of $400,000 and projected cash inflows of $110,000 for 5 years.

1. The payback model measures the time it will take to recover the project investment. Shorter paybacks are more desirable. Payback is the simplest and most widely

used model. Payback emphasizes cash flows, a key factor in business. Some managers use the payback model to eliminate unusually risky projects (those with lengthy payback periods). The major limitations of payback are that it ignores the time value of money, assumes cash inflows for the investment period (and not beyond), and does not consider profitability. The payback formula is

Payback period (yrs) = Estimated Project Cost/Annual Savings

Exhibit 2.3 compares the payback for Project A and Project B. The payback for Project A is 3.1 years and for Project B is 3.6 years. Using the payback method, both projects are acceptable since both return the initial investment in less than five years and have returns on the investment of 32.1 and 27.5 percent. Payback provides especially useful information for firms concerned with liquidity and having sufficient resources to manage their financial obligations.

Exhibit 2.3A presents the payback method.

2. The net present value (NPV) model uses management's minimum desired rate-of-return (discount rate, for example, 20 percent) to compute the present value of all net cash inflows. If the result is positive (the project meets the minimum desired rate

EXHIBIT 2.3A
Example Comparing Two Projects Using Payback Method

	A	B	C	D	E	F	G	H	I	J	K	L	M
1					Exhibit 2.3A								
2													
3					Example Comparing Two Projects Using the Payback Method								
4													
5				Project A		Project B				Formulas			
6													
7													
8		Investment	$700,000		$400,000				Project A: Payback = (D8/D9)				
9		Annual savings	$225,000		$110,000				Project B: Payback = (F8/F9)				
10													
11		Payback period*	3.1 years		3.6 years								
12													
13		Rate of return **	32.1%		27.5%				Project A: Rate of return = (D9/D8)				
14										Project B: Rate of return = (F9/F8)				
15	Project A: Accept. Less than 5 years and exceeds 15% desired rate.												
16													
17	Project B: Accept. Less than 5 years and exceeds 15% desired rate.												
18													
19	*	Note: Payback does not use the time value of money.											
20	**	Note: Rate of return is reciprocal of Payback.											
21													
22													

EXHIBIT 2.3B
Example Comparing Two Projects Using Net Present Value Method

	A	B	C	D	E	F	G	H	I	J	K	L	M
1													
2					Exhibit 2.3B								
3													
4					Example Comparing Two Projects Using NPV								
5	Project A		Year 0	Year 1	Year 2	Year 3	Year 4	Year 5	Total		Formulas		
6	Required	15%											
7	Outflows		-$700,000						-$700,000				
8	Inflows			$225,000	$225,000	$225,000	$225,000	$225,000	$1,125,000				
9	Net inflows			$225,000	$225,000	$225,000	$225,000	$225,000	$425,000	Project A: =C7+NPV(B6,D9:H9)			
10	NPV	$54,235											
11													
12													
13	Project B												
14	Required	15%											
15	Outflows		-$400,000						-$400,000				
16	Inflows			$110,000	$110,000	$110,000	$110,000	$110,000	$550,000				
17	Net inflows			$110,000	$110,000	$110,000	$110,000	$110,000	$150,000	Project B: =C15+NPV(B14,D17:H17)			
18	NPV	-$31,263											
19													
20													
21													
22	NPV comparison: Accept Project A---NPV is positive.												
23	Reject Project B---NPV is negative.												

of return), it is eligible for further consideration. If the result is negative, the project is rejected. Thus, higher positive NPVs are desirable. Excel uses this formula:

$$\text{Project NPV} = I_0 + \sum_{t=1}^{n} \frac{F_t}{(1 + k)^t}$$

where

I_0 = Initial investment (since it is an outflow, the number will be negative)

F_t = Net cash inflow for period t

k = Required rate of return

Exhibit 2.3B presents the NPV model using Microsoft Excel software. The NPV model accepts Project A, which has a *positive* NPV of $54,235. Project B is rejected since the NPV is *negative* $31,263. Compare the NPV results with the payback results. The NPV model is more realistic because it considers the time value of money, cash flows, and profitability.

When using the NPV model, the discount rate (return on investment hurdle rate) can differ for different projects. For example, the expected ROI on strategic projects is frequently set higher than operational projects. Similarly, ROIs can differ for riskier versus safer projects. The criteria for setting the ROI hurdle rate should be clear and applied consistently.

Unfortunately, pure financial models fail to include many projects where financial return is impossible to measure and/or other factors are vital to the accept or reject decision. One research study by Foti showed that companies using predominantly financial models to prioritize projects yielded unbalanced portfolios and projects that aren't strategically oriented (2003).

Nonfinancial Criteria

Financial return, while important, does not always reflect strategic importance. The past saw firms become overextended by diversifying too much. Now the prevailing thinking is that long-term survival is dependent upon developing and maintaining core competencies. Companies have to be disciplined in saying no to potentially profitable projects that are outside the realm of their core mission. This requires other criteria be considered beyond direct financial return. For example, a firm may support projects that do not have high profit margins for other strategic reasons including:

To capture larger market share

To make it difficult for competitors to enter the market

To develop an enabler product, which by its introduction will increase sales in more profitable products

To develop core technology that will be used in next-generation products

To reduce dependency on unreliable suppliers

To prevent government intervention and regulation

Less tangible criteria may also apply. Organizations may support projects to restore corporate image or enhance brand recognition. Many organizations are committed to corporate citizenship and support community development projects.

Two Multi-Criteria Selection Models

Since no single criterion can reflect strategic significance, portfolio management requires multi-criteria screening models. Two models, the checklist and multi-weighted scoring models, are described next.

EXHIBIT 2.4
Sample Selection Questions Used in Practice

Topic	Question
Strategy/alignment	What specific organization strategy does this project align with?
Driver	What business problem does the project solve?
Sponsorship	Who is the project sponsor?
Risk	What is the impact of not doing this project?
Risk	What is the project risk to our organization?
Benefits, value, ROI	What is the value of the project to this organization?
Benefits, value, ROI	When will the project show results?
Objectives	What are the project objectives?
Organization culture	Is our organization culture right for this type of project?
Resources	Will internal resources be available for this project?
Approach	Will we build or buy?
Schedule	How long will this project take?
Schedule	Is the time line realistic?
Training/resources	Will staff training be required?
Finance/portfolio	What is the estimated cost of the project?
Portfolio	Is this a new initiative or part of an existing initiative?
Portfolio	How does this project interact with current projects?
Technology	Is the technology available or new?

LO 2-5

Understand how multi-criteria models can be used to select projects.

Checklist Models   The most frequently used method in selecting projects has been the checklist. This approach basically uses a list of questions to review potential projects and to determine their acceptance or rejection. Several of the typical questions found in practice are listed in Exhibit 2.4. One large, multiproject organization has 250 different questions!

A justification of checklist models is that they allow great flexibility in selecting among many different types of projects and are easily used across different divisions and locations. Although many projects are selected using some variation of the checklist approach, this approach has serious shortcomings. Major shortcomings of this approach are that it fails to answer the relative importance or value of a potential project to the organization and fails to allow for comparison with other potential projects. Each potential project will have a different set of positive and negative answers. How do you compare? Ranking and prioritizing projects by their importance is difficult, if not impossible. This approach also leaves the door open to the potential opportunity for power plays, politics, and other forms of manipulation. To overcome these serious shortcomings experts recommend the use of a multi-weighted scoring model to select projects, which is examined next.

Multi-Weighted Scoring Models   A weighted scoring model typically uses several weighted selection criteria to evaluate project proposals. Weighted scoring models will generally include qualitative and/or quantitative criteria. Each selection criterion is assigned a weight. Scores are assigned to each criterion for the project, based on its importance to the project being evaluated. The weights and scores are multiplied to get a total weighted score for the project. Using these multiple screening criteria, projects can then be compared using the weighted score. Projects with higher weighted scores are considered better.

Selection criteria need to mirror the critical success factors of an organization. For example, 3M set a target that 25 percent of the company's sales would come from products fewer than four years old versus the old target of 20 percent. Their priority

SNAPSHOT FROM PRACTICE 2.2   Crisis IT

In May 2007, Frontier Airlines Holdings hired Gerry Coady as chief information officer (CIO). Nearly a year later the airline filed for bankruptcy under Chapter 11. In an interview Coady describes how he managed IT projects during the bankruptcy and recession crisis of 2008–2009.

Fundamentally, Coady faced a situation of too many projects and too few resources. Coady used a strategy of focusing on reducing the number of projects in the portfolio. He put together a steering committee of senior management that reviewed several hundred projects. The end result was a reduction to less than 30 projects remaining in the portfolio.

© PRNewsFoto/Genesis, Inc.

How Can You Get to a Backlog of over 100 Projects?

"There are never enough resources to get everything done." Backlogs build over time. Sacred cow projects get included in the selection system. Projects proposed from people who have left the airline still reside in the project portfolio. Non-value-added projects somehow make their way into the project portfolio. Soon the queue gets longer. With everyone in IT working on too many projects concurrently, project completion and productivity are slow.

Which Projects Remain?

To cut the number of projects, the steering committee used a weighting scheme that reflected the airline's priorities, which were: fly safe, generate revenue, reduce costs, and customer service. The weighting scheme easily weeded out the fluff. Coady noted that "by the time you get to the 20s the margin of differentiation gets narrower and narrower." Of the remaining projects, project sponsors had to have solid justification why their project is important. Reduction of the number of projects places emphasis on high value projects.

What Advice Does Coady Have for Crisis Management?

In times of crisis, it is easier to take bold steps to make changes. But you need to have a clear vision of what you should be focusing on with the resources available. Coady suggests, "It comes back to really having a good idea of what the initial business case for a project is and what resources it is consuming, both people and otherwise."

Source: Worthen, B., "Crisis IT," *The Wall Street Journal,* April 20, 2009, p. 6.

system for project selection strongly reflects this new target. On the other hand, failure to pick the right factors will render the screening process "useless" in short order. See Snapshot from Practice 2.2: Crisis IT.

Figure 2.3 represents a project scoring matrix using some of the factors found in practice. The screening criteria selected are shown across the top of the matrix (e.g., stay within core competencies . . . ROI of 18 percent plus). Management weights each criterion (a value of 0 to a high of, say, 3) by its relative importance to the organization's objectives and strategic plan. Project proposals are then submitted to a project **priority team** or project office.

Each project proposal is then evaluated by its relative contribution/value added to the selected criteria. Values of 0 to a high of 10 are assigned to each criterion for each project. This value represents the project's fit to the specific criterion. For example, project 1 appears to fit well with the strategy of the organization since it is given a value of 8. Conversely, project 1 does nothing to support reducing defects (its value is 0). Finally, this model applies the management weights to each criterion by importance using a value of 1 to 3. For example, ROI and strategic fit have a weight of 3, while urgency and core competencies have weights of 2. Applying the weight to each

FIGURE 2.3   Project Screening Matrix

Criteria Weight	Stay within core competencies	Strategic fit	Urgency	25% of sales from new products	Reduce defects to less than 1%	Improve customer loyalty	ROI of 18% plus	Weighted total
	2.0	3.0	2.0	2.5	1.0	1.0	3.0	
Project 1	1	8	2	6	0	6	5	66
Project 2	3	3	2	0	0	5	1	27
Project 3	9	5	2	0	2	2	5	56
Project 4	3	0	10	0	0	6	0	32
Project 5	1	10	5	10	0	8	9	102
Project 6	6	5	0	2	0	2	7	55
⋮								
Project n	5	5	7	0	10	10	8	83

criterion, the priority team derives the weighted total points for each project. For example, project 5 has the highest value of 102 [$(2 \times 1) + (3 \times 10) + (2 \times 5) + (2.5 \times 10) + (1 \times 0) + (1 \times 8) + (3 \times 9) = 102$] and project 2 has a low value of 27. If the resources available create a cutoff threshold of 50 points, the priority team would eliminate projects 2 and 4. (Note: Project 4 appears to have some urgency, but it is not classified as a "must" project. Therefore, it is screened with all other proposals.) Project 5 would receive first priority, project n second, and so on. In rare cases where resources are severely limited and project proposals are similar in weighted rank, it is prudent to pick the project placing less demand on resources. Weighted multiple criteria models similar to this one are rapidly becoming the dominant choice for prioritizing projects.

At this point in the discussion it is wise to stop and put things into perspective. While selection models like the one above may yield numerical solutions to project selection decisions, models should not make the final *decisions*—the people using the models should. No model, no matter how sophisticated, can capture the total reality it is meant to represent. Models are tools for guiding the evaluation process so that the decision makers will consider relevant issues and reach a meeting of the minds as to which projects should be supported and not supported. This is a much more subjective process than calculations suggest.

2.5 Applying a Selection Model

LO 2-6

Apply an objective priority system to project selection.

Project Classification

It is not necessary to have exactly the same criteria for the different types of projects discussed above (strategic and operations). However, experience shows most organizations use similar criteria across all types of projects, with perhaps one or two criteria specific to the type of project—e.g., strategic breakthrough versus operational.

Regardless of criteria differences among different types of projects, the most important criterion for selection is the project's fit to the organization strategy. Therefore, this criterion should be consistent across all types of projects and carry a high priority relative to other criteria. This uniformity across all priority models used can keep departments from suboptimizing the use of organization resources. Project proposals should be classified by type, so the appropriate criteria can be used to evaluate them.

Selecting a Model

In the past, financial criteria were used almost to the exclusion of other criteria. However, in the last two decades we have witnessed a dramatic shift to include multiple criteria in project selection. Concisely put, profitability alone is simply not an adequate measure of contribution; however, it is still an important criterion, especially for projects that enhance revenue and market share such as breakthrough R&D projects.

Today, senior management is interested in identifying the potential mix of projects that will yield the best use of human and capital resources to maximize return on investment in the long run. Factors such as researching new technology, public image, ethical position, protection of the environment, core competencies, and strategic fit might be important criteria for selecting projects. Weighted scoring criteria seem the best alternative to meet this need.

Weighted scoring models result in bringing projects to closer alignment with strategic goals. If the scoring model is published and available to everyone in the organization, some discipline and credibility are attached to the selection of projects. The number of wasteful projects using resources is reduced. Politics and "sacred cow" projects are exposed. Project goals are more easily identified and communicated using the selection criteria as corroboration. Finally, using a weighted scoring approach helps project managers understand how their project was selected, how their project contributes to organization goals, and how it compares with other projects. Project selection is one of the most important decisions guiding the future success of an organization.

Criteria for project selection are the area where the power of your portfolio starts to manifest itself. New projects are aligned with the strategic goals of the organization. With a clear method for selecting projects in place, project proposals can be solicited.

Sources and Solicitation of Project Proposals

As you would guess, projects should come from anyone who believes his or her project will add value to the organization. However, many organizations restrict proposals from specific levels or groups within the organization. This could be an opportunity lost. Good ideas are not limited to certain types or classes of organization stakeholders. Encourage and keep solicitations open to all sources—internal and external sponsors.

Figure 2.4A provides an example of a proposal form for an automatic vehicular tracking (Automatic Vehicle Location) public transportation project. Figure 2.4B presents a preliminary risk analysis for a 500-acre wind farm. Many organizations use risk analysis templates to gain a quick insight of a project's inherent risks. Risk factors depend on the organization and type of projects. This information is useful in balancing the project portfolio and identifying major risks when executing the project. Project risk analysis is the subject of Chapter 7.

FIGURE 2.4A
A Proposal Form for an Automatic Vehicular Tracking (AVL) Public Transportation Project

Project Proposal Form

Date: Jan 22, 2xxx   Proposal # 11   Sponsor J. Moran

Project classification?
Strategic_____ Infrastructure __X__ Compliance_____

What business problem does the project solve?
Increase customer satisfaction through kiosk and Web site for bus, streetcar, and fast rail
Enhance driver and traveler safety   Hyperlink to: AVL.tri-met.org

How does this project align with our organization strategy?
Increase customer ridership through better passenger travel planning & scheduling decisions
Faster response to accidents

What are the major deliverables of the project?
GPS vehicle tracking system, Internet access, schedule screen

What is the impact of not doing this project?
Not meeting ridership goals

What are the three major risks for this project?
Cost overruns   Integration of fast rail, bus, and streetcar systems
Hacking system

How will we measure success?   Increased ridership
Customer satisfaction
Meeting budget and schedule

Yes [X] No [ ] Will this project require internal resources?
Yes [X] No [ ] Available?

What is the estimated cost of the project? $10 million

How long will this project take? __22__ Weeks

Oversight action: Accept [X]   Return [ ]

Signature __XXXXXX__   Date: Feb. 7, 2xxx

In some cases organizations will solicit ideas for projects when the knowledge requirements for the project are not available in the organization. Typically, the organization will issue an RFP (Request for Proposal) to contractors/vendors with adequate experience to implement the project. In one example, a hospital published an RFP that asked for a bid to design and build a new operating room that uses the latest technology. Several architecture firms submitted bids to the hospital. The bids for the project were evaluated internally against other potential projects. When the project was accepted as a go, other criteria were used to select the best qualified bidder.

FIGURE 2.4B
Risk Analysis for a 500-Acre Wind Farm

Brief Risk Assessment

Purpose: To draw attention to apparent project risks that will need management attention.

What are the four major risks of this project?
1. *Government incentives curtailed*
2. *Land use injunction*
3. *Energy price decrease*
4. *New import tax*

Rank risks above by "probability" and "impact" on the chart below by High, Medium or Low.

Risk Intensity Rating

Risk	Probability	Impact
1. *Government incentives curtailed*	*High*	*High*
2. *Land use injunction*	*Medium*	*High*
3. *Energy price decrease*	*Medium*	*Medium*
4. *New import tax*	*Low*	*High*

Check other project risk factors:

Complexity	Low ☐	Average ☒	High ☐
Resource skills	Good ☒	Okay ☐	Lacking ☐
Technology	Low ☐	Average ☒	High ☐

Reviewed by _____*Rachel*_____   **Date** _____*April 1, 2xxx*_____

Ranking Proposals and Selection of Projects

Culling through so many proposals to identify those that add the most value requires a structured process. Figure 2.5 shows a flow chart of a screening process beginning with the creation of an idea for a project. See Figure 12.3 for a template for evaluating contractors.

Data and information are collected to assess the value of the proposed project to the organization and for future backup. If the sponsor decides to pursue the project on the basis of the collected data, it is forwarded to the project priority team (or the project office). Note that the sponsor knows which criteria will be used to accept or reject the project. Given the selection criteria and current portfolio of projects, the priority team rejects or accepts the project. If the project is accepted, the priority team sets implementation in motion.

Figure 2.6 is a partial example of an evaluation form used by a large company to prioritize and select new projects. The form distinguishes between must and want objectives. If a project does not meet designated "must" objectives, it is not considered and is removed from consideration. Organization (or division) objectives have been ranked and weighted by their relative importance—for example, "Improve external customer service" carries a relative weight of 83 when compared to other want objectives. The want objectives are directly linked to objectives found in the strategic plan.

FIGURE 2.5
**Project Screening
Process**

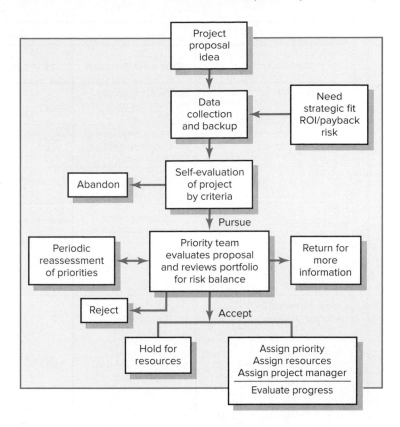

Impact definitions represent a further refinement to the screening system. They are developed to gauge the predicted impact a specific project would have on meeting a particular objective. A numeric scheme is created and anchored by defining criteria. To illustrate how this works, let's examine the $5 million in new sales objective. A "0" is assigned if the project will have no impact on sales or less than $100,000, a "1" is given if predicted sales are more than $100,000 but less than $500,000, a "2" if greater than $500,000. These impact assessments are combined with the relative importance of each objective to determine the predicted overall contribution of a project to strategic objectives. For example, project 26 creates an opportunity to fix field problems, has no effect on sales, and will have major impact on customer service. On these three objectives, project 26 would receive a score of 265 [99 + 0 + (2 × 83)]. Individual weighted scores are totaled for each project and are used to prioritize projects.

Responsibility for Prioritizing

Prioritizing can be an uncomfortable exercise for managers. But prioritizing projects is a major responsibility for senior management. Prioritizing means discipline, accountability, responsibility, constraints, reduced flexibility, and loss of power. Top management commitment means more than giving a blessing to the priority system; it means management will have to rank and weigh, in concrete terms, the objectives and strategies they believe to be most critical to the organization. This public declaration of commitment can be risky if the ranked objectives later prove to be poor choices, but setting the course for the organization is top management's job. The good news is, if management is truly trying to direct the organization to a strong future position, a good project priority system supports their efforts and develops a culture in which everyone is contributing to the goals of the organization.

FIGURE 2.6
Priority Screening Analysis

			Project number			
Must objectives		**Must meet if impacts**	**...26**	**27**	**28**	**29**
All activities meet current legal, safety, and environmental standards		Yes-Meets objective No-Does not meet obj N/A-No impact	n/a			
All new products will have a complete market analysis		Yes-Meets objective No-Does not meet obj N/A-No impact	yes			
Want objectives	**Relative Importance 1-100**	**Single project impact definitions**	Weighted score	Weighted score	Weighted score	Weighted score
Provides immediate response to field problems	99	0 Does not address 1 = Opportunity to fix 2 Urgent problem	99			
Create $5 million in new sales by 20xx	88	0 < $100,000 1 = $100,000–500,000 2 > $500,000	0			
Improve external customer service	83	0 Minor impact 1 = Significant impact 2 Major impact	166			
Total weighted score						
Priority						

2.6 Managing the Portfolio System

2-7

Understand the need to manage the project portfolio.

Managing the portfolio takes the selection system one step higher in that the merits of a particular project are assessed within the context of existing projects. At the same time it involves monitoring and adjusting selection criteria to reflect the strategic focus of the organization. This requires constant effort. The priority system can be managed by a small group of key employees in a small organization. Or, in larger organizations, the priority system can be managed by the project office or a governance team of senior managers.

Senior Management Input

Management of a portfolio system requires two major inputs from senior management. First, senior management must provide guidance in establishing selection criteria that strongly align with the current organization strategies. Second, senior management must annually decide how they wish to balance the available organizational resources (people and capital) among the different types of projects. A preliminary decision of balance must be made by top management (e.g., 20 percent compliance, 50 percent strategic, and 30 percent operational) before project selection takes place, although the balance may be changed when the projects submitted are reviewed. Given these inputs the priority team or project office can carry out its many responsibilities, which include supporting project sponsors and representing the interests of the total organization.

The Governance Team Responsibilities

The governance team, or project office, is responsible for publishing the priority of every project and ensuring the process is open and free of power politics. For example, most organizations using a governance team or project office use an electronic bulletin board to disperse the current portfolio of projects, the current status of each project, and current issues. This open communication discourages power plays. Over time the governance team evaluates the progress of the projects in the portfolio. If this whole process is managed well, it can have a profound impact on the success of an organization. See Snapshot from Practice 2.3: Project Code Names for the rationale behind titles given to projects.

SNAPSHOT FROM PRACTICE 2.3   Project Code Names*

 What do Yangtze, Operation Iceberg, and Get Blue have in common? They are all code names given to projects. Project code names are used for several reasons:

- To uniquely identify the project within the organization.

  Apple Corporation used to name major releases of MAC OS X after big cats such as **Jaguar, Tiger, Panther,** and **Leopard,** but now name them after national parks (i.e., **Yosemite**).

- To assist in maintaining secrecy of the project against rival concerns.

  Oxcart was used by U.S. Department of Defense during the height of the cold war for the secret development of super sonic fighter jet.

- As a public relations tool to garner support for project objectives

  Operation Just Cause was the name given by U.S. government for the 1989 invasion of Panama, which ousted corrupt leader Manual Noriega.

- To inspire and elevate performance.

  Revolution was used by Nintendo for groundbreaking Wii video game console.

© McGraw-Hill Education/Jill Braaten, photographer

Often on small projects names convey a playful sense of humor. For example, a set of interrelated software projects were all named after Smurf Characters (**Papa Smurf, Handy Smurf, Dreamy Smurf,...**). Other times the project name reflects an inside joke, for example, one software project was named ALINA, which was an acronym for At Least It Is Not Access.

*Sieminski, G. C., "The Art of Naming Operations," *Parameters,* Autumn 1995, pp. 81-98; "Operation Know-It-All: The Indispensable Guide to Choosing Good Project Names," articulatemarketing.com, accessed December 20, 2015.

Constant scanning of the external environment to determine if organizational focus and/or selection criteria need to be changed is imperative! Periodic priority review and changes need to keep current with the changing environment and keep a unified vision of organization focus. Regardless of the criteria used for selection, each project should be evaluated by the same criteria. If projects are classified by must do, operation, and strategic, each project in its class should be evaluated by the same criteria. Enforcing the project priority system is crucial. Keeping the whole system open and aboveboard is important to maintaining the integrity of the system and keeping new, young executives from going around the system. For example, communicating which projects are approved, project ranks, current status of in-process projects, and any changes in priority criteria will discourage people from bypassing the system.

Balancing the Portfolio for Risks and Types of Projects

A major responsibility of the priority team is to balance projects by type, risk, and resource demand. This requires a total organization perspective. Hence, a proposed project that ranks high on most criteria may not be selected because the organization portfolio already includes too many projects with the same characteristics—e.g., project risk level, use of key resources, high cost, nonrevenue producing, long durations. Balancing the portfolio of projects is as important as project selection. Organizations need to evaluate each new project in terms of what it adds to the project mix. Short-term needs need to be balanced with long-term potential. Resource usage needs to be optimized across all projects, not just the most important project.

Two types of risk are associated with projects. First are risks associated with the total portfolio of projects, which should reflect the organization's risk profile. Second are specific project risks that can inhibit the execution of a project, such as schedule, cost, and technical. In this chapter we look only to balancing the organizational risks inherent in the project portfolio, such as market risk, ability to execute, time to market, and technology advances. Project-specific risks will be covered in detail in Chapter 7.

David and Jim Matheson studied R&D organizations and developed a classification scheme that could be used for assessing a project portfolio.[7] They separated projects in terms of degree of difficulty and commercial value and came up with four basic types of projects:

> *Bread-and-butter* projects are relatively easy to accomplish and produce modest commercial value. They typically involve evolutionary improvements to current products and services. Examples include software upgrades and manufacturing cost reduction efforts.
>
> *Pearls* are low risk development projects with high commercial payoffs. They represent revolutionary commercial advances using proven technology. Examples include next-generation integrated circuit chip and subsurface imaging to locate oil and gas.
>
> *Oysters* are high risk, high value projects. These projects involve technological breakthroughs with tremendous commercial potential. Examples include embryonic DNA treatments and new kinds of metal alloys.
>
> *White elephants* are projects that at one time showed promise but are no longer viable. Examples include products for a saturated market or a potent energy source with toxic side-effects.

[7] Matheson, D., and J. Matheson, *The Smart Organization* (Boston: Harvard Business School Press, 1998), pp. 203–209.

The Mathesons report that organizations often have too many white elephants and too few pearls and oysters. To maintain strategic advantage they recommend that organizations capitalize on pearls, eliminate or reposition white elephants, and balance resources devoted to bread-and-butter and oyster projects to achieve alignment with overall strategy. Although their research centers on R&D organizations, their observations appear to hold true for all types of project organizations.

Summary

Multiple competing projects, limited skilled resources, dispersed virtual teams, time to market pressures, and limited capital serve as forces for the emergence of project portfolio management that provides the infrastructure for managing multiple projects and linking business strategy with project selection. The most important element of this system is the creation of a ranking system that utilizes multiple criteria that reflect the mission and strategy of the firm. It is critical to communicate priority criteria to all organizational stakeholders so that the criteria can be the source of inspiration for new project ideas.

Every significant project selected should be ranked and the results published. Senior management must take an active role in setting priorities and supporting the priority system. Going around the priority system will destroy its effectiveness. The project governance team needs to consist of seasoned managers who are capable of asking tough questions and distinguishing facts from fiction. Resources (people, equipment, and capital) for major projects must be clearly allocated and not conflict with daily operations or become an overload task.

The governance team needs to scrutinize significant projects in terms of not only their strategic value but also their fit with the portfolio of projects currently being implemented. Highly ranked projects may be deferred or even turned down if they upset the current balance among risks, resources, and strategic initiatives. Project selection must be based not only on the merits of the specific project but also on what it contributes to the current project portfolio mix. This requires a holistic approach to aligning projects with organizational strategy and resources.

The importance of aligning projects with organization strategy cannot be overstated. We have discussed two types of models found in practice. Checklist models are easy to develop and are justified primarily on the basis of flexibility across different divisions and locations. Unfortunately, questionnaire checklist models do not allow comparison of the relative value (rank) of alternative projects in contributing toward organization strategy. The latter is the major reason the authors prefer multi-weighted scoring models. These models keep project selection highly focused on alignment with organization strategy. Weighted scoring models require major effort in establishing the criteria and weights.

Key Terms

Implementation gap, *34*	Payback, *38*	Project sponsor, *35*
Net present value (NVP), *38*	Priority system, *34*	Sacred cow, *35*
	Priority team, *42*	Strategic management, *29*
Organization politics, *35*	Project portfolio, *34*	

Review Questions

1. Describe the major components of the strategic management process.
2. Explain the role projects play in the strategic management process.
3. How are projects linked to the strategic plan?
4. The portfolio of projects is typically represented by compliance, strategic, and operations projects. What impact can this classification have on project selection?
5. Why does the priority system described in this chapter require that it be open and published? Does the process encourage bottom-up initiation of projects? Does it discourage some projects? Why?
6. Why should an organization not rely only on ROI to select projects?
7. Discuss the pros and cons of the checklist versus the weighted factor method of selecting projects.

Exercises

1. You manage a hotel resort located on the South Beach on the Island of Kauai in Hawaii. You are shifting the focus of your resort from a traditional fun-in-the-sun destination to eco-tourism. (Eco-tourism focuses on environmental awareness and education.) How would you classify the following projects in terms of compliance, strategic, and operational?
   a. Convert the pool heating system from electrical to solar power.
   b. Build a four-mile nature hiking trail.
   c. Renovate the horse barn.
   d. Launch a new promotional campaign with Hawaii Airlines.
   e. Convert 12 adjacent acres into a wildlife preserve.
   f. Update all the bathrooms in condos that are 10 years old or older.
   g. Change hotel brochures to reflect eco-tourism image.
   h. Test and revise disaster response plan.
   i. Introduce wireless Internet service in café and lounge areas.

   How easy was it to classify these projects? What made some projects more difficult than others? What do you think you now know that would be useful for managing projects at the hotel?

2.* Two new software projects are proposed to a young, start-up company. The Alpha project will cost $150,000 to develop and is expected to have annual net cash flow of $40,000. The Beta project will cost $200,000 to develop and is expected to have annual net cash flow of $50,000. The company is very concerned about their cash flow. Using the payback period, which project is better from a cash flow standpoint? Why?

3. A five-year project has a projected net cash flow of $15,000, $25,000, $30,000, $20,000, and $15,000 in the next five years. It will cost $50,000 to implement the project. If the required rate of return is 20 percent, conduct a discounted cash flow calculation to determine the NPV.

4. You work for the 3T company, which expects to earn at least 18 percent on its investments. You have to choose between two similar projects. The following chart shows the cash information for each project. Which of the two projects would you fund if the decision is based only on financial information? Why?

*The solution to these exercises can be found in Appendix One.

Omega				Alpha			
Year	Inflow	Outflow	Netflow	Year	Inflow	Outflow	Netflow
Y0	0	$225,000	−225,000	Y0	0	$300,000	−300,000
Y1	0	190,000	−190,000	Y1	$ 50,000	100,000	−50,000
Y2	$ 150,000	0	150,000	Y2	150,000	0	150,000
Y3	220,000	30,000	190,000	Y3	250,000	50,000	200,000
Y4	215,000	0	215,000	Y4	250,000	0	250,000
Y5	205,000	30,000	175,000	Y5	200,000	50,000	150,000
Y6	197,000	0	197,000	Y6	180,000	0	180,000
Y7	100,000	30,000	70,000	Y7	120,000	30,000	90,000
Total	1,087,000	505,000	582,000	Total	1,200,000	530,000	670,000

5.* You are the head of the project selection team at SIMSOX. Your team is considering three different projects. Based on past history, SIMSOX expects at least a rate of return of 20 percent.

Given the following information for each project, which one should be SIMSOX's first priority? Should SIMSOX fund any of the other projects? If so, what should be the order of priority based on return on investment?

Project: **Dust Devils**

Year	Investment	Revenue Stream
0	$500,000	0
1		50,000
2		250,000
3		350,000

Project: **Osprey**

Year	Investment	Revenue Stream
0	$250,000	0
1		75,000
2		75,000
3		75,000
4		50,000

Project: **Voyagers**

Year	Investment	Revenue Stream
0	$75,000	0
1		15,000
2		25,000
3		50,000
4		50,000
5		150,000

*The solution to these exercises can be found in Appendix One.

6. You are the head of the project selection team at Broken Arrow records. Your team is considering three different recording projects. Based on past history, Broken Arrow expects at least a rate of return of 20 percent.

   Given the following information for each project, which one should be Broken Arrow's first priority? Should Broken Arrow fund any of the other projects? If so, what should be the order of priority based on return on investment?

Recording Project: **Time Fades Away**

Year	Investment	Revenue Stream
0	$600,000	0
1		600,000
2		75,000
3		20,000
4		15,000
5		10,000

Recording Project: **On the Beach**

Year	Investment	Revenue Stream
0	$400,000	0
1		400,000
2		100,000
3		25,000
4		20,000
5		10,000

Recording Project: **Tonight's the Night**

Year	Investment	Revenue Stream
0	$200,000	0
1		200,000
2		125,000
3		75,000
4		20,000
5		10,000

7. The Custom Bike Company has set up a weighted scoring matrix for evaluation of potential projects. Below are five projects under consideration.

   a. Using the scoring matrix in the following chart, which project would you rate highest? Lowest?

   b. If the weight for "Strong Sponsor" is changed from 2.0 to 5.0, will the project selection change? What are the three highest weighted project scores with this new weight?

   c. Why is it important that the weights mirror critical strategic factors?

Project Screening Matrix

Criteria Weight	Strong sponsor	Supports business strategy	Urgency	10% of sales from new products	Competition	Fill market gap	Weighted total
	2.0	5.0	4.0	3.0	1.0	3.0	
Project 1	9	5	2	0	2	5	
Project 2	3	7	2	0	5	1	
Project 3	6	8	2	3	6	8	
Project 4	1	0	5	10	6	9	
Project 5	3	10	10	1	8	0	

References

Adler, P. S., et al., "Getting the Most Out of Your Product Development Process," *Harvard Business Review,* vol. 74, no. 2, pp. 134–52.

Benko, C., and F. W. McFarlan, *Connecting the Dots: Aligning Projects With Objectives in Unpredictable Times* (Boston: Harvard Business School Press, 2003).

Bigelow, D., "Want to Ensure Quality? Think Project Portfolio Management," *PM Network,* vol. 16, no. 1 (April 2002), pp. 16–17.

Bloomberg Businessweek, "IBM Wants to Put Watson in Your Pocket," September 17–23, 2012, pp. 41–42.

Boyer, C., "Make Profit Your Priority," *PM Network,* vol. 15, no. 10 (October 2003), pp. 37–42.

Cohen, D., and R. Graham, *The Project Manager's MBA* (San Francisco: Jossey-Bass, 2001), pp. 58–59.

Crawford, L., B. Hobbs, and J. R. Turne, "Aligning Capability with Strategy: Categorizing of Projects to Do the Right Projects and Do Them Right," *Project Management Journal,* vol. 37, no. 2 (June 2006), pp. 38–50.

Descamps, J. P., "Mastering the Dance of Change: Innovation as a Way of Life," *Prism,* Second Quarter, 1999, pp. 61–67.

Doran, G. T., "There's a Smart Way to Write Management Goals and Objectives," *Management Review,* November 1981, pp. 35–36.

Floyd, S. W., and B. Woolridge, "Managing Strategic Consensus: The Foundation of Effectiveness Implementation," *Academy of Management Executives,* vol. 6, no. 4 (1992), pp. 27–39.

Foti, R., "Louder Than Words," *PM Network,* December 2002, pp. 22–29. Also see Foti, R., "Make Your Case, Not All Projects Are Equal," *PM Network,* vol. 31, no. 7 (2003), pp. 35–43.

Frank, L., "On Demand," *PM Network,* vol. 18, no. 4 (April 2004), pp. 58–62.

Friedman, Thomas L., *Hot, Flat, and Crowded* (New York: Farrar, Straus, and Giroux, 2008).

Fusco, J. C., "Better Policies Provide the Key to Implementing Project Management," *Project Management Journal,* vol. 28. no. 3 (1997), pp. 38–41.

Helm, J., and K. Remington, "Effective Project Sponsorship: An Evaluation of the Executive Sponsor in Complex Infrastructure Projects by Senior Project Managers," *Project Management Journal,* vol. 36, no. 1 (September 2005), pp. 51–61.

Hutchens, G., "Doing the Numbers," *PM Network,* vol. 16, no. 4 (March 2002), p. 20.

Johnson, R. E., "Scrap Capital Project Evaluations," *Chief Financial Officer,* May 1998, p. 14.

Kaplan, R. S., and D. P. Norton, "The Balanced Scorecard—Measures That Drive Performance," *Harvard Business Review,* January–February 1992, pp. 73–79. Also see Kaplan, Robert, http://balancedscorecard.org.

Kenny, J., "Effective Project Management for Strategic Innovation and Change in an Organizational Context," *Project Management Journal,* vol. 34, no. 1 (2003), pp. 45–53.

Kharbanda, O. P., and J. K. Pinto, *What Made Gertie Gallop: Learning from Project Failures* (New York: Van Nostrand Reinhold, 1996), pp. 106–11, 263–83.

Korte, R. F., and T. J. Chermack, "Changing Organizational Culture with Scenario Planning," *Futures,* vol. 39, no. 6 (August 2007), pp. 645–56.

Leifer, R., C. M. McDermott, G. C. O'Connor, L. S. Peters, M. Price, and R. W. Veryzer, *Radical Innovation: How Mature Companies Can Outsmart Upstarts* (Boston: Harvard Business School Press, 2000).

MacIntyre, J., *PM Network,* vol. 20, no. 11 (November 2006), pp. 32–35.

Magretta, Joan, *Understanding Michael Porter: The Essential Guide to Competition and Strategy* (Boston: Harvard Business Press Book, 2011).

Matheson, D., and J. Matheson, *The Smart Organization* (Boston: Harvard Business School Press, 1998), pp. 203–9.

Milosevic, D. Z., and S. Srivannaboon, "A Theoretical Framework for Aligning Project Management with Business Strategy," *Project Management Journal,* vol. 37, no. 3 (August 2006), pp. 98–110.

Morris, P. W., and A. Jamieson, "Moving from Corporate Strategy to Project Strategy," *Project Management Journal,* vol. 36, no. 4 (December 2005), pp. 5–18.

Motta, Silva, and Rogério Hermida Quintella, "Assessment of Non-Financial Criteria in the Selection of Investment Projects for Seed Capital Funding: The Contribution of Scientometrics and Patentometrics," *Journal of Technology Management Innovation,* vol. 7, no. 3 (2012).

PMI, "PMI's Pulse of the Profession," March 2012, Project Management Institute, p. 7.

Raskin, P., et al., *Great Transitions: The Promise and Lure of the Times Ahead,* retrieved June 3, 2008, *www.gtinitiative.org/documents/Great_Transitions.pdf*

Schwartz, Peter, and Doug Randall, "An Abrupt Climate Change Scenario and its Implications for United States National Security," Global Business Network, Inc., October 2003.

Shenhar, A., "Strategic Project Leadership: Focusing Your Project on Business Success," *Proceedings of the Project Management Institute Annual Seminars & Symposium,* San Antonio, Texas, October 3–10, 2002, CD. Also see Shenhar, Aaron, *Reinventing Project Management* (Harvard Business School, 2007).

Sieminski, G. C., "The Art of Naming Operations," *Parameters,* Autumn 1995, pp. 81–98.

Smith, D. K., and R. C. Alexander, *Fumbling the Future: How Xerox Invented, Then Ignored the First Personal Computer* (New York: Macmillan, 1988).

Swanson, S., "All Things Considered," *PM Network,* vol. 25, no. 2 (February 2011), pp. 36–40.

Woodward, H., "Winning in a World of Limited Project Spending," *Proceedings of the Project Management Institute Global Congress North America,* Baltimore, Maryland, September 18–12, 2003, CD.

Case 2.1

Hector Gaming Company

Hector Gaming Company (HGC) is an educational gaming company specializing in young children's educational games. HGC has just completed their fourth year of operation. This year was a banner year for HGC. The company received a large influx of capital for growth by issuing stock privately through an investment banking firm. It appears the return on investment for this past year will be just over 25 percent with zero debt! The growth rate for the last two years has been approximately 80 percent each year. Parents and grandparents of young children have been buying HGC's products almost as fast as they are developed. Every member of the 56-person firm is enthusiastic and looking forward to helping the firm grow to be the largest and best educational gaming company in the world. The founder of the firm, Sally Peters, has been written up in *Young Entrepreneurs* as "the young entrepreneur to watch." She has been able to develop an organization culture in which all stakeholders are committed to innovation, continuous improvement, and organization learning.

Last year, 10 top managers of HGC worked with McKinley Consulting to develop the organization's strategic plan. This year the same 10 managers had a retreat in Aruba to formulate next year's strategic plan using the same process suggested by McKinley Consulting. Most executives seem to have a consensus of where the firm should go in the intermediate and long term. But there is little consensus on how this should be accomplished. Peters, now president of HGC, feels she may be losing control. The frequency of conflicts seems to be increasing. Some individuals are always requested for any new project created. When resource conflicts occur among projects, each project manager believes his or her project is most important. More projects are not meeting deadlines and are coming in over budget. Yesterday's management meeting revealed some top HGC talent have been working on an international business game for college students. This project does not fit the organization vision or market niche. At times it seems everyone is marching to his or her own drummer. Somehow more focus is needed to ensure everyone agrees on *how* strategy should be implemented, given the resources available to the organization.

Yesterday's meeting alarmed Peters. These emerging problems are coming at a bad time. Next week HGC is ramping up the size of the organization, number of new products per year, and marketing efforts. Fifteen new people will join HGC next month. Peters is concerned that policies be in place that will ensure the new people are used most productively. An additional potential problem looms on the horizon. Other gaming companies have noticed the success HGC is having in their niche market; one company tried to hire a key product development employee away from HGC. Peters wants HGC to be ready to meet any potential competition head on and to discourage any new entries into their market. Peters knows HGC is project driven; however, she is not as confident that she has a good handle on how such an organization should be managed—especially with such a fast growth rate and potential competition closer to becoming a reality. The magnitude of emerging problems demands quick attention and resolution.

Peters has hired you as a consultant. She has suggested the following format for your consulting contract. You are free to use another format if it will improve the effectiveness of the consulting engagement.

What is our major problem?

Identify some symptoms of the problem.

What is the major cause of the problem?

Provide a detailed action plan that attacks the problem. Be specific and provide examples that relate to HGC.

Case 2.2

Film Prioritization

The purpose of this case is to give you experience in using a project priority system that ranks proposed projects by their contribution to the organization's objectives and strategic plan.

COMPANY PROFILE

The company is the film division for a large entertainment conglomerate. The main office is located in Anaheim, California. In addition to the feature film division, the conglomerate includes theme parks, home videos, a television channel, interactive games, and theatrical productions. The company has been enjoying steady growth over the past 10 years. Last year total revenues increased by 12 percent to $21.2 billion. The company is engaged in negotiations to expand its theme park empire to mainland China and Poland. The film division generated $274 million in revenues, which was an increase of 7 percent over the past year. Profit margin was down 3 percent to 16 percent because of the poor response to three of the five major film releases for the year.

COMPANY MISSION

The mission for the firm:

> Our overriding objective is to create shareholder value by continuing to be the world's premier entertainment company from a creative, strategic, and financial standpoint.

The film division supports this mission by producing four to six high-quality, family entertainment films for mass distribution each year. In recent years, the CEO of the company has advocated that the firm take a leadership position in championing environmental concerns.

COMPANY "MUST" OBJECTIVES

Every project must meet the must objectives as determined by executive management. It is important that selected film projects not violate such objectives of high strategic priority. There are three must objectives:

1. All projects meet current legal, safety, and environmental standards.
2. All film projects should receive a PG or lower advisory rating.
3. All projects should not have an adverse effect on current or planned operations within the larger company.

COMPANY "WANT" OBJECTIVES

Want objectives are assigned weights for their relative importance. Top management is responsible for formulating, ranking, and weighting objectives to ensure that projects support the company's strategy and mission. The following is a list of the company's want objectives:

1. Be nominated for and win an academy award for Best Animated Feature or Best Picture of the Year.
2. Generate additional merchandise revenue (action figures, dolls, interactive games, music CDs).
3. Raise public consciousness about environmental issues and concerns.
4. Generate profit in excess of 18 percent.
5. Advance the state of the art in film animation, and preserve the firm's reputation.
6. Provide the basis for the development of a new ride at a company-owned theme park.

ASSIGNMENT

You are a member of the priority team in charge of evaluating and selecting film proposals. Use the provided evaluation form to formally evaluate and rank each proposal. Be prepared to report your rankings and justify your decisions.

Assume that all of the projects have passed the estimated hurdle rate of 14 percent ROI. In addition to the brief film synopsis, the proposals include the following financial projections of theater and video sales: 80 percent chance of ROI, 50 percent chance of ROI, and 20 percent chance of ROI.

For example, for proposal #1 (Dalai Lama) there is an 80 percent chance that it will earn at least 8 percent return on investment (ROI), a 50-50 chance the ROI will be 18 percent, and a 20 percent chance that the ROI will be 24 percent.

FILM PROPOSALS

PROJECT PROPOSAL 1: MY LIFE WITH DALAI LAMA

An animated, biographical account of the Dalai Lama's childhood in Tibet based on the popular children's book *Tales from Nepal.* The Lama's life is told through the eyes of "Guoda," a field snake, and other local animals who befriend the Dalai and help him understand the principles of Buddhism.

Probability	80%	50%	20%
ROI	8%	18%	24%

PROJECT PROPOSAL 2: HEIDI

A remake of the classic children's story with music written by award-winning composers Syskle and Obert. The big-budget film will feature top-name stars and breathtaking scenery of the Swiss Alps.

Probability	80%	50%	20%
ROI	2%	20%	30%

PROJECT PROPOSAL 3: THE YEAR OF THE ECHO

A low-budget documentary that celebrates the career of one of the most influential bands in rock-and-roll history. The film will be directed by new-wave director Elliot Cznerzy and will combine concert footage and behind-the-scenes interviews spanning the 25-year history of the rock band the Echos. In addition to great music, the film will focus on the death of one of the founding members from a heroin overdose and reveal the underworld of sex, lies, and drugs in the music industry.

Probability	80%	50%	20%
ROI	12%	14%	18%

PROJECT PROPOSAL 4: ESCAPE FROM RIO JAPUNI

An animated feature set in the Amazon rainforest. The story centers around Pablo, a young jaguar who attempts to convince warring jungle animals that they must unite and escape the devastation of local clear cutting.

Probability	80%	50%	20%
ROI	15%	20%	24%

PROJECT PROPOSAL 5: NADIA!

The story of Nadia Comaneci, the famous Romanian gymnast who won three gold medals at the 1976 Summer Olympic Games. The low-budget film will document her life as a small child in Romania and how she was chosen by Romanian authorities to join their elite, state-run, athletic program. The film will highlight how Nadia maintained her independent spirit and love for gymnastics despite a harsh, regimented training program.

Probability	80%	50%	20%
ROI	8%	15%	20%

Project Priority Evaluation Form

Must objectives	Must meet if impacts	1	2	3	4	5	6	7
Meets all safety and environmental standards	Y = yes N = no N/A = not applicable							
PG or G rating	Y = yes N = no N/A = not applicable							
No adverse effect on other operations	Y = yes N = no N/A = not applicable							

Want objectives	Relative Importance 1–100	Single project impact definitions	Weighted Score	Weighted Score	Weighted Score	Weighted Score	Weighted Score	Weighted Score	Weighted Score
Win Best Picture of the Year	70	0 = No potential 1 = Low potential 2 = High potential							
Win Best Animated Feature Film	60	0 = No potential 1 = Low potential 2 = High potential							
Generate additional merchandise	10	0 = No potential 1 = Low potential 2 = High potential							
Raise environmental concerns	55	0 = No potential 1 = Low potential 2 = High potential							
Generate profit greater than 18%	70	0 < 18% 1 = 18–22% 2 > 22%							
Advance state of film animation	40	0 = No impact 1 = Some impact 2 = Great impact							
Provide basis for new theme ride	10	0 = No potential 1 = Low potential 2 = High potential							
Total weighted score									
Priority									

PROJECT PROPOSAL 6: KEIKO—ONE WHALE OF A STORY

The story of Keiko, the famous killer whale, will be told by an imaginary offspring Seiko, who in the distant future is telling her children about their famous grandfather. The big-budget film will integrate actual footage of the whale within a realistic animated environment using state-of-the-art computer imagery. The story will reveal how Keiko responded to his treatment by humans.

Probability	80%	50%	20%
ROI	6%	18%	25%

PROJECT PROPOSAL 7: GRAND ISLAND

The true story of a group of junior-high biology students who discover that a fertilizer plant is dumping toxic wastes into a nearby river. The moderate-budget film depicts how students organize a grassroots campaign to fight local bureaucracy and ultimately force the fertilizer plant to restore the local ecosystem.

Probability	80%	50%	20%
ROI	9%	15%	20%

Case 2.3

Fund Raising Project Selection case

The purpose of this "case exercise" is to provide you with experience in using a project selection process that ranks proposed projects by their contribution to an organization's mission and strategy.

FUND RAISING PROJECT

Assume you are a member of a class on project management. Each student will join a team of 5–7 students who will be responsible for creating, planning, and executing a fund raising project for a designated charity. The fund raising project has two goals: (1) raise money for a worthy cause and (2) provide an opportunity for all team members to practice project management skills and techniques.

In addition to completing the project a number of deliverables are required to complete this assignment. These deliverables include:

a. Project Proposal
b. Implementation Plan
c. Risk Management Plan
d. Status Report
e. Project Reflections Presentation
f. Project Retrospective/Audit

Approved projects will receive $250 seed money to be reimbursed upon completion of the project.

"MUST" OBJECTIVES

Every project must meet the "must" objectives as determined by the instructor. There are four must objectives:

1. All projects must be safe, legal and comply with university policies.
2. All projects must be capable of earning at least $500.
3. All projects must be able to be completed within nine weeks.
4. All projects must provide an opportunity for every member of the project team to experience and learn about project management.

Among the factors to consider for the last objective would be the extent there is meaningful work for every member of the team, the degree of coordination required, the extent the team will have to work with external stakeholders, and the complexity of the project.

"WANT" OBJECTIVES

In addition to the must objectives, there are "want" objectives that the instructor would like to achieve. The following is a list of these objectives:

1. Earn more than $500 for a charity
2. Increase public awareness of the charity
3. Provide a resume worthy experience for students
4. Be featured on local TV news
5. Be fun to do

ASSIGNMENT

You are a member of the class priority team in charge of evaluating and approving fund raising projects. Use the provided proposal evaluation form to formally evaluate and rank each proposal. Be prepared to report your rankings and justify your decision. You should assume that these projects would be held at your university or college.

FUND RAISING PROPOSALS

PROJECT PROPOSAL 1: HOOPS FOR HOPE

The project is a three-on-three basketball tournament to raise money for the Down Syndrome Association. The tournament will consist of three brackets: Co-ed, Male, and Female teams. There will be a $40 entry fee per team and additional funds will be derived from the sale of commemorative T-shirts ($10). Winning teams will receive gift baskets consisting of donations from local businesses and restaurants. The event will be held at the university recreational center.

PROJECT PROPOSAL 2: SINGING FOR SMILES

The project will hold a karaoke competition with celebrity judges at a popular campus night spot. Funds will be raised by $5 admission at the door and a raffle for prizes donated by local businesses. Funds will be donated to Smile Train, an international organization that performs cleft lip surgery at a cost of $250 per child. The event will feature pictures of children born with cleft lips and with every $50 earned a piece of a picture puzzle will be added until the original picture is covered with a smiling face.

PROJECT PROPOSAL 3: HALO FOR HEROES

The project will be a Halo video game competition to be held over the weekend utilizing the College's big screen electronic classrooms. Teams of 4 players will play each other in a single elimination tournament with the grand prize being a Sony Play Station 3 donated by a local video game store. Entry fee is 24$ per team and individual players will be able to play in a loser's bracket for 5$. All proceeds will go to the National Military Family Association.

PROJECT PROPOSAL 4: RAFFLE FOR LIFE

Organize a raffle contest. Raffle tickets will be sold for 3$ apiece with the winning ticket worth $300. Each of the six team members will be responsible for selling 50 raffle tickets. All profits will go to the American Cancer Society.

PROJECT PROPOSAL 5: HOLD'EM FOR HUNGER

Organize a Texas Hold'em poker tournament at a campus dining facility. It will cost $20 to enter the tournament with a $15 buy-in in fee. Prizes include $300, $150, and $50 gift certificates to a large department store. Gift certificates purchased from entry fees. All players will be eligible to win two donated tickets to Men and Women basketball games. Funds raised will go to local county food shelter.

PROJECT PROPOSAL 6: BUILD YOUR OWN BOX

The purpose of this project is to raise awareness of plight of homeless. Students will donate 10 dollars to participate in building and living in a cardboard city on the university quad for one night. Building materials will be provided by local recycling centers and hardware stores. Hot soup will be provided by the team at midnight to all participants. Proceeds go to the local homeless shelter.

Project Priority Evaluation Form

Must objectives	Must meet if impacts	1	2	3	4	5	6	7
Be safe, legal, & comply with University Policies	Y = yes N = no							
Earn at least $500	Y = yes N = no							
Can be completed within 9 weeks	Y = yes N = no							
Opportunity to learn Project Management	Y = yes N = no							

Want objectives	Relative Importance 1–100	Single project impact definitions	1	2	3	4	5	6	7
Earning potential	90	0: 500–750 1: 750–1500 2: >$1500 3: >$2000							
Fun	30	0: None 1: Some fun 2: A lot of fun							
Increase awareness of charity	30	0: No potential 1: Low potential 2: High potential							
Resume worthy	40	0: No potential 1: Low potential 2: High potential							
Be featured on local TV news	40	0: No potential 1: Low potential 2: High potential							
Total weighted score									
Priority									

3

Organization: Structure and Culture

LEARNING OBJECTIVES

After reading this chapter you should be able to:

3-1 Identify different project management structures and understand their strengths and weaknesses.

3-2 Distinguish three different types of matrix structures and understand their strengths and weaknesses.

3-3 Understand organizational and project considerations that should be considered in choosing an appropriate project management structure.

3-4 Appreciate the significant role that organizational culture plays in managing projects.

3-5 Interpret the culture of an organization.

3-6 Understand the interaction between project management structure and the culture of an organization.

OUTLINE

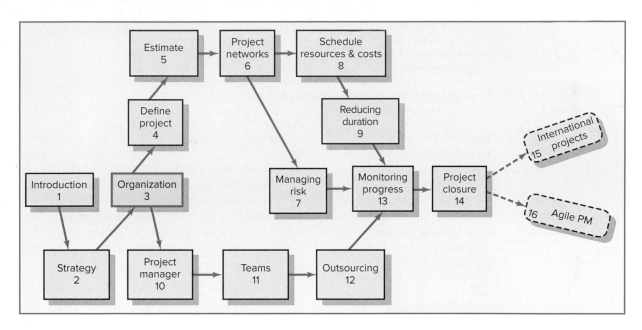

Matrix management works, but it sure is difficult at times. All matrix managers must keep up their health and take Stress-Tabs.

—*A Project Manager*

Once management approves a project, then the question becomes, how will the project be implemented? This chapter examines three different project management structures used by firms to implement projects: functional organization, dedicated project teams, and matrix structure. Although not exhaustive, these structures and their variant forms represent the major approaches for organizing projects. The advantages and disadvantages of each of these structures are discussed as well as some of the critical factors that might lead a firm to choose one form over others.

Whether a firm chooses to complete projects within the traditional functional organization or through some form of matrix arrangement is only part of the story. Anyone who has worked for more than one organization realizes that there are often considerable differences in how projects are managed within certain firms even with similar structures. Working in a matrix system at AT&T is different from working in a matrix environment at Hewlett-Packard. Many researchers attribute these differences to the organizational

FIGURE 3.1
Functional
Organizations

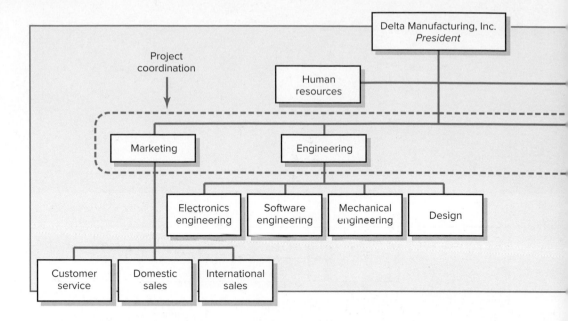

culture at AT&T and Hewlett-Packard. A simple explanation of *organizational culture* is that it reflects the "personality" of an organization. Just as each individual has a unique personality, so each organization has a unique culture. Toward the end of this chapter, we examine in more detail what organizational culture is and the impact that the culture of the parent organization has on organizing and managing projects.

Both the project management structure and the culture of the organization constitute major elements of the enterprise environment in which projects are implemented. It is important for project managers and participants to know the "lay of the land" so that they can avoid obstacles and take advantage of pathways to complete their projects.

3.1 Project Management Structures

LO 3-1

Identify different project management structures and understand their strengths and weaknesses.

A project management system provides a framework for launching and implementing project activities within a parent organization. A good system appropriately balances the needs of both the parent organization and the project by defining the interface between the project and parent organization in terms of authority, allocation of resources, and eventual integration of project outcomes into mainstream operations. With this in mind, we will start the discussion of project management structures.

Organizing Projects within the Functional Organization

One approach to organizing projects is to simply manage them within the existing functional hierarchy of the organization. Once management decides to implement a project, the different segments of the project are delegated to the respective functional units with each unit responsible for completing its segment of the project (see Figure 3.1). Coordination is maintained through normal management channels. For example, a tool manufacturing firm decides to differentiate its product line by offering a series of tools specially designed for left-handed individuals. Top management decides to implement the project, and different segments of the project are distributed to appropriate areas. The industrial design department is responsible for modifying specifications to conform

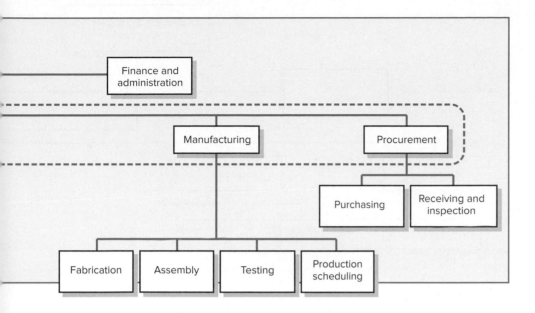

to the needs of left-handed users. The production department is responsible for devising the means for producing new tools according to these new design specifications. The marketing department is responsible for gauging demand and price as well as identifying distribution outlets. The overall project will be managed within the normal hierarchy, with the project being part of the working agenda of top management.

The functional organization is also commonly used when, given the nature of the project, one functional area plays a dominant role in completing the project or has a dominant interest in the success of the project. Under these circumstances, a high-ranking manager in that area is given the responsibility of coordinating the project. For example, the transfer of equipment and personnel to a new office would be managed by a top-ranking manager in the firm's facilities department. Likewise, a project involving the upgrading of the management information system would be managed by the information systems department. In both cases, most of the project work would be done within the specified department and coordination with other departments would occur through normal channels.

There are advantages and disadvantages for using the existing functional organization to administer and complete projects (Larson, 2004). The major advantages are the following:

1. **No Change.** Projects are completed within the basic functional structure of the parent organization. There is no radical alteration in the design and operation of the parent organization.

2. **Flexibility.** There is maximum flexibility in the use of staff. Appropriate specialists in different functional units can temporarily be assigned to work on the project and then return to their normal work. With a broad base of technical personnel available within each functional department, people can be switched among different projects with relative ease.

3. **In-Depth Expertise.** If the scope of the project is narrow and the proper functional unit is assigned primary responsibility, then in-depth expertise can be brought to bear on the most crucial aspects of the project.

FIGURE 3.2
Dedicated Project Team

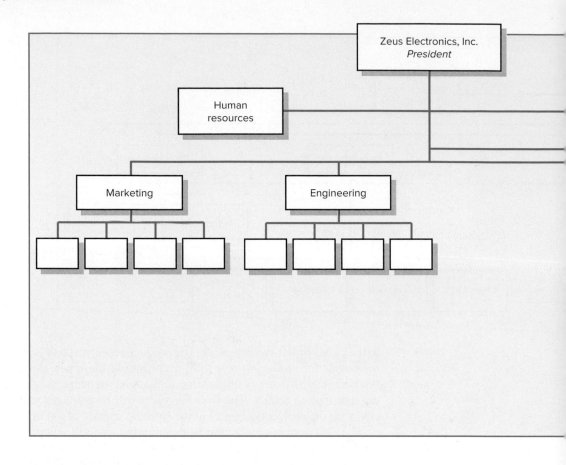

4. **Easy Post-Project Transition.** Normal career paths within a functional division are maintained. While specialists can make significant contributions to projects, their functional field is their professional home and the focus of their professional growth and advancement.

Just as there are advantages for organizing projects within the existing functional organization, there are also disadvantages. These disadvantages are particularly pronounced when the scope of the project is broad and one functional department does not take the dominant technological and managerial lead on the project:

1. **Lack of Focus.** Each functional unit has its own core routine work to do; sometimes project responsibilities get pushed aside to meet primary obligations. This difficulty is compounded when the project has different priorities for different units. For example, the marketing department may consider the project urgent while the operations people consider it only of secondary importance. Imagine the tension if the marketing people have to wait for the operations people to complete their segment of the project before they proceed.

2. **Poor Integration.** There may be poor integration across functional units. Functional specialists tend to be concerned only with their segment of the project and not with what is best for the total project.

3. **Slow.** It generally takes longer to complete projects through this functional arrangement. This is in part attributable to slow response time—project information and

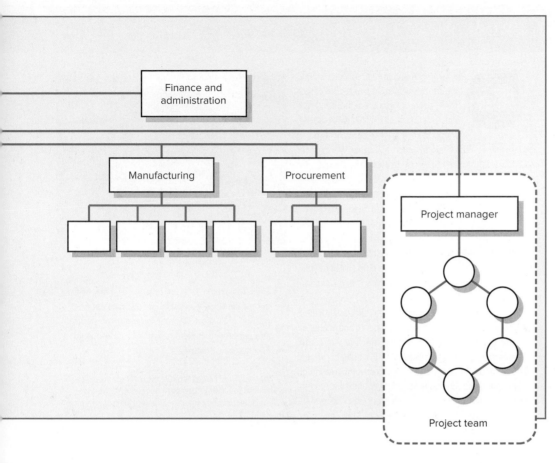

decisions have to be circulated through normal management channels. Furthermore, the lack of horizontal, direct communication among functional groups contributes to rework as specialists realize the implications of others' actions after the fact.

4. **Lack of Ownership.** The motivation of people assigned to the project can be weak. The project may be seen as an additional burden that is not directly linked to their professional development or advancement. Furthermore, because they are working on only a segment of the project, professionals do not identify with the project.

Organizing Projects as Dedicated Teams

At the other end of the structural spectrum is the creation of a **dedicated project team.** These teams operate as separate units from the rest of the parent organization. Usually a full-time project manager is designated to pull together a core group of specialists who work full time on the project. The project manager recruits necessary personnel from both within and outside the parent company. The subsequent team is physically separated from the parent organization and given marching orders to complete the project (see Figure 3.2).

The interface between the parent organization and the project teams will vary. In some cases, the parent organization maintains a tight rein through financial controls. In other cases, firms grant the project manager maximum freedom to get the project done as he

SNAPSHOT FROM PRACTICE 3.1 Skunk Works at Lockheed Martin*

In project management folklore, skunk works is code for a small, dedicated team assigned to a breakthrough project. The first skunk works was created more than a half a century ago by Clarence L. "Kelly" Johnson at Lockheed Aerospace Corporation. Kelly's project had two objectives: (1) to create a jet fighter, the Shooting Star, and (2) to do it as fast as possible. Kelly and a small band of engineering mavericks operated as a dedicated team unencumbered by red tape and the bureaucratic delays of the normal R&D process. The name was coined by team member Irvin Culver after the moonshine brewery deep in the forest in the popular cartoon strip Lil'Abner. The homemade whisky was euphemistically called kickapoo joy juice.

The project was a spectacular success. In just 43 days, Johnson's team of 23 engineers and teams of support personnel put together the first American fighter to fly at more than 500 miles per hour. Lockheed has continued to use skunk works to develop a string of high speed jets, including the F117 Nighthawk Stealth Fighter as well as jet drone prototypes. Lockheed Martin has an official Skunk Works Division. Their charter is:

© Monty Rakusen/Getty Images

The Skunk Works is a concentration of a few good people solving problems far in advance—and at a fraction of the cost—by applying the simplest, most straightforward methods possible to develop and produce new products.

*J. Miller, *Lockheed Martin's Skunk Works* (New York: Specialty Publications, 1996); "Lockheed Martin Skunk Works," www.lockheedmartin.com/us/aeronautics/skunkworks.html, accessed 1/22/2015.

sees fit. Lockheed Martin has used this approach to develop next-generation jet airplanes. See Snapshot from Practice 3.1: Skunk Works.

In the case of firms where projects are the dominant form of business, such as a construction firm or a consulting firm, the entire organization is designed to support project teams. Instead of one or two special projects, the organization consists of sets of quasi-independent teams working on specific projects. The main responsibility of traditional functional departments is to assist and support these project teams. For example, the marketing department is directed at generating new business that will lead to more projects, while the human resource department is responsible for managing a variety of personnel issues as well as recruiting and training new employees. This type of organization is referred to in the literature as a **projectized organization** and is graphically portrayed in Figure 3.3. It is important to note that not all projects are dedicated project teams; personnel can work part-time on several projects.

As in the case of functional organization, the dedicated project team approach has strengths and weaknesses (Larson, 2004). The following are recognized as strengths:

1. **Simple.** Other than taking away resources in the form of specialists assigned to the project, the functional organization remains intact with the project team operating independently.
2. **Fast.** Projects tend to get done more quickly when participants devote their full attention to the project and are not distracted by other obligations and duties. Furthermore, response time tends to be quicker under this arrangement because most decisions are made within the team and are not deferred up the hierarchy.

FIGURE 3.3 **Projectized Organization Structure**

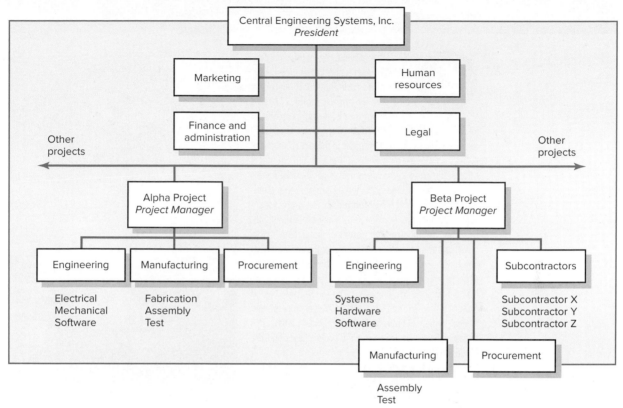

3. **Cohesive.** A high level of motivation and cohesiveness often emerges within the project team. Participants share a common goal and personal responsibility toward the project and the team.
4. **Cross-Functional Integration.** Specialists from different areas work closely together and, with proper guidance, become committed to optimizing the project, not their respective areas of expertise.

In many cases, the project team approach is the optimum approach for completing a project when you view it solely from the standpoint of what is best for completing the project. Its weaknesses become more evident when the needs of the parent organization are taken into account:

1. **Expensive.** Not only have you created a new management position (project manager), but resources are also assigned on a full-time basis. This can result in duplication of efforts across projects and a loss of economies of scale.
2. **Internal Strife.** Sometimes dedicated project teams become an entity in their own right and conflict emerges between the team and the remainder of the organization (see Snapshot from Practice 3.2: The Birth of the Mac). This divisiveness can undermine not only the integration of the eventual outcomes of the project into mainstream operations but also the assimilation of project team members back into their functional units once the project is completed.
3. **Limited Technological Expertise.** Creating self-contained teams inhibits maximum technological expertise being brought to bear on problems. Technical

SNAPSHOT FROM PRACTICE 3.2   The Birth of the Mac*

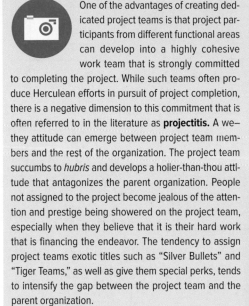

One of the advantages of creating dedicated project teams is that project participants from different functional areas can develop into a highly cohesive work team that is strongly committed to completing the project. While such teams often produce Herculean efforts in pursuit of project completion, there is a negative dimension to this commitment that is often referred to in the literature as **projectitis**. A we–they attitude can emerge between project team members and the rest of the organization. The project team succumbs to *hubris* and develops a holier-than-thou attitude that antagonizes the parent organization. People not assigned to the project become jealous of the attention and prestige being showered on the project team, especially when they believe that it is their hard work that is financing the endeavor. The tendency to assign project teams exotic titles such as "Silver Bullets" and "Tiger Teams," as well as give them special perks, tends to intensify the gap between the project team and the parent organization.

Such appears to have been the case with Apple's highly successful Macintosh development team. Steve Jobs, who at the time was both the chairman of Apple and the project manager for the Mac team, pampered his team with perks including at-the-desk massages, coolers stocked with freshly squeezed orange juice, a Bosendorfer grand piano, and first-class plane tickets. No other employees at Apple got to travel first class. Jobs considered his team to be the elite of Apple and had a tendency to refer to everyone else as "Bozos" who "didn't get it." Engineers from the Apple II division, which was the bread and butter of Apple's sales, became incensed with the special treatment their colleagues were getting.

One evening at Ely McFly's, a local watering hole, the tensions between Apple II engineers seated at one table and those of a Mac team at another boiled over. Aaron Goldberg, a long-time industry consultant, watched from his barstool as the squabbling escalated. "The Mac guys were screaming, 'We're the future!' The Apple II guys were screaming, 'We're the money!' Then

© McGraw-Hill Education/Jill Braaten

there was a geek brawl. Pocket protectors and pens were flying. I was waiting for a notebook to drop, so they would stop and pick up the papers."

Although comical from a distance, the discord between the Apple II and Mac groups severely hampered Apple's performance during the 1980s. John Sculley, who replaced Steve Jobs as chairman of Apple, observed that Apple had evolved into two "warring companies" and referred to the street between the Apple II and Macintosh buildings as "the DMZ" (demilitarized zone).

*J. Carlton, *Apple: The Inside Story of Intrigue, Egomania, and Business Blunders* (New York: Random House, 1997), pp. 13–14; J. Sculley, *Odyssey: Pepsi to Apple . . . A Journey of Adventure, Ideas, and the Future* (New York: Harper & Row, 1987), pp. 270–79.

expertise is limited somewhat to the talents and experience of the specialists assigned to the project. While nothing prevents specialists from consulting with others in the functional division, the we–they syndrome and the fact that such help is not formally sanctioned by the organization discourage this from happening.

4. **Difficult Post-Project Transition.** Assigning full-time personnel to a project creates the dilemma of what to do with personnel after the project is completed. If other project work is not available, then the transition back to their original functional departments may be difficult because of their prolonged absence and the need to catch up with recent developments in their functional area.

Organizing Projects within a Matrix Arrangement

One of the biggest management innovations to emerge in the past 40 years has been the matrix organization. **Matrix** management is a hybrid organizational form in which a horizontal project management structure is "overlaid" on the normal functional hierarchy. In a matrix system, there are usually two chains of command, one along functional lines and the other along project lines. Instead of delegating segments of a project to different units or creating an autonomous team, project participants report simultaneously to both functional and project managers.

Companies apply this matrix arrangement in a variety of different ways. Some organizations set up temporary matrix systems to deal with specific projects, while "matrix" may be a permanent fixture in other organizations. Let us first look at its general application and then proceed to a more detailed discussion of finer points. Consider Figure 3.4. There are three projects currently under way: A, B, and C. All three project managers (PM A-C) report to a director of project management, who supervises all projects. Each project has an administrative assistant, although the one for project C is only part time.

Project A involves the design and expansion of an existing production line to accommodate new metal alloys. To accomplish this objective, project A has assigned to it 3.5 people from manufacturing and 6 people from engineering. These individuals are assigned to the project on a part-time or full-time basis, depending on the project's needs during various phases of the project. Project B involves the development of a new product that requires the heavy representation of engineering, manufacturing, and marketing. Project C involves forecasting changing needs of an existing customer base. While these three projects, as well as others, are being completed, the functional divisions continue performing their basic, core activities.

The matrix structure is designed to optimally utilize resources by having individuals work on multiple projects as well as being capable of performing normal functional duties. At the same time, the matrix approach attempts to achieve greater integration by creating and legitimizing the authority of a project manager. In theory, the matrix approach provides a dual focus between functional/technical expertise and project requirements that is missing in either the project team or functional approach to project management. This focus can most easily be seen in the relative input of functional managers and project managers over key project decisions (see Table 3.1).

TABLE 3.1

Division of Project Manager and Functional Manager Responsibilities in a Matrix Structure

Project Manager	Negotiated Issues	Functional Manager
What has to be done?	Who will do the task?	How will it be done?
When should the task be done?	Where will the task be done?	
How much money is available to do the task?	Why will the task be done?	How will the project involvement impact normal functional activities?
How well has the total project been done?	Is the task satisfactorily completed?	How well has the functional input been integrated?

FIGURE 3.4
Matrix Organization
Structure

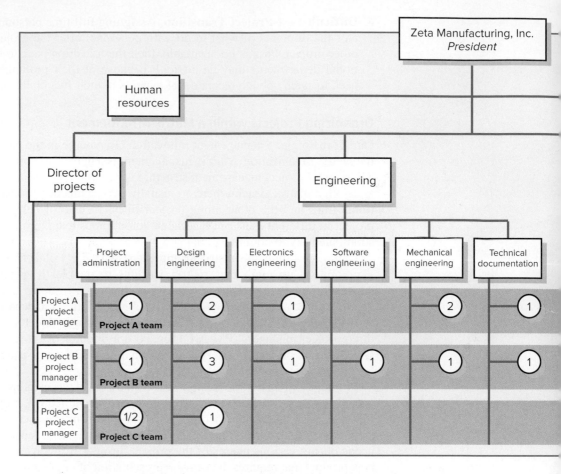

Different Matrix Forms

LO 3-2

Distinguish three different types of matrix structures and understand their strengths and weaknesses.

In practice there are really different kinds of matrix systems, depending on the relative authority of the project and functional managers (Larson & Gobeli, 1987; Bowen et al., 1994). Here is a thumbnail sketch of the three kinds of matrices:

- **Weak matrix**—This form is very similar to a functional approach with the exception that there is a formally designated project manager responsible for coordinating project activities. Functional managers are responsible for managing their segment of the project. The project manager basically acts as a staff assistant who draws the schedules and checklists, collects information on status of work, and facilitates project completion. The project manager has indirect authority to expedite and monitor the project. Functional managers call most of the shots and decide who does what and when the work is completed.
- **Balanced matrix**—This is the classic matrix in which the project manager is responsible for defining what needs to be accomplished while the functional managers are concerned with how it will be accomplished. More specifically, the project manager establishes the overall plan for completing the project, integrates the contribution of the different disciplines, sets schedules, and monitors progress. The functional managers are responsible for assigning personnel and executing their segment of the project according to the standards and schedules set by the project manager. The merger of "what and how" requires both parties to work closely together and jointly approve technical and operational decisions.

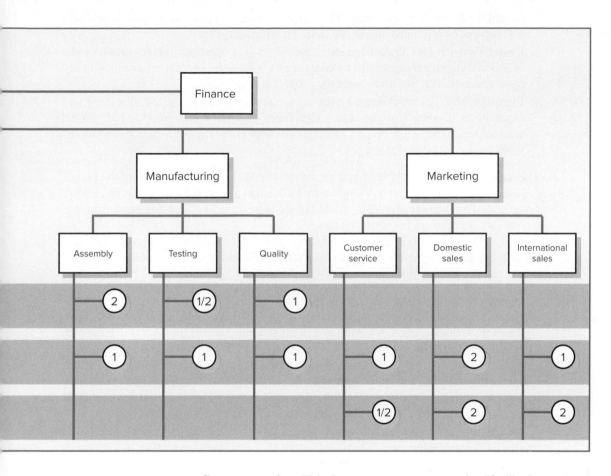

- **Strong matrix**—This form attempts to create the "feel" of a project team within a matrix environment. The project manager controls most aspects of the project, including scope trade-offs and assignment of functional personnel. The project manager controls when and what specialists do and has final say on major project decisions. The functional manager has title over her people and is consulted on a need basis. In some situations a functional manager's department may serve as a "subcontractor" for the project, in which case they have more control over specialized work. For example, the development of a new series of laptop computers may require a team of experts from different disciplines working on the basic design and performance requirements within a project matrix arrangement. Once the specifications have been determined, final design and production of certain components (i.e., power source) may be assigned to respective functional groups to complete.

Matrix management both in general and in its specific forms has unique strengths and weaknesses (Larson & Gobeli, 1987). The advantages and disadvantages of matrix organizations in general are noted below, while only briefly highlighting specifics concerning different forms:

1. **Efficient.** Resources can be shared across multiple projects as well as within functional divisions. Individuals can divide their energy across multiple projects on an as-needed basis. This reduces duplication required in a projectized structure.
2. **Strong Project Focus.** A stronger project focus is provided by having a formally designated project manager who is responsible for coordinating and integrating

contributions of different units. This helps sustain a holistic approach to problem solving that is often missing in the functional organization.

3. **Easier Post-Project Transition.** Because the project organization is overlaid on the functional divisions, specialists maintain ties with their functional group, so they have a homeport to return to once the project is completed.

4. **Flexible.** Matrix arrangements provide for flexible utilization of resources and expertise within the firm. In some cases functional units may provide individuals who are managed by the project manager. In other cases the contributions are monitored by the functional manager.

The strengths of the matrix structure are considerable. Unfortunately, so are the potential weaknesses. This is due in large part to the fact that a matrix structure is more complicated and the creation of multiple bosses represents a radical departure from the traditional hierarchical authority system.

Furthermore, one does not install a matrix structure overnight. Experts argue that it takes 3–5 years for a matrix system to fully mature. So many of the problems described below represent growing pains.

1. **Dysfunctional Conflict.** The matrix approach is predicated on tension between functional managers and project managers who bring critical expertise and perspectives to the project. Such tension is viewed as a necessary mechanism for achieving an appropriate balance between complex technical issues and unique project requirements. While the intent is noble, the effect is sometimes analogous to opening Pandora's box. Legitimate conflict can spill over to a more personal level, resulting from conflicting agendas and accountabilities. Worthy discussions can degenerate into heated arguments that engender animosity among the managers involved.

2. **Infighting.** Any situation in which equipment, resources, and people are being shared across projects and functional activities lends itself to conflict and competition for scarce resources. Infighting can occur among project managers, who are primarily interested in what is best for their project.

3. **Stressful.** Matrix management violates the management principle of unity of command. Project participants have at least two bosses—their functional head and one or more project managers. Working in a matrix environment can be extremely stressful. Imagine what it would be like to work in an environment in which you are being told to do three conflicting things by three different managers.

4. **Slow.** In theory, the presence of a project manager to coordinate the project should accelerate the completion of the project. In practice, decision making can get bogged down as agreements have to be forged across multiple functional groups. This is especially true for the balanced matrix.

When the three variant forms of the matrix approach are considered, we can see that advantages and disadvantages are not necessarily true for all three forms of matrix. The Strong matrix is likely to enhance project integration, diminish internal power struggles, and ultimately improve control of project activities and costs. On the downside, technical quality may suffer because functional areas have less control over their contributions. Finally, projectitis may emerge as the members develop a strong team identity.

The Weak matrix is likely to improve technical quality as well as provide a better system for managing conflict across projects because the functional manager assigns personnel to different projects. The problem is that functional control is often maintained at the expense of poor project integration. The Balanced matrix can achieve better balance between technical and project requirements, but it is a very delicate system to manage and is more likely to succumb to many of the problems associated with the matrix approach.

3.2 What Is the Right Project Management Structure?

 LO 3-3

Understand organizational and project considerations that should be considered in choosing an appropriate project management structure.

There is empirical evidence that project success is directly linked to the amount of autonomy and authority project managers have over their projects (Gray et al., 1990; Larson & Gobeli, 1988; Larson & Gobeli, 1987). However, most of this research is based on what is best for managing specific projects. It is important to remember what was stated in the beginning of the chapter—that the best system balances the needs of the project with those of the parent organization. So what project structure should an organization use? This is a complicated question with no precise answers. A number of issues need to be considered at both the organization and project level.

Organization Considerations

At the organization level, the first question that needs to be asked is how important is project management to the success of the firm? What percentage of core work involves projects? If over 75 percent of work involves projects, then an organization should consider a fully projectized organization. If an organization has both standard products and projects, then a matrix arrangement would appear to be appropriate. If an organization has very few projects, then a less formal arrangement is probably all that is required. Dedicated teams could be created on an as-needed basis and the organization could outsource project work.

A second key question is resource availability. Remember, matrix evolved out of the necessity to share resources across multiple projects and functional domains while at the same time creating legitimate project leadership. For organizations that cannot afford to tie up critical personnel on individual projects, a matrix system would appear to be appropriate. An alternative would be to create a dedicated team but outsource project work when resources are not available internally.

Within the context of the first two questions, an organization needs to assess current practices and what changes are needed to more effectively manage projects. A strong project matrix is not installed overnight. The shift toward a greater emphasis on projects has a host of political implications that need to be worked through, requiring time and strong leadership. For example, we have observed many companies that make the transition from a functional organization to a matrix organization begin with a weak functional matrix. This is due in part to resistance by functional and department managers toward transferring authority to project managers. With time, these matrix structures eventually evolve into a project matrix. Many organizations have created Project Management Offices to support project management efforts. See Snapshot from Practice 3.3: POs: Project Offices.

Project Considerations

At the project level, the question is how much autonomy the project needs in order to be successfully completed. Hobbs and Ménard (1993) identify seven factors that should influence the choice of project management structure:

- Size of project.
- Strategic importance.

SNAPSHOT FROM PRACTICE 3.3   POs: Project Offices*

Project offices (POs) were originally developed as a response to the poor track record many companies had in completing projects on time, within budget, and according to plan. They were often established to help matrix systems mature into more effective project delivery platforms.

Today, POs come in many different shapes and forms. One interesting way of classifying POs was set forth by Casey and Peck, who describe certain POs in terms of being (1) a weather station, (2) a control tower, or (3) a resource pool. Each of these models performs a very different function for its organization.

- **Weather Station.** The primary function of the weather station PO is to track and monitor project performance. It is typically created to satisfy top management's need to stay on top of the portfolio of projects under way in the firm. Staff provides an independent forecast of project performance. The questions answered for specific projects include:

  - How are our projects progressing? Which ones are on track? Which ones are not?

- How are we doing in terms of cost? Which projects are over or under budget?

- What are the major problems confronting projects? Are contingency plans in place? What can the organization do to help the project?

- **Control Tower.** The primary function of the control tower PO is to improve project execution. It considers project management as a profession to be protected and advanced. Staff at the PO identify best practices and standards for project management excellence. They work as consultants and trainers to support project managers and their teams.

- **Resource Pool.** The goal of the resource pool PO is to provide the organization with a cadre of trained project managers and professionals. It operates like an academy for continually upgrading the skills of a firm's project professionals. In addition to training, this kind of PO also serves to elevate the stature of project management within the organization.

* W. Casey and W. Peck, "Choosing the Right PMO Setup," *PM Network,* vol. 15, no. 2 (2001), pp. 40–47.

- Novelty and need for innovation.
- Need for integration (number of departments involved).
- Environmental complexity (number of external interfaces).
- Budget and time constraints.
- Stability of resource requirements.

The higher the levels of these seven factors, the more autonomy and authority the project manager and project team need to be successful.[1] This translates into using either a dedicated project team or a project matrix structure. For example, these structures should be used for large projects that are strategically critical and are new to the company, thus requiring much innovation. These structures would also be appropriate for complex, multidisciplinary projects that require input from many departments, as well as for projects that require constant contact with customers to assess their expectations. Dedicated project teams should also be used for urgent projects in which the nature of the work requires people working steadily from beginning to end.

Many firms that are heavily involved in project management have created a flexible management system that organizes projects according to project requirements. For example, Chaparral Steel, a mini-mill that produces steel bars and beams from scrap

[1] For a more sophisticated discussion of contingency factors related to managing specific projects see: A. J. Shenhar and D. Dvir, *Reinventing Project Management: The Diamond Approach to Successful Growth and Innovation* (Boston: Harvard Press, 2007).

metal, classifies projects into three categories: advanced development, platform, and incremental. Advanced development projects are high-risk endeavors involving the creation of a breakthrough product or process. Platform projects are medium-risk projects involving system upgrades that yield new products and processes. Incremental projects are low-risk, short-term projects that involve minor adjustments in existing products and processes. At any point in time, Chaparral might have 40–50 projects under way, of which only one or two are advanced, three to five are platform projects, and the remainder are small, incremental projects. The incremental projects are almost all done within a weak matrix with the project manager coordinating the work of functional subgroups. A strong matrix is used to complete the platform projects, while dedicated project teams are typically created to complete the advanced development projects. More and more companies are using this "mix and match" approach to managing projects.

3.3 Organizational Culture

LO 3-4

Appreciate the significant role that organizational culture plays in managing projects.

The decision for combining a discussion of project management structures and organizational cultures in this chapter can be traced to a conversation we, the authors, had with two project managers who work for a medium-sized information technology firm.

The managers were developing a new operating platform that would be critical to the future success of their company. When they tried to describe how this project was organized, one manager began to sketch out on a napkin a complicated structure involving 52 different teams, each with a project leader and a technical leader! In response to our further probing to understand how this system worked, the manager stopped short and proclaimed, "The key to making this structure work is the culture in our company. This approach would never work at company Y, where I worked before. But because of our culture here we are able to pull it off."

This comment, our observations of other firms, and research suggest there is a strong connection between project management structure, organizational culture, and project success.[2] We have observed organizations successfully manage projects within the traditional functional organization because the culture encouraged cross-functional integration. Conversely we have seen matrix structures break down because the culture of the organization did not support the division of authority between project managers and functional managers. We have also observed companies relying on independent project teams because the dominant culture would not support the innovation and speed necessary for success.

What Is Organizational Culture?

LO 3-5

Interpret the culture of an organization.

Organizational culture refers to a system of shared norms, beliefs, values, and assumptions which binds people together, thereby creating shared meanings (Deal & Kennedy, 1982). This system is manifested by customs and habits that exemplify the values and beliefs of the organization. For example, egalitarianism may be expressed in the informal dress worn at a high-tech firm. Conversely, mandated uniforms at a department store reinforce respect for the hierarchy.

---

[2] See, for example: Kerzner, H., *In Search of Excellence in Project Management* (New York: Von Nostrand Reinhold, 1997); Yazici, H. "The Role of Project Management Maturity and Organizational Culture in Perceived Performance", *Project Management Journal,* 2009.

Culture reflects the personality of the organization and, similar to an individual's personality, can enable us to predict attitudes and behaviors of organizational members. Culture is also one of the defining aspects of an organization that sets it apart from other organizations even in the same industry.

Research suggests that there are 10 primary characteristics which, in aggregate, capture the essence of an organization's culture:[3]

1. **Member identity**—the degree to which employees identify with the organization as a whole rather than with their type of job or field of professional expertise.
2. **Team emphasis**—the degree to which work activities are organized around groups rather than individuals.
3. **Management focus**—the degree to which management decisions take into account the effect of outcomes on people within the organization.
4. **Unit integration**—the degree to which units within the organization are encouraged to operate in a coordinated or interdependent manner.
5. **Control**—the degree to which rules, policies, and direct supervision are used to oversee and control employee behavior.
6. **Risk tolerance**—the degree to which employees are encouraged to be aggressive, innovative, and risk seeking.
7. **Reward criteria**—the degree to which rewards such as promotion and salary increases are allocated according to employee performance rather than seniority, favoritism, or other nonperformance factors.
8. **Conflict tolerance**—the degree to which employees are encouraged to air conflicts and criticisms openly.
9. **Means versus end orientation**—the degree to which management focuses on outcomes rather than on techniques and processes used to achieve those results.
10. **Open-systems focus**—the degree to which the organization monitors and responds to changes in the external environment.

As shown in Figure 3.5, each of these dimensions exists on a continuum. Assessing an organization according to these 10 dimensions provides a composite picture of the organization's culture. This picture becomes the basis for feelings of shared understanding that the members have about the organization, how things are done, and the way members are supposed to behave.

Culture performs several important functions in organizations. An organization's culture *provides a sense of identity* for its members. The more clearly an organization's shared perceptions and values are stated, the more strongly people can identify with their organization and feel a vital part of it. Identity generates commitment to the organization and reasons for members to devote energy and loyalty to the organization.

A second important function is that culture *helps legitimize the management system* of the organization. Culture helps clarify authority relationships. It provides reasons why people are in a position of authority and why their authority should be respected.

---

[3] Harrison, M. T., and J. M. Beyer, *The Culture of Organizations* (Englewood Cliffs, NJ: Prentice Hall, 1993); O'Reilly, C. A., J. Chatman, and D. F. Caldwell, "People and Organizational Culture: A Profile Comparison Approach to Assessing Person-Organization Fit," *Academy of Management Journal,* vol. 34, no. 3 (September 1991), pp. 487–516; and Schein, E., *Organizational Culture and Leadership: A Dynamic* View (San Francisco, CA: Jossey-Bass, 2010).

FIGURE 3.5
Key Dimensions Defining an Organization's Culture

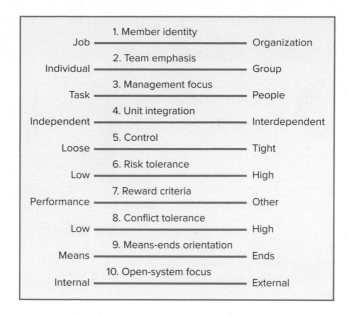

Most importantly, organizational culture *clarifies and reinforces standards of behavior.* Culture helps define what is permissible and inappropriate behavior. These standards span a wide range of behavior from dress code and working hours to challenging the judgment of superiors and collaborating with other departments. Ultimately, culture *helps create social order* within an organization. Imagine what it would be like if members didn't share similar beliefs, values, and assumptions—chaos! The customs, norms, and ideals conveyed by the culture of an organization provide the stability and predictability in behavior that is essential for an effective organization. See Snapshot from Practice 3.4: Google-y for an example of this.

Although our discussion of organizational culture may appear to suggest one culture dominates the entire organization, in reality this is rarely the case. "Strong" or "thick" are adjectives used to denote a culture in which the organization's core values and customs are widely shared within the entire organization. Conversely, a "thin" or "weak" culture is one that is not widely shared or practiced within a firm.

Even within a strong organizational culture, there are likely to be subcultures often aligned within specific departments or specialty areas. As noted earlier in our discussion of project management structures, it is not uncommon for norms, values, and customs to develop within a specific field or profession such as marketing, finance, or operations. People working in the marketing department may have a different set of norms and values than those working in finance.

Countercultures sometimes emerge within organizations that embody a different set of values, beliefs, and customs—often in direct contradiction with the culture espoused by top management. How pervasive these subcultures and countercultures are affects the strength of the culture of the organization and the extent to which culture influences members' actions and responses.

Identifying Cultural Characteristics

Deciphering an organization's culture is a highly interpretative, subjective process that requires assessment of both current and past history. The student of culture cannot

SNAPSHOT FROM PRACTICE 3.4 Google-y*

In 2016 Google Inc. topped *Fortune* magazine's list of best companies to work at for the seventh time in the past ten years. When one enters the 24-hour Googleplex located in Mountain View, California, you feel that you are walking through a new-age college campus rather than the corporate office of a billion-dollar business. The collection of interconnected low-rise buildings with colorful, glass-encased offices feature upscale trappings—free gourmet meals three times a day, free use of an outdoor wave pool, indoor gym and large child care facility, private shuttle bus service to and from San Francisco and other residential areas— that are the envy of workers across the Bay area. These perks and others reflect Google's culture of keeping people happy and thinking in unconventional ways.

The importance of corporate culture is no more evident than in the fact that the head of Human Resources, Stacy Savides Sullivan, also has the title of Chief Culture Officer. Her task is to try to preserve the innovative culture of a start-up as Google quickly evolves into a mammoth international corporation. Sullivan characterizes Google culture as "team-oriented, very collaborative and encouraging people to think nontraditionally, different from where they ever worked before—work with integrity and for the good of the company and for the good of the world, which is tied to our overall mission of making information accessible to the world." Google goes to great lengths to screen new employees to not only make sure that they have outstanding technical capabilities but also that they are going to fit Google's culture. Sullivan goes on to define a Google-y employee as somebody who is "flexible, adaptable, and not focusing on titles and hierarchy, and just gets stuff done."

Google's culture is rich with customs and traditions not found in corporate America. For example, project

© Caiaimage/Glow Images

teams typically have daily "stand-up" meetings seven minutes after the hour. Why seven minutes after the hour? Because Google cofounder Sergey Brin once estimated that it took seven minutes to walk across the Google campus. Everybody stands to make sure no one gets too comfortable and no time is wasted during the rapid-fire update. As one manager noted, "The whole concept of the stand-up is to talk through what everyone's doing, so if someone is working on what you're working on, you can discover and collaborate not duplicate."

Another custom is "dogfooding." This is when a project team releases the functional prototype of a future product to Google employees for them to test drive. There is a strong norm within Google to test new products and provide feedback to the developers. The project team receives feedback from thousands of Google-ys. The internal focus group can log bugs or simply comment on design or functionality. Fellow Google-ys do not hold back on their feedback and are quick to point out things they don't like. This often leads to significant product improvements.

* Walters, H., "How Google Got Its New Look," *BusinessWeek,* May 10, 2010; Goo, S. K., "Building a 'Googley' Workforce," *Washington Post,* October 21, 2006; Mills, E., "Meet Google's Culture Czar," *CNET News.com,* April 27, 2007.

simply rely on what people report about their culture. The physical environment in which people work, as well as how people act and respond to different events that occur, must be examined. Figure 3.6 contains a worksheet for diagnosing the culture of an organization. Although by no means exhaustive, the checklist often yields clues about the norms, customs, and values of an organization:

1. **Study the physical characteristics of an organization.** What does the external architecture look like? What image does it convey? Is it unique? Are the buildings

FIGURE 3.6
Organizational Culture Diagnosis Worksheet

Power Corp.

I. Physical Characteristics:
Architecture, office layout, décor, attire

Corporate HQ is 20 story modern building—president on top floor. Offices are bigger in the top floors than lower floors. Formal business attire (white shirts, ties, power suits, . . .). Power appears to increase the higher up you are.

II. Public Documents:
Annual reports, internal newsletters, vision statements

At the heart of the Power Corp. way is our vision . . . to be the global energy company most admired for its people, partnership, and performance.

Integrity. We are honest with others and ourselves. We meet the highest ethical standards in all business dealings. We do what we say we will do.

III. Behavior:
Pace, language, meetings, issues discussed, decision-making style, communication patterns, rituals

Hierarchical decision making, pace brisk but orderly, meetings start on time and end on time, subordinates choose their words very carefully when talking to superiors, people rarely work past 6:00 p.m., president takes top performing unit on a boat cruise each year . . .

IV. Folklore:
Stories, anecdotes, heroines, heroes, villains

Young project manager was fired after going over his boss's head to ask for additional funds.

Stephanie C. considered a hero for taking complete responsibility for a technical error.

Jack S. was labeled a traitor for joining chief competitor after working for Power Corp. for 15 years.

and offices the same quality for all employees? Or are modern buildings and fancier offices reserved for senior executives or managers from a specific department? What are the customs concerning dress? What symbols does the organization use to signal authority and status within the organization? These physical characteristics can shed light on who has real power within the organization, the extent to which the organization is internally differentiated, and how formal the organization is in its business dealings.

2. **Read about the organization.** Examine annual reports, mission statements, press releases, and internal newsletters. What do they describe? What principles are espoused in these documents? Do the reports emphasize the people who work for the organization and what they do or the financial performance of the firm? Each emphasis reflects a different culture. The first demonstrates concern for the people who make up the company. The second may suggest a concern for results and the bottom line.

3. **Observe how people interact within the organization.** What is their pace—is it slow and methodical or urgent and spontaneous? What rituals exist within the organization? What values do they express? Meetings can often yield insightful information. Who are the people at the meetings? Who does the talking? To whom do they talk? How candid is the conversation? Do people speak for the organization or for the individual department? What is the focus of the meetings? How much time is spent on various issues? Issues that are discussed repeatedly and at length are clues about the values of the organization's culture.

4. **Interpret stories and folklore surrounding the organization.** Look for similarities among stories told by different people. The subjects highlighted in recurring stories often reflect what is important to an organization's culture. For example, many of the stories that are repeated at Versatec, a Xerox subsidiary that makes graphic plotters for computers, involve their flamboyant cofounder, Renn Zaphiropoulos. According to company folklore, one of the very first things Renn did when the company was formed was to assemble the top management team at his home. They then devoted the weekend to handmaking a beautiful teak conference table around which all future decisions would be made. This table came to symbolize the importance of teamwork and maintaining high standards of performance, two essential qualities of the culture at Versatec. Try to identify who the heroes and villains are in company folklore. What do they suggest about the culture's ideals? Returning to the Versatec story, when the company was eventually purchased by Xerox many employees expressed concern that Versatec's informal, play hard/work hard culture would be overwhelmed by the bureaucracy at Xerox. Renn rallied the employees to superior levels of performance by arguing that if they exceeded Xerox's expectations they would be left alone. Autonomy has remained a fixture of Versatec's culture long after Renn's retirement.

It is also important to pay close attention to the basis for promotions and rewards. What do people see as the keys to getting ahead within the organization? What contributes to downfalls? These last two questions can yield important insights into the qualities and behaviors which the organization honors as well as the cultural taboos and behavioral land mines that can derail a career. For example, one project manager confided that a former colleague was sent to project management purgatory soon after publicly questioning the validity of a marketing report. From that point on, the project manager was extra careful to privately consult the marketing department whenever she had questions about their data.

With practice an observer can assess how strong the dominant culture of an organization is and the significance of subcultures and countercultures. Furthermore, learners can discern and identify where the culture of an organization stands on the 10 cultural dimensions presented earlier and, in essence, begin to build a cultural profile for a firm. Based on this profile, conclusions can be drawn about specific customs and norms that need to be adhered to as well as those behaviors and actions that violate the norms of a firm.

3.4 Implications of Organizational Culture for Organizing Projects

Understand the interaction between project management structure and the culture of an organization.

Project managers have to be able to operate in several, potentially diverse, organizational cultures. First, they have to interact with the culture of their parent organization as well as the subcultures of various departments (e.g., marketing, accounting). Second, they have to interact with the project's client or customer organizations. Finally, they have to interact in varying degrees with a host of other organizations connected to the project. These organizations include suppliers and vendors, subcontractors, consulting firms, government and regulatory agencies, and, in many cases, community groups. Many of these organizations are likely to have very different cultures. Project managers have to be able to read and speak the culture they are working in to develop strategies, plans, and responses that are likely to be understood and accepted. Still, the emphasis of this chapter is on the relationship between organizational culture and project management structure, and it is necessary to defer further discussion of these

FIGURE 3.7
Cultural Dimensions of an Organization Supportive of Project Management

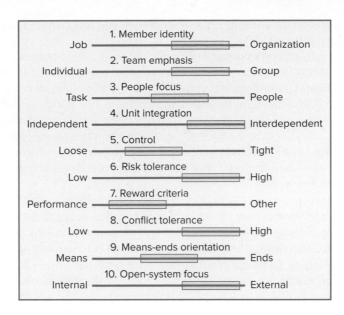

implications until Chapters 10–12, which focus on leadership, team building, and outsourcing.

Earlier we stated that we believe there are strong relationships among project management structure, organizational culture, and successful project management. To explore these relationships further, let us return to the dimensions that can be used to characterize the culture of an organization. When examining these dimensions we could hypothesize that certain aspects of the culture of an organization would support successful project management while other aspects would deter or interfere with effective management. Figure 3.7 attempts to identify which cultural characteristics create an environment conducive to completing most complex projects involving people from different disciplines.

Note that, in many cases, the ideal culture is not at either extreme. For example, a fertile project culture would likely be one in which management balances its focus on the needs of both the task and the people. An optimal culture would balance concern with output (ends) and processes to achieve those outcomes (means). In other cases, the ideal culture would be on one end of a dimension or the other. For example, because most projects require collaboration across disciplines, it would be desirable that the culture of the organization emphasize working in teams and identifying with the organization, not just the professional domain. Likewise, it is important that the culture support a certain degree of risk taking and a tolerance for constructive conflict.

One organization that appears to fit this ideal profile is 3M. 3M has received acclaim for creating an entrepreneurial culture within a large corporate framework. The essence of its culture is captured in phrases that have been chanted often by 3Mers throughout its history: "Encourage experimental doodling." "Hire good people and leave them alone." "If you put fences around people, you get sheep. Give people the room they need." Freedom and autonomy to experiment are reflected in the "15 percent rule," which encourages technical people to spend up to 15 percent of their time on projects of their own choosing and initiative. This fertile culture has contributed to

3M's branching out into more than 60,000 products and 35 separate business units (Collins & Porras, 1994).

The metaphor we choose to describe the relationship between organizational culture and project management is that of a riverboat trip. Culture is the river and the project is the boat. Organizing and completing projects within an organization in which the culture is conducive to project management is like paddling downstream: much less effort is required. In many cases, the current can be so strong that steering is all that is required. Such is the case for projects that operate in a project-friendly environment where teamwork and cross-functional cooperation are the norms, where there is a deep commitment to excellence, and where healthy conflict is voiced and dealt with quickly and effectively.

Conversely, trying to complete a project in a toxic culture is like paddling upstream: much more time, effort, and attention are needed to reach the destination. This would be the situation in cultures that discourage teamwork and cooperation, that have a low tolerance for conflict, and where getting ahead is based less on performance and more on cultivating favorable relationships with superiors. In such cases, the project manager and her people not only have to overcome the natural obstacles of the project but also have to overcome the prevailing negative forces inherent in the culture of the organization.

The implications of this metaphor are important. Greater project authority and time are necessary to complete projects that encounter a strong, negative cultural current. Conversely, less formal authority and fewer dedicated resources are needed to complete projects in which the cultural currents generate behavior and cooperation essential to project success.

The key issue is the degree of interdependency between the parent organization and the project team. In cases where the prevalent organizational culture supports the behaviors essential to project completion, a weaker, more flexible project management structure can be effective. For example, one of the major reasons Chaparral Steel is able to use a functional matrix to successfully complete incremental projects is that its culture contains strong norms for cooperation (Bowen et al., 1994). See Research Highlight 3.1: The Secret of Success for another example of how culture supports successful project management.

When the dominant organizational culture inhibits collaboration and innovation, it is advisable to insulate the project team from the dominant culture. Here it becomes necessary to create a self-sufficient project team. If a dedicated project team is impossible because of resource constraints, then at least a project matrix should be used where the project manager has dominant control over the project. In both cases, the managerial strategy is to create a distinct team subculture in which a new set of norms, customs, and values evolves that will be conducive to project completion.

Under extreme circumstances this project culture could even represent a counterculture in that many of the norms and values are the antithesis of the dominant, parent culture. Such was the case when IBM decided to develop their personal computer quickly in 1980 (Smith & Reinertsen, 1995). They knew that the project could get bogged down by the overabundance of computer knowledge and bureaucracy in the company. They also realized that they would have to work closely with suppliers and make use of many non-IBM parts if they were to get to the market quickly. This was not the IBM way at the time, so IBM established the PC project team in a warehouse in Boca Raton, Florida, far from corporate headquarters and other corporate development facilities that existed within the organization.

In *The Secret of Success: The Double Helix of Formal and Informal Structures in an R&D Laboratory* Polly Rizova revealed the results of a year-long investigation into the inner workings of a Fortune 500 R&D Lab. Through interviews with key participants and analysis of social networking data, Rizova assessed the efficacy of six high-tech development projects.

Four critical success factors emerged from her research. One element that is crucial to success is a heavy reliance on open and unrestricted patterns of communication, coupled with a low degree of formal reporting. In other words, team members freely interacted with each other regardless of title, experience, or discipline. A second key is having individuals on the project who are highly respected across the laboratory for their exceptional technical skills and experience. Similarly, it is also vital to have individuals involved in the project who are highly respected for their organizational expertise and experience. Having both "technical stars" and "organizational stars" on the project team was essential to success. The final factor is a strong and sustained support for the project from the company's corporate management. What's more, her analysis revealed the interactive nature of the four conditions, namely, that no one condition was likely to produce successful outcomes on its own, but only when put together in a way in which they reinforce each other. Here the culture of the laboratory was seen as the key catalyst.

Rizova describes a matrix system in which people work on multiple projects simultaneously but with a different wrinkle. Individuals occupy different positions and play different roles depending upon the project. For example, it is common for a senior engineer to be the manager of one project and a researcher on another that is led by his or her subordinate. In essence one must "boss" his or her own boss. At first glance this formal structure should create destructive tensions. However, Rizova argues that the organizational culture of the lab is the glue that keeps things running smoothly.

She describes a culture in which the social norms of cooperation, respect, and civility are upheld and reproduced. It is a culture characterized by trust and a strong drive toward superior individual and organizational learning and achievement. The culture is captured in the comments of researchers:

> That is one of the nicest things around here. Your opinions are listened to. Superiors consider our advice. You will find that most of the projects here are a team effort.
>
> What I like most is the positive thinking and the "whatever it takes" attitude. Personality conflicts can be devastating. Here everyone helps you and supports you. There is no "I" in the word team.
>
> Very friendly environment. . . . I met new people and learned a lot from them. They do not mind sharing their expertise.

* Polly S. Rizova, *The Secret of Success: The Double Helix of Formal and Informal Structures in an R&D Laboratory* (Stanford, CA: Stanford University Press, 2007).

Summary

This chapter examined two major characteristics of the parent organization that affect the implementation and completion of projects. The first is the formal structure of the organization and how it chooses to organize and manage projects. Although the individual project manager may have very little say as to how the firm chooses to manage projects, he or she must be able to recognize the options available as well as the inherent strengths and weaknesses of different approaches.

Three basic project management structures were described and assessed as to their weaknesses and strengths. Only under unique circumstances can a case be made for managing a project within the normal functional hierarchy. When thinking only in terms of what is best for the project, the creation of an independent project team is clearly favored. However, the most effective project management system appropriately balances the needs of the project with those of the parent organization. Matrix structures emerged out of the parent organization's need to share personnel and resources across multiple projects and operations while creating legitimate project focus. The matrix approach is a hybrid organizational form that combines elements of both the functional and project team forms in an attempt to realize the advantages of both.

The second major characteristic of the parent organization that was discussed in this chapter is the concept of organizational culture. Organizational culture is the pattern of beliefs and expectations shared by an organization's members. Culture includes the behavioral norms, customs, shared values, and the "rules of the game" for getting along and getting ahead within the organization. It is important for project managers to be "culture sensitive" so that they can develop appropriate strategies and responses and avoid violating key norms that would jeopardize their effectiveness within the organization.

The interaction between project management structure and organizational culture is a complicated one. We have suggested that in certain organizations, culture encourages the implementation of projects. In this environment the project management structure used plays a less decisive role in the success of the project. Conversely, for other organizations in which the culture stresses internal competition and differentiation, just the opposite may be true. The prevailing norms, customs, and attitudes inhibit effective project management, and the project management structure plays a more decisive role in the successful implementation of projects. At a minimum, under adverse cultural conditions, the project manager needs to have significant authority over the project team; under more extreme conditions firms should physically relocate dedicated project teams to complete critical projects. In both cases, the managerial strategy should be insulate project work from the dominant culture so that a more positive "subculture" can emerge among project participants.

The project management structure of the organization and the culture of the organization are major elements of the environment in which a project is initiated. Subsequent chapters will examine how project managers and professionals work within this environment to successfully complete projects.

Key Terms

Balanced matrix, *76*
Dedicated project team, *71*
Matrix, *75*
Organizational culture, *81*
Projectitis, *74*
Projectized organization, *72*
Project office, *80*
Strong matrix, *77*
Weak matrix, *76*

Review Questions

1. What are the relative advantages and disadvantages of the functional, matrix, and dedicated team approaches to managing projects?
2. What distinguishes a weak matrix from a strong matrix?
3. Under what conditions would it be advisable to use a strong matrix instead of a dedicated project team?
4. How can project management offices (POs) support effective project management?
5. Why is it important to assess the culture of an organization before deciding what project management structure should be used to complete a project?
6. Other than culture, what other organizational factors should be used to determine which project management structure should be used?
7. What do you believe is more important for successfully completing a project—the formal project management structure or the culture of the parent organization?

Exercises

1. Going to college is analogous to working in a matrix environment in that most students take more than one class and must distribute their time across multiple classes. What problems does this situation create for you? How does it affect your performance? How could the system be better managed to make your life less difficult and more productive?

2. You work for LL Company, which manufactures high-end optical scopes for hunting rifles. LL Company has been the market leader for the past 20 years and has decided to diversify by applying its technology to develop a top-quality binocular. What kind of project management structure would you recommend they use for this project? What information would you like to have to make this recommendation, and why?

3. You work for Barbata Electronics. Your R&D people believe they have come up with an affordable technology that will double the capacity of existing MP3 players and use audio format that is superior to MP3. The project is code named KYSO (Knock Your Socks Off). What kind of project management structure would you recommend they use for the KYSO project? What information would you like to have to make this recommendation and why?

4. This chapter discussed the role of values and beliefs in forming an organization's culture. The topic of organizational culture is big business on the Internet. Many companies use their Web pages to describe their mission, vision, and corporate values and beliefs. There also are many consulting firms that advertise how they help organizations to change their culture. The purpose of this exercise is for you to obtain information pertaining to the organizational culture for two different companies. You can go about this task by very simply searching on the key words "organizational culture" or "corporate vision and values." This search will identify numerous companies for you to use to answer the following questions. You may want to select companies that you would like to work for in the future.

   a. What are the espoused values and beliefs of the companies?

   b. Use the worksheet in Figure 3.6 to assess the Web page. What does the Web page reveal about the culture of this organization? Would this culture be conducive to effective project management?

5. Use the cultural dimensions listed in Figure 3.5 to assess the culture of your school. Instead of employees, consider students, and instead of management, use faculty. For example, member identity refers to the degree to which students identify with the school as a whole rather than their major or option. Either as individuals or in small groups rate the culture of your school on the 10 dimensions.

   a. What dimensions were easy to evaluate and which ones were not?

   b. How strong is the culture of your school?

   c. What functions does the culture serve for your school?

   d. Do you think the culture of your school is best suited to maximizing your learning? Why or why not?

   e. What kind of projects would be easy to implement in your school and what kind of projects would be difficult given the structure and culture of your school? Explain your answer.

6. You work as an analyst in the marketing department for Springfield International (SI). SI uses a weak matrix to develop new services. Management has created an extremely competitive organizational culture that places an emphasis upon achieving results above everything else. One of the project managers that you have been assigned to

help has been pressuring you to make his project your number one priority. He also wants you to expand the scope of your work on his project beyond what your marketing manager believes is necessary or appropriate. The project manager is widely perceived as a rising star within SI. Up to now you have been resisting the project manager's pressure and complying with your marketing manager's directives. However, your most recent interchange with the project manager ended by his saying, "I'm not happy with the level of help I am getting from you and I will remember this when I become VP of Marketing." How would you respond and why?

References

Block, T. R., and J. D. Frame, *The Project Office—A Key to Managing Projects Effectively* (Menlo Park, CA: Crisp Publications, 1998).

Block, T. R., and J. D. Frame, "Today's Project Office: Gauging Attitudes," *PM Network,* August 2001.

Bowen, H. K., K. B. Clark, C. A. Holloway, and S. C. Wheelwright, *The Perpetual Enterprise Machine* (New York: Oxford University Press, 1994).

Brown, S., and K. R. Eisenhardt, "Product Development: Past Research, Present Findings, and Future Directions," *Academy of Management Review,* vol. 20, no. 2 (1995), pp. 343–78.

Cameron, K. S., and R. E. Quinn, *Diagnosing and Changing Organizational Culture: Based on the Competing Values Framework* (Upper Saddle River, NJ: Prentice Hall, 2011).

Carlton, J., *Apple: The Inside Story of Intrigue, Egomania, and Business Blunders* (New York: Random House, 1997), pp. 13–14.

Casey, W., and W. Peck, "Choosing the Right PMO Setup," *PM Network,* vol. 15, no. 2 (2001), pp. 40–47.

Collins, J. C., and J. I. Porras, *Built to Last: The Successful Habits of Visionary Companies* (New York: HarperCollins, 1994), pp. 150–58.

Deal, T. E., and A. A. Kennedy, *Corporate Cultures: The Rites and Rituals of Corporate Life* (Reading, MA: Addison-Wesley, 1982).

De Laat, P. B., "Matrix Management of Projects and Power Struggles: A Case Study of an R&D Laboratory," *IEEE Engineering Management Review,* Winter 1995.

Filipczak, B., "Beyond the Gates of Microsoft," *Training,* September 1992, pp. 37–44.

Gallagher, R. S., *The Soul of an Organization: Understanding the Values That Drive Successful Corporate Cultures* (Chicago: Dearborn Trade Publishing, 2002).

Graham, R. J., and R. L. Englund, *Creating an Environment for Successful Projects: The Quest to Manage Project Management* (San Francisco: Jossey-Bass, 1997).

Gray, C., S. Dworatschek, D. H. Gobeli, H. Knoepfel, and E. W. Larson, "International Comparison of Project Organization Structures: Use and Effectiveness," *International Journal of Project Management,* vol. 8, no. 1 (February 1990), pp. 26–32.

Harrison, M. T., and J. M. Beyer, *The Culture of Organizations* (Englewood Cliffs, NJ: Prentice Hall, 1993).

Hobbs, B., and P. Ménard, "Organizational Choices for Project Management," in Paul Dinsmore (ed.), *The AMA Handbook of Project Management* (New York: AMACOM, 1993).

Hobday, M., "The Project-Based Organization: An Ideal Form for Managing Complex Products and Systems?" *Research Policy,* vol. 29, no. 17 (2000).

Jassawalla, A. R., and H. C. Sashittal, "Cultures that Support Product-Innovation Processes," *Academy of Management Executive,* vol. 15, no. 3 (2002), pp. 42–54.

Johnson, C. L., M. Smith, and L. K. Geary, *More Than My Share in All* (Washington, D.C.: Smithsonian Institute Publications, 1990).

Kerzner, H., *In Search of Excellence in Project Management* (New York: Von Nostrand Reinhold, 1997).

Kerzner, H., "Strategic Planning for the Project Office," *Project Management Journal,* vol. 34, no. 2 (2003), pp. 13–25.

Larson, E. W., "Project Management Structures" in *The Wiley Handbook for Managing Projects,* P. Morris & J. Pinto (eds.) (New York: Wiley, 2004), pp. 48–66.

Larson, E. W., and D. H. Gobeli, "Matrix Management: Contradictions and Insights," *California Management Review,* vol. 29, no. 4 (Summer 1987), p. 137.

Larson, E. W., and D. H. Gobeli, "Organizing for Product Development Projects," *Journal of Product Innovation Management,* vol. 5 (1988), pp. 180–90.

Larsson, U. (ed.), *Cultures of Creativity: The Centennial Exhibition of the Nobel Prize* (Canton, MA: Science History Publications, 2001).

Laslo, Z., and A. I. Goldberg, "Matrix Structures and Performance: The Search for Optimal Adjustments to Organizational Objectives?" *IEEE Transactions in Engineering Management,* vol. 48, no. 12 (2001).

Lawrence, P. R., and J. W. Lorsch, *Organization and Environment* (Homewood, IL: Irwin, 1969).

Majchrzak, A., and Q. Wang, "Breaking the Functional Mind-Set in Process Organizations," *Harvard Business Review,* September–October 1996, pp. 93–99.

Miller, J., *Lockheed Martin's Skunk Works* (New York: Speciality Publications, 1996).

Olson, E. M., O. C. Walker, Jr., and R. W. Ruekert, "Organizing for Effective New Product Development: The Moderating Role of Product Innovativeness," *Journal of Marketing,* vol. 59 (January 1995), pp. 48–62.

O'Reilly, C. A., J. Chatman, and D. F. Caldwell, "People and Organizational Culture: A Profile Comparison Approach to Assessing Person-Organization Fit," *Academy of Management Journal,* vol. 34, no. 3 (September 1991), pp. 487–516.

Pettegrew, A. M., "On Studying Organizational Culture," *Administrative Science Quarterly,* vol. 24, no. 4 (1979), pp. 570–81.

Powell, M., and J. Young, "The Project Management Support Office" in *The Wiley Handbook for Managing Projects,* P. Morris and J. Pinto (eds.) (New York: Wiley, 2004), pp. 937–69.

Rebello, K., "Inside Microsoft," *Business Weekly,* July 15, 1996, pp. 56–67.

time on the application until it was completed while the other engineers would work on multiple projects as needed. Likewise, GUI designers would work on the project at certain key stages in the product development cycle when their expertise was needed.

The head of Graphics managed the GUI designers' schedule while the head of Software managed the software engineer assignments. At the end of each project Account Managers submitted performance reviews of their team. The Director of Sales was responsible for the Account Managers' performance reviews based on customer satisfaction, generation of sales, and project performance.

Horizon believed in iterative development, and every two to three weeks Account Managers were expected to demonstrate the latest version of applications to clients. This led to useful feedback and in many cases redefining the scope of the project. Often clients wanted to add more functionality to their application once they realized what the software could do. Depending upon the complexity of the application and changes introduced once the project was under way, it typically took Horizon two to four months to deliver a finished product to a client.

Patti was currently working on three projects. One was for Shanghai Wok, a busy Chinese mom and pop restaurant located in downtown Charlotte, North Carolina. The owners of Shanghai Wok wanted Horizon to create a smartphone app that would allow customers to order and pay in advance for meals they would simply pick up at a walk-up window. The second project was for Taste of India that operated in Kannapolis, North Carolina. They wanted Horizon to create a phone app that would allow staff at the nearby bio-tech firms to order food that would be delivered on-site during lunch and dinner hours. The last project was for Nearly Normal, a vegetarian restaurant which wanted to send out e-mail alerts to subscribers that would describe in detail their daily fresh specials.

James Thrasher was an admirer of Google and encouraged a playful but focused environment at work. Employees were allowed to decorate their work spaces, bring pets to work, and play ping-pong or pool when they needed a break. Horizon paid its employees well but the big payoff was the annual Christmas bonus. This bonus was based on overall company profits, which were distributed proportionately based on pay grade and performance reviews. It was not uncommon for employees to receive a 10–15 percent boost in pay at the end of the year.

STATUS REPORT MEETING

As was her habit Patti entered the status report meeting room early. David Briggs was in the midst of describing the game-winning catch John Lorsch had made in last night's softball game. Horizon sponsored a co-ed city league softball team which most of the Account Managers played on. Patti had been coaxed to play to ensure that the requisite number of "females" were on the field. She balked at the idea at first; softball wasn't really her sport, but she was glad she did. Not only was it fun, but it gave her a chance to get to know the other managers.

James Thrasher entered the room and everyone settled down to business. He started off as he always did by asking if anybody had important news to bring to everyone's attention. Jackson Browne slowly raised his hand and said, "I am afraid I do. I just received notification from Apple IOS that they have rejected our TAT app." TAT was a phone app that Jackson was the project lead on that allowed subscribers to reserve and see in real time what swimming lanes were available at a prestigious athletic club. This announcement was followed by a collective groan. Before an Apple app could go operational it had to be submitted and approved by Apple. Usually this was not a problem, but lately Apple had been rejecting apps for a variety of reasons. Jackson went on to circulate the list of changes that had to be made before Apple would approve the app. The group studied the list, and in some cases ridiculed the new requirements.

Ultimately, James Thrasher asked Jackson how long it would take to make the necessary changes and resubmit the app for approval. Jackson felt it would probably take two to three weeks at most. Thrasher asked who the engineers that worked on this project were. Patti's heart fell. One of the app engineers who had developed the TAT app was working on her Shanghai Wok project. She knew what was going to happen next. Thrasher announced, "OK everyone, it only makes sense that these engineers are the best ones to finish what they had started so they are all going to have to be reassigned back to the TAT project. Those affected are going to have to get together after this meeting and figure how you are going to replace them." The meeting then proceeded as planned with all the account managers reporting the status of their projects, and sharing relevant issues with the group.

POST-MEETING

As everyone filed out, Patti looked around to see who else was in her same boat. There were three other Account Managers as well as Jackson Browne. Resource assignments were a reoccurring issue at Horizon given the nature of their work. Horizon had developed a policy where decisions were made based on project priority. Each project was assigned a Green, Blue or Purple designation based on the company priority. Priority status was based on the extent the project contributed to the mission of the firm. The Shanghai Wok project given its limited size and scope was a Purple project, which was the lowest ranking. The list of available software engineers was displayed on the big screen. Patti was only familiar with a few of the names.

Leigh Taylor who had the only Green project immediately selected Jason Wheeler from the list. She had used him before and was confident in his work. Tom Watson and Samantha Stewart both had Blue Projects and both needed to replace a mobile app engineer. They both immediately jumped on the name of Prem Mathew, claiming he was the best person for their project. After some friendly jousting, Tom said, "OK, Sam, you can have him; I remember when you helped me out on the Argos project; besides my project is just beginning. I'll take Shin Chen." Everyone looked at Patti; she started by saying, "You know, I am only familiar with a few of these names; I guess I'll go with Mike Thu." Jackson interjected, "Hey everyone, I am really sorry this happened, and I am sure Mike is a good programmer, but I recommend you work with Axel Gerthoff. I have used him before, and he is a very quick study and a joy to work with." This was a relief to Patti and she quickly took his advice. They left to submit a report to Thrasher detailing the decisions they each had made and the impact on their projects.

1. How successful was the post-meeting?
2. What factors contributed to the success or failure of this meeting?
3. What kind of project management structure does Horizon use? Is it the right structure? Explain.

4 Defining the Project

LEARNING OBJECTIVES

After reading this chapter you should be able to:

4-1 Identify key elements of a project scope statement and understand why a complete scope statement is critical to project success.

4-2 Understand why it is important to establish project priorities in terms of cost, time, and performance.

4-3 Demonstrate the importance of a work breakdown structure (WBS) to the management of projects and how it serves as a data base for planning and control.

4-4 Demonstrate how the organization breakdown structure (OBS) establishes accountability to organizational units.

4-5 Describe a process breakdown structure (PBS) and when to use it.

4-6 Create responsibility matrices for small projects.

4-7 Create a communication plan for a project.

OUTLINE

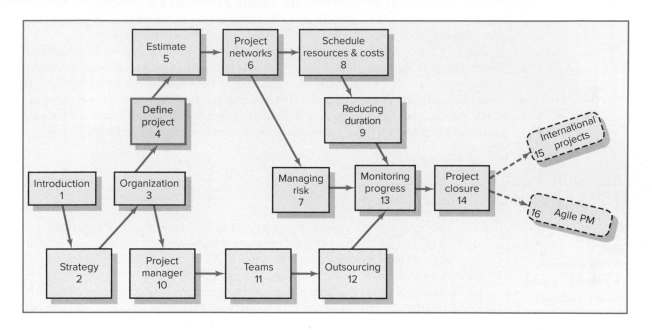

Select a dream
Use your dream to set a goal
Create a plan
Consider resources
Enhance skills and abilities
Spend time wisely
Start! Get organized and go
. . . it is one of those acro-whatevers, said Pooh. *

Project managers in charge of a single small project can plan and schedule the project tasks without much formal planning and information. However, when the project manager must manage several small projects or a large complex project, a threshold is quickly reached in which the project manager can no longer cope with the detail.

* Roger E. Allen and Stephen D. Allen, *Winnie-the-Pooh on Success* (New York: Penguin, 1997), p. 10.

This chapter describes a disciplined, structured method for selectively collecting information to use through all phases of the project life cycle, to meet the needs of all stakeholders (e.g., customer, project manager), and to measure performance against the strategic plan of the organization. The method suggested is a selective outline of the project called the *work breakdown structure.* The early stages of developing the outline serve to ensure that all tasks are identified and that participants of the project have an understanding of what is to be done. Once the outline and its detail are defined, an integrated information system can be developed to schedule work and allocate budgets. This baseline information is later used for control.

In addition, the chapter presents a variant of the work breakdown structure called the *process breakdown structure* as well as responsibility matrices that are used for smaller, less complex projects. With the work of the project defined through the *work breakdown structure,* the chapter concludes with the process of creating a communication plan used to help coordinate project activities and follow progress.

The five generic steps described herein provide a structured approach for collecting the project information necessary for developing a work breakdown structure. These steps and the development of project networks found in the next chapters all take place concurrently, and several iterations are typically required to develop dates and budgets that can be used to manage the project. The old saying "We can control only what we have planned" is true; therefore, defining the project is the first step.

4.1 Step 1: Defining the Project Scope

LO 4-1

Identify key elements of a project scope statement and understand why a complete scope statement is critical to project success.

Defining the project scope sets the stage for developing a project plan. Project scope is a definition of the end result or mission of your project—a product or service for your client/customer. The primary purpose is to define as clearly as possible the deliverable(s) for the end user and to focus project plans.

Research clearly shows that a poorly defined scope or mission is the most frequently mentioned barrier to project success. In a study involving more than 1,400 project managers in the United States and Canada, Gobeli and Larson (1990) found that approximately 50 percent of the planning problems relate to unclear definition of scope and goals. This and other studies suggest a strong correlation between project success and clear scope definition (Ashley et al., 1987; Pinto and Slevin, 1988; Standish Group, 2009). The scope document directs focus on the project purpose throughout the life of the project for the customer and project participants.

The scope should be developed under the direction of the project manager, customer, and other significant stakeholders. The project manager is responsible for seeing that there is agreement with the owner on project objectives, deliverables at each stage of the project, technical requirements, and so forth. For example, a deliverable in the early stage might be specifications; for the second stage, three prototypes for production; for the third, a sufficient quantity to introduce to market; and finally, marketing promotion and training.

Your project scope definition is a document that will be published and used by the project owner and project participants for planning and measuring project success. *Scope* describes what you expect to deliver to your customer when the project is complete. Your project scope should define the results to be achieved in specific, tangible, and measurable terms.

Employing a Project Scope Checklist

Clearly, project scope is the keystone interlocking all elements of a project plan. To ensure that scope definition is complete, you may wish to use the following checklist:

Project Scope Checklist

---

1. Project objective
2. Deliverables
3. Milestones
4. Technical requirements
5. Limits and exclusions
6. Reviews with customer

---

1. **Project objective.** The first step of project scope definition is to define the overall objective to meet your customer's need(s). For example, as a result of extensive market research a computer software company decides to develop a program that automatically translates verbal sentences in English to Russian. The project should be completed within three years at a cost not to exceed $1.5 million. Another example is to design and construct a portable, hazardous-waste thermal treatment system in 13 months at a cost not to exceed $13 million. The project objective answers the questions of what, when, how much, and at times, where.

2. **Deliverables.** The next step is to define major deliverables—the expected, measurable outputs over the life of the project. For example, deliverables in the early design phase of a project might be a list of specifications. In the second phase deliverables could be software coding and a technical manual. The next phase could be the prototype. The final phase could be final tests and approved software. Note: Deliverables and requirements are often used interchangeably.

3. **Milestones.** A milestone is a significant event in a project that occurs at a point in time. The milestone schedule shows only major segments of work; it represents first, rough-cut estimates of time, cost, and resources for the project. The milestone schedule is built using the deliverables as a platform to identify major segments of work and an end date—for example, testing complete and finished by July 1 of the same year. Milestones should be natural, important control points in the project. Milestones should be easy for all project participants to recognize.

4. **Technical requirements.** More frequently than not, a product or service will have technical requirements to ensure proper performance. Technical requirements typically clarify either the deliverables or define the performance specifications. For example, a technical requirement for a personal computer might be the ability to accept 120-volt alternating current or 240-volt direct current without any adapters or user switches. Another well-known example is the ability of 911 emergency systems to identify the caller's phone number and location of the phone. Examples from information systems projects include speed and capacity of database systems and connectivity with alternative systems. For understanding the importance of key requirements, see Snapshot from Practice 4.1: Big Bertha.

5. **Limits and exclusions.** The limits of scope should be defined. Failure to do so can lead to false expectations and to expending resources and time on the wrong problem. Examples of limits are: work on site is allowed only between the hours of 8:00 pm - 5:00 am; system maintenance and repair will be done only up to one month after final inspection; client will be billed for additional training beyond that

SNAPSHOT FROM PRACTICE 4.1

Big Bertha II versus the USGA's COR Requirement*

© Les Jorgensen/Getty

In 1991 Callaway Golf Equipment introduced their Big Bertha driver and revolutionized the golf equipment business. Big Bertha—named after the World War I German long-distance cannon—was much larger than conventional woods and lacked a hosel (the socket in the head of the club into which the shaft is inserted) so that the weight could be better distributed throughout the head. This innovative design gave the clubhead a larger sweet spot, which allowed a player to strike the golf ball off-center and not suffer much loss in distance or accuracy. Callaway has maintained its preeminent position in the golf industry by utilizing space-age technology to extend the accuracy and distance of golf equipment.

In 2000 Callaway introduced the Big Bertha ERC II forged titanium driver. The driver was technologically superior to any driver on the market. However, there was one big problem. The new version of Bertha did not conform to the coefficient of restitution (COR) requirement established by the United States Golf Association (USGA). As a result it was barred from use by golfers in North America who intended to play by the USGA's Rules of Golf.

The USGA believed that the rapid technological advances in golf equipment made by Callaway Golf and other golf manufacturers were threatening the integrity of the game. Players were hitting balls so much farther and straighter that golf courses around the world were being redesigned to make them longer and more difficult.

So in 1998 the USGA established performance thresholds for all new golf equipment. In order to prevent manufacturers from developing more powerful clubs, the USGA limited the COR of new golf equipment to 0.83. The COR was calculated by firing a golf ball at a driver out of a cannon-like machine at 109 miles per hour. The speed that the ball returned to the cannon could not exceed 83 percent of its initial speed (90.47 mph). The USGA called the ratio of incoming to outgoing velocity the coefficient of restitution (COR). The intent of the USGA COR threshold was to limit the distance that golf balls could be hit since studies indicated that 0.01 increase in COR resulted in two extra yards of carry. The Big Bertha ERC II's COR was 0.86.

After numerous efforts to get USGA to change its technical requirements, Callaway's engineers went back to the drawing board and in 2002 introduced Great Big Bertha II, which conformed to USGA's 0.83 COR restriction.

* John E. Gamble, "Callaway Golf Company: Sustaining Advantage in a Changing Industry," in A. A. Thompson, J. E. Gamble, and A. J. Strickland, *Strategy: Winning in the Marketplace* (Boston: McGraw-Hill/Irwin, 2004), pp. C204–C228.

SNAPSHOT FROM PRACTICE 4.2   Scope Statement

PROJECT OBJECTIVE

To construct a high-quality, custom home within five months at cost not to exceed $700,000 on lot 42A in Greendale, Oregon.

DELIVERABLES

- A 2,200-square-foot, 2½-bath, 3-bedroom, finished home.
- A finished garage, insulated and sheetrocked.
- Kitchen appliances to include range, oven, microwave, and dishwasher.
- High-efficiency gas furnace with programmable thermostat.

MILESTONES

1. Permits approved—March 5
2. Foundation poured—March 14
3. Drywall in. Framing, sheathing, plumbing, electrical, and mechanical inspections passed—May 25
4. Final inspection—June 7

TECHNICAL REQUIREMENTS

1. Home must meet local building codes.
2. All windows and doors must pass NFRC class 40 energy ratings.
3. Exterior wall insulation must meet an "R" factor of 21.
4. Ceiling insulation must meet an "R" factor of 38.
5. Floor insulation must meet an "R" factor of 25.
6. Garage will accommodate two large-size cars and one 20-foot Winnebago.
7. Structure must pass seismic stability codes.

LIMITS AND EXCLUSIONS

1. The home will be built to the specifications and design of the original blueprints provided by the customer.
2. Owner is responsible for landscaping.
3. Refrigerator is not included among kitchen appliances.
4. Air conditioning is not included but prewiring is included.
5. Contractor reserves the right to contract out services.
6. Contractor is responsible for subcontracted work.
7. Site work limited to Monday through Friday, 8:00 a.m. to 6:00 p.m.

CUSTOMER REVIEW

John and Joan Smith

---

prescribed in the contract. Exclusions further define the boundary of the project by stating what is not included. Examples include: data will be collected by the client, not the contractor; a house will be built, but no landscaping or security devices added; software will be installed, but no training given.

6. **Reviews with customer.** Completion of the scope checklist ends with a review with your customer—internal or external. The main concern here is the understanding of and agreement to expectations. Is the customer getting what he or she desires in deliverables? Does the project definition identify key accomplishments, budgets, timing, and performance requirements? Are questions of limits and exclusions covered? Clear communication in all these issues is imperative to avoid claims or misunderstanding.

Scope definition should be as brief as possible but complete; one or two pages are typical for small projects. See Snapshot from Practice 4.2: Scope Statement.

The project scope checklist in Step 1 is generic. Different industries and companies will develop unique checklists and templates to fit their needs and specific kinds of projects. A few companies engaged in contracted work refer to scope statements as "statements of work" (SOW). Other organizations use the term *project charter*. However, the term **project charter** has emerged to have a special meaning in the world of project management. A project charter refers to a document that authorizes the project manager to initiate and lead the project. This document is issued by upper management and provides the project manager with written authority to use organizational resources for project activities. Often the charter will include a brief scope description as well as such items as risk limits, business case, spending limits, and even team composition.

Many projects suffer from **scope creep,** which is the tendency for the project scope to expand over time—usually by changing requirements, specifications, and priorities. Scope creep can be reduced by carefully writing your scope statement. A scope statement that is too broad is an invitation for scope creep. Scope creep can have a positive or negative effect on the project, but in most cases scope creep means added costs and possible project delays. Changes in requirements, specifications, and priorities frequently result in cost overruns and delays. Examples are abundant—Denver airport baggage handling system; Boston's new freeway system ("The Big Dig"); Sochi Winter Olympics; and the list goes on. On software development projects, scope creep is manifested in bloated products in which added functionality undermines ease of use.

If the project scope needs to change, it is critical to have a sound change control process in place that records the change and keeps a log of all project changes. The log identifies the change, impact, and those responsible for accepting or rejecting a proposed change.

Change control is one of the topics of Chapter 7. Project managers in the field constantly suggest that dealing with changing requirements is one of their most challenging problems.

4.2 Step 2: Establishing Project Priorities

Understand why it is important to establish project priorities in terms of cost, time, and performance.

Quality and the ultimate success of a project are traditionally defined as meeting and/ or exceeding the expectations of the customer and/or upper management in terms of cost (budget), time (schedule), and performance (scope) of the project (see Figure 4.1). The interrelationship among these criteria varies. For example, sometimes it is necessary to compromise the performance and scope of the project to get the project done quickly or less expensively. Often the longer a project takes, the more expensive it becomes. However, a positive correlation between cost and schedule may not always be true. Other times project costs can be reduced by using cheaper, less efficient labor or equipment that extends the duration of the project. Likewise, as will be seen in Chapter 9, project managers are often forced to expedite or "crash" certain key activities by adding additional labor, thereby raising the original cost of the project.

One of the primary jobs of a project manager is to manage the trade-offs among time, cost, and performance. To do so, project managers must define and understand the nature of the priorities of the project. They need to have a candid discussion with the project customer and upper management to establish the relative importance of

FIGURE 4.1
Project Management Trade-offs

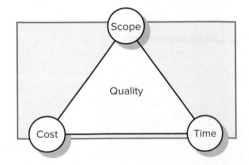

each criterion. For example, what happens when the customer keeps adding requirements? Or if, midway through the project, a trade-off must be made between cost and expediting, which criterion has priority?

One technique found in practice that is useful for this purpose is completing a **priority matrix** for the project to identify which criterion is constrained, which should be enhanced, and which can be accepted:

Constrain. The original parameter is fixed. The project must meet the completion date, specifications and scope of the project, or budget.

Enhance. Given the scope of the project, which criterion should be optimized? In the case of time and cost, this usually means taking advantage of opportunities to either reduce costs or shorten the schedule. Conversely, with regard to performance, enhancing means adding value to the project.

Accept. For which criterion is it tolerable not to meet the original parameters? When trade-offs have to be made, is it permissible for the schedule to slip, to reduce the scope and performance of the project, or to go over budget?

Figure 4.2 displays the priority matrix for the development of a new wireless router. Because *time* to market is important to sales, the project manager is instructed to take advantage of every opportunity to reduce completion time. In doing so, going over *budget* is acceptable though not desirable. At the same time, the original *performance* specifications for the modem as well as reliability standards cannot be compromised.

Priorities vary from project to project. For example, for many software projects time to market is critical, and companies like Microsoft may defer original scope requirements to later versions in order to get to the market first. Alternatively, for special event projects (conferences, parades, tournaments) time is constrained once the date has been announced, and if the budget is tight, the project manager will compromise the scope of the project in order to complete the project on time.

Some would argue that all three criteria are always constrained and that good project managers should seek to optimize each criterion. If everything goes well on a project and no major problems or setbacks are encountered, their argument may be valid. However, this situation is rare, and project managers are often forced to make tough decisions that benefit one criterion while compromising the other two. The purpose of this exercise is to define and agree on what the priorities and constraints of the project are so that when "push comes to shove," the right decisions can be made.

FIGURE 4.2
Project Priority Matrix

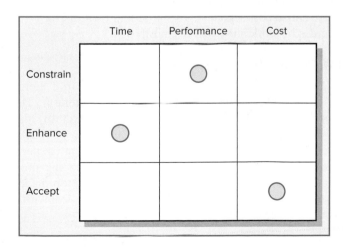

There are likely to be natural limits to the extent managers can constrain, optimize, or accept any one criterion. It may be acceptable for the project to slip one month behind schedule but no further or to exceed the planned budget by as much as $20,000. Likewise, it may be desirable to finish a project a month early, but after that cost conservation should be the primary goal. Some project managers document these limits as part of creating the priority matrix.

In summary, developing a priority matrix for a project *before the project begins* is a useful exercise. It provides a forum for clearly establishing priorities with customers and top management so as to create shared expectations and avoid misunderstandings. The priority information is essential to the planning process, where adjustments can be made in the scope, schedule, and budget allocation. Finally, the matrix is useful midway in the project for approaching a problem that must be solved.

One caveat must be mentioned; during the course of a project, priorities may change. The customer may suddenly need the project completed one month sooner, or new directives from top management may emphasize cost saving initiatives. The project manager needs to be vigilant in order to anticipate and confirm changes in priorities and make appropriate adjustments.

4.3 Step 3: Creating the Work Breakdown Structure

LO 4-3

Demonstrate the importance of a work breakdown structure (WBS) to the management of projects and how it serves as a data base for planning and control.

Major Groupings Found in a WBS

Once the scope and deliverables have been identified, the work of the project can be successively subdivided into smaller and smaller work elements. The outcome of this hierarchical process is called the **work breakdown structure (WBS).** Use of a WBS helps to assure project managers that all products and work elements are identified, to integrate the project with the current organization, and to establish a basis for control. Basically, the WBS is an outline of the project with different levels of detail.

Figure 4.3 shows the major groupings commonly used in the field to develop a hierarchical WBS. The WBS begins with the project as the final deliverable. Major project work deliverables/systems are identified first; then the subdeliverables necessary to accomplish the larger deliverables are defined. The process is repeated until the subdeliverable detail is small enough to be manageable and where one person can be responsible. This subdeliverable is further divided into work packages. Because the lowest subdeliverable usually includes several work packages, the work packages are grouped by type of work—for example, design and testing. These groupings within a subdeliverable are called cost accounts. This grouping facilitates a system for monitoring project progress by work, cost, and responsibility.

How WBS Helps the Project Manager

The WBS defines all the elements of the project in a hierarchical framework and establishes their relationships to the project end item(s). Think of the project as a large work package that is successively broken down into smaller work packages; the total project is the summation of all the smaller work packages. This hierarchical structure facilitates evaluation of cost, time, and technical performance at all levels in the organization over the life of the project. The WBS also provides management with information appropriate to each level. For example, top management deals primarily with major deliverables, while first-line supervisors deal with smaller subdeliverables and work packages.

FIGURE 4.3
Hierarchical Breakdown of the WBS

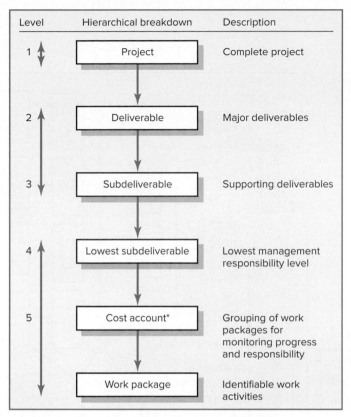

Level	Hierarchical breakdown	Description
1	Project	Complete project
2	Deliverable	Major deliverables
3	Subdeliverable	Supporting deliverables
4	Lowest subdeliverable	Lowest management responsibility level
5	Cost account*	Grouping of work packages for monitoring progress and responsibility
	Work package	Identifiable work activities

* This breakdown groups work packages by type of work within a deliverable and allows assignment of responsibility to an organizational unit. This extra step facilitates a system for monitoring project progress (discussed in Chapter 13).

Each item in the WBS needs a time and cost estimate. With this information it is possible to plan, schedule, and budget your project. The WBS also serves as a framework for tracking cost and work performance.

As the WBS is developed, organizational units and individuals are assigned responsibility for executing work packages. This integrates the work and the organization. In practice, this process is sometimes called the organization breakdown structure (OBS), which will be further discussed later in the chapter.

Use of the WBS provides the opportunity to "roll up" (sum) the budget and actual costs of the smaller work packages into larger work elements so that performance can be measured by organizational units and work accomplishment.

The WBS can also be used to define communication channels and assist in understanding and coordinating many parts of the project. The structure shows the work and organizational units responsible and suggests where written communication should be directed. Problems can be quickly addressed and coordinated because the structure integrates work and responsibility.

A Simple WBS Development

Figure 4.4 shows a simplified WBS to develop a new prototype tablet computer. At the top of the chart (level 1) is the project end item—the E-Slim Tablet x-13 Prototype. The subdeliverables levels (2–5) below level 1 represent further decomposition of work. The levels of the structure can also represent information for different levels of

FIGURE 4.4 Work Breakdown Structure

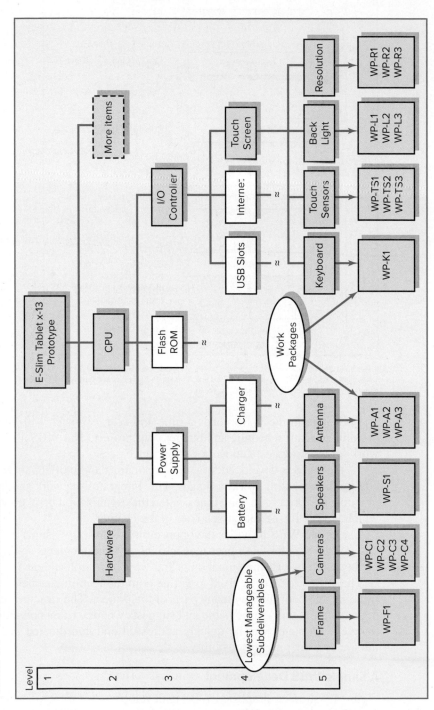

management. For example, level 1 information represents the total project objective and is useful to top management; levels 2, 3, and 4 are suitable for middle management; and level 5 is for first-line managers.

In Figure 4.4 level 2 indicates there are two major deliverables—Hardware and CPU, or central processing unit. (There are likely to be other major deliverables such as software, but for illustrative purposes we are limiting our focus to just two major deliverables.) At level 3, the CPU is connected to three deliverables—Power Supply, Flash ROM, and I/O Controller. The I/O Controller has three subdeliverables at level 4—USB Slots, Internet, and Touch Screen. The many subdeliverables for USB Slots and Internet have not been decomposed. The Touch Screen (shaded) has been decomposed down to level 5 and to the work package level.

Note that level 2, Hardware, skips levels 3 and 4 because the final subdeliverables can be pushed down to the lowest manageable level 5; skipping levels 3 and 4 suggests little coordination is needed and skilled team members are already familiar with the work needed to complete the level 5 subdeliverables. For example, Hardware requires four subdeliverables at level 5—Frame, Cameras, Speakers, and Antenna. Each subdeliverable includes work packages that will be completed by an assigned organizational unit. Observe that the Cameras subdeliverable includes four work packages—WP-C1, 2, 3, and 4. The Back Light, a subdeliverable of Touch Screen, includes three work packages—WP-L 1, 2, and 3.

The lowest level of the WBS is called a **work package.** Work packages are short-duration tasks that have a definite start and stop point, consume resources, and represent cost. Each work package is a control point. A work package manager is responsible for seeing that the package is completed on time, within budget, and according to technical specifications. Practice suggests a work package should not exceed 10 workdays or one reporting period. If a work package has a duration exceeding 10 days, check or monitoring points should be established within the duration, say, every three to five days, so progress and problems can be identified before too much time has passed. Each work package of the WBS should be as independent of other packages of the project as possible. No work package is described in more than one subdeliverable of the WBS.

There is an important difference from start to finish between the last work breakdown subdeliverable and a work package. Typically, a work breakdown subdeliverable includes the outcomes of more than one work package from perhaps two or three departments. Therefore, the subdeliverable does not have a duration of its own and does not consume resources or cost money directly. (In a sense, of course, a duration for a particular work breakdown element can be derived from identifying which work package must start first [earliest] and which package will be the latest to finish; the difference from start to finish becomes the duration for the subdeliverable.) The higher elements are used to identify deliverables at different phases in the project and to develop status reports during the execution stage of the project life cycle. Thus, the work package is the basic unit used for planning, scheduling, and controlling the project.

To review, each work package in the WBS

1. Defines work (what).
2. Identifies time to complete a work package (how long).
3. Identifies a time-phased budget to complete a work package (cost).
4. Identifies resources needed to complete a work package (how much).
5. Identifies a single person responsible for units of work (who).
6. Identifies monitoring points for measuring progress (how well).

SNAPSHOT FROM PRACTICE 4.3   Creating a WBS

Figure 4.4 represents the classic WBS in which the project is broken down to the lowest manageable deliverable and subsequent work packages. Many situations do not require this level of detail. This begs the question of how far you should break down the work.

There is no set answer to this question. However, here are some tips given by project managers:

Break down the work until you can do an estimate that is accurate enough for your purposes. If you are doing a ball-park estimate to see if the project is worthy of serious consideration, you probably do not need to break it down beyond major deliverables. On the other hand, if you are pricing a project to submit a competitive bid, then you are likely to go down to the work package level.

The WBS should conform to how you are going to schedule work. For example, if assignments are made in terms of days, then tasks should be limited as best as possible to one day or more to complete. Conversely, if hours are the smallest unit for scheduling, then work can be broken down to one-hour increments.

Final activities should have clearly defined start/end events. Avoid open-ended tasks like "research" or "market analysis." Take it down to the next level in which deliverables/outcomes are more clearly defined.

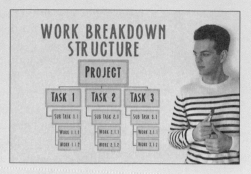

© astephan/Shutterstock

Instead of ending with market analysis include items such as identify market share, list user requirements, or write a problem statement.

If accountability and control are important, then break the work down so that one individual is clearly responsible for the work. For example, instead of stopping at product design, take it to the next level and identify specific components of the design (i.e., electrical schematics, power source, etc.) that different individuals will be responsible for creating.

The bottom line is that the WBS should provide the level of detail needed to manage the specific project successfully.

Creating a WBS from scratch can be a daunting task. Project managers should take advantage of relevant examples from previous projects to begin the process.

WBSs are products of group efforts. If the project is small, the entire project team may be involved breaking down the project into its components. For large, complex projects, the people responsible for the major deliverables are likely to meet to establish the first two levels of deliverables. In turn, further detail would be delegated to the people responsible for the specific work. Collectively this information would be gathered and integrated into a formal WBS by a project support person. The final version would be reviewed by the inner echelon of the project team. Relevant stakeholders (most notably customers) would be consulted to confirm agreement and revise when appropriate.

Project teams developing their first WBS frequently forget that the structure should be end-item, output oriented. First attempts often result in a WBS that follows the organization structure—design, marketing, production, finance. If a WBS follows the organization structure, the focus will be on the organization function and processes rather than the project output or deliverables. In addition, a WBS with a process focus will become an accounting tool that records costs by function rather than a tool for "output" management. Every effort should be made to develop a WBS that is output oriented in order to concentrate on concrete deliverables. See Snapshot from Practice 4.3: Creating a WBS.

4.4 Step 4: Integrating the WBS with the Organization

LO 4-4

Demonstrate how the organization breakdown structure (OBS) establishes accountability to organizational units.

The WBS is used to link the organizational units responsible for performing the work. In practice, the outcome of this process is the **organization breakdown structure (OBS).** The OBS depicts how the firm has organized to discharge work responsibility. The purposes of the OBS are to provide a framework to summarize organization unit work performance, identify organization units responsible for work packages, and tie the organizational unit to cost control accounts. Recall, cost accounts group similar work packages (usually under the purview of a department). The OBS defines the organization subdeliverables in a hierarchical pattern in successively smaller and smaller units. Frequently, the traditional organization structure can be used. Even if the project is completely performed by a team, it is necessary to break down the team structure for assigning responsibility for budgets, time, and technical performance.

As in the WBS, the OBS assigns the lowest organizational unit the responsibility for work packages within a cost account. Herein lies one major strength of using WBS and OBS; they can be *integrated* as shown in Figure 4.5. The intersection of work packages and the organizational unit creates a project control point **(cost account)** that integrates work and responsibility. For example, at level 5 Touch Sensors has three work packages that have been assigned to the Design, Quality Control Test, and Production departments. The intersection of the WBS and OBS represents the set of work packages necessary to complete the subdeliverable located immediately above and the organizational unit on the left responsible for accomplishing the packages at the intersection. Note that the design department is responsible for five different work packages across the Hardware and Touch Screen deliverables.

Later we will use the intersection as a cost account for management control of projects. For example, the Cameras element requires completion of work packages whose primary responsibility will include the design, QC test, production, and outsourcing departments. Control can be checked from two directions—outcomes and responsibility. In the execution phase of the project, progress can be tracked vertically on deliverables (client's interest) and tracked horizontally by organization responsibility (owner's interest).

4.5 Step 5: Coding the WBS for the Information System

Gaining the maximum usefulness of a breakdown structure depends on a coding system. The codes are used to define levels and elements in the WBS, organization elements, work packages, and budget and cost information. The codes allow reports to be consolidated at any level in the structure. The most commonly used scheme in practice is numeric indention. A portion of the E-Slim Tablet x-13 Prototype project is presented in Exhibit 4.1.

Note the project identification is 1.0. Each successive indention represents a lower element or work package. Ultimately the numeric scheme reaches down to the work package level, and all tasks and elements in the structure have an identification code. The "cost account" is the focal point because all budgets, work assignments, time, cost, and technical performance come together at this point.

This coding system can be extended to cover large projects. Additional schemes can be added for special reports. For example, adding a "23" after the code could indicate a site location, an elevation, or a special account such as labor. Some letters can be used as special identifiers such as "M" for materials or "E" for engineers. You are not

FIGURE 4.5 **Integration of WBS and OBS**

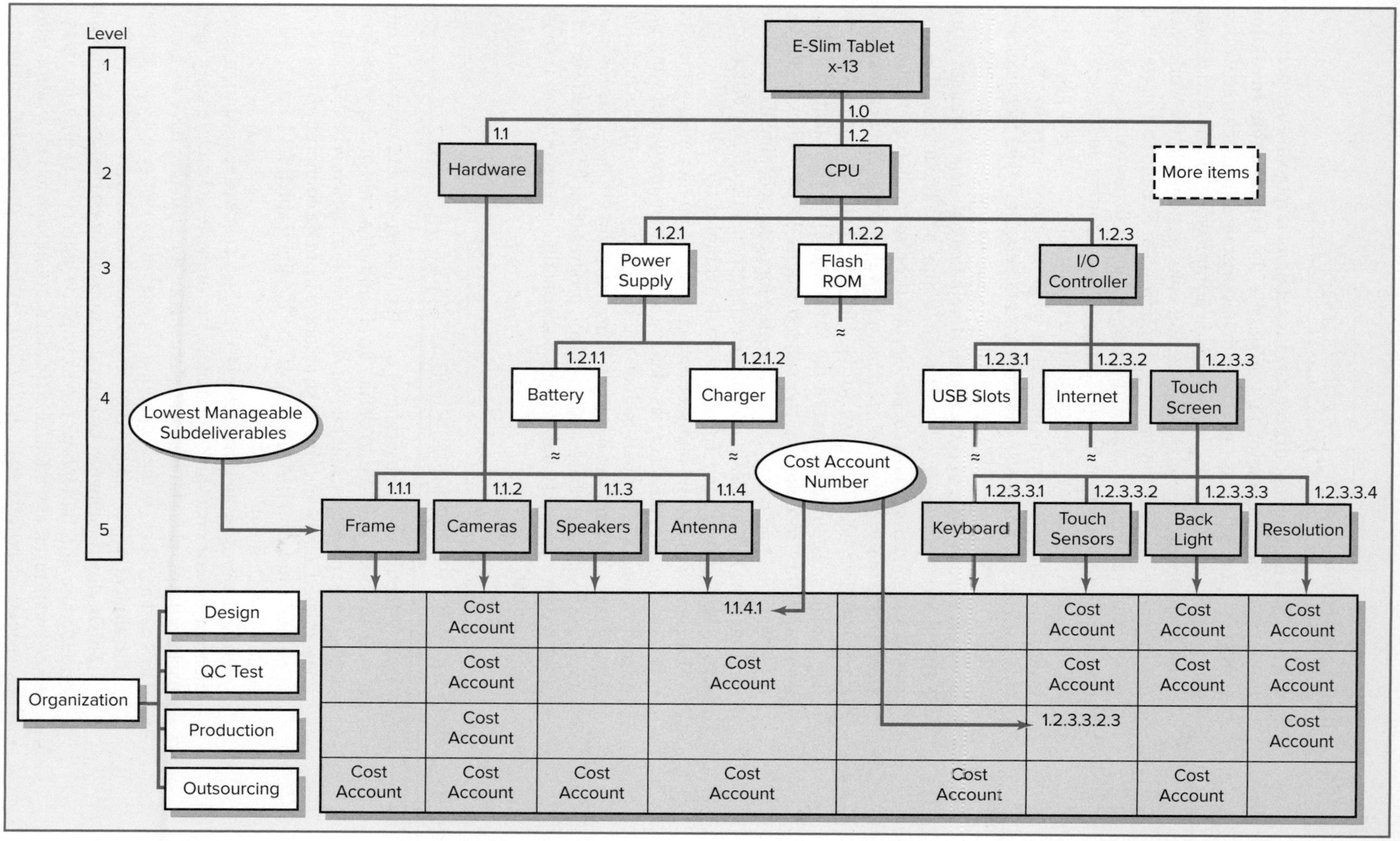

EXHIBIT 4.1
Coding the WBS

		Task Mode ▾	Task Name ▾
1			⊟ **1 E-Slim Tablet x-13 Prototype**
2			⊟ **1.1 Hardware**
3			1.1.1 Cameras
4			1.1.2 Speakers
5			1.1.3 Antenna
6			⊟ **1.2 CPU**
7			⊟ **1.2.1 Power supply**
8			1.2.1.1 Battery (more items)
9			1.2.1.2 Charger (more items)
10			⊟ **1.2.2 Flash Rom (more items)**
11			1.2.2.1 I/O controller
12			1.2.2.2 USB slots (more items)
13			1.2.2.3 Internet (more items)
14			⊟ **1.2.3 Touch screen**
15			⊟ **1.2.3.1 Keyboard**
16			1.2.3.1.1 Work package
17			⊟ **1.2.3.2 Touch sensors**
18			1.2.3.2.1 Work package
19			1.2.3.2.2 Work package
20			1.2.3.2.3 Work package
21			1.2.3.3 Back light (more items)
22			1.2.3.4 Resolution (more items)

limited to only 10 subdivisions (0–9); you can extend each subdivision to large numbers—for example, .1–.99 or .1–.9999. If the project is small, you can use whole numbers. The following example is from a large, complex project:

$$3R-237A-P2-33.6$$

where 3R identifies the facility, 237A represents elevation and the area, P2 represents pipe two inches wide, and 33.6 represents the work package number. In practice most organizations are creative in combining letters and numbers to minimize the length of WBS codes.

On larger projects, the WBS is further supported with a **WBS dictionary** that provides detailed information about each element in the WBS. The dictionary typically includes the work package level (code), name, and functional description. In some cases the description is supported with specifications. The availability of detailed descriptions has an added benefit of dampening scope creep.

4.6 Process Breakdown Structure

LO 4-5

Describe a process breakdown structure (PBS) and when to use it.

The WBS is best suited for design and build projects that have tangible outcomes such as an offshore mining facility or a new car prototype. The project can be decomposed or broken down into major deliverables, subdeliverables, further subdeliverables, and ultimately to work packages. It is more difficult to apply WBS to less tangible, *process-oriented* projects in which the final outcome is a product of a series of steps or phases. Here, the big difference is that the project evolves over time with each phase affecting the next phase. Information systems projects typically fall in this category—for example, creating an extranet website or an internal software database system. Process projects are driven by performance requirements, not by plans/blueprints. Some practitioners choose to utilize what we refer to as a **process breakdown structure (PBS)** instead of the classic WBS.

Figure 4.6 provides an example of a PBS for a software development project. Instead of being organized around deliverables, the project is organized around phases. Each of the five major phases can be broken down into more specific activities until a sufficient level of detail is achieved to communicate what needs to be done to complete that phase. People can be assigned to specific activities, and a complementary OBS can be created just as is done for the WBS. Deliverables are not ignored but are defined as outputs required to move to the next phase. The software industry often refers to PBS as the "waterfall method" since progress flows downward through each phase.[1]

[1] The limitations of the waterfall method for software development have led to the emergence of Agile project management methods that are the subject of Chapter 17.

FIGURE 4.6 **PBS for Software Development Project**

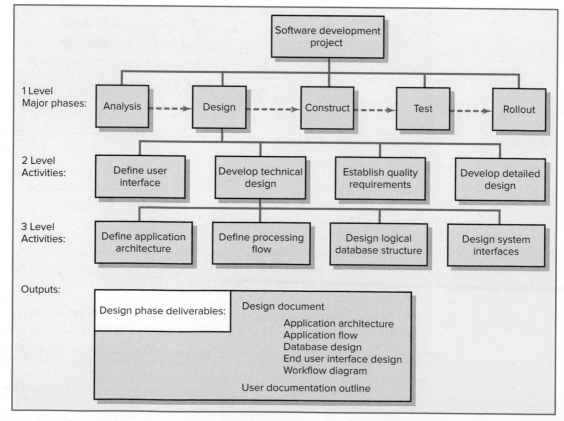

Checklists that contain the phase exit requirements are developed to manage project progress. These checklists provide the means to support phase walk-throughs and reviews. Checklists vary depending upon the project and activities involved but typically include the following details:

- Deliverables needed to exit a phase and begin a new one.
- Quality checkpoints to ensure that deliverables are complete and accurate.
- Sign-offs by all responsible stakeholders to indicate that the phase has been successfully completed and that the project should move on to the next phase.

As long as exit requirements are firmly established and deliverables for each phase are well defined, the PBS provides a suitable alternative to the standard WBS for projects that involve extensive development work.

4.7 Responsibility Matrices

 LO 4-6

Create responsibility matrices for small projects.

In many cases, the size and scope of the project do not warrant an elaborate WBS or OBS. One tool that is widely used by project managers and task force leaders of small projects is the **responsibility matrix** (RM). The RM (sometimes called a linear responsibility chart) summarizes the tasks to be accomplished and who is responsible for what on a project. In its simplest form an RM consists of a chart listing all the project activities and the participants responsible for each activity. For example, Figure 4.7 illustrates an RM for a market research study. In this matrix the R is used to identify the committee member who is responsible for coordinating the efforts of other team members assigned to the task and making sure that the task is completed. The S is used to identify members of the five-person team who will support and/or assist the individual responsible. Simple RMs like this one are useful not only for organizing and assigning responsibilities for small projects but also for subprojects of large, more complex projects.

More complex RMs not only identify individual responsibilities but also clarify critical interfaces between units and individuals that require coordination. For

FIGURE 4.7   Responsibility Matrix for a Market Research Project

	Project Team				
Task	Richard	Dan	Dave	Linda	Elizabeth
Identify target customers	R	S		S	
Develop draft questionnaire	R	S	S		
Pilot-test questionnaire		R		S	
Finalize questionnaire	R	S	S	S	
Print questionnaire					R
Prepare mailing labels					R
Mail questionnaires					R
Receive and monitor returned questionnaires				R	S
Input response data			R		
Analyze results		R	S	S	
Prepare draft of report	S	R	S	S	
Prepare final report	R		S		

R = Responsible
S = Supports/assists

FIGURE 4.8 Responsibility Matrix for the Conveyor Belt Project

Deliverables	Organization							
	Design	Development	Documentation	Assembly	Testing	Purchasing	Quality Assur.	Manufacturing
Architectural designs	1	2			2		3	3
Hardware specifications	2	1				2	3	
Kernel specifications	1	3			3			3
Utilities specifications	2	1						
Hardware design	1			3		3		3
Disk drivers	3	1	2					
Memory management	1	3			3			
Operating system documentation	2	2	1					3
Prototypes	5		4	1	3	3	3	4
Integrated acceptance test	5	2	2		1		5	5

1 Responsible
2 Support
3 Consult
4 Notification
5 Approval

example, Figure 4.8 is an RM for a larger, more complex project to develop a new piece of automated equipment. Notice that within each cell a numeric coding scheme is used to define the nature of involvement on that specific task. Such an RM extends the WBS/OBS and provides a clear and concise method for depicting responsibility, authority, and communication channels.

Responsibility matrices provide a means for all participants in a project to view their responsibilities and agree on their assignments. They also help clarify the extent or type of authority exercised by each participant in performing an activity in which two or more parties have overlapping involvement. By using an RM and by defining authority, responsibility, and communications within its framework, the relationship between different organizational units and the work content of the project is made clear.

4.8 Project Communication Plan

LO 4-7

Create a communication plan for a project.

Once the project deliverables and work are clearly identified, following up with an internal communication plan is vital. Stories abound of poor communication as a major contributor to project failure. Having a robust communications plan can go a long way toward mitigating project problems and can ensure that customers, team members, and other stakeholders have the information to do their jobs.

The communication plan is usually created by the project manager and/or the project team in the early stage of project planning.

Communication is a key component in coordinating and tracking project schedules, issues, and action items. The plan maps out the flow of information to different stakeholders and becomes an integral part of the overall project plan. The purpose of a project communication plan is to express what, who, how, and when information will be transmitted to project stakeholders so schedules, issues, and action items can be tracked.

Project communication plans address the following core questions:

- What information needs to be collected and when?
- Who will receive the information?
- What methods will be used to gather and store information?
- What are the limits, if any, on who has access to certain kinds of information?
- When will the information be communicated?
- How will it be communicated?

Developing a communication plan that answers these questions usually entails the following basic steps:

1. **Stakeholder analysis.** Identify the target groups. Typical groups could be the customer, sponsor, project team, project office, or anyone who needs project information to make decisions and/or contribute to project progress. A common tool found in practice to initially identify and analyze major project stakeholders' communication needs is presented in Figure 4.9.[2] How and what is communicated is influenced by the stakeholder interest and power. Some of these stakeholders may have the power either to block or enhance your project. By identifying stakeholders and prioritizing them on the "Power/Interest" map, you can plan the type and frequency of communications needed. (More on stakeholders will be discussed in Chapter 10.)

[2] For a more elaborate scheme for assessing stakeholders, see: Lynda Bourne, *Stakeholder Relationship Management* (Farnham, U.K.: Gower Publishing Ltd., 2009).

FIGURE 4.9
Stakeholder
Communications

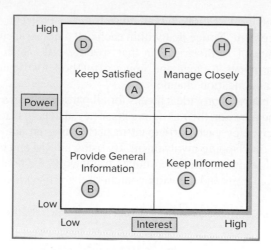

For example, on a typical project you want to manage closely the professionals doing the work, while you want to satisfy senior management and project sponsor with periodic updates. Unions and operation managers interested in capacity would be someone you would want to keep informed, while you would only need to provide general information to the legal, public relations, and other departments.

2. **Information needs.** What information is pertinent to stakeholders who contribute to the project's progress? The simplest answer to this question can be obtained by asking the different people what information they need and when they need it. For example, top management needs to know how the project is progressing, whether it is encountering critical problems, and the extent to which project goals are being realized. This information is required so that they can make strategic decisions and manage the portfolio of projects. Project team members need to see schedules, task lists, specifications, and the like, so they know what needs to be done next. External groups need to know any changes in the schedule and performance requirements of the components they are providing. Frequent information needs found in communication plans are:

Project status reports	Deliverable issues
Changes in scope	Team status meetings
Gating decisions	Accepted request changes
Action items	Milestone reports

3. **Sources of information.** When the information needs are identified, the next step is to determine the sources of information. That is, where does the information reside? How will it be collected? For example, information relating to the milestone report, team meetings, and project status meetings would be found in the minutes and reports of various groups.

4. **Dissemination modes.** In today's world, traditional status report meetings are being supplemented by e-mail, teleconferencing, SharePoint, and a variety of database sharing programs to circulate information. In particular, many companies are using the Web to create a "virtual project office" to store project information. Project management software feeds information directly to the website so that different people have immediate access to relevant project information. In some cases, appropriate information is routed automatically to key stakeholders. Backup paper hardcopy to specific stakeholders is still critical for many project changes and action items.

FIGURE 4.10   Shale Oil Research Project Communication Plan

What Information	Target Audience	When?	Method of Communication	Provider
Milestone report	Senior management and project manager	Bimonthly	E-mail and hardcopy	Project office
Project status reports & agendas	Staff and customer	Weekly	E-mail and hardcopy	Project manager
Team status reports	Project manager and project office	Weekly	E-mail	Team recorder
Issues report	Staff and customer	Weekly	E-mail	Team recorder
Escalation reports	Staff and customer	When needed	Meeting and hardcopy	Project manager
Outsourcing performance	Staff and customer	Bimonthly	Meeting	Project manager
Accepted change requests	Project office, senior mgmt., customer, staff, and project mgr.	Anytime	E-mail and hardcopy	Design department
Oversight gate decisions	Senior management and project manager	As required	E-mail meeting report	Oversight group or project office

5. **Responsibility and timing.** Determine who will send out the information. For example, a common practice is to have secretaries of meetings forward the minutes or specific information to the appropriate stakeholders. In some cases the responsibility lies with the project manager or project office. Timing and frequency of distribution appropriate to the information need to be established.

The advantage of establishing a communication plan is that instead of responding to information requests, you are controlling the flow of information. This reduces confusion and unnecessary interruptions, and it can provide project managers greater autonomy. Why? By reporting on a regular basis how things are going and what is happening, you allow senior management to feel more comfortable about letting the team complete the project without interference. See Figure 4.10 for a sample Shale Oil Research Project Communication Plan.

The importance of establishing up-front a plan for communicating important project information cannot be overstated. Many of the problems that plague a project can be traced back to insufficient time devoted to establishing a well-grounded internal communication plan.

Summary

The project scope definition, priorities, and breakdown structure are the keys to nearly every aspect of managing the project. The scope definition provides focus and emphasis on the end item(s) of the project. Establishing project priorities allows managers to make appropriate trade-off decisions. The WBS structure helps ensure all tasks of the project are identified and provides two views of the project—one on deliverables and one on organization responsibility. The WBS avoids having the project driven by organization function or by a finance system. The structure forces attention to realistic requirements of personnel, hardware, and budgets. Use of the structure provides a powerful framework for project control that identifies deviations from plan, identifies responsibility, and spots areas for improved performance. No well-developed project plan or control system is possible without a disciplined, structured approach. The WBS, OBS, and cost account codes provide this discipline. The WBS will serve as the database for developing the project network which establishes the timing of work, people, equipment, and costs.

PBS is often used for process-based projects with ill-defined deliverables. In small projects responsibility matrices may be used to clarify individual responsibility.

Clearly defining your project is the first and most important step in planning. The absence of a clearly defined project plan consistently shows up as the major reason for project failures. Whether you use a WBS, PBS, or responsibility matrix will depend primarily on the size and nature of your project. Whatever method you use, definition of your project should be adequate to allow for good control as the project is being implemented. Follow-up with a clear communication plan for coordinating and tracking project progress will help keep important stakeholders informed and avoid some potential problems.

Key Terms

Cost account, *113*	Process breakdown	Scope statement, *105*
Milestone, *103*	structure (PBS), *116*	WBS dictionary, *115*
Organization breakdown	Project charter, *105*	Work breakdown
structure (OBS), *113*	Responsibility matrix, *117*	structure (WBS), *108*
Priority matrix, *107*	Scope creep, *106*	Work package, *111*

Review Questions

1. What are the six elements of a typical scope statement?
2. What questions does a project objective answer? What would be an example of a good project objective?
3. What does it mean if the priorities of a project include: Time-constrain, Scope-accept, and Cost-enhance?
4. What kinds of information are included in a work package?
5. When would it be appropriate to create a responsibility matrix rather than a full-blown WBS?
6. How does a communication plan benefit management of projects?

Exercises

1. You are in charge of organizing a dinner-dance concert for a local charity. You have reserved a hall that will seat 30 couples and have hired a jazz combo.
   a. Develop a scope statement for this project that contains examples of all the elements. Assume that the event will occur in four weeks and provide your best guess estimate of the dates for milestones.
   b. What would the priorities likely be for this project?
2. In small groups, identify real life examples of a project that would fit each of the following priority scenarios:
   a. Time-constrain, Scope-enhance, Cost-accept
   b. Time-accept, Scope-constrain, Cost-accept
   c. Time-constrain, Scope-accept, Cost-enhance

3. Develop a WBS for a project in which you are going to build a bicycle. Try to identify all of the major components and provide three levels of detail.

4. You are the father or mother of a family of four (kids ages 13 and 15) planning a weekend camping trip. Develop a responsibility matrix for the work that needs to be done prior to starting your trip.

5. Develop a WBS for a local stage play. Be sure to identify the deliverables and organizational units (people) responsible. How would you code your system? Give an example of the work packages in one of your cost accounts. Develop a corresponding OBS which identifies who is responsible for what.

6. Use an example of a project you are familiar with or are interested in. Identify the deliverables and organizational units (people) responsible. How would you code your system? Give an example of the work packages in one of your cost accounts.

7. Develop a communication plan for an airport security project. The project entails installing the hardware and software system that (1) scans a passenger's eyes, (2) fingerprints the passenger, and (3) transmits the information to a central location for evaluation.

8. Go to an Internet search engine (e.g., Google) and type in "project communication plan." Check three or four that have ".gov" as their source. How are they similar or dissimilar? What would be your conclusion concerning the importance of an internal communication plan?

9. Your roommate is about to submit a scope statement for a spring concert sponsored by the entertainment council at Western Evergreen State University (WESU). WESU is a residential university with over 22,000 students. This will be the first time in six years since WESU sponsored a spring concert. The entertainment council has budgeted $40,000 for the project. The event is to occur on June 5th. Since your roommate knows you are taking a class on project management she has asked you to review her scope statement and make suggestions for improvement. She considers the concert a resume-building experience and wants to be as professional as possible. Below is a draft of her scope statement. What suggestions would you make and why?

WESU Spring Music Concert

Project Objective

    To organize and deliver a 6-hour music concert

Deliverables

- Concert security
- Contact local newspapers and radio stations
- Separate beer garden
- Six hours of musical entertainment
- Design a commemorative concert T-shirt
- Local sponsors
- Food venues
- Event insurance
- Safe environment

Milestones

1. Secure all permissions and approvals
2. Sign big-name artist
3. Contact secondary artists
4. Secure vendor contracts

5. Advertising campaign
6. Plan set-up
7. Concert
8. Clean-up

Technical Requirements

1. Professional sound stage and system
2. At least five performing acts
3. Restroom facilities
4. Parking
5. Compliance with WESU and city requirements/ordinances

Limits and Exclusions

- Seating capacity for 8,000 students
- Performers are responsible for travel arrangement to and from WESU
- Performers must provide own liability insurance
- Performers and security personnel will be provided lunch and dinner on the day of the concert
- Vendors contribute 25 percent of sales to concert fund
- Concert must be over at 12:15 a.m.

Customer Review: WESU

References

Ashley, D. B., et al., "Determinants of Construction Project Success," *Project Management Journal,* vol. 18, no. 2 (June 1987), p. 72.

Chilmeran, A. H., "Keeping Costs on Track," *PM Network,* vol. 19, no. 2 (2004), pp. 45–51.

Gary, L. "Will Project Scope Cost You—Or Create Value?" *Harvard Management Update,* January 2005.

Gobeli, D. H., and E. W. Larson, "Project Management Problems," *Engineering Management Journal,* vol. 2 (1990), pp. 31–36.

Ingebretsen, M., "Taming the Beast," *PM Network,* July 2003, pp. 30–35.

Katz, D. M., "Case Study: Beware 'Scope Creep' on ERP Projects," *CFO.com,* March 27, 2001.

Kerzner, H., *Project Management: A Systems Approach to Planning,* 8th ed. (New York: Van Nostrand Reinhold, 2003).

Lewis, J. P., *Project Planning, Scheduling and Controlling,* 3rd ed. (Burr Ridge, IL: McGraw-Hill, 2000).

Luby, R. E., D. Peel, and W. Swahl, "Component-Based Work Breakdown Structure," *Project Management Journal,* vol. 26, no. 2 (December 1995), pp. 38–44.

Murch, R., *Project Management: Best Practices for IT Professionals* (Upper Darby, NJ: Prentice Hall, 2001).

Pinto, J. K., and D. P. Slevin, "Critical Success Factors Across the Project Life Cycle," *Project Management Journal,* vol. 19, no. 3 (June 1988), p. 72.

Pitagorsky, G., "Realistic Project Planning Promotes Success," *Engineer's Digest,* vol. 29, no. 1 (2001).

PMI Standards Committee, *Guide to the Project Management Body of Knowledge* (Newton Square, PA: Project Management Institute, 2000).

Posner, B. Z., "What It Takes to Be a Good Project Manager," *Project Management Journal,* vol. 18, no. 1 (March 1987), p. 52.

Raz, T., and S. Globerson, "Effective Sizing and Content Definition of Work Packages," *Project Management Journal,* vol. 29, no. 4 (1998), pp. 17–23.

The Standish Group, *CHAOS Summary 2009*, pp. 1–4.

Tate, K., and K. Hendrix, "Chartering IT Projects," *Proceedings, 30th Annual, Project Management Institute* (Philadelphia, PA. 1999), CD.

Case 4.1

Manchester United Soccer Club

Nicolette Larson was loading the dishwasher with her husband, Kevin, and telling him about the first meeting of the Manchester United Tournament Organizing Committee. Nicolette, a self-confessed "soccer mom," had been elected tournament director and was responsible for organizing the club's first summer tournament.

Manchester United Soccer Club (MUSC), located in Manchester, New Hampshire, was formed in 1992 as a way of bringing recreational players to a higher level of competition and preparing them for the State Olympic Development Program and/or high school teams. The club currently has 24 boys and girls (ranging in age from under 9 to 16) on teams affiliated with the New Hampshire Soccer Association and the Granite State Girls Soccer League. The club's board of directors decided in the fall to sponsor a summer invitational soccer tournament to generate revenue. Given the boom in youth soccer, hosting summer tournaments has become a popular method for raising funds. MUSC teams regularly compete in three to four tournaments each summer at different locales in New England. These tournaments have been reported to generate between $50,000 and $70,000 for the host club.

MUSC needs additional revenue to refurbish and expand the number of soccer fields at the Rock Rimmon soccer complex. Funds would also be used to augment the club's scholarship program, which provides financial aid to players who cannot afford the $450 annual club dues.

Nicolette gave her husband a blow-by-blow account of what transpired during the first tournament committee meeting that night. She started the meeting by having everyone introduce themselves and by proclaiming how excited she was that the club was going to sponsor its own tournament. She then suggested that the committee brainstorm what needed to be done to pull off the event; she would record their ideas on a flipchart.

What emerged was a free-for-all of ideas and suggestions. One member immediately stressed the importance of having qualified referees and spent several minutes describing in detail how his son's team was robbed in a poorly officiated championship game. This was followed by other stories of injustice on the soccer field. Another member suggested that they needed to quickly contact the local colleges to see if they could use their fields. The committee spent more than 30 minutes talking about how they should screen teams and how much they should charge as an entry fee. An argument broke out over whether they should reward the winning teams in each age bracket with medals or trophies. Many members felt that medals were too cheap, while others thought the trophies would be too expensive. Someone suggested that they seek local corporate sponsors to help fund the tournament. The proposed sale of tournament T-shirts and sweatshirts was followed by a general critique of the different shirts parents had acquired at different tournaments. One member advocated that they recruit an artist he knew to develop a unique silk-screen design for the tournament. The meeting adjourned 30 minutes late with only half of the members remaining until the end. Nicolette drove home with seven sheets of ideas and a headache.

As Kevin poured a glass of water for the two aspirin Nicolette was about to take, he tried to comfort her by saying that organizing this tournament would be a big project not unlike the projects he worked on at his engineering and design firm. He offered to sit down with her the next night and help her plan the project. He suggested that the first thing they needed to do was to develop a WBS for the project.

1. Make a list of the major deliverables for the project and use them to develop a draft of the work breakdown structure for the tournament that contains at least three levels of detail. What are the major deliverables associated with hosting an event such as a soccer tournament?
2. How would developing a WBS alleviate some of the problems that occurred during the first meeting and help Nicolette organize and plan the project?
3. Where can Nicolette find additional information to help her develop a WBS for the tournament?
4. How could Nicolette and her task force use the WBS to generate cost estimates for the tournament? Why would this be useful information?

Case 4.2

The Home Improvement Project

Lukas Nelson and his wife, Anne, and their three daughters had been living in their house for over five years when they decided it was time to make some modest improvements. One area they both agreed needed an upgrade was the bathtub. Their current house had one standard shower bathtub combination. Lukas was 6 feet four, and could barely squeeze into it. In fact, he had taken only one bath since they moved in. He and Anne both missed soaking in the older, deep bathtubs they enjoyed when they lived back East.

Fortunately, the previous owners that built the house had plumbed the corner of a large exercise room in the basement for a hot tub. They contacted a trusted remodeling contractor who assured them it would be relatively easy to install a new bathtub and it shouldn't cost more than $1,500. They decided to go ahead with the project.

First the Nelsons went to the local plumbing retailer to pick out a tub. They soon realized that for a few hundred dollars more they could buy a big tub with water jets (a Jacuzzi). With old age on the horizon a Jacuzzi seemed like a luxury that was worth the extra money.

Originally the plan was to install the tub using the simple plastic frame the bath came with and install a splash guard around the tub. Once Anne saw the tub, frame, and splashguard in the room she balked. She did not like how it looked with the cedar paneling in the exercise room. After significant debate, Ann won out, and the Nelsons agreed to pay extra to have a cedar frame built for the tub and use attractive tile instead of the plastic splashguard. Lukas rationalized the changes would pay for themselves when they tried to sell the house.

The next hiccup occurred when it came time to address the flooring issue. The exercise room was carpeted, which wasn't ideal when getting out of a bathtub. The original idea was to install relatively cheap laminated flooring in the drying and undressing area adjacent to the tub. However, the Nelsons couldn't agree on the pattern to use. One of Anne's friends said it would be a shame to put such cheap flooring in such a nice room. She felt they should consider using tile. The contractor agreed and said he knew a tile installer who needed work and would give them a good deal.

Lukas reluctantly agreed that the laminated options just didn't fit the style or quality of the exercise room. Unlike the laminated floor debate both Anne and Lukas immediately liked a tile pattern that matched the tile used around the tub. Anxious not to delay the project, they agreed to pay for the tile flooring.

Once the tub was installed and the framing was almost completed, Anne realized that something had to be done about the lighting. One of her favorite things to do was to read while soaking in the tub. The existing lights didn't provide sufficient illumination for doing so. Lukas knew this was "non-negotiable" and they hired an electrician to install additional lighting over the bathtub.

While the lighting was being installed and the tile was being laid, another issue came up. The original plan was to tile only the exercise room and use remnant rugs to cover the area away from the tub where the Nelsons did their exercises. The Nelsons were very happy with how the tile looked and fit with the overall room. However, it clashed with the laminated flooring in the adjacent bathroom. Lukas agreed with Ann, that it really made the adjacent bathroom look cheap and ugly. He also felt the bathroom was so small it wouldn't cost much more.

After a week the work was completed. Both Lukas and Anne were quite pleased with how everything turned out. It cost much more than they had planned, but they planned to live in the house until the girls graduated from college so they felt it was a good long-term investment.

Anne had the first turn using the bathtub followed by their three girls. Everyone enjoyed the Jacuzzi. It was 10:00 p.m. when Lukas began running water for his first bath. At first the water was steaming hot, but by the time he was about to get in, it was lukewarm at best. Lukas groaned, "After paying all of that money I still can't enjoy a bath."

The Nelsons rationed bathing for a couple weeks, until they decided to find out what if anything could be done about the hot water problem. They asked a reputable heating contractor to assess the situation. The contractor reported that the hot water tank was insufficient to service a family of five. This had not been discovered before because baths were rarely taken in the past. The contractor said it would cost $2,200 to replace the existing water heater with a larger one that would meet their needs. The heating contractor also said if they wanted to do it right they should replace the existing furnace with a more energy efficient one. A new furnace would not only heat the house but also indirectly heat the water tank. Such a furnace would cost $7,500, but with the improved efficiency and savings in the gas bill, the furnace would pay for itself in 10 years. Besides, the Nelsons would likely receive tax credits for the more fuel-efficient furnace.

Three weeks later, after the new furnace was installed, Lukas settled into the new bathtub. He looked around the room at all the changes that had been made and muttered to himself, "And to think that all I wanted was to soak in a nice, hot bath."

1. What factors and forces contributed to scope creep in this case?
2. Is this an example of good or bad scope creep? Explain.
3. How could scope creep have been better managed by the Nelsons?

5

Estimating Project Times and Costs

LEARNING OBJECTIVES

After reading this chapter you should be able to:

5-1 Understand estimating project times and costs are the foundation for project planning and control.

5-2 Describe guidelines for estimating time, costs, and resources.

5-3 Describe the methods, uses, and advantages and disadvantages of top-down and bottom-up estimating methods.

5-4 Distinguish different kinds of costs associated with a project.

5-5 Suggest a scheme for developing an estimating database for future projects.

5-6 Understand the challenge of estimating mega projects and describe steps that lead to better informed decisions.

5-7 Define a "white elephant" in project management and provide examples.

OUTLINE

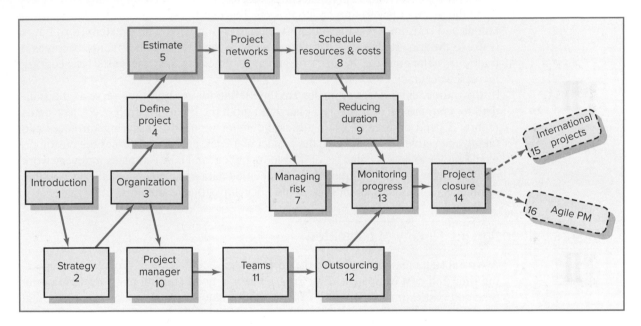

Project estimation is indeed a yardstick for project cost control. And if the yardstick is faulty, you start on the "wrong foot." . . . We exhort you not to underestimate the estimate. *

Given the urgency to start work on the project, managers sometimes minimize or avoid the effort to follow through on estimating project time and cost. This attitude is a huge mistake and costly. There are important reasons to make the effort and incur the cost of estimating for your project. Exhibit 5.1 summarizes some key reasons.

Estimating is the process of forecasting or approximating the time and cost of completing project deliverables. Estimating processes are frequently classified as top-down and bottom-up. Top-down estimates are usually done by senior management. Management will often derive estimates from analogy, group consensus, or mathematical relationships. Bottom-up estimates are typically performed by the people who are

LO 5-1

Understand estimating project times and costs are the foundation for project planning and control.

* O. P. Kharbanda and J. K. Pinto, *What Made Gertie Gallop: Learning from Project Failures* (New York: Von Nostrand Reinhold, 1996), p. 73.

EXHIBIT 5.1
Why Estimating Time and Cost Is Important

- Estimates are needed to support good decisions.
- Estimates are needed to schedule work.
- Estimates are needed to determine how long the project should take and its cost.
- Estimates are needed to determine whether the project is worth doing.
- Estimates are needed to develop cash flow needs.
- Estimates are needed to determine how well the project is progressing.

Source: O. P. Kharbanda and J. K. Pinto, *What Made Gertie Gallop: Learning from Project Failures* (New York: Von Nostrand Reinhold, 1996), p. 73.

doing the work. Their estimates are based on estimates of elements found in the work breakdown structure.

All project stakeholders prefer accurate cost and time estimates, but they also understand the inherent uncertainty in all projects. Inaccurate estimates lead to false expectations and consumer dissatisfaction. Accuracy is improved with greater effort, but is it worth the time and cost?—estimating costs money! Project estimating becomes a trade-off, balancing the benefits of better accuracy against the costs for securing increased accuracy.

Cost, time, and budget estimates are the lifeline for control; they serve as the standard for comparison of actual and plan throughout the life of the project. Project status reports depend on reliable estimates as the major input for measuring variances and taking corrective action. Ideally, the project manager, and in most cases the customer, would prefer to have a database of detailed schedule and cost estimates for every work package in the project. Regrettably, such detailed data gathering is not always possible or practical and other methods are used to develop project estimates.

5.1 Factors Influencing the Quality of Estimates

A typical statement in the field is the desire to "have a 95 percent probability of meeting time and cost estimates." *Past experience* is a good starting point for developing time and cost estimates. But past experience estimates must almost always be refined by other considerations to reach the 95 percent probability level. Factors related to the uniqueness of the project will have a strong influence on the accuracy of estimates. Project, people, and external factors all need to be considered to improve quality of estimates for project times and costs.

Planning Horizon

The quality of the estimate depends on the *planning horizon;* estimates of current events are close to 100 percent accurate but are reduced for more distant events. For example, cost estimates for a party you are organizing this weekend should be much more accurate than the estimates for a party that will take place in six months. The accuracy of time and cost estimates should improve as you move from the conceptual phase to the point where individual work packages are defined. Long-duration projects increase the uncertainty in estimates.

Project Complexity

Time to implement new *technology* has a habit of expanding in an increasing, nonlinear fashion. Sometimes poorly written scope specifications for new technology result in errors in estimating times and costs.

People

The *people* factor can influence the quality of time and cost estimates. For example, accuracy of estimates depends on the skills of the people making the estimates. How familiar are they with the task they are estimating?

Project Structure and Organization

Which *project structure* is chosen to manage the project will influence time and cost estimates. One of the major advantages of a dedicated project team discussed earlier is the speed gained from concentrated focus and localized project decisions. This speed comes at an additional cost of tying up personnel full time. Conversely, projects operating in a matrix environment may reduce costs by more efficiently sharing personnel across projects but may take longer to complete since attention is divided and coordination demands are higher.

Padding Estimates

In some cases people are inclined to *pad estimates*. For example, if you are asked how long it takes you to drive to the airport, you might give an average time of 30 minutes, assuming a 50/50 chance of getting there in 30 minutes. If you are asked the fastest you could possibly get there, you might reduce the driving time to 20 minutes. Finally, if you are asked how long the drive would take if you absolutely had to be there to meet with the president, it is likely you would increase the estimate to say 50 minutes to ensure not being late. In work situations where you are asked for time and cost estimates, most of us are inclined to add a little padding to increase the probability and reduce the risk of being late. If everyone at all levels of the project adds a little padding to reduce risk, the project duration and cost are seriously overstated. This phenomenon causes some managers or owners to call for a 10–15 percent cut in time and/or cost for the project. Of course the next time the game is played, the person estimating cost and/or time will pad the estimate to 20 percent or more. Clearly such games defeat chances for realistic estimates, which is what is needed to be competitive.

Organization Culture

Organization culture can significantly influence project estimates. In some organizations padding estimates is tolerated and even privately encouraged. Other organizations place a premium on accuracy and strongly discourage estimating gamesmanship. Organizations vary in the importance they attach to estimates. The prevailing belief in some organizations is that detailed estimating takes too much time and is not worth the effort or that it's impossible to predict the future. Other organizations subscribe to the belief that accurate estimates are the bedrock of effective project management. Organization culture shapes every dimension of project management; estimating is not immune to this influence.

Other Factors

Finally, *nonproject factors* can impact time and cost estimates. For example, equipment down-time can alter time estimates. National holidays, vacations, and legal limits can influence project estimates. Project priority can influence resource assignment and impact time and cost.

Project estimating is a complex process. The quality of time and cost estimates can be improved when these variables are considered in making the estimates. Estimates of time and cost together allow the manager to develop a time-phased budget, which is imperative for project control. Before discussing macro and micro estimating methods for times and costs, a review of estimating guidelines will remind us of some of the important "rules of the game" that can improve estimating.

5.2 Estimating Guidelines for Times, Costs, and Resources

LO 5-2

Describe guidelines for estimating time, costs, and resources.

Managers recognize time, cost, and resource estimates must be accurate if project planning, scheduling, and controlling are to be effective. However, there is substantial evidence suggesting poor estimates are a major contributor to projects that have failed. Therefore, every effort should be made to see that initial estimates are as accurate as possible since the choice of no estimates leaves a great deal to luck and is not palatable to serious project managers. Even though a project has never been done before, a manager can follow seven guidelines to develop useful work package estimates.

1. **Responsibility.** At the work package level, estimates should be made by the person(s) most familiar with the task. Draw on their expertise! Except for supertechnical tasks, those responsible for getting the job done on schedule and within budget are usually first-line supervisors or technicians who are experienced and familiar with the type of work involved. These people will not have some preconceived, imposed duration for a deliverable in mind. They will give an estimate based on experience and best judgment. A secondary benefit of using those responsible is the hope they will "buy in" to seeing that the estimate materializes when they implement the work package. If those involved are not consulted, it will be difficult to hold them responsible for failure to achieve the estimated time. Finally, drawing on the expertise of team members who will be responsible helps to build communication channels early.

2. **Use several people to estimate.** It is well known that a cost or time estimate usually has a better chance of being reasonable and realistic when several people with relevant experience and/or knowledge of the task are used (sometimes called "crowdsourcing"). True, people bring different biases based on their experience. But discussion of the individual differences in their estimate leads to consensus and tends to eliminate extreme estimate errors.

3. **Normal conditions.** When task time, cost, and resource estimates are determined, they are based on certain assumptions. *Estimates should be based on normal conditions, efficient methods, and a normal level of resources.* Normal conditions are sometimes difficult to discern, but it is necessary to have a consensus in the organization as to what normal conditions mean in this project. If the normal workday is eight hours, the time estimate should be based on an eight-hour day. Similarly, if the normal workday is two shifts, the time estimate should be based on a two-shift workday. Any time estimate should reflect efficient methods for the resources normally available. The time estimate should represent the normal level of resources—people or equipment. For example, if three programmers are available for coding or two road graders are available for road construction, time and cost estimates should be based on these normal levels of resources unless it is anticipated the project will

change what is currently viewed as "normal." In addition, possible conflicts in demand for resources on parallel or concurrent activities should not be considered at this stage. The need for adding resources will be examined when resource scheduling is discussed in a later chapter.

4. **Time units.** Specific time units to use should be selected early in the development phase of the project network. *All task time estimates need consistent time units.* Estimates of time must consider whether normal time is represented by calendar days, workdays, workweeks, person days, single shift, hours, minutes, etc. In practice the use of workdays is the dominant choice for expressing task duration. However, in projects such as a heart transplant operation, minutes probably would be more appropriate as a time unit. One such project that used minutes as the time unit was the movement of patients from an old hospital to an elegant new one across town. Since there were several life-endangering moves, minutes were used to ensure patient safety so proper emergency life-support systems would be available if needed. The point is, network analysis requires a standard unit of time. When computer programs allow more than one option, some notation should be made of any variance from the standard unit of time. If the standard unit of time is a five-day workweek and the estimated activity duration is in calendar days, it must be converted to the normal workweek.

5. **Independence.** Estimators should treat each task as independent of other tasks that might be integrated by the WBS. Use of first-line managers usually results in considering tasks independently; this is good. Top managers are prone to aggregate many tasks into one time estimate and then deductively make the individual task time estimates add to the total. If tasks are in a chain and performed by the same group or department, it is best not to ask for all the time estimates in the sequence at once to avoid the tendency for a planner or a supervisor to look at the whole path and try to adjust individual task times in the sequence to meet an arbitrary imposed schedule or some rough "guesstimate" of the total time for the whole path or segment of the project. This tendency does not reflect the uncertainties of individual activities and generally results in optimistic task time estimates. In summary, each task time estimate should be considered independently of other activities.

6. **Contingencies.** *Work package estimates should not include allowances for contingencies.* The estimate should assume normal or average conditions even though every work package will not materialize as planned. For this reason top management needs to create an extra fund for contingencies that can be used to cover unforeseen events.

7. **Adding risk assessment to the estimate helps to avoid surprises to stakeholders.** It is obvious some tasks carry more time and cost risks than others. For example, a new technology usually carries more time and cost risks than a proven process. Simply identifying the degree of risk lets stakeholders consider alternative methods and alter process decisions. A simple breakdown by optimistic, most likely, and pessimistic for task time could provide valuable information regarding time and cost. See Chapter 7 for further discussion of project risk.

Where applicable, these guidelines will greatly help to avoid many of the pitfalls found so often in practice. See Snapshot from Practice 5.1: Reducing Estimating Errors for a similar set of guidelines.

SNAPSHOT FROM PRACTICE 5.1 — Reducing Estimating Errors*

Complexity is the major source of estimating error, says Kerry Willis, Project Management Sr. Director at the healthcare services organization Cigna, in Hartford, Connecticut. "Project managers cannot possibly be experts in all areas and therefore need to rely on the stakeholders for their expertise when estimating," Willis notes. To minimize errors he recommends treating estimating as a living process and not a one-time event.

He follows the same approach on all of his projects:

1. **Identify all of the stakeholders** based on the scope of the project and organizational history.

2. **Involve the stakeholders when creating the estimates.** "You can't hold people accountable for estimates they didn't help create," Willis says.

3. **Aggregate the estimates by comparing several models** (resource based, parametric, etc.).

4. **Manage the project against the estimates.** This includes making adjustments based on changes in project scope.

5. **Track projects closely** using tools such as earned value to gauge progress toward estimates.

6. **Track actual costs and time at a granular level** to recalibrate the model for future projects.

"The initial estimate could be perfect, but if it is not managed, then the end result will be bad and people will point to the estimating process," Willis argues.

* S. Swanson, "Estimating Errors," *PMNetwork*, October 2011, pp. 62–66.

5.3 Top-Down versus Bottom-Up Estimating

LO 5-3

Describe the methods, uses, and advantages and disadvantages of top-down and bottom-up estimating methods.

Since estimating efforts cost money, the time and detail devoted to estimating are important decisions. Yet, when estimating is considered, you as a project manager may hear statements such as these:

> *Rough order of magnitude is good enough. Spending time on detailed estimating wastes money.*

> *Time is everything; our survival depends on getting there first! Time and cost accuracy is not an issue.*

> *The project is internal. We don't need to worry about cost.*

> *The project is so small, we don't need to bother with estimates. Just do it.*

However, there are sound reasons for using top-down or bottom-up estimates. Table 5.1 depicts conditions that suggest when one approach is preferred over another.

Top-down estimates usually are derived from someone who uses experience and/or information to determine the project duration and total cost. However, these estimates are sometimes made by top managers who have very little knowledge of the component activities used to complete the project. For example, a mayor of a major

TABLE 5.1
Conditions for Preferring Top-Down or Bottom-Up Time and Cost Estimates

Condition	Top-Down Estimates	Bottom-Up Estimates
Strategic decision making	X	
Cost and time important		X
High uncertainty	X	
Internal, small project	X	
Fixed-price contract		X
Customer wants details		X
Unstable scope	X	

SNAPSHOT FROM PRACTICE 5.2

Council Fumes as Tram Tale Unfolds*

Portland, Oregon's, Willamette riverfront development has exploded with seven condominium towers and a new health sciences center under construction. The health science complex is to be linked with Oregon Health Sciences University (OHSU), which is high on a nearby hill, with an aerial cable tram.

The aerial tram linking the waterfront district to OHSU is to support the university expansion, to increase biotechnology research, and to become Portland's icon equivalent to Seattle's Space Needle. All of the hype turned south when news from a hearing suggested that the real budget for the tram construction, originally estimated at $15 million, is going to be about $55–$60 million, more than triple the original estimate. The estimate could even go higher.

Commissioners want to find out why city staff knowingly relied on flawed estimates. Mike Lindberg, president of the nonprofit Aerial Transportation Inc., acknowledged "the $15 million number was not a good number. It was simply a guesstimate." Commissioner

© Spaces Images/Blend Images LLC

Erik Sten said, "Those numbers were presented as much more firm than they appear to have been. . . . It appears the actual design wasn't costed out. That's pretty shoddy."

* *The Oregonian,* January 13, 2006, by Frank Ryan, pages A1 and A14, and April 2, 2006, page A1.

city making a speech noted that a new law building would be constructed at a cost of $23 million and would be ready for occupancy in two and one-half years. Although the mayor probably asked for an estimate from someone, the estimate could have come from a luncheon meeting with a local contractor who wrote an estimate (guesstimate) on a napkin. This is an extreme example, but in a relative sense this scenario is frequently played out in practice. See Snapshot from Practice 5.2: Council Fumes, for another example of this. The question actually is, *do these estimates represent low-cost, efficient methods?* Seldom. The fact that the estimate came from the top can influence people responsible to "do what it takes to make the estimate."

If possible and practical, you want to push the estimating process down to the work package level for **bottom-up estimates** that establish low-cost, efficient methods. This process can take place after the project has been defined in detail. Good sense suggests project estimates should come from the people most knowledgeable about the estimate needed. The use of several people with relevant experience with the task can improve the time and cost estimate. The bottom-up approach at the work package level can serve as a check on cost elements in the WBS by rolling up the work packages and associated cost accounts to major deliverables. Similarly, resource requirements can be checked. Later, the time, resource, and cost estimates from the work packages can be consolidated into time-phased networks, resource schedules, and budgets that are used for control.

The bottom-up approach also provides the customer with an opportunity to compare the low-cost, efficient method approach with any imposed restrictions. For example, if the project completion duration is imposed at two years and your bottom-up analysis tells you the project will take two and one-half years, the client can now consider the trade-off of the low-cost method versus compressing the project to two years—or in rare cases canceling the project. Similar trade-offs can be compared for different levels of resources or increases in technical performance. The assumption is any movement away from the low-cost, efficient method will increase costs—e.g., overtime. The preferred approach in defining the project is to make rough top-down estimates, develop the WBS/OBS, make bottom-up estimates, develop schedules and budgets, and reconcile differences between top-down and bottom-up estimates. Hopefully, these steps will be done *before* final negotiation with either an internal or external customer. In conclusion, the ideal approach is for the project manager to allow enough time for both the top-down and bottom-up estimates to be worked out so a complete plan based on reliable estimates can be offered to the customer. In this way false expectations are minimized for all stakeholders and negotiation is reduced.

5.4 Methods for Estimating Project Times and Costs

Top-Down Approaches for Estimating Project Times and Costs

At the strategic level top-down estimating methods are used to evaluate the project proposal. Sometimes much of the information needed to derive accurate time and cost estimates is not available in the initial phase of the project—for example, design is not finalized. In these situations top-down estimates are used until the tasks in the WBS are clearly defined.

Consensus Methods

This method simply uses the pooled experience of senior and/or middle managers to estimate the total project duration and cost. This typically involves a meeting where experts discuss, argue, and ultimately reach a decision as to their best guess estimate. Firms seeking greater rigor will use the Delphi Method to make these macro estimates. See Snapshot from Practice 5.3: The Delphi Method.

SNAPSHOT FROM PRACTICE 5.3　　The Delphi Method

Originally developed by the RAND Corporation in 1969 for technological forecasting, the **Delphi Method** is a group decision process about the likelihood that certain events will occur. The Delphi Method makes use of a panel of experts familiar with the kind of project in question. The notion is that well-informed individuals, calling on their insights and experience, are better equipped to estimate project costs/times than theoretical approaches or statistical methods. Their responses to estimate questionnaires are anonymous, and they are provided with a summary of opinions.

Experts are then encouraged to reconsider, and if appropriate, to change their previous estimate in light of the replies of other experts. After two or three rounds it is believed that the group will converge toward the "best" response through this consensus process. The midpoint of responses is statistically categorized by the median score. In each succeeding round of questionnaires, the range of responses by the panelists will presumably decrease and the median will move toward what is deemed to be the "correct" estimate.

One distinct advantage of the Delphi Method is that the experts never need to be brought together physically. The process also does not require complete agreement by all panelists, since the majority opinion is represented by the median. Since the responses are anonymous, the pitfalls of ego, domineering personalities, and the "bandwagon or halo effect" in responses are all avoided. On the other hand, future developments are not always predicted correctly by iterative consensus nor by experts, but at times by creative, "off the wall" thinking.

It is important to recognize that these first top-down estimates are only a rough cut and typically occur in the "conceptual" stage of the project. The top-down estimates are helpful in initial development of a complete plan. However, such estimates are sometimes significantly off the mark because little detailed information is gathered. At this level individual work items are not identified. Or, in a few cases, the top-down estimates are not realistic because top management "wants the project." Nevertheless, the initial top-down estimates are helpful in determining whether the project warrants more formal planning, which would include more detailed estimates. Be careful that macro estimates made by senior managers are not dictated to lower level managers who might feel compelled to accept the estimates even if they believe resources are inadequate.

Although your authors prefer to avoid the top-down approach if possible, we have witnessed surprising accuracy in estimating project duration and cost in isolated cases. Some examples are building a manufacturing plant, building a distribution warehouse, developing air control for skyscraper buildings, and road construction. However, we have also witnessed some horrendous miscalculations, usually in areas where the technology is new and unproven. Top-down methods can be useful if experience and judgment have been accurate in the past.

Ratio Methods

Top-down methods (sometimes called parametric) usually use ratios, or surrogates, to estimate project times or costs. Top-down approaches are often used in the concept or "need" phase of a project to get an initial duration and cost estimate for the project. For example, contractors frequently use number of square feet to estimate the cost and time to build a house; that is, a house of 2,700 square feet might cost $160 per square foot (2,700 feet × $160 per foot equals $432,000). Likewise, knowing the square feet and dollars per square foot, experience suggests it should take approximately 100 days to complete. Two other common examples of top-down cost estimates are the cost for a new plant estimated by capacity size, or a software product estimated by features and complexity.

Apportion Methods

This method is an extension to the ratio method. **Apportionment** is used when projects closely follow past projects in features and costs. Given good historical data, estimates can be made quickly with little effort and reasonable accuracy. This method is very common in projects that are relatively standard but have some small variation or customization.

Anyone who has borrowed money from a bank to build a house has been exposed to this process. Given an estimated total cost for the house, banks and the FHA (Federal Housing Authority) authorize pay to the contractor by completion of specific segments of the house. For example, foundation might represent 3 percent of the total loan, framing 25 percent, plumbing and heating 15 percent, etc. Payments are made as these items are completed. An analogous process is used by some companies that apportion costs to deliverables in the WBS—given average cost percentages from past projects. Figure 5.1 presents an example similar to one found in practice. Assuming the total project cost is estimated, using a top-down estimate, to be $500,000, the costs are apportioned as a percentage of the total cost. For example, the costs apportioned to the "Document" deliverable are 5 percent of the total, or $25,000. The subdeliverables "Doc-1 and Doc-2" are allocated 2 and 3 percent of the total—$10,000 and $15,000, respectively.

FIGURE 5.1   **Apportion Method of Allocating Project Costs Using the Work Breakdown Structure**

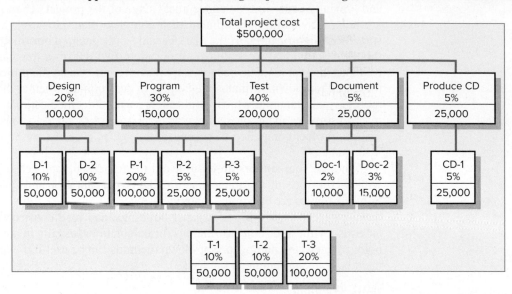

Function Point Methods for Software and System Projects

In the software industry, software development projects are frequently estimated using weighted macro variables called **"function points"** or major parameters such as number of inputs, number of outputs, number of inquiries, number of data files, and number of interfaces. These weighted variables are adjusted for a complexity factor and added. The total adjusted count provides the basis for estimating the labor effort and cost for a project (usually using a regression formula derived from data of past projects). This latter method assumes adequate historical data by type of software project for the industry—for example, MIS systems. In the U.S. software industry, one person-month represents on average five function points. A person working one month can generate on average (across all types of software projects) about five function points. Of course each organization needs to develop its own average for its specific type of work. Such historical data provide a basis for estimating the project duration. Variations of this top-down approach are used by companies such as IBM, Bank of America, Sears Roebuck, HP, AT&T, Ford Motors, GE, DuPont, and many others. See Table 5.2 and Table 5.3 for a simplified example of function point count methodology.

From historical data the organization developed the weighting scheme for complexity found in Table 5.2. Function points are derived from multiplying the number of kinds of elements by weighted complexity.

TABLE 5.2
Simplified Basic Function Point Count Process for a Prospective Project or Deliverable

	Complexity Weighting			
Element	Low	Average	High	Total
Number of *inputs*	____ × 2 +	____ × 3 +	____ × 4	= ____
Number of *outputs*	____ × 3 +	____ × 6 +	____ × 9	= ____
Number of *inquiries*	____ × 2 +	____ × 4 +	____ × 6	= ____
Number of *files*	____ × 5 +	____ × 8 +	____ × 12	= ____
Number of *interfaces*	____ × 5 +	____ × 10 +	____ × 15	= ____

TABLE 5.3
Example: Function Point Count Method

Software Project 13: Patient Admitting and Billing			
15	Inputs	Rated complexity as low	(2)
5	Outputs	Rated complexity as average	(6)
10	Inquiries	Rated complexity as average	(4)
30	Files	Rated complexity as high	(12)
20	Interfaces	Rated complexity as average	(10)

Application of Complexity Factor					
Element	**Count**	**Low**	**Average**	**High**	**Total**
Inputs	15	× 2			= 30
Outputs	5		× 6		= 30
Inquiries	10		× 4		= 40
Files	30			× 12	= 360
Interfaces	20		× 10		= 200
				Total	660

Table 5.3 shows the data collected for a specific task or deliverable: Patient Admitting and Billing—the number of inputs, outputs, inquiries, files, and interfaces along with the expected complexity rating. Finally, the application of the element count is applied and the function point count total is 660. Given this count and the fact that one person-month has historically been equal to 5 function points, the job will require 132 person-months (660/5 = 132). Assuming you have 10 programmers who can work on this task, the duration would be approximately 13 months. The cost is easily derived by multiplying the labor rate per month times 132 person-months. For example, if the monthly programmer rate is $4,000, then the estimated cost would be $528,000 (132 × 4,000). Although function point metrics are useful, their accuracy depends on adequate historical data, currency of data, and relevancy of the project/deliverable to past averages.

Learning Curves

Some projects require that the same task, group of tasks, or product be repeated several times. Managers know intuitively that the time to perform a task improves with repetition. This phenomenon is especially true of tasks that are labor intensive. In these circumstances the pattern of improvement phenomenon can be used to predict the reduction in time to perform the task. From empirical evidence across *all* industries, the pattern of this improvement has been quantified in the **learning curve** (also known as improvement curve, experience curve, and industrial progress curve), which is described by the following relationship:

Each time the output quantity doubles, the unit labor hours are reduced at a constant rate.

In practice the improvement ratio may vary from 60 percent, representing very large improvement, to 100 percent, representing no improvement at all. Generally, as the difficulty of the work decreases the expected improvement also decreases and the improvement ratio that is used becomes greater. One significant factor to consider is the proportion of labor in the task in relation to machine-paced work. Obviously, a lower percentage of improvement can occur only in operations with high labor content. Appendix 5.1 at the end of the chapter provides a detailed example of how the improvement phenomenon can be used to estimate time and cost for repetitive tasks.

The main disadvantage of top-down approaches to estimating is simply that the time and cost for a specific task are not considered. Grouping many tasks into a common basket encourages errors of omission and the use of imposed times and costs.

Micro estimating methods are usually more accurate than macro methods.

Bottom-Up Approaches for Estimating Project Times and Costs

Template Methods

If the project is similar to past projects, the costs from past projects can be used as a starting point for the new project. Differences in the new project can be noted and past times and costs adjusted to reflect these differences. For example, a ship repair dry-dock firm has a set of standard repair projects (i.e., templates for overhaul, electrical, mechanical) that are used as starting points for estimating the cost and duration of any new project. Differences from the appropriate standardized project are noted (for times, costs, and resources) and changes are made. This approach enables the firm to develop a potential schedule, estimate costs, and develop a budget in a very short time span. Development of such templates in a database can quickly reduce estimate errors.

Parametric Procedures Applied to Specific Tasks

Just as parametric techniques such as cost per square foot can be the source of top-down estimates, the same technique can be applied to specific tasks. For example, as part of an MS Office conversion project, 36 different computer workstations needed to be converted. Based on past conversion projects, the project manager determined that on average one person could convert three workstations per day. Therefore the task of converting the 36 workstations would take three technicians four days [(36/3)/3]. Similarly, to estimate the wallpapering allowance on a house remodel, the contractor figured a cost of $5 per square yard of wallpaper and $2 per yard to install it, for a total cost of $7. By measuring the length and height of all the walls she was able to calculate the total area in square yards and multiply it by $7.

Range Estimating

When do you use range estimating? **Range estimating** works best when work packages have significant uncertainty associated with the time or cost to complete. If the work package is routine and carries little uncertainty, using a person most familiar with the work package is usually the best approach. She is likely to know best how to estimate work packages durations and costs. However, when work packages have significant uncertainty associated with the time or cost to complete, it is a prudent policy to require three time estimates—low, average, and high (borrowed from PERT methodology that uses probability distributions). The low to high give a range within which the average estimate will fall. Determining the low and high estimates for the activity is influenced by factors such as complexity, technology, newness, familiarity.

How do you get the estimates? Since range estimating works best for work packages that have significant uncertainty, having a group determine the low, average, and high cost or duration gives best results. Group estimating tends to refine extremes by bringing more evaluative judgments to the estimate and potential risks. The judgment of others in a group helps to moderate extreme perceived risks associated with a time or cost estimate. Involving others in making activity estimates gains buy-in and credibility to the estimate.

Figure 5.2 presents an abridged estimating template using three time estimates for work packages developed by a cross functional group(s) of project stakeholders. The group estimates show the low, average, and high for each work package. The Risk

FIGURE 5.2
Range Estimating Template

	A	B	C	D	E	F	G	H
1	Project number: 18				Project Manager: Dawn O'Connor			
2	Project description: New Organic Wine Launch				Date: 2/17/2xxx			
3			Organic Wine Launch Project					
4			Range Estimates					
5								
6	WBS	Description	Low	Average	High	Range	Risk	
7	ID		Estimate	Estimate	Estimate		Level	
8			Days	Days	Days	Days		
9								
10	102	Approval	1	1	3	2	low	
11	103	Design packaging	4	7	12	8	medium	
12	104	ID potential customers	14	21	35	21	high	
13	105	Design bottle logo	5	7	10	5	low	
14	106	Contract kiosk space	8	10	15	7	medium	
15	107	Construct kiosk	4	4	8	4	medium	
16	108	Design fair brochure	6	7	12	6	high	
17	109	Trade journal advertising	10	12	15	5	medium	
18	110	Production test	10	14	20	10	high	
19	111	Produce to inventory	5	5	10	5	high	
20	112	Business card scanner hookup	1	2	3	2	low	
21	113	Video hook up	2	2	4	2	medium	
22	114	Event rehearsal	2	2	5	3	high	

Level column is the group's independent assessment of the degree of confidence that the actual time will be very close to the estimate. In a sense this number represents the group's evaluation of many factors (e.g., complexity, technology) that might impact the average time estimate. In our example, the group feels work packages 104, 108, 110, 111, and 114 have a high chance that the average time may vary from expected. Likewise, the group's confidence feels the risk of work packages 102, 105, and 112 not materializing as expected is low.

How do you use the estimate? Group range estimating gives the project manager and owner an opportunity to assess the confidence associated with project times (and/or costs). For example, a contractor responsible for building a high rise apartment building can tell the owner that the project will cost between 3.5 and 4.1 million dollars and take between six and nine months to complete. The approach helps to reduce surprises as the project progresses. The range estimating method also provides a basis for assessing risk, managing resources, and determining the project contingency fund. (See Chapter 7 for a discussion of contingency funds.) Range estimating is popular in software and new product projects where up-front requirements are fuzzy and not well known. Group range estimating is often used with phase estimating, which is discussed next.

A Hybrid: Phase Estimating

This approach begins with a top-down estimate for the project and then refines estimates for phases of the project as it is implemented. Some projects by their nature cannot be rigorously defined because of the uncertainty of design or the final product. Although rare, such projects do exist. These projects are often found in aerospace projects, IT projects, new technology projects, and construction projects where design is incomplete. In these projects, phase or life-cycle estimating is frequently used.

Phase estimating is used when an unusual amount of uncertainty surrounds a project and it is impractical to estimate times and costs for the entire project. Phase estimating uses a two-estimate system over the life of the project. A detailed estimate is developed for the immediate phase and a macro estimate is made for the remaining phases of the project. Figure 5.3 depicts the phases of a project and the progression of estimates over its life.

FIGURE 5.3
Phase Estimating over Project Life Cycle

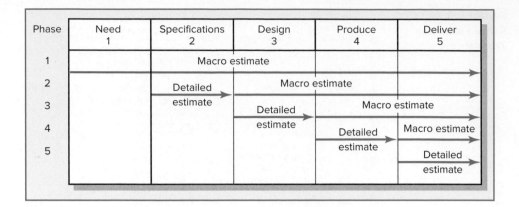

Phase	Need 1	Specifications 2	Design 3	Produce 4	Deliver 5
1		Macro estimate			
2		Detailed estimate	Macro estimate		
3			Detailed estimate	Macro estimate	
4				Detailed estimate	Macro estimate
5					Detailed estimate

For example, when the project need is determined, a macro estimate of the project cost and duration is made so analysis and decisions can be made. Simultaneously a detailed estimate is made for deriving project specifications and a macro estimate for the remainder of the project. As the project progresses and specifications are solidified, a detailed estimate for design is made and a macro estimate for the remainder of the project is computed. Clearly, as the project progresses through its life cycle and more information is available, the reliability of the estimates should be improving. See Snapshot from Practice 5.4: Estimate Accuracy.

Phase estimating is preferred by those working on projects where the final product is not known and the uncertainty is very large—for example, the integration of wireless phones and computers. The commitment to cost and schedule is only necessary over the next phase of the project and commitment to unrealistic future schedules and costs based on poor information is avoided. This progressive macro/micro method provides a stronger basis for using schedule and cost estimates to manage progress during the next phase.

SNAPSHOT FROM PRACTICE 5.4   Estimate Accuracy

The smaller the element of a work package, the more accurate the overall estimate is likely to be. The extent of this improvement varies by type of project. The table below is developed to reflect this observation. For example, information technology projects that determine their time and cost estimates in the conceptual stage can expect their "actuals" to err up to 200 percent over cost and duration and, perhaps, as much as 30 percent under estimates. Conversely, estimates for buildings, roads, etc., made after the work packages are clearly defined, have a smaller error in actual costs and times of 15 percent over estimate and 5 percent less than estimate. Although these estimates vary by project, they can serve as ballpark numbers for project stakeholders selecting how project time and cost estimates will be derived.

Time and Cost Estimate Accuracy by Type of Project

	Bricks and Mortar	Information Technology
Conceptual stage	+60% to −30%	+200% to −30%
Deliverables defined	+30% to −15%	+100% to −15%
Work packages defined	+15% to −5%	+50% to −5%

FIGURE 5.4
**Top-Down and
Bottom-Up Estimates**

Top-Down Estimates
Intended Use
Feasibility/conceptual phase
Rough time/cost estimate
Fund requirements
Resource capacity planning
Preparation Cost
1/10 to 3/10
of a percent
of total project cost
Accuracy
Minus 20%,
to plus 60%
Method
Consensus
Ratio
Apportion
Function point
Learning curves

Bottom-Up Estimates
Intended Use
Budgeting
Scheduling
Resource requirements
Fund timing
Preparation Cost
3/10 of a percent
to 1.0 percent
of total project cost
Accuracy
Minus 10%,
to plus 30%
Method
Template
Parametric
WBS packages
Range estimates

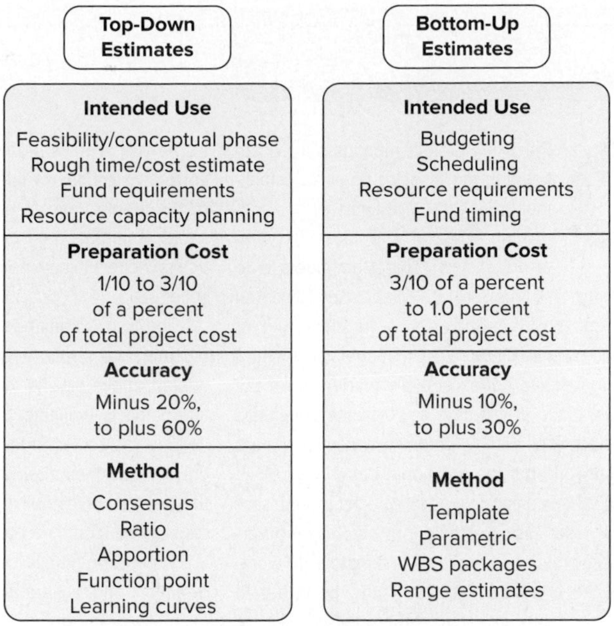

Unfortunately your customer—internal or external—will want an accurate estimate of schedule and cost the moment the decision is made to implement the project. Additionally, the customer who is paying for the project often perceives phase estimating as a blank check because costs and schedules are not firm over most of the project life cycle. Even though the reasons for phase estimating are sound and legitimate, most customers have to be sold on its legitimacy. A major advantage for the customer is the opportunity to change features, re-evaluate, or even cancel the project in each new phase. In conclusion, phase estimating is very useful in projects that possess huge uncertainties concerning the final nature (shape, size, features) of the project.

See Figure 5.4 for a summary of the differences between top-down and bottom-up estimates.

Obtaining accurate estimates is a challenge. Committed organizations accept the challenge of coming up with meaningful estimates and invest heavily in developing their capacity to do so. Accurate estimates reduce uncertainty and support a discipline for effectively managing projects.

5.5 Level of Detail

Level of detail is different for different levels of management. At any level the detail should be no more than is necessary and sufficient. Top management interests usually center on the total project and major milestone events that mark major accomplishments—e.g., "Build Oil Platform in the North Sea" or "Complete Prototype." Middle management might center on one segment of the project or one milestone. First-line managers' interests may be limited to one task or work package. One of the beauties of WBS is the ability to aggregate network information so each level of management can have the kind of information necessary to make decisions.

Getting the level of detail in the WBS to match management needs for effective implementation is crucial, but the delicate balance is difficult to find. See Snapshot from Practice 5.5: Level of Detail. The level of detail in the WBS varies with the

SNAPSHOT FROM PRACTICE 5.5 — Level of Detail—Rule of Thumb

Practicing project managers advocate keeping the level of detail to a minimum. But there are limits to this suggestion. One of the most frequent errors of new project managers is to forget that the task time estimate will be used to control schedule and cost performance. A frequent rule of thumb used by practicing project managers says that a task duration should not exceed 5 workdays or at the most 10 workdays, if workdays are the time units used for the project. Such a rule probably will result in a more detailed network, but the additional detail pays off in controlling schedule and cost as the project progresses.

Suppose the task is "build prototype computer-controlled conveyor belt," the time estimate is 40 workdays, and the budget $300,000. It may be better to divide the task into seven or eight smaller tasks for control purposes. If one of the smaller tasks gets behind because of problems or a poor time estimate, it will be possible to take corrective action quickly and avoid delaying successive tasks and the project. If the

single task of 40 workdays is used, it is possible that no corrective action would be taken until day 40, since many people have a tendency to "wait and see" or avoid admitting they are behind or passing on bad news; the result may mean far more than 5 days behind schedule.

The 5- to 10-day rule of thumb applies to cost and performance goals. If using the rule of thumb suggested above results in too many network tasks, an alternative is available, but it has conditions. The activity time can be extended beyond the 5- to 10-day rule only *IF* control monitoring checkpoints for segments of the task can be established so clear measures of progress can be identified by a specific percent complete.

This information is invaluable to the control process of measuring schedule and cost performance—for example, payments for contract work are paid on "percent complete" basis. Defining a task with clear definable start and end points and intermediate points enhances the chances of early detection of problems, corrective action, and on-time project completion.

complexity of the project; the need for control; the project size, cost, duration; and other factors. If the structure reflects excessive detail, there is a tendency to break the work effort into department assignments. This tendency can become a barrier to success, since the emphasis will be on departmental outcomes rather than on deliverable outcomes. Excessive detail also means more unproductive paperwork. Note that if the level of the WBS is increased by one, the number of cost accounts may increase geometrically. On the other hand, if the level of detail is not adequate, an organization unit may find the structure falls short of meeting its needs. Fortunately, the WBS has built-in flexibility. Participating organization units may expand their portion of the structure to meet their special needs. For example, the engineering department may wish to further break their work on a deliverable into smaller packages by electrical, civil, and mechanical. Similarly, the marketing department may wish to break their new product promotion into TV, radio, periodicals, and newspapers.

5.6 Types of Costs

LO 5-4

Distinguish different kinds of costs associated with a project.

Assuming work packages are defined, detailed cost estimates can be made. Here are typical kinds of costs found in a project:

1. Direct costs
   a. Labor   c. Equipment
   b. Materials   d. Other
2. Direct project overhead costs
3. General and administrative (G&A) overhead costs

The total project cost estimate is broken down in this fashion to sharpen the control process and improve decision making.

Direct Costs

These costs are clearly chargeable to a specific work package. **Direct costs** can be influenced by the project manager, project team, and individuals implementing the work package. These costs represent real cash outflows and must be paid as the project progresses; therefore, direct costs are usually separated from overhead costs. Lower-level project rollups frequently include only direct costs.

Direct Project Overhead Costs

Direct overhead rates more closely pinpoint which resources of the organization are being used in the project. Direct project **overhead costs** can be tied to project deliverables or work packages. Examples include the salary of the project manager and temporary rental space for the project team. Although overhead is not an immediate out-of-pocket expense, it is *real* and must be covered in the long run if the firm is to remain viable. These rates are usually a ratio of the dollar value of the resources used—e.g., direct labor, materials, equipment. For example, a direct labor burden rate of 20 percent would add a direct overhead charge of 20 percent to the direct labor cost estimate. A direct charge rate of 50 percent for materials would carry an additional 50 percent charge to the material cost estimate. Selective direct overhead charges provide a more accurate project (job or work package) cost, rather than using a blanket overhead rate for the whole project.

General and Administrative (G&A) Overhead Costs

These represent organization costs that are not directly linked to a specific project. These costs are carried for the duration of the project. Examples include organization costs across all products and projects such as advertising, accounting, and senior management above the project level. Allocation of G&A costs varies from organization to organization. However, G&A costs are usually allocated as a percent of total direct cost, or a percent of the total of a specific direct cost such as labor, materials, or equipment.

Given the totals of direct and overhead costs for individual work packages, it is possible to cumulate the costs for any deliverable or for the entire project. A percentage can be added for profit if you are a contractor. A breakdown of costs for a proposed contract bid is presented in Figure 5.5.

Perceptions of costs and budgets vary depending on their users. The project manager must be very aware of these differences when setting up the project budget and when communicating these differences to others. Figure 5.6 depicts these different

FIGURE 5.5
Contract Bid Summary Costs

Direct costs	$80,000
Direct overhead	$20,000
Total direct costs	$100,000
G&A overhead (20%)	$20,000
Total costs	$120,000
Profit (20%)	$24,000
Total bid	$144,000

FIGURE 5.6
Three Views of Cost

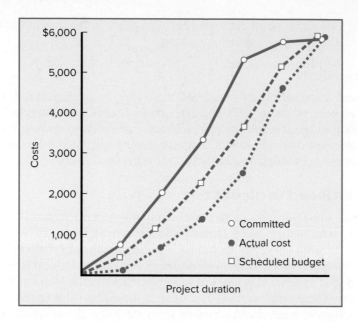

perceptions. The project manager can commit costs months before the resource is used. This information is useful to the financial officer of the organization in forecasting future cash outflows. The project manager is interested in when the budgeted cost is expected to occur, and when the budgeted cost actually is charged (earned); the respective timings of these two cost figures are used to measure project schedule and cost variances.

5.7 Refining Estimates

As described earlier in Chapter 4, detailed work package estimates are aggregated and "rolled up" by deliverable to estimate the total direct cost of the project. Similarly, estimated durations are entered into the project network to establish the project schedule and determine the overall duration of the project. Experience tells us that for many projects the total estimates do not materialize and the actual costs and schedule of some projects significantly exceed original work package–based estimates. In order to compensate for the problem of actual cost and schedule exceeding estimates, some project managers adjust total costs by some multiplier (i.e., total estimated costs × 1.20).

The practice of adjusting original estimates by 20 percent or even 100 percent begs the question of why, after investing so much time and energy on detailed estimates, the numbers could be so far off. There are a number of reasons for this, most of which can be traced to the estimating process and the inherent uncertainty of predicting the future. Some of these reasons are discussed below.

- **Interaction costs are hidden in estimates.** According to the guidelines, each task estimate is supposed to be done independently. However, tasks are rarely completed in a vacuum. Work on one task is dependent upon prior tasks, and the hand-offs between tasks require time and attention. For example, people working on prototype development need to interact with design engineers after the design is completed, whether to simply ask clarifying questions or to make adjustments in the original design. Similarly, the time necessary to coordinate activities is typically not reflected in independent estimates. Coordination is reflected in meetings and briefings as well as time necessary to resolve disconnects between tasks. Time, and therefore cost, devoted to managing interactions rises exponentially as the number of people and different disciplines involved increases on a project.

- **Normal conditions do not apply.** Estimates are supposed to be based on normal conditions. While this is a good starting point, it rarely holds true in real life. This is especially true when it comes to the availability of resources. Resource shortages, whether in the form of people, equipment, or materials, can extend original estimates. For example, under normal conditions four bulldozers are typically used to clear a certain site size in five days, but the availability of only three bulldozers would extend the task duration to eight days. Similarly, the decision to outsource certain tasks can increase costs as well as extend task durations since time is added to acclimating outsiders to the particulars of the project and the culture of the organization.

- **Things go wrong on projects.** Design flaws are revealed after the fact, extreme weather conditions occur, accidents happen, and so forth. Although you shouldn't plan for these risks to happen when estimating a particular task, the likelihood and impact of such events need to be considered.

- **Changes in project scope and plans.** As one gets further and further into the project, a manager obtains a better understanding of what needs to be done to accomplish the project. This may lead to major changes in project plans and costs. Likewise, if the project is a commercial project, changes often have to be made midstream to respond to new demands by the customer and/or competition. Unstable project scopes are a major source of cost overruns. While every effort should be made up front to nail down the project scope, it is becoming increasingly difficult to do so in our rapidly changing world.

- **Overly optimistic.** There is solid research indicating that there is a tendency in people to overestimate how quickly they can get things done and underestimate how long it will take them to complete tasks (Lovallo, D., and D. Kahneman, 2003; Buehler, R., D. Griffin, and M. Ross, 1994).

- **Strategic misrepresentation.** There is growing evidence that some project promoters underestimate the costs of projects and overestimate project benefits in order to win approval. This appears to be particularly true for large-scale public works projects which have a notorious habit of coming in way over budget (remember the earlier Snapshot from Practice 5.2: Council Fumes).

The reality is that for many projects not all of the information needed to make accurate estimates is available, and it is impossible to predict the future. The challenge is further compounded by human nature and the political dynamics associated with gaining project approval. The dilemma is that without solid estimates, the credibility of the project plan is eroded. Deadlines become meaningless, budgets become rubbery, and accountability becomes problematic.

Challenges similar to those described above will influence the final time and cost estimates. Even with the best estimating efforts, it may be necessary to revise estimates based on relevant information *prior* to establishing a baseline schedule and budget.

Effective organizations adjust estimates of specific tasks once risks, resources, and particulars of the situation have been more clearly defined. They recognize that the rolled-up estimates generated from a detailed estimate based on the WBS are just the starting point. As they delve further into the project-planning process, they make appropriate revisions both in the time and cost of specific activities. They factor the final assignment of resources into the project budget and schedule. For example, when they realize that only three instead of four bulldozers are available to clear a site, they adjust both the time and cost of that activity. They adjust estimates to account for specific actions to mitigate potential risks on the project. For example, to reduce the chances of design code errors, they would add the cost of independent testers to the schedule and budget. Finally, organizations adjust estimates to take into account abnormal conditions. For example, if soil samples reveal excessive ground water, then they adjust foundation costs and times.

There will always be some mistakes, omissions, and adjustments that will require additional changes in estimates. Fortunately every project should have a change management system in place to accommodate these situations and any impact on the project baseline. Change management and contingency funds will be discussed later in Chapter 7.

5.8 Creating a Database for Estimating

LO 5-5

Suggest a scheme for developing an estimating database for future projects.

The best way to improve estimates is to collect and archive data on past project estimates and actuals. Saving historical data—estimates and actuals—provides a knowledge base for improving project time and cost estimating. Creating an estimating database is a "best practice" among leading project management organizations.

Some organizations have large estimating departments of professional estimators—e.g., Boeing, IBM—that have developed large **time and cost databases.** Others collect these data through the project office. This database approach allows the project estimator to select a specific work package item from the database for inclusion. The estimator then makes any necessary adjustments concerning the materials, labor, and equipment. Of course any items not found in the database can be added to the project—and ultimately to the database if desired. Again, the quality of the database estimates depends on the experience of the estimators, but over time the data quality should improve. Such structured databases serve as feedback for estimators and as benchmarks for cost and time for each project. In addition, comparison of estimate and actual for different projects can suggest the degree of risk inherent in estimates. See Figure 5.7 for the structure of a database similar to those found in practice.

FIGURE 5.7
Estimating Database Templates

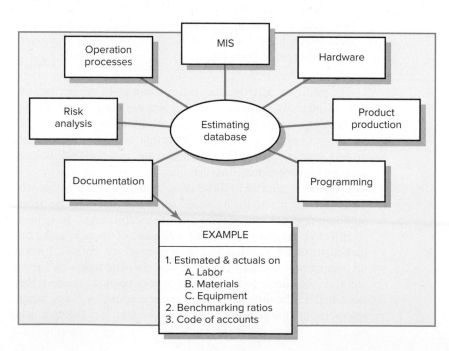

5.9 Mega Projects: A Special Case

LO 5-6

Understand the challenge of estimating mega projects and describe steps that lead to better informed decisions.

Mega projects are large-scale, complex ventures that typically cost $1 billion or more, take many years to complete, and involve multiple private and public stakeholders. They are often transformational, and impact millions of people (Flyvbjerg, 2014). Examples include high-speed rail lines, airports, healthcare reform, the Olympics, development of new aircraft, and so forth. What do these projects have in common beyond scope and complexity? They all tend to go way over budget and fall behind schedule. For example, the new Denver airport that opened in 1995 had cost overrun of 200 percent and was completed two years later than planned. The "Chunnel," the 31-mile-plus tunnel that connects France with England, was 80 percent over budget. These are but two examples of many public works and other large-scale projects in which costs came in way over than planned. In a study of government infrastructure projects, Flyvbjerg found costs for bridges and tunnels, road, and rail to be underestimated 34 percent, 20 percent, and 45 percent, respectively, from baseline estimates (Flyvbjerg, Bruzelius, and Rothengatter, 2003)!

Mega projects often involve a double whammy. Not only did they cost much more than expected, but they underdelivered on benefits they were to provide. The Denver Airport realized only 55 percent of forecasted traffic during its first year of operation. The Chunnel traffic revenues have been one-half of what was predicted with internal rate of return of −14.5 percent! Again Flyvbjerg's study revealed a consistent pattern of underusage on most infrastructure projects (Flyvbjerg et al., 2003), including only a 5 percent forecasted usage for the Kolkata metro!

So why does there appear to be a consistent pattern of overestimating benefits and underestimating costs? Many argue the sheer complexity and long time horizon make it impossible to accurately estimate costs and benefits. While this is certainly true, Flyvbjerg and his colleagues' research suggests that other factors come in to play. They concluded that in most cases project promoters use deception to promote projects not for public good but for personal gain, political or economic. Deception may be deliberate, or may be the product of overzealousness, optimism, and ignorance (Flyvbjerg et al., 2003). In some cases, promoters rationalize that nothing great would ever get built if people knew in advance what the real costs and challenges involved were (Hirschman, 1967).

On some mega projects, there is a triple whammy. Not only are they over budget and under value, but the cost of maintaining them exceeds the benefits received. These kinds of projects are called **white elephants.**

LO 5-7

Define a "white elephant" in project management and provide examples.

A "white elephant" suggests a valuable, but burdensome, possession which the owner cannot easily dispose of and whose cost (particularly upkeep) is out of proportion with its usefulness. The term derives from the story that the Kings of Siam (now Thailand) would often make a present of a white elephant to courtiers who had fallen out of favor with the king. At first glance, it was a great honor to receive such a revered beast from the king. However, the true intent was to ruin the recipient by forcing him to absorb the costs of taking care of the animal.

Examples of white elephants abound. While traveling across southern China one of the authors was struck by the palatial stature of the Trade Expo buildings each city had. It was as if each city tried to outdo its neighbor in terms of grandeur. When asked how often they were used, city officials would say once or twice a year. The 2015 FIFA scandal brought attention to the hidden costs of hosting the World Cup. South Africa built six new world class stadiums for the 2010 competition. None of the post-World Cup revenue generated from these stadiums exceeds their maintenance cost (Molloy and Chetty, 2015).

White elephants are not limited to buildings and stadiums. Air France had to mothball the Concorde, the world's fastest commercial airline, because maintenance costs and noise restrictions did not justify a three-flights-a-week schedule. It is not uncommon in our personal lives to acquire white elephants, such as underutilized vacation homes or yachts.

Flyvbjerg and others argue that cost overrun is not the price of doing big things and that we are capable of making better informed decisions on mega projects. The first step is to assume there is optimism bias and even deception on the part of promoters. Proposals should require a thorough review by impartial observers who do not have vested interest in the project. Some if not all financial risk should be absorbed by promoters and those who benefit financially from the project. Sustainable business practices should be used and maintenance costs be integrated into the forecasted cost/benefit analyses of projects. See Snapshot from Practice 5.6: London 2012 Olympics to see how British organizers tried to avoid the curse of the white elephant in the 2012 Olympic games.

SNAPSHOT FROM PRACTICE 5.6 — London 2012 Olympics: Avoiding White Elephant Curse*

Once hosting the Olympics was considered the crown prize and a tremendous source of national and local pride. Seven cities competed to host the 1992 Winter Olympics. For the 2022 Winter Olympics only Beijing and Almaty (Kazakhstan) submitted bids. Oslo (Norway), the favorite, withdrew application due to a lack of public support. Likewise, Boston withdrew application for the 2024 Summer Olympics in the face of public outcry. Why the outcry? Because of the legacy of exorbitant cost overruns and draining maintenance costs. The Olympics has a long history of expensive white elephants. For example, the Beijing National Stadium, nicknamed the *Bird's Nest,* built at cost of $480 million for the 2008 Olympic games, requires over $10 million each year to maintain, and has no regular tenant. Some have attributed the Greek economic meltdown to exorbitant debt accrued from hosting the 2004 summer games (Flyvbjerg, 2014). Perhaps the most infamous example is the "Big Owe," Montreal's Olympic Stadium, which took Canadian taxpayers over thirty years to pay off and was not even finished in time for the 1976 Olympics!

The London 2012 organizers were committed to turning this around. In particular, they were well aware of hidden post-Olympic maintenance costs of buildings that were no longer in demand. One advantage they had over less developed countries is that the infrastructure and many of the arenas were already in place and the Olympics provided a necessary upgrade. They built temporary arenas for less popular sports. For example, after the games the water polo arena was deconstructed and

© Sophie Vigneault /123RF

materials recycled. The 12,000-seat basketball arena was designed to be portable so it could be used in future Olympics. Scalability was another key consideration. For example, during the Olympics over 17,000 people watched swimming events in the newly constructed aquatic center. The aquatic center was downsized to a 2,500-person capacity after the Olympics and is now open to the public.

In recognition of its achievements, London 2012 Olympics won Gold in the Environmental and Sustainability category of the 6th International Sports Events awards. "We set out with a huge promise to the world, to deliver the most sustainable Olympic Games of modern times," says David Stubbs, London 2012's Head of Sustainability. "Seven years, nine million visitors, and 2,484 medals later, that's exactly what we achieved."

* "London 2012's Sustainability Legacy Lives On," Olympic .org, accessed October 10, 2015.

In particular, Flyvbjerg advocates an external view based on the outcome of similar projects completed in the past. It is called **reference class forecasting (RCF)** and involves three major steps:

1. Select a reference class of projects similar to your potential project, for example, cargo ships or bridges.
2. Collect and arrange outcome data as a distribution. Create a distribution of cost overruns as a percentage of the original project estimate (low to high).
3. Use the distribution data to arrive at a realistic forecast. Compare the original cost estimate for the project with the reference class projects. (For example, ask an advocate of rail tunnel what strong evidence do you have that your project will not follow the tunnel projects in the reference class?)

The benefits of RCF are compelling:

* Outside empirical data mitigates human bias.
* Political, strategic, and promoter forces have difficulty ignoring outside RCF information.
* Serves as reality check for funding large projects.
* Helps executives avoid unsound optimism.
* Leads to improved accountability.
* Provides basis for project contingency funds.

The use of RCF is increasing as governments and organizations require this method be used to temper project promoters' estimates and reduce cost/benefit inaccuracies.

Summary

Quality time and cost estimates are the bedrock of project control. Past experience is the best starting point for these estimates. The quality of estimates is influenced by other factors such as people, technology, and downtimes. The key for getting estimates that represent realistic average times and costs is to have an organization culture that allows errors in estimates without incriminations. If times represent average time, we should expect that 50 percent will be less than the estimate and 50 percent will exceed the estimate. The use of teams that are highly motivated can help in keeping task times and costs near the average. For this reason, it is crucial to get the team to buy into time and cost estimates.

Using top-down estimates is good for initial and strategic decision making or in situations where the costs associated with developing better estimates have little benefit. However, in most cases the bottom-up approach to estimating is preferred and more reliable because it assesses each work package, rather than the whole project, section, or deliverable of a project. Estimating time and costs for each work package facilitates development of the project schedule and a time-phased budget, which are needed to control the project as it is implemented. Using the estimating guidelines will help eliminate many common mistakes made by those unacquainted with estimating times and costs for project control. Establishing a time and cost estimating database fits well with the learning organization philosophy.

The level of time and cost detail should follow the old saying of "no more than is necessary and sufficient." Managers must remember to differentiate between committed outlays, actual costs, and scheduled costs. It is well known that up-front efforts in clearly defining project objectives, scope, and specifications vastly improve time and cost estimate accuracy.

How estimates are gathered and how they are used can affect their usefulness for planning and control. The team climate, organization culture, and organization structure can strongly influence the importance attached to time and cost estimates and how they are used in managing projects.

Finally, large-scale mega projects like subway systems or football stadiums often suffer from underestimated costs and overestimated benefits. They also can evolve into "white elephants" in which the cost of maintenance exceeds benefits. Steps must be taken to remove bias and compare mega project estimates with similar projects that have been done in the past.

Key Terms

Apportionment, *137*
Bottom-up estimates, *135*
Delphi Method, *136*
Direct costs, *145*
Function points, *138*
Learning curve, *139*

Overhead costs, *145*
Phase estimating, *141*
Range estimating, *140*
Ratio methods, *137*
Reference class
    forecasting (RCF), *151*

Template method, *140*
Time and cost
    databases, *148*
Top-down estimates, *134*
White elephant, *149*

Review Questions

1. Why are accurate estimates critical to effective project management?
2. How does the culture of an organization influence the quality of estimates?
3. What are the differences between bottom-up and top-down estimating approaches? Under what conditions would you prefer one over the other?
4. What are the major types of costs? Which costs are controllable by the project manager?
5. Why is it difficult to estimate mega project (e.g., airports, stadiums, etc.) costs and benefits?
6. Define what a "white elephant" is in project management. Provide a real-life example.

Exercises

1. Calculate the direct cost of labor for a project team member using the following data:

    Hourly rate: $40/hr

    Hours needed: 80

    Overhead rate: 40%

2. Mrs. Tolstoy and her husband, Serge, are planning their dream house. The lot for the house sits high on a hill with a beautiful view of the Appalachian Mountains. The plans show the size of the house to be 2,900 square feet. The average price for a lot and house similar to this one has been $120 per square foot. Fortunately, Serge is a retired plumber and feels he can save money by installing the plumbing himself. Mrs. Tolstoy feels she can take care of the interior decorating.

The following average cost information is available from a local bank that makes loans to local contractors and dispenses progress payments to contractors when specific tasks are verified as complete.

24%	Excavation and framing complete
8%	Roof and fireplace complete
3%	Wiring roughed in
6%	Plumbing roughed in
5%	Siding on
17%	Windows, insulation, walks, plaster, and garage complete
9%	Furnace installed
4%	Plumbing fixtures installed
10%	Exterior paint, light fixtures installed, finish hardware installed
6%	Carpet and trim installed
4%	Interior decorating
4%	Floors laid and finished

a. What is the estimated cost for the Tolstoys' house if they use contractors to complete all of the house?

b. Estimate what the cost of the house would be if the Tolstoys use their talents to do some of the work themselves.

3. Exercise Figure 5.1 is a project WBS with cost apportioned by percentages. If the total project cost is estimated to be $600,000, what are the estimated costs for the following deliverables?

a. Design

b. Programming

c. In-house testing

What weaknesses are inherent in this estimating approach?

EXERCISE FIGURE 5.1
WBS Figure

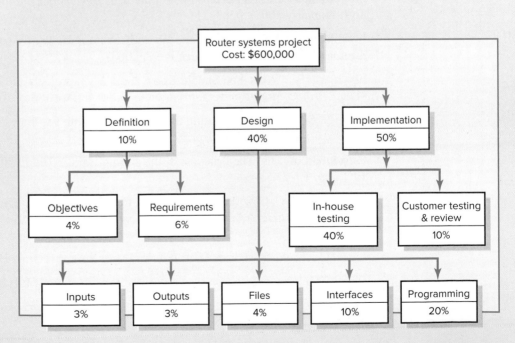

4. Firewall Project XT. Using the "complexity weighting" scheme shown in Table 5.3 and the function point complexity weight table shown below, estimate the total function point count. Assume historical data suggest five function points equal one person a month and six people can work on the project.

Complexity Weight Table		
Number of inputs	10	Rated complexity low
Number of outputs	20	Rated complexity average
Number of inquiries	10	Rated complexity average
Number of files	30	Rated complexity high
Number of interfaces	50	Rated complexity high

a. What is the estimated project duration?

b. If 20 people are available for the project, what is the estimated project duration?

c. If the project must be completed in six months, how many people will be needed for the project?

References

Buehler, R., D. Griffin, and M. Ross, "Exploring the 'Planning Fallacy': Why People Underestimate Their Task Completion Times," *Journal of Personality and Social Psychology,* vol. 67, no. 3 (1994), pp. 366–81.

Dalkey, N. C., D. L. Rourke, R. Lewis, and D. Snyder, *Studies in the Quality of Life: Delphi and Decision Making* (Lexington, MA: Lexington Books, 1972).

Flyvbjerg, Bent, "From Nobel Prize to Project Management: Getting Risks Right," *Project Management Journal,* August 2006, pp. 5–15.

Flyvbjerg, Bent, "Curbing Optimism Bias and Strategic Misrepresentation in Planning: Reference Class Forecasting in Practice," *European Planning Studies,* vol. 16, no. 1 (January 2008), pp. 3–21.

Flyvbjerg, Bent, N. Bruzelius, and W. Rothengatter, *Mega Projects and Risk: An Anatomy of Ambition* (Cambridge Press, 2003).

Flyvbjerg, B., "What You Should Know about Megaprojects and Why: An Overview," *Project Management Journal*, vol. 45, no. 2 (April/May 2014), pp. 6–19.

Gray, N. S., "Secrets to Creating the Elusive 'Accurate Estimate,'" *PM Network,* vol. 15, no. 8 (August 2001), p. 56.

Hirschman. A. O., "The Principle of the Hiding Hand," *The Public Interest,* Winter 1967, pp. 10–23.

Jeffery, R., G. C. Low, and M. Barnes, "A Comparison of Function Point Counting Techniques," *IEEE Transactions on Software Engineering,* vol. 19, no. 5 (1993), pp. 529–32.

Jones, C., *Applied Software Measurement* (New York: McGraw-Hill, 1991).

Jones, C., *Estimating Software Costs* (New York: McGraw-Hill, 1998).

Kharbanda, O. P., and J. K. Pinto, *What Made Gertie Gallop: Learning from Project Failures* (New York: Von Nostrand Reinhold, 1996).

Lovallo, D., and D. Kahneman, "Delusions of Success: How Optimism Undermines Executives' Decisions," *Harvard Business Review,* July 2003, pp. 56–63.

Magne, E., K. Emhjellenm, and P. Osmundsen, "Cost Estimation Overruns in the North Sea," *Project Management Journal,* vol. 34, no. 1 (2003), pp. 23–29.

McLeod, G., and D. Smith, *Managing Information Technology Projects* (Cambridge, MA: Course Technology, 1996).

Molloy, E., and T. Chetty, "The Rocky Road to Legacy: Lessons from the 2010 FIFA World Cup South Africa Stadium Program," *Project Management Journal,* vol. 46, no. 3 (June/July 2015), pp. 88–107.

Milosevic, D. Z., *Project Management ToolBox* (Upper Saddle River, NJ: John Wiley, 2003), p. 229.

Pressman, R. S., *Software Engineering: A Practitioner's Approach,* 4th ed. (New York: McGraw-Hill, 1997).

Symons, C. R., "Function Point Analysis: Difficulties and Improvements," *IEEE Transactions on Software Engineering,* vol. 14, no. 1 (1988), pp. 2–11.

Case 5.1

Sharp Printing, AG

Three years ago the Sharp Printing (SP) strategic management group set a goal of having a color laser printer available for the consumer and small business market for less than $200. A few months later the senior management met off-site to discuss the new product. The results of this meeting were a set of general technical specifications along with major deliverables, a product launch date, and a cost estimate based on prior experience.

Shortly afterward, a meeting was arranged for middle management explaining the project goals, major responsibilities, the project start date, and importance of meeting the product launch date within the cost estimate. Members of all departments involved attended the meeting. Excitement was high. Although everyone saw the risks as high, the promised rewards for the company and the personnel were emblazoned in their minds. A few participants questioned the legitimacy of the project duration and cost estimates. A couple of R&D people were worried about the technology required to produce the high-quality product for less than $200. But given the excitement of the moment, everyone agreed the project was worth doing and doable. The color laser printer project was to have the highest project priority in the company.

Lauren was selected to be the project manager. She had 15 years of experience in printer design and manufacture, which included successful management of several projects related to printers for commercial markets. Since she was one of those uncomfortable with the project cost and time estimates, she felt getting good bottom-up time and cost estimates for the deliverables was her first concern. She quickly had a meeting with the significant stakeholders to create a WBS identifying the work packages and organizational unit responsible for implementing the work packages. Lauren stressed she wanted time and cost estimates from those who would do the work or were the most knowledgeable, if possible. Getting estimates from more than one source was encouraged. Estimates were due in two weeks.

The compiled estimates were placed in the WBS/OBS. The corresponding cost estimate seemed to be in error. The cost estimate was $1,250,000 over the top-down senior management estimate; this represented about a 20 percent overrun! Furthermore the bottom-up time estimate based on the project network was four months longer than the top management time estimate. Another meeting was scheduled with the significant stakeholders to check the estimates and to brainstorm for alternative solutions. At this meeting everyone agreed the bottom-up cost and time estimates appeared to be accurate. Some of the suggestions for the brainstorming session are listed below.

- Change scope.
- Outsource technology design.
- Use the priority matrix (found in Chapter 4) to get top management to clarify their priorities.
- Partner with another organization or build a research consortium to share costs and to share the newly developed technology and production methods.
- Cancel the project.
- Commission a break-even study for the laser printer.

Very little in the way of concrete savings was identified, although there was consensus that time could be compressed to the market launch date, but at additional costs.

Lauren met with the marketing (Connor), production (Kim), and design (Gage) managers who yielded some ideas for cutting costs, but nothing significant enough to have a large impact. Gage remarked, "I wouldn't want to be the one to deliver the message to top management that their cost estimate is $1,250,000 off! Good luck, Lauren."

1. At this point, what would you do if you were the project manager?
2. Was top management acting correctly in developing an estimate?
3. What estimating techniques should be used for a mission critical project such as this?

Case 5.2

Post Graduation Adventure

Josh and Mike met each other as roommates during freshman year at MacAlister College in St. Paul, Minnesota. Despite a rocky start they became best friends. They are planning on going on a two-week adventure together to celebrate their graduation in June. Josh has never been to Europe and wants to visit France or Spain. Mike spent a semester abroad in Aarhus, Denmark, and traveled extensively in northern Europe. Even though he never went to France or Spain, Mike wants to go to someplace more exotic like South Africa or Vietnam. For the past week they have been arguing back and forth over where they should go. Josh argues that it will cost too much to fly to South Africa or Vietnam, while Mike counters that it will be much cheaper to travel in Vietnam or South Africa once they are there. Each of them agreed that they can spend no more than $3,500 each on the trip and could be gone for only two weeks.

One evening when they were arguing with each other over beers with friends, Sara said, "Why don't you use what you learned in your project management class

to decide what to do?" Josh and Mike looked at each other and ag
perfect sense.

1. Assume you are either Mike or Josh; how would you go about ma
   using project management methodology?
2. Looking first at only cost, what decision would you make?
3. After cost, what other factors should be considered before making a decision?

Appendix 5.1

LEARNING OBJECTIVES

After reading this appendix you should be able to:

A5-1 Use learning curves to improve task estimates.

Learning Curves for Estimating

LO A5-1

Use learning curves to
improve task estimates.

A forecast estimate of the time required to perform a work package or task is a basic
necessity for scheduling the project. In some cases, the manager simply uses judgment
and past experience to estimate work package time, or may use historical records of
similar tasks.

Most managers and workers intuitively know that improvement in the amount of
time required to perform a task or group of tasks occurs with repetition. A worker can
perform a task better/quicker the second time and each succeeding time she/he performs it (without any technological change). It is this pattern of improvement that is
important to the project manager and project scheduler.

This improvement from repetition generally results in a reduction of labor hours for
the accomplishment of tasks and results in lower project costs. From empirical evidence across *all* industries, the pattern of this improvement has been quantified in the
learning curve (also known as improvement curve, experience curve, and industrial
progress curve), which is described by the following relationship:

Each time the output quantity doubles, the unit labor hours are reduced at a constant rate.

For example, assume that a manufacturer has a new contract for 16 prototype units
and a total of 800 labor hours were required for the first unit. Past experience has indicated that on similar types of units the improvement rate was 80 percent. This relationship of improvement in labor hours is shown below:

Unit		Labor Hours
1		800
2	800 × .80 =	640
4	640 × .80 =	512
8	512 × .80 =	410
16	410 × .80 =	328

By using Table A5.1 unit values, similar labor hours per unit can be determined.
Looking across the 16 unit level and down the 80 percent column, we find a ratio

TABLE A5.1
**Learning Curves
Unit Values**

Units	60%	65%	70%	75%	80%	85%	90%	95%
1	1.0000	1.0000	1.0000	1.0000	1.0000	1.0000	1.0000	1.0000
2	.6000	.6500	.7000	.7500	.8000	.8500	.9000	.9500
3	.4450	.5052	.5682	.6338	.7021	.7729	.8462	.9219
4	.3600	.4225	.4900	.5625	.6400	.7225	.8100	.9025
5	.3054	.3678	.4368	.5127	.5956	.6857	.7830	.8877
6	.2670	.3284	.3977	.4754	.5617	.6570	.7616	.8758
7	.2383	.2984	.3674	.4459	.5345	.6337	.7439	.8659
8	.2160	.2746	.3430	.4219	.5120	.6141	.7290	.8574
9	.1980	.2552	.3228	.4017	.4930	.5974	.7161	.8499
10	.1832	.2391	.3058	.3846	.4765	.5828	.7047	.8433
12	.1602	.2135	.2784	.3565	.4493	.5584	.6854	.8320
14	.1430	.1940	.2572	.3344	.4276	.5386	.6696	.8226
16	.1296	.1785	.2401	.3164	.4096	.5220	.6561	.8145
18	.1188	.1659	.2260	.3013	.3944	.5078	.6445	.8074
20	.1099	.1554	.2141	.2884	.3812	.4954	.6342	.8012
22	.1025	.1465	.2038	.2772	.3697	.4844	.6251	.7955
24	.0961	.1387	.1949	.2674	.3595	.4747	.6169	.7904
25	.0933	.1353	.1908	.2629	.3548	.4701	.6131	.7880
30	.0815	.1208	.1737	.2437	.3346	.4505	.5963	.7775
35	.0728	.1097	.1605	.2286	.3184	.4345	.5825	.7687
40	.0660	.1010	.1498	.2163	.3050	.4211	.5708	.7611
45	.0605	.0939	.1410	.2060	.2936	.4096	.5607	.7545
50	.0560	.0879	.1336	.1972	.2838	.3996	.5518	.7486
60	.0489	.0785	.1216	.1828	.2676	.3829	.5367	.7386
70	.0437	.0713	.1123	.1715	.2547	.3693	.5243	.7302
80	.0396	.0657	.1049	.1622	.2440	.3579	.5137	.7231
90	.0363	.0610	.0987	.1545	.2349	.3482	.5046	.7168
100	.0336	.0572	.0935	.1479	.2271	.3397	.4966	.7112
120	.0294	.0510	.0851	.1371	.2141	.3255	.4830	.7017
140	.0262	.0464	.0786	.1287	.2038	.3139	.4718	.6937
160	.0237	.0427	.0734	.1217	.1952	.3042	.4623	.6869
180	.0218	.0397	.0691	.1159	.1879	.2959	.4541	.6809
200	.0201	.0371	.0655	.1109	.1816	.2887	.4469	.6757
250	.0171	.0323	.0584	.1011	.1691	.2740	.4320	.6646
300	.0149	.0289	.0531	.0937	.1594	.2625	.4202	.5557
350	.0133	.0262	.0491	.0879	.1517	.2532	.4105	.6482
400	.0121	.0241	.0458	.0832	.1453	.2454	.4022	.6419
450	.0111	.0224	.0431	.0792	.1399	.2387	.3951	.6363
500	.0103	.0210	.0408	.0758	.1352	.2329	.3888	.6314
600	.0090	.0188	.0372	.0703	.1275	.2232	.3782	.6229
700	.0080	.0171	.0344	.0659	.1214	.2152	.3694	.6158
800	.0073	.0157	.0321	.0624	.1163	.2086	.3620	.6098
900	.0067	.0146	.0302	.0594	.1119	.2029	.3556	.6045
1,000	.0062	.0137	.0286	.0569	.1082	.1980	.3499	.5998
1,200	.0054	.0122	.0260	.0527	.1020	.1897	.3404	.5918
1,400	.0048	.0111	.0240	.0495	.0971	.1830	.3325	.5850
1,600	.0044	.0102	.0225	.0468	.0930	.1773	.3258	.5793
1,800	.0040	.0095	.0211	.0446	.0895	.1725	.3200	.5743
2,000	.0037	.0089	.0200	.0427	.0866	.1683	.3149	.5698
2,500	.0031	.0077	.0178	.0389	.0606	.1597	.3044	.5605
3,000	.0027	.0069	.0162	.0360	.0760	.1530	.2961	.5530

of .4096. By multiplying this ratio times the labor hours for the first unit, we obtain the per unit value:

$$.4096 \times 800 = 328 \text{ hours or } 327.68$$

That is, the 16th unit should require close to 328 labor hours, assuming an 80 percent improvement ratio.

Obviously, a project manager may need more than a single unit value for estimating the time for some work packages. The cumulative values in Table A5.2 provide factors for computing the cumulative total labor hours of all units. In the previous example, for the first 16 units, the total labor hours required would be

$$800 \times 8.920 = 7,136 \text{ hours}$$

By dividing the total cumulative hours (7,136) by the units, the average unit labor hours can be obtained:

$$7,136 \text{ labor hours}/16 \text{ units} = 446 \text{ average labor hours per unit}$$

Note how the labor hours for the 16th unit (328) differs from the average for all 16 units (446). The project manager, knowing the average labor costs and processing costs, could estimate the total prototype costs. (The mathematical derivation of factors found in Tables A5.1 and A5.2 can be found in Jelen, F. C., and J. H. Black, *Cost and Optimization Engineering,* 2nd ed. (New York: McGraw-Hill, 1983.)

FOLLOW-ON CONTRACT EXAMPLE

Assume the project manager gets a follow-on order of 74 units; how should she estimate labor hours and cost? Going to the cumulative Table A5.2 we find at the 80 percent ratio and 90 total units intersection—a 30.35 ratio.

$800 \times 30.35 =$	24,280 labor hours for 90 units
Less previous 16 units =	7,136
Total follow-on order =	17,144 labor hours
17,144/74 equals 232 average labor hours per unit	

Labor hours for the 90th unit can be obtained from Table A5.1: $.2349 \times 800 = 187.9$ labor hours. (For ratios between given values, simply estimate.)

Exercise A5.1

Norwegian Satellite Development Company
Cost Estimates
for
World Satellite Telephone Exchange Project

NSDC has a contract to produce eight satellites to support a worldwide telephone system (for Alaska Telecom, Inc.) that allows individuals to use a single, portable telephone in any location on earth to call in and out. NSDC will develop and produce the eight units. NSDC has estimated that the R&D costs will be NOK (Norwegian Krone) 12,000,000. Material costs are expected to be NOK 6,000,000. They have estimated the design and production of the first satellite will require 100,000 labor hours and an

TABLE A5.2

Learning Curves Cumulative Values

Units	60%	65%	70%	75%	80%	85%	90%	95%
1	1.000	1.000	1.000	1.000	1.000	1.000	1.000	1.000
2	1.600	1.650	1.700	1.750	1.800	1.850	1.900	1.950
3	2.045	2.155	2.268	2.384	2.502	2.623	2.746	2.872
4	2.405	2.578	2.758	2.946	3.142	3.345	3.556	3.774
5	2.710	2.946	3.195	3.459	3.738	4.031	4.339	4.662
6	2.977	3.274	3.593	3.934	4.299	4.688	5.101	5.538
7	3.216	3.572	3.960	4.380	4.834	5.322	5.845	6.404
8	3.432	3.847	4.303	4.802	5.346	5.936	6.574	7.261
9	3.630	4.102	4.626	5.204	5.839	6.533	7.290	8.111
10	3.813	4.341	4.931	5.589	6.315	7.116	7.994	8.955
12	4.144	4.780	5.501	6.315	7.227	8.244	9.374	10.62
14	4.438	5.177	6.026	6.994	8.092	9.331	10.72	12.27
16	4.704	5.541	6.514	7.635	8.920	10.38	12.04	13.91
18	4.946	5.879	6.972	8.245	9.716	11.41	13.33	15.52
20	5.171	6.195	7.407	8.828	10.48	12.40	14.64	17.13
22	5.379	6.492	7.819	9.388	11.23	13.38	15.86	18.72
24	5.574	6.773	8.213	9.928	11.95	14.33	17.10	20.31
25	5.668	6.909	8.404	10.19	12.31	14.80	17.71	21.10
30	6.097	7.540	9.305	11.45	14.02	17.09	20.73	25.00
35	6.478	8.109	10.13	12.72	15.64	19.29	23.67	28.86
40	6.821	8.631	10.90	13.72	17.19	21.43	26.54	32.68
45	7.134	9.114	11.62	14.77	18.68	23.50	29.37	36.47
50	7.422	9.565	12.31	15.78	20.12	25.51	32.14	40.22
60	7.941	10.39	13.57	17.67	22.87	29.41	37.57	47.65
70	8.401	11.13	14.74	19.43	25.47	33.17	42.87	54.99
80	8.814	11.82	15.82	21.09	27.96	36.80	48.05	62.25
90	9.191	12.45	16.83	22.67	30.35	40.32	53.14	69.45
100	9.539	13.03	17.79	24.18	32.65	43.75	58.14	76.59
120	10.16	14.16	19.57	27.02	37.05	50.39	67.93	90.71
140	10.72	15.08	21.20	29.67	41.22	56.78	77.46	104.7
160	11.21	15.97	22.72	32.17	45.20	62.95	86.80	118.5
180	11.67	16.79	24.14	34.54	49.03	68.95	95.96	132.1
200	12.09	17.55	25.48	36.80	52.72	74.79	105.0	145.7
250	13.01	19.28	28.56	42.08	61.47	88.83	126.9	179.2
300	13.81	20.81	31.34	46.94	69.66	102.2	148.2	212.2
350	14.51	22.18	33.89	51.48	77.43	115.1	169.0	244.8
400	15.14	23.44	36.26	55.75	84.85	127.6	189.3	277.0
450	15.72	24.60	38.48	59.80	91.97	139.7	209.2	309.0
500	16.26	25.68	40.58	63.68	98.85	151.5	228.8	340.6
600	17.21	27.67	44.47	70.97	112.0	174.2	267.1	403.3
700	18.06	29.45	48.04	77.77	124.4	196.1	304.5	465.3
800	18.82	31.09	51.36	84.18	136.3	217.3	341.0	526.5
900	19.51	32.60	54.46	90.26	147.7	237.9	376.9	587.2
1,000	20.15	34.01	57.40	96.07	158.7	257.9	412.2	647.4
1,200	21.30	36.59	62.85	107.0	179.7	296.6	481.2	766.6
1,400	22.32	38.92	67.85	117.2	199.6	333.9	548.4	884.2
1,600	23.23	41.04	72.49	126.8	218.6	369.9	614.2	1001.
1,800	24.06	43.00	76.85	135.9	236.8	404.9	678.8	1116.
2,000	24.83	44.84	80.96	144.7	254.4	438.9	742.3	1230.
2,500	26.53	48.97	90.39	165.0	296.1	520.8	897.0	1513.
3,000	27.99	52.62	98.90	183.7	335.2	598.9	1047.	1791.

80 percent improvement curve is expected. Skilled labor cost is NOK 300 per hour. Desired profit for all projects is 25 percent of total costs.

A. How many labor hours should the eighth satellite require?

B. How many labor hours for the whole project of eight satellites?

C. What price would you ask for the project? Why?

D. Midway through the project your design and production people realize that a 75 percent improvement curve is more appropriate. What impact does this have on the project?

E. Near the end of the project, Deutsch Telefon AG has requested a cost estimate for four satellites identical to those you have already produced. What price will you quote them? Justify your price.

6

Developing a Project Plan

LEARNING OBJECTIVES

After reading this chapter you should be able to:

6-1 Understand the linkage between WBS and the project network.

6-2 Diagram a project network using AON methods.

6-3 Calculate early, late, and slack activity times.

6-4 Identify and understand the importance of managing the critical path.

6-5 Distinguish free slack from total slack.

6-6 Demonstrate understanding and application of lags in compressing projects or constraining the start or finish of an activity.

OUTLINE

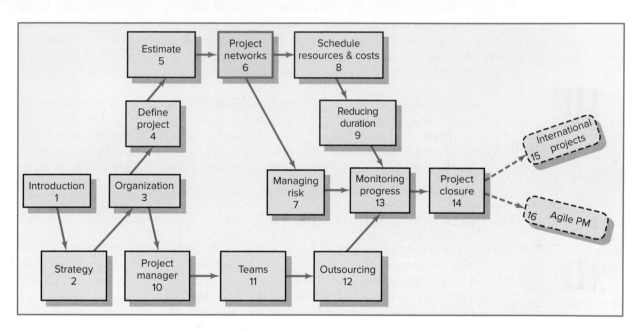

I keep six honest serving-men (they taught me all I knew); their names are What and Why and When and How and Where and Who.

—*Rudyard Kipling*

6.1 Developing the Project Network

The project network is the tool used for planning, scheduling, and monitoring project progress. The network is developed from the information collected for the WBS and is a graphic flow chart of the project job plan. The network depicts the project activities that must be completed, the logical sequences, the interdependencies of the activities to be completed, and in most cases the times for the activities to start and finish along with the longest path(s) through the network—the *critical path*. The network is the framework for the project information system that will be used by the project managers to make decisions concerning project time, cost, and performance.

Developing the project networks takes time for someone or some group to develop; therefore, they cost money! Are networks really worth the struggle? The answer is definitely yes, except in cases where the project is considered trivial or very short in duration.[1] The network is easily understood by others because the network presents a graphic display of the flow and sequence of work through the project. Once the network is developed, it is very easy to modify or change when unexpected events occur as the project progresses. For example, if materials for an activity are delayed, the impact can be quickly assessed and the whole project revised in only a few minutes with the computer. These revisions can be communicated to all project participants quickly (for example, via e-mail or project website).

The project network provides other invaluable information and insights. It provides the basis for scheduling labor and equipment. It enhances communication that melds all managers and groups together in meeting the time, cost, and performance objectives of the project. It provides an estimate of project duration rather than picking a project completion date from a hat or someone's preferred date. The network gives the times when activities can start and finish and when they can be delayed. It provides the basis for budgeting the cash flow of the project. It identifies which activities are "critical" and, therefore, should not be delayed if the project is to be completed as planned. It highlights which activities to consider if the project needs to be compressed to meet a deadline.

There are other reasons project networks are worth their weight in gold. Basically, project networks minimize surprises by getting the plan out early and allowing corrective feedback. A commonly heard statement from practitioners is that the project network represents three-quarters of the planning process. Perhaps this is an exaggeration, but it signals the perceived importance of the network to project managers in the field.

6.2 From Work Package to Network

 LO 6-1

Understand the linkage between WBS and the project network.

Project networks are developed from the WBS. The project network is a visual flow diagram of the sequence, interrelationships, and dependencies of all the activities that must be accomplished to complete the project. *An **activity** is an element in the project that consumes time—for example, work or waiting.* Work packages from the WBS are used to build the activities found in the project network. An activity can include one or more work packages. The activities are placed in a sequence that provides for orderly completion of the project. Networks are built using nodes (boxes) and arrows (lines).

Integrating the work packages and the network represents a point where the management process often fails in practice. The primary explanations for this failure are that (1) different groups (people) are used to define work packages and activities and (2) the WBS is poorly constructed and not deliverable/output oriented. Integration of the WBS and project network is crucial to effective project management. The project manager must be careful to guarantee continuity by having some of the same people who defined the WBS and work packages develop the network activities.

Networks provide the project schedule by identifying dependencies, sequencing, and timing of activities, which the WBS is not designed to do. The primary inputs for developing a project network plan are work packages. Remember, a work package is defined independently of other work packages, has definite start and finish points, requires specific resources, includes technical specifications, and has cost estimates for the package. However, dependency, sequencing, and timing of each of these factors are not included in the work package. A network activity can include one or more work packages.

---

[1] This process could be clarified and improved by using a simple responsibility matrix (see Chapter 4).

FIGURE 6.1
WBS/Work Packages to Network

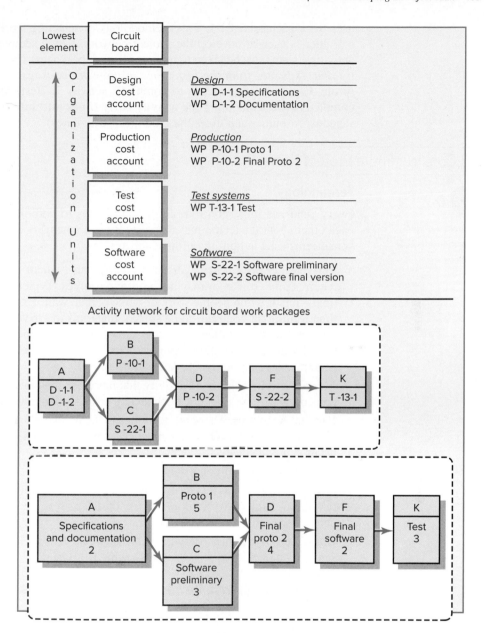

Figure 6.1 shows a segment of the WBS example and how the information is used to develop a project network. The lowest level deliverable in Figure 6.1 is "circuit board." The cost accounts (design, production, test, software) denote project work, organization unit responsible, and time-phased budgets for the work packages. Each cost account represents one or more work packages. For example, the design cost account has two work packages (D-1-1 and D-1-2)—specifications and documentation. The software and production accounts also have two work packages. Developing a network requires sequencing tasks from all work packages that have measurable work.

Figure 6.1 traces how work packages are used to develop a project network. You can trace the use of work packages by the coding scheme. For example, activity A uses work packages D-1-1 and D-1-2 (specifications and documentation), while activity C uses work package S-22-1. This methodology of selecting work packages to describe activities is used to develop the project network, which sequences and times project activities. Care must be taken to include all work packages. *The manager derives activity time estimates from the task times in the work package.* For example, activity B (proto 1) requires five weeks to complete; activity K (test) requires three weeks to complete. After computing the activity **early times and late times,** the manager can schedule resources and time-phase budgets (with dates).

6.3 Constructing a Project Network

LO 6-2

Diagram a project network using AON methods.

Terminology

Every field has its jargon that allows colleagues to communicate comfortably with each other about the techniques they use. Project managers are no exception. Here are some terms used in building project networks.

> **Activity.** For project managers, an *activity* is an element of the project that requires time. It may or may not require resources. Typically an activity consumes time—either while people work or while people wait. Examples of the latter are time waiting for contracts to be signed, materials to arrive, drug approval by the government, budget clearance, etc. Activities usually represent one or more tasks from a work package. Descriptions of activities should use a verb/noun format: for example, develop product specifications.
>
> **Merge Activity.** This is an activity that has more than one activity immediately preceding it (more than one dependency arrow flowing to it).
>
> **Parallel Activities.** These are activities that can take place at the same time, if the manager wishes. However, the manager may choose to have parallel activities *not* occur simultaneously.
>
> **Path.** A sequence of connected, dependent activities.
>
> **Critical Path.** When this term is used, it means the path(s) with the longest duration through the network; if an activity on the path is delayed, the project is delayed the same amount of time.
>
> **Burst Activity.** This activity has more than one activity immediately following it (more than one dependency arrow flowing from it).

Basic Rules to Follow in Developing Project Networks

The following eight rules apply in general when developing a project network:

1. Networks flow typically from left to right.
2. An activity cannot begin until all preceding connected activities have been completed.
3. Arrows on networks indicate precedence and flow. Arrows can cross over each other.
4. Each activity should have a unique identification number.
5. An activity identification number must be larger than that of any activities that precede it.
6. Looping is not allowed (in other words, recycling through a set of activities cannot take place).
7. Conditional statements are not allowed (that is, this type of statement should not appear: If successful, do something; if not, do nothing).
8. Experience suggests that when there are multiple starts, a common start node can be used to indicate a clear project beginning on the network. Similarly, a single project end node can be used to indicate a clear ending.

SNAPSHOT FROM PRACTICE 6.1

The Yellow Sticky Approach (for Constructing a Project Network)

In practice small project networks (25 to 100 activities) are frequently developed using yellow Post-it® stickers. The meeting requirements and process for the project team are described herein.

The following are the requirements for such a project:

1. Project team members and a facilitator.
2. One yellow sticker (3 × 4 inches or larger) for each activity with the description of the activity printed on the sticker.
3. Erasable whiteboard with marker pen (a long, 4-foot-wide piece of butcher paper can be used in place of the whiteboard).

All of the yellow stickers are placed in easy view of all team members. The team begins by identifying those activity stickers that have no predecessors. Each of these activity stickers is then attached to the whiteboard. A start node is drawn, and a dependency arrow is connected to each activity.

Given the initial network start activities, each activity is examined for immediate successor activities. These activities are attached to the whiteboard and dependency arrows drawn. This process is continued until all of the yellow stickers are attached to the whiteboard with dependency arrows. (Note: The process can be reversed, beginning with those activities that have no successor activities and connecting them to a project end node. The predecessor activities are selected for each activity and attached to the whiteboard with dependency arrows marked.)

When the process is complete, the dependencies are recorded in the project software, which develops a computer-designed network along with the critical path(s) and early, late, and slack times. This methodology sensitizes team members early to the interdependencies among activities of the project. But more importantly, the methodology empowers team members by giving them input to the important decisions that they must implement later.

© Image Source/Alamy

Read the Snapshot from Practice 6.1: The Yellow Sticky Approach to see how these rules are used to create project networks.

6.4 Activity-on-Node (AON) Fundamentals

Historically, two methods have been used to develop project networks: **Activity-on-node (AON)** and **Activity-on-arrow (AOA).** Over time the availability of advanced computer graphics improved the clarity and visual appeal of the AON method. Today, the activity-on-node method has come to dominate nearly all project network plans. For this reason, we have limited our discussion to AON methods. Figure 6.2 shows a few typical uses of building blocks for the AON network

FIGURE 6.2
Activity-on-Node
Network
Fundamentals

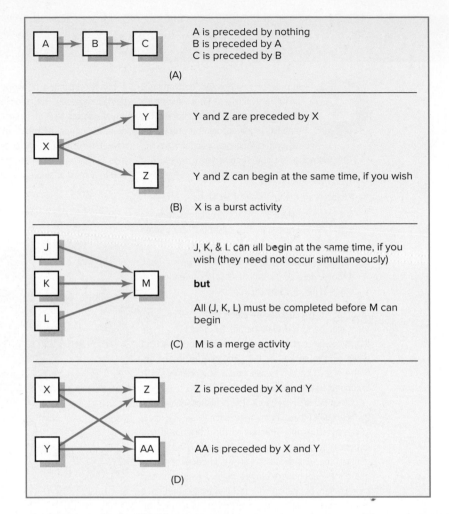

A is preceded by nothing
B is preceded by A
C is preceded by B

(A)

Y and Z are preceded by X

Y and Z can begin at the same time, if you wish

(B)   X is a burst activity

J, K, & L can all begin at the same time, if you wish (they need not occur simultaneously)

but

All (J, K, L) must be completed before M can begin

(C)   M is a merge activity

Z is preceded by X and Y

AA is preceded by X and Y

(D)

construction. An **activity** is represented by a *node* (box). The node can take many forms, but in recent years the node represented as a rectangle (box) has dominated. The dependencies among activities are depicted by *arrows* between the rectangles (boxes) on the AON network. The arrows indicate how the activities are related and the sequence in which things must be accomplished. The length and slope of the arrow are arbitrary and set for convenience of drawing the network. The letters in the boxes serve here to identify the activities while you learn the fundamentals of network construction and analysis. In practice, activities have identification numbers and descriptions.

There are three basic relationships that must be established for activities included in a project network. The relationships can be found by answering the following three questions for each activity:

1. Which activities must be completed immediately *before* this activity? These activities are called *predecessor* activities.
2. Which activities must immediately *follow* this activity? These activities are called *successor* activities.
3. Which activities can occur *while* this activity is taking place? This is known as a *concurrent* or *parallel* relationship.

Sometimes a manager can use only questions 1 and 3 to establish relationships. This information allows the network analyst to construct a graphic flow chart of the sequence and logical interdependencies of project activities.

Figure 6.2A is analogous to a list of things to do where you complete the task at the top of the list first and then move to the second task, etc. This figure tells the project manager that activity A must be completed before activity B can begin, and activity B must be completed before activity C can begin.

Figure 6.2B tells us that activities Y and Z cannot begin until activity X is completed. This figure also indicates that activities Y and Z can occur concurrently or simultaneously if the project manager wishes; however, it is not a necessary condition. For example, pouring a concrete driveway (activity Y) can take place while landscape planting (activity Z) is being accomplished, but land clearing (activity X) must be completed before activities Y and Z can start. Activities Y and Z are considered *parallel* activities. Parallel paths allow concurrent effort, which may shorten time to do a series of activities. Activity X is sometimes referred to as a *burst* activity because more than one arrow bursts from the node. The number of arrows indicates how many activities immediately follow activity X.

Figure 6.2C shows us activities J, K, and L can occur simultaneously if desired, and activity M cannot begin until activities J, K, and L are all completed. Activities J, K, and L are parallel activities. Activity M is called a *merge* activity because more than one activity must be completed before M can begin. Activity M could also be called a milestone—a significant accomplishment.

In Figure 6.2D, activities X and Y are parallel activities that can take place at the same time; activities Z and AA are also parallel activities. But activities Z and AA cannot begin until activities X and Y are both completed. Given these fundamentals of AON, we can practice developing a simple network. Remember, the arrows can cross over each other (e.g., Figure 6.2D), be bent, or be any length or slope. Neatness is not a criterion for a valid, useful network—only accurate inclusion of all project activities, their dependencies, and time estimates.

Information for a simplified project network is given in Table 6.1. This project represents a new automated warehouse system for picking frozen food package orders and moving them to a staging area for delivery to stores.

Figure 6.3 shows the first steps in constructing the AON project network from the information in Table 6.1. We see that activity A (define requirements) has nothing preceding it; therefore, it is the first node to be drawn. Next, we note that activities B and C (assign team and design hardware) are both preceded by activity A. We draw two arrows and connect them to activities B and C. This segment shows

TABLE 6.1
Network Information

AUTOMATED WAREHOUSE Order Picking System		
Activity	**Description**	**Preceding Activity**
A	Define Requirements	None
B	Assign Team	A
C	Design Hardware	A
D	Code Software	B
E	Build and Test Hardware	C
F	Develop Patent Request	C
G	Test Software	D
H	Integrate Systems	E, F, G

FIGURE 6.3
Automated
Warehouse—Partial
Network

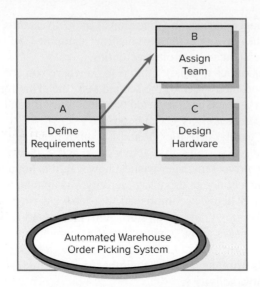

the project manager that activity A must be completed before activities B and C can begin. After A is completed, B and C can take place concurrently, if desired. Figure 6.4 shows the completed network with all of the activities sequences and dependencies.

The information in Figure 6.4 is tremendously valuable to those managing the project. However, estimating the duration for each activity will further increase the value of the network. A realistic project plan and schedule require reliable time estimates for project activities. The addition of time to the network allows us to estimate how long the project will take. When activities can or must start, when resources must be available, which activities can be delayed, and when the project is estimated to be complete are all determined from the times assigned. Deriving an activity time estimate necessitates early assessment of resource needs in terms of material, equipment, and people. In essence the project network with activity time estimates links planning, scheduling, and controlling of projects.

FIGURE 6.4   Automated Warehouse—Completed Network

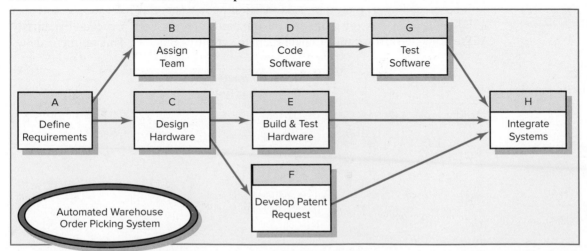

6.5 Network Computation Process

LO 6-3

Calculate early, late, and slack activity times.

Drawing the project network places the activities in the right seque... start and finish times of activities. Activity time estimates are taken in the work package and added to the network (review Figure 6.1). ...... simple computations allows the project manager to complete a process known as the forward and backward pass. Completion of the *forward and backward pass* will answer the following questions:

Forward Pass—Earliest Times

1. How soon can the activity start? (early start—ES)
2. How soon can the activity finish? (early finish—EF)
3. How soon can the project be finished? (expected time—TE)

Backward Pass—Latest Times

1. How late can the activity start? (late start—LS)
2. How late can the activity finish? (late finish—LF)
3. Which activities represent the critical path (CP)? This is the longest path in the network which, when delayed, will delay the project.
4. How long can the activity be delayed? (slack or float—SL)

The terms in parentheses represent the acronyms used in most texts and computer programs and by project managers. The forward and backward pass process is presented next.

Forward Pass—Earliest Times

The forward pass starts with the first project activity(ies) and traces each path (chain of sequential activities) through the network to the last project activity(ies). As you trace along the path, you *add* the activity times. The longest path denotes the project completion time for the plan and is called the critical path (CP). Table 6.2 lists the activity times in workdays for the Automated Warehouse project example we used for drawing a network.

Figure 6.5 shows the network with the activity time estimate found in the node (see "DUR" for duration in the legend). For example, activity A (define requirements) has an activity duration of 10 workdays, and activity E (build and test hardware) has a duration of 50 days. The forward pass begins with the project start time, which is usually time zero. (Note: Calendar times can be computed for the project later in the planning phase.)

TABLE 6.2
Network Information

AUTOMATED WAREHOUSE Order Picking System			
Activity	**Description**	**Preceding Activity**	**Activity Time**
A	Define Requirements	None	10 workdays
B	Assign Team	A	5
C	Design Hardware	A	25
D	Code Software	B	20
E	Build & Test Hardware	C	50
F	Develop Patent Request	C	15
G	Test Software	D	35
H	Integrate Systems	E, F, G	15

GURE 6.5   **Activity-on-Node Network**

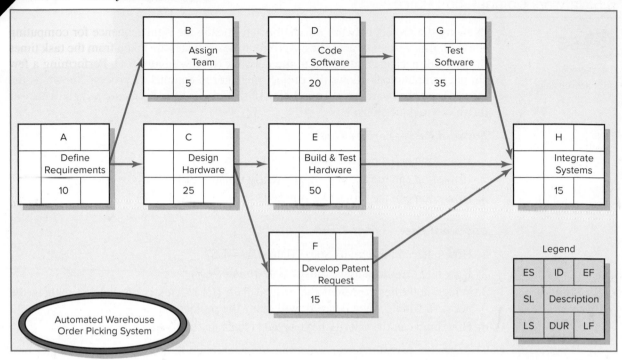

In our Automated Warehouse example, the early start time for the first activity (activity A) is zero. This time is found in the upper left corner of the activity A node in Figure 6.6. The early finish for activity A is 10 days ($EF = ES + DUR$ or $0 + 10 = 10$). Next, we see that activity A is the predecessor for activities B (assign team) and C (design hardware). Therefore, the earliest activities B and C can begin is the instant in time when activity A is completed; this time is 10 days. You can now see in Figure 6.6 that activities B and C have an early start (ES) of 10 days. Using the formula $EF = ES + DUR$, the early finish (EF) times for activities B and C are 15 and 35 days. Following the same process of moving along each network path, the early start and finish times for selected activities are shown here:

Activity D: ES = 15	EF = 15 + 20 = 35	Activity F: ES = 35	EF = 35 + 15 = 50
Activity E: ES = 35	EF = 35 + 50 = 85	Activity G: ES = 35	EF = 35 + 35 = 70

Activity H (integrate system) is a merge activity because it is preceded by more than one activity. The early start (ES) of a merge activity depends on the early finish (EF) of all activities that merge to it. In this project activity H is preceded by activities E, F, and G. Which activity controls the ES of activity H? The answer is activity E. In Figure 6.6 the EF times are 85, 50, and 70. Since 85 days is the largest EF time, activity E controls the ES for activity H, which is 85. If activity E is delayed, activity H will be delayed. The early finish for activity H or the project is 100 days ($EF = ES + DUR$ or $85 + 15 = 100$).

FIGURE 6.6   **Activity-on-Node Network Forward Pass**

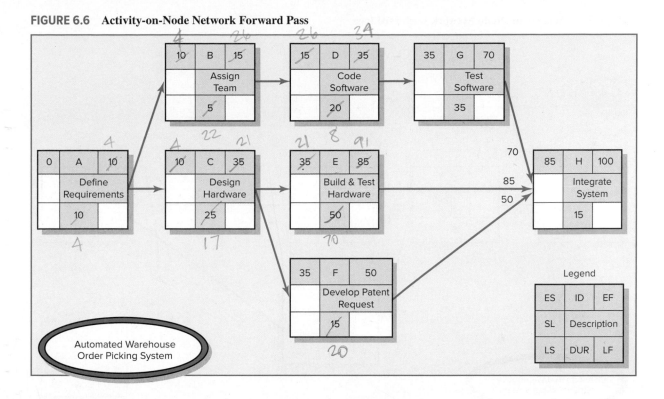

The forward pass requires that you remember just three things when computing early activity times:

1. You *add* activity times along each path in the network (ES + DUR = EF).
2. You carry the early finish (EF) to the next activity where it becomes its early start (ES), *or*
3. If the next succeeding activity is a *merge* activity, you select the *largest* early finish number (EF) of *all* its immediate predecessor activities.

The three questions derived from the forward pass have been answered; that is, early start (ES), early finish (EF), and the project expected duration (TE) times have been computed. The backward pass is the next process to learn.

Backward Pass—Latest Times

The backward pass starts with the last project activity(ies) on the network. You trace backward on each path *subtracting* activity times to find the late start (LS) and late finish (LF) times for each activity. Before the backward pass can be computed, the late finish for the last project activity(ies) must be selected. In early planning stages, this time is usually set equal to the early finish (EF) of the last project activity (or in the case of multiple finish activities, the activity with the largest EF). In some cases an imposed project duration deadline exists, and this date will be used. Let us assume for planning purposes we can accept the EF project duration (TE) equal to 100 workdays. The LF for activity H becomes 100 days (EF = LF) (see Figure 6.7).

FIGURE 6.7 **Activity-on-Node Network Backward Pass**

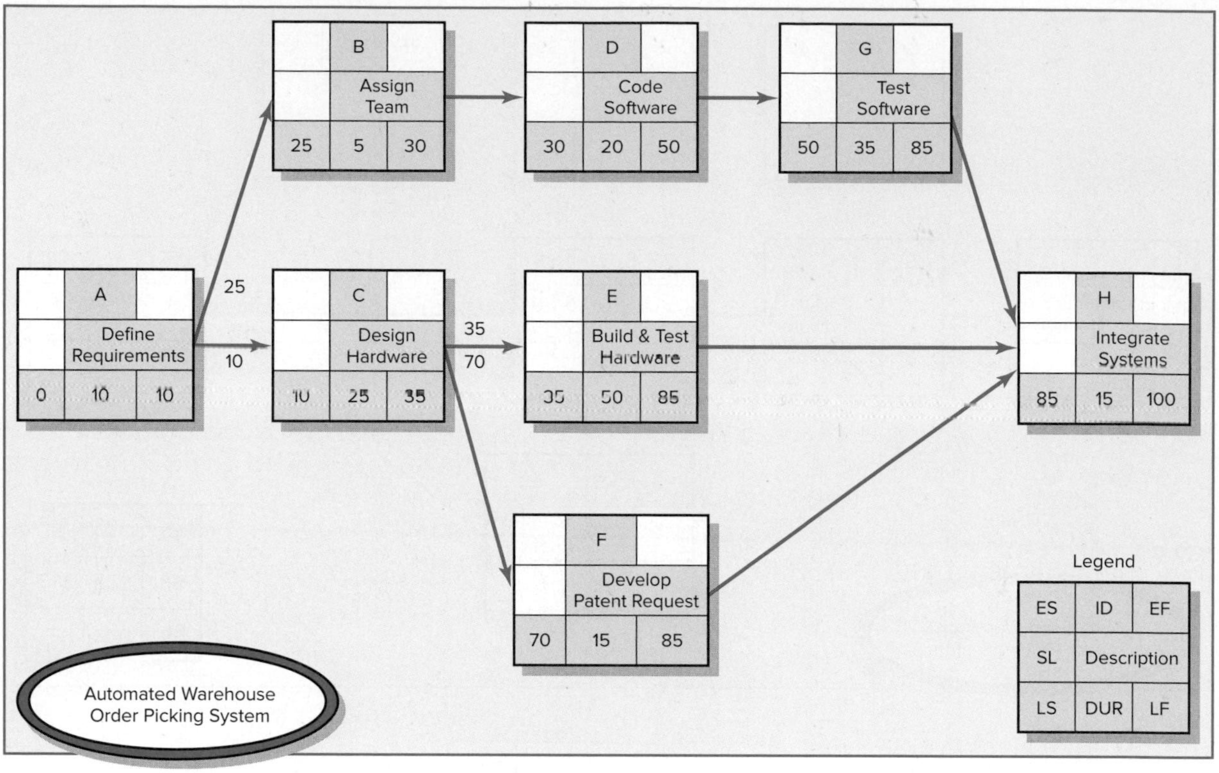

The backward pass is similar to the forward pass; you need to remember three things:

1. You *subtract* activity times along each path starting with the project end activity (LF − DUR = LS).
2. You carry the LS to the preceding activity to establish its LF, *or*
3. If the next preceding activity is a *burst* activity; in this case you select the *smallest* LS of all its immediate successor activities to establish its LF.

Let's apply these rules to our Automated Warehouse example. Beginning with activity H (integrate systems) and a LF of 100 workdays, the LS for activity H is 85 days (LF − DUR = LS or 100 − 15 = 85). The LS for activity H becomes the LF for activities E, F, and G. Moving backward on the network the late starts for E, F, and G are shown here (LS = LF − DUR):

Activity E: LS = 85 − 50 = 35	Activity G: 85 − 35 = 50
Activity F: LS = 85 − 15 = 70	

At this point we see that activity C is a *burst* activity that ties to (precedes) activities E and F. The late finish for activity C is controlled by the LS of activities E and F. The *smallest* LS of activities E and F (LS's = 35 and 70) is activity E. This establishes the LF for activity C. The LS for activity C becomes 10. Moving backward to the first project activity, we note it is also a *burst* activity that links to activities B and C. The

LF of activity A is controlled by activity C that has the smallest LS of 10 days. Given a LF of 10 days, the LS for activity is time period zero (LS = 10 − 10 = 0). The backward pass is complete, and the latest activity times are known. Figure 6.8 shows the completed network with all the early, late, and slack times included. Slack can be important to managing your project.

LO 6-4

Identify and understand the importance of managing the critical path.

Determining Slack (or Float)

Total Slack

When the forward and backward passes have been computed, it is possible to determine which activities can be delayed by computing "slack" or "float." **Total slack** *tells us the amount of time an activity can be delayed and not delay the project.* Stated differently, *total slack is the amount of time an activity can exceed its early finish date without affecting the project end date or an imposed completion date.*

Total slack or float for an activity is simply the difference between the LS and ES (LS − ES = SL) or between LF and EF (LF − EF = SL). For example, in Figure 6.8 the total slack for activity D is 15 workdays, for activity F is 35 days, and for activity E is zero. If total slack of one activity in a path is used, the ES for all activities that follow in the chain will be delayed and their slack reduced. Use of total slack *must be coordinated* with all participants in the activities that follow in the chain.

After slack for each activity is computed, the critical path(s) is (are) easily identified. When the LF = EF for the end project activity, the critical path can be identified

FIGURE 6.8 Forward and Backward Passes Completed with Slack Times

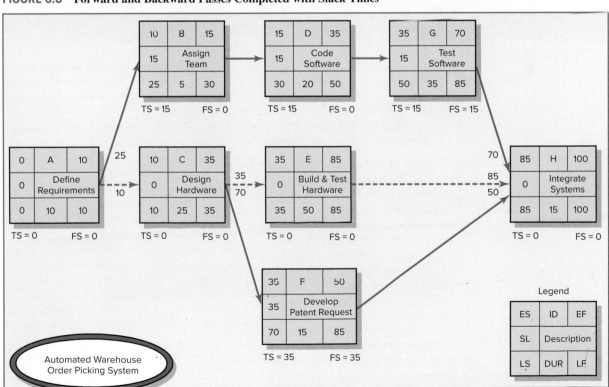

as those activities that also have LF = EF or a slack of zero (LF − EF = 0 or LS − ES = 0). *The critical path is the network path(s) that has (have) the least slack in common.* This awkward arrangement of words is necessary because a problem arises when the project finish activity has a LF that differs from the EF found in the forward pass—for example, an imposed duration date. If this is the case, the slack on the critical path will *not* be zero; it will be the difference between the project EF and the imposed LF of the last project activity. For example, if the EF for the project is 100 days, but the imposed LF or target date is set at 95 days, all activities on the critical path would have a slack of minus 5 days. Of course, this would result in a late start 5 days for the first project activity—a good trick if the project is to start now. Negative slack occurs in practice when the critical path is delayed.

In Figure 6.8 the critical path is marked with dashed arrows—activities A, C, E, and H. Delay of any of these activities will delay the total project by the same number of days. Since actual projects may have many critical activities with numerous preceding dependencies, coordination among those responsible for critical activities is crucial. Critical activities typically represent about 10 percent of the activities of the project. Therefore, project managers pay close attention to the critical path activities to be sure they are not delayed. See Snapshot from Practice 6.2: The Critical Path.

We use the term **sensitivity** to reflect the likelihood the original critical path(s) will change once the project is initiated. Sensitivity is a function of the number of critical or near-critical paths. A network schedule that has only one critical path and noncritical activities that enjoy significant slack would be labeled insensitive.

SNAPSHOT FROM PRACTICE 6.2   The Critical Path

The critical path method (CPM) has long been considered the "Holy Grail" of project management. Here are comments made by veteran project managers when asked about the significance of the critical path in managing projects:

- I try to make it a point whenever possible to put my best people on critical activities or on those activities that stand the greatest chance of becoming critical.

- I pay extra attention when doing risk assessment to identifying those risks that can impact the critical path, either directly or indirectly, by making a noncritical activity so late that it becomes critical. When I've got money to spend to reduce risks, it usually gets spent on critical tasks.

- I don't have time to monitor all the activities on a big project, but I make it a point to keep in touch with the people who are working on critical activities. When I have the time, they are the ones I visit to find out firsthand how things are going. It's amazing how much more I can find out from

talking to the rank and file who are doing the work and by reading the facial expressions of people—much more than I can gain from a number-driven status report.

- When I get calls from other managers asking to "borrow" people or equipment, I'm much more generous when it involves resources from working on noncritical activities. For example, if another project manager needs an electrical engineer who is assigned to a task with five days of slack, I'm willing to share that engineer with another project manager for two to three days.

- The most obvious reason the critical path is important is because these are the activities that impact completion time. If I suddenly get a call from above saying they need my project done two weeks earlier than planned, the critical path is where I schedule the overtime and add extra resources to get the project done more quickly. In the same way, if the project schedule begins to slip, it's the critical activities I focus on to get back on schedule.

Conversely, a sensitive network would be one with more than one critical path and/or noncritical activities with very little slack. Under these circumstances the original critical path is much more likely to change once work gets under way on the project. How sensitive is the Automated Warehouse schedule? Not very, since there is only one critical path and the two other noncritical paths have 15 and 35 days of slack, which suggests considerable flexibility. Project managers assess the sensitivity of their network schedules to determine how much attention they should devote to managing the critical path.

Free Slack (Float)

Free slack (FS) is unique. *It is the amount of time an activity can be delayed without delaying any immediately following (successor) activity. Or, free slack is the amount of time an activity can exceed its early finish date without affecting the early start date of any successor(s).* Free slack can never be negative. Only activities that occur at the end of a chain of activities, where you have a merge activity, can have free slack. See Figure 6.8, the Automated Warehouse project.

In Figure 6.8 activity G has free slack of 15 days, while activities B and D do not. In this case, activity G is the last activity in the upper path, and it merges to activity H. Hence, to delay activity G up to 15 days *does not delay any following activities and requires no coordination with managers of other activities.* Conversely, if either activity B or D is delayed, the managers of following activities need to be notified that the slack has been used so they can adjust their start schedules. For example, if activity B is delayed 5 days, the manager of activity B should notify those in charge of the following activities (D and G) that their slack has been reduced to 10 time units and their early start will be delayed 5 days. In this example, activity D cannot then start until day 20, which reduces activity D slack to 10 days (LS − ES = SL or 30 − 20 = 10). Free slack for activity G is also reduced to 10 days.

Free slack occurs at the last activity in a chain of activities. In some situations the "chain" has only one link. Activity F in Figure 6.8 is an example. It has free slack of 35 days. Note that it needs no coordination with other activities—unless a delay exceeds the free slack of 35 days. (Note: The moment you exceed all free slack available, you delay the project and must coordinate with others who are impacted.)

The distinction between free and total slack at first glance seems trivial, but in reality it is very important. When you are responsible for a late activity that has zero free slack you impact the schedules of subsequent activities. You should notify the managers of the remaining activities in the chain that you will be late. Again, note that total slack is shared across the whole path. Alternatively, if you are responsible for an activity that has free slack when you start, you do not need to notify anyone as long as your work does not absorb all of the slack!

LO 6-5

Distinguish free slack from total slack.

6.6 Using the Forward and Backward Pass Information

Returning to the Automated Warehouse project network in Figure 6.8, what does a slack of 35 days for activity F (develop patent request) mean for the project manager? In this specific case it means activity F can be delayed 35 days. In a larger sense the project manager soon learns that free slack is important because it allows flexibility in scheduling scarce project resources—personnel and equipment—that are used on more than one parallel activity or another project.

Knowing the four activity times of ES, LS, EF, and LF is invaluable for the planning, scheduling, and controlling phases of the project. The ES and LF tell the project manager the time interval in which the activity should be completed. For example, activity G (test software) must be completed within the time interval 35 and 85 days; the activity can start as early as day 35 or finish as late as day 85. Conversely, activity C (design hardware) must start on day 10, or the project will be delayed.

When the critical path is known, it is possible to tightly manage the resources of the activities on the critical path so no mistakes are made that will result in delays. In addition, if for some reason the project must be expedited to meet an earlier date, it is possible to select those activities, or combination of activities, that will cost the least to shorten the project. Similarly, if the critical path is delayed and the time must be made up by shortening some activity or activities on the critical path to make up any negative slack, it is possible to identify the activities on the critical path that cost the least to shorten. If there are other paths with very little slack, it may be necessary to shorten activities on those paths also.

6.7 Level of Detail for Activities

Time-phasing work and budgets of the project mandate careful definition of the activities that make up the project network. Typically an activity represents one or more tasks from a work package. How many tasks you include in each activity sets the level of detail. In some cases it is possible to end up with too much information to manage, and this can result in increased overhead costs. Managers of small projects have been able to minimize the level of detail by eliminating some of the preliminary steps to drawing networks. Larger firms also recognize the cost of information overload and are working to cut down the level of detail in networks and in most other dimensions of the project.

6.8 Practical Considerations

Network Logic Errors

Project network techniques have certain logic rules that must be followed. One rule is that conditional statements such as "if test successful build proto, if failure redesign" are not permitted. The network is not a decision tree; it is a project plan that we assume will materialize. If conditional statements were allowed, the forward and backward pass would make little sense. Although in reality a plan seldom materializes as we expect in every detail, it is a reasonable initial assumption. You shall see that once a network plan is developed, it is an easy step to make revisions to accommodate changes.

Another rule that defeats the project network and computation process is *looping*. Looping is an attempt by the planner to return to an earlier activity. Recall that the activity identification numbers should always be higher for the activities following an activity in question; this rule helps to avoid the illogical precedence relationships among the activities. An activity should only occur once; if it is to occur again, the activity should have a new name and identification number and should be placed in the right sequence on the network. Figure 6.9 shows an illogical loop. If this loop were allowed to exist, this path would perpetually repeat itself. Many computer programs catch this type of logic error.

FIGURE 6.9
Illogical Loop

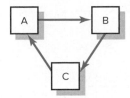

Activity Numbering

Each activity needs a unique identification code—a letter or a number. In practice very elegant schemes exist. Most schemes number activities in ascending order, that is, each succeeding activity has a larger number so that the flow of the project activities is toward project completion. It is customary to leave gaps between numbers (1, 5, 10, 15 . . .). Gaps are desirable so you can add missing or new activities later. Because it is nearly impossible to draw a project network perfectly, numbering networks is frequently not done until after the network is complete.

In practice you will find computer programs that accept numeric, alphabetic, or a combination of activity designations. Combination designations are often used to identify cost, work skill, departments, and locations. As a general rule, activity numbering systems should be ascending and as simple as possible. The intent is to make it as easy as you can for project participants to follow work through the network and locate specific activities.

Use of Computers to Develop Networks

All of the tools and techniques discussed in this chapter can be used with computer software currently available. Two examples are shown in Figures 6.10 and 6.11. Figure 6.10 presents a generic AON computer output for the Automated Warehouse Picking System project. Observe that these computer outputs use numbers to identify activities. The critical path is identified by the nodes (activities) 2, 4, 6, and 9. The activity description is shown on the top line of the activity node. The activity start time and identification are on the second line. The finish time and duration are on the third line of the node. The project starts on January 1 and is planned to finish May 20. Note this sample computer network has included non-workdays of holidays and weekends.

Figure 6.11 presents an early start **Gantt chart.**[2] Bar charts are popular because they present an easy-to-understand, clear picture on a time-scaled horizon. They are used during planning, resource scheduling, and status reporting. The format is a two-dimensional representation of the project schedule, with activities down the rows and time across the horizontal axis. In this computer output the shaded bars represent the activity durations. The extended lines from the bars represent slack. For example, "test software" (ID # 8) has a duration of 35 days (shaded area of the bar) and 15 days slack (represented by the extended line). The bar also indicates test software has an early start of February 19 and would finish April 8, but can finish as late as April 29 because it has 15 days of slack. When calendar dates are used on the time axis, Gantt charts provide a clear overview of the project schedule and can often be found posted on the walls of project offices. Unfortunately, when projects have many dependency relationships, the dependency lines soon become overwhelming and defeat the simplicity of the Gantt chart.

Project management software can be a tremendous help in the hands of those who understand and are familiar with the tools and techniques discussed in this text. However, there is nothing more dangerous than someone using the software with little or no

---

[2] Gantt charts were introduced over 100 years ago by Henry Gantt.

FIGURE 6.10   Automated Warehouse Order Picking System Network

Automated Warehouse
Order Picking System Network Diagram

Define Req.s		
Start: Tue 1/1	ID: 2	
Finish: Mon 1/14	Dur: 10 days	
Res:		

Assign Team		
Start: Tue 1/15	ID: 3	
Finish: Mon 1/21	Dur: 5 days	
Res:		

Design Hardware		
Start: Tue 1/15	ID: 4	
Finish: Mon 2/18	Dur: 25 days	
Res:		

Code Software		
Start: Tue 1/22	ID: 5	
Finish: Mon 2/18	Dur: 20 days	
Res:		

Build & Test HW		
Start: Tue 2/19	ID: 6	
Finish: Mon 4/29	Dur: 50 days	
Res:		

Dev. Patent Request		
Start: Tue 2/19	ID: 7	
Finish: Mon 3/11	Dur: 15 days	
Res:		

Test Software		
Start: Tue 2/19	ID: 8	
Finish: Mon 4/8	Dur: 35 days	
Res:		

Integrate Systems		
Start: Tue 4/30	ID: 9	
Finish: Mon 5/20	Dur: 15 days	
Res:		

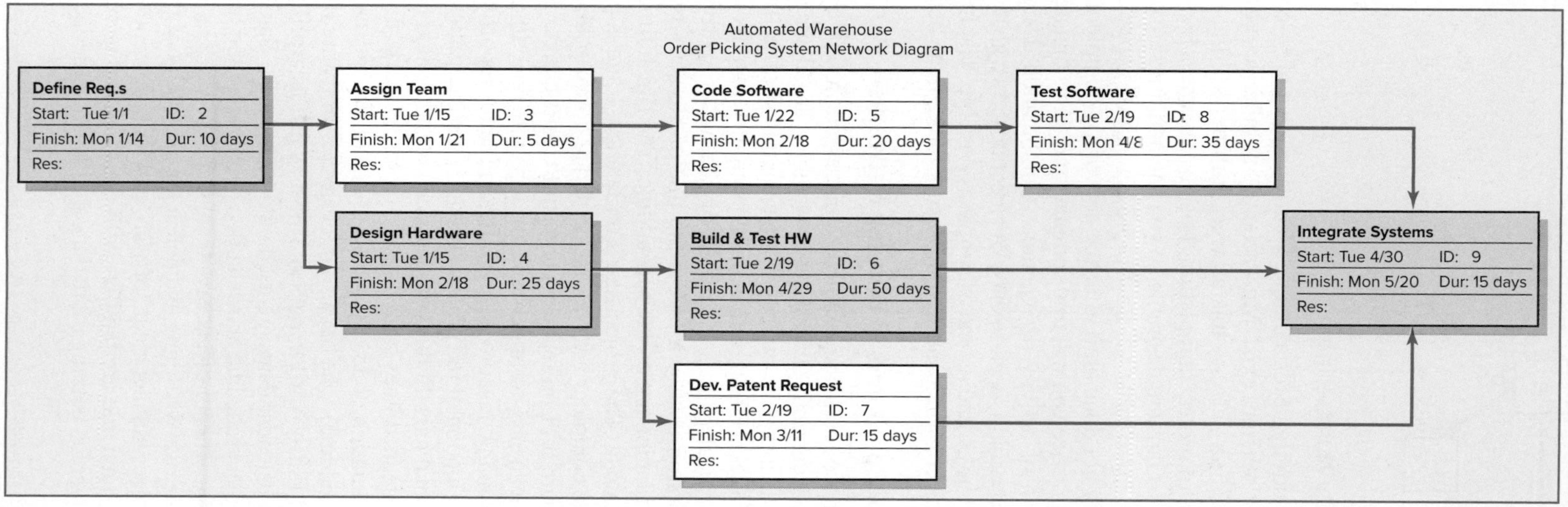

FIGURE 6.11   Automated Order Warehouse Picking System Bar Chart

ID	Duration	Task Name	Start	Finish	Late Start	Late Finish	Free Slack	Total Slack	Jan	Feb	Mar	Apr	May
						Automated Warehouse Order Picking System Schedule Table							
2	10	Define Req.s	Tue 1/1	Mon 1/14	Tue 1/1	Tue 1/15	0 days	0 days					
3	5	Assign Team	Tue 1/15	Mon 1/21	Tue 2/5	Mon 2/11	0 days	15 days					
4	25	Design Hardware	Tue 1/15	Mon 2/18	Tue 1/15	Mon 2/18	0 days	0 days					
5	20	Code Software	Tue 1/22	Mon 2/18	Tue 2/12	Mon 3/11	0 days	15 days					
6	50	Build and Test HW	Tue 2/19	Mon 4/29	Tue 2/19	Mon 4/29	0 days	0 days					
7	15	Dev. Patent Request	Tue 2/19	Mon 3/11	Tue 4/9	Mon 4/29	35 days	35 days					
8	35	Test Software	Tue 2/19	Mon 4/8	Tue 3/12	Mon 4/29	15 days	15 days					
9	15	Integrate Systems	Tue 4/30	Mon 5/20	Tue 4/30	Mon 5/20	0 days	0 days					

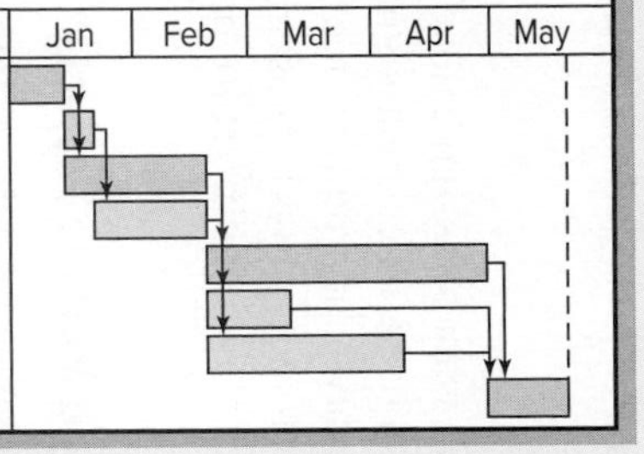

181

knowledge of how the software derives its output. Mistakes in input are very common and require someone skilled in the concepts, tools, and information system to recognize that errors exist so false actions are avoided.

Calendar Dates

Ultimately you will want to assign calendar dates to your project activities. If a computer program is not used, dates are assigned manually. Lay out a calendar of workdays (exclude non-workdays), and number them. Then relate the calendar workdays to the workdays on your project network. Most computer programs will assign calendar dates automatically after you identify start dates, time units, non-workdays, and other information.

Multiple Starts and Multiple Projects

Some computer programs require a common start and finish event in the form of a node—usually a circle or rectangle—for a project network. Even if this is not a requirement, it is a good idea because it avoids "dangler" paths. Dangler paths give the impression that the project does not have a clear beginning or ending. If a project has more than one activity that can begin when the project is to start, each path is a dangler path. The same is true if a project network ends with more than one activity; these unconnected paths are also called danglers. Danglers can be avoided by tying dangler activities to a common project start or finish node.

When several projects are tied together in an organization, using a common start and end node helps to identify the total planning period of all projects. Use of pseudo or dummy wait activities from the common start node allows different start dates for each project.

6.9 Extended Network Techniques to Come Closer to Reality

LO 6-6

Demonstrate understanding and application of lags in compressing projects or constraining the start or finish of an activity.

The method for showing relationships among activities in the last section is called the finish-to-start relationship because it assumes all immediate preceding connected activities must be completed before the next activity can begin. In an effort to come closer to the realities of projects, some useful extensions have been added. The use of *laddering* was the first obvious extension practitioners found very useful.

Laddering

The assumption that all immediate preceding activities must be 100 percent complete is too restrictive for some situations found in practice. This restriction occurs most frequently when one activity overlaps the start of another and has a long duration. Under the standard finish-to-start relationship, when an activity has a long duration and will delay the start of an activity immediately following it, the activity can be broken into segments and the network drawn using a *laddering* approach so the following activity can begin sooner and not delay the work. This segmenting of the larger activity gives the appearance of steps on a ladder on the network, thus the name. The classic example used in many texts and articles is laying pipe, because it is easy to visualize. The trench must be dug, pipe laid, and the trench refilled. If the pipeline is one mile long, it is not necessary to dig one mile of trench before the laying of pipe can begin or to lay one mile of pipe before refill can begin. Figure 6.12 shows how these overlapping activities might appear in an AON network using the standard finish-to-start approach.

FIGURE 6.12
Example of Laddering Using Finish-to-Start Relationship

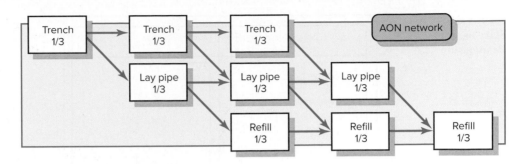

Use of Lags to Reduce Schedule Detail and Project Duration

The use of *lags* has been developed to offer greater flexibility in network construction. *A lag is the minimum amount of time a dependent activity must be delayed to begin or end.* The use of lags in project networks occurs for two primary reasons:

1. When activities of long duration delay the start or finish of successor activities, the network designer normally breaks the activity into smaller activities to avoid the long delay of the successor activity. Use of lags can avoid such delays and reduce network detail.

2. Lags can be used to constrain the start and finish of an activity.

The most commonly used relationship extensions are start-to-start, finish-to-finish, and combinations of these two. These relationship patterns are discussed in this section.

Finish-to-Start Relationship

The finish-to-start relationship represents the typical, generic network style used in the early part of the chapter. However, there are situations in which the next activity in a sequence must be delayed even when the preceding activity is complete. For example, removing concrete forms cannot begin until the poured cement has cured for two time units. Figure 6.13 shows this **lag relationship** for AON networks. Finish-to-start lags are frequently used when ordering materials. For example, it may take 1 day to place orders but take 19 days to receive the goods. The use of finish-to-start allows the activity duration to be only 1 day and the lag 19 days. This approach ensures the activity cost is tied to placing the order only rather than charging the activity for 20 days of work. This same finish-to-start lag relationship is useful to depict transportation, legal, and mail lags.

The use of finish-to-start lags should be carefully checked to ensure their validity. Conservative project managers or those responsible for completion of activities have been known to use lags as a means of building in a "slush" factor to reduce the risk of being late. A simple rule to follow is that the use of finish-to-start lags must be justified and approved by someone responsible for a large section of the project. The legitimacy of lags is not usually difficult to discern. The legitimate use of the additional relationship shown can greatly enhance the network by more closely representing the realities of the project.

Start-to-Start Relationship

An alternative to segmenting the activities as we did earlier is to use a start-to-start relationship. Typical start-to-start relationships are shown in Figure 6.14. Figure 6.14A

FIGURE 6.13
Finish-to-Start Relationship

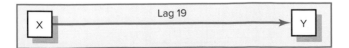

FIGURE 6.14
**Start-to-Start
Relationship**

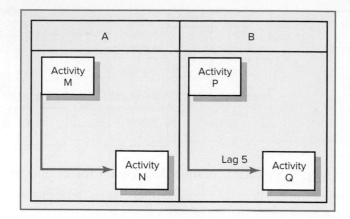

shows the start-to-start relationship with zero lag, while Figure 6.14B shows the same relationship with a lag of five time units. It is important to note that the relationship may be used with or without a lag. If time is assigned, it is usually shown on the dependency arrow of an AON network.

In Figure 6.14B, activity Q cannot begin until five time units after activity P begins. This type of relationship typically depicts a situation in which you can perform a portion of one activity and begin a following activity before completing the first. This relationship can be used on the pipe-laying project. Figure 6.15 shows the project using an AON network. The start-to-start relationship reduces network detail and project delays by using lag relationships.

It is possible to find compression opportunities by changing finish-to-start relations to start-to-start relationships. A review of finish-to-start critical activities may point out opportunities that can be revised to be parallel by using start-to-start relationships. For example, in place of a finish-to-start activity "design house, then build foundation," a start-to-start relationship could be used in which the foundation can be started, say, five days (lag) after design has started—assuming the design of the foundation is the first part of the total design activity. This start-to-start relationship with a small lag allows a sequential activity to be worked on in parallel and to compress the duration of the critical path. This same concept is frequently found in projects in which concurrent engineering is used to speed completion of a project. **Concurrent engineering,** which is highlighted in the Snapshot from Practice 6.3: Concurrent Engineering, basically breaks activities into smaller segments so that work can be done in parallel and the project

FIGURE 6.15
**Use of Lags to
Reduce Project
Duration**

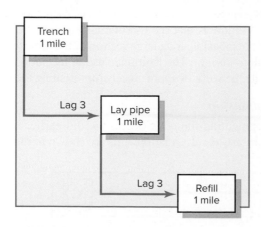

In the old days, when a new product development project was initiated by a firm, it would start its sequential journey in the research and development department. Concepts and ideas would be worked out and the results passed to the engineering department, which sometimes reworked the whole product. This result would be passed to manufacturing, where it might be reworked once more in order to ensure the product could be manufactured using existing machinery and operations. Quality improvements were initiated after the fact once defects and improvement opportunities were discovered during production. This sequential approach to product development required a great deal of time, and it was not uncommon for the final product to be totally unrecognizable when compared to original specifications.

Given the emphasis on speed to the market, companies have abandoned the sequential approach to product development and have adopted a more holistic approach titled concurrent engineering. In a nutshell, *concurrent engineering* entails the active involvement of all the relevant specialty areas throughout the design and development process. The traditional chainlike sequence of finish-to-start relationships is replaced by a series of start-to-start lag relationships as soon as meaningful work can be initiated for the next phase. Figure 6.16 summarizes the dramatic gains in time to market achieved by this approach.

Within the world of project management this approach is also called *Fast Tracking*. General Motors used this approach to design the very first American hybrid car, the Chevy Volt. From the very beginning specialists from marketing, engineering, design, manufacturing, quality assurance, and other relevant departments were involved in every stage of the project. Not only did the project meet all of its objectives, it was completed ahead of schedule.

*"Chevrolet Volt Hits Road, Ahead of Schedule," *The New York Times,* June 25, 2009; accessed online June 2, 2011.

FIGURE 6.16 **New Product Development Process**

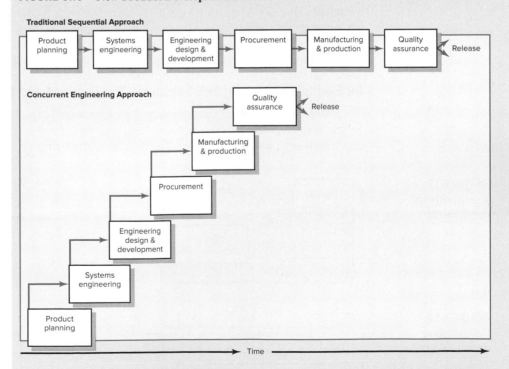

FIGURE 6.17
**Finish-to-Finish
Relationship**

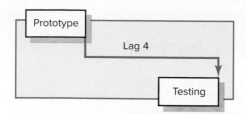

expedited (Turtle, 1994). Start-to-start relationships can depict the concurrent engineering conditions and reduce network detail. Of course, the same result can be accomplished by breaking an activity into small packages that can be implemented in parallel, but this latter approach increases the network and tracking detail significantly.

Finish-to-Finish Relationship

This relationship is found in Figure 6.17. The finish of one activity depends on the finish of another activity. For example, testing cannot be completed any earlier than four days after the prototype is complete. Note that this is not a finish-to-start relationship because the testing of subcomponents can begin before the prototype is completed, but four days of "system" testing is required after the prototype is finished.

Start-to-Finish Relationship

This relationship represents situations in which the finish of an activity depends on the start of another activity. For example, system documentation cannot end until three days after testing has started (see Figure 6.18). Here all the relevant information to complete the system documentation is produced after the first three days of testing.

Combinations of Lag Relationships

More than one lag relationship can be attached to an activity. These relationships are usually start-to-start and finish-to-finish combinations tied to two activities. For example, debug cannot begin until two time units after coding has started. Coding must be finished four days before debug can be finished (see Figure 6.19).

An Example Using Lag Relationships—The Forward and Backward Pass

The forward and backward pass procedures are the same as explained earlier in the chapter for finish-to-start relationships (without lags). The modifying technique lies in the need to check each new relationship to see if it alters the start or finish time of another activity.

FIGURE 6.18
**Start-to-Finish
Relationship**

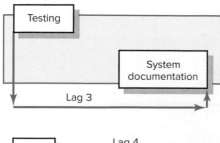

FIGURE 6.19
**Combination
Relationships**

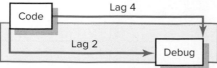

An example of the outcome of the forward and backward pass is shown in Figure 6.20. Order hardware depends upon the design of the system (start-to-start). Three days into the design of the system (activity A), it is possible to order the required hardware (activity B). It takes four days after the order is placed (activity B) for the hardware to arrive so it can begin to be installed (activity C). After two days of installing the software system (activity D), the testing of the system can begin (activity E). System testing (activity E) can be completed two days after the software is installed (activity D). Preparing system documentation (activity F) can begin once the design is completed (activity A), but it cannot be completed until two days after testing the system (activity E). This final relationship is an example of a finish-to-finish lag.

Note how an activity can have a critical finish and/or start. Activities E and F have critical finishes (zero slack), but their activity starts have 4 and 12 days of slack. It is only the finishes of activities E and F that are critical. Conversely, activity A has zero slack to start but has five days of slack to finish. The critical path follows activity start and finish constraints that occur due to the use of the additional relationships available and the imposed lags. You can identify the critical path in Figure 6.20 by following the dashed line on the network.

If a lag relationship exists, each activity must be checked to see if the start or finish is constrained. For example, in the forward pass the EF of activity E (test system) (18) is controlled by the finish of activity D (install software) and the lag of two time units (16 + lag 2 = 18). Finally, in the backward pass, the LS of activity A (design system) is controlled by activity B (order hardware) and the lag relationship to activity A (3 − 3 = 0).

FIGURE 6.20 **Network Using Lags**

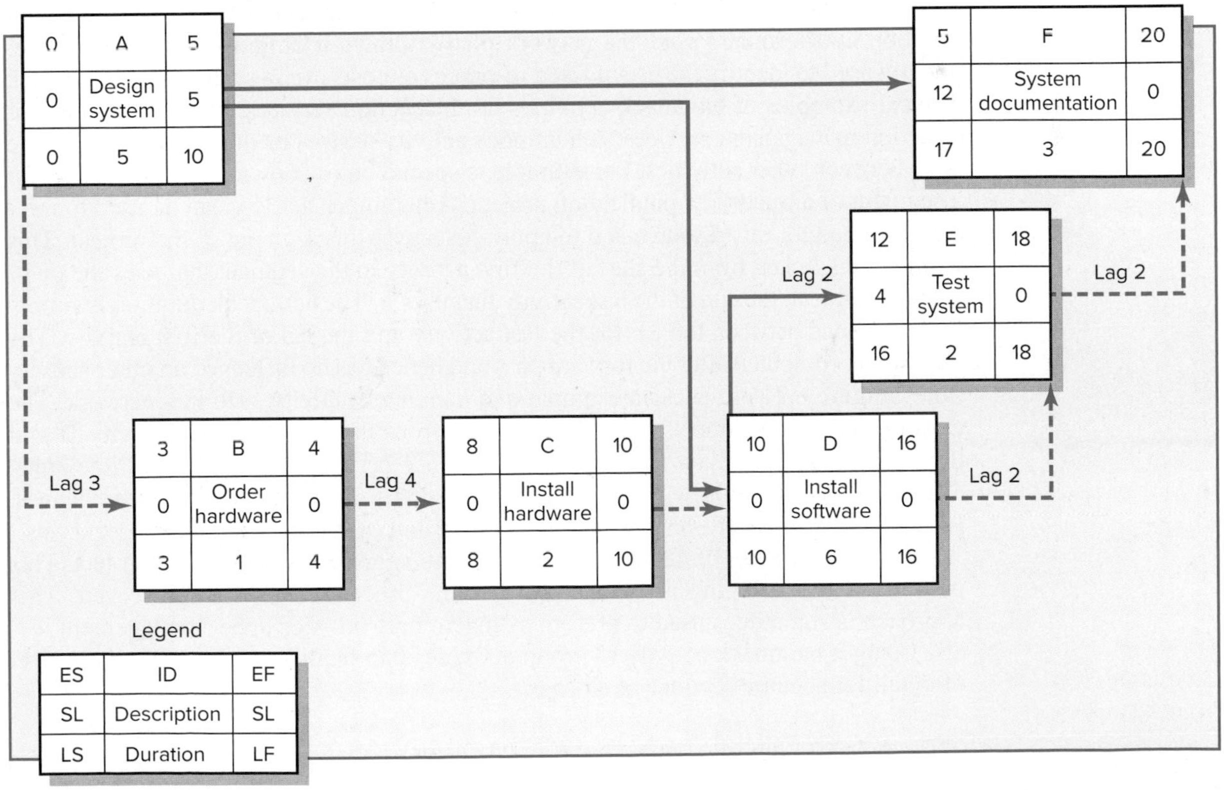

FIGURE 6.21 **Hammock Activity Example**

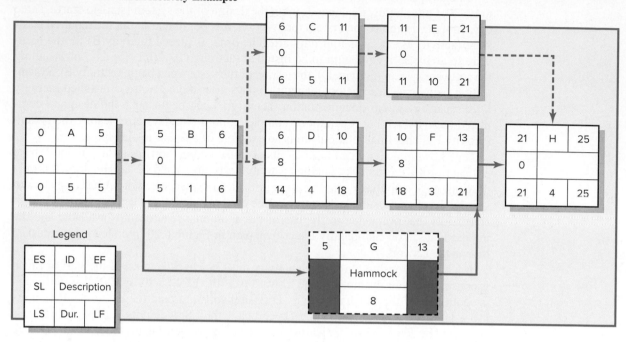

Hammock Activities

Another of the extended techniques uses a **hammock activity.** This type of activity derives its name because it spans over a segment of a project. The hammock activity duration is determined *after* the network plan is drawn. Hammock activities are frequently used to identify the use of fixed resources or costs over a segment of the project. Typical examples of hammock activities are inspection services, consultants, or construction management services. A hammock activity derives its duration from the time span between other activities. For example, a special color copy machine is needed for a segment of a tradeshow publication project. A hammock activity can be used to indicate the need for this resource and to apply costs over this segment of the project. This hammock is linked from the start of the first activity in the segment that uses the color copy machine to the end of the last activity that uses it. The hammock duration is simply the difference between the EF for the last activity and the ES of the first activity. The duration is computed after the forward pass and hence has no influence on other activity times. Figure 6.21 provides an example of a hammock activity used in a network. The duration for the hammock activity is derived from the early start of activity B and the early finish of activity F; that is, the difference between 13 and 5, or 8 time units. The hammock duration will change if any ES or EF in the chain-sequence changes. Hammock activities are very useful in assigning and controlling indirect project costs.[3]

Another major use of hammock activities is to aggregate sections of a project. This is similar to developing a subnetwork, but the precedence is still preserved. This approach is sometimes used to present a "macro network" for upper management levels. Using a hammock activity to group activities can facilitate getting the right level of detail for specific sections of a project.

---

[3] In order to designate G as a Hammock activity in MS Project 2012 you would copy and paste for activity G the start date of activity B and the finish date for activity F (http://support.microsoft.com/kb/141733).

Summary

Many project managers feel the project network is their most valuable exercise and planning document. Project networks sequence and time-phase the project work, resources, and budgets. Work package tasks are used to develop activities for networks. Every project manager should feel comfortable working in an AON environment. The AON method uses nodes (boxes) for activities and arrows for dependencies. The forward and backward passes establish early and late times for activities. Although most project managers use computers to generate networks and activity times, they find a keen understanding of network development and the ability to compute activity times is invaluable in the field. Computers break down; input errors give false information; some decisions must be made without computer "what if" analysis. Project managers who are well acquainted with network development and AON methods and who are able to compute activity times will encounter fewer problems than project managers less well acquainted. Project networks help to ensure there are no surprises.

Several extensions and modifications have been appended to the original AON method. Lags allow the project planner to more closely replicate the actual conditions found in practice. The use of lags can result in the start or finish of an activity becoming critical. Some computer software simply calls the whole activity critical rather than identifying the start or finish as being critical. Caution should be taken to ensure that lags are not used as a buffer for possible errors in estimating time. Finally, hammock activities are useful in tracking costs of resources used for a particular segment of a project. Hammock activities can also be used to reduce the size of a project network by grouping activities for simplification and clarity. All of the discussed refinements to the original AON methodology contribute toward better planning and control of projects.

Key Terms

Activity, 164, 166, 168
Activity-on-arrow (AOA), 167
Activity-on-node (AON), 167
Burst activity, 166
Concurrent engineering, 184

Critical path, 166
Early time, 166
Free slack (FS), 177
Gantt chart, 179
Hammock activity, 188
Lag relationship, 183

Late time, 166
Merge activity, 166
Parallel activity, 166
Path, 166
Sensitivity, 176
Total slack, 175

Review Questions

1. How does the WBS differ from the project network?
2. How are WBS and project networks linked?
3. Why bother creating a WBS? Why not go straight to a project network and forget the WBS?
4. Why is slack important to the project manager?
5. What is the difference between free slack and total slack?
6. Why are lags used in developing project networks?
7. What is a hammock activity, and when is it used?

Exercises

Creating a Project Network

1. Here is a partial work breakdown structure for a wedding. Use the method described in the Snapshot from Practice 6.1: The Yellow Sticky Approach to create a network for this project.

Note: Do not include summary tasks in the network (i.e., 1.3, Ceremony, is a summary task; 1.2, Marriage license, is not a summary task). Do not consider who would be doing the task in building the network. For example, do not arrange "hiring a band" to occur after "florist" because the same person is responsible for doing both tasks. Focus only on technical dependencies between tasks.

Hint: Start with the last activity (wedding reception), and work your way back to the start of the project. Build the logical sequence of tasks by asking the following question: In order to have or do this, what must be accomplished immediately before this? Once completed, check forward in time by asking this question: Is this task(s) the only thing that is needed immediately before the start of the next task?

Work Breakdown Structure

1. Wedding project

   1.1 Decide on date

   1.2 Marriage license

   1.3 Ceremony

   1.3.1 Rent church

   1.3.2 Florist

   1.3.3 Create/print programs

   1.3.4 Hire photographer

   1.3.5 Wedding ceremony

   1.4 Guests

   1.4.1 Develop guest list

   1.4.2 Order invitations

   1.4.3 Address and mail invitations

   1.4.4 Track RSVPs

   1.5 Reception

   1.5.1 Reserve reception hall

   1.5.2 Food and beverage

   1.5.2.1 Choose caterer

   1.5.2.2 Decide on menu

   1.5.2.3 Make final order

   1.5.3 Hire DJ

   1.5.4 Decorate reception hall

   1.5.5 Wedding reception

Drawing AON Networks

2. Draw a project network from the following information. What activity(ies) is a burst activity? What activity(ies) is a merge activity?

ID	Description	Predecessor
A	Survey site	None
B	Excavate site	A
C	Install power lines	B
D	Install drainage	B
E	Pour foundation	C, D

3.*Draw a project network from the following information. What activity(ies) is a burst activity? What activity(ies) is a merge activity?

ID	Description	Predecessor
A	Identify topic	None
B	Research topic	A
C	Draft paper	B
D	Edit paper	C
E	Create graphics	C
F	References	C
G	Proof paper	D, E, F
H	Submit paper	G

4. Draw a project network from the following information. What activity(ies) is a burst activity? What activity(ies) is a merge activity?

ID	Description	Predecessor
A	Contract signed	None
B	Survey designed	A
C	Target market identified	B
D	Data collection	B, C
E	Develop presentation	B
F	Analyze results	D
G	Demographics	C
H	Presentation	E, F, G

5. Draw a project network from the following information. What activity(ies) is a burst activity? What activity(ies) is a merge activity?

ID	Description	Predecessor
A	Order review	None
B	Order standard parts	A
C	Produce standard parts	A
D	Design custom parts	A
E	Software development	A
F	Manufacture custom parts	C, D
G	Assemble	B, F
H	Test	E, G

* The solution to this exercise can be found in Appendix One.

AON Network Times

6. From the following information, develop an AON project network. Complete the forward and backward pass, compute activity slack, and identify the critical path. How many days will the project take?

ID	Description	Predecessor	Time
A	Survey site	None	2
B	Excavate site	A	4
C	Install power lines	B	3
D	Install drainage	B	5
E	Pour foundation	C, D	3

7. The project information for the custom order project of the Air Control Company is presented here. Draw a project network for this project. Compute the early and late activity times and the slack times. Identify the critical path.

ID	Description	Predecessor	Time
A	Order review	None	2
B	Order standard parts	A	3
C	Produce standard parts	A	10
D	Design custom parts	A	13
E	Software development	A	18
F	Manufacture custom hardware	C, D	15
G	Assemble	B, F	10
H	Test	E, G	5

8. You have signed a contract to build a garage for the Simpsons. You will receive a $500 bonus for completing the project within 17 working days. The contract also contains a penalty clause in which you will lose $100 for each day the project takes longer than 17 working days.

Draw a project network given the information below. Complete the forward and backward pass, compute the activity slack, and identify the critical path. Do you expect to receive a bonus or a penalty on this project?

ID	Description	Predecessor	Time (days)
A	Prepare site	None	2
B	Pour foundation	B	3
C	Erect frame	C	4
D	Roof	C	4
E	Windows	C	1
	Doors	C	1
G	Electrical	D, E, F, G	3
H	Rough-in frame	F, G	2
I	Door opener	H, I	1
J	Paint	J	2
K	Cleanup		1

9. You are creating a customer database for the Hillsboro Hops minor league baseball team. Draw a project network given the information in the table that follows. Complete the forward and backward pass, compute activity slack, and identify the critical path.

How long will this project take? How sensitive is the network schedule? Calculate the free slack and total slack for all noncritical activities.

ID	Description	Predecessor	Time (days)
A	Systems design	None	2
B	Subsystem A design	A	1
C	Subsystem B design	A	1
D	Subsystem C design	A	1
E	Program A	B	2
F	Program B	C	2
G	Program C	D	2
H	Subsystem A test	E	1
I	Subsystem B test	F	1
J	Subsystem C test	G	1
K	Integration	H, I, J	3
L	Integration test	K	1

10. K. Nelson, project manager of Print Software, Inc., wants you to prepare a project network; compute the early, late, and slack activity times; determine the planned project duration; and identify the critical path. His assistant has collected the following information for the Color Printer Drivers Software Project:

ID	Description	Predecessor	Time
A	External specifications	None	8
B	Review design features	A	2
C	Document new features	A	3
D	Write software	A	60
E	Program and test	B	40
F	Edit and publish notes	C	2
G	Review manual	D	2
H	Alpha site	E, F	20
I	Print manual	G	10
J	Beta site	H, I	10
K	Manufacture	J	12
L	Release and ship	K	3

11. *A large Southeast city is requesting federal funding for a park-and-ride project. One of the requirements in the request application is a network plan for the design phase of the project. Sophie Kim, the chief engineer, wants you to develop a project network plan to meet this requirement. She has gathered the activity time estimates and their dependencies shown here. Show your project network with the activity early, late, and slack times. Mark the critical path.

ID	Description	Predecessor	Time
A	Survey	None	5
B	Soils report	A	20
C	Traffic design	A	30
D	Lot layout	A	5
E	Approve design	B, C, D	80
F	Illumination	E	15
G	Drainage	E	30
H	Landscape	E	25
I	Signage	E	15
J	Bid proposal	F, G, H, I	10

* The solution to this exercise can be found in Appendix One.

12. You are creating a customer database for the Lehigh Valley IronPigs minor league baseball team. Draw a project network given the information below. Complete the forward and backward pass, compute activity slack, and identify the critical path.

How long will this project take? How sensitive is the network schedule? Calculate the free slack and total slack for all noncritical activities.

ID	Description	Predecessor	Time (days)
A	Systems design	None	2
B	Subsystem A design	A	1
C	Subsystem B design	A	2
D	Subsystem C design	A	1
E	Program A	B	2
F	Program B	C	10
G	Program C	D	3
H	Subsystem A test	E	1
I	Subsystem B test	F	1
J	Subsystem C test	G	1
K	Integration	H, I, J	3
L	Integration test	K	1

13. *You are completing a group term paper. Given the project network that follows, complete the forward and backward pass, compute activity slack, and identify the critical path. Use this information to create a Gantt chart for the project. Be sure to show slack for noncritical activities.

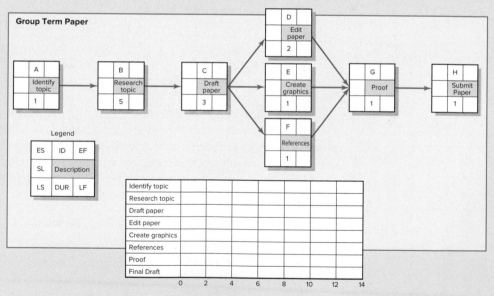

* The solution to this exercise can be found in Appendix One.

14. You are managing a product upgrade project for Bangkokagogo. Given the project network that follows, complete the forward and backward pass, compute activity slack, and identify the critical path. Use this information to create a Gantt chart for the project. Be sure to show slack for noncritical activities.

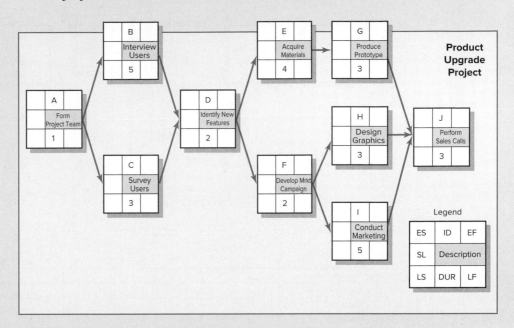

Product Upgrade Project Gantt Chart

	1	2	3	4	5	6	7	8	9	10	11	12	13	14	15	16	17	18
Project Team																		
Interview Users																		
Survey Users																		
ID New Features																		
Acquire Materials																		
Dev Mrkt Campaign																		
Produce Prototypes																		
Design Graphics																		
Conduct Marketing																		
Perform Sales Calls																		

15. You are creating a database for the Oklahoma City Thunder NBA Basketball team. Given the project network that follows, complete the forward and backward pass, compute activity slack, and identify the critical path. Use this information to create a Gantt chart for the project.

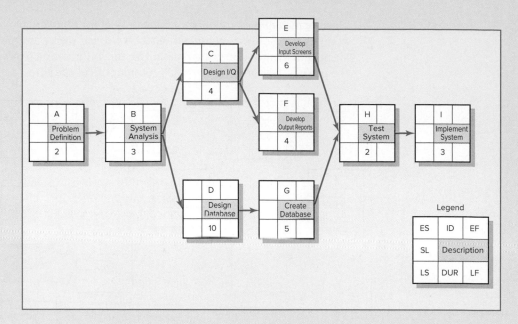

	0	1	2	3	4	5	6	7	8	9	10	11	12	13	14	15	16	17	18	19	20	21	22	23	24	25
Problem Definition																										
System Analysis																										
Design I/Q																										
Design Database																										
Develop Input Screens																										
Develop Input Reports																										
Create Database																										
Test System																										
Implement System																										

Computer Exercises

16. The planning department of an electronics firm has set up the activities for developing and production of a new MP3 Player. Given the information below, develop a project network using Microsoft Project. Assume a five-day workweek and the project starts on January 4, 2017.

Activity ID	Description	Activity Predecessor	Activity Time (weeks)
1	Staff	None	2
2	Develop market program	1	3
3	Select channels of distribution	1	8
4	Patent	1	12
5	Pilot production	1	4
6	Test market	5	4
7	Ad promotion	2	4
8	Set up for production	4, 6	16

The project team has requested that you create a network for the project, and determine if the project can be completed in 45 weeks.

17. Using Microsoft Project, set up the network and determine the critical path for Phase 1 of the Whistler Ski Resort project. The project workweek will be 5 days (M–F).

Whistler Ski Resort Project

Given the fact that the number of skiing visitors to Whistler, B.C., Canada, has been increasing at an exciting rate, thanks to the 2010 Winter Olympics, the Whistler Ski Association has been considering construction of another ski lodge and ski complex. The results of an economic feasibility study just completed by members of the staff show that a winter resort complex near the base of Whistler Mountain could be a very profitable venture. The area is accessible by car, bus, train, and air. The board of directors has voted to build the 10-million-dollar complex recommended in the study. Unfortunately, due to the short summer season, the complex will have to be built in stages. The first stage (year 1) will contain a day lodge, chair lift, rope tow, generator house (for electricity), and a parking lot designed to accommodate 400 cars and 30 buses. The second and third stages will include a hotel, ice rink, pool, shops, two additional chair lifts, and other attractions. The board has decided that stage one should begin no later than April 1 and be completed by October 1, in time for the next skiing season. You have been assigned the task of project manager, and it is your job to coordinate the ordering of materials and construction activities to ensure the project's completion by the required date.

After looking into the possible sources of materials, you are confronted with the following time estimates. Materials for the chair lift and rope tow will take 30 days and 12 days, respectively, to arrive once the order is submitted. Lumber for the day lodge, generator hut, and foundations will take 9 days to arrive. The electrical and plumbing materials for the day lodge will take 12 days to arrive. The generator will take 12 days to arrive. Before actual construction can begin on the various facilities, a road to the site must be built; this will take 6 days. As soon as the road is in, clearing can begin concurrently on the sites of the day lodge, generator house, chair lift, and rope tow. It is estimated that the clearing task at each site will take 6 days, 3 days, 36 days, and 6 days, respectively. The clearing of the main ski slopes can begin after the area for the chair lift has been cleared; this will take 84 days.

The foundation for the day lodge will take 12 days to complete. Construction of the main framework will take an additional 18 days. After the framework is completed, electrical wiring and plumbing can be installed concurrently. These should take 24 and 30 days, respectively. Finally, the finishing construction on the day lodge can begin; this will take 36 days.

Installation of the chair lift towers (67 days) can begin once the site is cleared, lumber delivered, and the foundation completed (6 days). Also, when the chair lift site has been cleared, construction of a permanent road to the upper towers can be started; this will take 24 days. While the towers are being installed, the electric motor to drive the chair lift can be installed; the motor can be installed in 24 days. Once the towers are completed and the motor installed, it will take 3 days to install the cable and an additional 12 days to install the chairs.

Installation of the towers for the rope tow can begin once the site is cleared and the foundation is built and poured; it takes 4 days to build the foundation, pour the concrete and let it cure, and 20 days to install the towers for the rope tow. While the towers are being erected, installation of the electric motor to drive the rope tow can begin; this activity will take 24 days. After the towers and motor are installed, the rope tow can be strung in 1 day. The parking lot can be cleared once the rope tow is finished; this task will take 18 days.

The foundation for the generator house can begin at the same time as the foundation for the lodge; this will take 6 days. The main framework for the generator house can begin once the foundation is completed; framing will take 12 days. After the house is framed, the diesel generator can be installed in 18 days. Finishing construction on the generator house can now begin and will take 12 more days.

Assignment:

1. Identify the critical path on your network.
2. Can the project be completed by October 1?

Optical Disk Preinstallation Project

18. The optical disk project team has started gathering the information necessary to develop the project network—predecessor activities and activity times in weeks. The results of their meeting are found in the following table.

Activity	Description	Duration	Predecessor
1	Define scope	6	None
2	Define customer problems	3	1
3	Define data records and relationships	5	1
4	Mass storage requirements	5	2, 3
5	Consultant needs analysis	10	2, 3
6	Prepare installation network	3	4, 5
7	Estimate costs and budget	2	4, 5
8	Design section "point" system	1	4, 5
9	Write request proposal	5	4, 5
10	Compile vendor list	3	4, 5
11	Prepare mgmt. control system	5	6, 7
12	Prepare comparison report	5	9, 10
13	Compare system "philosophies"	3	8, 12
14	Compare total installation	2	8, 12
15	Compare cost of support	3	8, 12
16	Compare customer satisfaction level	10	8, 12
17	Assign philosophies points	1	13
18	Assign installation cost	1	14
19	Assign support cost	1	15
20	Assign customer satisfaction points	1	16
21	Select best system	1	11, 17, 18, 19, 20
22	Order system	1	21

The project team has requested that you create a network for the project, and determine if the project can be completed in 45 weeks.

Lag Exercises

19. From the following information, compute the early, late, and slack times for each activity. Identify the critical path.

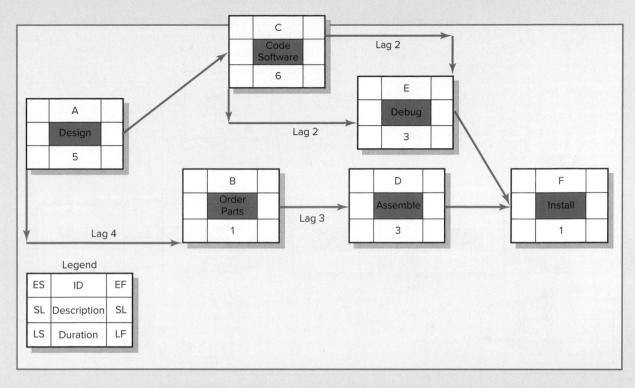

20. Given the following information, compute the early, late, and slack times for the project network. Which activities on the critical path have only the start or finish of the activity on the critical path?

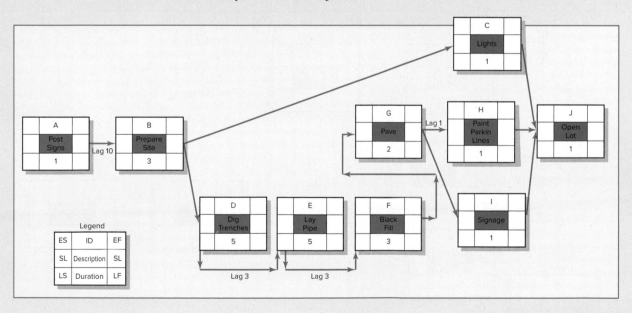

21. *Given the information in the following lag exercises, compute the early, late, and slack times for the project network. Which activities on the critical path have only the start or finish of the activity on the critical path?

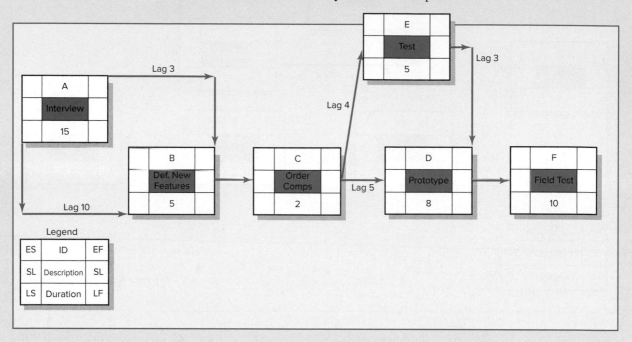

22. Given the network below, compute the early, late, and slack time for each activity. Clearly identify the critical path.

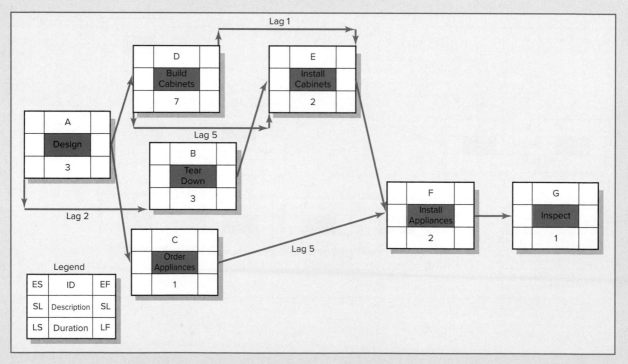

* The solution to this exercise can be found in Appendix One.

CyClon Project

23. The CyClon project team has started gathering information necessary to develop a project network—predecessor activities and activity time in days. The results of their meeting are found in the following table:

Activity	Description	Duration	Predecessor
1	**CyClon Project**		
2	Design	10	
3	Procure prototype parts	10	2
4	Fabricate parts	8	2
5	Assemble prototype	4	3, 4
6	Laboratory test	7	5
7	Field test	10	6
8	Adjust design	6	7
9	Order stock components	10	8
10	Order custom components	15	8
11	Assemble test production unit	10	9, 10
12	Test unit	5	11
13	Document results	3	12

Part A. Create a network based on the above information. How long will the project take? What is the critical path?

Part B. Upon further review the team recognizes that they missed three finish-to-start lags. Procure prototype parts will involve only 2 days of work but it will take 8 days for the parts to be delivered. Likewise, Order stock components will take 2 days of work and 8 days for delivery and Order custom components 2 days of work and 13 days for delivery.

Reconfigure the CyClon schedule by entering the three finish-to-start lags. What impact did these lags have on the original schedule? On the amount of work required to complete the project?

Part C. Management is still not happy with the schedule and wants the project completed as soon as possible. Unfortunately, they are not willing to approve additional resources. One team member pointed out that the network contained only finish-to-start relationships and that it might be possible to reduce project duration by creating start-to-start lags. After much deliberation the team concluded that the following relationships could be converted into start-to-start lags:

- Procure prototype parts could start 6 days after the start of Design.
- Fabricate parts could start 9 days after the start of Design.
- Laboratory test could begin 1 day after the start of Assemble prototype.
- Field test could start 5 days after the start of Laboratory test.
- Adjust design could begin 7 days after the start of Field test.
- Order stock and Order custom components could begin 5 days after Adjust design.
- Test unit could begin 9 days after the start of Assemble test production unit.
- Document results could start 3 days after the start of Test unit.

Reconfigure the CyClon schedule by entering all nine start-to-start lags. What impact did these lags have on the original schedule (Part A)? How long will the project take? Is there a change in the critical path? Is there a change in the sensitivity of the network? Why would management like this solution?

References

Gantt, H. L., *Work, Wages and Profit*, published by *The Engineering Magazine*, New York, 1910; republished as *Work, Wages and Profits* (Easton, PA: Hive Publishing Company, 1974).

Kelly, J. E., "Critical Path Planning and Scheduling: Mathematical Basis," *Operations Research,* vol. 9, no. 3 (May–June 1961), pp. 296–321.

Levy, F. K., G. L. Thompson, and J. D. West, "The ABCs of the Critical Path Method," *Harvard Business Review,* vol. 41, no. 5 (1963), pp. 98–108.

Rosenblatt, A., and G. Watson, "Concurrent Engineering," *IEEE Spectrum,* July 1991, pp. 22–37.

Turtle, Q. C., *Implementing Concurrent Project Management* (Englewood Cliffs, NJ: Prentice Hall, 1994).

Case 6.1

Advantage Energy Technology Data Center Migration*—Part A

Brian Smith, network administrator at Advanced Energy Technology (AET), has been given the responsibility of implementing the migration of a large data center to a new office location. Careful planning is needed because AET operates in the highly competitive petroleum industry. AET is one of five national software companies that provide an accounting and business management package for oil jobbers and gasoline distributors. A few years ago, AET jumped into the "application service provider" world. Their large data center provides clients with remote access to AET's complete suite of application software systems. Traditionally, one of AET's primary competitive advantages has been the company's trademark IT reliability. Due to the complexity of this project, Brian will have to use a parallel method of implementation. Although this will increase project costs, a parallel approach is essential if reliability is not to be compromised.

Currently, AET's data center is located on the second floor of a renovated old bank building in downtown Corvallis, Oregon. The company is moving to a new, one-level building located in the recently developed industrial complex at the Corvallis International Airport. On February 1, Brian is formally assigned the task by the Vice President of Operations, Dan Whitmore, with the following guidelines:

- From start to finish, it is anticipated the entire project will take three to four months to complete.

- It is essential that AET's 235 clients suffer no downtime.

Whitmore advises Brian to come back to the Executive Committee on February 15, with a presentation on the scope of the project that includes costs, "first-cut" timeline, and proposed project team members.

Brian had some preliminary discussions with some of AET's managers and directors from each of the functional departments and then arranged for a full-day scope

---

*Prepared by James Moran, a project management instructor at the College of Business, Oregon State University

meeting on February 4 with a few of the managers and technical representatives from operations, systems, facilities, and applications. The scope team determined the following:

- Three to four months is a feasible project timeline and first-cut cost estimate is $80,000–$90,000 (this includes the infrastructure upgrade of the new site).
- Critical to the "no-downtime" requirement is the need to completely rely on AET's remote disaster recovery "hot" site for full functionality.
- Brian will serve as project manager of a team consisting of one team member each from facilities, operations/systems, operations/telecommunications, systems & applications, and customer service.

Brian's Executive Committee report was positively received and, after a few modifications and recommendations, he was formally charged with responsibility for the project. Brian recruited his team and scheduled their first team meeting (March 1) as the initial task of his project planning process.

Once the initial meeting is conducted Brian can hire the contractors to renovate the new data center. During this time Brian will figure out how to design the network. Brian estimates that screening and hiring a contractor will take about one week and that the network design will take about two weeks. The new center requires a new ventilation system. The manufacturer's requirements include an ambient temperature of 67 degrees to keep all of the data servers running at optimal speeds. The ventilation system has a lead time of three weeks. Brian will also need to order new racks to hold the servers, switches, and other network devices. The racks have a two-week delivery time.

The data center supervisor requested that Brian replace all of the old power supplies and data cables. Brian will need to order these as well. Because Brian has a great relationship with the vendor, they guarantee that it will take only one week lead time for the power supplies and the data cables. Once the new ventilation system and racks arrive, Brian can begin installing them. It will take one week to install the ventilation system and three weeks to install the racks. The renovation of the new data center can begin as soon as the contractors have been hired. The contractors tell Brian that construction will take 20 days. Once the construction begins and after Brian installs the ventilation system and racks, the city inspector must approve the construction of the raised floor.

The city inspector will take two days to approve the infrastructure. After the city inspection and after the new power supplies and cables have arrived, Brian can install the power supplies and run the cables. Brian estimates that it will take five days to install the power supplies and one week to run all of the data cables. Before Brian can assign an actual date for taking the network off line and switching to the hot remote site, he must get approval from each of the functional units ("Switchover Approval"). Meetings with each of the functional units will require one week. During this time he can initiate a power check to ensure that each of the racks has sufficient voltage. This will require only one day.

Upon completion of the power check, he can take one week to install his test servers. The test servers will test all of the primary network functions and act as a safeguard before the network is taken off line. The batteries must be charged, ventilation installed, and test servers up and running before management can be assured that the new infrastructure is safe, which will take two days. Then they will sign off the Primary Systems check, taking one day of intense meetings. They will also set an official date for the network move.

Brian is happy that everything has gone well thus far and is convinced that the move will go just as smoothly. Now that an official date is set, the network will be shut down for a day. Brian must move all of the network components to the new data center. Brian will do the move over the weekend—two days—when user traffic is at low point.

ASSIGNMENT

1. Generate a priority matrix for AET's system move.
2. Develop a WBS for Brian's project. Include duration (days) and predecessors.
3. Using a project planning tool, generate a network diagram for this project.

   Note: Base your plan on the following guidelines: eight-hour days, five-day weeks except for when Brian moves the network components over a weekend, no holiday breaks, March 1, 2010, is the project start date. Ordering Ventilation System, New Racks, and Power Supplies/Cables takes only one actual day of work. The remaining days are the time necessary for the vendors to fill and ship the order to Brian. So use Finish to Start lags here. Assume that five days after the start of the Renovation of the Data Center that the raised floor will be ready for inspection (a Start-to-Start lag).

Case 6.2

Shoreline Stadium Case

The G&E Company is preparing a bid to build the new 47,000-seat Shoreline baseball stadium. The construction must start on July 3, 2017, and be completed in time for the start of the 2020 season. A penalty clause of $250,000 per day of delay beyond April 3 is written into the contract.

Percival Young, the president of the company, expressed optimism at obtaining the contract and revealed that the company could net as much as $3 million on the project. He also said if they were successful, the prospects of future projects are bright since there is a projected renaissance in building classic ball parks with modern luxury boxes.

ASSIGNMENT

Given the information provided in Table 6.3, construct a network schedule for the stadium project and answer the following questions:

1. Will the project be able to be completed by the April 3 deadline? How long will it take?
2. What is the critical path for the project?
3. Based on the schedule would you recommend that G&E pursue this contact? Why? Include a one-page Gantt chart for the stadium schedule.

TABLE 6.3   **Shoreline Stadium Case**

ID	Activity	Duration	Predecessor(s)
1	*Baseball Stadium*		
2	Clear stadium site	70 days	—
3	Demolish building	30 days	2
4	Set up construction site	70 days	3
5	Drive support piling	120 days	4
6	Pour lower concrete bowl	120 days	5
7	Pour main concourse	120 days	6
8	Install playing field	90 days	6
9	Construct upper steel bowl	120 days	6
10	Install seats	140 days	9
11	Build luxury boxes	90 days	9
12	Install jumbotron	30 days	9
13	Stadium infrastructure	120 days	9
14	Construct steel canopy	75 days	10
15	Light installation	30 days	10
16	Build roof supports	90 days	4
17	Construct roof	180 days	16
18	Install roof tracks	90 days	14
19	Install roof	90 days	17, 18
20	Inspection	20 days	8, 11, 13, 15, 19

Case Appendix

Technical Details For The Shoreline Baseball Stadium

For purposes of this case assume the following:

1. The following holidays are observed: January 1, Martin Luther King Day (third Monday in January), Memorial Day (last Monday in May), July 4th, Labor Day (first Monday in September), Thanksgiving Day (4th Thursday in November), December 25 and 26.

2. If a holiday falls on a Saturday then Friday will be given as an extra day off, and if it falls on a Sunday then Monday will be given as a day off.

3. The construction crew work Monday through Friday.

7 Managing Risk

LEARNING OBJECTIVES

After reading this chapter you should be able to:

7-1 Describe the risk management process.

7-2 Understand how to identify project risks.

7-3 Assess the significance of different project risks.

7-4 Describe the four different responses to managing risks.

7-5 Understand the role contingency plans play in risk management process.

7-6 Understand opportunity management and describe the four different approaches to responding to opportunities in a project.

7-7 Understand how contingency funds and time buffers are used to manage risks on a project.

7-8 Recognize the need for risk management being an ongoing activity.

7-9 Describe the change control process.

OUTLINE

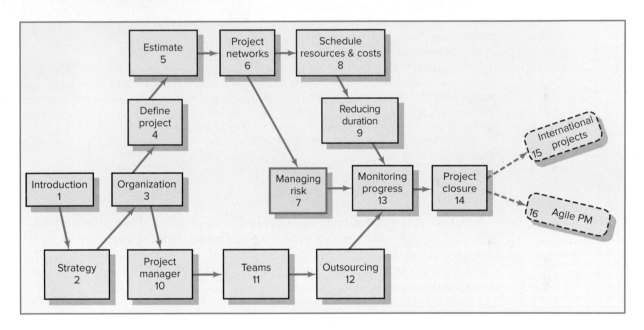

You've got to go out on a limb sometimes because that's where the fruit is.

—Will Rogers

Every project manager understands risks are inherent in projects, deliveries are delayed, accidents happen, people get sick, etc. No amount of planning can overcome *risk,* or the inability to control chance events. In the context of projects, **risk** is an uncertain event or condition that, if it occurs, has a positive or negative effect on project objectives. A risk has a cause and, if it occurs, a consequence. For example, a cause may be a flu virus or change in scope requirements. The event is that team members get stricken with the flu or the product has to be redesigned. If either of these uncertain events occurs, it will impact the cost, schedule, and quality of the project.

Some potential risk events can be identified before the project starts—such as equipment malfunction or change in technical requirements. Risks can be anticipated consequences, like schedule slippages or cost overruns. Risks can be beyond imagination like the 2008 financial meltdown.

While risks can have positive consequences such as unexpected price reduction in materials, the primary focus of this chapter is on what can go wrong and the risk management process.

SNAPSHOT FROM PRACTICE 7.1 Giant Popsicle Gone Wrong*

An attempt to erect the World's Largest Popsicle in New York City ended with a scene straight out of a disaster film, but much stickier.

The 25-foot-tall, 17½-ton treat of frozen juice melted faster than expected, flooding Union Square in downtown Manhattan with kiwi-strawberry–flavored fluid.

Bicyclists wiped out in the stream of goo. Pedestrians slipped. Traffic was, well, frozen. Firefighters closed off several streets and used hoses to wash away the thick, sweet slime.

The Snapple Company, a leading maker of soft beverages, had been trying to promote a new line of frozen treats by setting a record for the World's Largest Popsicle, but called off the stunt before the frozen giant was pulled fully upright by a construction crane.

Authorities said they were worried the 2½-story popsicle would collapse.

© Brian Smith/Zuma Press, Inc.

Organizers were not sure why it melted so quickly. "We planned for it. We just didn't expect for it to happen so fast," said Snapple spokeswoman Lauren Radcliffe. She said the company would offer to pay the city for the clean-up costs.

* Associated Press, June 23, 2005.

Risk management attempts to recognize and manage potential and unforeseen trouble spots that may occur when the project is implemented. Risk management identifies as many risk events as possible (what can go wrong), minimizes their impact (what can be done about the event before the project begins), manages responses to those events that do materialize (contingency plans), and provides contingency funds to cover risk events that actually materialize.

For a humorous, but ultimately embarrassing example of poor risk management see Snapshot from Practice 7.1: Giant Popsicle Gone Wrong.

7.1 Risk Management Process

LO 7-1

Describe the risk management process.

Figure 7.1 presents a graphic model of the risk management challenge. The chances of a risk event occurring (e.g., an error in time estimates, cost estimates, or design technology) are greatest during the early stages of a project. This is when uncertainty is highest and many questions remain unanswered. As the project progresses toward completion, risk declines as the answers to critical issues (Will the technology work? Is the timeline feasible?) are resolved. The cost impact of a risk event, however, increases over the life of the project. For example, the risk event of a design flaw occurring after a prototype has been made has a greater cost or time impact than if the flaw were discovered during the planning phase of the project.

The cost of mismanaged risk control early on in the project is exemplified by the ill-fated 1999 NASA Mars Climate Orbiter. Investigations revealed that Lockheed Martin botched the design of critical navigation software. While flight computers on the ground did calculations based on pounds of thrust per second, the spacecraft's

FIGURE 7.1
Risk Event Graph

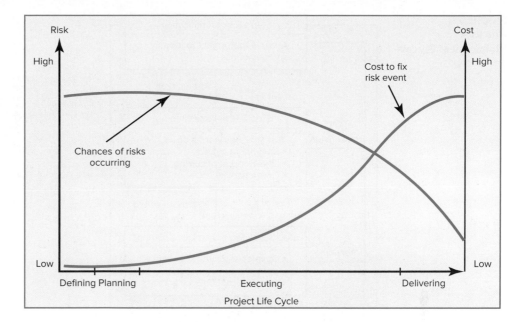

computer software used metric units called newtons. A check to see if the values were compatible was never done.

"Our check and balances processes did not catch an error like this that should have been caught," said Ed Weiler, NASA's associate administrator for space science. "That is the bottom line" (*Orlando Sentinel,* 1999). If the error had been discovered early the correction would have been relatively simple and inexpensive. Instead the error was never discovered, and after the nine-month journey to the Red Planet, the $125-million probe approached Mars at too low an altitude and burned up in the planet's atmosphere.

Following the 1999 debacle, NASA instituted a more robust risk management system which has produced a string of successful missions to Mars, including the dramatic landing of the *Curiosity* rover in August 2012.[1]

Risk management is a proactive approach rather than reactive. It is a preventive process designed to ensure that surprises are reduced and that negative consequences associated with undesirable events are minimized. It also prepares the project manager to take action when a time, cost, and/or technical advantage is possible. Successful management of project risk gives the project manager better control over the future and can significantly improve chances of reaching project objectives on time, within budget, and meeting required technical (functional) performance.

The sources of project risks are unlimited. There are external sources, such as inflation, market acceptance, exchange rates, and government regulations. In practice, these risk events are often referred to as "threats" to differentiate them from those that are not within the project manager's or team's responsibility area. (Later we will see budgets for such risk events are placed in a "management reserve" contingency budget.) Since such external risks are usually considered before the decision to go ahead with the project, they will be excluded from the discussion of project risks. However, external risks are extremely important and must be addressed.

The major components of the risk management process are depicted in Figure 7.2. Each step will be examined in more detail in the remainder of the chapter.

[1] E. Landau, "Mars Landing Went 'Flawlessly,' Scientists Say," *CNN.com*, accessed August 14, 2012.

FIGURE 7.2
The Risk
Management Process

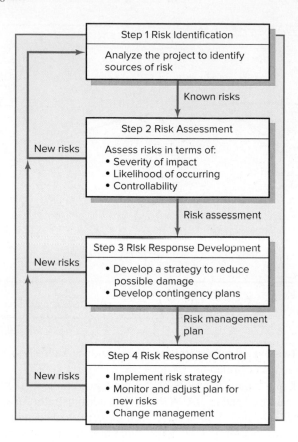

7.2 Step 1: Risk Identification

Understand how to
identify project risks.

The risk management process begins by trying to generate a list of all the possible risks that could affect the project. Typically the project manager pulls together, during the planning phase, a risk management team consisting of core team members and other relevant stakeholders. Research has demonstrated that groups make more accurate judgments about risks than individuals do (Snizek and Henry, 1989). The team uses brainstorming and other problem identifying techniques to identify potential problems. Participants are encouraged to keep an open mind and generate as many probable risks as possible. More than one project has been bushwhacked by an event that members thought was preposterous in the beginning. Later during the assessment phase, participants will have a chance to analyze and filter out unreasonable risks.

One common mistake that is made early in the risk identification process is to focus on objectives and not on the events that could produce consequences. For example, team members may identify failing to meet schedule as a major risk. What they need to focus on are the events that could cause this to happen (i.e., poor estimates, adverse weather, shipping delays, etc.). Only by focusing on actual events can potential solutions be found.

Organizations use **risk breakdown structures** (RBSs) in conjunction with work breakdown structures (WBSs) to help management teams identify and eventually analyze risks. Figure 7.3 provides a generic example of a RBS. The focus at the beginning should be on risks that can affect the whole project as opposed to a specific section of the project or network. For example, the discussion of funding may lead the team to identify the possibility of the project budget being cut after the project has started as a

FIGURE 7.3   The Risk Breakdown Structure (RBS)

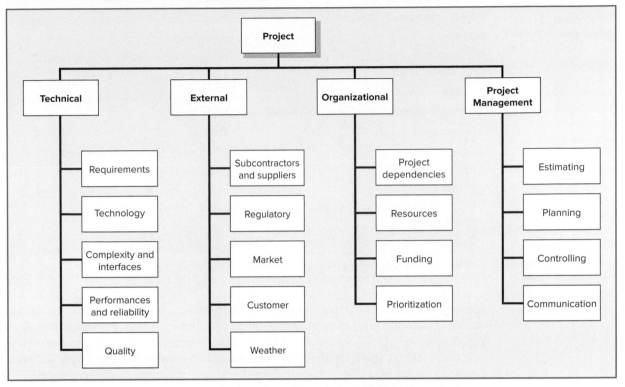

significant risk event. Likewise, when discussing the market the team may identify responding to new product releases by competitors as a risk event.

After the macro risks have been identified, specific areas can be checked. An effective tool for identifying specific risks is the work breakdown structure. Use of the RBS reduces the chance a risk event will be missed. On large projects multiple risk teams are organized around specific deliverables and submit their risk management reports to the project manager.

A risk profile is another useful tool. A **risk profile** is a list of questions that address traditional areas of uncertainty on a project. These questions have been developed and refined from previous, similar projects. Figure 7.4 provides a partial example of a risk profile.

Good risk profiles, like RBSs, are tailored to the type of project in question. For example, building an information system is different from building a new car. They are organization specific. Risk profiles recognize the unique strengths and weaknesses of the firm. Finally, risk profiles address both technical and management risks. For example, the profile shown in Figure 7.4 asks questions about design such as, Does the design depend upon unrealistic assumptions? The questions may lead the team to identify that the technology will not work under extreme conditions as a risk. Similarly, questions about work environment (Do people cooperate across functional boundaries?) may lead to the identification of potential communication breakdowns between marketing and R&D as a risk.

Risk profiles are generated and maintained usually by personnel from the project office. They are updated and refined during the postproject audit (see Chapter 14). These profiles, when kept up to date, can be a powerful resource in the risk management process. The collective experience of the firm's past projects resides in their questions.

Historical records can complement or be used when formal risk profiles are not available. Project teams can investigate what happened on similar projects in the past to

FIGURE 7.4
Partial Risk Profile for Product Development Project

Technical Requirements Are the requirements stable?	**Quality** Are quality considerations built into the design?
Design Does the design depend on unrealistic or optimistic assumptions?	**Management** Do people know who has authority for what?
Testing Will testing equipment be available when needed?	**Work Environment** Do people work cooperatively across functional boundaries?
Development Is the development process supported by a compatible set of procedures, methods, and tools?	**Staffing** Is staff inexperienced or understaffed?
Schedule Is the schedule dependent upon the completion of other projects?	**Customer** Does the customer understand what it will take to complete the project?
Budget How reliable are the cost estimates?	**Contractors** Are there any ambiguities in contractor task definitions?

identify potential risks. For example, a project manager can check the on-time performance of selected vendors to gauge the threat of shipping delays. IT project managers can access "best practices" papers detailing other companies' experiences converting software systems. Inquiries should not be limited to recorded data. Savvy project managers tap the wisdom of others by seeking the advice of veteran project managers.

The risk identification process should not be limited to just the core team. Input from customers, sponsors, subcontractors, vendors, and other stakeholders should be solicited. Relevant stakeholders can be formally interviewed or included on the risk management team. Not only do these players have a valuable perspective, but by involving them in the risk management process they also become more committed to project success.[2]

One of the keys to success in risk identification is attitude. While a "can do" attitude is essential during implementation, project managers have to encourage critical thinking when it comes to risk identification. The goal is to find potential problems before they happen.

The RBS and risk profiles are useful tools for making sure no stones are left unturned. At the same time, when done well the number of risks identified can be overwhelming and a bit discouraging. Initial optimism can be replaced with griping and cries of "what have we gotten ourselves into?" It is important that project managers set the right tone and complete the risk management process so members regain confidence in themselves and the project.

7.3 Step 2: Risk Assessment

 LO 7-3

Assess the significance of different project risks.

Step 1 produces a list of potential risks. Not all of these risks deserve attention. Some are trivial and can be ignored, while others pose serious threats to the welfare of the project. Managers have to develop methods for sifting through the list of risks, eliminating inconsequential or redundant ones and stratifying worthy ones in terms of importance and need for attention.

---

[2] The Delphi Method (see Snapshot from Practice 5.3) is a popular technique for involving stakeholders.

Scenario analysis is the easiest and most commonly used technique for analyzing risks. Team members assess the significance of each risk event in terms of:

- Probability of the event.
- Impact of the event.

Simply stated, risks need to be evaluated in terms of the likelihood the event is going to occur and the impact or consequences of its occurrence. The risk of a project manager being struck by lightning at a work site would have major negative impact on the project, but the likelihood is so low it is not worthy of consideration. Conversely, people do change jobs, so an event like the loss of key project personnel would have not only an adverse impact but also a high likelihood of occurring in some organizations. If so, then it would be wise for that organization to be proactive and mitigate this risk by developing incentive schemes for retaining specialists and/or engaging in cross-training to reduce the impact of turnover.

The quality and credibility of the risk analysis process require that different levels of risk probabilities and impacts be defined. These definitions vary and should be tailored to the specific nature and needs of the project. For example, a relatively simple scale ranging from "very unlikely" to "almost certainly" may suffice for one project, whereas another project may use more precise numerical probabilities (e.g., 0.1, 0.3, 0.5, . . .).

Impact scales can be a bit more problematic since adverse risks affect project objectives differently. For example, a component failure may cause only a slight delay in project schedule but a major increase in project cost. If controlling cost is a high priority, then the impact would be severe. If, on the other hand, time is more critical than cost, then the impact would be minor.

Because impact ultimately needs to be assessed in terms of project priorities, different kinds of impact scales are used. Some scales may simply use rank-order descriptors, such as "low," "moderate," "high," and "very high," whereas others use numeric weights (e.g., 1–10). Some may focus on the project in general while others focus on specific project objectives. The risk management team needs to establish up front what distinguishes a 1 from a 3 or "moderate" impact from "severe" impact. Figure 7.5 provides an example of how impact scales could be defined given the project objectives of cost, time, scope, and quality.

Documentation of scenario analyses can be seen in various risk assessment forms used by companies. Figure 7.6 is a partial example of a risk assessment form used on an IS project involving the upgrade from Windows 10 to Windows 11.

Notice that in addition to evaluating the severity and probability of risk events the team also assesses when the event might occur and its detection difficulty. Detection difficulty is a measure of how easy it would be to detect that the event was going to occur in time to take mitigating action, that is, how much warning would we have? So in the Windows 11 conversion example, the detection scale would range from 5 = no warning to 1 = lots of time to react.

Often organizations find it useful to categorize the severity of different risks into some form of risk assessment matrix. The matrix is typically structured around the impact and likelihood of the risk event. For example, the risk matrix presented in Figure 7.7 consists of a 5×5 array of elements with each element representing a different set of impact and likelihood values.

The matrix is divided into red, yellow, and green zones representing major, moderate, and minor risks, respectively. The red zone is centered on the top right corner of the matrix (high impact/high likelihood), while the green zone is centered on the

FIGURE 7.5 **Defined Conditions for Impact Scales of a Risk on Major Project Objectives (examples for negative impacts only)**

Project Objective	Relative or Numerical Scale				
	1 Very Low	2 Low	3 Moderate	4 High	5 Very High
Cost	Insignificant cost increase	< 10% cost increase	10–20% cost increase	20–40% cost increase	> 40% cost increase
Time	Insignificant time increase	< 5% time increase	5–10% time increase	10–20% time increase	> 20% time increase
Scope	Scope decrease barely noticeable	Minor areas of scope affected	Major areas of scope affected	Scope reduction unacceptable to sponsor	Project end item is effectively useless
Quality	Quality degradation barely noticeable	Only very demanding applications are affected	Quality reduction requires sponsor approval	Quality reduction unacceptable to sponsor	Project end item is effectively useless

bottom left corner (low impact/low likelihood). The moderate risk, yellow zone extends down the middle of the matrix. Since impact is generally considered more important than likelihood (a 10 percent chance of losing $1,000,000 is usually considered a more severe risk than a 90 percent chance of losing $1,000), the red zone (major risk) extends farther down the high impact column.

Using the Windows 11 project again as an example, interface problems and system freezing would be placed in the red zone (major risk), while user backlash and hardware malfunctioning would be placed in the yellow zone (moderate risk).

The **risk severity matrix** provides a basis for prioritizing which risks to address. Red zone risks receive first priority followed by yellow zone risks. Green zone risks are typically considered inconsequential and ignored unless their status changes.

FIGURE 7.6
Risk Assessment Form

Risk Event	Likelihood	Impact	Detection Difficulty	When
Interface problems	4	4	4	Conversion
System freezing	2	5	5	Start-up
User backlash	4	3	3 .	Postinstallation
Hardware malfunctioning	1	5	5	Installation

FIGURE 7.7
Risk Severity Matrix

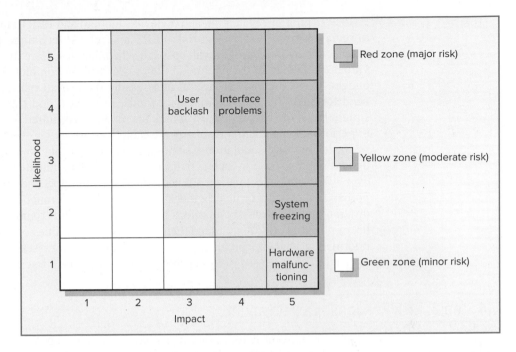

Failure Mode and Effects Analysis (FMEA) extends the risk severity matrix by including ease of detection in the equation:

$$\text{Impact} \times \text{Probability} \times \text{Detection} = \text{Risk Value}$$

Each of the three dimensions is rated according to a five-point scale. For example, detection is defined as the ability of the project team to discern that the risk event is imminent. A score of 1 would be given if even a chimpanzee could spot the risk coming. The highest detection score of 5 would be given to events that could only be discovered after it is too late (i.e., system freezing). Similar anchored scales would be applied for severity of impact and the probability of the event occurring. The weighting of the risks is then based on their overall score. For example, a risk with an impact in the "1" zone with a very low probability and an easy detection score might score a 1 ($1 \times 1 \times 1 = 1$). Conversely, a high-impact risk with a high probability and impossible to detect would score 125 ($5 \times 5 \times 5 = 125$). This broad range of numerical scores allows for easy stratification of risk according to overall significance.

No assessment scheme is absolutely foolproof. For example, the weakness of the FMEA approach is that a risk event rated Impact = 1, Probability = 5, and Detection = 5 would receive the same weighted score as an event rated Impact = 5, Probability = 5, and Detection = 1! This underscores the importance of *not* treating risk assessment as simply an exercise in mathematics. There is no substitute for thoughtful discussion of key risk events.

Probability Analysis

There are many statistical techniques available to the project manager that can assist in assessing project risk. Decision trees have been used to assess alternative courses of action using expected values. Statistical variations of net present value (NPV) have been used to assess cash flow risks in projects. Correlations between past projects' cash flow and S-curves (cumulative project cost curve—baseline—over the life of the project) have been used to assess cash flow risks.

PERT (program evaluation and review technique) and PERT simulation can be used to review activity and project risk. PERT and related techniques take a more macro perspective by looking at overall cost and schedule risks. Here the focus is not on individual events but on the likelihood the project will be completed on time and within budget. These methods are useful in assessing the overall risk of the project and the need for such things as contingency funds, resources, and time. The use of PERT simulation is increasing because it uses the same data required for PERT, and software to perform the simulation is readily available.

Basically PERT simulation assumes a statistical distribution (range between optimistic and pessimistic) for each activity duration; it then simulates the network (perhaps over 1,000 simulations) using a random number generator. The outcome is the relative probability, called a criticality index, of an activity becoming critical under the many different, possible activity durations for each activity. PERT simulation also provides a list of potential critical paths and their respective probabilities of occurring. Having this information available can greatly facilitate identifying and assessing schedule risk. (See Appendix 7.1 at the end of this chapter for a more detailed description and discussion.)

7.4 Step 3: Risk Response Development

LO 7-4

Describe the four different responses to managing risks.

When a risk event is identified and assessed, a decision must be made concerning which response is appropriate for the specific event. Responses to risk can be classified as mitigating, avoiding, transferring, or retaining.

Mitigating Risk

Reducing risk is usually the first alternative considered. There are basically two strategies for **mitigating risk**: (1) reduce the likelihood that the event will occur and/or (2) reduce the impact that the adverse event would have on the project. Most risk teams focus first on reducing the likelihood of risk events since, if successful, this may eliminate the need to consider the potentially costly second strategy.

Testing and prototyping are frequently used to prevent problems from surfacing later in a project. An example of testing can be found in an information systems project. The project team was responsible for installing a new operating system in their parent company. Before implementing the project, the team tested the new system on a smaller isolated network. By doing so they discovered a variety of problems and were able to come up with solutions prior to implementation. The team still encountered problems with the installation but the number and severity were greatly reduced.

Often identifying the root causes of an event is useful. For example, the fear that a vendor will be unable to supply customized components on time may be attributable to (1) poor vendor relationships, (2) design miscommunication, and (3) lack of motivation. As a result of this analysis the project manager may decide to take his counterpart to lunch to clear the air, invite the vendor to attend design meetings, and restructure the contract to include incentives for on-time delivery.

Other examples of reducing the probability of risks occurring are scheduling outdoor work during the summer months, investing in up-front safety training, and choosing high-quality materials and equipment.

When the concerns are that duration and costs have been underestimated, managers will augment estimates to compensate for the uncertainties. It is common to use a ratio between old and new project to adjust time or cost. The ratio typically serves as a constant. For example, if past projects have taken 10 minutes per line of computer code, a constant of 1.10 (which represents a 10 percent increase) would be used for the proposed project time estimates because the new project is more difficult than prior projects.

An alternative mitigation strategy is to reduce the impact of the risk if it occurs. For example, a bridge-building project illustrates risk reduction. A new bridge project for a coastal port was to use an innovative, continuous cement-pouring process developed by an Australian firm to save large sums of money and time. The major risk was that the continuous pouring process for each major section of the bridge could not be interrupted. Any interruption would require that the whole cement section (hundreds of cubic yards) be torn down and started over. An assessment of possible risks centered on delivery of the cement from the cement factory. Trucks could be delayed, or the factory could break down. Such risks would result in tremendous rework costs and delays. Risk was reduced by having two additional portable cement plants built nearby on different highways within 20 miles of the bridge project in case the main factory supply was interrupted. These two portable plants carried raw materials for a whole bridge section, and extra trucks were on immediate standby each time continuous pouring was required. Similar risk reduction scenarios are apparent in system and software development projects where parallel innovation processes are used in case one fails.

Snapshot from Practice 7.2: From Dome to Dust details the steps Controlled Demolition took to minimize damage when they imploded the Seattle Kingdome.

Avoiding Risk

Risk avoidance is changing the project plan to eliminate the risk or condition. Although it is impossible to eliminate all risk events, some specific risks may be avoided before you launch the project. For example, adopting proven technology instead of experimental technology can eliminate technical failure. Choosing an Australian supplier as opposed to an Indonesian supplier would virtually eliminate the chance that political unrest would disrupt the supply of critical materials. Likewise, one could eliminate the risk of choosing the wrong software by developing web applications using both ASAP.NET and PHP. Choosing to move a concert indoors would eliminate the threat of inclement weather.

Transferring Risk

Passing risk to another party is common; this transfer does not change risk. Passing risk to another party almost always results in paying a premium for this exemption. Fixed-price contracts are the classic example of transferring risk from an owner to a contractor. The contractor understands his or her firm will pay for any risk event that materializes; therefore, a monetary risk factor is added to the contract bid price. Before deciding to transfer risk, the owner should decide which party can best control activities that would lead to the risk occurring. Also, is the contractor capable of absorbing the risk? Clearly identifying and documenting responsibility for absorbing risk is imperative.

Another more obvious way to transfer risk is insurance. However, in most cases this is impractical because defining the project risk event and conditions to an insurance broker who is unfamiliar with the project is difficult and usually expensive. Of course, low-probability and high-consequence risk events such as acts of God are more easily defined and insured. Performance bonds, warranties, and guarantees are other financial instruments used to transfer risk.

On large, international construction projects like petrochemical plants and oil refineries, host countries are insisting on contracts that enforce Build-Own-Operate-Transfer (BOOT) provisions. Here the prime project organization is expected not only to build the facility, but also to take over ownership until its operation capacity has been proven and all the debugging has occurred before final transfer of ownership to

SNAPSHOT FROM PRACTICE 7.2　From Dome to Dust*

On March 26, 2000, the largest concrete domed structure in the world was reduced to a pile of rubble in a dramatic implosion lasting less than 20 seconds. According to Mark Loizeaux, whose Maryland-based Controlled Demolition Inc. was hired to bring the 24-year-old Seattle Kingdome down, "We don't blow things up. We use explosives as an engine, but gravity is the catalyst that will bring it down."

Destroying the Kingdome was the most complicated of the 7,000 demolitions Loizeaux's company has undertaken. Nearly three months of preparations were needed to implode the dome at a total cost of $9 million. The Kingdome was considered to be one of the strongest structures in the world containing over 25,000 tons of concrete with each of its 40 vaulted ribs incorporating seven lengths of two-and-one-quarter-inch reinforcing steel bar.

Strands of orange detonating cord—basically dynamite in a string that explodes at the lightning pace of 24,000 feet per second—connected six pielike divisions of the Kingdome to a nearby control center.

Throughout each section, Controlled Demolition workers drilled nearly 1,000 holes and packed them with high-velocity gelatin explosives the size of hot dogs. Large charges were placed about one-third of the way up each dome rib; smaller charges were put farther up the ribs. When the detonation button was pushed, blasting caps set off a chain reaction of explosions in each section reducing the stadium to rubble.

While the actual implosion was a technical tour-de-force, risk management was a critical part of the project's success. To minimize damage to surrounding buildings, the explosive charges were wrapped in a layer of chain-link fencing covered with thick sheets of geotextile polypropylene fabric to contain flying concrete. Nearby buildings were protected in various manners depending on the structure and proximity to the

© Tim Matsui/Getty Images

Dome. Measures included sealing air-handling units, taping seams on doors and windows, covering floors and windows with plywood and draping reinforced polyethylene sheeting around the outside.

To help absorb the impact, air-conditioning units removed from the interior were stacked with other material to create a barrier around the perimeter of the work area.

Hundreds of police officers and security personnel were used to cordon off an area extending roughly 1,000 feet from the Dome from overzealous spectators. Traffic was closed for a larger area. Accommodations were provided for people and pets who lived within the restricted zone.

Eight water trucks, eight sweeper units, and more than 100 workers were deployed immediately after the blast to control dust and begin the cleanup.

As a side note, one-third of the concrete will be crushed and used in the foundation of a new $430-million outdoor football stadium which is being built in its place. The rest of the concrete will be carted away and used in roadbeds and foundations throughout the Seattle area.

* *New York Times*—Sunday Magazine (March 19, 2000); *Seattle Times* (March 27, 2000) website.

the client. In such cases, the host country has transferred financial risk of ownership until the project has been completed and capabilities proven.

Accept Risk

In some cases a conscious decision is made to accept the risk of an event occurring. Some risks are so large it is not feasible to consider transferring or reducing the event (e.g., an earthquake or flood). The project owner assumes the risk because the chance of such an event occurring is slim. In other cases risks identified in the budget reserve can simply be absorbed if they materialize. The risk is retained by developing a contingency plan to implement if the risk materializes. In a few cases a risk event can be ignored and a cost overrun accepted should the risk event occur.

The more effort given to risk response before the project begins, the better the chances are for minimizing project surprises. Knowing that the response to a risk event will be retained, transferred, or mitigated greatly reduces stress and uncertainty. Again, control is possible with this structured approach.

7.5 Contingency Planning

LO 7-5

Understand the role contingency plans play in risk management process.

A **contingency plan** is an alternative plan that will be used if a possible foreseen risk event becomes a reality. The contingency plan represents actions that will reduce or mitigate the negative impact of the risk event. A key distinction between a risk response and a contingency plan is that a response is part of the actual implementation plan and action is taken before the risk can materialize, while a contingency plan is not part of the initial implementation plan and only goes into effect after the risk is recognized.

Like all plans, the contingency plan answers the questions of what, where, when, and how much action will take place. The absence of a contingency plan, when a risk event occurs, can cause a manager to delay or postpone the decision to implement a remedy. This postponement can lead to panic, and acceptance of the first remedy suggested. Such after-the-event decision making under pressure can be potentially dangerous and costly. Contingency planning evaluates alternative remedies for possible foreseen events before the risk event occurs and selects the best plan among alternatives. This early contingency planning facilitates a smooth transition to the remedy or work-around plan. The availability of a contingency plan can significantly increase the chances for project success.

Conditions for activating the implementation of the contingency plan should be decided and clearly documented. The plan should include a cost estimate and identify the source of funding. All parties affected should agree to the contingency plan and have authority to make commitments. Because implementation of a contingency plan embodies disruption in the sequence of work, all contingency plans should be communicated to team members so that surprise and resistance are minimized.

Here is an example: A high-tech niche computer company intends to introduce a new "platform" product at a very specific target date. The project's 47 teams all agree delays will not be acceptable. Their contingency plans for two large component suppliers demonstrate how seriously risk management is viewed. One supplier's plant sits on the San Andreas Fault, which is prone to earthquakes. The contingency plan has an alternative supplier, who is constantly updated, producing a replica of the component in another plant. Another key supplier in Toronto, Canada, presents a delivery risk on their due date because of potential bad weather. This contingency plan calls for a chartered plane (already contracted to be on standby) if overland transportation presents a delay problem. To outsiders these plans must seem a bit extreme, but in high-tech industries where time to market is king, risks of identified events are taken seriously.

Risk response matrices such as the one shown in Figure 7.8 are useful for summarizing how the project team plans to manage risks that have been identified. Again, the Windows 11 project is used to illustrate this kind of matrix. The first step is to identify whether to reduce, share, transfer, or accept the risk. The team decided to reduce the chances of the system freezing by experimenting with a prototype of the system. Prototype experimentation not only allows them to identify and fix conversion "bugs" before the actual installation, but it also yields information that could be useful in enhancing acceptance by end-users. The project team is then able to identify and document changes between the old and new system that will be incorporated in the training the users receive. The risk of equipment malfunctioning is transferred by choosing a reliable supplier with a strong warranty program.

FIGURE 7.8 **Risk Response Matrix**

Risk Event	Response	Contingency Plan	Trigger	Who Is Responsible
Interface problems	Mitigate: Test prototype	Work around until help comes	Not solved within 24 hours	Nils
System freezing	Mitigate: Test prototype	Reinstall OS	Still frozen after one hour	Emmylou
User backlash	Mitigate: Prototype demonstration	Increase staff support	Call from top management	Eddie
Equipment malfunctions	Mitigate: Select reliable vendor Transfer: Warranty	Order replacement	Equipment fails	Jim

The next step is to identify contingency plans in case the risk still occurs. For example, if interface problems prove insurmountable, then the team would attempt a work-around until vendor experts arrived to help solve the problem. If the system freezes after installation, the team will first try to reinstall the software. If user dissatisfaction is high, then the IS department will provide more staff support. If the team is unable to get reliable equipment from the original supplier, then it will order a different brand from a second dealer. The team also needs to discuss and agree what would "trigger" implementation of the contingency plan. In the case of the system freezing, the trigger is not being able to unfreeze the system within one hour or, in the case of user backlash, an angry call from top management. Finally, the individual responsible for monitoring the potential risk and initiating the contingency plan needs to be assigned. Smart project managers establish protocols for contingency responses before they are needed. For an example of the importance of establishing protocols see Snapshot from Practice 7.3: Risk Management at the Top of the World.

Some of the most common methods for handling risk are discussed here.

Technical Risks

Technical risks are problematic; they can often be the kind that cause the project to be shut down. What if the system or process does not work? Contingency or backup plans are made for those possibilities that are foreseen. For example, Carrier Transicold was involved in developing a new Phoenix refrigeration unit for truck-trailer applications. This new unit was to use rounded panels made of bonded metals, which at the time was new technology for Transicold. Furthermore, one of its competitors had tried unsuccessfully to incorporate similar bonded metals in their products. The project team was eager to make the new technology work, but it wasn't until the very end of the project that they were able to get the new adhesives to bond adequately to complete the project. Throughout the project, the team maintained a welded-panel fabrication approach just in case they were unsuccessful. If this contingency approach had been needed, it would have increased production costs, but the project still would have been completed on time.

In addition to backup strategies, project managers need to develop methods to quickly assess whether technical uncertainties can be resolved. The use of sophisticated CAD programs has greatly helped resolve design problems. At the same time, Smith and Reinertsen (1995), in their book *Developing Products in Half the Time,* argue that there is no substitute for making something and seeing how it works, feels, or looks. They suggest that one should first identify the high-risk technical areas, then

SNAPSHOT FROM PRACTICE 7.3

Risk Management at the Top of the World*

The gripping account in the 2015 film *Everest* of an ill-fated attempt to climb Mount Everest in which six climbers died provides testimony to the risks of extreme mountain climbing.

Accounts of Mount Everest expeditions provide insights into project risk management. First, most climbers spend more than three weeks acclimating their bodies to high-altitude conditions. Native Sherpas are used extensively to carry supplies and set up each of the four base camps that will be used during the final stages of the climb. To reduce the impact of hypoxia, lightheadness, and disorientation caused by shortage of oxygen, most climbers use oxygen masks and bottles during the final ascent. If lucky enough not to be one of the first expeditions of the season, the path to the summit should be staked out and roped by previous climbers. Climbing guides receive last-minute weather reports by radio to confirm whether the weather conditions warrant the risk. Finally, for added insurance, most climbers join their Sherpas in an elaborate *puja* ritual intended to summon the divine support of the gods before beginning their ascent.

All of these efforts pale next to the sheer physical and mental rigors of making the final climb from base camp IV to the summit. This is what climbers refer to as the "death zone" because beyond 26,000 feet the mind and body begin to quickly deteriorate despite supplemental oxygen. Under fair conditions it takes around 18 hours to make the round-trip to the top and back to the base camp. Climbers leave as early as 1:00 a.m. in order to make it back before night falls and total exhaustion sets in.

The greatest danger in climbing Mount Everest is not in reaching the summit but in making it back to the base camp. One out of every five climbers who make it to the summit dies during their descent. The key is establishing a contingency plan in case the climbers encounter hard

© Bobby Model/National Geographic Stock/Getty Images

going or the weather changes. Guides establish a predetermined turnaround time (i.e., 2:00 p.m.) to ensure a safe return no matter how close the climbers are to the summit. Many lives have been lost by failing to adhere to the turnaround time and pushing forward to the summit. As one climber put it, "With enough determination, any bloody idiot can get to the top of the hill. The trick is to get back alive."

One climber who faced the 2:00 p.m. deadline was Goran Krupp. After cycling 8,000 miles from Stockholm to Katmandu he turned back 1,000 feet from the summit.

* Jon Krakauer, *Into Thin Air* (New York: Doubleday, 1997), p. 190; Broughton Coburn, *Everest: Mountain without Mercy* (New York: National Geographic Society, 1997).

build models or design experiments to resolve the risk as quickly as possible. Technology offers many methods for early testing and validation, ranging from 3-D printing and holographic imagery for model building to focus groups and early design usability testing for market testing (Thamhain, 2013). By isolating and testing the key technical questions early on in a project, project feasibility can be quickly determined and necessary adjustments made such as reworking the process or in some cases closing down the project.[3]

[3] This is a key principle of Agile project management, which is discussed in Chapter 17.

Schedule Risks

Often organizations will defer the threat of a project coming in late until it surfaces. Here contingency funds are set aside to expedite or "crash" the project to get it back on track. Crashing, or reducing project duration, is accomplished by shortening (compressing) one or more activities on the critical path. This comes with additional costs and risk. Techniques for managing this situation are discussed in Chapter 9. Some contingency plans can avoid costly procedures. For example, schedules can be altered by working activities in parallel or using start-to-start lag relationships. Also, using the best people for high-risk tasks can relieve or lessen the chance of some risk events occurring.

Cost Risks

Projects of long duration need some contingency for price changes—which are usually upward. The important point to remember when reviewing price is to avoid the trap of using one lump sum to cover price risks. For example, if inflation has been running about 3 percent, some managers add 3 percent for all resources used in the project. This lump-sum approach does not address exactly where price protection is needed and fails to provide for tracking and control. On cost sensitive projects, price risks should be evaluated item by item. Some purchases and contracts will not change over the life of the project. Those that may change should be identified and estimates made of the magnitude of change. This approach ensures control of the contingency funds as the project is implemented.

Funding Risks

What if the funding for the project is cut by 25 percent or completion projections indicate that costs will greatly exceed available funds? What are the chances of the project being canceled before completion? Seasoned project managers recognize that a complete risk assessment must include an evaluation of funding supply. This is especially true for publicly funded projects. Case in point was the ill-fated ARH-70 Arapaho helicopter which was being developed for the U.S. Army by BellAircraft. Over 300-million dollars had been invested to develop a new age combat and reconnaissance helicopter, when in October 2008, the Defense Department recommended that the project be canceled. The cancellation reflected a need to cut costs and a switch toward using unmanned aircraft for surveillance as well as attack missions.

Just as government projects are subject to changes in strategy and political agenda, business firms frequently undergo changes in priorities and top management. The pet projects of the new CEO replace the pet projects of the former CEO. Resources become tight and one way to fund new projects is to cancel other projects.

Severe budget cuts or lack of adequate funding can have a devastating effect on a project. Typically, when such a fate occurs, there is a need to scale back the scope of the project to what is possible. "All-or-nothing projects" are ripe targets to budget cutters. This was the case of the Arapaho helicopter once the decision was made to move away from manned reconnaissance aircraft. Here the "chunkability" of the project can be an advantage. For example, freeway projects can fall short of the original intentions but still add value for each mile completed.

On a much smaller scale, similar funding risks may exist for more mundane projects. For example, a building contractor may find that due to a sudden downturn in the stock market the owners can no longer afford to build their dream house. Or an IS consulting firm may be left empty handed when a client files for bankruptcy. In the former case the contractor may have as a contingency selling the house on the open market, while unfortunately the consulting firm will have to join the long line of creditors.

7.6 Opportunity Management

LO 7-6

Understand opportunity management and describe the four different approaches to responding to opportunities in a project.

For the sake of brevity, this chapter has focused on negative risks—what can go wrong on a project. There is a flip side—what could go right on a project? This is commonly referred to as a positive risk or opportunity. An **opportunity** is an event that can have a positive impact on project objectives. For example, unusually favorable weather can accelerate construction work, or a drop in fuel prices may create savings that could be used to add value to a project. Essentially the same process that is used to manage negative risks is applied to positive risks. Opportunities are identified, assessed in terms of likelihood and impact, responses are determined, and even contingency plans and funds can be established to take advantage of the opportunity if it occurs. The major exception between managing negative risks and opportunity is in the responses. The project management profession has identified four different types of response to an opportunity:[4]

Exploit. This tactic seeks to eliminate the uncertainty associated with an opportunity to ensure that it definitely happens. Examples include assigning your best personnel to a critical burst activity to reduce the time to completion or revising a design to enable a component to be purchased rather than developed internally.

Share. This strategy involves allocating some or all of the ownership of an opportunity to another party who is best able to capture the opportunity for the benefit of the project. Examples include establishing continuous improvement incentives for external contractors or joint ventures.

Enhance. Enhance is the opposite of mitigation in that action is taken to increase the probability and/or the positive impact of an opportunity. Examples include choosing site location based on favorable weather patterns or choosing raw materials that are likely to decline in price.

Accept. Accepting an opportunity is being willing to take advantage of it if it occurs, but not taking action to pursue it.

While it is only natural to focus on negative risks, it is sound practice to engage in active opportunity management as well.

7.7 Contingency Funding and Time Buffers

LO 7-7

Understand how contingency funds and time buffers are used to manage risks on a project.

Contingency funds are established to cover project risks—identified and unknown. When, where, and how much money will be spent is not known until the risk event occurs. Project "owners" are often reluctant to set up project contingency funds that seem to imply the project plan might be a poor one. Some perceive the contingency fund as an add-on slush fund. Others say they will face the risk when it materializes. Usually such reluctance to establish contingency reserves can be overcome with documented risk identification, assessment, contingency plans, and plans for when and how funds will be disbursed.

The size and amount of contingency reserves depend on uncertainty inherent in the project. Uncertainty is reflected in the "newness" of the project, inaccurate time and cost estimates, technical unknowns, unstable scope, and problems not anticipated. In practice, contingencies run from 1 to 10 percent in projects similar to past projects.

[4] PMBOK, 5th ed. (Newton Square, PA: PMI, 2013), pp. 345-46.

However, in unique and high-technology projects it is not uncommon to find contingencies running in the 20 to 60 percent range. Use and rate of consumption of reserves must be closely monitored and controlled. Simply picking a percentage of the baseline, say, 5 percent, and calling it the contingency reserve is not a sound approach. Also, adding up all the identified contingency allotments and throwing them into one pot is not conducive to sound control of the reserve fund.

In practice, the contingency reserve fund is typically divided into budget and management reserve funds for control purposes. **Budget reserves** are set up to cover identified risks; these reserves are those allocated to specific segments or deliverables of the project. **Management reserves** are set up to cover unidentified risks and are allocated to risks associated with the total project. The risks are separated because their use requires approval from different levels of project authority. Because all risks are probabilistic, the reserves are not included in the baseline for each work package or activity; they are only activated when a risk occurs. If an identified risk does not occur and its chance of occurring is past, the fund allocated to the risk should be deducted from the budget reserve. (This removes the temptation to use budget reserves for other issues or problems.) Of course if the risk does occur, funds are removed from the reserve and added to the cost baseline.

It is important that contingency allowances be independent of the original time and cost estimates. These allowances need to be clearly distinguished to avoid time and budget game playing.

Budget Reserves

These reserves are identified for specific work packages or segments of a project found in the baseline budget or work breakdown structure. For example, a reserve amount might be added to "computer coding" to cover the risk of "testing" showing a coding problem. The reserve amount is determined by costing out the accepted contingency or recovery plan. The budget reserve should be communicated to the project team. This openness suggests trust and encourages good cost performance. However, distributing budget reserves should be the responsibility of both the project manager and the team members responsible for implementing the specific segment of the project. If the risk does not materialize, the funds are removed from the budget reserve. Thus, budget reserves decrease as the project progresses.

Management Reserves

These reserve funds are needed to cover major unforeseen risks and, hence, are applied to the total project. For example, a major scope change may appear necessary midway in the project. Because this change was not anticipated, it is covered from the management reserve. Management reserves are established *after* budget reserves are identified and funds established. These reserves are independent of budget reserves and are controlled by the project manager and the "owner" of the project. The "owner" can be internal (top management) or external to the project organization. Most management reserves are set using historical data and judgments concerning the uniqueness and complexity of the project.

Placing technical contingencies in the management reserve is a special case. Identifying possible technical (functional) risks is often associated with a new, untried, innovative process or product. Because there is a chance the innovation may not work out, a fallback plan is necessary. This type of risk is beyond the control of the project manager. Hence, technical reserves are held in the management reserve and controlled by

TABLE 7.1
Contingency Fund Estimate

Activity	Budget Baseline	Budget Reserve	Project Budget
Design	$500,000	$15,000	$515,000
Code	900,000	80,000	980,000
Test	20,000	2,000	22,000
Subtotal	$1,420,000	$97,000	$1,517,000
Management reserve	—	—	50,000
Total	$1,420,000	$97,000	$1,567,000

the owner or top management. The owner and project manager decide when the contingency plan will be implemented and the reserve funds used. It is assumed there is a high probability these funds will never be used.

Table 7.1 shows the development of a contingency fund estimate for a hypothetical project. Note how budget and management reserves are kept separate; control is easily tracked using this format.

Time Buffers

Just as contingency funds are established to absorb unplanned costs, managers use time buffers to cushion against potential delays in the project. And like contingency funds, the amount of time is dependent upon the inherent uncertainty of the project. The more uncertain the project the more time should be reserved for the schedule. The strategy is to assign extra time at critical moments in the project. For example, buffers are added to

A. Activities with severe risks.
B. Merge activities that are prone to delays due to one or more preceding activities being late.
C. Noncritical activities to reduce the likelihood that they will create another critical path.
D. Activities that require scarce resources to ensure that the resources are available when needed.

In the face of overall schedule uncertainty, buffers are sometimes added to the end of the project. For example, a 300-working-day project may have a 30-day project buffer. While the extra 30 days would not appear on the schedule, it is available if needed. Like management reserves, this buffer typically requires the authorization of top management. A more systematic approach to buffer management is discussed in the Chapter 8 appendix on critical chain project management.

7.8 Step 4: Risk Response Control

Typically the results of the first three steps of the risk management process are summarized in a formal document often called the risk register. A **risk register** details all identified risks, including descriptions, category, and probability of occurring, impact, responses, contingency plans, owners, and current status. The register is the backbone for the last step in the risk management process: risk control. Risk control involves executing the risk response strategy, monitoring triggering events, initiating contingency plans, and watching for new risks. Establishing a change management system to deal with events that require formal changes in the scope, budget, and/or schedule of the project is an essential element of risk control.

Recognize the need for risk management being an ongoing activity.

Project managers need to monitor risks just like they track project progress. Risk assessment and updating needs to be part of every status meeting and progress report system. The project team needs to be on constant alert for new, unforeseen risks. Thamhain studied 35 major product development efforts and found that over half of contingencies that occurred were not anticipated (Thamhain, 2013)! Readiness to respond to the unexpected is a critical element of risk management.

Management needs to be sensitive that others may not be forthright in acknowledging new risks and problems. Admitting that there might be a bug in the design code or that different components are not compatible reflects poorly on individual performance. If the prevailing organizational culture is one where mistakes are punished severely, then it is only human nature to protect oneself. Similarly, if bad news is greeted harshly and there is a propensity to "kill the messenger," then participants will be reluctant to speak freely. The tendency to suppress bad news is compounded when individual responsibility is vague and the project team is under extreme pressure from top management to get the project done quickly.

Project managers need to establish an environment in which participants feel comfortable raising concerns and admitting mistakes. The norm should be that mistakes are acceptable, hiding mistakes is intolerable. Problems should be embraced not denied. Participants should be encouraged to identify problems and new risks. Here a positive attitude by the project manager toward risks is a key.

On large, complex projects it may be prudent to repeat the risk identification/assessment exercise with fresh information. Risk profiles should be reviewed to test to see if the original responses held true. Relevant stakeholders should be brought into the discussion and the risk register needs to be updated. While this may not be practical on an ongoing basis, project managers should touch base with them on a regular basis or hold special stakeholder meetings to review the status of risks on the project.

A second key for controlling the cost of risks is documenting responsibility. This can be problematic in projects involving multiple organizations and contractors. Responsibility for risk is frequently passed on to others with the statement, "That is not my worry." This mentality is dangerous. Each identified risk should be assigned (or shared) by mutual agreement of the owner, project manager, and the contractor or person having line responsibility for the work package or segment of the project. It is best to have the line person responsible approve the use of budget reserve funds and monitor their rate of usage. If management reserve funds are required, the line person should play an active role in estimating additional costs and funds needed to complete the project. Having line personnel participate in the process focuses attention on the management reserve, control of its rate of usage, and early warning of potential risk events. If risk management is not formalized, responsibility and responses to risk will be ignored—*it is not my area.*

The bottom line is that project managers and team members need to be vigilant in monitoring potential risks and identify new land mines that could derail a project. Risk assessment has to be part of the working agenda of status meetings, and when new risks emerge they need to be analyzed and incorporated into the risk management process.

7.9 Change Control Management

Describe the change control process.

A major element of the risk control process is change management. Every detail of a project plan will not materialize as expected. Coping with and controlling project changes present a formidable challenge for most project managers. Changes come from many sources such as the project customer, owner, project manager, team members, and occurrence of risk events. Most changes easily fall into three categories:

1. Scope changes in the form of design or additions represent big changes; for example, customer requests for a new feature or a redesign that will improve the product.
2. Implementation of contingency plans, when risk events occur, represent changes in baseline costs and schedules.
3. Improvement changes suggested by project team members represent another category.

Because change is inevitable, a well-defined change review and control process should be set up early in the project planning cycle.

Change management systems involve reporting, controlling, and recording changes to the project baseline. (Note: Some organizations consider change control systems part of configuration management.) In practice most change management systems are designed to accomplish the following:

1. Identify proposed changes.
2. List expected effects of proposed change(s) on schedule and budget.
3. Review, evaluate, and approve or disapprove changes formally.
4. Negotiate and resolve conflicts of change, conditions, and cost.
5. Communicate changes to parties affected.
6. Assign responsibility for implementing change.
7. Adjust master schedule and budget.
8. Track all changes that are to be implemented.

FIGURE 7.9
Change Control Process

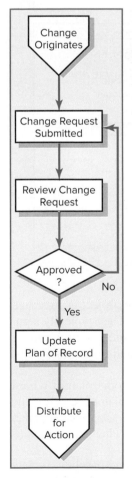

As part of the project communication plan, stakeholders define up front the communication and decision-making process that will be used to evaluate and accept changes. The process can be captured in a flow diagram like the one presented in Figure 7.9. On small projects this process may simply entail approval of a small group of stakeholders. On larger projects more elaborate decision-making processes are established, with different processes being used for different kinds of change. For example, changes in performance requirements may require multiple sign-offs, including the project sponsor and client, while switching suppliers may be authorized by the project manager. Regardless of the nature of the project, the goal is to establish the process for introducing necessary changes in the project in a timely and effective manner.

Of particular importance is assessing the impact of the change on the project. Often solutions to immediate problems have adverse consequences on other aspects of a project. For example, in overcoming a problem with the exhaust system for a hybrid automobile, the design engineers contributed to the prototype exceeding weight parameters. It is important that the implications of changes are assessed by people with appropriate expertise and perspective. On construction projects this is often the responsibility of the architecture firm, while "software architects" perform a similar function on software development efforts.

Organizations use change request forms and logs to track proposed changes. An example of a simplified change request form is depicted in Figure 7.10. Typically change request forms include a description of the change, the impact of not approving the change, the impact of the change on project scope/schedule/cost, and defined signature paths for review as well as a tracking log number.

FIGURE 7.10
Sample Change Request

Project name   *Irish/Chinese culture exchange*   Project sponsor   *Irish embassy*

Request number   _12_   Date   *June 6, 2xxx*

Originator   *Jennifer McDonald*   Change requested by   *Chinese culture office*

Description of requested change

1. Request river dancers to replace small Irish dance group.
2. Request one combination dance with river dancers and China ballet group.

Reason for change

River dancers will enhance stature of event. The group is well known and loved by Chinese people.

Areas of impact of proposed change—describe each on separate sheet

[X] Scope   [X] Cost   [ ] Other _____

[ ] Schedule   [ ] Risk

Disposition	Priority	Funding Source
[ ] Approve	[ ] Emergency	[ ] Mgmt. reserve
[X] Approve as amended	[X] Urgent	[ ] Budget reserve
[ ] Disapprove	[ ] Low	[X] Customer
[ ] Deferred		[ ] Other

Sign-off Approvals

Project manager   *William O'Mally*   Date   *June 12, 2xxx*

Project sponsor   *Kenneth Thompson*   Date   *June 13, 2xxx*

Project customer   *Hong Lee*   Date   *June 18, 2xxx*

Other   _____   Date   _____

An abridged version of a change request log for a construction project is presented in Figure 7.11. These logs are used to monitor change requests. They typically summarize the status of all outstanding change requests and include such useful information as source and date of the change, document codes for related information, cost estimates, and the current status of the request.

Every approved change must be identified and integrated into the plan of record through changes in the project WBS and baseline schedule. The plan of record is the current official plan for the project in terms of scope, budget, and schedule. The plan of record serves as a change management benchmark for future change requests as well as the baseline for evaluating project progress.

If the change control system is not integrated with the WBS and baseline, project plans and control will soon self-destruct. Thus, one of the keys to a successful change

FIGURE 7.11 **Change Request Log**

Owner Requested Change Status Report—Open Items							OSU—Weatherford
Rc#	Description	Reference Document	Dates		Amount	Status	Comments
			Date Rec'd	Date Submit			
51	Sewer work offset				−188,129	OPEN	FUNDING FROM OTHER SOURCE
52	Stainless Plates at restroom Shower Valves	ASI 56	1/5/2013	3/30/2013	9,308	APPROVED	
53	Waterproofing Options	ASI 77	1/13/2013		169,386	OPEN	
54	Change Electrical floor box spec change	RFI 113	12/5/2013	3/29/2013	2,544	SUBMIT	
55	VE Option for Style and rail doors	Door samples	1/14/2013		−20,000	ROM	
56	Pressure Wash C tower	Owner request	3/15/2013	3/30/2013	14,861	SUBMIT	
57	Fire Lite glass in stairs	Owner request			8,000	QUOTE	ROM BASED ON FIRELITE NT
58	Cyber Café added tele /OFOI equipment	ASI 65	1/30/2013	3/29/2013	4,628	APPROVED	
59	Additional Dampers In C wing	ASI 68	2/4/2013	3/29/2013	1,085	SUBMIT	
60	Revise Corridor ceilings	ASI 72	2/13/2013	3/31/2013	−3,755	SUBMIT	

OPEN—Requires estimate SUBMIT—RC letter submitted ASI—Architect's supplemental instructions
ROM—Rough order magnitude APPROVED—RC letter approved RFI—Request for information
QUOTE—Subcontractor quotes REVISE—RC letter to be reviewed

control process is document, document, document! The benefits derived from change control systems are the following:

1. Inconsequential changes are discouraged by the formal process.
2. Costs of changes are maintained in a log.
3. Integrity of the WBS and performance measures is maintained.
4. Allocation and use of budget and management reserve funds are tracked.
5. Responsibility for implementation is clarified.
6. Effect of changes is visible to all parties involved.
7. Implementation of change is monitored.
8. Scope changes will be quickly reflected in baseline and performance measures.

Clearly, change control is important and requires that someone or some group be responsible for approving changes, keeping the process updated, and communicating changes to the project team and relevant stakeholders. Project control depends heavily on keeping the change control process current. This historical record can be used for satisfying customer inquiries, identifying problems in post-project audits, and estimating future project costs.

Summary

To put the processes discussed in this chapter in proper perspective one should recognize that the essence of project management is risk management. Every technique in this book is really a risk management technique. Each in its own way tries to prevent something bad from happening. Project selection systems try to reduce the likelihood that projects will not contribute to the mission of the firm. Project scope statements, among other things, are designed to avoid costly misunderstandings and reduce scope creep. Work breakdown structures reduce the likelihood that some vital part of the project will be omitted or that the budget estimates are unrealistic. Teambuilding reduces the likelihood of dysfunctional conflict and breakdowns in coordination. All of the techniques try to increase stakeholder satisfaction and increase the chances of project success.

From this perspective managers engage in risk management activities to compensate for the uncertainty inherent in project management and that things never go according to plan. Risk management is proactive not reactive. It reduces the number of surprises and prepares people for the unexpected.

Although many managers believe that in the final analysis, risk assessment and contingency depend on subjective judgment, some standard method for identifying, assessing, and responding to risks should be included in all projects. The very process of identifying project risks forces some discipline at all levels of project management and improves project performance.

Contingency plans increase the chance that the project can be completed on time and within budget. Contingency plans can be simple "work-arounds" or elaborate detailed plans. Responsibility for risks should be clearly identified and documented. It is desirable and prudent to keep a reserve as a hedge against project risks. Budget reserves are linked to the WBS and should be communicated to the project team. Control of management reserves should remain with the owner, project manager, and line person responsible. Use of contingency reserves should be closely monitored, controlled, and reviewed throughout the project life cycle.

Experience clearly indicates that using a formal, structured process to handle possible foreseen and unforeseen project risk events minimizes surprises, costs, delays, stress, and misunderstandings. Risk management is an iterative process that occurs throughout the lifespan of the project. When risk events occur or changes are necessary, using an effective change control process to quickly approve and record changes will facilitate measuring performance against schedule and cost. Ultimately successful risk management requires a culture in which threats are embraced not denied and problems are identified not hidden.

Key Terms

Accept risk, 218
Avoiding risk, 217
Budget reserve, 224
Change management
system, 227
Contingency plan, 219
Management reserve, 224
Mitigating risk, 216

Opportunity, 223
Risk, 207
Risk breakdown
structure (RBS), 210
Risk profile, 211
Risk register, 225
Risk severity matrix, 214
Scenario analysis, 213

Time buffer, 225
Transferring risk, 217

Review Questions

1. Project risks can/cannot be eliminated if the project is carefully planned. Explain.
2. The chances of risk events occurring and their respective costs increasing change over the project life cycle. What is the significance of this phenomenon to a project manager?
3. What is the difference between avoiding a risk and accepting a risk?
4. What is the difference between mitigating a risk and contingency planning?
5. Explain the difference between budget reserves and management reserves.
6. How are the work breakdown structure and change control connected?
7. What are the likely outcomes if a change control process is not used? Why?
8. What are the major differences between managing negative risks versus positive risks (opportunities)?

Exercises

1. Gather a small team of students. Think of a project most students would understand; the kinds of tasks involved should also be familiar. Identify and assess major and minor risks inherent to the project. Decide on a response type. Develop a contingency plan for two to four identified risks. Estimate costs. Assign contingency reserves. How much reserve would your team estimate for the whole project? Justify your choices and estimates.

2. You have been assigned to a project risk team of five members. Because this is the first time your organization has formally set up a risk team for a project, it is hoped that your team will develop a process that can be used on all future projects. Your first team meeting is next Monday morning. Each team member has been asked to prepare for the meeting by developing, in as much detail as possible, an outline that describes how you believe the team should proceed in handling project risks. Each of the team members will hand out their proposed outline at the beginning of the meeting. Your outline should include but not be limited to the following information:

   a. Team objectives.
   b. Process for handling risk events.
   c. Team activities.
   d. Team outputs.

3. The Manchester United Soccer Tournament project team (review the Manchester United case at the end of Chapter 4) has identified the following potential risks to their project:

   a. Referees failing to show up at designated games.
   b. Fighting between teams.
   c. Pivotal error committed by a referee that determines the outcome of a game.
   d. Abusive behavior along the sidelines by parents.
   e. Inadequate parking.
   f. Not enough teams sign up for different age brackets.
   g. Serious injury.

   How would you recommend that they respond (i.e., avoid, accept, . . .) to these risks and why?

4. Search the Web using the key words: "best practices, project management." What did you find? How might this information be useful to a project manager?

References

Atkinson, W., "Beyond the Basics," *PM Network,* May 2003, pp. 38–43.

Baker, B., and R. Menon, "Politics and Project Performance: The Fourth Dimension of Project Management," *PM Network,* vol. 9, no. 11 (November 1995), pp. 16–21.

Carr, M. J., S. L. Konda, I. Monarch, F. C. Ulrich, and C. F. Walker, "Taxonomy-Based Risk Identification," *Technical Report CMU/SEI-93-TR 6, Software Engineering Institute,* Carnegie Mellon University, Pittsburgh, 1993.

Ford, E. C., J. Duncan, A. G. Bedeian, P. M. Ginter, M. D. Rousculp, and A. M. Adams, "Mitigating Risks, Visible Hands, Inevitable Disasters, and Soft Variables: Management Research That Matters to Managers," *Academy of Management Executive,* vol. 19, no. 4 (November 2005), pp. 24–38.

Gray, C. F., and R. Reinman, "PERT Simulation: A Dynamic Approach to the PERT Technique," *Journal of Systems Management,* March 1969, pp. 18–23.

Hamburger, D. H., "The Project Manager: Risk Taker and Contingency Planner," *Project Management Journal,* vol. 21, no. 4 (1990), pp. 11–16.

Hulett, D. T., "Project Schedule Risk Assessment," *Project Management Journal,* 26 (1) 1995, pp. 21–31.

Ingebretson, M., "In No Uncertain Terms," *PM Network,* 2002, pp. 28–32.

Meyer, A. D., C. H. Loch, and M. T. Pich, "Managing Project Uncertainty: From Variation to Chaos," *MIT Sloan Management Review,* Winter 2002, pp. 60–67.

Orlando Sentinel, "Math Mistake Proved Fatal to Mars Orbiter," November 23, 1999.

Pavlik, A., "Project Troubleshooting: Tiger Teams for Reactive Risk Management," *Project Management Journal,* vol. 35, no. 4 (December 2004), pp. 5–14.

Pinto, J. K., *Project Management: Achieving Competitive Advantage* (Upper Saddle River, NJ: Pearson, 2007).

Project Management Body of Knowledge (Newton Square, PA: Project Management Institute, 2013).

Schuler, J. R., "Decision Analysis in Projects: Monte Carlo Simulation," *PM Network,* vol. 7, no. 1 (January 1994), pp. 30–36.

Skelton, T. and H. Thamhain, "Managing Risk in New Product Development Projects: Beyond Analytical Methods," *Project Perspectives*, vol. 27, no. 1 (2006), pp. 12–20.

Skelton, T. and H. Thamhain, "Success Factors for Effective R&D Risk Management," *International Journal of Technology Intelligence and Planning,* vol. 3, no. 4 (2007), pp. 376–386.

Smith, P. G., and G. M. Merritt, *Proactive Risk Management: Controlling Uncertainty in Product Development* (New York: Productivity Press, 2002).

Smith, P. G., and D. G. Reinertsen, *Developing Products in Half the Time* (New York: Van Nostrand Reinhold, 1995).

Snizek, J. A., and R. A. Henry, "Accuracy and Confidence in Group Judgment," *Organizational Behavior and Human Decision Processes,* vol. 4, no. 3 (1989), pp. 1–28.

Thamhain, H., "Managing Risks in Complex Projects," *Project Management Journal*, vol. 44, no. 20 (2013), pp. 20–35.

Case 7.1

Alaska Fly-Fishing Expedition[*]

You are sitting around the fire at a lodge in Dillingham, Alaska, discussing a fishing expedition you are planning with your colleagues at Great Alaska Adventures (GAA). Earlier in the day you received a fax from the president of BlueNote, Inc. The president wants to reward her top management team by taking them on an all-expense-paid fly-fishing adventure in Alaska. She would like GAA to organize and lead the expedition.

You have just finished a preliminary scope statement for the project (see below). You are now brainstorming potential risks associated with the project.

1. Brainstorm potential risks associated with this project. Try to come up with at least five different risks.
2. Use a risk assessment form similar to Figure 7.6 to analyze identified risks.
3. Develop a risk response matrix similar to Figure 7.8 to outline how you would deal with each of the risks.

PROJECT SCOPE STATEMENT

PROJECT OBJECTIVE

To organize and lead a five-day fly-fishing expedition down the Tikchik River system in Alaska from June 21 to 25 at a cost not to exceed $35,000.

DELIVERABLES

- Provide air transportation from Dillingham, Alaska, to Camp I and from Camp II back to Dillingham.
- Provide river transportation consisting of two eight-man drift boats with outboard motors.
- Provide three meals a day for the five days spent on the river.
- Provide four hours fly-fishing instruction.
- Provide overnight accommodations at the Dillingham lodge plus three four-man tents with cots, bedding, and lanterns.
- Provide four experienced river guides who are also fly fishermen.
- Provide fishing licenses for all guests.

MILESTONES

1. Contract signed January 22.
2. Guests arrive in Dillingham June 20.
3. Depart by plane to Base Camp I June 21.
4. Depart by plane from Base Camp II to Dillingham June 25.

[*] This case was prepared with the assistance of Stuart Morigeau.

TECHNICAL REQUIREMENTS

1. Fly in air transportation to and from base camps.
2. Boat transportation within the Tikchik River system.
3. Digital cellular communication devices.
4. Camps and fishing conform to state of Alaska requirements.

LIMITS AND EXCLUSIONS

1. Guests are responsible for travel arrangements to and from Dillingham, Alaska.
2. Guests are responsible for their own fly-fishing equipment and clothing.
3. Local air transportation to and from base camps will be outsourced.
4. Tour guides are not responsible for the number of King Salmon caught by guests.

CUSTOMER REVIEW

The president of BlueNote, Inc.

Case 7.2

Silver Fiddle Construction

You are the president of Silver Fiddle Construction (SFC), which specializes in building high-quality, customized homes in the Grand Junction, Colorado, area. You have just been hired by the Czopeks to build their dream home. You operate as a general contractor and employ only a part-time bookkeeper. You subcontract work to local trade professionals. Housing construction in Grand Junction is booming. You are tentatively scheduled to complete 11 houses this year. You have promised the Czopeks that the final costs will range from $450,000 to $500,000 and that it will take five months to complete the house once groundbreaking has begun. The Czopeks are willing to have the project delayed in order to save costs.

You have just finished a preliminary scope statement for the project (see below). You are now brainstorming potential risks associated with the project.

1. Identify potential risks associated with this project. Try to come up with at least five different risks.
2. Use a risk assessment form similar to Figure 7.6 to analyze identified risks.
3. Develop a risk response matrix similar to Figure 7.8 to outline how you would deal with each of the risks.

PROJECT SCOPE STATEMENT

PROJECT OBJECTIVE

To construct a high-quality, custom home within five months at a cost not to exceed $500,000.

DELIVERABLES

- A 2,500-square-foot, 2½-bath, 3-bedroom, finished home.
- A finished garage, insulated and sheetrocked.

- Kitchen appliances to include range, oven, microwave, and dishwasher.
- High-efficiency gas furnace with programmable thermostat.

MILESTONES

1. Permits approved July 5.
2. Foundation poured July 12.
3. "Dry in"—framing, sheathing, plumbing, electrical, and mechanical inspections—passed September 25.
4. Final inspection November 7.

TECHNICAL REQUIREMENTS

1. Home must meet local building codes.
2. All windows and doors must pass NFRC class 40 energy ratings.
3. Exterior wall insulation must meet an "R" factor of 21.
4. Ceiling insulation must meet an "R" factor of 38.
5. Floor insulation must meet an "R" factor of 25.
6. Garage will accommodate two cars and one 28-foot-long Winnebago.
7. Structure must pass seismic stability codes.

LIMITS AND EXCLUSIONS

1. The home will be built to the specifications and design of the original blueprints provided by the customer.
2. Owner is responsible for landscaping.
3. Refrigerator is not included among kitchen appliances.
4. Air conditioning is not included, but house is prewired for it.
5. SFC reserves the right to contract out services.

CUSTOMER REVIEW

"Bolo" and Izabella Czopek.

Case 7.3

Trans LAN Project

Trans Systems is a small information systems consulting firm located in Meridian, Louisiana. Trans has just been hired to design and install a local area network (LAN) for the city of Meridian's social welfare agency. You are the manager for the project, which includes one Trans professional and two interns from a local university. You have just finished a preliminary scope statement for the project (see below). You are now brainstorming potential risks associated with the project.

1. Identify potential risks associated with this project. Try to come up with at least five different risks.
2. Use a risk assessment form similar to Figure 7.6 to analyze identified risks.
3. Develop a risk response matrix similar to Figure 7.8 to outline how you would deal with each of the risks.

PROJECT SCOPE STATEMENT

PROJECT OBJECTIVE

To design and install a new local area network (LAN) within one month with a budget not to exceed $90,000 for the Meridian Social Service Agency with minimum disruption to ongoing operations.

DELIVERABLES

- Twenty workstations and twenty laptop computers.
- Server with dual-core processors.
- Two color laser printers.
- Windows R2 server and workstation operating system (Windows 10).
- Migration of existing databases and programs to new system.
- Four hours of introduction training for client's personnel.
- Sixteen hours of training for client network administrator.
- Fully operational LAN system.

MILESTONES

1. Hardware January 22.
2. Setting users' priority and authorization January 26.
3. In-house whole network test completed February 1.
4. Client site test completed February 2.
5. Training completed February 16.

TECHNICAL REQUIREMENTS

1. Workstations with 17-inch flat panel monitors, dual-core processors, 4 GB RAM, 8X DVD+RW, wireless card, Ethernet card, 500 GB hard drive.
2. Laptops with 12-inch display monitor, dual-core processors, 2GB RAM, 8X DVD+RW, wireless card, Ethernet card, 500 GB hard drive and weigh less than 4½ lbs.
3. Wireless network interface cards and Ethernet connections.
4. System must support Windows 11 platforms.
5. System must provide secure external access for field workers.

LIMITS AND EXCLUSIONS

1. On-site work to be done after 8:00 p.m. and before 7:00 a.m. Monday through Saturday.
2. System maintenance and repair only up to one month after final inspection.
3. Warranties transferred to client.
4. Only responsible for installing software designated by the client two weeks before the start of the project.
5. Client will be billed for additional training beyond that prescribed in the contract.

CUSTOMER REVIEW

Director of the city of Meridian's Social Service Agency.

Case 7.4

XSU Spring Concert

You are a member of the X State University (XSU) student body entertainment committee. Your committee has agreed to sponsor a spring concert. The motive behind this concert is to offer a safe alternative to Hasta Weekend. Hasta Weekend is a spring event in which students from XSU rent houseboats and engage in heavy partying. Traditionally this occurs during the last weekend in May. Unfortunately, the partying has a long history of getting out of hand, sometimes leading to fatal accidents. After one such tragedy last spring, your committee wants to offer an alternative experience for those who are eager to celebrate the change in weather and the pending end of the school year.

You have just finished a preliminary scope statement for the project (see below). You are now brainstorming potential risks associated with the project.

1. Identify potential risks associated with this project. Try to come up with at least five different risks.
2. Use a risk assessment form similar to Figure 7.6 to analyze identified risks.
3. Develop a risk response matrix similar to Figure 7.8 to outline how you would deal with each of the risks.

PROJECT SCOPE STATEMENT

PROJECT OBJECTIVE

To organize and deliver an eight-hour concert at Wahoo Stadium at a cost not to exceed $50,000 on the last Saturday in May.

DELIVERABLES

- Local advertising.
- Concert security.
- Separate Beer Garden.
- Eight hours of music and entertainment.
- Food venues.
- Souvenir concert T-shirts.
- Secure all licenses and approvals.
- Secure sponsors.

MILESTONES

1. Secure all permissions and approvals by January 15.
2. Sign big-name artist by February 15.
3. Complete artist roster by April 1.
4. Secure vendor contracts by April 15.
5. Setup completed on May 27.
6. Concert on May 28.
7. Cleanup completed by May 31.

TECHNICAL REQUIREMENTS

1. Professional sound stage and system.
2. At least one big-name artist.
3. At least seven performing acts.
4. Restroom facilities for 10,000 people.
5. Parking available for 1,000 cars.
6. Compliance with XSU and city requirements/ordinances.

LIMITS AND EXCLUSIONS

1. Performers responsible for travel arrangements to and from XSU.
2. Vendors contribute a set percentage of sales.
3. Concert must be over by 11:30 p.m.

CUSTOMER REVIEW

The president of XSU student body.

Case 7.5

Sustaining Project Risk Management during Implementation

BACKGROUND

Bill (Senior VP of product development): Carlos [project manager], we have to talk. I am concerned about the way we manage project risk here at Futuronics. I just came from an international "Future Mote Devices" meeting at UC Berkeley. [Note: A *mote* is a very small [e.g., 2–3mm square], wireless sensing pod that may be placed on land or in water to measure and communicate data.] The project management sessions receiving most attention addressed risk in product development projects. They described our management of project risk to the letter—failure to sustain risk management *after the project gets rolling*. It seems someone has to get burned before risk management is taken seriously.

Much to my surprise, almost every project manager there admitted their firms have a problem sustaining team members' interest in managing risk after the project is on its way. The old saying, "If you don't manage risk, you pay the price later," generated horror stories from a few who paid the price. We spent some time brainstorming ways to handle the problem at the project level, but there were very few concrete suggestions. The meeting gave me a wakeup call. Carlos, we need to tackle this problem or some new or known risk event could put us both out of a job. The similarities between their horror stories and some of our past mistakes are scary.

Since here at Futuronics we only develop new products that are at least seven years beyond anything on the market, the level of both "known risk events and unknown risk" is far higher than in most other organizations. Managing project risk is important to every project, but here at Futuronics every new product project is loaded with risks. Carlos, I'm willing to work with you to improve our management of project risk at Futuronics.

Carlos: Bill, I am aware of the problem. The PMI Roundtables I attend also talk to the difficulty of keeping teams and other stakeholders willing to revisit risk once the project is on its way. [PMI Roundtables are monthly meetings of practicing PMs across industries designed to address project management problems.] I also heard war stories at a recent project management roundtable meeting. I have some notes from the meeting right here.

It all started with the leader's question: "How many project managers actually manage risk over the complete project life cycle?"

PM 1: We all work through the risk management process well before the project begins. We have the process template of risk identification, assessment, response, control, risk register, and contingency down pat. We just don't follow through after the project begins. I think interest dies. Have you ever tried to get project stakeholders to come to a risk meeting when the project is moving relatively well?

PM 2: A recent e-mail from one of our stakeholders said, "We'll deal with it [risk] when it happens."

PM 3: I agree. Interest seems to move from future oriented to reactionary. Also, risk management seems to degenerate into issue (concerns and problems) management versus real risk management.

PM 4: I ask team members, "What is the risk of not managing risk over the life of the project?" Sometimes this question nudges a few to respond positively, especially if risks have changed or new ones are perceived. I use a failed project where a solid risk management process would have avoided the project failure. I explain all of the risk management processes that would have helped to improve the risk elements—risk identification, triggers, responsibility, transfer, accept, etc.

PM 5: Risk is not a line item in the budget or schedule. Maybe it is in the contingency budget to cover "unknowns of unknowns." I have to watch that management doesn't try to squeeze out the contingency budget for something else.

Carlos continued to share with his boss that there were many more comments, but very few gave much guidance. Carlos then shared his idea:

Carlos: Colette is our best trainer, especially in transition management, and she would be a great choice for following through on this problem. Her training classes on upfront risk management are excellent. Should we ask her to present a session?

Bill: You are right, Carlos, Colette is ideal. She is smart and a great team motivator. Ask her, but give her some kind of direction for focus.

A few days later, Carlos sent out a memo:

Colette, this is to follow up on our lunch conversation yesterday discussing sustaining risk management after the project is on its way. Given the nature of our futuristic company, we should stress the point that our product development projects carry many more inherent risks than do traditional projects. I suggest the training classes should drill down on concrete actions and policies that will encourage interest of team members and other project stakeholders in sustaining risk management practices during project execution.

Colette, we appreciate your taking on this project. When you have developed your training session, please give me a copy so I can schedule and support your efforts.

Regards, Carlos

CHALLENGE

Divide the class into teams of three or more participants.

Colette needs your help to develop her training program. You may wish to consider the questions listed below to initiate ideas.

- Why do project stakeholders lose interest in project risk after the project is under way?
- What are the dangers of not keeping on top of risk management during implementation?
- What kind of business is Futuronics in?

Brainstorm specific actions that will encourage project stakeholders to continue to scan and track the project environment for risk events. Suggest three concrete actions or scenarios that will encourage project stakeholders to change their behavior and truly support risk management while projects are being implemented. The following outline headings may be helpful in developing possible actions that would improve/enhance stakeholder support.

- Improving the risk management process
- Organization actions
- Motivating participation

Appendix 7.1

PERT and PERT Simulation

LEARNING OBJECTIVES

After reading this appendix you should be able to:

A7-1 Calculate basic Pert Simulation projections.

PERT—PROGRAM EVALUATION AND REVIEW TECHNIQUE

LO A7-1

Calculate basic Pert Simulation projections.

In 1958 the Special Office of the Navy and the Booze, Allen, and Hamilton consulting firm developed PERT (program evaluation and review technique) to schedule the more than 3,300 contractors of the Polaris submarine project and to cover uncertainty of activity time estimates.

PERT is almost identical to the critical path method (CPM) technique except it assumes each activity duration has a range that follows a statistical distribution. PERT uses three time estimates for each activity. Basically, this means each activity duration can range from an optimistic time to a pessimistic time, and a weighted average can be computed for each activity. Because project activities usually represent work, and because work tends to stay behind once it gets behind, the PERT developers chose an approximation of the *beta distribution* to represent activity durations. This distribution is known to be flexible and can accommodate empirical data that do not follow a normal distribution. The activity durations can be skewed more toward the high or low end of the data range. Figure A7.1A depicts a *beta distribution* for activity durations that is skewed toward the right and is representative of work that tends to stay late once it is behind. The distribution for the project duration is represented by a normal

FIGURE A7.1   Activity and Project Frequency Distributions

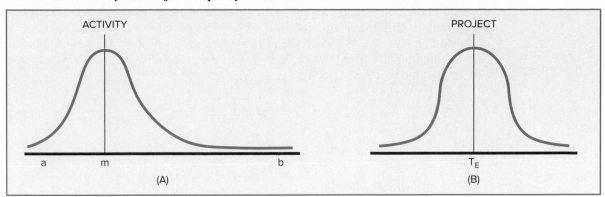

(symmetrical) distribution shown in Figure A7.1B. The project distribution represents the sum of the weighted averages of the activities on the critical path(s).

Knowing the weighted average and variances for each activity allows the project planner to compute the probability of meeting different project durations. Follow the steps described in the hypothetical example given next. (The jargon is difficult for those not familiar with statistics, but the process is relatively simple after working through a couple of examples.)

The weighted average activity time is computed by the following formula:

$$t_e = \frac{a + 4m + b}{6} \tag{7.1}$$

where

t_e = weighted average activity time
a = optimistic activity time (1 chance in 100 of completing the activity earlier under *normal* conditions)
b = pessimistic activity time (1 chance in 100 of completing the activity later under *normal* conditions)
m = most likely activity time

When the three time estimates have been specified, this equation is used to compute the weighted average duration for each activity. The average (deterministic) value is placed on the project network as in the CPM method and the early, late, slack, and project completion times are computed as they are in the CPM method.

The variability in the activity time estimates is approximated by the following equations: Equation 7.2 represents the standard deviation for the *activity*. Equation 7.3 represents the standard deviation for the *project*. Note the standard deviation of the activity is squared in this equation; this is also called variance. This sum includes only activities on the critical path(s) or path being reviewed.

$$\sigma_{t_e} = \left(\frac{b - a}{6} \right) \tag{7.2}$$

$$\sigma_{T_E} = \sqrt{\Sigma \sigma_{t_e}^2} \tag{7.3}$$

Finally, the average project duration (T_E) is the sum of all the average activity times along the critical path (sum of t_e), and it follows a normal distribution.

Knowing the average project duration and the variances of activities allows the probability of completing the project (or segment of the project) by a specific time to be computed using standard statistical tables. The equation below (Equation 7.4) is used to compute the "*Z*" value found in statistical tables (*Z* = number of standard deviations from the mean), which, in turn, tells the probability of completing the project in the time specified.

$$Z = \frac{T_S - T_E}{\sqrt{\Sigma \sigma^2_{t_e}}} \tag{7.4}$$

where

T_E = critical path duration
T_S = scheduled project duration
Z = probability (of meeting scheduled duration) found in statistical Table A7.2

A HYPOTHETICAL EXAMPLE USING THE PERT TECHNIQUE

The activity times and variances are given in Table A7.1. The project network is presented in Figure A7.2. This figure shows the project network as AOA and AON. The AON network is presented as a reminder that PERT can use AON networks as well as AOA.

The expected project duration (T_E) is 64 time units; the critical path is 1-2-3-5-6. With this information, the probability of completing the project by a specific date can easily be computed using standard statistical methods. For example, what is the probability the project will be completed before a scheduled time (T_S) of 67? The normal curve for the project would appear as shown in Figure A7.3.

Using the formula for the *Z* value, the probability can be computed as follows:

$$Z = \frac{T_S - T_E}{\sqrt{\Sigma \sigma^2_{t_e}}}$$

$$= \frac{67 - 64}{\sqrt{25 + 9 + 1 + 1}}$$

$$= \frac{+3}{\sqrt{36}}$$

$$= +0.50$$

$$P = 0.69$$

Reading from Table A7.2, a Z value of +0.5 gives a probability of 0.69, which is interpreted to mean there is a 69 percent chance of completing the project on or before 67 time units.

TABLE A7.1
Activity Times and Variances

Activity	a	m	b	t_e	$[(b-a)/6]^2$
1–2	17	29	47	30	25
2–3	6	12	24	13	9
2–4	16	19	28	20	4
3–5	13	16	19	16	1
4–5	2	5	14	6	4
5–6	2	5	8	5	1

**FIGURE A7.2
Hypothetical
Network**

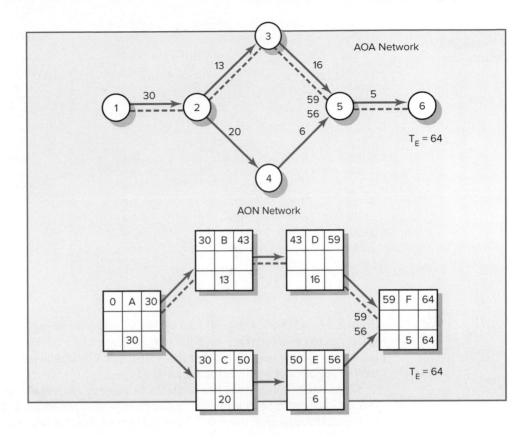

Conversely, the probability of completing the project by time period 60 is computed as follows:

$$Z = \frac{60 - 64}{\sqrt{25 + 9 + 1 + 1}}$$
$$= \frac{-4}{\sqrt{36}}$$
$$= -0.67$$
$$P \approx 0.26$$

**FIGURE A7.3
Possible Project
Durations**

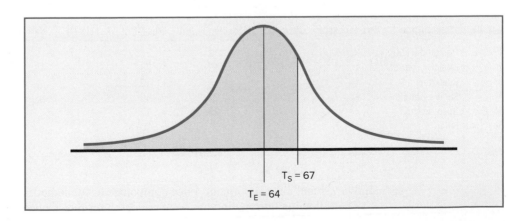

TABLE A7.2
Z Values and
Probabilities

Z Value	Probability	Z Value	Probability
−3.0	.001	+0.0	.500
−2.8	.003	+0.2	.579
−2.6	.005	+0.4	.655
−2.4	.008	+0.6	.726
−2.2	.014	+0.8	.788
−2.0	.023	+1.0	.841
−1.8	.036	+1.2	.885
−1.6	.055	+1.4	.919
−1.4	.081	+1.6	.945
−1.2	.115	+1.8	.964
−1.0	.159	+2.0	.977
−0.8	.212	+2.2	.986
−0.6	.274	+2.4	.992
−0.4	.345	+2.6	.995
−0.2	.421	+2.8	.997

From Table A7.2, a Z value of −0.67 gives an approximate probability of 0.26, which is interpreted to mean there is about a 26 percent chance of completing the project on or before 60 time units. Note that this same type of calculation can be made for any path or segment of a path in the network.

When such probabilities are available to management, trade-off decisions can be made to accept or reduce the risk associated with a particular project duration. For example, if the project manager wishes to improve the chances of completing the project by 64 time units, at least two choices are available. First, management can spend money up front to change conditions that will reduce the duration of one or more activities on the critical path. A more prudent, second alternative would be to allocate money to a contingency fund and wait to see how the project is progressing as it is implemented.

EXERCISES

1. Given the project information below, what is the probability of completing the National Holiday Toy project in 93 time units?

Act. ID	Description	Predecessor	Optm. (a)	Most likely (m)	Pess. (b)	Act time t_e	Variance $[(b - a)/6]^2$	Critical
1	Design package	None	6	12	24			
2	Design product	1	16	19	28			
3	Build package	1	4	7	10			
4	Secure patent	2	24	27	36			
5	Build product	2	17	29	47			
6	Paint	3, 4, 5	4	7	10			
7	Test market	6	13	16	19			

2. The Global Tea and Organic Juice companies have merged.
   The following information has been collected for the "Consolidation Project."

Activity	Description	Predecessor	*a* opt	*m* ml	*b* pess
1	Codify accounts	None	16	19	28
2	File articles of unification	None	30	30	30
3	Unify price and credit policy	None	60	72	90
4	Unify personnel policies	None	18	27	30
5	Unify data processing	1	17	29	47
6	Train accounting staff	1	4	7	10
7	Pilot run data processing	5	12	15	18
8	Calculate P & L and balance sheet	6, 7	6	12	24
9	Transfer real property	2	18	27	30
10	Train salesforce	3	20	35	50
11	Negotiate with unions	4	40	55	100
12	Determine capital needs	8	11	20	29
13	Explain personnel policies	11	14	23	26
14	Secure line of credit	9, 12	13	16	19
15	End	10, 13, 14	0	0	0

1. Compute the expected time for each activity.
2. Compute the variance for each activity.
3. Compute the expected project duration.
4. What is the probability of completing the project by day 112? Within 116 days?
5. What is the probability of completing "Negotiate with Unions" by day 90?

3. The expected times and variances for the project activities are given below. What is the probability of completing the project in 25 periods?

ID	Description	Predecessor	t_e	Variance $[(b-a)/6]^2$
1	Pilot production	None	6	3
2	Select channels of distrib.	None	7	4
3	Develop mktg. program	None	4	2
4	Test market	1	4	2
5	Patent	1	10	5
6	Full production	4	16	10
7	Ad promotion	3	3	2
8	Release	2, 5, 6, 7	2	1

Case A7.1

International Capital, Inc.—Part A

International Capital, Inc. (IC), is a small investment banking firm that specializes in securing funds for small- to medium-sized firms. IC is able to use a standardized project format for each engagement. Only activity times and unusual circumstances change the standard network. Beth Brown has been assigned to this client as project manager partner and has compiled the network information and activity times for the latest client as follows:

Activity	Description	Immediate Predecessor
A	Start story draft using template	—
B	Research client firm	—
C	Create "due diligence" rough draft	A, B
D	Coordinate needs proposal with client	C
E	Estimate future demand and cash flows	C
F	Draft future plans for client company	E
G	Create and approve legal documents	C
H	Integrate all drafts into first-draft proposal	D, F, G
I	Line up potential sources of capital	G, F
J	Check, approve, and print final legal proposal	H
K	Sign contracts and transfer funds	I, J

	Time in Workdays		
Activity	Optimistic	Most Likely	Pessimistic
A	4	7	10
B	2	4	8
C	2	5	8
D	16	19	28
E	6	9	24
F	1	7	13
G	4	10	28
H	2	5	14
I	5	8	17
J	2	5	8
K	17	29	45

MANAGERIAL REPORT

Brown and other broker partners have a policy of passing their plan through a project review committee of colleagues. This committee traditionally checks that all details are covered, times are realistic, and resources are available. Brown wishes you to develop a report that presents a planned schedule and expected project completion time in workdays. Include a project network in your report. The average duration for a sourcing capital project is 70 workdays. IC partners have agreed it is good business to set up projects with a 95 percent chance of attaining the plan. How does this project stack up with the average project? What would the average have to be to ensure a 95 percent chance of completing the project in 70 workdays?

Case A7.2

Advantage Energy Technology Data Center Migration—Part B

In Chapter 6, Brian Smith, network administrator at Advanced Energy Technology (AET), was given the responsibility of implementing the migration of a large data center to a new office location.

| | Time in Workdays | | | | |
Task Name	Optimistic Dur.	Most Likely Dur.	Pessimistic Dur.	Immediate Predecessor	Critical Path
1 AET DATA CENTER MIGRATION	54	68	92		✓
2 Team meeting	0.5	1	1.5		
3 Hire contractors	6	7	8	2	
4 Network design	12	14	16	2	
5 Ventilation system	—	—	—	—	
6 Order ventilation system	18	21	30	2	
7 Install ventilation system	5	7	9	6	
8 New racks	—	—	—	—	
9 Order new racks	13	14	21	2	✓
10 Install racks	17	21	25	9	✓
11 Power supplies and cables	—	—	—	—	
12 Order power supplies & cables	6	7	8	2	
13 Install power supplies	5	5	11	12, 16	
14 Install cables	6	8	10	12, 16	✓
15 Renovation of data center	19	20	27	3, 4	
16 City inspection	1	2	3	3, 7, 10	✓
17 Switchover Meetings	—	—	—	—	
18 Facilities	7	8	9	14	
19 Operations/systems	5	7	9	14	
20 Operations/telecommunications	6	7	8	14	
21 Systems & applications	7	7	13	14	
22 Customer service	5	6	13	14	✓
23 Power check	0.5	1	1.5	13, 14, 15	✓
24 Install test servers	5	7	9	18, 19, 20, 21, 22, 23	✓
25 Management safety check	1	2	3	7, 23, 24	✓
26 Primary systems check	1.5	2	2.5	25	✓
27 Set date for move	1	1	1	26	✓
28 Complete move	1	2	3	27	✓

Careful planning was needed because AET operates in the highly competitive petroleum industry. AET is one of five national software companies that provide an accounting and business management package for oil jobbers and gasoline distributors. A few years ago, AET jumped into the "application service provider" world. Their large data center provides clients with remote access to AET's complete suite of application software systems. Traditionally, one of AET's primary competitive advantages has been the company's trademark IT reliability. Due to the complexity of this project, the Executive Committee insisted that preliminary analysis of the anticipated completion date be conducted.

Brian compiled the following information, in preparation for some PERT analysis:

1. Based on these estimates and the resultant expected project duration of 69 days, the executive committee wants to know what the probability is of completing the project before a scheduled time (T_S) of 68 days.

2. The significance of this project has the executive committee very concerned. The committee has decided that more analysis of the duration of each activity is needed. Prior to conducting that effort, they asked Brian to calculate what the expected project duration would have to be to ensure a 93 percent chance of completion within 68 days.

ADVANTAGE ENERGY TECHNOLOGY (AET)—ACCOUNTS PAYABLE SYSTEM

The AET sales department has been concerned about a new start-up company that is about to release an accounts payable system. Their investigation indicates that this new package will provide features which will seriously compete with AET's current Accounts Payable system and in some cases exceed what AET offers.

Tom Wright, senior applications developer at AET, has been given the responsibility of analyzing, designing, developing, and delivering a new accounts payable system (A/P) for AET customers.

Complicating the issue is the concern of the sales department about AET's recent inability to meet promised delivery dates. They have convinced CEO (Larry Martain) that a significant marketing effort will have to be expended to convince the clients they should wait for the AET product rather than jump to a package provided by a new entry to the petroleum software business. Companion to this effort is the importance of the performance of the software development group.

Consequently, Tom has decided to take the following action: tighten up the estimating effort by his developers; incorporate some new estimating procedures; and use some PERT techniques to generate probabilities associated with his delivery dates.

Tom's planning team made a first-cut at the set of activities and associated durations:

	Task Name	Time in Workdays			Immediate Predecessor	Critical Path
		Optimistic Dur.	Most Likely Dur.	Pessimistic Dur.		
1	**ACCOUNTS PAYABLE SYSTEM**					
2	Planning meeting	1	1	2		✓
3	Team assignments	3	4	5	2	✓
4	**Program specification**					
5	Customer requirements	8	10	12	3	✓
6	Feasibility study	3	5	7	5	
7	Systems analysis	6	8	10	5	✓
8	Prelim budget & schedule	1	2	3	7	✓
9	Functional specification	3	5	7	7	✓
10	Prelim design	10	12	14	9	✓
11	Configuration & perf needs	3	4	5	10	✓
12	Hardware requirements	4	6	8	11	✓
13	System specification	5	7	9	10	
14	Detailed design	12	14	16	12, 13	✓
15	Program specification	8	10	12	14	✓
16	Programming—first phase	27	32	37	15	✓
17	Documentation	14	16	18	10	
18	**Prototype**					
19	Development	5	7	9	16	✓
20	User testing & feedback	12	14	16	19	✓
21	Programming—second phase	10	12	14	16	
22	Beta testing	18	20	22	21	
23	Final documentation pkg	9	10	11	17, 20	✓
24	Training pkg	4	5	6	21SS, 23	✓
25	Product release	3	5	7	22, 23, 24	✓

SS = Start to Start lag

3. Based on these estimates and the critical path, the project duration is estimated at 149 days. But an AET salesperson in the Southeast Region has discovered that the competing A/P package (with significant improvements) is scheduled for delivery in approximately 145 days. The sales force is very anxious to beat that delivery time. The executive committee asks Tom for an estimated probability of reducing his expected project duration by two days.

4. The executive committee is advised by Tom that after all the estimating was completed, he determined that one of his two critical systems analysts might have to move out of the area for critical family reasons. Tom is still very confident that with some staff rearrangements, assistance from a subcontractor, and some "hands on" activities on his part he can still meet the original delivery date, based on 149 days.

   This news is very disconcerting to the committee and the sales staff. At this point, the committee decides that based on the most recent delivery performance of AET, a modified, comfortable delivery date should be communicated to AET clients—one that Tom and his staff are very likely to meet. Consequently, Tom is asked to calculate what the expected project duration would have to be to ensure a 98 percent chance of completion within 160 days—that is a "published, drop dead date" that can be communicated to the clients.

8

Scheduling Resources and Costs

LEARNING OBJECTIVES

After reading this chapter you should be able to:

8-1 Understand the differences between time-constrained and resource-constrained schedules.

8-2 Identify different types of resource constraints.

8-3 Describe how the smoothing approach is used on time-constrained projects.

8-4 Describe how leveling approach is used for resource-constrained projects.

8-5 Understand how project management software creates resource-constrained schedules.

8-6 Understand when and why splitting tasks should be avoided.

8-7 Identify general guidelines for assigning people to specific tasks.

8-8 Identify common problems with multiproject resource scheduling.

8-9 Explain why a time-phased budget baseline is needed.

8-10 Create a time-phased project budget baseline.

OUTLINE

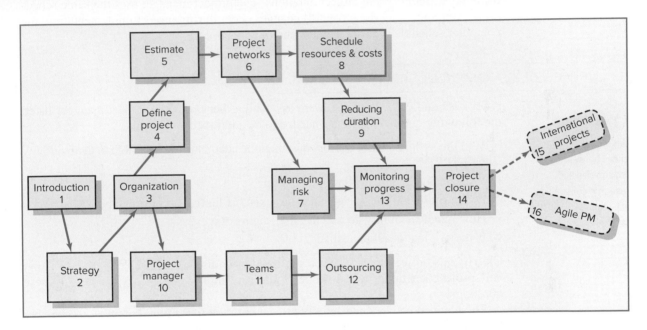

Project network times are not a schedule until resources have been assigned. Cost estimates are not a budget until they have been time-phased.

We have consistently stressed that up-front planning results in big payoffs. For those who have diligently worked through the earlier planning processes chapters, you are nearly ready to launch your project. This chapter completes the final two planning tasks that become the master plan for your project—resource and cost scheduling. (See Figure 8.1.) This process uses the resource schedule to assign *time-phased* costs that provide the project budget *baseline*. Given this time-phased baseline, comparisons can be made with actual and planned schedule and costs. This chapter first discusses the process for developing the project resource schedule. This resource schedule will be used to assign the time-phased budgeted values to create a project budget baseline.

There are always more project proposals than there are available resources. The priority system needs to select projects that best contribute to the organization's objectives, within the constraints of the resources available. If all projects and their respective resources are computer scheduled, the feasibility and impact of adding a new project to those in process can be quickly assessed. With this information the project

FIGURE 8.1
Project Planning Process

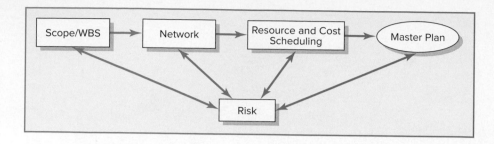

priority team will add a new project only if resources are available. This chapter examines methods of scheduling resources so the team can make realistic judgments of resource availability and project durations. The project manager uses the same schedule for implementing the project. If changes occur during project implementation, the computer schedule is easily updated and the effects easily assessed.

8.1 Overview of the Resource Scheduling Problem

 8-1

Understand the differences between time-constrained and resource-constrained schedules.

After staff and other resources were assigned to her project, a project manager listed the following questions that still needed to be addressed:

- Will the assigned labor and/or equipment be adequate and available to deal with my project?
- Will outside contractors have to be used?
- Do unforeseen resource dependencies exist? Is there a new critical path?
- How much flexibility do we have in using resources?
- Is the original deadline realistic?

Clearly, this project manager has a good understanding of the problems she is facing. Any project scheduling system should facilitate finding quick, easy answers to these questions.

The planned network and activity project duration times found in previous chapters fail to deal with resource usage and availability. The time estimates for the work packages and network times were made independently with the implicit assumption that resources would be available. This may or may not be the case.

If resources are adequate but the demand varies widely over the life of the project, it may be desirable to even out resource demand by delaying noncritical activities (using slack) to lower peak demand and, thus, increase resource utilization. This process is called **resource smoothing.**

On the other hand, if resources are not adequate to meet peak demands, the late start of some activities must be delayed, and the duration of the project may be increased. This process is called *resource-constrained scheduling.* One research study of more than 50 projects by Woodworth and Willie (1975) found that planned project network durations were increased 38 percent when resources were scheduled.

The consequences of failing to schedule limited resources are costly and project delays usually manifest themselves midway in the project when quick corrective action is difficult. An additional consequence of failing to schedule resources is ignoring the peaks and valleys of resource usage over the duration of the project. Because project resources are usually overcommitted and because resources seldom line up by availability and need, procedures are needed to deal with these problems. This chapter

FIGURE 8.2
Constraint Examples

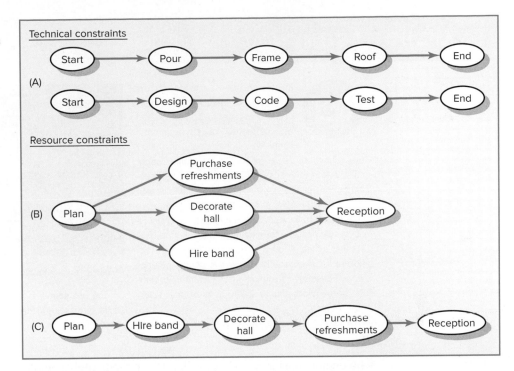

addresses methods available to project managers for dealing with resource utilization and availability through resource leveling and resource-constrained scheduling.

Up to now the start and sequence of activities has been based solely on technical or logical considerations. For example, a project network for framing a house might show three activities in a sequence: (1) pour foundation, (2) build frame, and (3) cover roof. A network for a new software project could place the activities in the network, as a sequence of (1) design, (2) code, and (3) test. In other words, you cannot logically perform activity 2 until 1 is completed, and so on. The project network depicts technical constraints (see Figure 8.2A). The network assumes the personnel and equipment are available to perform the required work. This is often not the case!

The absence or shortage of resources can drastically alter technical constraints. A project network planner may assume adequate resources and show activities occurring in parallel. However, parallel activities hold potential for resource conflicts. For example, assume you are planning a wedding reception that includes four activities—(1) plan, (2) hire band, (3) decorate hall, and (4) purchase refreshments. Each activity takes one day. Activities 2, 3, and 4 could be done in parallel by different people. There is no technical reason or dependency of one on another (see Figure 8.2B). However, if one person must perform all activities, the resource constraint requires the activities be performed in sequence or series. Clearly the consequence is a delay of these activities and a very different set of network relationships (see Figure 8.2C). Note that the resource dependency takes priority over the technological dependency but *does not violate the technological dependency;* that is, hire, decorate, and purchase may now have to take place in sequence rather than concurrently, but they must all be completed before the reception can take place.

The interrelationships and interactions among time and resource constraints are complex for even small project networks. Some effort to examine these interactions before the project begins frequently uncovers surprising problems. Project managers

SNAPSHOT FROM PRACTICE 8.1   Working in Tight Places

In rare situations, physical factors cause activities that would normally occur in parallel to be constrained by contractual or environmental conditions. For example, in theory the renovation of a sailboat compartment might involve four to five tasks that can be done independently. However, since space allows only one person to work at one time, all tasks have to be performed sequentially. Likewise, on a mining project it may be physically possible for only two miners to work in a shaft at a time. Another example would be the erection of a communication tower and nearby groundwork. For safety considerations, the contract prohibits groundwork within 2,000 feet of the tower construction.

© Getty Images/iStockphoto

The procedures for handling physical factors are similar to those used for resource constraints.

who do not consider resource availability in moderately complex projects usually learn of the problem when it is too late to correct. A deficit of resources can significantly alter project dependency relationships, completion dates, and project costs. Project managers must be careful to schedule resources to ensure availability in the right quantities and at the right time. Fortunately, there are computer software programs that can identify resource problems during the early project planning phase when corrective changes can be considered. These programs only require activity resource needs and availability information to schedule resources.

See the Snapshot from Practice 8.1: Working in Tight Places for a third constraint that impinges on project schedules.

8.2 Types of Resource Constraints

LO 8-2

Identify different types of resource constraints.

Resources are people, equipment, and material that can be drawn on to accomplish something. In projects the availability or unavailability of resources will often influence the way projects are managed.

1. People. This is the most obvious and important project resource. Human resources are usually classified by the skills they bring to the project—for example, programmer, mechanical engineer, welder, inspector, marketing director, supervisor. In rare cases some skills are interchangeable, but usually with a loss of productivity. The many differing skills of human resources add to the complexity of scheduling projects.

2. Materials. Project materials cover a large spectrum: for example, chemicals for a scientific project, concrete for a road project, survey data for a marketing project.

Material availability and shortages have been blamed for the delay of many projects. When it is known that a lack of availability of materials is important and probable, materials should be included in the project network plan and schedule. For example, delivery and placement of an oil rig tower in a Siberian oil field has a very small time window during one summer month. Any delivery delay means a one-year, costly delay.

Another example in which material was the major resource scheduled was the resurfacing and replacement of some structures on the Golden Gate Bridge in San Francisco. Work on the project was limited to the hours between midnight and 5:00 a.m. with a penalty of $1,000 per minute for any work taking place after 5:00 a.m. Scheduling the arrival of replacement structures was an extremely important part of managing the five-hour work-time window of the project. Scheduling materials has also become important in developing products where time-to-market can result in loss of market share.

3. Equipment. Equipment is usually presented by type, size, and quantity. In some cases equipment can be interchanged to improve schedules, but this is not typical. Equipment is often overlooked as a constraint. The most common oversight is to assume the resource pool is more than adequate for the project. For example, if a project needs one earthmoving tractor six months from now and the organization owns four, it is common to assume the resource will not delay the pending project. However, when the earthmoving tractor is due on-site in six months, all four machines in the pool might be occupied on other projects. In multiproject environments it is prudent to use a common resource pool for all projects. This approach forces a check of resource availability across all projects and reserves the equipment for specific project needs in the future. Recognition of equipment constraints before the project begins can avoid high crashing or delay costs.

8.3 Classification of a Scheduling Problem

Most of the scheduling methods available today require the project manager to classify the project as either *time constrained* or *resource constrained*. Project managers need to consult their priority matrix (see Figure 4.2) to determine which case fits their project. One simple test to determine if the project is time or resource constrained is to ask, "If the critical path is delayed, will resources be added to get back on schedule?" If the answer is yes, assume the project is time constrained; if no, assume the project is resource constrained.

A **time-constrained project** is one that must be completed by an imposed date. If required, resources can be added to ensure the project is completed by a specific date. Although time is the critical factor, resource usage should be no more than is necessary and sufficient.

A **resource-constrained project** is one that assumes the level of resources available cannot be exceeded. If the resources are inadequate, it will be acceptable to delay the project, but as little as possible.

In scheduling terms, time constrained means time (project duration) is fixed and resources are flexible, while resource constrained means resources are fixed and time is flexible. Methods for scheduling these projects are presented in the next section.

8.4 Resource Allocation Methods

Assumptions

Ease of demonstrating the allocation methods available requires some limiting assumptions to keep attention on the heart of the problem. The rest of the chapter depends entirely on the assumptions noted here. First, splitting activities will not be allowed. This means once an activity is placed in the schedule, assume it will be worked on continuously until it is finished; hence, an activity cannot be started, stopped for a period of time, and then finished. Second, the level of resources used for an activity cannot be changed. These limiting assumptions do not exist in practice, but simplify learning. It is easy for new project managers to deal with the reality of splitting activities and changing the level of resources when they meet them on the job.

LO 8-3

Describe how the smoothing approach is used on time-constrained projects.

Time-Constrained Projects: Smoothing Resource Demand

Scheduling time-constrained projects focuses on resource *utilization*. When demand for a specific resource type is erratic, it is difficult to manage, and utilization may be very poor. Practitioners have attacked the utilization problem using resource leveling techniques that balance demand for a resource. Basically, all **leveling** techniques delay noncritical activities by using positive slack to reduce peak demand and fill in the valleys for the resources. An example will demonstrate the basic procedure for a time-constrained project. See Figure 8.3.

For the purpose of demonstration, the Botanical Garden project uses only one resource (backhoes); all backhoes are interchangeable. The top bar chart shows the activities on a time scale. The dependencies are shown with the vertical connecting

FIGURE 8.3 **Botanical Garden**

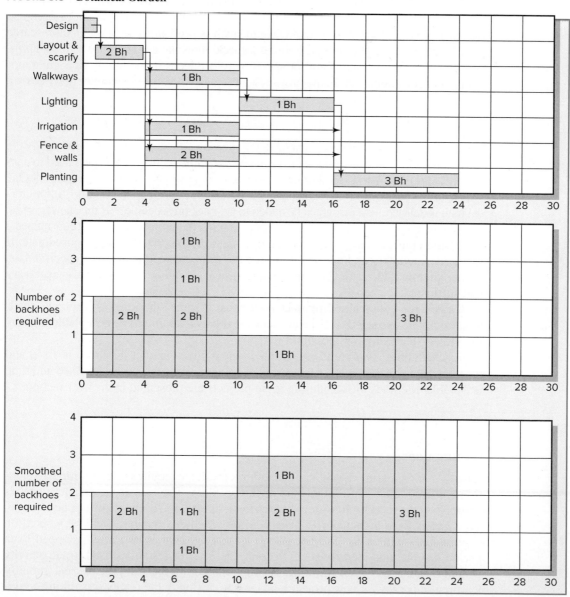

arrows. The horizontal arrows following activities represent activity slack (for example, irrigation requires six days to complete and has six days slack). The number of backhoes needed for each task is shown in the shaded activity duration block (rectangle). After the land has been scarified and the plan laid out, work can begin on the walkways, irrigation, and fencing and retaining walls simultaneously. The middle chart shows the resource profile for the backhoes. For periods 4 through 10, four backhoes are needed.

Because this project is declared time constrained, the goal will be to reduce the peak requirement for the resource and thereby increase the utilization of the resource. A quick examination of the ES (early start) resource load chart suggests only two activities have slack that can be used to reduce the peak—fence and walls provide the best choice for smoothing the resource needs. Another choice could be irrigation, but it would result in an up and down resource profile. The choice will probably center on the activity that is perceived as having the least risk of being late. The smoothed resource loading chart shows the results of delaying the fence and walls activity. Note the differences in the resource profiles. The important point is the resources needed over the life of the project have been reduced from four to three (25 percent). In addition the profile has been smoothed, which should be easier to manage.

The Botanical Garden project schedule reached the three goals of smoothing:

- The peak of demand for the resource was reduced.
- The number of resources over the life of the project have been reduced.
- The fluctuations in resource demand were minimized.

The latter improves the utilization of resources. Backhoes are not easily moved from location to location. There are costs associated with changing the level of resources needed. The same analogy applies to the movement of people back and forth among projects. It is well known that people are more efficient if they can focus their effort on one project rather than multitasking their time among, say, three projects.

The downside of leveling is a loss of flexibility that occurs from reducing slack. The risk of activities delaying the project also increases because slack reduction can create more critical activities and/or near-critical activities. Pushing leveling too far for a perfectly level resource profile is risky. Every activity then becomes critical.

The Botanical Garden example gives a sense of the time-constrained problem and the smoothing approach. However, in practice the magnitude of the problem is very complex for even small projects. Manual solutions are not practical. Fortunately, the software packages available today have very good routines for leveling project resources. Typically, they use activities that have the most slack to level project resources. The rationale is those activities with the most slack pose the least risk. Although this is generally true, other risk factors such as reduction of flexibility to use reassigned resources on other activities or the nature of the activity (easy, complex) are not addressed using such a simple rationale. It is easy to experiment with many alternatives to find the one that best fits your project and minimizes risk of delaying the project.

Resource-Constrained Projects

LO 8-4

Describe how leveling approach is used for resource-constrained projects.

When the number of people and/or equipment is not adequate to meet peak demand requirements and it is impossible to obtain more, the project manager faces a resource-constrained problem. Something has to give. The trick is to prioritize and allocate resources to minimize project delay without exceeding the resource limit or altering the technical network relationships.

FIGURE 8.6 EMR Project Network View Schedule before Resources Leveled

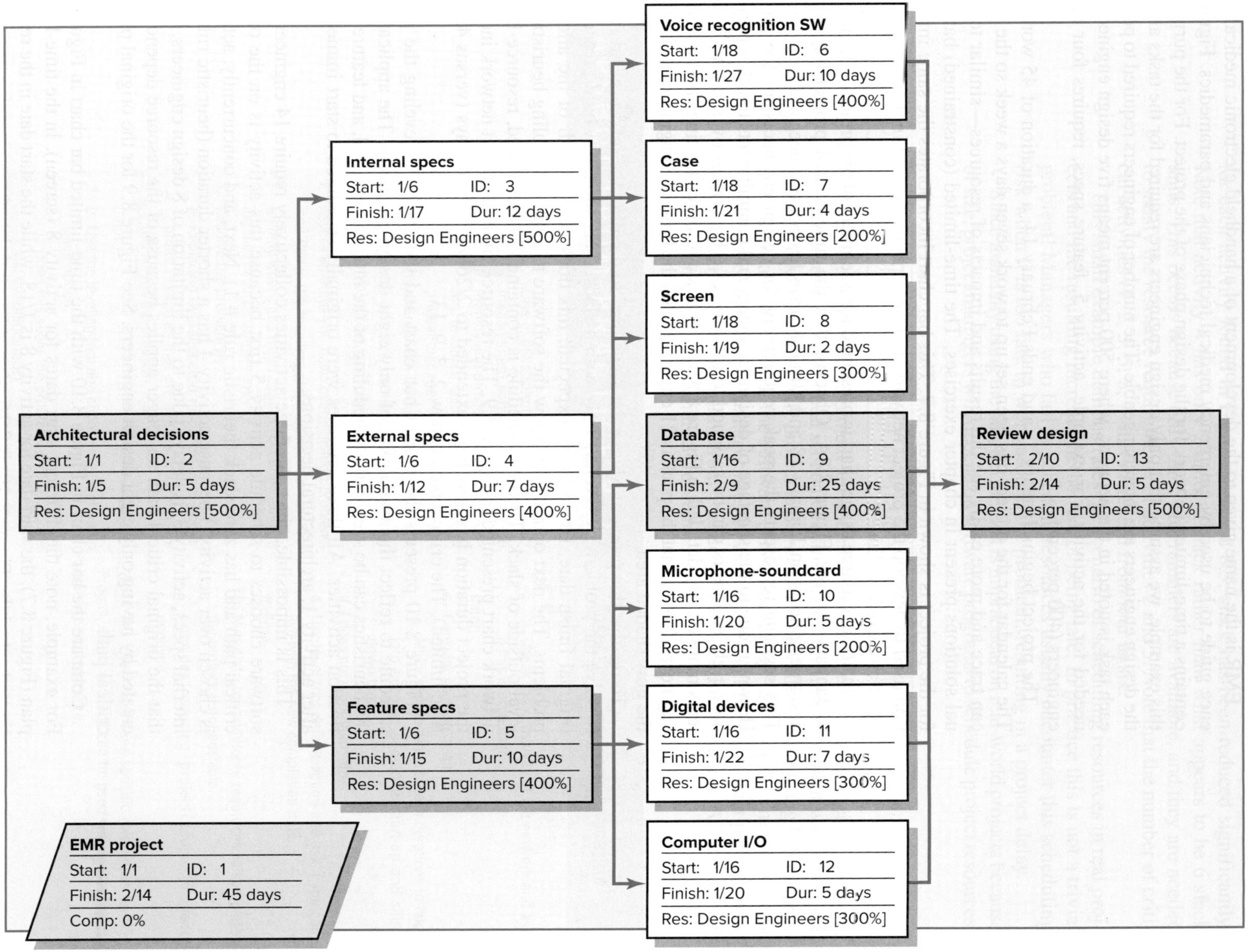

EMR project
Start: 1/1   ID: 1
Finish: 2/14   Dur: 45 days
Comp: 0%

Architectural decisions
Start: 1/1   ID: 2
Finish: 1/5   Dur: 5 days
Res: Design Engineers [500%]

Internal specs
Start: 1/6   ID: 3
Finish: 1/17   Dur: 12 days
Res: Design Engineers [500%]

External specs
Start: 1/6   ID: 4
Finish: 1/12   Dur: 7 days
Res: Design Engineers [400%]

Feature specs
Start: 1/6   ID: 5
Finish: 1/15   Dur: 10 days
Res: Design Engineers [400%]

Voice recognition SW
Start: 1/18   ID: 6
Finish: 1/27   Dur: 10 days
Res: Design Engineers [400%]

Case
Start: 1/18   ID: 7
Finish: 1/21   Dur: 4 days
Res: Design Engineers [200%]

Screen
Start: 1/18   ID: 8
Finish: 1/19   Dur: 2 days
Res: Design Engineers [300%]

Database
Start: 1/16   ID: 9
Finish: 2/9   Dur: 25 days
Res: Design Engineers [400%]

Microphone-soundcard
Start: 1/16   ID: 10
Finish: 1/20   Dur: 5 days
Res: Design Engineers [200%]

Digital devices
Start: 1/16   ID: 11
Finish: 1/22   Dur: 7 days
Res: Design Engineers [300%]

Computer I/O
Start: 1/16   ID: 12
Finish: 1/20   Dur: 5 days
Res: Design Engineers [300%]

Review design
Start: 2/10   ID: 13
Finish: 2/14   Dur: 5 days
Res: Design Engineers [500%]

FIGURE 8.7 EMR Project before Resources Added

ID	Task Name	Start	Finish	Late Start	Late Finish	Free Slack	Total Slack
1	**EMR project**	**Tue 1/1**	**Thu 2/14**	**Tue 1/1**	**Thu 2/14**	**0 days**	**0 days**
2	Architectural decisions	Tue 1/1	Sat 1/5	Tue 1/1	Sat 1/5	0 days	0 days
3	Internal specs	Sun 1/6	Thu 1/17	Sat 1/19	Wed 1/30	0 days	13 days
4	External specs	Sun 1/6	Sat 1/12	Thu 1/24	Wed 1/30	5 days	18 days
5	Feature specs	Sun 1/6	Tue 1/15	Sun 1/6	Tue 1/15	0 days	0 days
6	Voice recognition SW	Fri 1/18	Sun 1/27	Thu 1/31	Sat 2/9	13 days	13 days
7	Case	Fri 1/18	Mon 1/21	Wed 2/6	Sat 2/9	19 days	19 days
8	Screen	Fri 1/18	Sat 1/19	Fri 2/8	Sat 2/9	21 days	21 days
9	Database	Wed 1/16	Sat 2/9	Wed 1/16	Sat 2/9	0 days	0 days
10	Microphone-soundcard	Wed 1/16	Sun 1/20	Tue 2/5	Sat 2/9	20 days	20 days
11	Digital devices	Wed 1/16	Tue 1/22	Sun 2/3	Sat 2/9	18 days	18 days
12	Computer I/O	Wed 1/16	Sun 1/20	Tue 2/5	Sat 2/9	20 days	20 days
13	Review design	Sun 2/10	Thu 2/14	Sun 2/10	Thu 2/14	0 days	0 days

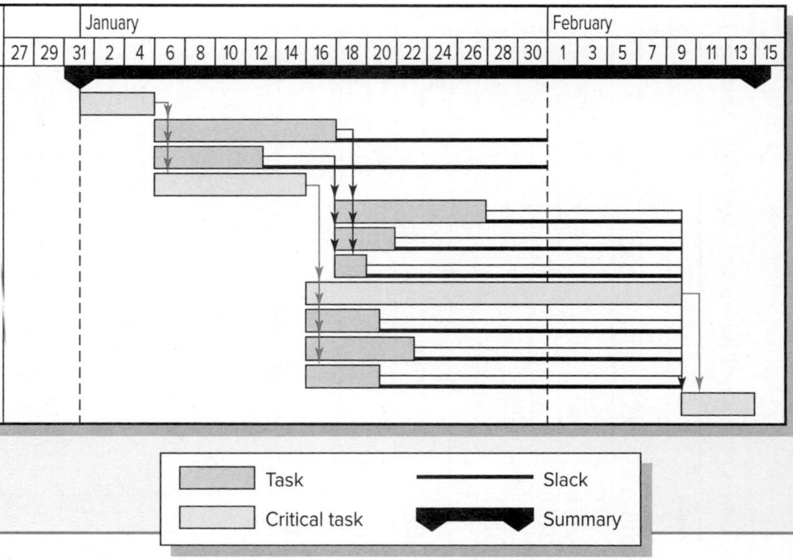

265

FIGURE 8.8A   EMR Project—Time-Constrained Resource Usage View, January 15–23

Resource Name	Work	Jan 15						Jan 21		
		T	W	T	F	S	S	M	T	W
Design engineers	**3,024 hrs**	72h	136h	136h	168h	168h	144h	104h	88h	64h
Architectural decisions	200 hrs									
Internal specs	480 hrs	40h	40h	40h						
External specs	224 hrs									
Feature specs	320 hrs	32h								
Voice recognition SW	320 hrs				32h	32h	32h	32h	32h	32h
Case	64 hrs				16h	16h	16h	16h		
Screen	48 hrs				24h	24h				
Database	800 hrs		32h	32h	32h	32h	32h	32h	32h	32h
Microphone-soundcard	80 hrs		16h	16h	16h	16h	16h			
Digital devices	168 hrs		24h	24h	24h	24h	24h	24h	24h	
Computer I/O	120 hrs		24h	24h	24h	24h	24h			
Review design	200 hrs									

FIGURE 8.8B
Resource Loading
Chart for
EMR Project,
January 15–23

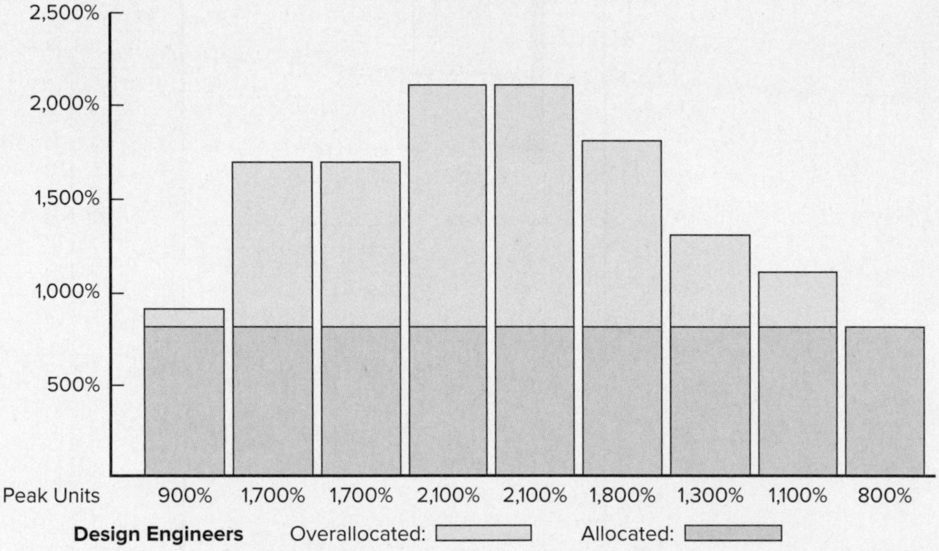

Peak Units	900%	1,700%	1,700%	2,100%	2,100%	1,800%	1,300%	1,100%	800%

Design Engineers   Overallocated: ▭   Allocated: ▭

While resource bar graphs are commonly used to illustrate overallocation problems, we prefer to view resource usage tables like the one presented in Figure 8.8A. This table tells you when you have an overallocation problem and identifies activities that are causing the overallocation.

The Impacts of Resource-Constrained Scheduling

Like leveling schedules, the limited resource schedule usually reduces slack, reduces flexibility by using slack to ensure delay is minimized, and increases the number of critical and near-critical activities. Scheduling complexity is increased because resource constraints are added to technical constraints; start times may now have two constraints. The traditional critical path concept of sequential activities from the start to the end of the project is no longer meaningful. The resource constraints can break the sequence and leave the network with a set of disjointed critical activities.[1]

[1] See the appendix at the end of this chapter for more on how resource constraints affect project schedule.

FIGURE 8.9 EMR Project Network View Schedule after Resources Leveled

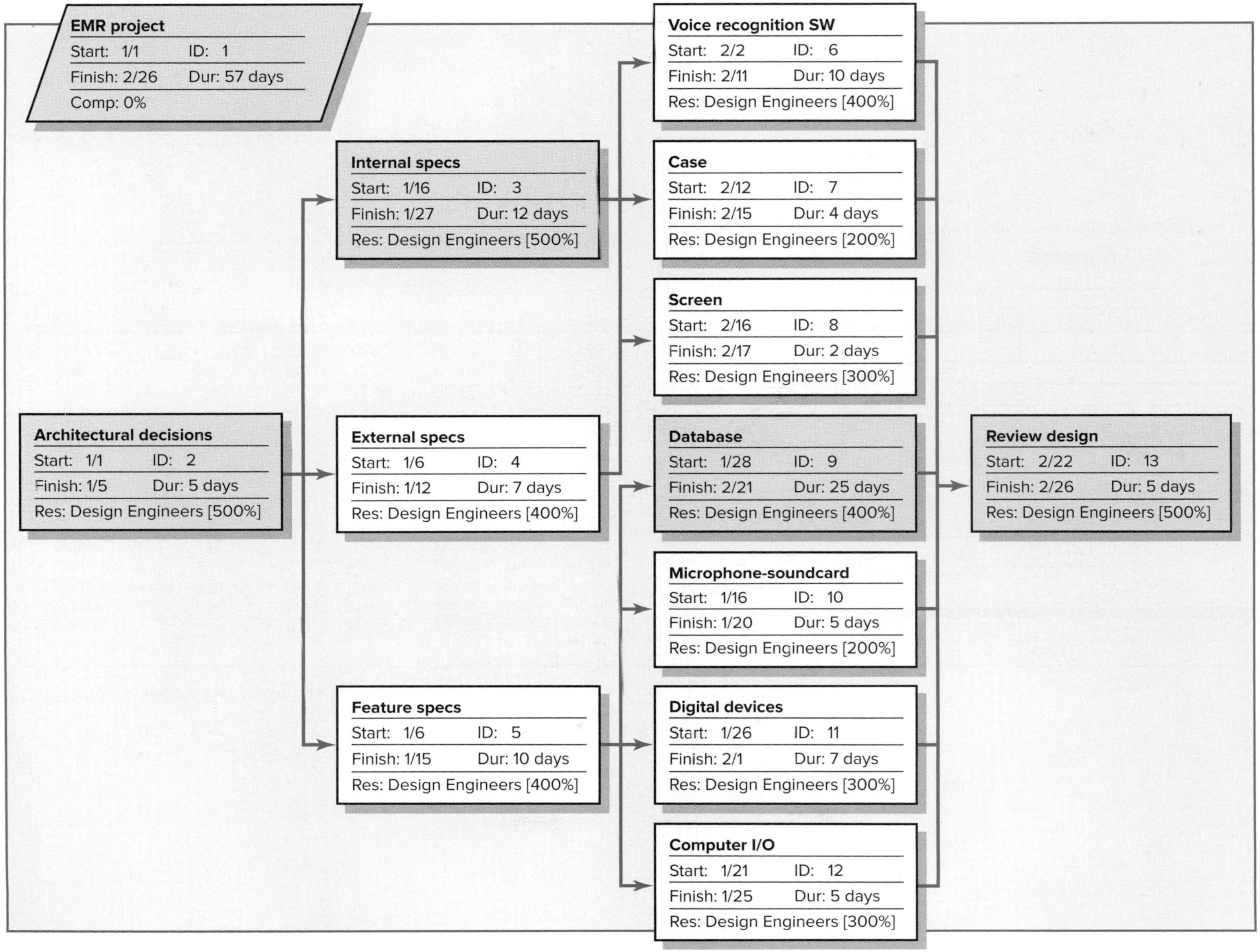

EMR project

Start: 1/1	ID: 1
Finish: 2/26	Dur: 57 days
Comp: 0%	

Internal specs

Start: 1/16	ID: 3
Finish: 1/27	Dur: 12 days
Res: Design Engineers [500%]	

External specs

Start: 1/6	ID: 4
Finish: 1/12	Dur: 7 days
Res: Design Engineers [400%]	

Feature specs

Start: 1/6	ID: 5
Finish: 1/15	Dur: 10 days
Res: Design Engineers [400%]	

Architectural decisions

Start: 1/1	ID: 2
Finish: 1/5	Dur: 5 days
Res: Design Engineers [500%]	

Voice recognition SW

Start: 2/2	ID: 6
Finish: 2/11	Dur: 10 days
Res: Design Engineers [400%]	

Case

Start: 2/12	ID: 7
Finish: 2/15	Dur: 4 days
Res: Design Engineers [200%]	

Screen

Start: 2/16	ID: 8
Finish: 2/17	Dur: 2 days
Res: Design Engineers [300%]	

Database

Start: 1/28	ID: 9
Finish: 2/21	Dur: 25 days
Res: Design Engineers [400%]	

Microphone-soundcard

Start: 1/16	ID: 10
Finish: 1/20	Dur: 5 days
Res: Design Engineers [200%]	

Digital devices

Start: 1/26	ID: 11
Finish: 2/1	Dur: 7 days
Res: Design Engineers [300%]	

Computer I/O

Start: 1/21	ID: 12
Finish: 1/25	Dur: 5 days
Res: Design Engineers [300%]	

Review design

Start: 2/22	ID: 13
Finish: 2/26	Dur: 5 days
Res: Design Engineers [500%]	

FIGURE 8.10 EMR Project Resources Leveled

ID	Task Name	Start	Finish	Late Start	Late Finish	Free Slack	Total Slack
1	**EMR project**	**Tue 1/1**	**Thu 2/26**	**Tue 1/1**	**Tue 2/26**	**0 days**	**0 days**
2	Architectural decisions	Tue 1/1	Sat 1/5	Tue 1/1	Sat 1/5	0 days	0 days
3	Internal specs	Wed 1/16	Sun 1/27	Sun 1/20	Thu 1/31	0 days	4 days
4	External specs	Sun 1/6	Sat 1/12	Fri 1/25	Thu 1/31	15 days	19 days
5	Feature specs	Sun 1/6	Tue 1/15	Sun 1/6	Tue 1/15	0 days	0 days
6	Voice recognition SW	Sat 2/2	Mon 2/11	Tue 2/12	Thu 2/21	10 days	10 days
7	Case	Tue 2/12	Fri 2/15	Mon 2/18	Thu 2/21	6 days	6 days
8	Screen	Sat 2/16	Sun 2/17	Wed 2/20	Thu 2/21	4 days	4 days
9	Database	Mon 1/28	Thu 2/21	Mon 1/28	Thu 2/21	0 days	0 days
10	Microphone-soundcard	Wed 1/16	Sun 1/20	Sun 2/17	Thu 2/21	32 days	32 days
11	Digital devices	Sat 1/26	Fri 2/1	Fri 2/15	Thu 2/21	20 days	20 days
12	Computer I/O	Mon 1/21	Fri 1/25	Sun 2/17	Thu 2/21	27 days	27 days
13	Review design	Fri 2/22	Tue 2/26	Fri 2/22	Tue 2/26	0 days	0 days

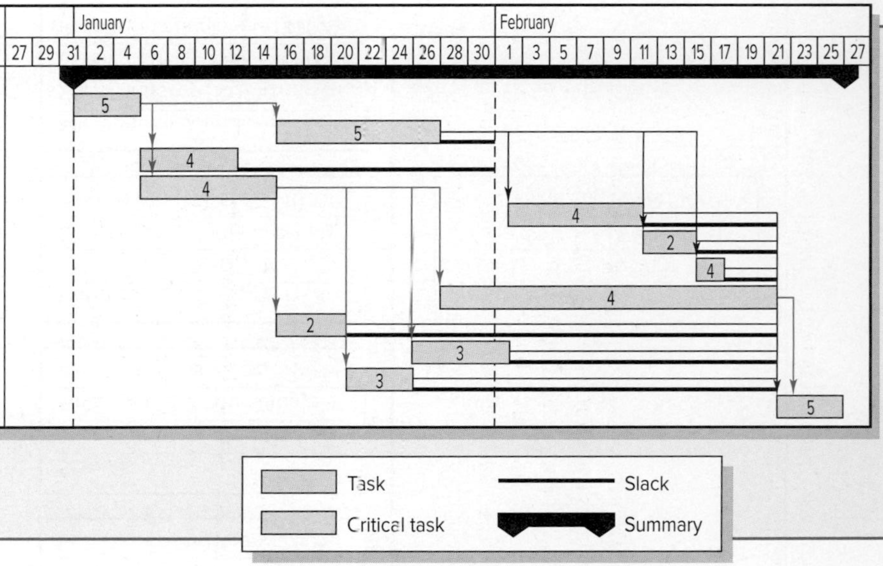

Conversely, parallel activities can become sequential. Activities with slack on a time-constrained network can change from critical to noncritical.

8.6 Splitting Activities

LO 8-6

Understand when and why splitting tasks should be avoided.

Splitting tasks is a scheduling technique used to get a better project schedule and/or to increase resource utilization. A planner splits the continuous work included in an activity by interrupting the work and sending the resource to another activity for a period of time and then having the resource resume work on the original activity. Splitting can be a useful tool if the work involved does not include large start-up or shutdown costs—for example, moving equipment from one activity location to another. The most common error is to interrupt "people work," where there are high conceptual start-up and shutdown costs. For example, having a bridge designer take time off to work on the design problem of another project may cause this individual to lose four days shifting conceptual gears in and out of two activities. The cost may be hidden, but it is real. Figure 8.11 depicts the nature of the splitting problem. The original activity has been split into three separate activities: A, B, and C. The shutdown and start-up times lengthen the time for the original activity. One study reported that task switching can cost from 20 percent to 40 percent loss in efficiency (Rubinstein, Meyer, and Evans, 2001).

Some have argued that the propensity to deal with resource shortages by splitting is a major reason why projects fail to meet schedule (c.f., Goldratt, 1997; Newbold, 1997). We agree. Planners should avoid the use of splitting as much as possible, except in situations where splitting costs are known to be small or when there is no alternative for resolving the resource problem. Computer software offers the splitting option for each activity; use it sparingly. See Snapshot from Practice 8.2: Assessing Resource Allocation.

FIGURE 8.11
Splitting Activities

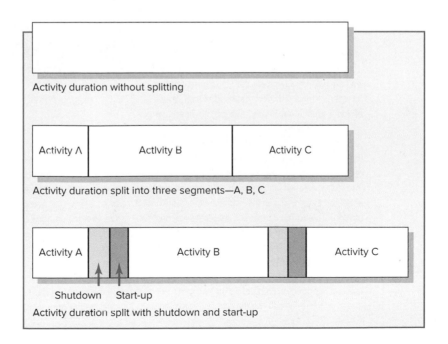

Activity duration without splitting

| Activity A | Activity B | Activity C |

Activity duration split into three segments—A, B, C

| Activity A | Activity B | Activity C |

Shutdown   Start-up

Activity duration split with shutdown and start-up

8.7 Benefits of Scheduling Resources

It is important to remember that, if resources are truly limited and activity time estimates are accurate, the resource-constrained schedule *will* materialize as the project is implemented—*not* the time-constrained schedule! Therefore, failure to schedule limited resources can lead to serious problems for a project manager. The benefit of creating this schedule *before* the project begins leaves time for considering reasonable alternatives. If the scheduled delay is unacceptable or the risk of being delayed too high, the assumption of being resource constrained can be reassessed. Cost-time trade-offs can be considered. In some cases priorities may be changed. See Snapshot from Practice 8.3: U.S. Forest Service Resource Shortage.

Resource schedules provide the information needed to prepare time-phased work package budgets with dates. Once established, they provide a quick means for a project manager to gauge the impact of unforeseen events such as turnover, equipment breakdowns, or transfer of project personnel. Resource schedules also allow project managers to assess how much flexibility they have over certain resources. This is useful when they receive requests from other managers to borrow or share resources. Honoring such requests creates goodwill and an "IOU" that can be cashed in during a time of need.

SNAPSHOT FROM PRACTICE 8.3 — U.S. Forest Service Resource Shortage

A major segment of work in managing U.S. Forest Service (USFS) forests is selling mature timber to logging companies that harvest the timber under contract conditions monitored by the Service. The proceeds are returned to the federal government. The budget allocated to each forest depends on the two-year plan submitted to the U.S. Department of Agriculture.

Olympic Forest headquarters in Olympia, Washington, was developing a two-year plan as a basis for funding. All of the districts in the forest submitted their timber sale projects (numbering more than 50) to headquarters, where they were compiled and aggregated into a project plan for the whole forest. The first computer run was reviewed by a small group of senior managers to determine if the plan was reasonable and "doable." Management was pleased and relieved to note all projects appeared to be doable in the two-year time frame until a question was raised concerning the computer printout. "Why are all the columns in these projects labeled 'RESOURCE' blank?" The response from an engineer was, "We don't use that part of the program."

The discussion that ensued recognized the importance of resources in completing the two-year plan and ended with a request to "try the program with resources

© Seth Lazar/Alamy

included." The new output was startling. The two-year program turned into a three-and-a-half-year plan because of the shortage of specific labor skills such as road engineer and environmental impact specialist. Analysis showed that adding only three skilled people would allow the two-year plan to be completed on time. In addition, further analysis showed hiring only a few more skilled people, beyond the three, would allow an extra year of projects to also be compressed into the two-year plan. This would result in additional revenue of more than $3 million. The Department of Agriculture quickly approved the requested extra dollars for additional staff to generate the extra revenue.

8.8 Assigning Project Work

LO 8-7

Identify general guidelines for assigning people to specific tasks.

When making individual assignments, project managers should match, as best they can, the demands and requirements of specific work with the qualifications and experience of available participants. In doing so, there is a natural tendency to assign the best people the most difficult tasks. Project managers need to be careful not to overdo this. Over time these people may grow to resent the fact that they are always given the toughest assignments. At the same time, less experienced participants may resent the fact that they are never given the opportunity to expand their skill/knowledge base. Project managers need to balance task performance with the need to develop the talents of people assigned to the project.

Project managers not only need to decide who does what but who works with whom. A number of factors need to be considered in deciding who should work together. First, to minimize unnecessary tension, managers should pick people with compatible work habits and personalities but who complement each other (i.e., one person's weakness is the other person's strength). For example, one person may be brilliant at solving complex problems but sloppy at documenting his or her progress. It would be wise to pair this person with an individual who is good at paying attention to details. Experience is another factor. Veterans should be teamed up with new hires—not only so they can share their experience but also to help socialize the newcomers to the customs and norms of the organization. Finally, future needs should be considered. If managers have some people who have never worked together before but who have to later on in the project, they may be wise to take advantage of opportunities to have these people work together early on so that they can become familiar with each other. Finally, see the Snapshot in Practice 8.4: Managing Geeks for some interesting thoughts from the former CEO of Google on how to put together teams.

SNAPSHOT FROM PRACTICE 8.4   Managing Geeks*

Eric Schmidt, after a successful career at Sun Microsystems, took over struggling Novell, Inc., and helped turn it around within two years. Four years later he became the CEO of Google. One of the keys to his success is his ability to manage the technical wizards who develop the sophisticated systems, hardware, and software that are the backbone of electronically driven companies. He uses the term "geek" (and he can, since he is one, with a Ph.D. in computer science) to describe this group of technologists who rule the cyberworld.

Schmidt has some interesting ideas about assigning geeks to projects. He believes that putting geeks together in project teams with other geeks creates productive peer pressure. Geeks care a great deal about how other geeks perceive them. They are good at judging the quality of technical work and are quick to praise as well as criticize each other's work. Some geeks can be unbearably arrogant, but Schmidt claims that having them work together on projects is the best way to control them—by letting them control each other.

At the same time, Schmidt argues that too many geeks spoil the soup. By this he means that, when there are too many geeks on a development team, there is a tendency for intense technical navel gazing. Members lose sight of deadlines, and delays are inevitable. To combat this tendency, he recommends using geeks only in small groups. He urges breaking up large projects into smaller, more manageable projects so that small teams of geeks can be assigned to them. This keeps the project on time and makes the teams responsible to each other.

*Russ Mitchell, "How to Manage Geeks," *Fast Company*, May 31, 1999, pp. 175–80.

8.9 Multiproject Resource Schedules

LO 8-8

Identify common problems with multiproject resource scheduling.

For clarity we have discussed key resource allocation issues within the context of a single project. In reality resource allocation generally occurs in a multiproject environment where the demands of one project have to be reconciled with the needs of other projects. Organizations must develop and manage systems for efficiently allocating and scheduling resources across several projects with different priorities, resource requirements, sets of activities, and risks. The system must be dynamic and capable of accommodating new projects as well as reallocating resources once project work is completed. While the same resource issues and principles that apply to a single project also apply to this multiproject environment, application and solutions are more complex, given the interdependency among projects.

The following lists three of the more common problems encountered in managing multiproject resource schedules. Note that these are macro manifestations of single-project problems that are now magnified in a multiproject environment:

1. **Overall schedule slippage.** Because projects often share resources, delays in one project can have a ripple effect and delay other projects. For example, work on one software development project can grind to a halt because the coders scheduled for the next critical task are late in completing their work on another development project.

2. **Inefficient resource utilization.** Because projects have different schedules and requirements, there are peaks and valleys in overall resource demands. For example, a firm may have a staff of 10 electricians to meet peak demands when, under normal conditions, only 5 electricians are required.

3. **Resource bottlenecks.** Delays and schedules are extended as a result of shortages of critical resources that are required by multiple projects. For example, at one Lattice Semiconductor facility, project schedules were delayed because of competition over access to test equipment necessary to debug programs. Likewise, several projects at a U.S. forest area were extended because there was only one silviculturist on the staff.

To deal with these problems, more and more companies create project offices or departments to oversee the scheduling of resources across multiple projects. One approach to multiple project resource scheduling is to use a first come–first served rule. A project queue system is created in which projects currently under way take precedence over new projects. New project schedules are based on the projected availability of resources. This queuing tends to lead to more reliable completion estimates and is preferred on contracted projects that have stiff penalties for being late. The disadvantages of this deceptively simple approach are that it does not optimally utilize resources or take into account the priority of the project. See the Snapshot from Practice 8.5: Multiple Project Resource Scheduling.

Many companies utilize more elaborate processes for scheduling resources to increase the capacity of the organization to initiate projects. Most of these methods approach the problem by treating individual projects as part of one big project and adapting the scheduling heuristics previously introduced to this "megaproject." Project schedulers monitor resource usage and provide updated schedules based on progress and resource availability across all projects. One major improvement in project management software in recent years is the ability to prioritize resource allocation to specific projects. Projects can be prioritized in ascending order (e.g., 1, 2, 3, 4,…), and these priorities will override scheduling heuristics so that resources go to the project highest on the priority list. (Note: This improvement fits perfectly with organizations that use project priority models similar to those described in Chapter 2.) Centralized project scheduling also makes it easier to identify resource bottlenecks that stifle progress on projects. Once identified, the impact

SNAPSHOT FROM PRACTICE 8.5

Multiple Project Resource Scheduling

The case for a central source to oversee project resource scheduling is well known by practitioners. Here is a synopsis of a conversation with one middle manager.

Interviewer: Congratulations on acceptance of your multiproject scheduling proposal. Everyone tells me you were very convincing.

Middle Manager: Thanks. Gaining acceptance was easy this time. The board quickly recognized we have no choice if we are to keep ahead of competition by placing our resources on the right projects.

Interviewer: Have you presented this to the board before?

Middle Manager: Yes, but not this company. I presented the same spiel to the firm I worked for two years ago. For their annual review meeting I was charged to present a proposal suggesting the need and benefits of central capacity resource planning for managing the projects of the firm.

I tried to build a case for bringing projects under one umbrella to standardize practices and to forecast and assign key people to mission critical projects. I explained how benefits such as resource demands would be aligned with mission critical projects, proactive resource planning, and a tool for catching resource bottlenecks and resolving conflicts.

Almost everyone agreed the idea was a good one. I felt good about the presentation and felt confident something was going to happen. But the idea never really got off the ground; it just faded into the sunset.

With hindsight, managers really did not trust colleagues in other departments, so they only gave half-hearted support to central resource planning. Managers wanted to protect their turf and ensure that they would not have to give up power. The culture there was simply too inflexible for the world we live in today. They are still struggling with constant conflicts among projects.

I'm glad I made the switch to this firm. The culture here is much more team-oriented. Management is committed to improving performance.

of the bottlenecks can be documented and used to justify acquiring additional equipment, recruiting critical personnel, or delaying the project.

Finally, many companies are using outsourcing as a means for dealing with their resource allocation problems. In some cases, a company will reduce the number of projects they have to manage internally to only core projects and outsource noncritical projects to contractors and consulting firms. In other cases, specific segments of projects are outsourced to overcome resource deficiencies and scheduling problems. Companies may hire temporary workers to expedite certain activities that are falling behind schedule or contract project work during peak periods when there are insufficient internal resources to meet the demands of all projects. The ability to more efficiently manage the ebbs and flows of project work is one of the major driving forces behind outsourcing today.

8.10 Using the Resource Schedule to Develop a Project Cost Baseline

Once resource assignments have been finalized we are able to develop a baseline budget schedule for the project. Using your project schedule, you can *time-phase* work packages and assign them to their respective scheduled activities to develop a budget schedule over the life of your project. Understanding the reason for time-phasing your budget is very important. Without a time-phased budget good project schedule and cost control are impossible.

LO 8-9

Explain why a time-phased budget baseline is needed.

Why a Time-Phased Budget Baseline Is Needed

The need for a **time-phased budget baseline** is demonstrated in the following scenario. The development of a new product is to be completed in 10 weeks at an estimated cost

FIGURE 8.14
Two Time-Phased Work Packages (labor cost only)

Time-Phased Work Package Budget
Labor cost only

Work Package Description ___Software___   Page ____1____ of ____1____

Work Package ID **1.1.3.2.4.1 and 1.1.3.2.4.2**   Project _____PC Prototype_____

Deliverable _____Circuit board_____   Date _____3/24/xx_____

Responsible organization unit _Software_   Estimator _____LGG_____

Work Package Duration ___4___ weeks   Total labor cost _$180,000_

Time-Phased Labor Budget ($000)

Work Package	Resource	Labor rate	Work Periods--Weeks					
			1	2	3	4	5	Total
Code 1.1.3.2.4.1	Program'rs	$2,000/ week	$20	$15	$15			$50
Integration 1.1.3.2.4.2	System/ program'rs	$2,500/ week			$60	$70		$130
Total			$20	$15	$75	$70		$180

activity and the process of distributing costs is relatively simple. That is, the relationship is one-for-one. Such budget timing is directly from the work package to the activity.

In a few instances an activity will include more than one work package, where the packages are assigned to *one responsible person or department and deliverable*. In this case the work packages are consolidated into one activity. As seen in Figure 8.14, this activity includes two WPs. The first, WP-1.1.3.2.4.1 (Code), is distributed over the first three weeks. The second, WP-1.1.3.2.4.2 (Integration), is sequenced over weeks 3 and 4. The activity duration is four weeks. When the activity is placed in the schedule, the costs are distributed starting with the schedule start—$20,000, $15,000, $75,000, and $70,000, respectively.

These time-phased budgets for work packages are lifted from your WBS and are placed in your project schedule as they are expected to occur over the life of the project. The outcome of these budget allocations is the project *cost* baseline (also called **planned value—PV**), which is used to determine cost and schedule variances as the project is implemented.

Figure 8.15 shows the Patient Entry Project network schedule, which is used to place the time-phased work packages' budgets in the baseline. Figure 8.16 presents the project time-phased budget for the Patient Entry Project and the cumulative graph of the project budget baseline. In this figure you can see how the time-phased work package costs were placed into the network and how the cumulative project budget graph for a project is developed. Notice that costs do not have to be distributed linearly, but the costs should be placed as you expect them to occur.

You have now developed complete time and cost plans for your project. These project baselines will be used to compare planned schedule and costs using an integrative system called *earned value*. The application and use of project baselines to measure performance are discussed in detail in Chapter 13. With your project budget baseline established, you are also able to generate cash flow statements for your project like the one presented in Figure 8.17. Such statements prepare the firm to cover costs over the lifespan of the project. Finally, with resource assignments finalized you are able to generate resource usage schedules for your project (see Figure 8.18). These schedules map out the full deployment of personnel and equipment and can be used to generate individual work schedules.

FIGURE 8.15   **Patient Entry Project Network**

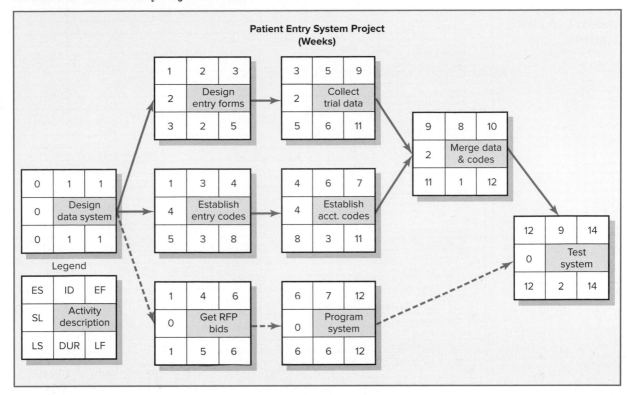

FIGURE 8.16
Patient Entry Time-Phased Work Packages Assigned

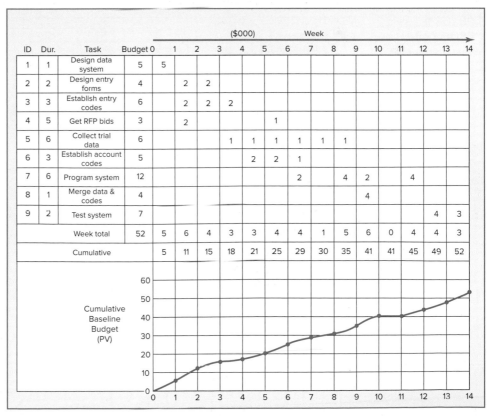

FIGURE 8.17
CEBOO Project Monthly Cash Flow Statement

	January	February	March	April	May	June	July
CEBOO Project							
Hardware							
Hardware specifications	$11,480.00	$24,840.00	$3,360.00				
Hardware design			$23,120.00	$29,920.00	$14,960.00		
Hardware documentation					$14,080.00	$24,320.00	
Prototypes							
Order GXs							
Assemble preproduction models							
Operating system							
Kernel specifications	$5,320.00	$9,880.00					
Drivers							
OC drivers				$3,360.00	$12,320.00	$11,760.00	$12,880.00
Serial VO drivers							
Memory management							
Operating system documentation		$10,240.00	$21,760.00				
Network interface							
Utilities							
Utilities specifications				$8,400.00			
Routine utilities				$5,760.00	$21,120.00	$20,160.00	$10,560.00
Complex utilities							
Utilities documentation				$7,680.00	$17,920.00		
Shell							
System integration							
Architectural decisions	$20,400.00						
Integration first phase							
System H/S test							
Project documentation							
Integration acceptance test							
Total	$37,200.00	$44,960.00	$48,240.00	$55,120.00	$80,400.00	$56,240.00	$23,440.00

FIGURE 8.18
CEBOO Project Weekly Resource Usage Schedule

	12/30	1/6	1/13	1/20	1/27	2/03
I. Suzuki	24 hrs	40 hrs	40 hrs	40 hrs	40 hrs	40 hrs
Hardware specifications				24 hrs	40 hrs	40 hrs
Hardware design						
Hardware documentation						
Operating system documentation						
Utilities documentation						
Architectural decisions	24 hrs	40 hrs	40 hrs	16 hrs		
J. Lopez	24 hrs	40 hrs	40 hrs	40 hrs	40 hrs	40 hrs
Hardware specifications				12 hrs	20 hrs	20 hrs
Hardware design						
Prototypes						
Kernel specifications				12 hrs	20 hrs	20 hrs
Utilities specifications						
Architectural decisions	24 hrs	40 hrs	40 hrs	16 hrs		
Integration first phase						
J.J. Putz				24 hrs	40 hrs	40 hrs
Hardware documentation						
Kernel specifications				24 hrs	40 hrs	40 hrs
Operating system documentation						
Utilities documentation						
Project documentation						
R. Sexon				24 hrs	40 hrs	40 hrs
Hardware specifications				24 hrs	40 hrs	40 hrs
Prototypes						
Assemble preproduction models						
OC drivers						
Complex utilities						
Integration first phase						
System H/S test						
Integration acceptance test						

Summary

Usage and availability of resources are major problem areas for project managers. Attention to these areas in developing a project schedule can point out resource bottlenecks before the project begins. Project managers should understand the ramifications of failing to schedule resources. The results of resource scheduling are frequently significantly different from the results of the standard CPM method.

With the rapid changes in technology and emphasis on time-to-market, catching resource usage and availability problems before the project starts can save the costs of crashing project activities later. Any resource deviations from plan and schedule that occur when the project is being implemented can be quickly recorded and the effect noted. Without this immediate update capability, the real negative effect of a change may not be known until it happens. Tying resource availability to a multiproject, multiresource system supports a project priority process that selects projects by their contribution to the organization's objectives and strategic plan.

Assignment of individuals to projects may not fit well with those assigned by computer software routines. In these cases overriding the computer solution to accommodate individual differences and skills is almost always the best choice.

The project resource schedule is important because it serves as your time baseline, which is used for measuring time differences between plan and actual. The resource schedule serves as the basis for developing your time-phased project cost budget baseline. The baseline (planned value, PV) is the sum of the cost accounts, and each cost account is the sum of the work packages in the cost account. Remember, if your budgeted costs are not time-phased, you really have no reliable way to measure performance. Although there are several types of project costs, the cost baseline is usually limited to direct costs (such as labor, materials, equipment) that are under the control of the project manager; other indirect costs can be added to project costs separately.

Key Terms

Heuristics, *258*
Leveling, *256*
Planned value (PV), *276*

Resource-constrained project, *255*
Resource smoothing, *252*
Splitting, *269*

Time-constrained project, *255*
Time-phased budget baseline, *273*

Review Questions

1. How does resource scheduling tie to project priority?
2. How does resource scheduling reduce flexibility in managing projects?
3. Present six reasons scheduling resources is an important task.
4. How can outsourcing project work alleviate the three most common problems associated with multiproject resource scheduling?
5. Explain the risks associated with leveling resources, compressing or crashing projects, and imposed durations or "catch-up" as the project is being implemented.
6. Why is it critical to develop a time-phased baseline?

Exercises

1. Given the network plan that follows, compute the early, late, and slack times. What is the project duration? Using any approach you wish (e.g., trial and error), develop a loading chart for resources, Electrical Engineers (EE), and resource, Mechanical Engineers (ME). Assume only one of each resource exists. Given your resource schedule, compute the early, late, and slack times for your project. Which activities are now critical? What is the project duration now? Could something like this happen in real projects?

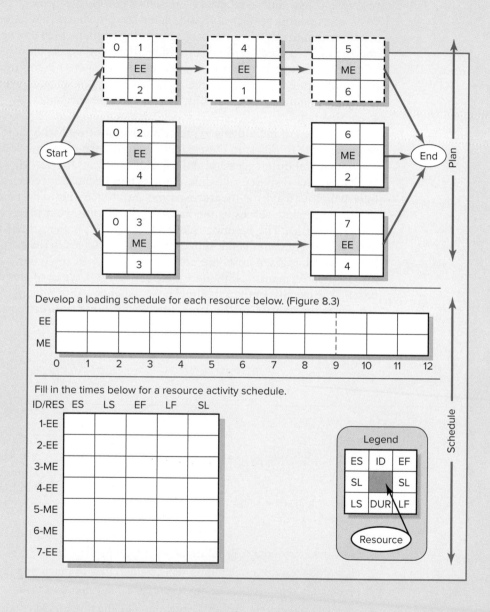

2. Given the network plan that follows, compute the early, late, and slack times. What is the project duration? Using any approach you wish (e.g., trial and error), develop a loading chart for resources Carpenters (C) and Electricians (E). Assume only one

Carpenter is available and two Electricians are available. Given your resource schedule, compute the early, late, and slack times for your project. Which activities are now critical? What is the project duration now?

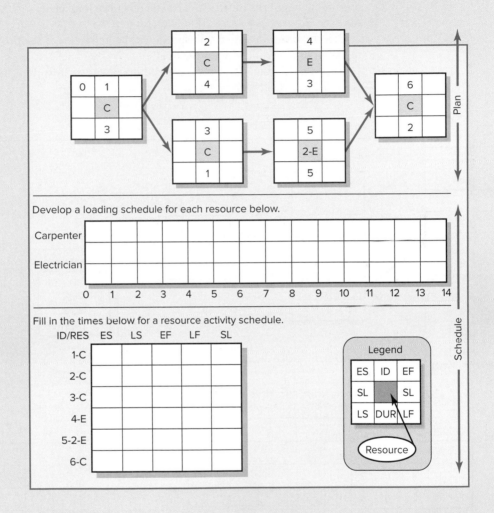

3. Compute the early, late, and slack times for the activities in the network that follows, assuming a time-constrained network. Which activities are critical? What is the time-constrained project duration?

   Note: Recall, in the schedule resource load chart the *time-constrained* scheduling interval (ES through LF) has been shaded. Any resource scheduled beyond the shaded area will delay the project.

   Assume you have only three resources and you are using a computer that uses software that schedules projects by the parallel method and following heuristics. Schedule only one period at a time!

   Minimum slack
   Smallest duration
   Lowest identification number

Keep a log of each activity change and update you make each period—e.g., period 0–1, 1–2, 2–3, etc. (Use a format similar to the one on page 259.) The log should include any changes or updates in ES and slack times each period, activities scheduled, and activities delayed. (Hint: Remember to maintain the technical dependencies of the network.) Use the resource load chart to assist you in scheduling (see Figures 8.4 and 8.5).

List the order in which you scheduled the activities of the project. Which activities of your schedule are now critical?

Recompute your slack for each activity given your new schedule. What is the slack for activity 1? 4? 5?

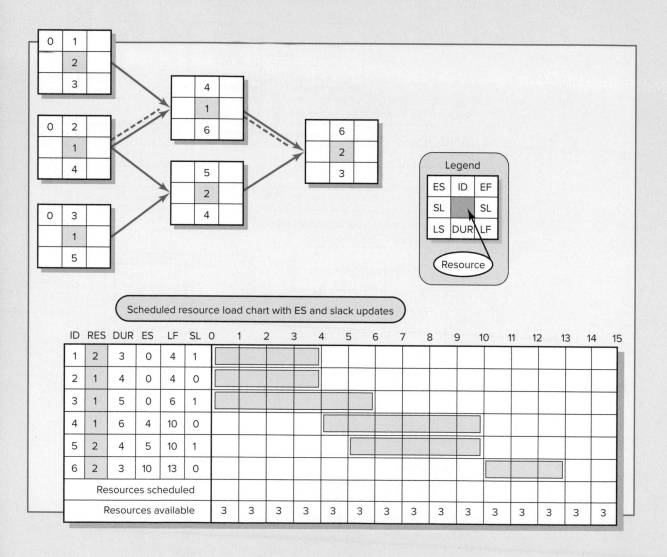

Scheduled resource load chart with ES and slack updates

ID	RES	DUR	ES	LF	SL	0	1	2	3	4	5	6	7	8	9	10	11	12	13	14	15
1	2	3	0	4	1																
2	1	4	0	4	0																
3	1	5	0	6	1																
4	1	6	4	10	0																
5	2	4	5	10	1																
6	2	3	10	13	0																
Resources scheduled																					
Resources available						3	3	3	3	3	3	3	3	3	3	3	3	3	3	3	3

4. *You have prepared the following schedule for a project in which the key resource is a tractor(s). There are three tractors available to the project. Activities A and D require one tractor to complete while activities B, C, E, and F require 2 tractors.

   Develop a resource-constrained schedule in the loading chart that follows. Use the parallel method and heuristics given. Be sure to update each period as the computer would do. Record the early start (ES), late finish (LF), and slack (SL) for the new schedule.

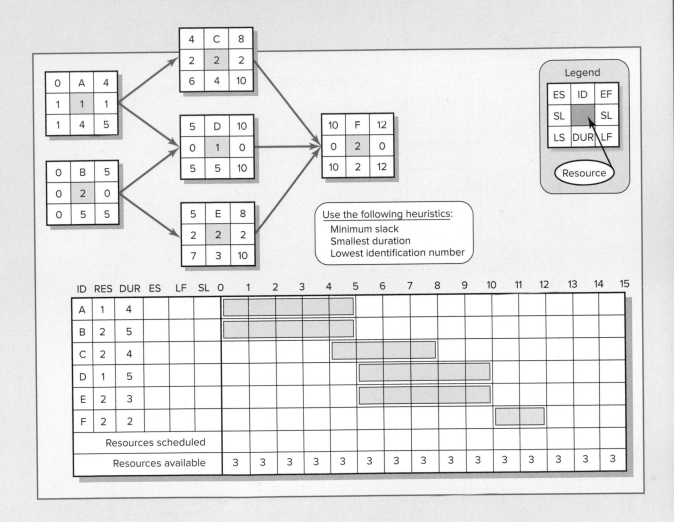

5. Develop a resource schedule in the loading chart that follows. Use the parallel method and heuristics given. Be sure to update each period as the computer would do. Note: activities 2, 3, 5, and 6 use two of the resource skills. Three of the resource skills are available. How has slack changed for each activity? Has the risk of being late changed? How?

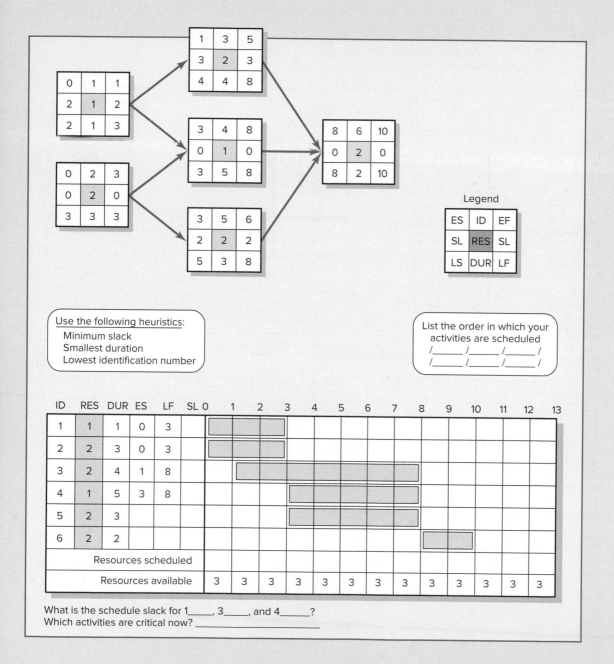

Use the following heuristics:
  Minimum slack
  Smallest duration
  Lowest identification number

List the order in which your activities are scheduled
/_____ /_____ /_____ /
/_____ /_____ /_____ /

What is the schedule slack for 1_____, 3_____, and 4_____?
Which activities are critical now? _____

6. You have prepared the following schedule for a project in which the key resource is a backhoe(s). This schedule is contingent on having 3 backhoes. You receive a call from your partner, Brooker, who desperately needs one of your backhoes. You tell

Brooker you would be willing to let him have the backhoe if you are still able to complete your project in 11 months.

Develop a resource schedule in the loading chart that follows to see if it is possible to complete the project in 11 months with only 2 backhoes. Be sure to record the order in which you schedule the activities using scheduling heuristics. Activities 5 and 6 require 2 backhoes, while activities 1, 2, 3, and 4 require 1 backhoe. No splitting of activities is possible. Can you say yes to Brooker's request?

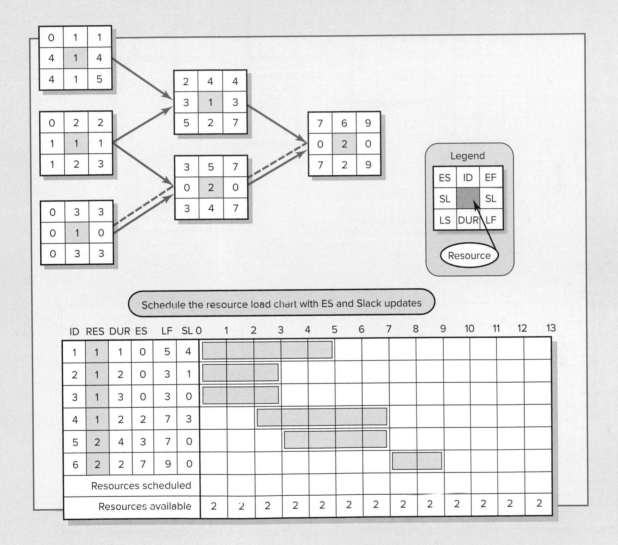

7. *You are one of three carpenters assigned to complete a short construction project. Right before the start of the project, one of your fellow carpenters was hospitalized and will not be available to work on the project.

Develop a resource-constrained schedule in the loading chart that follows to see how long the project will take with only 2 carpenters. Be sure to record the order in

*The solution to this exercise can be found in Appendix 1.

which you schedule the activities using the scheduling heuristics. Activities A, B, C, D, E, G, and H require 2 carpenters to complete. Activity F requires only 1 carpenter. No splitting of activities is possible.

You will receive a bonus if the project is completed within 15 days. Should you start planning how you will spend your bonus?

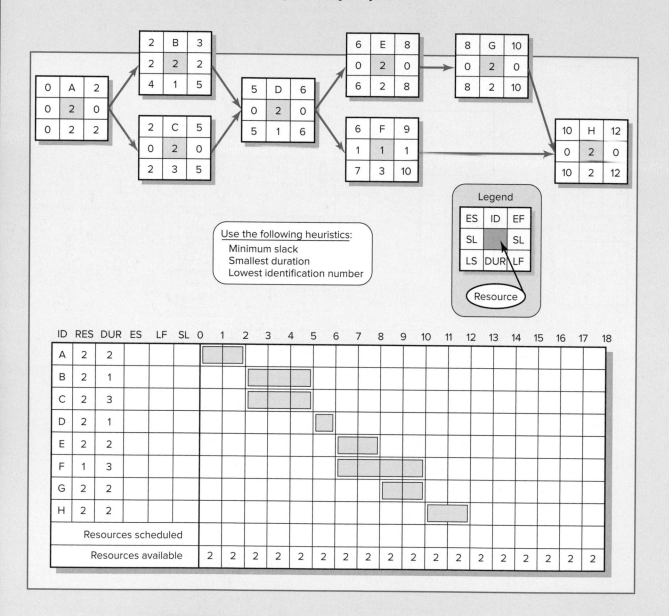

8. Given the time-phased work packages, complete the baseline budget form for the project.

Time-phased budget ($ 000)

Task	Budget	0	1	2	3	4	5	6	7	8	9	10
Activity 1	4	4										
Activity 2	6		1	3	2							
Activity 3	10		2	4	2	2						
Activity 4	8						2	3	3			
Activity 5	3									2	1	
Total	31											
Cumulative												

9. Given the time-phased work packages and network, complete the baseline budget form for the project.

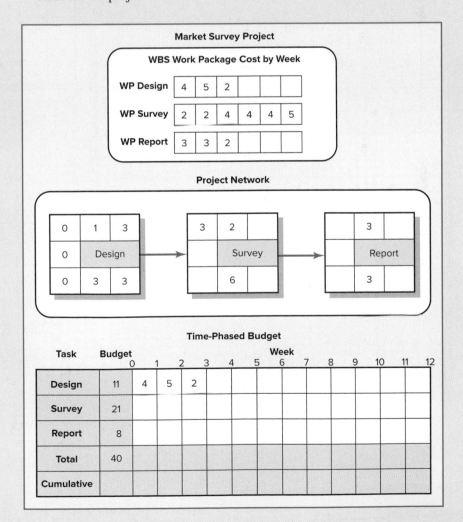

Market Survey Project

WBS Work Package Cost by Week

WP Design	4	5	2			
WP Survey	2	2	4	4	4	5
WP Report	3	3	2			

Project Network

0	1	3
0	Design	
0	3	3

3	2	
	Survey	
	6	

	3	
	Report	
	3	

Time-Phased Budget

Task	Budget	0	1	2	3	4	5	6	7	8	9	10	11	12
Design	11	4	5	2										
Survey	21													
Report	8													
Total	40													
Cumulative														

10. *Given the time-phased work packages and network, complete the baseline budget form for the project.

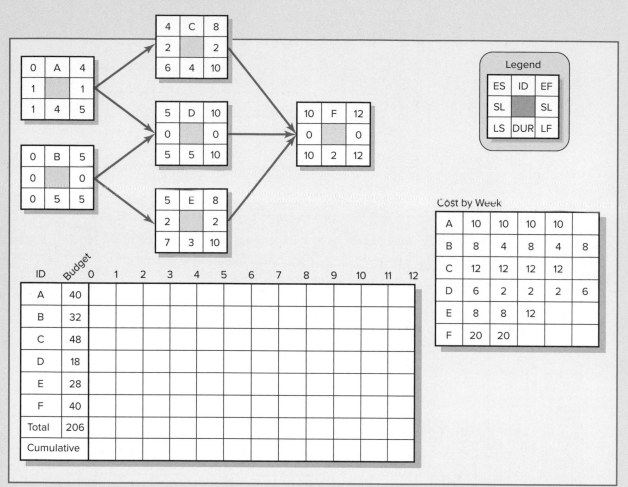

Cost by Week

A	10	10	10	10	
B	8	4	8	4	8
C	12	12	12	12	
D	6	2	2	2	6
E	8	8	12		
F	20	20			

ID	Budget	0	1	2	3	4	5	6	7	8	9	10	11	12
A	40													
B	32													
C	48													
D	18													
E	28													
F	40													
Total	206													
Cumulative														

*The solution to this exercise can be found in Appendix 1.

11. Given the time-phased work packages and network, complete the baseline budget form for the project.

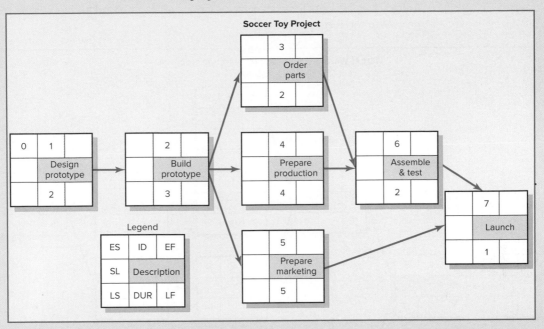

Soccer Toy Project

Cost by Week ($000)

	←1	←2	←3	←4	←5
Design prototype	12	12			
Build prototype	10	10	10		
Order parts	5	5			
Prepare production	16	10	22	16	
Prepare marketing	6	6	0	6	12
Assemble & test	18	18			
Launch	12				

Time-phased Budget ($000)

Week

Budget		0	1	2	3	4	5	6	7	8	9	10	11	12	13
Design prototype	24														
Build prototype	30														
Order parts	10														
Prepare prod'n	64														
Prepare market'g	30														
Assemble & test	36														
Launch	12														
Total	206														
Cumulative															

12. The National Oceanic Research Institute is planning a research study on global warming in Antarctica. The 16-month network schedule is presented below. It is followed by budgets for each activity. Create a time-phased budget for the research project in the form provided.

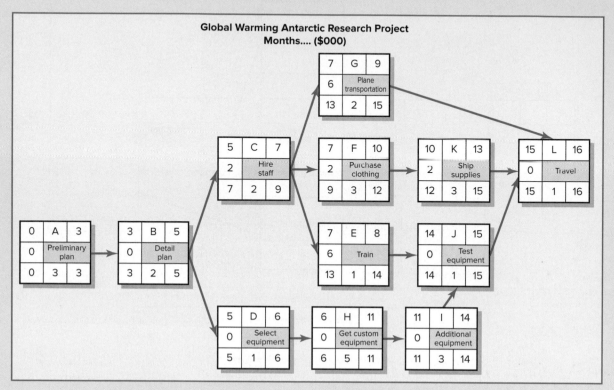

Global Warming Antarctic Research Project
Months.... ($000)

Global Warming Antarctic Research Project
Activity Time Phased Work Packages by Month ($000)

	Task	Duration	Budget	0	1	2	3	4	5	6
A	Preliminary plan	3	3	1	1	1				
B	Detail plan	2	2	1	1					
C	Hire staff	2	4	4						
D	Select equipment	1	5	5						
E	Train	1	3	3						
F	Purchase clothing	3	9	3	0	6				
G	Plane transportation	2	60	5	55					
H	Get custom equipment	5	36	5	5	10	10	6		
I	Additional equipment	3	20	10	5	5				
J	Test equipment	1	6	6						
K	Ship all supplies	5	15	3	3	0	0	9		
L	Travel	1	9	9						
	Total budget		172							

References

Arrow, K. J., and L. Hurowicz, *Studies in Resource Allocation Process* (New York: Cambridge University Press, 1997).

Brucker, P., A. Drexl, R. Mohring, L. Newmann, and E. Pesch, "Resource-constrained Project Scheduling: Notation, Classification, Models and Methods," *European Journal of Operational Research,* vol. 112 (1999), pp. 3–42.

Burgess, A. R., and J. B. Kellebrew, "Variations in Activity Level on Cyclical Arrow Diagrams," *Journal of Industrial Engineering,* vol. 13 (March–April 1962), pp. 76–83.

Charnes, A., and W. W. Cooper, "A Network Interpretation and Direct Sub Dual Algorithm for Critical Path Scheduling," *Journal of Industrial Engineering,* July–August 1962.

Davis, E. W., and J. Patterson, "A Comparison of Heuristic and Optimum Solutions in Resource-Constrained Project Scheduling," *Management Science*, April 1975, pp. 944–955.

Demeulemeester, E. L., and W. S. Herroelen, *Project Scheduling: A Research Handbook* (Norwell, MA: Kluwer Academic Publishers, 2002).

Fendly, L. G., "Towards the Development of a Complete Multi Project Scheduling System," *Journal of Industrial Engineering,* vol. 19 (1968), pp. 505–15.

Goldratt, E., *Critical Chain* (Great Barrington, MA: North River Press, 1997).

Kurtulus, I., and E. W. Davis, "Multi-project Scheduling: Categorization of Heuristic Rules Performance," *Management Science,* February 1982, pp. 161–72.

Newbold, R. C., "Leveraging Project Resources: Tools for the Next Century," *Proceedings of 28th Annual Project Management Institute, 1997 Seminars and Symposium* (Newtown, PA: Project Management Institute, 1997), pp. 417–21.

Pascoe, T. L., "An Experimental Comparison of Heuristic Methods for Allocating Resources," Ph.D. dissertation, University of Cambridge, United Kingdom, 1965.

Reinersten, D., "Is It Always a Bad Idea to Add Resources to a Late Project?" *Electric Design,* October 30, 2000, pp. 17–18.

Rubinstein, J., D. Meyer, and J. Evans, "Executive Control of Cognitive Processes in Task Switching," *Journal of Experimental Psychology: Human Perception and Performance,* vol. 27, no. 4 (2001), pp. 763–97.

Talbot, B. F., and J. H. Patterson, "Optimal Methods for Scheduling Under Resource Constraints," *Project Management Journal,* December 1979.

Wiest, J. D., "A Heuristic Model for Scheduling Large Projects with Unlimited Resources," *Management Science,* vol. 18 (February 1967), pp. 359–77.

Woodworth, B. M., and C. J. Willie, "A Heuristic Algorithm for Resource Leveling in Multiproject, Multiresource Scheduling," *Decision Sciences,* vol. 6 (July 1975), pp. 525–40.

Woodworth, B. M., and S. Shanahan, "Identifying the Critical Sequence in a Resource Constrained Project," *International Journal of Project Management,* vol. 6 (1988), pp. 89–96.

Case 8.1

Blue Mountain Cabin

Jack and Jill Smith have just retired and want to build a small, basic cabin in the Blue Mountains of Vermont. They have hired Daryl Hannah as the general contractor for the project. She has assembled a team of three workers to complete the project: Tom, Dick, and Harry. Daryl has negotiated a cost-plus contract with the Smiths whereby she will receive 15 percent beyond the cost of labor and materials.

Before they sign the contract the Smiths want an estimate of how much the project is likely to cost and how long it will take.

Darryl has estimated that the cost for materials, permits, etc., will total $40,000. She wants to determine labor costs as well as how long the project will take. This is one of several projects Daryl is managing, and other than occasionally helping out, her role is strictly limited to supervising. She has devised the following master plan and assignments.

Note that Dick is the only skilled plumber in the group while Harry is the only skilled electrician. Tom is a general carpenter and can assist them with their work. Dick and Harry each get paid $300 a day while Tom gets paid $200 per day.

Darryl has negotiated a 10 percent management reserve to deal with unexpected problems. Unused funds will be returned to the Smiths.

ID	Task	Predecessor	Time (days)	Assignment
A	Prepare Site	none	2	Tom, Dick, Harry
B	Pour Foundation	A	2	Tom, Dick, Harry
C	Erect Frame	B	4	Tom, Dick, Harry
D	Roof	C	3	Tom, Dick, Harry
E	Windows/Doors	D	2	Tom, Dick
F	Electrical	D	2	Harry, Tom
G	Plumbing	D	2	Dick, Tom
H	Rough-in-frame	E, F,G	2	Tom, Dick, Harry
I	Clean up	H	1	Tom, Dick, Harry

Prepare a short proposal for the Smiths that includes a Gantt chart with resources assigned, and cost estimates if the project starts on 8/1/16. Did resource limitations affect the final schedule? If so, how? What financial risks does this project face? What can the Smiths do to protect themselves against those risks?

Case 8.2

Power Train, Ltd.

We have smashing systems for reporting, tracking, and controlling costs on design projects. Our planning of projects is better than any I have seen at other companies. Our scheduling seemed to serve us well when we were small and we had only a few projects. Now that we have many more projects and schedule using multiproject software, there are too many occasions when the right people are not assigned to the projects deemed important to our success. This situation is costing us big money, headaches, and stress!

Claude Jones, VP, Design and Operations

HISTORY

Power Train, Ltd. (PT), was founded in 1970 by Daniel Gage, a skilled mechanical engineer and machinist. Prior to founding PT he worked for three years as design engineer for a company that designed and built transmissions for military tanks and trucks. It was a natural transition for Dan to start a company designing and building power trains for farm tractor companies. Today, Dan is no longer active in the management of PT but is still revered as its founder. He and his family still own 25 percent of the company, which went public in 1998. PT has been growing at a 6 percent clip for the last five years but expects industry growth to level off as supply exceeds demand.

Today, PT continues its proud tradition of designing and building the best-quality power trains for manufacturers of farm tractors and equipment. The company employs 178 design engineers and has about 1,800 production and support staff. Contract design projects for tractor manufacturers represent a major portion of PT's revenue. At any given time, about 45 to 60 design projects are going on concurrently. A small portion of their design work is for military vehicles. PT only accepts military contracts that involve very advanced, new technology and are cost plus.

A new phenomenon has attracted management of PT to look into a larger market. Last year a large Swedish truck manufacturer approached PT to consider designing power trains for its trucks. As the industry consolidates, the opportunities for PT should increase because these large firms are moving to more outsourcing to cut infrastructure costs and stay very flexible. Only last week a PT design engineer spoke to a German truck manufacturing manager at a conference. The German manager was already exploring outsourcing of drive trains to Porsche and was very pleased to be reminded of PT's expertise in the area. A meeting is set up for next month.

CLAUDE JONES

Claude Jones joined PT in 1999 as a new MBA from the University of Edinburgh. He worked as a mechanical engineer for U.K. Hydraulics for five years prior to returning to school for the MBA. "I just wanted to be part of the management team and where the action is." Jones moved quickly through the ranks. Today he is the vice president of design and operations. Sitting at his desk, Jones is pondering the conflicts and confusion that seem to be increasing in scheduling people to projects. He gets a real rush at the thought of designing power trains for large trucks; however, given their current project scheduling problems, a large increase in business would only compound their problems. Somehow these conflicts in scheduling have to be resolved before any serious thought can be given to expanding into design of power transmissions for truck manufacturers.

Jones is thinking of the problems PT had in the last year. The MF project is the first to come to mind. The project was not terribly complex and did not require their best design engineers. Unfortunately, the scheduling software assigned one of the most creative and expensive engineers to the MF project. A similar situation, but reversed, happened on the Deer project. This project involved a big customer and new hydrostatic technology for small tractors. In this project the scheduling software assigned engineers who were not familiar with small tractor transmissions. Somehow, thinks Jones, the right people need to be scheduled to the right projects. Upon reflection, this problem with scheduling has been increasing since PT went to multiproject scheduling. Maybe a project office is needed to keep on top of these problems.

A meeting with the information technology team and software vendors was positive but not very helpful because these people are not really into detailed scheduling problems. The vendors provided all sorts of evidence suggesting the heuristics used—least

Appendix Summary

Regardless of where one stands in the debate, the CCPM approach deserves credit for bringing resource dependency to the forefront, highlighting the modern ills of multitasking, and forcing us to rethink conventional methods of project scheduling.

Appendix Review Questions

1. Explain how time is wasted in management of projects.
2. Distinguish between project and feeder buffers.
3. Buffers are not the same as slack. Explain.

Appendix Exercises

1. Check out the Goldratt Institute's homepage at *http://www.goldratt.com* for current information on the application of critical-chain techniques to project management.
2. Apply critical-chain scheduling principles to the Print Software, Inc., project (Exercise 10) presented in Chapter 6. Revise the estimated time durations by 50 percent except round up the odd time durations (i.e., 3 becomes 4). Draw a CCPM network diagram similar to the one contained in Figure A8.3 for the Print Software project as well as a Gantt chart similar to Figure A8.4. How would these diagrams differ from the ones generated using the traditional scheduling technique?

Appendix References

Budd, C. S., and M. J. Cooper, "Improving On-time Service Delivery: The Case of Project as Product," *Human Systems Management,* vol. 24, no. 1 (2005), pp. 67–81.

Button, S., "A Critical Look at Critical Chain", EM 540 research Paper, March 2011.

Goldratt, E., *Critical Chain* (Great Barrington, MA: North River Press, 1997).

Herroelen, W., R. Leus, and E. Demeulemeester, "Critical Chain Project Scheduling: Do Not Oversimplify," *Project Management Journal,* vol. 33, no. 4 (2002), pp. 48–60.

Leach, L. P., "Critical Chain Project Management," *Proceedings of 29th Annual Project Management Institute, 1998, Seminars and Symposium* (Newtown, PA: Project Management Institute, 1998), pp. 1239–44.

Levine, H. A., "Shared Contingency: Exploring the Critical Chain," *PM Network,* October 1999, pp. 35–38.

Newbold, R. C., *Project Management in the Fast Lane: Applying the Theory of Constraints* (Boca Raton, FL: St. Lucie Press, 1998).

Noreen, E., D. Smith, and J. Mackey, *The Theory of Constraints and Its Implication for Management Accounting* (Great Barrington, MA: North River Press, 1995).

Pinto, J., "Some Constraints on the Theory of Constraints: Taking a Critical Look at Critical Chain," *PM Network*, vol. 13, no. 8 (1999), pp. 49–51.

Raz, T., R. Barnes, and D. Dvir, "A Critical Look at Critical Chain Project Management," *Project Management Journal,* December 2003, pp. 24–32.

Sood, S., "Taming Uncertainty: Critical-Chain Buffer Management Helps Minimize Risk in the Project Equation," *PM Network,* March 2003, pp. 57–59.

Steyn, H., "An Investigation into the Fundamentals of Critical Chain Scheduling," *International Journal of Project Management*, vol. 19 (2000), pp. 363–69.

Zalmanson, E., "Readers Feedback," *PM Network,* vol. 15, no. 1 (2001), p. 4.

Case A8.1

The CCPM Dilemma

Pinyarat worked in the IT department of a diversified IT firm. She was describing the firm's early encounters with critical-chain scheduling to a friend in another IT firm.

Three years ago management decided to add 10 percent time to all activity estimates because almost all projects were coming in late. One thought was people were simply working too hard and needed some relief. This approach did not work! Projects still came in late. Next, management decided to take away the extra time for activities and add 10 percent for project estimates to ensure project durations would be met. Again, nothing improved and projects continued to come in late. Recently, the firm hired a consultant who promoted critical-chain scheduling, which was implemented for all projects in her division. Almost all failed to perform.

Pinyarat explained, "The estimates were basically impossible. The activity durations got squeezed down to less than the 50 percent guideline. We were late on nearly every task. In addition, I was not allowed to put in a big enough project buffer, which only added to projects being late. One colleague who was working on six projects gave up and quit; he said he was killing himself and saw no hope of things getting better. My projects are not the only ones having big problems. Some people had no idea why anyone would use CCPM scheduling. To quote one of my best programmers: 'They ask for an estimate and then they cut it 50 percent or more.' What kind of game is this? Apparently they don't trust us."

A week later, to Pinyarat's surprise, she was called to the IT manager's office. Pinyarat imagined numerous bad scenarios of how the meeting would go—even to the remote possibility of being fired! The manager wanted the division to straighten out their project management practices and stop this business of nearly all IT projects being late. There were rumors of cleaning house or outsourcing IT work.

The manager believed Pinyarat, who passed the PMP exam, had the best chance of turning things around. He said, "Pinyarat, I'm nearing the desperate level; top management is reaching the end of the rope with our division. We need to turn this around for both our sakes. Give me a plan that I can sponsor within the week."

Pinyarat explained to her friend a few of her ideas—like squeezing estimates too far. But she said she would take any ideas she could get from anyone.

Give Pinyarat a report that identifies the key problems and a plan of action she can present to her sponsor. Limit your report to 800 words or less.

9

Reducing Project Duration

LEARNING OBJECTIVES

After reading this chapter you should be able to:

9-1   Understand the different reasons for crashing a project.

9-2   Identify the different options for crashing an activity when resources are not constrained.

9-3   Identify the different options for crashing an activity when resources are constrained.

9-4   Determine the optimum cost-time point in a project network.

9-5   Understand the risks associated with compressing or crashing a project.

9-6   Identify different options for reducing the costs of a project.

OUTLINE

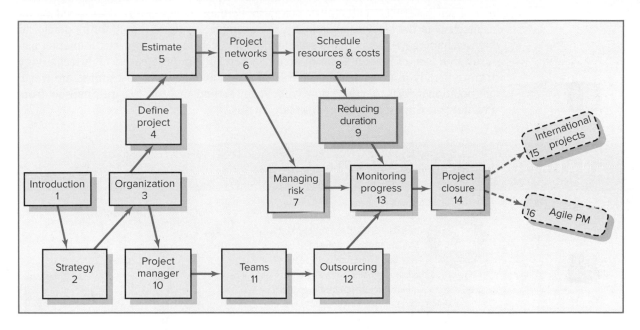

In skating over thin ice our safety is in our speed.

—Ralph Waldo Emerson

Imagine the following scenarios:

    —After finalizing your project schedule, you realize the estimated completion date is two months beyond what your boss publicly promised an important customer.

    —Five months into the project, you realize that you are already three weeks behind the drop-dead date for the project.

    —Four months into a project top management changes its priorities and now tells you that money is not an issue. Complete the project ASAP!

What do you do?

    This chapter addresses strategies for reducing project duration either prior to setting the baseline for the project or in the midst of project execution. Choice of options is based on the constraints surrounding the project. Here the project priority matrix introduced in Chapter 4 comes into play. For example, there are many more options available for reducing project time if you are not resource constrained than if you cannot spend more than your original budget. We will begin first by examining the reasons for reducing project duration followed by a discussion of different options for accelerating project completion. The chapter will conclude with the classic time-cost framework for selecting which activities to "crash." Crash is a term that has emerged in the Project Management lexicon for shortening the duration of an activity or project beyond when it can be normally done.

9.1 Rationale for Reducing Project Duration

LO 9-1

Understand the different reasons for crashing a project.

There are many good reasons for attempting to reduce the duration of a project. One of the more important reasons today is time to market. Intense global competition and rapid technological advances have made speed a competitive advantage. To succeed, companies have to spot new opportunities, launch project teams, and bring new products or services to the marketplace in a flash. Perhaps in no industry does speed matter as much as in the electronics industry. For example, a rule of thumb for moderate- to high-technology firms is that a six-month delay in bringing a product to market can result in a loss of market share of about 35 percent. In these cases, high-technology firms typically assume that the time savings and avoidance of lost profits are worth any additional costs to reduce time without any formal analysis. See the Snapshot from Practice 9.1: Smartphone Wars for more on this.

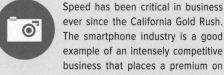

SNAPSHOT FROM PRACTICE 9.1 Smartphone Wars*

Speed has been critical in business ever since the California Gold Rush. The smartphone industry is a good example of an intensely competitive business that places a premium on speed and innovation. Analysts forecast over 14 different new smartphones on the market in 2016 including Acer Predator 6, Samsung Galaxy 7, and Iphone 7.

In order to survive, RIM, Samsung, Apple, and other smartphone manufacturers have become masters at project management. They have been able to cut the market release time of new phones from 12–18 months to 6–9 months. What is at stake is over $1 billion in forecasted sales of new smartphones.

* Hall, C., and B. O'Boyle, "Best Smartphones to Look Forward to in 2016," pocket-lint.com, accessed January 11, 2015.

© Rex Features/AP Images

Business survival depends not only on rapid innovation but also on adaptability. Global recession and energy crises have stunned the business world, and those companies that survive will be those that can quickly adapt to new challenges. This requires speedy project management! For example, the fate of the U.S. auto industry depends in part on how quickly they shift their efforts to develop fuel-efficient, alternative forms of transportation.

Another common reason for reducing project time occurs when unforeseen delays—for example, adverse weather, design flaws, and equipment breakdown—cause substantial delays midway in the project. Getting back on schedule usually requires compressing the time on some of the remaining critical activities. The additional costs of getting back on schedule need to be compared with the consequences of being late. This is especially true when time is a top priority.

Incentive contracts can make reduction of project time rewarding—usually for both the project contractor and owner. For example, a contractor finished a bridge across a lake 18 months early and received more than $6 million for the early completion. The availability of the bridge to the surrounding community 18 months early to reduce traffic gridlock made the incentive cost to the community seem small to users. In another example, in a continuous improvement arrangement, the joint effort of the owner and contractor resulted in early completion of a river lock and a 50/50 split of the savings to the owner and contractor. See Snapshot from Practice 9.2: Northridge Earthquake for a classic example of a contractor who went to great lengths to quickly complete a project with a big payoff.

"Imposed deadlines" is another reason for accelerating project completion. For example, a politician makes a public statement that a new law building will be available in two years. Or the president of a software company remarks in a speech that new advanced software will be available in one year. Such statements too often become imposed project duration dates—without any consideration of the problems or cost of meeting such a date. The project duration time is set while the project is in its "concept" phase before or without any detailed scheduling of all the activities in the project. This phenomenon occurs very frequently in practice! Unfortunately, this practice almost always leads to a higher-cost project than one that is planned using low-cost and detailed planning. In addition, quality is sometimes compromised to meet deadlines. More important, these increased costs of imposed duration dates are seldom recognized or noted by project participants.

Sometimes very high overhead costs are recognized before the project begins. For example, it may cost $80,000 per day to simply house and feed a construction crew in the farthest reaches of Northern Alaska. In these cases it is prudent to examine the direct costs of shortening the critical path versus the overhead cost savings. Usually there are opportunities to shorten a few critical activities at less than the daily overhead rate. Under specific conditions (which are not rare), huge savings are possible with little risk.

Finally there are times when it is important to reassign key equipment and/or people to new projects. Under these circumstances, the cost of compressing the project can be compared with the opportunity costs of not releasing key equipment or people.

9.2 Options for Accelerating Project Completion

Managers have several effective methods for crashing specific project activities when resources are not constrained. Several of these are summarized below.

SNAPSHOT FROM PRACTICE 9.2

Responding to the
Northridge Earthquake*

On January 17, 1994, a 6.8-magnitude earthquake struck the Los Angeles basin, near suburban Northridge, causing 60 deaths, thousands of injuries, and billions of dollars in property damage. Nowhere was the destructive power of nature more evident than in the collapsed sections of the freeway system that disrupted the daily commute of an estimated 1 million Los Angelenos. The Northridge earthquake posed one of the greatest challenges to the California Department of Transportation (CalTrans) in its nearly 100-year history. To expedite the recovery process, Governor Pete Wilson signed an emergency declaration allowing CalTrans to streamline contracting procedures and offer attractive incentives for completing work ahead of schedule. For each day that the schedule was beaten, a sizable bonus was to be awarded. Conversely, for each day over the deadline, the contractor would be penalized the same amount. The amount ($50,000 to $200,000) varied depending on the importance of the work.

The incentive scheme proved to be a powerful motivator for the freeway reconstruction contractors. C. C. Myers, Inc., of Rancho Cordova, California, won the contract for the reconstruction of the Interstate 10 bridges. Myers pulled out all stops to finish the project in a blistering 66 days—a whopping 74 days ahead of schedule—and earning a $14.8 million bonus! Myers took every opportunity to save time and streamline operations. They greatly expanded the workforce. For example, 134 iron-workers were employed instead of the normal 15. Special lighting equipment was set up so that work could be performed around the clock. Likewise, the sites were prepared and special materials were used so that work could continue despite inclement weather that would normally shut down construction. The work was scheduled much like an assembly line so that critical activities were followed by

© David Butow/Corbis SABA

the next critical activity. A generous incentive scheme was devised to reward teamwork and reach milestones early. Carpenters and iron-workers competed as teams against each other to see who could finish first.

Although C. C. Myers received a substantial bonus for finishing early, they spent a lot of money on overtime, bonuses, special equipment, and other premiums to keep the job rolling along. CalTrans supported Myers's efforts. With reconstruction work going on 24 hours a day, including jackhammering and pile-driving, CalTrans temporarily housed many families in local motels. CalTrans even erected a temporary plastic soundwall to help reduce the construction noise traveling to a nearby apartment complex. The double-layer curtain, 450 feet long and 20 feet high, was designed to reduce construction noise by 10 decibels.

Despite the difficulties and expense incurred by around-the-clock freeway building, most of Los Angeles cheered CalTrans's quake recovery efforts. The Governor's Office of Planning and Research issued a report concluding that for every day the Santa Monica Freeway was closed, it cost the local economy more than $1 million.

* Jerry B. Baxter, "Responding to the Northridge Earthquake,"
PM Network (November 1994), pp. 13–22.

Options When Resources Are Not Constrained

Adding Resources

LO 9-2

Identify the different options for crashing an activity when resources are not constrained.

The most common method for shortening project time is to assign additional staff and equipment to activities. There are limits, however, as to how much speed can be gained by adding staff. Doubling the size of the workforce will not necessarily reduce completion time by half. The relationship would be correct only when tasks can be partitioned so minimal communication is needed between workers, as in harvesting a crop by hand or repaving a highway. Most projects are not set up that way; additional

SNAPSHOT FROM PRACTICE 9.3

Outsourcing in Bio-Tech Picks Up Speed*

In the face of increasing time-to-market pressures, many bio-tech firms are turning to outsourcing to expedite the drug development process. Panos Kalaritis, vice president of operations for Irix Pharmaceuticals, says that outsourcing process development can accelerate a drug's evolution by allowing a pharmaceutical company to continue research while a contractor works on process optimization. Susan Dexter of Lonza Biologics identified different types of outsourcing contracts including agreements for product development, clinical trial supplies, in-market or commercial supplies, and technology transfer. Often, she said, a given project can encompass more than one of the above stages over a period of several years.

Using a contractor, said Paul Henricks, business manager for Patheon Inc., gives the client company access to specialized knowledge and infrastructure as well as flexible resources and capacity. The sponsoring company can also manage risks by sharing responsibilities through outsourcing.

"Communication is key to a successful outsourcing relationship," said Dan Gold, vice president of process development for Covance, which was formerly Corning Bio. "Contractors and sponsors should both assign project managers, and the two must work together to maintain, track, and document project completion. There must be a concerted effort on the part of both parties to work as partners to complete the project."

* Mathew Lerner, "Outsourcing in Bio-Technology Picks Up Speed," *Chemical Market Reporter,* vol. 251, no. 14 (2002), p. 17.

---

workers increase the communication requirements to coordinate their efforts. For example, doubling a team by adding two workers requires six times as much pairwise intercommunication than is required in the original two-person team. Not only is more time needed to coordinate and manage a larger team; there is the additional delay of training the new people and getting them up to speed on the project. The end result is captured in Brooks's law: *Adding manpower to a late software project makes it later.*[1]

Frederick Brooks formulated this principle based on his experience as a project manager for IBM's System/360 software project during the early 1960s. While subsequent research confirmed Brooks's prediction, it also discovered that adding more people to a late project does not always cause the project to be later.[2] The key is whether the new staff is added early so there is sufficient time to make up for lost ground once the new members have been fully assimilated.

Outsourcing Project Work

A common method for shortening the project time is to subcontract an activity. The subcontractor may have access to superior technology or expertise that will accelerate the completion of the activity. For example, contracting for a backhoe can accomplish in two hours what it can take a team of laborers two days to do. Likewise, by hiring a consulting firm that specializes in ADSI programming, a firm may be able to cut in half the time it would take for less experienced, internal programmers to do the work. Subcontracting also frees up resources that can be assigned to a critical activity and will ideally result in a shorter project duration. See Snapshot from Practice 9.3: Outsourcing in Bio-Tech. Outsourcing will be addressed more fully in Chapter 12.

---

[1] Brooks's *The Mythical Man-Month* (Reading, MA: Addison-Wesley, 1994) is considered a classic on software project management.

[2] R. L. Gordon and J. C. Lamb, "A Close Look at Brooks' Law," *Datamation,* June 1977, pp. 81–86.

Scheduling Overtime

The easiest way to add more labor to a project is not to add more people, but to schedule overtime. If a team works 50 hours a week instead of 40, it might accomplish 20 percent more. By scheduling overtime you avoid the additional costs of coordination and communication encountered when new people are added. If people involved are salaried workers, there may be no real additional cost for the extra work. Another advantage is that there are fewer distractions when people work outside normal hours.

Overtime has disadvantages. First, hourly workers are typically paid time and a half for overtime and double time for weekends and holidays. Sustained overtime work by salaried employees may incur intangible costs such as divorce, burnout, and turnover. The latter is a key organizational concern when there is a shortage of workers. Furthermore, it is an oversimplification to assume that, over an extended period of time, a person is as productive during his or her eleventh hour at work as during his or her third hour of work. There are natural limits to what is humanly possible, and extended overtime may actually lead to an overall decline in productivity when fatigue sets in (DeMarco, 2002).

Overtime and working longer hours is the preferred choice for accelerating project completion, especially when the project team is salaried. The key is to use overtime judiciously. Remember a project is a marathon not a sprint! You do not want to run out of energy before the finish line.

Establish a Core Project Team

As discussed in Chapter 3, one of the advantages of creating a dedicated core team to complete a project is speed. Assigning professionals full time to a project avoids the hidden cost of multitasking in which people are forced to juggle the demands of multiple projects. Professionals are allowed to devote their undivided attention to a specific project. This singular focus creates a shared goal that can bind a diverse set of professionals into a highly cohesive team capable of accelerating project completion. Factors that contribute to the emergence of high-performing project teams will be discussed in detail in Chapter 11.

Do It Twice—Fast and Correctly

If you are in a hurry, try building a "quick and dirty" short-term solution, then go back and do it the right way. For example, pontoon bridges are used as temporary solutions to damaged bridges in combat. In business, software companies are notorious for releasing version 1.0 of products that are not completely finished and tested. Subsequent versions 1.1 . . . x correct bugs and add intended functionality to the product. The additional costs of doing it twice are often more than compensated for by the benefits of satisfying the deadline.

Options When Resources Are Constrained

Identify the different options for crashing an activity when resources are constrained.

A project manager has fewer options for accelerating project completion when additional resources are either not available or the budget is severely constrained. This is especially true once the schedule has been established. Below are some of these options, which are also available when resources are not constrained.

Improve the Efficiency of the Project Team

The project team may be able to improve productivity by implementing more efficient ways to do their work. This can be achieved by improving the planning and organization of the project or eliminating barriers to productivity such as excessive bureaucratic interference and red tape.

Fast-Tracking

Sometimes it is possible to rearrange the logic of the project network so that critical activities are done in parallel (concurrently) rather than sequentially. This alternative is commonly referred to as **fast tracking** and is a good one if the project situation is right. When this alternative is given serious attention, it is amazing to observe how creative project team members can be in finding ways to restructure sequential activities in parallel. As noted in Chapter 6, one of the most common methods for restructuring activities is to change a finish-to-start relationship to a start-to-start relationship. For example, instead of waiting for the final design to be approved, manufacturing engineers can begin building the production line as soon as key specifications have been established. Changing activities from sequential to parallel is not without risk. Late design changes can produce wasted effort and rework. Fast tracking requires close coordination among those responsible for the activities affected and confidence in the work that has been completed.

Critical-Chain

Critical-chain project management (CCPM) is designed to accelerate project completion. As discussed in Appendix 8.1, it would be difficult to apply CCPM midstream in a project. CCPM requires considerable training and a shift in habits and perspectives that takes time to adopt. Although there have been reports of immediate gains, especially in terms of completion times, a long-term management commitment is probably necessary to reap full benefits. See the Snapshot from Practice 9.4: The Fastest House in the World for an extreme example of CCPM application.

Reducing Project Scope

Probably the most common response for meeting unattainable deadlines is to reduce or scale back the scope of the project. This invariably leads to a reduction in the functionality of the project. For example, the new car will average only 25 mpg instead of 30, or the software product will have fewer features than originally planned. While scaling back the scope of the project can lead to big savings in both time and money, it may come at a cost of reducing the value of the project. If the car gets lower gas mileage, will it stand up to competitive models? Will customers still want the software minus the features?

The key to reducing a project scope without reducing value is to reassess the true specifications of the project. Often requirements are added under best-case, blue-sky scenarios and represent desirables, but not essentials. Here it is important to talk to the customer and/or project sponsors and explain the situation—you can get it your way but not until February. This may force them to accept an extension or to add money to expedite the project. If not, then a healthy discussion of what the essential requirements are and what items can be compromised in order to meet the deadline needs to take place. More intense reexamination of requirements may actually improve the value of the project by getting it done more quickly and for a lower cost.

Calculating the savings of reduced project scope begins with the work breakdown structure. Reducing functionality means certain tasks, deliverables, or requirements can be reduced or even eliminated. These tasks need to be found and the schedule adjusted. Focus should be on changes in activities on the critical path.

Compromise Quality

Reducing quality is always an option, but it is rarely acceptable or used. If quality is sacrificed, it may be possible to reduce the time of an activity on the critical path.

SNAPSHOT FROM PRACTICE 9.4   The Fastest House in the World*

December 17, 2002—After revving up their power tools and lining up volunteers, Shelby County Habitat for Humanity broke the world record for the fastest house ever built, clocking in at 3 hours, 26 minutes, and 34 seconds. Former record holder New Zealand's Habitat Affiliate Mannakau held the record for three years at 3 hours, 44 minutes, and 59 seconds. The Alabama project beat the New Zealand record by 18 minutes.

© Blend Images/Ariel Skelley/Getty Images

"This was different than any construction project that I've ever been a part of," said Project Manager Chad Calhoun. "The minute-by-minute schedule, the planning of each precise movement, the organization of all the teams and materials, could not have gone more smoothly on build day. All the long hours of planning definitely paid off."

In preparation for the build, Habitat volunteers put the foundation in place and constructed prefabricated wall panels. Once the whistle blew at 11:00 a.m. on December 17th, the exterior wall panels were raised into place, followed by the interior panel, which took only 16 minutes. Special color coded teams of workers connected the wiring and plumbing, put in insulation, installed appliances, laid carpet and tile, installed light fixtures, painted the house inside, applied vinyl siding outside, and attached assembled front and back porches.

At the same time, the roof was constructed on the ground next to the house. Once the roof was completed—approximately 1½ hours later—a Steel City crane lifted the 14,000-pound roof assembly into place. Crews attached the roof while others completed the interior work. There was even time to lay sod, plant shrubbery, and decorate a Christmas tree in the front yard—all within the official build time of 3 hours, 26 minutes, and 34 seconds.

The recipient of this wonderful holiday gift was Bonnie Lilly, a single mother and nursing technician who had applied to Habitat for Humanity three times before she was selected to receive the three-bedroom, two-bath home. "It's amazing," Lilly said. "Who am I to have this happen for me? A world record, hundreds of people coming together to build my house—I still can't believe it."

Habitat for Humanity is an international charitable organization that builds simple, affordable houses and sells them on a no-interest, no-profit basis to needy families.

* "The house that love built, really FAST—and just in time for Christmas kicker: Habitat for Humanity breaks world record set by New Zealand," Erin Drummond, www.csre.com. "Shelby County, Ala. Builds fastest Habitat House in three and a half hours," www.habitat.org/newsroom/2002archive.

In practice the methods most commonly used to crash projects are scheduling overtime, outsourcing, and adding resources. Each of these maintains the essence of the original plan. Options that depart from the original project plan include do it twice and fast-tracking. Rethinking of project scope, customer needs, and timing become major considerations for these techniques.

9.3 Project Cost–Duration Graph

Nothing on the horizon suggests that the need to shorten project time will change. In fact, if anything the pressure to get projects done quicker and sooner is likely to increase in importance. The challenge for the project manager is to use a quick, logical method to compare the benefits of reducing project time with the cost. When sound, logical methods are absent, it is difficult to isolate those activities that will have the greatest impact on reducing project time at least cost. This section describes a procedure for identifying the costs of reducing project time so that comparisons can be made with the benefits of getting the project completed sooner. The method requires gathering direct and indirect costs for specific project durations. Critical activities are searched to find the lowest direct-cost activities that will shorten the project duration. Total cost for specific project durations are computed and then compared with the benefits of reducing project time—before the project begins or while it is in progress.

Explanation of Project Costs

LO 9-4

Determine the optimum cost-time point in a project network.

The general nature of project costs is illustrated in Figure 9.1, **Project Cost–Duration Graph.** The total cost for each duration is the sum of the indirect and direct costs. Indirect costs continue for the life of the project. Hence, any reduction in project duration means a reduction in indirect costs. Direct costs on the graph grow at an increasing rate as the project duration is reduced from its original planned duration. With the information from a graph such as this for a project, managers can quickly judge any alternative such as meeting a time-to-market deadline. Further discussion of indirect and direct costs is necessary before demonstrating a procedure for developing the information for a graph similar to the one depicted in Figure 9.1.

Project Indirect Costs

Indirect costs generally represent overhead costs such as supervision, administration, consultants, and interest. Indirect costs cannot be associated with any particular work

FIGURE 9.1
Project Cost–Duration Graph

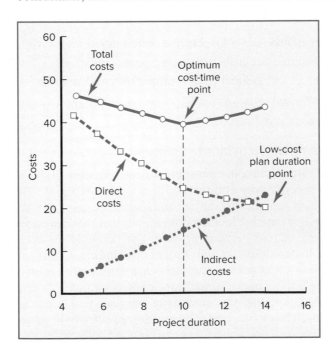

package or activity, hence the term. Indirect costs vary directly with time. That is, any reduction in time should result in a reduction of indirect costs. For example, if the daily costs of supervision, administration, and consultants are $2,000, any reduction in project duration would represent a savings of $2,000 per day. If indirect costs are a significant percentage of total project costs, reductions in project time can represent very real savings (assuming the indirect resources can be utilized elsewhere).

Project Direct Costs

Direct costs commonly represent labor, materials, equipment, and sometimes subcontractors. Direct costs are assigned directly to a work package and activity, hence the term. The ideal assumption is that direct costs for an activity time represent normal costs, which typically mean low-cost, efficient methods for a normal time. When project durations are imposed, direct costs may no longer represent low-cost, efficient methods. Costs for the imposed duration date will be higher than for a project duration developed from ideal normal times for activities. Because direct costs are assumed to be developed from normal methods and time, any reduction in activity time should add to the costs of the activity. The sum of the costs of all the work packages or activities represents the total direct costs for the project.

The major challenge faced in creating the information for a graph similar to Figure 9.1 is computing the direct cost of shortening individual critical activities and then finding the total direct cost for each project duration as project time is compressed; the process requires selecting those critical activities that cost the least to shorten. (Note: The graph implies that there is always an optimum cost-time point. This is only true if shortening a schedule has incremental indirect cost savings exceeding the incremental direct cost incurred. However, in practice there are almost always several activities in which the direct costs of shortening are less than the indirect costs.)

9.4 Constructing a Project Cost–Duration Graph

There are three major steps required to construct a project cost–duration graph:

1. Find total direct costs for selected project durations.
2. Find total indirect costs for selected project durations.
3. Sum direct and indirect costs for these selected durations.

The graph is then used to compare additional cost alternatives for benefits. Details of these steps are presented here.

Determining the Activities to Shorten

The most difficult task in constructing a cost–duration graph is finding the total direct costs for specific project durations over a relevant range. The central concern is to decide which activities to shorten and how far to carry the shortening process. Basically, managers need to look for critical activities that can be shortened with the *smallest increase in cost per unit of time*. The rationale for selecting critical activities depends on identifying the activity's normal and crash times and corresponding costs. *Normal time* for an activity represents low-cost, realistic, efficient methods for completing the activity under normal conditions. Shortening an activity is called **crashing.** The shortest possible time an activity can realistically be completed in is called its **crash time.** The direct cost for completing an activity in its crash time is called *crash cost.* Both normal and crash times and costs are collected from personnel most familiar

FIGURE 9.2
Activity Graph

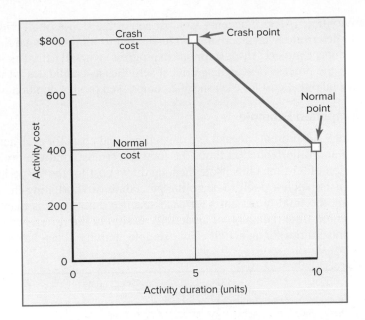

with completing the activity. Figure 9.2 depicts a hypothetical cost–duration graph for an activity.

The normal time for the activity is 10 time units, and the corresponding cost is $400. The crash time for the activity is five time units and $800. The intersection of the normal time and cost represents the original low-cost, early-start schedule. The **crash point** represents the maximum time an activity can be compressed. The heavy line connecting the normal and crash points represents the slope, which assumes the cost of reducing the time of the activity is constant *per unit of time*. The assumptions underlying the use of this graph are as follows:

1. The cost-time relationship is linear.
2. Normal time assumes low-cost, efficient methods to complete the activity.
3. Crash time represents a limit—the greatest time reduction possible under realistic conditions.
4. Slope represents cost per unit of time.
5. All accelerations must occur within the normal and crash times.

Knowing the slope of activities allows managers to compare which critical activities to shorten. The less steep the cost slope of an activity, the less it costs to shorten one time period; a steeper slope means it will cost more to shorten one time unit. The cost per unit of time or slope for any activity is computed by the following equation:

$$\text{Cost slope} = \frac{\text{Rise}}{\text{Run}} = \frac{\text{Crash cost} - \text{Normal cost}}{\text{Normal time} - \text{Crash time}}$$

$$= \frac{\text{CC} - \text{NC}}{\text{NT} - \text{CT}} = \frac{\$800 - \$400}{10 - 5}$$

$$= \frac{\$400}{5} = \$80 \text{ per unit of time}$$

In Figure 9.2 the rise is the *y* axis (cost) and the run is the *x* axis (duration). The slope of the cost line is $80 for each time unit the activity is reduced; the limit reduction of the activity time is five time units. Comparison of the slopes of all critical activities allows us to determine which activity(ies) to shorten to minimize total direct cost. Given the preliminary project schedule (or one in progress) with all activities set to their early-start times, the process of searching critical activities as candidates for reduction can begin. The total direct cost for each specific compressed project duration must be found.

A Simplified Example

Figure 9.3A presents normal and crash times and costs for each activity, the computed slope and time reduction limit, the total direct cost, and the project network with a duration of 25 time units. Note the total direct cost for the 25-period duration is $450. This is an anchor point to begin the procedure of shortening the critical path(s) and finding the total direct costs for each specific duration less than 25 time units. The maximum time reduction of an activity is simply the difference between the normal and crash times for an activity. For example, activity D can be reduced from a normal

FIGURE 9.3
Cost–Duration
Trade-off Example

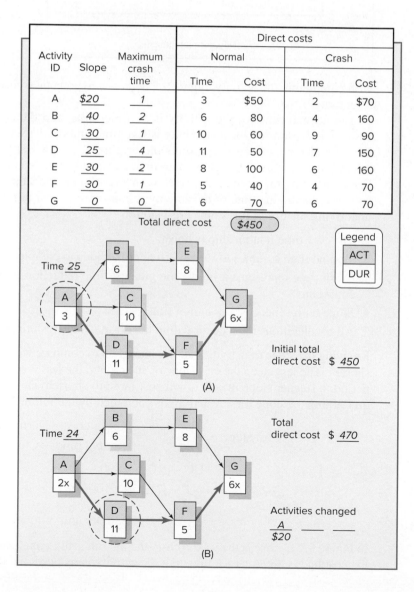

Activity ID	Slope	Maximum crash time	Direct costs			
			Normal		Crash	
			Time	Cost	Time	Cost
A	$20	1	3	$50	2	$70
B	40	2	6	80	4	160
C	30	1	10	60	9	90
D	25	4	11	50	7	150
E	30	2	8	100	6	160
F	30	1	5	40	4	70
G	0	0	6	70	6	70

Total direct cost $450

Legend
ACT
DUR

Time 25

B 6   E 8
A 3   C 10   G 6x
D 11   F 5

Initial total
direct cost $ 450

(A)

Time 24

B 6   E 8
A 2x   C 10   G 6x
D 11   F 5

Total
direct cost $ 470

Activities changed
A
$20

(B)

time of 11 time units to a crash time of 7 time units, or a maximum of 4 time units. The positive slope for activity D is computed as follows:

$$\text{Slope} = \frac{\text{Crash cost} - \text{Normal cost}}{\text{Normal time} - \text{Crash time}} = \frac{\$150 - \$50}{11 - 7}$$

$$= \frac{\$100}{4} = \$25 \text{ per period reduced}$$

The network shows the critical path to be activities A, D, F, G. Because it is impossible to shorten activity G ("x" is used to indicate this), activity A is circled because it is the least-cost candidate; that is, its slope ($20) is less than the slopes for activities D and F ($25 and $30). Reducing activity A one time unit cuts the project duration to 24 time units but increases the total direct costs to $470 ($450 + $20 = $470). Figure 9.3B reflects these changes. The duration of activity A has been reduced to two time units; the "x" indicates the activity cannot be reduced any further. Activity D is circled because it costs the least ($25) to shorten the project to 23 time units. Compare the cost of activity F. The total direct cost for a project duration of 23 time units is $495 (see Figure 9.4A).

FIGURE 9.4
Cost–Duration
Trade-off Example
(continued)

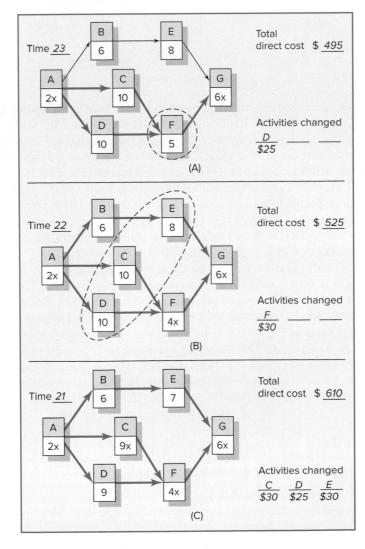

FIGURE 9.5 **Summary Costs by Duration**

Project duration	Direct costs	+	Indirect costs	=	Total costs
25	450		400		$850
24	470		350		820
23	495		300		795
22	525		250		775
21	610		200		810

FIGURE 9.6 **Project Cost–Duration Graph**

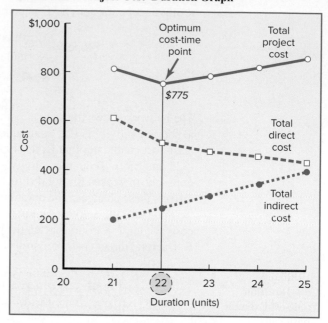

Observe that the project network in Figure 9.4A now has two critical paths—A, C, F, G and A, D, F, G. Reducing the project to 22 time units will require that activity F be reduced; thus, it is circled. This change is reflected in Figure 9.4B. The total direct cost for 22 time units is $525. This reduction has created a third critical path—A, B, E, G; all activities are critical. The least-cost method for reducing the project duration to 21 time units is the combination of the circled activities C, D, E which cost $30, $25, $30, respectively, and increase total direct costs to $610. The results of these changes are depicted in Figure 9.4C. Although some activities can still be reduced (those without the "x" next to the activity time), no activity or combination of activities will result in a reduction in the project duration.

With the total direct costs for the array of specific project durations found, the next step is to collect the indirect costs for these same durations. These costs are typically a rate per day and are easily obtained from the accounting department. Figure 9.5 presents the total direct costs, total indirect costs, and total project costs. These same costs are plotted in Figure 9.6. This graph shows that the optimum cost-time duration is 22 time units and $775. Assuming the project will actually materialize as planned, any movement away from this time duration will increase project costs. The movement from 25 to 22 time units occurs because, in this range, the absolute slopes of the indirect costs are greater than the direct cost slopes.

9.5 Practical Considerations

Using the Project Cost–Duration Graph

This graph, as presented in Figures 9.1 and 9.6, is valuable to compare any proposed alternative or change with the optimum cost and time. More importantly, the creation of such a graph keeps the importance of indirect costs in the forefront of decision making. Indirect costs are frequently forgotten in the field when the pressure for action is intense. Finally, such a graph can be used before the project begins or while the project is in progress.

Creating the graph in the preproject planning phase without an imposed duration is the first choice because normal time is more meaningful. Creating the graph in the project planning phase with an imposed duration is less desirable because normal time is made to fit the imposed date and is probably not low cost. Creating the graph after the project has started is the least desirable because some alternatives may be ruled out of the decision process. Managers may choose not to use the formal procedure demonstrated. However, regardless of the method used, the principles and concepts inherent in the formal procedure are highly applicable in practice and should be considered in any cost–duration trade-off decision.

Crash Times

Collecting crash times for even a moderate-size project can be difficult. The meaning of crash time is difficult to communicate. What is meant when you define crash time as "the shortest time you can realistically complete an activity"? Crash time is open to different interpretations and judgments. Some estimators feel very uncomfortable providing crash times. Regardless of the comfort level, the accuracy of crash times and costs is frequently rough at best, when compared with normal time and cost.

Linearity Assumption

Because the accuracy of compressed activity times and costs is questionable, the concern of some theorists—that the relationship between cost and time is not linear but curvilinear—is seldom a concern for practicing managers. Reasonable, quick comparisons can be made using the linear assumption.[3] The simple approach is adequate for most projects. There are rare situations in which activities cannot be crashed by single time units. Instead, crashing is "all or nothing." For example, activity A will take 10 days (for say $1,000) or it will take 7 days (for say $1,500), but no options exist in which activity A will take 8 or 9 days to complete. In a few rare cases of very large, complex, long-duration projects, the use of present value techniques may be useful; such techniques are beyond the scope of this text.

Choice of Activities to Crash Revisited

LO 9-5

Understand the risks associated with compressing or crashing a project.

The cost–time crashing method relies on choosing the cheapest method for reducing the duration of the project. There are other factors that should be assessed beyond simply cost. First, the inherent risks involved in crashing particular activities need to be considered. Some activities are riskier to crash than others. For example, accelerating the completion of a software design code may not be wise if it increases the likelihood of errors surfacing downstream. Conversely, crashing a more expensive activity may be wise if fewer inherent risks are involved.

Second, the timing of activities needs to be considered. Crashing an early activity may be prudent if there is concern that subsequent activities are likely to be delayed, and absorb the time gained. Then the manager would still have the option of crashing final activities to get back on schedule.

Third, crashing frequently results in overallocation of resources. The resources required to accelerate a cheaper activity may suddenly not be available. Resource availability, not cost, may dictate which activities are crashed.

---

[3] Linearity assumes that the cost for crashing each day is constant.

SNAPSHOT FROM PRACTICE 9.5   I'll Bet You . . .

The focus of this chapter has been on how project managers crash activities by typically assigning additional manpower and equipment to cut significant time off of scheduled tasks. Project managers often encounter situations in which they need to motivate individuals to accelerate the completion of a specific, critical task. Imagine the following scenario.

Bruce Young just received a priority assignment from corporate headquarters. The preliminary engineering sketches that were due tomorrow need to be e-mailed to the West Coast by 4:00 p.m. today so that the model shop can begin construction of a prototype to present to top management. He approaches Danny Whitten, the draftsman responsible for the task, whose initial response is, "That's impossible!" While he agrees that it would be very difficult he does not believe that it is as impossible as Danny suggests or that Danny truly believes that. What should he do?

He tells Danny that he knows this is going to be a rush job, but he is confident that he can do it. When Danny balks, he responds, "I tell you what, I'll make a bet with you. If you are able to finish the design by 4:00, I'll make sure you get two of the company's tickets to tomorrow night's Celtics–Knicks basketball game." Danny accepts the challenge, works feverishly to complete the assignment, and is able to take his daughter to her first professional basketball game.

Conversations with project managers reveal that many use bets like this one to motivate extraordinary performance. These bets range from tickets to sporting and entertainment events to gift certificates at high-class restaurants to a well-deserved afternoon off. For bets to work they need to adhere to the principles of expectancy theory of motivation.* Boiled down to simple terms, expectancy theory rests on three key questions:

1. Can I do it (Is it possible to meet the challenge)?
2. Will I get it (Can I demonstrate that I met the challenge and can I trust the project manager will deliver his/her end of the bargain)?
3. Is it worth it (Is the payoff of sufficient personal value to warrant the risk and extra effort)?

If in the mind of the participant the answer to any of these three questions is no, then the person is unlikely to accept the challenge. However, when the answers are affirmative, then the individual is likely to accept the bet and be motivated to meet the challenge.

Bets can be effective motivational tools and add an element of excitement and fun to project work. But, the following practical advice should be heeded:

1. The bet has greater significance if it also benefits family members or significant others. Being able to take a son or daughter to a professional basketball game allows that individual to "score points" at home through work. These bets also recognize and reward the support project members receive from their families and reinforces the importance of their work to loved ones.

2. Bets should be used sparingly; otherwise everything can become negotiable. They should be used only under special circumstances that require extraordinary effort.

3. Individual bets should involve clearly recognizable individual effort, otherwise others may become jealous and discord may occur within a group. As long as others see it as requiring truly remarkable, "beyond the call of duty" effort, they will consider it fair and warranted.

* Expectancy Theory is considered one of the major theories of human motivation and was first developed by V. H. Vroom, *Work and Motivation* (New York: John Wiley & Sons, 1964).

Finally, the impact crashing would have on the morale and motivation of the project team needs to be assessed. If the least-cost method repeatedly signals a subgroup to accelerate progress, fatigue and resentment may set in. Conversely, if overtime pay is involved, other team members may resent not having access to this benefit. This situation can lead to tension within the entire project team. Good project managers gauge the response that crashing activities will have on the entire project team. See Snapshot from Practice 9.5: I'll Bet You… for a novel approach to motivating employees to work faster.

Time Reduction Decisions and Sensitivity

Should the project owner or project manager go for the optimum cost-time? The answer is, "It depends." Risk must be considered. Recall from our example that the optimum project time point represented a reduced project cost and was less than the original normal project time (review Figure 9.6). The project direct-cost line near the normal point is usually relatively flat. Because indirect costs for the project are usually greater in the same range, the optimum cost-time point is less than the normal time point. Logic of the cost-time procedure suggests managers should reduce the project duration to the lowest total cost point and duration.

How far to reduce the project time from the normal time toward the optimum depends on the *sensitivity* of the project network. A network is sensitive if it has several critical or near-critical paths. In our example project movement toward the optimum time requires spending money to reduce critical activities, resulting in slack reduction and/or more critical paths and activities. Slack reduction in a project with several near-critical paths increases the risk of being late. The practical outcome can be a higher total project cost if some near-critical activities are delayed and become critical; the money spent reducing activities on the original critical path would be wasted. Sensitive networks require careful analysis. The bottom line is that compression of projects with several near-critical paths reduces scheduling flexibility and increases the risk of delaying the project. The outcome of such analysis will probably suggest only a partial movement from the normal time toward the optimum time.

There is a positive situation where moving toward the optimum time can result in very real, large savings—this occurs when the network is *insensitive*. A project network is insensitive if it has a dominant critical path, that is, no near-critical paths. In this project circumstance, movement from the normal time point toward the optimum time will *not* create new or near-critical activities. The bottom line here is that the reduction of the slack of noncritical activities increases the risk of their becoming critical only slightly when compared with the effect in a sensitive network. Insensitive networks hold the greatest potential for real, sometimes large, savings in total project costs with a minimum risk of noncritical activities becoming critical.

Insensitive networks are not a rarity in practice; they occur in perhaps 25 percent of all projects. For example, a light rail project team observed from their network a dominant critical path and relatively high indirect costs. It soon became clear that by spending some dollars on a few critical activities, very large savings of indirect costs could be realized. Savings of several million dollars were spent extending the rail line and adding another station. The logic found in this example is just as applicable to small projects as large ones. Insensitive networks with high indirect costs can produce large savings.

Ultimately, deciding if and which activities to crash is a judgment call requiring careful consideration of the options available, the costs and risks involved, and the importance of meeting a deadline.

9.6 What If Cost, Not Time, Is the Issue?

LO 9-6

Identify different options for reducing the costs of a project.

In today's fast-paced world, there appears to be a greater emphasis on getting things done quickly. Still, organizations are always looking for ways to get things done cheaply. This is especially true for fixed-bid projects, where profit margin is derived from the difference between the bid and actual cost of the project. Every dollar saved is a dollar in your pocket. Sometimes, in order to secure a contract, bids are tight, which puts added pressure on cost containment. In other cases, there are financial incentives tied to cost containment.

Even in situations where cost is transferred to customers there is pressure to reduce cost. Cost overruns make for unhappy customers and can damage future business opportunities. Budgets can be fixed or cut, and when contingency funds are exhausted, then cost overruns have to be made up with remaining activities.

As discussed earlier, shortening project duration may come at the expense of overtime, adding additional personnel, and using more expensive equipment and/or materials. Conversely, sometimes cost savings can be generated by extending the duration of a project. This may allow for a smaller workforce, less-skilled (expensive) labor, and even cheaper equipment and materials to be used. Below are some of the more commonly used options for cutting costs.

Reduce Project Scope

Just as scaling back the scope of the project can gain time, delivering less than what was originally planned also produces significant savings. Again, calculating the savings of a reduced project scope begins with the work breakdown structure. However, since time is not the issue, you do not need to focus on critical activities. For example, on over-budget movie projects it is not uncommon to replace location shots with stock footage to cut costs.

Have Owner Take on More Responsibility

One way of reducing project costs is identifying tasks that customers can do themselves. Homeowners frequently use this method to reduce costs on home improvement projects. For example, to reduce the cost of a bathroom remodel, a homeowner may agree to paint the room instead of paying the contractor to do it. On IS projects, a customer may agree to take on some of the responsibility for testing equipment or providing in-house training. Naturally, this arrangement is best negotiated before the project begins. Customers are less receptive to this idea if you suddenly spring it on them. An advantage of this method is that, while costs are lowered, the original scope is retained. Clearly this option is limited to areas in which the customer has expertise and the capability to pick up the tasks.

Outsourcing Project Activities or Even the Entire Project

When estimates exceed budget, it not only makes sense to re-examine the scope but also search for cheaper ways to complete the project. Perhaps instead of relying on internal resources, it would be more cost effective to outsource segments or even the entire project, opening up work to external price competition. Specialized subcontractors often enjoy unique advantages, such as material discounts for large quantities, as well as equipment that not only gets the work done more quickly but also less expensively. They may have lower overhead and labor costs. For example, to reduce costs of software projects, many American firms outsource work to firms overseas where the salary of a software engineer is one-third that of an American software engineer. However, outsourcing means you have less control over the project and will need to have clearly definable deliverables.

Brainstorming Cost Savings Options

Just as project team members can be a rich source of ideas for accelerating project activities, they can offer tangible ways for reducing project costs. For example, one project manager reported that his team was able to come up with over $75,000 worth of cost saving suggestions without jeopardizing the scope of the project. Project managers should not underestimate the value of simply asking if there is a cheaper, better way.

Summary

The need for reducing the project duration occurs for many reasons such as imposed duration dates, time-to-market considerations, incentive contracts, key resource needs, high overhead costs, or simply unforeseen delays. These situations are very common in practice and are known as cost-time trade-off decisions. This chapter presented a logical, formal process for assessing the implications of situations that involve shortening the project duration. Crashing the project duration increases the *risk* of being late. How far to reduce the project duration from the normal time toward the optimum depends on the *sensitivity* of the project network. A sensitive network is one that has several critical or near-critical paths. Great care should be taken when shortening sensitive networks to avoid increasing project risks. Conversely, insensitive networks represent opportunities for potentially large project cost savings by eliminating some overhead costs with little downside risk.

Alternative strategies for reducing project time were discussed within the context of whether or not the project is resource limited. Project acceleration typically comes at a cost of either spending money for more resources or compromising the scope of the project. If the latter is the case, then it is essential that all relevant stakeholders be consulted so that everyone accepts the changes that have to be made. One other key point is the difference in implementing time-reducing activities in the midst of project execution versus incorporating them into the project plan. You typically have far fewer options once the project is under way than before it begins. This is especially true if you want to take advantage of the new scheduling methodologies such as fast-tracking and critical-chain. Time spent up front considering alternatives and developing contingency plans will lead to time savings in the end.

Key Terms

Crashing, *314*	Direct costs, *314*	Project Cost–Duration
Crash point, *315*	Fast-tracking, *311*	Graph, *313*
Crash time, *314*	Indirect costs, *313*	

Review Questions

1. What are five common reasons for crashing a project?
2. What are the advantages and disadvantages of reducing project scope to accelerate a project? What can be done to reduce the disadvantages?
3. Why is scheduling overtime a popular choice for getting projects back on schedule? What are the potential problems for relying on this option?
4. Identify four indirect costs you might find on a moderately complex project. Why are these costs classified as indirect?
5. How can a cost–duration graph be used by the project manager? Explain.
6. Reducing the project duration increases the risk of being late. Explain.
7. It is possible to shorten the critical path and save money. Explain how.

Exercises

1. Use the information contained below to compress one time unit per move using the least cost method. Reduce the schedule until you reach the crash point of the network. For each move identify what activity(ies) was crashed and the adjusted total cost.

   Note: The correct normal project duration, critical path, and total direct cost are provided.

Act.	Crash Cost (Slope)	Maximum Crash Time	Normal Time	Normal Cost
A	50	1	3	150
B	100	1	3	100
C	60	2	4	200
D	60	2	3	200
E	70	1	4	200
F	0	0	1	150

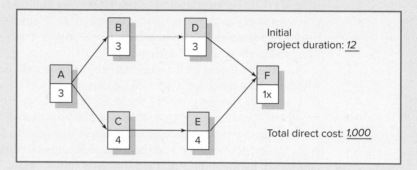

2. *Use the information contained below to compress one time unit per move using the least cost method. Reduce the schedule until you reach the crash point of the network. For each move identify what activity(ies) was crashed and the adjusted total cost.

   Note: Choose B instead of C and E (equal costs) because it is usually smarter to crash early rather than late AND one activity instead of two activities

Act.	Crash Cost (Slope)	Maximum Crash Time	Normal Time	Normal Cost
A	0		2	150
B	100	1	3	100
C	50	2	4	200
D	40	1	4	200
E	50	1	3	200
F	0		1	150

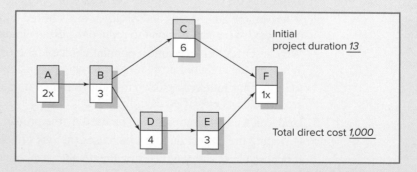

3. Use the information contained below to compress one time unit per move using the least cost method. Reduce the schedule until you reach the crash point of the network. For each move identify what activity(ies) was crashed and the adjusted total cost.

Act.	Crash Cost (Slope)	Maximum Crash Time	Normal Time	Normal Cost
A	100	1	2	150
B	80	1	3	100
C	60	1	2	200
D	40	1	5	200
E	40	2	5	200
F	40	2	3	150
G	20	1	5	200
H			1	200

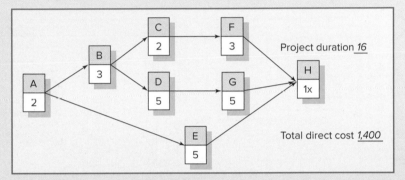

Project duration *16*

Total direct cost *1,400*

4. Given the data and information that follow, compute the total direct cost for each project duration. If the indirect costs for each project duration are $90 (15 time units), $70 (14), $50 (13), $40 (12), and $30 (11), compute the total project cost for each duration. What is the optimum cost-time schedule for the project? What is this cost?

Act.	Crash Cost (Slope)	Maximum Crash Time	Normal Time	Normal Cost
A	30	1	5	50
B	60	2	3	60
C	0	0	4	70
D	10	1	2	50
E	60	3	5	100
F	100	1	2	90
G	30	1	5	50
H	40	0	2	60
I	200	1	3	200
				$730

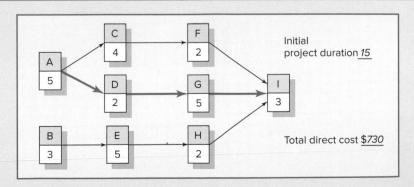

Initial project duration *15*

Total direct cost $*730*

5. Use the information contained below to compress one time unit per move using the least cost method. Assume the total indirect cost for the project is $700 and there is a savings of $50 per time unit reduced. Record the total direct, indirect, and project costs for each duration. What is the optimum cost-time schedule for the project? What is the cost?

   Note: The correct normal project duration and total direct cost are provided.

Act.	Crash Cost (Slope)	Maximum Crash Time	Normal Time	Normal Cost
A		0	2	100
B	100	1	3	200
C	40	1	5	200
D	60	2	3	200
E	20	1	5	200
F	40	1	4	150
G		0	2	150

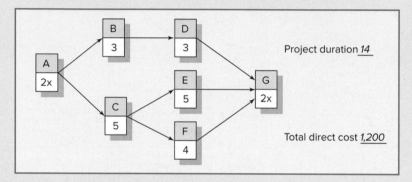

Project duration *14*

Total direct cost *1,200*

6. If the indirect costs for each duration are $300 for 27 days, $240 for 26 days, $180 for 25 days, $120 for 24 days, $60 for 23 days, and $50 for 22 days, compute the direct, indirect, and total costs for each duration. What is the optimum cost-time schedule? The customer offers you $10 for every day you shorten the project from your original network. Would you take it? If so for how many days?

Act.	Crash Cost (Slope)	Maximum Crash Time	Normal Time	Normal Cost
A	80	2	10	40
B	30	3	8	10
C	40	1	5	80
D	50	2	11	50
E	100	4	15	100
F	30	1	6	20
				$300

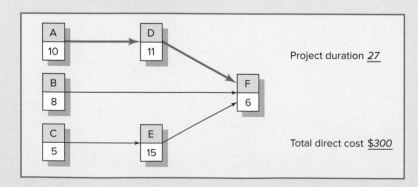

Project duration *27*

Total direct cost *$300*

7. Use the information contained below to compress one time unit per move using the least cost method. Assume the total indirect cost for the project is $2,000 and there is a savings of $100 per time unit reduced. Calculate the total direct, indirect, and project costs for each duration. Plot these costs on a graph. What is the optimum cost-time schedule for the project?

   Note: The correct normal project duration and total direct cost are provided.

Act.	Crash Cost (Slope)	Maximum Crash Time	Normal Time	Normal Cost
A		0	2	200
B	50	1	4	1000
C	200	2	5	800
D	200	2	5	1000
E	100	1	3	800
F	40	1	5	1000
G	40	1	4	1000
H		0	1	200

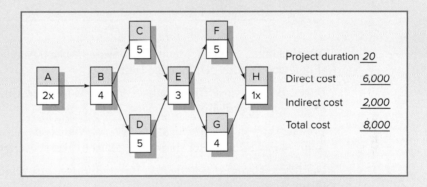

Project duration _20_

Direct cost _6,000_

Indirect cost _2,000_

Total cost _8,000_

8.*Use the information contained below to compress one time unit per move using the least cost method. Reduce the schedule until you reach the crash point of the network. For each move identify what activity(ies) was crashed, the adjusted total cost, and explain your choice if you have to choose between activities that cost the same.

   If the indirect cost for each duration is $1,500 for 17 weeks, $1,450 for 16 weeks, $1,400 for 15 weeks, $1,350 for 14 weeks, $1,300 for 13 weeks, $1,250 for 12 weeks, $1,200 for 11 weeks, and $1,150 for 10 weeks, what is the optimum cost-time schedule for the project? What is the cost?

* The solution to this exercise can be found in Appendix One.

Act.	Crash Cost (Slope)	Maximum Crash Time	Normal Time	Normal Cost
A	0	0	3	150
B	100	1	4	200
C	60	1	3	250
D	40	1	4	200
E	0	0	2	250
F	30	2	3	200
G	20	1	2	250
H	60	2	4	300
I	200	1	2	200

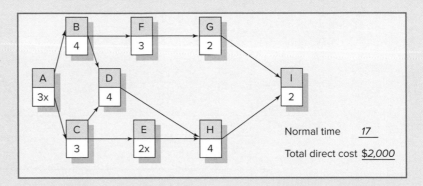

Normal time   _17_

Total direct cost $2,000

References

Abdel-Hamid, T., and S. Madnick, *Software Project Dynamics: An Integrated Approach* (Englewood Cliffs, NJ: Prentice Hall, 1991).

Baker, B. M., "Cost/Time Trade-off Analysis for the Critical Path Method," *Journal of the Operational Research Society,* vol. 48, no. 12 (1997), pp. 1241–44.

Brooks, F. P., Jr., *The Mythical Man-Month: Essays on Software Engineering Anniversary Edition* (Reading, MA: Addison-Wesley Longman, Inc., 1994), pp. 15–26.

DeMarco, T., *Slack: Getting Past Burnout, Busywork, and the Myth of Total Efficiency* (New York: Broadway, 2002).

Gordon, R. I. and J. C. Lamb, "A Closer Look at Brooke's Law," *Datamation,* June 1977, pp. 81–86.

Ibbs, C. W., S. A. Lee, and M. I. Li, "Fast-Tracking's Impact on Project Change," *Project Management Journal,* vol. 29, no. 4 (1998), pp. 35–42.

Khang, D. B., and M.Yin, "Time, Cost, and Quality Trade-off in Project Management," *International Journal of Project Management,* vol. 17, no. 4 (1999), pp. 249–56.

Perrow, L. A., *Finding Time: How Corporations, Individuals, and Families Can Benefit From New Work Practices* (Ithaca, NY: Cornell University Press, 1997).

Roemer, T. R., R. Ahmadi, and R. Wang, "Time-Cost Trade-offs in Overlapped Product Development," *Operations Research,* vol. 48, no. 6 (2000), pp. 858–65.

Smith, P. G., and D. G. Reinersten, *Developing Products in Half the Time* (New York: Van Nostrand Reinhold, 1995).

Verzuh, E., *The Fast Forward MBA in Project Management,* 4th ed. (New York: John Wiley, 2012).

Vroom, V. H., *Work and Motivation* (New York: John Wiley & Sons, 1964).

Case 9.1

International Capital, Inc.—Part B

Given the project network derived in Part A of the case from Chapter 7, Brown also wants to be prepared to answer any questions concerning compressing the project duration. This question will almost always be entertained by the accounting department, review committee, and the client. To be ready for the compression question, Brown has prepared the following data in case it is necessary to crash the project. (Use your weighted average times (t_e) computed in Part A of the International Capital case found in Chapter 7.)

Activity	Normal Cost	Maximum Crash Time	Crash Cost/Day
A	$ 3,000	3	$ 500
B	5,000	2	1,000
C	6,000	0	—
D	20,000	3	3,000
E	10,000	2	1,000
F	7,000	1	1,000
G	20,000	2	3,000
H	8,000	1	2,000
I	5,000	1	2,000
J	7,000	1	1,000
K	12,000	6	1,000
Total normal costs = $103,000			

Using the data provided, determine the activity crashing decisions and best-time cost project duration. Given the information you have developed, what suggestions would you give Brown to ensure she is well prepared for the project review committee? Assume the overhead costs for this project are $700 per workday. Will this alter your suggestions?

Case 9.2

Whitbread World Sailboat Race

Each year countries enter their sailing vessels in the nine-month Round the World Whitbread Sailboat Race. In recent years, about 14 countries entered sailboats in the race. Each year's sailboat entries represent the latest technologies and human skills each country can muster.

Bjorn Ericksen has been selected as a project manager because of his past experience as a master helmsman and because of his recent fame as the "best designer of racing sailboats in the world." Bjorn is pleased and proud to have the opportunity to design, build, test, and train the crew for next year's Whitbread entry for his country. Bjorn has picked Karin Knutsen (as chief design engineer) and Trygve Wallvik (as master helmsman) to be team leaders responsible for getting next year's entry ready for the traditional parade of all entries on the Thames River in the United Kingdom, which signals the start of the race.

As Bjorn begins to think of a project plan, he sees two parallel paths running through the project—design and construction and crew training. Last year's boat will be used for training until the new entry can have the crew on board to learn maintenance tasks. Bjorn calls Karin and Trygve together to develop a project plan. All three agree the major goal is to have a winning boat and crew ready to compete in next year's competition at a cost of $3.2 million. A check of Bjorn's calendar indicates he has 45 weeks before next year's vessel must leave port for the United Kingdom to start the race.

THE KICKOFF MEETING

Bjorn asks Karin to begin by describing the major activities and the sequence required to design, construct, and test the boat. Karin starts by noting that design of the hull, deck, mast, and accessories should only take six weeks—given the design prints from past race entries and a few prints from other countries' entries. After the design is complete, the hull can be constructed, the mast ordered, sails ordered, and accessories ordered. The hull will require 12 weeks to complete. The mast can be ordered and will require a lead time of eight weeks; the seven sails can be ordered and will take six weeks to get; accessories can be ordered and will take 15 weeks to receive. As soon as the hull is finished, the ballast tanks can be installed, requiring two weeks. Then the deck can be built, which will require five weeks. Concurrently, the hull can be treated with special sealant and friction-resistance coating, taking three weeks. When the deck is completed and mast and accessories received, the mast and sails can be installed, requiring two weeks; the accessories can be installed, which will take six weeks. When all of these activities have been completed, the ship can be sea-tested, which should take five weeks. Karin believes she can have firm cost estimates for the boat in about two weeks.

Trygve believes he can start selecting the 12-man or woman crew and securing their housing immediately. He believes it will take six weeks to get a committed crew on-site and three weeks to secure housing for the crew members. Trygve reminds Bjorn that last year's vessel must be ready to use for training the moment the crew is on-site until the new vessel is ready for testing. Keeping the old vessel operating will cost $4,000 per week as long as it is used. Once the crew is on-site and housed, they can develop and implement a routine sailing and maintenance training program, which will take 15 weeks (using the old vessel). Also, once the crew is selected and on-site, crew equipment can be selected, taking only two weeks. Then crew equipment can be ordered; it will take five weeks to arrive. When the crew equipment and maintenance training program are complete, crew maintenance on the new vessel can begin; this should take 10 weeks. But crew maintenance on the new vessel cannot begin until the deck is complete and the mast, sails, and accessories have arrived. Once crew maintenance on the new vessel begins, the new vessel will cost $6,000 per week until sea training is complete. After the new ship maintenance is complete and while the boat is being tested, initial sailing training can be implemented; training should take seven weeks. Finally, after the boat is tested and initial training is complete, regular sea training can be implemented—weather permitting; regular sea training requires eight weeks. Trygve believes he can put the cost estimates together in a week, given last year's expenses.

Bjorn is pleased with the expertise displayed by his team leaders. But he believes they need to have someone develop one of those critical path networks to see if they can safely meet the start deadline for the race. Karin and Trygve agree. Karin suggests the cost estimates should also include crash costs for any activities that can be compressed and the resultant costs for crashing. Karin also suggests the team complete the following priority matrix for project decision making:

FIGURE C9.1
Project Priority
Matrix: Whitbread
Project

	Time	Performance	Cost
Constrain			
Enhance			
Accept			

TWO WEEKS LATER

Karin and Trygve submit the following cost estimates for each activity and corresponding crash costs to Bjorn (costs are in thousands of dollars):

Activity		Normal Time	Normal Cost	Crash Time	Crash Cost
A	Design	6	$ 40	2	$ —
B	Build hull	12	1,000	2	—
C	Install ballast tanks	2	100	0	—
D	Order mast	8	100	1	200
E	Order sails	6	40	0	—
F	Order accessories	15	600	2	100
G	Build deck	5	200	0	—
H	Coat hull	3	40	0	—
I	Install accessories	6	300	1	100
J	Install mast and sails	2	40	1	40
K	Test	5	60	1	40
L	Sea trials	8	200	1	250
M	Select crew	6	10	1	10
N	Secure housing	3	30	0	—
O	Select crew equipment	2	10	0	—
P	Order crew equipment	5	30	0	—
Q	Routine sail/maintenance	15	40	3	30
R	Crew maintenance training	10	100	1	240
S	Initial sail training	7	50	2	150
	Total direct cost		$2,990		

Bjorn reviews the materials and wonders if the project will come in within the budget of $3.2 million and in 45 weeks. Advise the Whitbread team of their situation.

Case 9.3

Nightingale Project—A

You are the assistant project manager to Rassy Brown, who is in charge of the Nightingale project. Nightingale was the code name given to the development of a handheld electronic medical reference guide. Nightingale would be designed for emergency medical technicians and paramedics who need a quick reference guide to use in emergency situations.

Rassy and her project team were developing a project plan aimed at producing 30 working models in time for MedCON, the biggest medical equipment trade show each year. Meeting the MedCON October 25 deadline was critical to success. All the major medical equipment manufacturers demonstrated and took orders for new products at MedCON. Rassy had also heard rumors that competitors were considering developing a similar product, and she knew that being first to market would have a significant sales advantage. Besides, top management made funding contingent upon developing a workable plan for meeting the MedCON deadline.

The project team spent the morning working on the schedule for Nightingale. They started with the WBS and developed the information for a network, adding activities when needed. Then the team added the time estimates they had collected for each activity. Following is the preliminary information for activities with duration time and predecessors:

Activity	Description	Duration	Predecessor
1	Architectural decisions	10	None
2	Internal specifications	20	1
3	External specifications	18	1
4	Feature specifications	15	1
5	Voice recognition	15	2,3
6	Case	4	2,3
7	Screen	2	2,3
8	Speaker output jacks	2	2,3
9	Tape mechanism	2	2,3
10	Database	40	4
11	Microphone/soundcard	5	4
12	Pager	4	4
13	Barcode reader	3	4
14	Alarm clock	4	4
15	Computer I/O	5	4
16	Review design	10	5,6,7,8,9,10,11,12,13,14,15
17	Price components	5	5,6,7,8,9,10,11,12,13,14,15
18	Integration	15	16,17
19	Document design	35	16
20	Procure prototype components	20	18
21	Assemble prototypes	10	20
22	Lab test prototypes	20	21
23	Field test prototypes	20	19,22
24	Adjust design	20	23
25	Order stock parts	15	24
26	Order custom parts	2	24
27	Assemble first production unit	10	25, FS—8 time units 26, FS—13 time units
28	Test unit	10	27
29	Produce 30 units	15	28
30	Train sales representatives	10	29

Use any project network computer program available to you to develop the schedule for activities (see Case Appendix for further instructions)—noting late and early times, the critical path, and estimated completion for the project.

Prepare a short memo that addresses the following questions:

1. Will the project as planned meet the October 25th deadline?
2. What activities lie on the critical path?
3. How sensitive is this network?

Case 9.4

Nightingale Project—B

Rassy and the team were concerned with the results of your analysis. They spent the afternoon brainstorming alternative ways for shortening the project duration. They rejected outsourcing activities because most of the work was developmental in nature and could only be done in-house. They considered altering the scope of the project by eliminating some of the proposed product features. After much debate, they felt they could not compromise any of the core features and be successful in the marketplace. They then turned their attention to accelerating the completion of activities through overtime and adding additional technical manpower. Rassy had built into her proposal a discretionary fund of $200,000. She was willing to invest up to half of this fund to accelerate the project, but wanted to hold onto at least $100,000 to deal with unexpected problems. After a lengthy discussion, her team concluded that the following activities could be reduced at the specified cost:

- Development of voice recognition system could be reduced from 15 days to 10 days at a cost of $15,000.
- Creation of database could be reduced from 40 days to 35 days at a cost of $35,000.
- Document design could be reduced from 35 days to 30 days at a cost of $25,000.
- External specifications could be reduced from 18 days to 12 days at a cost of $20,000.
- Procure prototype components could be reduced from 20 days to 15 days at a cost of $30,000.
- Order stock parts could be reduced from 15 days to 10 days at a cost of $20,000.

Ken Clark, a development engineer, pointed out that the network contained only finish-to-start relationships and that it might be possible to reduce project duration by creating start-to-start lags. For example, he said that his people would not have to wait for all of the field tests to be completed to begin making final adjustments in the design. They could start making adjustments after the first 15 days of testing. The project team spent the remainder of the day analyzing how they could introduce lags into the network to hopefully shorten the project. They concluded that the following finish-to-start relationships could be converted into lags:

- Document design could begin 5 days after the start of the review design.
- Adjust design could begin 15 days after the start of field test prototypes.
- Order stock parts could begin 5 days after the start of adjust design.
- Order custom parts could begin 5 days after the start of adjust design.

10 Being an Effective Project Manager

LEARNING OBJECTIVES

After reading this chapter you should be able to:

10-1 Understand the difference between leading and managing a project.

10-2 Understand the need to manage project stakeholders.

10-3 Identify and apply different "influence currencies" to build positive relations with others.

10-4 Create a stakeholder map and develop strategies for managing project dependencies.

10-5 Understand the need for a highly interactive management style on projects.

10-6 More effectively manage project expectations.

10-7 Develop strategies for managing upward relations.

10-8 Understand the importance of building trust and acting in an ethical manner while working on a project.

10-9 Identify the qualities of an effective project manager.

OUTLINE

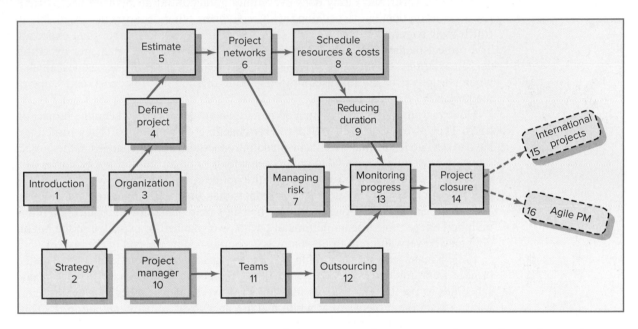

I couldn't wait to be the manager of my own project and run the project the way I thought it should be done. Boy, did I have a lot to learn!

—First-time project manager

This chapter is based on the premise that one of the keys to being an effective project manager is building cooperative relationships among different groups of people to complete projects. Project success does not just depend on the performance of the project team. Success or failure often depends on the contributions of top management, functional managers, customers, suppliers, contractors, and others.

The chapter begins with a brief discussion of the differences between leading and managing a project. The importance of managing project stakeholders is then introduced. Managers require a broad influence base to be effective in this area. Different sources of influence are discussed and are used to describe how project managers build social capital. This management style necessitates constant interacting with different groups of people whom project managers depend on. Special attention is devoted to managing the critical relationship with top management and the importance of leading by example. The importance of gaining cooperation in ways that build and sustain the trust of others is emphasized. The chapter concludes by identifying personal attributes associated with being an effective project manager. Subsequent chapters will expand on these ideas in a discussion of managing the project team and working with people outside the organization.

10.1 Managing versus Leading a Project

 10-1

Understand the difference between leading and managing a project.

In a perfect world, the project manager would simply implement the project plan and the project would be completed. The project manager would work with others to formulate a schedule, organize a project team, keep track of progress, and announce what needs to be done next, and then everyone would charge along. Of course no one lives in a perfect world, and rarely does everything go according to plan. Project participants get testy; they fail to get along with each other; other departments are unable to fulfill their commitments; technical glitches arise; work takes longer than expected. The project manager's job is to get the project back on track. A manager expedites certain activities; figures out ways to solve technical problems; serves as peacemaker when tensions rise; and makes appropriate trade-offs among time, cost, and scope of the project.

However, project managers often do more than put out fires and keep the project on track. They also innovate and adapt to ever-changing circumstances. They sometimes have to deviate from what was planned and introduce significant changes in the project scope and schedule to respond to unforeseen threats or opportunities. For example, customers' needs may change, requiring significant design changes midway through the project. Competitors may release new products that dictate crashing project deadlines. Working relationships among project participants may break down, requiring a reformulation of the project team. Ultimately, what was planned or expected in the beginning may be very different from what was accomplished by the end of the project.

Project managers are responsible for integrating assigned resources to complete the project according to plan. At the same time they need to initiate changes in plans and schedules as persistent problems make plans unworkable. In other words, managers want to keep the project going while making necessary adjustments along the way. According to Kotter (1990) these two different activities represent the distinction between management and leadership. Management is about coping with complexity, while leadership is about coping with change.

Good management brings about order and stability by formulating plans and objectives, designing structures and procedures, monitoring results against plans, and taking corrective action when necessary. Leadership involves recognizing and articulating the need to significantly alter the direction and operation of the project, aligning people to the new direction, and motivating them to work together to overcome hurdles produced by the change and to realize new objectives.

Strong leadership, while usually desirable, is not always necessary to successfully complete a project. Well-defined projects that encounter no significant surprises require little leadership, as might be the case in constructing a conventional apartment building in which the project manager simply administrates the project plan. Conversely, the higher the degree of uncertainty encountered on a project—whether in terms of changes in project scope, technological stalemates, breakdowns in coordination between people, and so forth—the more leadership is required. For example, strong leadership would be needed for a software development project in which the parameters are always changing to meet developments in the industry.

It takes a special person to perform both roles well. Some individuals are great visionaries who are good at exciting people about change. Too often though, these same people lack the discipline or patience to deal with the day-to-day drudgeries of managing. Likewise, there are other individuals who are very well organized and methodical but lack the ability to inspire others.

Strong leaders can compensate for their managerial weaknesses by having trusted assistants who oversee and manage the details of the project. Conversely, a weak leader can complement his or her strengths by having assistants who are good at sensing the need to change and rallying project participants. Still, one of the things that make good project managers so valuable to an organization is that they have the ability to both manage and lead a project. In doing so they recognize the need to create a social network that allows them to find out what needs to be done and obtain the cooperation necessary to achieve it.

10.2 Managing Project Stakeholders

 LO 10-2

Understand the need to manage project stakeholders.

First-time project managers are eager to implement their own ideas and manage their people to successfully complete their project. What they soon find out is that project success depends on the cooperation of a wide range of individuals, many of whom do not directly report to them. For example, during the course of a system integration project, a project manager was surprised by how much time she was spending negotiating and working with vendors, consultants, technical specialists, and other functional managers:

> Instead of working with my people to complete the project, I found myself being constantly pulled and tugged by demands of different groups of people who were not directly involved in the project but had a vested interest in the outcome.

Too often when new project managers do find time to work directly on the project, they adopt a hands-on approach to managing the project. They choose this style not because they are power-hungry egomaniacs but because they are eager to achieve results. They become quickly frustrated by how slowly things operate, the number of people that have to be brought on board, and the difficulty of gaining cooperation. Unfortunately, as this frustration builds, the natural temptation is to exert more pressure and get more heavily involved in the project. These project managers quickly earn the reputation of "micro managing" and begin to lose sight of the real role they play on guiding a project.

Some new managers never break out of this vicious cycle. Others soon realize that authority does not equal influence and that being an effective project manager involves managing a much more complex and expansive set of interfaces than they had previously anticipated. They encounter a web of relationships that requires a much broader spectrum of influence than they felt was necessary or even possible.

For example, a significant project, whether it involves renovating a bridge, creating a new product, or installing a new information system, will likely involve in one way or another working with a number of different groups of stakeholders. First, there is the core group of specialists assigned to complete the project. This group is likely to be supplemented at different times by professionals who work on specific segments of the project. Second, there are the groups of people within the performing organization who are either directly or indirectly involved with the project. The most notable is top management, to whom the project manager is accountable. There are also other

FIGURE 10.1
Network of
Stakeholders

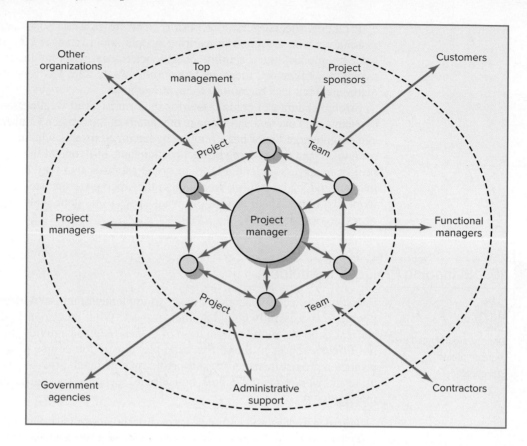

managers who provide resources and/or may be responsible for specific segments of the project, and administrative support services such as human resources, finance, etc. Depending on the nature of the project, there are a number of different groups outside the organization that influence the success of the project; the most important is the customer for which the project is designed (see Figure 10.1).

Each of these groups of stakeholders brings different expertise, standards, priorities, and agendas to the project. **Stakeholders** are people and organizations that are actively involved in the project, or whose interests may be positively or negatively affected by the project (PMBOK, 2013). The sheer breadth and complexity of stakeholder relationships distinguish project management from regular management. To be effective, a project manager must understand how stakeholders can affect the project and develop methods for managing the dependency. The nature of these dependencies is identified here:

- The **project team** manages and completes project work. Most participants want to do a good job, but they are also concerned with their other obligations and how their involvement on the project will contribute to their personal goals and aspirations.

- **Project managers** naturally compete with each other for resources and the support of top management. At the same time they often have to share resources and exchange information.

- **Administrative support** groups, such as human resources, information systems, purchasing agents, and maintenance, provide valuable support services. At the same time they impose constraints and requirements on the project such as the documentation of expenditures and the timely and accurate delivery of information.

- **Functional managers,** depending on how the project is organized, can play a minor or major role toward project success. In matrix arrangements, they may be responsible for assigning project personnel, resolving technical dilemmas, and overseeing the completion of significant segments of the project work. Even in dedicated project teams, the technical input from functional managers may be useful, and acceptance of completed project work may be critical to in-house projects. Functional managers want to cooperate up to a point, but only up to a certain point. They are also concerned with preserving their status within the organization and minimizing the disruptions the project may have on their own operations.

- **Top management** approves funding of the project and establishes priorities within the organization. They define success and adjudicate rewards for accomplishments. Significant adjustments in budget, scope, and schedule typically need their approval. They have a natural vested interest in the success of the project, but at the same time have to be responsive to what is best for the entire organization.

- **Project sponsors** champion the project and use their influence to gain approval of the project. Their reputation is tied to the success of the project, and they need to be kept informed of any major developments. They defend the project when it comes under attack and are a key project ally.

- **Contractors** may do all the actual work, in some cases, with the project team merely coordinating their contributions. In other cases, they are responsible for ancillary segments of the project scope. Poor work and schedule slips can affect work of the core project team. While contractors' reputations rest with doing good work, they must balance their contributions with their own profit margins and their commitments to other clients.

- **Government agencies** place constraints on project work. Permits need to be secured. Construction work has to be built to code. New drugs have to pass a rigorous battery of U.S. Food and Drug Administration tests. Other products have to meet safety standards, for example, Occupational Safety and Health Administration standards.

- **Other organizations,** depending on the nature of the project, may directly or indirectly affect the project. For example, suppliers provide necessary resources for completion of the project work. Delays, shortages, and poor quality can bring a project to a standstill. Public interest groups may apply pressure on government agencies. Customers often hire consultants and auditors to protect their interests on a project.

- **Customers** define the scope of the project, and ultimate project success rests in their satisfaction. Project managers need to be responsive to changing customer needs and requirements and to meeting their expectations. Customers are primarily concerned with getting a *good deal* and, as will be elaborated in Chapter 11, this naturally breeds tension with the project team.

These relationships are interdependent in that a project manager's ability to work effectively with one group will affect her ability to manage other groups. For example, functional managers are likely to be less cooperative if they perceive that top management's commitment to the project is waning. Conversely, the ability of the project manager to buffer the team from excessive interference from a client is likely to increase her standing with the project team.

The project management structure being used will influence the number and degree of external dependencies that will need to be managed. One advantage of creating a

SNAPSHOT FROM PRACTICE 10.1 The Project Manager as Conductor

Metaphors convey meaning beyond words. For example, a meeting can be described as being difficult or "like wading through molasses." A popular metaphor for the role of a project manager is that of *conductor*. The conductor of an orchestra integrates the divergent sounds of different instruments to perform a given composition and make beautiful music. Similarly, the project manager integrates the talents and contributions of different specialists to complete the project. Both have to be good at understanding how the different players contribute to the performance of the whole. Both are almost entirely dependent upon the expertise and know-how of the players. The conductor does not have command of all the musical instruments. Likewise, the project manager usually possesses only a small proportion of the technical knowledge to make decisions. As such, the conductor and project manager both facilitate the performance of others rather than actually perform.

Conductors use their arms, baton, and other nonverbal gestures to influence the pace, intensity, and involvement of different musicians. Likewise, project managers orchestrate the completion of the project by

© JGI/Jamie Grill/Blend Images LLC

managing the involvement and attention of project members. Project managers balance time and process and induce participants to make the right decisions at the right time just as the conductor induces the wind instruments to perform at the right moment in a movement. Each controls the rhythm and intensity of work by managing the tempo and involvement of the players. Finally, each has a vision that transcends the music score or project plan. To be successful they must both earn the confidence, respect, and trust of their players.

dedicated project team is that it reduces dependencies, especially within the organization, because most of the resources are assigned to the project. Conversely, a functional matrix structure increases dependencies, with the result that the project manager is much more reliant upon functional colleagues for work and staff.

The old-fashioned view of managing projects emphasized planning and directing the project team; the new perspective emphasizes managing project stakeholders and anticipating change as the most important jobs. Project managers need to be able to assuage concerns of customers, sustain support for the project at higher levels of the organization, quickly identify problems that threaten project work, while at the same time defend the integrity of the project and the interests of the project participants.[1]

Within this web of relationships, the project manager must find out what needs to be done to achieve the goals of the project and build a cooperative network to accomplish it. Project managers must do so without the requisite authority to expect or demand cooperation. Doing so requires sound communication skills, political savvy, and a broad influence base. See the Snapshot from Practice 10.1: The Project Manager as Conductor for more on what makes project managers special. See Research Highlight 10.1: Give and Take for an interesting finding regarding this concept.

[1] For a systematic treatise on stakeholder management, see: Lynda Bourne, *Stakeholder Relationship Management* (Farnham, England: Gower Publishing Ltd., 2009).

Adam Grant from the University of Pennsylvania identified three fundamental styles of social interaction with regard to the law of reciprocity:

Takers: Like to get more than give and put their own interests ahead of others.

Givers: Prefer to give more than they get and pay more attention to what others need.

Matchers: Strive to preserve an equal balance between giving and getting and operate on the principle of fairness.

While Grant admits that people will shift from one style to another, he cites research that indicates that most people develop a primary interaction style. He goes on to review research on the relationship between interaction style and professional success. Not surprisingly, he found *Givers* tend to sink to the bottom of the success ladder. They make others better off but sacrifice their own success in the process.

Guess who was at the very top of the success ladder? It was *Givers* again! Grant goes on to explain this paradox by arguing that while it is true that many *Givers* are too caring and too timid, there are other *Givers* who are willing to give more than they receive, and still keep their own interests in sight, using them as a guide for choosing when, how, and to whom to give. These kind of *Givers* are able to create much bigger and more powerful social networks than *Takers* and *Matchers*. The good will they are able to generate is a major factor behind the success of this kind of *Givers*.

Grant claims that Abraham Lincoln is a perfect example of a *Giver* that climbed to the top. When he won the presidency in 1860, he recruited bitter competitors whom he had earlier defeated to join his management team (Cabinet) in key positions. Grant predicts a *Taker* would have protected his ego and invited only "yes men" and a *Matcher* would have offered appointments to allies. Lincoln reported he needed the best men possible to run the country and by always focusing on what was best for the country he was able to forge an effective management team.

* Adam Grant, *Give and Take: A Revolutionary Approach to Success* (New York: Viking Press, 2013).

10.3 Influence as Exchange

LO 10-3

Identify and apply different "influence currencies" to build positive relations with others.

To successfully manage a project, a manager must adroitly build a cooperative network among divergent allies. Networks are mutually beneficial alliances that are generally governed by the **law of reciprocity** (Kaplan, 1984; Grant, 2013). The basic principle is that "one good deed deserves another, and likewise, one bad deed deserves another." The primary way to gain cooperation is to provide resources and services for others in exchange for future resources and services. This is the age-old maxim: "Quid pro quo (something for something)." Or in today's vernacular: "You scratch my back, I'll scratch yours."

Cohen and Bradford (1990) described the exchange view of influence as "currencies." If you want to do business in a given country, you have to be prepared to use the appropriate currency, and the exchange rates can change over time as conditions change. In the same way, what is valued by a marketing manager may be different from what is valued by a veteran project engineer, and you are likely to need to use different influence currency to obtain the cooperation of each individual. Although this analogy is a bit of an oversimplification, the key premise holds true that in the long run, "debit" and "credit" accounts must be balanced for cooperative relationships to work. Table 10.1 presents the commonly traded organizational currencies identified by Cohen and Bradford; they are then discussed in more detail in the following sections.

Task-Related Currencies

This form of influence comes in different forms and is based on the project manager's ability to contribute to others' accomplishing their work. Probably the most significant form of this currency is the ability to respond to subordinates' requests for additional

TABLE 10.1
Commonly Traded Organizational Currencies

Source: Adapted from A. R. Cohen and David L. Bradford, *Influence without Authority* (New York: John Wiley & Sons, 1990).

Task-related currencies

Resources	Lending or giving money, budget increases, personnel, etc.
Assistance	Helping with existing projects or undertaking unwanted tasks.
Cooperation	Giving task support, providing quicker response time, or aiding implementation.
Information	Providing organizational as well as technical knowledge.

Position-related currencies

Advancement	Giving a task or assignment that can result in promotion.
Recognition	Acknowledging effort, accomplishments, or abilities.
Visibility	Providing a chance to be known by higher-ups or significant others in the organization.
Network/contacts	Providing opportunities for linking with others.

Inspiration-related currencies

Vision	Being involved in a task that has larger significance for the unit, organization, customer, or society.
Excellence	Having a chance to do important things really well.
Ethical correctness	Doing what is "right" by a higher standard than efficiency.

Relationship-related currencies

Acceptance	Providing closeness and friendship.
Personal support	Giving personal and emotional backing.
Understanding	Listening to others' concerns and issues.

Personal-related currencies

Challenge/learning	Sharing tasks that increase skills and abilities.
Ownership/involvement	Letting others have ownership and influence.
Gratitude	Expressing appreciation.

manpower, money, or time to complete a segment of a project. This kind of currency is also evident in sharing resources with another project manager who is in need. At a more personal level, it may simply mean providing direct assistance to a colleague in solving a technical problem.

Providing a good word for a colleague's proposal or recommendation is another form of this currency. Because most work of significance is likely to generate some form of opposition, the person who is trying to gain approval for a plan or proposal can be greatly aided by having a "friend in court."

Another form of this currency includes extraordinary effort. For example, fulfilling an emergency request to complete a design document in two days instead of the normal four days is likely to engender gratitude. Finally, sharing valuable information that would be useful to other managers is another form of this currency.

Position-Related Currencies

This form of influence stems from the manager's ability to enhance others' positions within their organization. A project manager can do this by giving someone a challenging assignment that can aid their advancement by developing their skills and abilities. Being given a chance to prove yourself naturally generates a strong sense of gratitude. Sharing the glory and bringing to the attention of higher-ups the efforts and accomplishments of others generate goodwill.

Project managers confide that a useful strategy for gaining the cooperation of professionals in other departments/organizations is figuring out how to make these people look good to their bosses. For example, a project manager worked with a subcontractor whose organization was heavily committed to total quality management (TQM). The project manager made it a point in top-level briefing meetings to point out how quality improvement processes initiated by the contractor contributed to cost control and problem prevention.

Another variation of recognition is enhancing the reputation of others within the firm. "Good press" can pave the way for lots of opportunities, while "bad press" can quickly shut a person off and make it difficult to perform. This currency is also evident in helping to preserve someone's reputation by coming to the defense of someone unjustly blamed for project setbacks.

Finally, one of the strongest forms of this currency is sharing contacts with other people. Helping individuals expand their own networks by introducing them to key people naturally engenders gratitude. For example, suggesting to a functional manager that he should contact Sally X if he wants to find out what is really going on in that department or to get a request expedited is likely to engender a sense of indebtedness.

Inspiration-Related Currencies

Perhaps the most powerful form of influence is based on inspiration. Most sources of inspiration derive from people's burning desire to make a difference and add meaning to their lives. Creating an exciting, bold vision for a project can elicit extraordinary commitment. For example, many of the technological breakthroughs associated with the introduction of the original Macintosh computer were attributed to the feeling that the project members had a chance to change the way people approached computers. A variant form of vision is providing an opportunity to do something really well. Being able to take pride in your work often drives many people.

Often the very nature of the project provides a source of inspiration. Discovering a cure for a devastating disease, introducing a new social program that will help those in need, or simply building a bridge that will reduce a major traffic bottleneck can provide opportunities for people to feel good about what they are doing and that they are making a difference. Inspiration operates as a magnet—pulling people as opposed to pushing people toward doing something.

Relationship-Related Currencies

These currencies have more to do with strengthening the relationship with someone than directly accomplishing the project tasks. The essence of this form of influence is forming a relationship that transcends normal professional boundaries and extends into the realm of friendship. Such relationships develop by giving personal and emotional backing. Picking people up when they are feeling down, boosting their confidence, and providing encouragement naturally breed goodwill. Sharing a sense of humor and making difficult times fun is another form of this currency. Similarly, engaging in non-work-related activities such as sports and family outings is another way relationships are naturally enhanced.

Perhaps the most basic form of this currency is simply listening to other people. Psychologists suggest that most people have a strong desire to be understood and that relationships break down because the parties stop listening to each other. Sharing personal secrets/ambitions and being a wise confidant also creates a special bond between individuals.

Personal-Related Currencies

This last form of currency deals with individual needs and an overriding sense of self-esteem. Some argue that self-esteem is a primary psychological need; the extent to which we can help others feel a sense of importance and personal worth will naturally generate goodwill. A project manager can enhance a colleague's sense of worth by asking for help and seeking opinions, delegating authority over work and allowing individuals to feel comfortable stretching their abilities. This form of currency can also be seen in sincere expressions of gratitude for the contributions of others. Care, though, must be exercised in expressing gratitude since it is easily devalued when overused. That is, the first *thank you* is likely to be more valued than the fiftieth.

The bottom line is that a project manager will be influential only insofar as she can offer something that others value. Furthermore, given the diverse cast of people a project manager depends on, it is important that she be able to acquire and exercise different influence currencies. The ability to do so will be constrained in part by the nature of the project and how it is organized. For example, a project manager who is in charge of a dedicated team has considerably more to offer team members than a manager who is given the responsibility of coordinating the activities of different professionals across different departments and organizations. In such cases, that manager will probably have to rely more heavily on personal and relational bases of influence to gain the cooperation of others.

10.4 Social Network Building

LO 10-4

Create a stakeholder map and develop strategies for managing project dependencies.

Mapping Stakeholder Dependencies

The first step to **social network building** is identifying those stakeholders on whom the project depends for success. The project manager and his or her key assistants need to ask the following questions:

- Whose cooperation will we need?
- Whose agreement or approval will we need?
- Whose opposition would keep us from accomplishing the project?

Many project managers find it helpful to draw a map of these dependencies. For example, Figure 10.2 contains the dependencies identified by a project manager responsible for installing a new financial software system in her company.

It is always better to overestimate rather than underestimate dependencies. All too often, otherwise talented and successful project managers have been derailed because they were blindsided by someone whose position or power they had not anticipated. After identifying the stakeholders associated with your project, it is important to assess their significance. Here the power/interest matrix introduced in Chapter 3 becomes useful. Those individuals with the most power over and interest in the project are the most significant stakeholders and deserve the greatest attention. In particular, you need to "step into their shoes" and see the project from their perspective:

- What differences exist between myself and the people on whom I depend (goals, values, pressures, working styles, risks)?
- How do these different people view the project (supporters, indifferents, antagonists)?

FIGURE 10.2
Stakeholder Map for Financial Software Installation Project

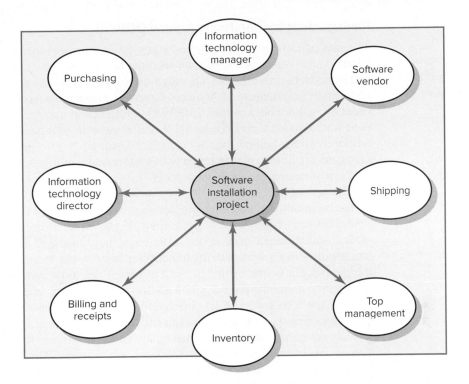

- What is the current status of the relationship I have with the people I depend on?
- What sources of influence do I have relative to those on whom I depend?

Once you start this analysis you can begin to appreciate what others value and what currencies you might have to offer as a basis on which to build a working relationship. You begin to realize where potential problems lie—relationships in which you have a current debit or no convertible currency. Furthermore, diagnosing another's point of view as well as the basis for their positions will help you anticipate their reactions and feelings about your decisions and actions. This information is vital for selecting the appropriate influence strategy and tactics and producing win/win solutions.

For example, after mapping her dependency network, the project manager who was in charge of installing the software system realized that she was likely to have serious problems with the manager of the receipts department, who would be one of the primary users of the software. She had no previous history of working with this individual but had heard through the grapevine that the manager was upset with the choice of software and that he considered this project to be another unnecessary disruption of his department's operation.

Prior to project initiation the project manager arranged to have lunch with the manager, where she sat patiently and listened to his concerns. She invested additional time and attention to educate him and his staff about the benefits of the new software. She tried to minimize the disruptions the transition would cause in his department. She altered the implementation schedule to accommodate his preferences as to when the actual software would be installed and the subsequent training would occur. In turn, the receipts manager and his people were much more accepting of the change, and the transition to the new software went more smoothly than anticipated.

LO 10-5

Understand the need for a highly interactive management style on projects.

Management by Wandering Around (MBWA)

The preceding example illustrates a key point - project management is a "contact sport." Once you have established who the key players are, then you initiate contact and begin to build a relationship with those players. Building this relationship requires an interactive management style employees at Hewlett-Packard refer to as **"management by wandering around" (MBWA)** to reflect that managers spend the majority of their time outside their offices. MBWA is somewhat of a misnomer in that there is a purpose/pattern behind the "wandering." Through face-to-face interactions, project managers are able to stay in touch with what is really going on in the project and build cooperation essential to project success.

Effective project managers initiate contact with key players to keep abreast of developments, anticipate potential problems, provide encouragement, and reinforce the objectives and vision of the project. They are able to intervene to resolve conflicts and prevent stalemates from occurring. In essence, they "manage" the project. By staying in touch with various aspects of the project they become the focal point for information on the project. Participants turn to them to obtain the most current and comprehensive information about the project which reinforces their central role as project manager.

We have also observed less-effective project managers who eschew MBWA and attempt to manage projects from their offices and computer terminals. Such managers proudly announce an open-door policy and encourage others to see them when a problem or an issue comes up. To them no news is good news. This allows their contacts to be determined by the relative aggressiveness of others. Those who take the initiative and seek out the project manager get too high a proportion of the project manager's attention. Those people less readily available (physically removed) or more passive get ignored. This behavior contributes to the adage, "Only the squeaky wheel gets greased," which breeds resentment within the project team.

Effective project managers also find the time to regularly interact with more distal stakeholders. They keep in touch with suppliers, vendors, top management, and other functional managers. In doing so they maintain familiarity with different parties, sustain friendships, discover opportunities to do favors, and understand the motives and needs of others. They remind people of commitments and champion the cause of their project. They also shape people's expectations (see Snapshot from Practice 10.2: Managing Expectations). Through frequent communication they alleviate people's concerns about the project, dispel rumors, warn people of potential problems, and lay the groundwork for dealing with setbacks in a more effective manner.

Unless project managers take the initiative to build a supportive network up front, they are likely to see a manager (or other stakeholder) only when there is bad news or when they need a favor (e.g., they don't have the data they promised or the project has slipped behind schedule). Without prior, frequent, easy give-and-take interactions around nondecisive issues, the encounter prompted by the problem is likely to provoke excess tension. The parties are more likely to act defensively, interrupt each other, and lose sight of the common goal.

Experienced project managers recognize the need to build relationships before they need them. They initiate contact with the key stakeholders at times when there are no outstanding issues or problems and therefore no anxieties and suspicions. On these social occasions, they naturally engage in small talk and responsive banter. They respond to others' requests for aid, provide supportive counsel, and exchange information. In doing so they establish good feelings which will allow them to deal with more serious problems down the road. When one person views another as pleasant, credible,

LO 10-6

More effectively manage project expectations.

SNAPSHOT FROM PRACTICE 10.2 — Managing Expectations*

Dorothy Kirk, a project management consultant and program manager with Financial Solutions Group of Mynd, offers several keen insights about the art of managing stakeholder expectations:

. . . expectations are hardy. All they need to take root is the absence of evidence to the contrary. Once rooted, the unspoken word encourages growth. They can develop and thrive without being grounded in reality. For this reason, project managers do daily battle with unrealistic expectations.

She goes on to offer several tips for managing expectations:

- The way you present information can either clarify or muddy expectations. For example, if you estimate that a task will take 317 hours, you are setting high expectations by your precision. The stakeholder is likely to be unhappy if it takes 323 hours. The stakeholder will not be unhappy with 323 hours if you quoted an estimate of 300–325 hours.
- Recognize that it is only human nature to interpret a situation in one's best interest. For example, if you tell someone it will be done by January, you are inclined to interpret it to your advantage and assume you have to the end of January, while the other person believes it will be done January 1st.
- Seize every opportunity to realign expectations with reality. Too often we avoid opportunities to adjust expectations because we hold onto a false hope that things will somehow work out.
- Do not ask for stakeholder suggestions for improvement if you do not intend to do something with their input. Asking for their input raises expectations.
- State the obvious. What is obvious to you may be obscure to others.
- Don't avoid delivering bad news. Communicate openly and in person. Expect some anger and frustration. Do not get defensive in return. Be prepared to explain the impact of the problems. For example, never say the project is going to be late without being able to give a new date. Explain what you are doing to see that this does not continue to happen.

All stakeholders have expectations about the schedule, cost, and project benefits. Project managers need to listen for, understand, and manage these expectations.

* D. Kirk, "Managing Expectations," *PM Network,* August 2000, pp. 59–62.

and helpful based on past contact, he or she is much more likely to be responsive to requests for help and less confrontational when problems arise.[2]

Managing Upward Relations

Research consistently points out that project success is strongly affected by the degree to which a project has the support of top management.[3] Such support is reflected in an appropriate budget, responsiveness to unexpected needs, and a clear signal to others in the organization of the importance of the project and the need to cooperate.

Visible top management support is not only critical for securing the support of other managers within an organization, but it also is a key factor in the project manager's ability to motivate the project team. Nothing establishes a manager's right to

LO 10-7

Develop strategies for managing upward relations.

[2] This discussion is based on Leonard R. Sayles, *Leadership: Managing in Real Organizations* (New York: McGraw-Hill, 1989) pp. 70–78.

[3] See, for example: J. L. Pinto and S. K. Mantel, "The Causes of Project Failure," *IEEE Transactions in Engineering Management,* vol. 37, no. 4 (1990), pp. 269–76.

lead more than her ability to defend. To win the loyalty of team members, project managers have to be effective advocates for their projects. They have to be able to get top management to rescind unreasonable demands, provide additional resources, and recognize the accomplishments of team members. This is more easily said than done.

Working relationships with upper management are a common source of consternation. Laments like the following are often made by project managers about upper management:

> They don't know how much it sets us back losing Neil to another project.
> I would like to see them get this project done with the budget they gave us.
> I just wish they would make up their minds as to what is really important.

While it may seem counterintuitive for a subordinate to "manage" a superior, smart project managers devote considerable time and attention to influencing and garnering the support of top management. Project managers have to accept profound differences in perspective and become skilled at the art of persuading superiors.

Many of the tensions that arise between upper management and project managers are a result of differences in perspective. Project managers become naturally absorbed with what is best for their project. To them the most important thing in the world is their project. Top management should have a different set of priorities. They are concerned with what is best for the entire organization. It is only natural for these two interests to conflict at times. For example, a project manager may lobby intensively for additional personnel only to be turned down because top management believes that the other departments cannot afford a reduction in staff. Although frequent communication can minimize differences, the project manager has to accept the fact that top management is inevitably going to see the world differently.

Once project managers accept that disagreements with superiors are more a question of perspective than substance, they can focus more of their energy on the art of persuading upper management. But before they can persuade superiors, they must first prove loyalty.[4] Loyalty in this context simply means that most of the time project managers have to show that they consistently follow through on requests and adhere to the parameters established by top management without a great deal of grumbling or fuss. Once managers have proven loyalty to upper management, senior management is much more receptive to their challenges and requests.

Project managers have to cultivate strong ties with upper managers who are sponsoring the project. As noted earlier, these are high-ranking officials who championed approval and funding of the project; as such, their reputations are aligned with the project. Sponsors are also the ones who defend the project when it is under attack in upper circles of management. They shelter the project from excessive interference (see Figure 10.3). Project managers should *always* keep such people informed of any problems that may cause embarrassment or disappointment. For example, if costs are beginning to outrun the budget or a technical glitch is threatening to delay the completion of the project, managers make sure that the sponsors are the first to know.

Timing is everything. Asking for additional budget the day after disappointing third-quarter earnings are reported is going to be much more difficult than making a similar request four weeks later. Good project managers pick the optimum time to appeal to top management. They enlist their project sponsors to lobby their cause. They also realize there are limits to top management's accommodations. Here, the Lone Ranger analogy is appropriate—you have only so many silver bullets, so use them wisely.

FIGURE 10.3

The Significance of a Project Sponsor

[4] Sayles, *Leadership,* pp. 136–45.

Project managers need to adapt their communication pattern to that of the senior group. For example, one project manager recognized that top management had a tendency to use sports metaphors to describe business situations, so she framed a recent slip in schedule by admitting that "we lost five yards, but we still have two plays to make a first down." Smart project managers learn the language of top management and use it to their advantage.

Finally, a few project managers admit ignoring chains of command. If they are confident that top management will reject an important request and that what they want to do will benefit the project, they do it without asking permission. While acknowledging that this is very risky, they claim that bosses typically won't argue with success.

Leading by Example

A highly visible, interactive management style is not only essential to building and sustaining cooperative relationships, it also allows project managers to utilize their most powerful leadership tool—their own behavior (Peters, 1988; Kouznes & Posner, 2012). Often, when faced with uncertainty, people look to others for cues as to how to respond and demonstrate a propensity to mimic the behavior of people they respect. A project manager's behavior symbolizes how other people should work on the project. Through her behavior a project manager can influence how others act and respond to a variety of issues related to the project. (See Snapshot from Practice 10.3: Leading at the Edge for a dramatic example of this.)

To be effective, project managers must "walk the talk" (see Figure 10.4). Six aspects of leading by example are discussed next.

Priorities

Actions speak louder than words. Subordinates and others discern project managers' priorities by how they spend their time. If a project manager claims that this project is critical and then is perceived as devoting more time to other projects, then all his verbal reassurances are likely to fall on deaf ears. Conversely, a project manager who takes the time to observe a critical test instead of simply waiting for a report affirms

FIGURE 10.4
Leading by Example

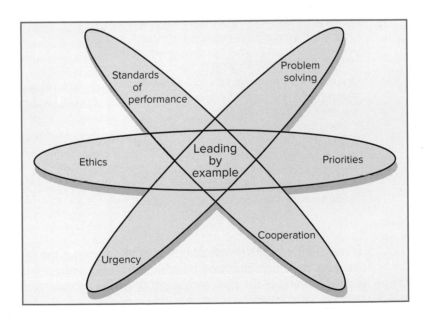

SNAPSHOT FROM PRACTICE 10.3   Leading at the Edge*

In 1914, the intrepid explorer Ernest Shackleton embarked on the *Endurance* with his team of seamen and scientists, intent upon crossing the unexplored Antarctic continent. What happened in the two years between their departure and their ultimate incredible rescue has rarely been matched in the annals of survival: a ship crushed by expanding ice pack . . . a crew stranded on the floes of the frozen Weddell Sea . . . two perilous treks in open boats across a raging Southern Ocean . . . a team marooned on the wild, forlorn Elephant Island, stretched to the limits of human endurance.

This adventure provided the basis for the book *Leading at the Edge: Leadership Lessons from the Extraordinary Saga of Shackleton's Antarctic Expedition* written by Dennis Perkins. Perkins provides numerous incidents of how Shackleton's personal example influenced the behavior of his beleaguered crew. For example, from the beginning of the Trans-Atlantic expedition to its end, Shackleton consistently encouraged behavior that emphasized caring and respect:

> After the destruction of the *Endurance* Shackleton heated hot milk for the crew and went from tent to tent with the "life giving" drink. After the sail to the island of South Georgia, when the exhausted crew had landed, Shackleton took the first watch, which he kept for three hours instead of the usual one.

Crew members emulated the caring behaviors that Shackleton modeled. A good example of this occurred during one of the most dramatic moments in the *Endurance* saga. The food supply had dwindled to perilously low levels. Less than a week's supply remained, and the tiny ration of seal steak usually served at breakfast was eliminated. The waste meat generally used to feed the dogs was inspected for edible scraps.

Under these wretched conditions, and after a wet sleepless night, an argument broke out among some of the team members. Caught in the middle, one crew member (Greenstreet) spilled his tiny ration of powdered milk and shouted at the biologist (Clark). Alfred Lansing described what happened next:

© Topham/The Image Works

> Greenstreet paused to get his breath, and in that instant his anger was spent and he suddenly fell silent. Everyone else in the tent became quiet, too, and looked at Greenstreet, shaggy-haired, bearded, and filthy with blubber soot, holding his empty mug in his hand and looking helplessly down into the snow that had thirstily soaked up his precious milk. The loss was so tragic he seemed almost on the point of weeping. Without speaking, Clark reached out and poured some milk into Greenstreet's mug. Then Worsely, then Macklin, and Rickerson and Kerr, Orde-Lees, and finally Blackborrow. They finished in silence.

* Adapted from Dennis N. T. Perkins, *Leading at the Edge: Leadership Lessons from the Extraordinary Saga of Shackleton's Antarctica Expedition* (New York: AMACOM Press, 2000), pp. 94–95; and Alfred Lansing, *Endurance: Shackleton's Incredible Voyage* (New York: Carroll & Graf, 1998), p. 127.

the importance of the testers and their work. Likewise, the types of questions project managers pose communicate priorities. By repeatedly asking how specific issues relate to satisfying the customer, a project manager can reinforce the importance of customer satisfaction.

Urgency

Through their actions project managers can convey a sense of urgency, which can permeate project activities. This urgency in part can be conveyed through stringent deadlines, frequent status report meetings, and aggressive solutions for expediting the project. The project manager uses these tools like a metronome to pick up the beat of the project. At the same time, such devices will be ineffective if there is not also a corresponding change in the project manager's behavior. If they want others to work faster and solve problems quicker, then they need to work faster. They need to hasten the pace of their own behavior. They should accelerate the frequency of their interactions, talk and walk more quickly, get to work sooner, and leave work later. By simply increasing the pace of their daily interaction patterns, project managers can reinforce a sense of urgency in others.

Problem Solving

How project managers respond to problems sets the tone for how others tackle problems. If bad news is greeted by verbal attacks, then others will be reluctant to be forthcoming.[5] If the project manager is more concerned with finding out who is to blame instead of how to prevent problems from happening again, then others will tend to cover their tracks and cast the blame elsewhere. If, on the other hand, project managers focus more on how they can turn a problem into an opportunity or what can be learned from a mistake, then others are more likely to adopt a more proactive approach to problem solving.

Cooperation

How project managers act toward outsiders influences how team members interact with outsiders. If a project manager makes disparaging remarks about the "idiots" in the marketing department, then this oftentimes becomes the shared view of the entire team. If project managers set the norm of treating outsiders with respect and being responsive to their needs, then others will more likely follow suit.

Standards of Performance

Veteran project managers recognize that if they want participants to exceed project expectations then they have to exceed others' expectations of a good project manager. They establish a high standard for project performance through the quality of their daily interactions. They respond quickly to the needs of others, carefully prepare and run crisp meetings, stay on top of all the critical issues, facilitate effective problem solving, and stand firm on important matters.

Ethics

How others respond to ethical dilemmas that arise in the course of a project will be influenced by how the project manager has responded to similar dilemmas. In many cases, team members base their actions on how they think the project manager would respond. If project managers deliberately distort or withhold vital information from customers or top management, then they are signaling to others that this kind of behavior is acceptable. Project management invariably creates a variety of ethical dilemmas; this would be an appropriate time to delve into this topic in more detail.

---

[5] This is the classic "kill the messenger" syndrome. This and other forces that contribute to distorting information can be found in Erik Larson and Jon King "The Systemic Distortion of Information: An On-going Management Challenge," *Organizational Dynamics*, Winter 1996, pp. 49–62.

10.5 Ethics and Project Management

LO 10-8

Understand the importance of building trust and acting in an ethical manner while working on a project.

Questions of ethics have already arisen in previous chapters that discussed padding of cost and time estimations, exaggerating pay-offs of project proposals, and so forth. Ethical dilemmas involve situations where it is difficult to determine whether conduct is right or wrong.

In a survey of project managers, 81 percent reported that they encounter ethical issues in their work.[6] These dilemmas range from being pressured to alter status reports, backdate signatures, compromising safety standards to accelerate progress, and approving shoddy work. The more recent work of Müller and colleagues suggests that the most common dilemma project managers face involves *transparency* issues related to project performance (Müller et al., 2013, 2014). For example, is it acceptable to falsely assure customers that everything is on track when in reality you are doing so to prevent them from panicking and making matters even worse?

Project management is complicated work, and, as such, ethics invariably involve gray areas of judgment and interpretation. For example, it is difficult to distinguish deliberate falsification of estimates from genuine mistakes or the willful exaggeration of project payoffs from genuine optimism. It becomes problematic to determine whether unfulfilled promises were deliberate deception or an appropriate response to changing circumstances.

To provide greater clarity to business ethics, many companies and professional groups publish a code of conduct. Cynics see these documents as simply window dressing, while advocates argue that they are important, albeit limited, first steps. In practice, personal ethics do not lie in formal statutes but at the intersection of one's work, family, education, profession, religious beliefs, and daily interactions. Most project managers report that they rely on their own private sense of right and wrong— what one project manager called his "internal compass." One common rule of thumb for testing whether a response is ethical is to ask, "Imagine that whatever you did was going to be reported on the front page of your local newspaper. How would you like that? Would you be comfortable?"

Unfortunately, scandals at Enron, Worldcom, and Arthur Andersen have demonstrated the willingness of highly trained professionals to abdicate personal responsibility for illegal actions and to obey the directives of superiors (see Snapshot from Practice 10.4: The Collapse of Arthur Andersen). Top management and the culture of an organization play a decisive role in shaping members' beliefs of what is right and wrong. Many organizations encourage ethical transgressions by creating a "win at all cost" mentality. The pressures to succeed obscure consideration of whether the ends justify the means. Other organizations place a premium on "fair play" and command a market position by virtue of being trustworthy and reliable.[7]

Many project managers claim that ethical behavior is its own reward. By following your own internal compass your behavior expresses your personal values. Others suggest that ethical behavior is doubly rewarding. You not only are able to fall asleep at night but you also develop a sound and admirable reputation. As will be explored in the next section, such a reputation is essential to establishing the trust necessary to exercise influence effectively.

[6] While this survey is a bit old, our conversations with project managers suggest that the results hold true today (J. Cabanis, "A Question of Ethics: The Issues Project Managers Face and How They Resolve Them," *PM Network,* December 1995, pp. 8–28).

[7] For a more in-depth discussion of ethics, see: L. Trevino and K. Nelson, *Managing Business Ethics: Straight Talk about How to Do It Right,* 5th ed. (Hoboken, NJ: John Wiley & Sons, 2011).

SNAPSHOT FROM PRACTICE 10.4 — The Collapse of Arthur Andersen*

"Think straight and talk straight" was the principle on which Arthur E. Andersen built his accounting firm in the early 1900s. It was a phrase his mother taught him and became the firm's motto. The commitment to integrity and a systematic, planned approach to work were instrumental in Arthur Andersen becoming one of the largest and best-known accounting firms in the world.

According to the book, *Inside Arthur Anderson* by Susan Squires and colleagues:

> Working for Arthur Andersen was not for everyone. It could be a tough culture. It was much too hierarchical and top down for the more free spirited. Many people left after less than two years, believing the rewards did not warrant the demands that were made on them. Others learned to play by the rules and some even thrived. To remain in the firm, staff members were expected to work hard, respect authority of rank, and maintain a high level of conformity. In return they were rewarded with support, promotion, and the possibility of making partner. Those individuals who made a career with the firm grew old together, professionally and personally, and most had never worked anywhere else. To these survivors, Andersen was their second family, and they developed strong loyalties to the firm and its culture. (p. 133)

On October 23, 2001, David Duncan told his Enron project team that they needed to start complying with Andersen's new policy on handling audit documents. The policy had been instituted to make sure that the firm's extraneous paperwork could not be used in court cases. Although the document retention policy required that papers supporting the firm's opinions and audit be retained, it allowed a broad category of secondary documents to be destroyed. The team reacted with

© Stephen J. Carrera/AP Photo

stunned silence to Duncan's directive. Then everyone got up and began racing to do what they had been told to do. No one asked Duncan to explain further. None asked whether what they were doing was wrong. No one questioned whether what he or she were doing might be illegal. Andersen's Houston staff just reacted, following orders without question.

On November 9, 2001, the day after the Securities Exchange Commission (SEC) issued a subpoena to Andersen, the shredding stopped. More than one ton of documents had been destroyed and 30,000 e-mails and Enron-related computer files erased. According to Andersen's legal defense team, the shredding was business as usual. The lawyers claimed that the shredding was standard practice for eliminating unnecessary files. To the SEC, it appeared to be the start of a deep cover-up operation. Subsequently one of the most respected accounting firms in the world closed its doors.

* Susan E. Squires, Cynthia J. Smith, Lorna McDougall, and William R. Yeak, *Inside Arthur Andersen: Shifting Values, Unexpected Consequences* (Upper Saddle River, NJ: Prentice Hall, 2004).

10.6 Building Trust: The Key to Exercising Influence

The significance of trust can be discerned by its absence. Imagine how different a working relationship is when you distrust the other party as opposed to trusting them. Here is what one line manager had to say about how he reacted to a project manager he did not trust:

> Whenever Jim approached me about something, I found myself trying to read between the lines to figure what was really going on. When he made a request, my initial reaction was "no" until he proved it.

taught stress and time management techniques. However, we know of no workshop or magic potion that can transform a pessimist into an optimist or provide a sense of purpose when there is not one. These qualities get at the very soul or being of a person. Optimism, integrity, and even being proactive are not easily developed if there is not already a predisposition to display them.

Summary

To be successful, project managers must build a cooperative network among a diverse set of allies. They begin by identifying who the key stakeholders on a project are, followed by a diagnosis of the nature of the relationships, and the basis for exercising influence. Effective project managers are skilled at acquiring and exercising a wide range of influence. They use this influence and a highly interactive management style to monitor project performance and initiate appropriate changes in project plans and direction. They do so in a manner that generates trust, which is ultimately based on others' perceptions of their character and competence.

Project managers are encouraged to keep in mind the following suggestions:

- *Build relationships before you need them.* Identify key players and what you can do to help them before you need their assistance. It is always easier to receive a favor after you have granted one. This requires the project manager to see the project in systems terms and to appreciate how it affects other activities and agendas inside and outside the organization. From this perspective they can identify opportunities to do good deeds and garner the support of others.

- *Trust is sustained through frequent face-to-face contact.* Trust withers through neglect. This is particularly true under conditions of rapid change and uncertainty that naturally engender doubt, suspicion, and even momentary bouts of paranoia. Project managers must maintain frequent contact with key stakeholders to keep abreast of developments, assuage concerns, engage in reality testing, and focus attention on the project. Frequent face-to-face interactions either directly or by teleconferencing affirm mutual respect and trust in each other.

Ultimately, exercising influence in an effective and ethical manner begins and ends with how you view the other parties. Do you view them as potential partners or obstacles to your goals? If obstacles, then you wield your influence to manipulate and gain compliance and cooperation. If partners, you exercise influence to gain their commitment and support. People who view social network building as building partnerships see every interaction with two goals: resolving the immediate problem/concern and improving the working relationship so that next time it will be even more effective. Experienced project managers realize that "what goes around comes around" and try at all cost to avoid antagonizing players for quick success.

Key Terms

Emotional intelligence (EQ), *361*
Inspiration-related currencies, *347*
Law of reciprocity, *345*
Leading by example, *353*
Management by wandering around (MBWA), *350*

Personal-related currencies, *348*
Position-related currencies, *346*
Proactive, *360*
Relationship-related currencies, *347*

Social network building, *348*
Stakeholder, *342*
Systems thinking, *360*
Task-related currencies, *345*

**Review
Questions**

1. What is the difference between leading and managing a project?

2. Why is a conductor of an orchestra an appropriate metaphor for being a project manager? What aspects of project managing are not reflected by this metaphor? Can you think of other metaphors that would be appropriate?

3. What does the exchange model of influence suggest you do to build cooperative relationships to complete a project?

4. What differences would you expect to see between the kinds of influence currencies that a project manager in a functional matrix would use and the influence a project manager of a dedicated project team would use?

5. Why is it important to build a relationship before you need it?

6. Why is it critical to keep the project sponsor informed?

7. Why is trust a function of both character and competence?

8. Which of the eight traits/skills associated with being an effective project manager is the most important? The least important? Why?

Exercises

1. Do an Internet search for the Keirsey Temperament Sorter Questionnaire and find a site that appears to have a reputable self-assessment questionnaire. Respond to the questionnaire to identify your temperament type. Read supportive documents associated with your type. What does this material suggest are the kinds of projects that would best suit you? What does it suggest your strengths and weaknesses are as a project manager? How can you compensate for your weaknesses?

2. Access the Project Management Institute website and review the standards contained in the PMI Member Ethical Standards section. How useful is the information for helping someone decide what behavior is appropriate and inappropriate?

3. You are organizing a benefit concert in your hometown that will feature local heavy metal rock groups and guest speakers. Draw a dependency map identifying the major groups of people that are likely to affect the success of this project. Who do you think will be most cooperative? Who do you think will be the least cooperative? Why?

4. You are the project manager responsible for the overall construction of a new international airport. Draw a dependency map identifying the major groups of people that are likely to affect the success of this project. Who do you think will be most cooperative? Who do you think will be the least cooperative? Why?

5. Identify an important relationship (co-worker, boss, friend) in which you are having trouble gaining cooperation. Assess this relationship in terms of the influence currency model. What kinds of influence currency have you been exchanging in this relationship? Is the "bank account" for this relationship in the "red" or the "black"? What kinds of influence would be appropriate for building a stronger relationship with that person?

6. Each of the following seven mini-case scenarios involves ethical dilemmas associated with project management. How would you respond to each situation, and why?

Jack Nietzche

You returned from a project staffing meeting in which future project assignments were finalized. Despite your best efforts, you were unable to persuade the director of project management to promote one of your best assistants, Jack Nietzche, to a project manager position. You feel a bit guilty because you dangled the prospect of this promotion to motivate Jack. Jack responded by putting in extra hours to ensure that his segments of the project were completed on time. You wonder how Jack will react to this disappointment. More importantly, you wonder how his reaction might affect your project. You have five days remaining to meet a critical deadline for a very important customer. While it won't be easy, you believed you would be able to complete the project on time. Now you're not so sure. Jack is halfway through completing the documentation phase, which is the last critical activity. Jack can be pretty emotional at times, and you are worried that he will blow up once he finds he didn't get the promotion. As you return to your office, you wonder what you should do. Should you tell Jack that he isn't going to be promoted? What should you say if he asks about whether the new assignments were made?

Seaburst Construction Project

You are the project manager for the Seaburst construction project. So far the project is progressing ahead of schedule and below budget. You attribute this in part to the good working relationship you have with the carpenters, plumbers, electricians, and machine operators who work for your organization. More than once you have asked them to give 110 percent, and they have responded.

One Sunday afternoon you decide to drive by the site and show it to your son. As you point out various parts of the project to your son, you discover that several pieces of valuable equipment are missing from the storage shed. When you start work again on Monday you are about to discuss this matter with a supervisor when you realize that all the missing equipment is back in the shed. What should you do? Why?

The Project Status Report Meeting

You are driving to a project status report meeting with your client. You encountered a significant technical problem on the project that has put your project behind schedule. This is not good news because completion time is the number one priority for the project. You are confident that your team can solve the problem if they are free to give their undivided attention to it and that with hard work you can get back on schedule. You also believe if you tell the client about the problem, she will demand a meeting with your team to discuss the implications of the problem. You can also expect her to send some of her personnel to oversee the solution to the problem. These interruptions will likely further delay the project. What should you tell your client about the current status of the project?

Gold Star LAN project

You work for a large consulting firm and were assigned to the Gold Star LAN project. Work on the project is nearly completed and your clients at Gold Star appear to be pleased with your performance. During the course of the project, changes in the original scope had to be made to accommodate specific needs of managers at Gold Star. The costs of these changes were documented as well as overhead and submitted to the centralized accounting department. They processed the information and submitted a change order bill for your signature. You are surprised to see the bill is 10 percent higher than what you submitted. You contact Jim Messina in the accounting office and ask if a mistake has been made. He curtly replies that no mistake was made and that management adjusted the bill. He recommends that you sign the document. You talk to another project manager about this and she tells you off the record that overcharging clients on change orders is common practice in your firm. Would you sign the document? Why? Why not?

Cape Town Bio-Tech

You are responsible for installing the new Double E production line. Your team has collected estimates and used the WBS to generate a project schedule. You have confidence in the schedule and the work your team has done. You report to top management that you believe that the project will take 110 days and be completed by March 5. The news is greeted positively. In fact, the project sponsor confides that orders do not have to be shipped until April 1. You leave the meeting wondering whether you should share this information with the project team or not.

Ryman Pharmaceuticals

You are a test engineer on the Bridge project at Ryman Pharmaceuticals in Nashville, Tennessee. You have just completed conductivity tests of a new electrochemical compound. The results exceeded expectations. This new compound should revolutionize the industry. You are wondering whether to call your stockbroker and ask her to buy $20,000 worth of Ryman stock before everyone else finds out about the results. What would you do and why?

Princeton Landing

You are managing the renovation of the Old Princeton Landing Bar and Grill. The project is on schedule despite receiving a late shipment of paint. The paint was supposed to arrive on 1/30, but instead arrived on 2/1. The assistant store manager apologizes profusely for the delay and asks if you would be willing to sign the acceptance form and backdate it to 1/30. He says he won't qualify for a bonus that he has worked hard to meet for the past month if the shipment is reported late. He promises to make it up to you on future projects. What would you do and why?

References

Abrashoff, D. M., *It's Your Ship* (New York: Business Plus, 2002).

Anand, V., B. E. Ashforth, and M. Joshi, "Business as Usual: The Acceptance and Perpetuation of Corruption in Organizations," *Academy of Management Executive,* vol. 19, no. 4 (2005), pp. 9–23.

Ancona, D. G., and D. Caldwell, "Improving the Performance of New-Product Teams," *Research Technology Management,* vol. 33, no. 2 (March-April 1990), pp. 25–29.

Badaracco, J. L., Jr., and A. P. Webb, "Business Ethics: A View from the Trenches," *California Management Review,* vol. 37, no. 2 (Winter 1995), pp. 8–28.

Baker, B., "Leadership and the Project Manager," *PM Network,* December 2002, p. 20.

Baker, W. E., *Network Smart: How to Build Relationships for Personal and Organizational Success* (New York: McGraw-Hill, 1994).

Bennis, W., *On Becoming a Leader* (Reading, MA: Addison-Wesley, 1989).

Bertsche, R., "Seven Steps to Stronger Relationships between Project Managers and Sponsors," *PM Network*, September 2014, pp. 50–55.

Bourne, L., *Stakeholder Relationship Management* (Farnham, England: Gower Publishing Ltd., 2009).

Bradberry, T., and J. Graves, *The Emotional Intelligence Quick Book: How to Put Your EQ to Work* (New York: Simon & Schuster, 2005).

Cabanis, J., "A Question of Ethics: The Issues Project Managers Face and How They Resolve Them," *PM Network,* December 1996, pp. 19–24.

Cabanis-Brewin, J., "The Human Task of a Project Leader: Daniel Goleman on the Value of High EQ," *PM Network,* November 1999, pp. 38–42.

Cohen, A. R., and D. L. Bradford, *Influence Without Authority* (New York: John Wiley & Sons, 1990).

Covey, S. R., *The Seven Habits of Highly Effective People* (New York: Simon & Schuster, 1989).

Dinsmore, P. C., "Will the Real Stakeholders Please Stand Up?" *PM Network,* December 1995, pp. 9–10.

Einsiedel, A. A., "Profile of Effective Project Managers," *Project Management Journal,* vol. 31, no. 3 (1987), pp. 51–56.

Ferrazzi, K., *Never Eat Alone and Other Secrets to Success One Relationship at a Time* (Crown Publishers, 2005).

Gabarro, S. J., *The Dynamics of Taking Charge* (Boston: Harvard Business School Press, 1987).

Grant, A., *Give and Take: A Revolutionary Approach to Success* (New York: Viking Press, 2013).

Hill, L. A., *Becoming a Manager: Mastery of a New Identity* (Boston: Harvard Business School Press, 1992).

Kanter, R. M., "Power Failures in Management Circuits," *Harvard Business Review*, July–August, 1979, pp. 65–79.

Kaplan, R. E., "Trade Routes: The Manager's Network of Relationships," *Organizational Dynamics,* vol. 12, no. 4 (Spring 1984), pp. 37–52.

Kirk, D., "Managing Expectations," *PM Network,* August 2000, pp. 59–62.

Kotter, J. P., "What Leaders Really Do," *Harvard Business Review,* vol. 68, no. 3 (May–June 1990), pp. 103–11.

Kouzes, J. M., and B. Z. Posner, *Credibility: How Leaders Gain and Lose It, Why People Demand It* (San Francisco: Jossey-Bass, 1993).

Kouzes, J. M., and B. Z. Posner, *The Leadership Challenge,* 5th ed. (San Francisco: Jossey-Bass, 2012).

Larson, E. W., and J. B. King, "The Systemic Distortion of Information: An Ongoing Management Challenge," *Organizational Dynamics,* vol. 24, no. 3 (Winter 1996), pp. 49–62.

Lewis, M. W., M. A. Welsh, G. E. Dehler, and S. G. Green, "Product Development Tensions: Exploring Contrasting Styles of Project Management," *Academy of Management Journal,* vol. 45, no. 3 (2002), pp. 546–64.

Müller, R., and R. Turner, "Leadership Competency Profiles of Successful Project Managers," *International Journal of Project Management,* vol. 28, no. 5 (July 2010), pp. 437–48.

Müller R., Erling S. Andersen, Ø. Kvalnes, J. Shao, S. Sankaran, J. R. Turner, C. Biesenthal, D. Walker, and S. Gudergan, "The Interrelationship of Governance, Trust, and Ethics in Temporary Organizations," *Journal of Project Management*, vol. 44, no. 4 (August 2013), pp. 26-44.

Müller, R., R. Turner, E. Andersen, J. Shao, and O. Kvalnes, "Ethics, Trust, and Goverance in Temporary Organizations," *Journal of Project Management*, vol. 45, no. 4 (August/September 2014), pp. 39–54.

Peters, L. H., "A Good Man in a Storm: An Interview with Tom West," *Academy of Management Executive,* vol. 16, no. 4 (2002), pp. 53–63.

Peters, L. H., "Soulful Ramblings: An Interview with Tracy Kidder," *Academy of Management Executive,* vol. 16, no. 4 (2002), pp. 45–52.

Peters, T., *Thriving on Chaos: Handbook for a Management Revolution* (New York: Alfred A. Knopf, 1988).

Pinto, J. K., and S. K. Mantel, "The Causes of Project Failure," *IEEE Transactions in Engineering Management,* vol. 37, no. 4 (1990), pp. 269–76.

Pinto, J. K., and D. P. Sleven, "Critical Success Factors in Successful Project Implementation," *IEEE Transactions in Engineering Management,* vol. 34, no. 1 (1987), pp. 22–27.

Posner, B. Z., "What It Takes to Be an Effective Project Manager," *Project Management Journal,* March 1987, pp. 51–55.

Project Management Institute, *Leadership in Project Management Annual* (Newtown Square, PA: PMI Publishing, 2006).

Project Management Institute, *PMBOK Guide,* 5th ed. (Newtown Square, PA: Project Management Institute, 2013).

Robb, D. J., "Ethics in Project Management: Issues, Practice, and Motive," *PM Network,* December 1996, pp. 13–18.

Sayles, L. R., *Leadership: Managing in Real Organizations* (New York: McGraw-Hill, 1989), pp. 70–78.

Sayles, L. R., *The Working Leader* (New York: Free Press, 1993).

Senge, P. M., *The Fifth Discipline* (New York: Doubleday, 1990).

Shenhar, A. J., and B. Nofziner, "A New Model for Training Project Managers," *Proceedings of the 28th Annual Project Management Institute Symposium,* 1997, pp. 301–6.

Shtub, A., J. F. Bard, and S. Globerson, *Project Management: Engineering, Technology, and Implementation* (Englewood Cliffs, NJ: Prentice Hall, 1994).

Trevino, L. K., and K. A. Nelson, *Managing Business Ethics: Straight Talk about How to Do It Right,* 5th ed. (Hoboken, NJ: John Wiley & Sons, 2011).

Turner, J. R., and R. Müller, "The Project Manager Leadership Style as a Success Factor on Projects: A Literature Review," *Project Management Journal,* vol. 36, no. 2 (2005), pp. 49–61.

Case 10.1

The Blue Sky Project*

Garth Hudson was a 29-year-old graduate of Eastern State University (ESU) with a B.S. degree in management information systems. After graduation he worked for seven years at Bluegrass Systems in Louisville, Kentucky. While at ESU he worked part time for an oceanography professor, Ahmet Green, creating a customized database for a research project he was conducting. Green was recently appointed director of Eastern Oceanography Institute (EOI), and Hudson was confident that this prior experience was instrumental in his getting the job as information services (IS) director at the Institute. Although he took a significant pay cut, he jumped at the opportunity to return to his alma mater. His job at Bluegrass Systems had been very demanding. The long hours and extensive traveling had created tension in his marriage. He was looking forward to a normal job with reasonable hours. Besides, Jenna, his wife, would be busy

* Prepared by Erik Larson and V. T. Raja, senior instructor at the College of Business, Oregon State University.

pursuing her MBA at Eastern State University. While at Bluegrass, Hudson worked on a wide range of IS projects. He was confident that he had the requisite technical expertise to excel at his new job.

Eastern Oceanography Institute was an independently funded research facility aligned with Eastern State University. Approximately 50 full- and part-time staff worked at the Institute. They worked on research grants funded by the National Science Foundation (NSF) and the United Nations (UN), as well as research financed by private industry. There were typically 7 to 9 major research projects under way at any one time as well as 20 to 25 smaller projects. One-third of the Institute's scientists had part-time teaching assignments at ESU and used the Institute to conduct their own basic research.

FIRST YEAR AT EOI

Hudson made a point of introducing himself to the various groups of people upon his arrival at the Institute. Still, his contact with the staff had been limited. He spent most of his time becoming familiar with EOI's information system, training his staff, responding to unexpected problems, and working on various projects. Hudson suffered from food allergies and refrained from informal staff lunches at nearby restaurants. He stopped regularly attending the biweekly staff meetings in order to devote more time to his work. He now only attended the meetings when there was a specific agenda item regarding his operation.

The IS staff at EOI consisted of two full-time assistants, Tom Jackson and Grant Hill. They were supported by five part-time student assistants from the computer science department. Grant Hill was assigned full-time to a large five-year NSF grant aimed at creating a virtual library of oceanographic research. Hill worked out of the project leader's office and had very little interaction with Hudson or Jackson. Hudson's relationship with Jackson was awkward from the start. He found out, after the fact, that Jackson thought he would get the job as director. They never talked about it, but he sensed tension the first couple of months on the job. One of the problems was that he and Jackson were totally different personalities. Jackson was gregarious and very talkative. He had a habit of after lunch walking around the Institute talking to different scientists and researchers. Often this would lead to useful information. Hudson, on the other hand, preferred to stay in his office working on various assignments and ventured out only when called upon. While Hudson felt Jackson was not on top of the latest developments as he was, he respected Jackson's work.

Last month the system was corrupted by a virus introduced over the Internet. Hudson devoted an entire weekend to restoring the system to operation. A recurring headache was one of the servers, code-named "Poncho," that would occasionally shut down for no apparent reason. Instead of replacing it, he decided to nurse Poncho along until it could be replaced. His work was frequently interrupted by frantic calls from staff researchers who needed immediate help on a variety of computer-related problems. He was shocked at how computer illiterate some of the researchers were and how he had to guide them through some of the basics of e-mail management and database configuration. He did find time to help Assistant Professor Amanda Johnson on a project. Johnson was the only researcher to respond to Hudson's e-mail announcing that the IS staff was available to help on projects. Hudson created a virtual project office on the Internet so that Johnson could collaborate with colleagues from institutes in Italy and Thailand on a UN research grant. He looked forward to the day when he could spend more time on fun projects like that.

THE BLUE SKY CONVERSION PROJECT

The "Blue Sky" conversion project began in earnest four months ago. Ahmet Green returned from Washington, D.C., with grim news. The economic downturn was going to lead to a dramatic reduction in funding. He anticipated as much as a 25 percent reduction in annual budget over the next three to five years. This would lead to staff reductions and cutting operating costs. One cost-cutting measure was moving IT operations to the "cloud." Green had first proposed the idea to Hudson after attending a meeting with several directors of other institutes who faced similar financial challenges.

The basic strategy was to move all of the Institute's databases, software, and even hardware to a "private cloud." Staff would use their current PCs to simply access more powerful machines over the Internet. These powerful machines could be partitioned and configured differently as per the needs of research staff, giving each staff their own virtual machine (VM). Staff could also access, use, and share virtual servers over the Internet as needed. Hudson worked with the Institute's accountant on a cost/benefit analysis. From their standpoint it made perfect sense. First, the Institute would not have to replace or upgrade aging computers and servers. Second, the Institute would enjoy significant IT savings since they would pay for only IT resources actually used. They would not have to make any major IT capital expenditures. Third, cloud computing would provide scientists greater flexibility by accessing desired resources or software from anywhere at any time. And finally, once the system was up and running, the Institute would no longer need the services of at least one full-time IT worker. Green decided to name the project "Blue Sky" to put a positive spin on the conversion.

At first the associate directors balked at the idea. Some had a hard time conceptualizing what cloud computing meant. Others were worried about security and reliability. In the end they reluctantly signed off on the project when given alternative cost-cutting initiatives. Hudson assured them that cloud computing was the wave of the future and setting up or accessing virtual machines on the "cloud" was as simple as setting up or accessing their g-mail account.

The conversion project would be completed in stages. The first stage was selecting a provider. The next stage was migrating non–mission critical information to the cloud. The next stages would entail migrating each of the six big grant projects in waves to the cloud. The final stage would focus on the remaining smaller projects. Training would be an integral part of each stage. The Institute would maintain a back-up for all the data until 6 months after complete conversion. After that the cloud service provider would be responsible for backing up the data.

At first Jackson was excited about the project. He was savvy enough to realize that this was the future of computing and he was intrigued with how the whole system would work. His feelings soon changed when he started thinking about the potential ramifications for his job. He asked Hudson more than once what the department would look like after the conversion. Hudson replied vaguely that they would figure it out once the system was up and running.

A task force was formed, headed by Hudson, to select a cloud service provider. Hudson was surprised by how many choices there were. Plans and cost structures varied considerably. After much deliberation the committee narrowed the choices to three. The first two were among the bigger providers in the industry, VMWARE and Microsoft. The third choice was a relatively new company, OpenRange, which offered a cheaper solution. Jackson argued that even though the bigger providers would cost more, they were a much safer bet. Hudson responded that he had confidence in OpenRange and cutting costs was the primary goal behind the project. In the end, Hudson persuaded the committee to choose OpenRange. Not only would cost be significantly cheaper, but OpenRange would help in the training of the personnel. Hudson liked this idea; training was not his strength, and he wasn't looking forward to holding senior scientists' hands through the process.

It took Hudson and Jackson six weeks to identify non-critical data. Hudson worked on the back end while Jackson met with staff to identify non-critical information. The motto was when in doubt, leave it out. The actual migration only took a couple of days. Training proved to be more problematic. The staff sent by OpenRange appeared to be straight out of college. While enthusiastic, they were inexperienced in the art of getting older staff to accept and use new technology. Many trainers had the habit of simply doing things for the staff instead of showing them how to do it themselves. It all came to a head when a power outage at the OpenRange storage system shut down and disrupted operations at the Institute for 36 hours.

Ahmet held an emergency meeting. Hudson reported that the power outage occurred in North East India and that OpenRange was expanding their back-up systems. Several members argued that the Institute should switch to one of the bigger providers. When this came up Hudson looked at Jackson and was relieved when he remained silent. In the end, Ahmet announced that it would be too costly to switch providers and Hudson and his staff would have to make the conversion work. Jackson stepped forward and volunteered to manage the training. Everyone agreed that the Institute should hire 3 more part-time assistants to help the staff with the transition.

Hudson worked behind the scenes, coordinating with his counterparts at OpenRange and planning the conversion of the next segment of the project. Jackson worked closely with the OpenRange trainers and refocused their attention on teaching. Resistance was pretty high at first. Jackson used his personal contacts within the Institute to rally support for the change. He persuaded Hudson to change the conversion schedule to begin with those projects in which the leads were most supportive of the change. Training improved and Jackson created some useful training materials, including short videos on how to access the virtual machines.

One problem that occurred early in the process involved a graduate research assistant who mistakenly hit the wrong commands and terminated her virtual machine instead of logging off. This resulted in complete loss of that machine's data in the cloud. Fortunately, the Institute still had back-up and Jackson was able recover the work. Collaborating with some programmers at OpenRange, Jackson wrote a program that triggered a pop-up message on the screen warning users not to terminate their virtual machine when logging off.

CLOSING OUT THE BLUE SKY PROJECT

It took almost a year to complete the Blue Sky project. After the rocky beginning things went relatively smoothly. Acceptance was slow, but Jackson and his staff worked with the staff to demonstrate how the new system would make their work easier. Two student assistants were always on call to address any problem or question. Hudson spent most of his time interacting with the OpenRange counterparts and rarely ventured out of his office. He had his student assistants collect information from staff so he could configure the new virtual machines to exactly match staff needs. He put in long hours so that customized databases would work in the new environment. This proved to be a very difficult task and he was quite pleased with his work. Twice OpenRange experienced momentary power shortages at their server facility which disrupted work at the Institute. Hudson was happy to report that OpenRange was breaking ground on an alternative server system in Ukraine.

When the Institute conducted a retrospective (project review) on the Blue Sky project, some still questioned the choice of OpenRange as a cloud service provider, but praised Jackson's work on helping the staff make the transition. Despite the criticism over the choice of OpenRange, Hudson felt good about the project. The system was up and running and the staff was beginning to enjoy the flexibility it provided. Besides, the Institute would achieve real savings from the new system.

Soon after the retrospective, Hudson was surprised when Ahmet walked into his office and closed the door. Ahmet began by thanking Hudson for his work on the project. He then cleared his throat and said, "You know, Garth, one of the consequences of Blue Sky is reducing our IT staff. Grant Hill is needed for the data library project. So it comes down to you or Jackson. Frankly there is general agreement among the Associate Directors that Jackson is essential to the Institute. I know this might come as a surprise to you, and before I make a decision I want to give you a chance to change my mind."

1. If you were Hudson, how would you respond to the director?
2. What mistakes did Hudson make?
3. What are the lessons to be learned from this case?

Case 10.2

Tom Bray

Tom Bray was mulling over today's work schedule as he looked across the bay at the storm that was rolling in. It was the second official day of the Pegasus project and now the real work was about to begin.

Pegasus was a two-month renovation project for AtlantiCorp, a major financial institution headquartered in Boston, Massachusetts. Tom's group was responsible for installing the furniture and equipment in the newly renovated accounts receivable department on the third floor. The Pegasus project was a dedicated project team formed out of AtlantiCorp facilities department with Tom as the project lead.

Tom was excited because this was his first *major league* project and he was looking forward to practicing a new management style—MBWA, aka management by wandering around. He had been exposed to MBWA in a business class in college, but it wasn't until he attended an AtlantiCorp leadership training seminar that he decided to change how he managed people. The trainer was a devout MBWA champion ("You can't manage people from a computer!"). Furthermore, the testimonies from his peers reinforced the difference that MBWA can make when it comes to working on projects.

Tom had joined the facilities group at AtlantiCorp five years earlier after working for EDS for six years. He quickly demonstrated technical competences and good work habits. He was encouraged to take all the internal project management workshops offered by AtlantiCorp. On his last two projects he served as assistant project manager responsible for procurement and contract management.

He had read books about the soft side of project management and MBWA made sense—after all, people not tools get projects done. His boss had told him he needed to refine his people skills and work on developing rapport with team members. MBWA seemed like a perfect solution.

Tom reviewed the list of team member names; some of the foreign names were real tongue twisters. For example, one of his better workers was from Thailand and her name was Pinyarat Sirisomboonsuk. He practiced saying "Pin-ya-răt See-rē-som-boon-sook."

He got up, tucked in his shirt, and walked out of his office and down to the floor where his team was busy unloading equipment.

Tom said "Hi" to the first few workers he met until he encountered Jack and three other workers. Jack was busy pulling hardware out of a box while his teammates were standing around talking. Tom blurted, "Come on guys, we've got work to do." They quickly separated and began unloading boxes.

The rest of the visit seemed to go well. He helped Shari unload a heavy box and managed to get an appreciative grin from Pinyarat when he almost correctly pronounced her name. Satisfied, Tom went back up to his office thinking that MBWA wouldn't be that tough to do.

After responding to e-mail and calling some vendors, Tom ventured back out to see how things were going downstairs. When he got there, the floor was weirdly quiet. People were busy doing their work and his attempts at generating conversation elicited stiff responses. He left thinking that maybe MBWA is going to be tougher than he thought.

1. What do you think is going on at the end of this case?
2. What should Tom do next and why?
3. What can be learned from this case?

Case 10.3

Cerberus Corporation*

Cerberus is a successful producer of specialty chemicals. It operates nine large campus sites in the United States, with a number of different business units on each site. These business units operate independently, with direct reporting to corporate headquarters. Site functions such as safety, environmental, and facilities management report to a host organization—typically the business unit that is the largest user of their services.

SUSAN STEELE

Susan Steele has worked in the Facilities group at the Cerberus Richmond site for the last two years. The Facilities manager, Tom Stern, reports to the General Manager of the largest business unit on site, the highly profitable Adhesives and Sealants Division. Susan started with Cerberus when she graduated with her business degree from Awsum University. She was excited about her new assignment—leading a project for the first time. She remembered Tom saying, "We've got office furniture dating back to the 80s. There are those ugly green-top desks that look like they came from military surplus! I'm especially concerned about computer workstation ergonomics—it's a major issue that we absolutely must fix! I want you to lead a project to transition our office furniture to the new corporate standard."

Susan assembled her project team: Jeff, the site safety/ergonomics engineer; Gretchen, the space planner; Cindy, the move coordinator; and Kari, the accounting liaison for Facilities. At their first meeting, everyone agreed that ergonomics was the most urgent concern. All five business units responded to a workstation survey that identified injury-causing ergonomics. The team was developing a plan to replace old desks with new, ergo-adjustable furniture by the end of the year. Susan asked Kari about the budget, and Kari responded, "Facilities should not pay for this. We want the individual business units to pay so that the costs will show where they are incurred."

* Courtesy of John Sloan, Oregon State University.

Gretchen spoke up: "You know, we've got lots of department moves going on constantly. Everybody is always jockeying for space and location as their business needs change. Besides the ergonomics, could we say that only corporate standard furniture gets moved? That would force changing some of the stuff that's just plain ugly." Everyone agreed that this was a great idea.

Susan presented the project plan to Tom and got a green light to proceed.

JON WOOD

Jon Wood is a planning manager, with 22 years experience at Cerberus. His business unit, Photographic Chemicals Division (PCD), is losing money. Digital photography is continuing to reduce the size of the market, and PCD is having trouble matching the competition's relentless price-cutting. Jon recently transferred to Richmond from corporate headquarters, where he ran the economic forecasting group. He is considered a new broom, and he is determined to sweep clean.

One of Jon's early actions was to negotiate with his general manager for a department move. Money was tight, and the site facilities function charged an arm and a leg for moves (covering all their fixed overhead, the operations people groused). However, Jon felt it was important to move from Building 4, where they were next to Production, to Building 6, where they could be close to Marketing, Forecasting, and Accounting. His General Manager agreed, and there was lots of excitement in his team about their upcoming move. Jon assigned one of his planners, Richard, to work with the Facilities team on the layout and move plan for the group. Things seemed to be going fine—Jon saw Richard sitting down with the move coordinator, and they seemed to be on track.

The day before the move, Jon hung up the phone from a particularly tense teleconference with a Canadian subcontractor. Production was not going well, and product availability would be tight for the rest of the quarter. Clustered around his desk were Richard, Cindy, and a person he hadn't met yet, Susan. After hurried introductions, Susan told Jon that his filing cabinets could not be moved. The cabinets are large lateral files, five feet wide and two feet deep, a combination of both filing cabinets and bookshelves. Jon brought them with him from Corporate because he thought they looked nice with their dark grey steel sides and wood veneer tops. Susan told him that he would have to replace them with new corporate standard cabinets, virtually the same size. Jon said, "You mean you want me to throw away perfectly good filing cabinets and spend another $2,000 on new ones, just so they match? I won't do it!"

Susan replied, "Then I won't authorize the movement of the old cabinets."

Jon said, "You're joking—these cabinets are grey, the new ones are grey—the only difference is the wood top! You'd throw away $2,000 for nothing?"

Susan replied stiffly, "I'm sorry, that's the policy."

Jon said, "I don't care what the policy is. If I have to move them myself, those cabinets are not going to the dump. My division is losing money and I'm not going to throw money away. If you don't like it, you're going to have to get your general manager to convince my general manager to make me do it. Now would you please leave so I can get some work done."

1. If you were Susan, what would you do?

2. What, if anything, could Susan have done differently to avoid this problem?

3. What could the management of Cerberus do to more effectively manage situations like this?

11 Managing Project Teams

LEARNING OBJECTIVES

After reading this chapter you should be able to:

11-1 Identify key characteristics of a high-performance project team.

11-2 Distinguish the different stages of team development.

11-3 Understand the impact situational factors have on project team development.

11-4 Identify strategies for developing a high-performance project team.

11-5 Distinguish functional conflict from dysfunctional conflict and describe strategies for encouraging functional conflict and discouraging dysfunctional conflict.

11-6 Understand the challenges of managing virtual project teams.

11-7 Recognize the different pitfalls that can occur in a project team.

OUTLINE

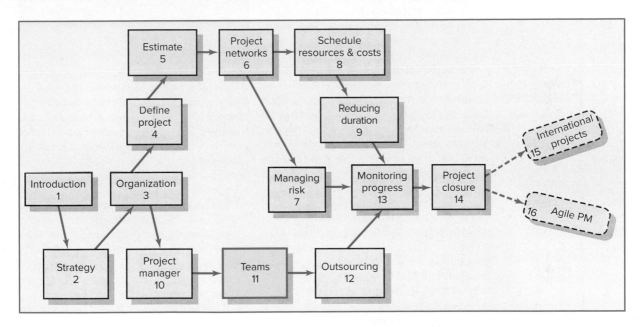

Coming together is a beginning. Keeping together is progress. Working together is success.

—*Henry Ford*

LO 11-1

Identify key characteristics of a high-performance project team.

The magic and power of teams is captured in the term "synergy," which is derived from the Greek word *sunergos:* "working together." There is positive and negative synergy. The essence of positive **synergy** can be found in the phrase "The whole is greater than the sum of the parts." Conversely, negative synergy occurs when the whole is less than the sum of the parts. Mathematically, these two states can be symbolized by the following equations:

$$\text{Positive Synergy } 1 + 1 + 1 + 1 + 1 = 10$$

$$\text{Negative Synergy } 1 + 1 + 1 + 1 + 1 = 2 \text{ (or even } -2)$$

Synergy perhaps can best be seen on a basketball court, a soccer pitch, or a football field where teammates play as one to defeat a superior foe (see Snapshot from Practice 11.1: The 2008 Olympic Redeem Team).

SNAPSHOT FROM PRACTICE 11.1   The 2008 Olympic Redeem Team*

In the 2004 Olympics in Athens, twelve years after Magic Johnson and Michael Jordan led the U.S. Dream Team to Olympic gold in Barcelona, the U.S. Basketball Team composed of NBA stars lost not once but three times to international competition. For the first time in Olympic history the U.S. settled for a bronze medal in men's basketball. Basketball was no longer America's game.

An autopsy of the debacle in Athens turned up a severe case of negative synergy. The causes were many. The team featured only three holdovers from the group that had qualified the previous summer. Seven of the original invitees withdrew. In the end some 14 players turned down Uncle Sam, invoking excuses from family obligations to nagging injuries to the security situation in Greece. As a result, coach Larry Brown took charge of a team with an average age of 23 years, and it showed. Behind the scenes, problems of dress and punctuality festered and on the eve of the games Brown wanted to send several players home. The million-dollar players were overconfident, and assumed that their individual brilliance would prevail. An overreliance on one-on-one basketball and poor team defense doomed them as they lost games to Puerto Rico, Lithuania, and Argentina.

Enter Jerry Colangelo, 68, former coach, player, and president of the Phoenix Suns. "The way they conducted themselves left a lot to be desired," he says of the 2004 team. "Watching and listening to how people reacted to our players, I knew we'd hit bottom." Colangelo told NBA commissioner David Stern that he would only assume duties as managing director if he was given complete control. As a measure of how abysmal the situation was, he immediately got what he asked for.

In 2005 Colangelo met face-to-face with every prospective national player, to hear in their own words why they wanted to represent their country. The few good men to set things right wouldn't be paid or guaranteed playing time, much less a starting spot. A key recruit was superstar LeBron James, who had been tagged "LeBronze" after his performance on the disappointing 2004 team. Colangelo says, "I got buy-in. Halfway through my talk with him, LeBron said, I'm in." Kobe Bryant soon followed and all but two of the 30 top NBA stars accepted Colangelo's offer.

Mike Kryzewski, the college coach at Duke, was hired with one project objective in mind—win the gold medal. To do so he had to change the attitude of team USA. They had to subordinate their superstar egos and buy in to the

© Dusan Vranic/AP Photo

concept of team ball. A blessing in disguise was being knocked out of the 2006 world championship by a Greek team. The players came away from that disappointment committed to team ball as extra passes became the staple in practices. The change in attitude was evident in more subtle ways. The USA on the uniforms was bright red, while the players' names were muted blue. The players no longer referred to hoops as "our game" and spoke about how it had become the world's game. Even the team's official slogan (United We Rise) and unofficial nickname (the Redeem Team) implied room for improvement.

The team bought into a common objective. Team USA marched to the final gold medal game by beating opponents by an average margin of 30+ points. Experts marveled not so much at the victory margin, but by how well they played as a team. "Our goal is to win a gold medal and be humble about it," said Jason Kidd, six-time all-pro point guard, "and if we do it by 50, to make sure it's because we're playing the right way." Nothing exemplified the right way more than a moment in the final, in which flawless ball movement from the Redeemers for 16 seconds, without a dribble being taken, culminated with Dwight Howard receiving a perfect pass for an uncontested dunk.

In the end, they didn't dominate the gold medal game. Spain proved to be inspired opponents. They simply closed the game out and for the first time since NBA players have come to the Olympics, the USA played as a team rather than showboating individuals.

* Alexander Wolff, "The Redeem Team: New Nickname, New Outlook for U.S. at Olympics," http://sportsillustrated.cnn .com/2008/writers/alexander_wolff/07/22/redeem.team0728 /index.html; and Greg Varkonyi, "The Redeem Team Played Like a Dream in the Olympic Basketball Final," http://www .sportingo.com/olympic-games/basketball/a10072_redeem -team-played-like-dream-olympic-basketball-final.

Although less visible than in team sports, positive and negative synergy can also be observed and felt in the daily operations of project teams. Here is a description from one team member we interviewed:

> Instead of operating as one big team we fractionalized into a series of subgroups. The marketing people stuck together as well as the systems guys. A lot of time was wasted gossiping and complaining about each other. When the project started slipping behind schedule, everyone started covering their tracks and trying to pass the blame on to others. After a while we avoided direct conversation and resorted to e-mail. Management finally pulled the plug and brought in another team to salvage the project. It was one of the worst project management experiences in my life.

This same individual fortunately was also able to recount a more positive experience:

> There was a contagious excitement within the team. Sure we had our share of problems and setbacks, but we dealt with them straight on and, at times, were able to do the impossible. We all cared about the project and looked out for each other. At the same time we challenged each other to do better. It was one of the most exciting times in my life.

The following is a set of characteristics commonly associated with high-performing teams that exhibit **positive synergy:**[1]

1. The team shares a sense of common purpose, and each member is willing to work toward achieving project objectives.
2. The team identifies individual talents and expertise and uses them, depending on the project's needs at any given time. At these times, the team willingly accepts the influence and leadership of the members whose skills are relevant to the immediate task.
3. Roles are balanced and shared to facilitate both the accomplishment of tasks and feelings of group cohesion and morale.
4. The team exerts energy toward problem solving rather than allowing itself to be drained by interpersonal issues or competitive struggles.
5. Differences of opinion are encouraged and freely expressed.
6. To encourage risk taking and creativity, mistakes are treated as opportunities for learning rather than reasons for punishment.
7. Members set high personal standards of performance and encourage each other to realize the objectives of the project.
8. Members identify with the team and consider it an important source of both professional and personal growth.

High-performing teams become champions, create breakthrough products, exceed customer expectations, and get projects done ahead of schedule and under budget. They are bonded together by mutual interdependency and a common goal or vision. They trust each other and exhibit a high level of collaboration.

11.1 The Five-Stage Team Development Model

LO 11-2

Distinguish the different stages of team development.

Just as infants develop in certain ways during their first months of life, many experts argue that groups develop in a predictable manner. One of the most popular models identifies five stages (see Figure 11.1) through which groups develop into effective teams (Tuchman, 1965; Tuchman and Jensen, 1977):

---

[1] See E. H. Schein, *Process Consultation,* 2nd ed. (Reading, MA: Addison-Wesley, 1988), pp. 42–43; and R. Likert, *New Patterns of Management* (New York: McGraw-Hill, 1961), pp. 162–77.

FIGURE 11.1

The Five-Stage Team Development Model

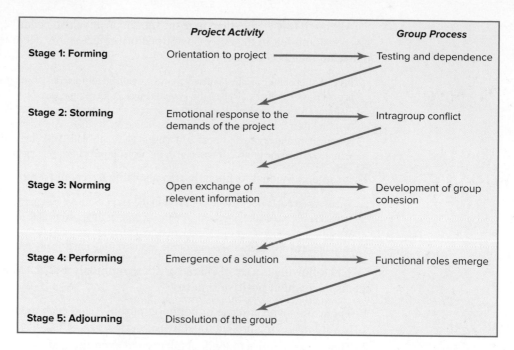

	Project Activity	Group Process
Stage 1: Forming	Orientation to project	Testing and dependence
Stage 2: Storming	Emotional response to the demands of the project	Intragroup conflict
Stage 3: Norming	Open exchange of relevent information	Development of group cohesion
Stage 4: Performing	Emergence of a solution	Functional roles emerge
Stage 5: Adjourning	Dissolution of the group	

1. **Forming.** During this initial stage the members get acquainted with each other and understand the scope of the project. They begin to establish ground rules by trying to find out what behaviors are acceptable with respect to both the project (what role they will play, what performance expectations are) and interpersonal relations (who's really in charge). This stage is completed once members begin to think of themselves as part of a group.

2. **Storming.** As the name suggests, this stage is marked by a high degree of internal conflict. Members accept that they are part of a project group but resist the constraints that the project and group put on their individuality. There is conflict over who will control the group and how decisions will be made. As these conflicts are resolved, the project manager's leadership becomes accepted, and the group moves to the next stage.

3. **Norming.** The third stage is one in which close relationships develop and the group demonstrates cohesiveness. Feelings of camaraderie and shared responsibility for the project are heightened. The norming phase is complete when the group structure solidifies and the group establishes a common set of expectations about how members should work together.

4. **Performing.** The team operating structure at this point is fully functional and accepted. Group energy has moved from getting to know each other and how the group will work together to accomplishing the project goals.

5. **Adjourning.** For conventional work groups, performing is the last stage of their development. However, for project teams, there is a completion phase. During this stage, the team prepares for its own disbandment. High performance is no longer a top priority. Instead attention is devoted to wrapping up the project. Responses of members vary in this stage. Some members are upbeat, basking in the project team's accomplishments. Others may be depressed over loss of camaraderie and friendships gained during the project's life.

This model has several implications for those working on project teams. The first is that the model provides a framework for the group to understand its own development. Project managers have found it useful to share the model with their teams. It helps members accept the tensions of the storming phase, and it directs their focus to moving toward the more productive phases. Another implication is that it stresses the importance of the norming phase, which contributes significantly to the level of productivity experienced during the performing phase. Project managers, as we shall see, have to take an active role in shaping group norms that will contribute to ultimate project success. For an alternative model of group development see Research Highlight 11.1: The Punctuated Equilibrium Model of Group Development.

11.2 Situational Factors Affecting Team Development

LO 11-3

Understand the impact situational factors have on project team development.

Experience and research indicate that high-performance project teams are much more likely to develop under the following conditions:[2]

- There are 10 or fewer members per team.
- Members volunteer to serve on the project team.
- Members serve on the project from beginning to end.
- Members are assigned to the project full time.
- Members are part of an organization culture that fosters cooperation and trust.
- Members report solely to the project manager.
- All relevant functional areas are represented on the team.
- The project involves a compelling objective.
- Members are located within conversational distance of each other.

In reality, it is rare that a project manager is assigned a project that meets all of these conditions. For example, many projects' requirements dictate the active involvement of more than 10 members and may consist of a complex set of interlocking teams comprising more than 100 professionals. In many organizations, functional managers or central manpower offices assign project members with little input from the project manager. To optimize resource utilization, team member involvement may be part time, and/or participants may move in and out of the project team on an as-needed basis. In the case of ad hoc task forces, no member of the team works full time on the project. In many corporations an NIH (not invented here) culture exists that discourages collaboration across functional boundaries.

Team members often report to different managers, and, in some cases, the project manager will have no direct input over performance appraisals and advancement opportunities of team members. Key functional areas may not be represented during the entire duration of the project but may only be involved in a sequential manner. Not all projects have a compelling objective. It can be hard to get members excited about mundane projects such as a simple product extension or a conventional apartment complex. Finally, team members are often scattered across different corporate offices and buildings or, in the case of a virtual project, across the entire globe.

[2] See, for example: G. C. Homans, *Social Behavior: Its Elementary Forms* (New York: Harcourt Brace Jovanovich, 1961); M. Sherif, *Group Conflict and Cooperation: Their Social Psychology* (Chicago: Aldine, 1967); J. J. Seta, P. B. Paulus, and J. Schkade, "Effects of Group Size and Proximity under Cooperative and Competitive Conditions," *Journal of Personality and Social Psychology,* vol. 98, no. 2 (1976), pp. 47–53; and A. Zander, *Making Groups Effective* (San Francisco: Jossey-Bass, 1994).

Gersick's research suggests that groups don't develop in a universal sequence of stages as suggested by the five-phase model. Her research, which is based on the systems concept of *punctuated equilibrium,* found that the *timing* of when groups form and actually change the way they work is highly consistent. What makes this research appealing is that it is based on studies of more than a dozen field and laboratory task forces assigned to complete a specific project. This research reveals that each group begins with a unique approach to accomplishing its project that is set in its first meeting and includes the behavior and roles that dominate phase I. Phase I continues until one-half of the allotted time for project completion has expired (regardless of actual amount of time). At this midpoint, a major transition occurs that includes the dropping of the group's old norms and behavior patterns and the emergence of new behavior and working relationships that contribute to increased progress toward completing the project. The last meeting is marked by accelerated activity to complete the project. These findings are summarized in Figure 11.2.

The remarkable discovery in these studies was that each group experienced its transition at the same point in its calendar—roughly halfway between the first meeting and the completion deadline—despite the fact that some groups spent as little as an hour on their project while others spent six months. It was as if the groups universally experienced a midlife crisis at this point. The midpoint appeared to work like an alarm clock, heightening members' awareness that time was limited and they needed to get moving.

Within the context of the five-stage model, it suggests that groups begin by combining the forming and norming stages, then go through a period of low performing, followed by storming, then a period of high performing, and finally adjourning.

Gersick's findings suggest that there are natural transition points during the life of teams in which the group is receptive to change and that such a moment naturally occurs at the midpoint of a project. However, a manager does not want to have to wait 6 months on a complicated 12-month project for a team to get its act together! Here it is important to note that Gersick's groups were working on relatively small-scale projects, i.e., a 4-person bank task force in charge of designing a new bank account in one month and a 12-person medical task force in charge of reorganizing two units of a treatment facility. In most cases no formal project plan was established. If anything, the results point to the importance of good project management and the need to establish deadlines and milestones. By imposing a series of deadlines associated with important milestones, it is possible to create multiple transition points for natural group development. For example, a 12-month construction project can be broken down into six to eight significant milestones with the challenge of meeting each deadline producing the prerequisite tension for elevating team performance.

* Connie J. Gersick, "Time and Transition in Work Teams: Toward a New Model of Group Development," *Academy of Management Journal,* vol. 31, no. 1 (March 1988), pp. 9–41; and Connie J. Gersick, "Making Time Predictable Transitions in Task Groups," *Academy of Management Journal,* vol. 32, no. 2 (June 1989), pp. 274–309.

FIGURE 11.2   The Punctuated Equilibrium Model of Group Development

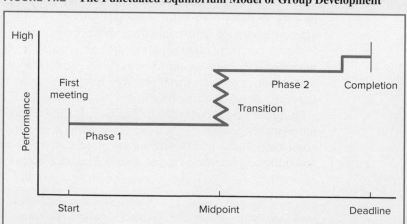

It is important for project managers and team members to recognize the situational constraints they are operating under and do the best they can. It would be naive to believe that every project team has the same potential to evolve into a high-performance team. Under less-than-ideal conditions, it may be a struggle just to meet project objectives. Ingenuity, discipline, and sensitivity to team dynamics are essential to maximizing the performance of a project team.

11.3 Building High-Performance Project Teams

 LO 11-4

Identify strategies for developing a high-performance project team.

Project managers play a key role in developing high-performance project teams. They recruit members, conduct meetings, establish a team identity, create a common sense of purpose or a shared vision, manage a reward system that encourages teamwork, orchestrate decision making, resolve conflicts that emerge within the team, and rejuvenate the team when energy wanes (see Figure 11.3). Project managers take advantage of situational factors that naturally contribute to team development while improvising around those factors that inhibit team development. In doing so they exhibit a highly interactive management style that exemplifies teamwork and, as discussed in the previous chapter, manage the interface between the team and the rest of the organization.

Recruiting Project Members

The process of selecting and recruiting project members will vary across organizations. Two important factors affecting recruitment are the importance of the project and the management structure being used to complete the project. Often for high-priority projects that are critical to the future of the organization, the project manager will be given virtual carte blanche to select whomever he or she deems necessary. For less significant projects, personnel will simply be assigned to the project.

In many matrix structures, the functional manager controls who is assigned to the project; the project manager will have to work with the functional manager to obtain necessary personnel. Even in a project team where members are selected and assigned full time to the project, the project manager has to be sensitive to the needs of others. There is no better way to create enemies within an organization than to be perceived as unnecessarily robbing other departments of essential personnel.

FIGURE 11.3
Creating a High-Performance Project Team

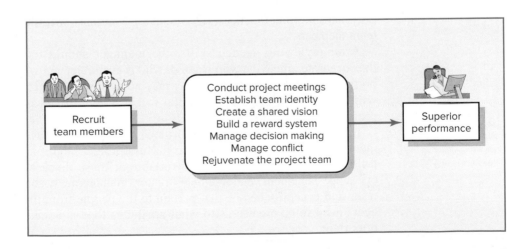

Recruit team members

Conduct project meetings
Establish team identity
Create a shared vision
Build a reward system
Manage decision making
Manage conflict
Rejuvenate the project team

Superior performance

Experienced project managers stress the importance of asking for volunteers. However, this desirable step oftentimes is outside the manager's control. Still, the value of having team members volunteer for the project as opposed to being assigned cannot be overlooked. Agreeing to work on the project is the first step toward building personal commitment to the project. Such commitment will be essential to maintain motivation when the project hits hard times and extra effort is required.

When selecting and recruiting team members, project managers naturally look for individuals with the necessary experience and knowledge/technical skills critical for project completion. At the same time, there are less obvious considerations that need to be factored into the recruitment process:

- *Problem-solving ability.* If the project is complex and fuzzy, then a manager wants people who are good at working under uncertainty and have strong problem-identification and problem-solving skills. These same people are likely to be bored and less productive working on straightforward projects that go by the book.

- *Availability.* Sometimes the people who are most available are not the ones wanted for the team. Conversely, if members recruited are already overcommitted, they may not be able to offer much.

- *Technological expertise.* Managers should be wary of people who know too much about a specific technology. They may be technology buffs who like to study but have a hard time settling down and doing the work.

- *Credibility.* The credibility of the project is enhanced by the reputation of the people involved in the project. Recruiting a sufficient number of "winners" lends confidence to the project.

- *Political connections.* Managers are wise to recruit individuals who already have a good working relationship with key stakeholders. This is particularly true for projects operating in a matrix environment in which a significant portion of the work will be under the domain of a specific functional department and not the core project team.

- *Ambition, initiative, and energy.* These qualities can make up for a lot of shortcomings in other areas and should not be underestimated.

- *Familiarity.* Research suggests repeat collaboration stifles creativity and innovation. On challenging, breakthrough projects it is wise to interject the team with experts who have little previous working experience with others. (Skilton and Dooley, 2010)

See Snapshot from Practice 11.2: Managing Martians for further advice on recruiting team members.

After reviewing needed skills, the manager should try to find out through the corporate grapevine who is good, who is available, and who might want to work on the project. Some organizations may allow direct interviews. Often a manager will have to expend political capital to get highly prized people assigned to the project.

In matrix environments, the project manager will have to request appointments with functional managers to discuss project requirements for staffing. The following documents should be available at these discussions: an overall project scope statement, endorsements of top management, and a description of the tasks and general schedule that pertain to the people from their departments. Managers need to be precise as to what attributes they are seeking and why they are important.

SNAPSHOT FROM PRACTICE 11.2   Managing Martians*

Donna Shirley's 35-year career as aerospace engineer reached a pinnacle in July 1997 when Sojourner—the solar-powered, self-guided, microwave-oven-sized rover—was seen exploring the Martian landscape in Pathfinder's spectacular images from the surface of the red planet. The event marked a milestone in space exploration: No vehicle had ever before roamed the surface of another planet. Shirley, a manager at the Jet Propulsion Laboratory's Mars Exploration Program, headed the mostly male team that designed and built Sojourner. In her insightful memoir, *Managing Martians,* written with Danelle Morton, she makes the following observation about managing creative teams:

Source: NASA/JPL

> When you are managing really brilliant, creative people, at some point you find it's impossible to command or control them because you can't understand what they are doing. Once they have gone beyond your ability to understand them, you have a choice to make as a manager. You can limit them and the project by your intelligence, which I think is the wrong way to do it. Or you can trust them and use your management skills to keep them focused on the goal.

A lot of bad managers get threatened when their "subordinates" know more than they do. They either hire people who are inferior to them so they can always feel in control or they bottleneck people who know something they don't so they can maintain control. The whole project suffers from the manager's insecurities.

* Donna Shirley and Danelle Morton, *Managing Martians* (New York: Broadway Books, 1998), pp. 88–89.

Conducting Project Meetings

The First Project Team Meeting

Research on team development confirms what we have heard from project managers: The first **project kick-off meeting** is critical to the early functioning of the project team. According to one veteran project manager:

> The first team meeting sets the tone for how the team will work together. If it is disorganized, or becomes bogged down with little sense of closure, then this can often become a self-fulfilling prophecy for subsequent group work. On the other hand, if it is crisply run, focusing on real issues and concerns in an honest and straightforward manner, members come away excited about being part of the project team.

There are typically three objectives project managers try to achieve during the first meeting of the project team. The first is to provide an overview of the project, including the scope and objectives, the general schedule, method, and procedures. The second is to begin to address some of the interpersonal concerns captured in the team development model: Who are the other team members? How will I fit in? Will I be able to work with these people? The third and most important objective is to begin to model how the team is going to work together to complete the project. The project manager must recognize that first impressions are important; her behavior will be carefully monitored and interpreted by team members. This meeting should serve as an exemplary role model for subsequent meetings and reflect the leader's style.

The meeting itself comes in a variety of shapes and forms. It is not uncommon in major projects for the kick-off meeting to involve one or two days, often at a remote site away from interruptions. This retreat provides sufficient time for preliminary introduction, to begin to establish ground rules, and to define the structure of the project. One advantage of off-site kick-off meetings is that they provide ample opportunity for informal interaction among members during breaks, meals, and evening activities; such informal interactions are critical to forming relationships.

However, many organizations do not have the luxury of holding elaborate retreats. In other cases the scope of a project does not warrant such an investment of time. In these cases, the key operating principle should be KISS (keep it simple, stupid!). Too often when constrained by time, project managers try to accomplish too much during the first meeting; in doing so, issues do not get fully resolved, and members come away with an information headache.

The project manager needs to remember that the primary goal is to run a productive meeting, and objectives should be realistic given the time available. If the meeting is only one hour, then the project manager should simply review the scope of the project, discuss how the team was formed, and provide an opportunity for members to introduce themselves to the team.

Establishing Ground Rules

Whether as part of an elaborate first meeting or during follow-up meetings, the project manager must quickly begin to establish operational ground rules for how the team will work together. These ground rules involve not only organizational and procedural issues but also normative issues on how the team will interact with each other. Although specific procedures will vary across organizations and projects, some of the major issues that need to be addressed include the following:

Planning Decisions

- How will the project plan be developed?
- Will a specific project management software package be used? If so, which one?
- What are the specific roles and responsibilities of all the participants?
- Who needs to be informed of decisions? How will they be kept informed?
- What is the relative importance of cost, time, and performance?
- What are the deliverables of the project planning process?
- Who will approve and sign off at the completion of each deliverable?
- Who receives each deliverable?

Tracking Decisions

- How will progress be assessed?
- At what level of detail will the project be tracked?
- How will team members get data from each other?
- How often will they get this data?
- Who will generate and distribute reports?
- Who needs to be kept informed about project progress, and how will they be informed?
- What content/format is appropriate for each audience?

- Meetings
  - Where will meetings be located?
  - What kind of meetings will be held?
  - Who will "run" these meetings?
  - How will agendas be produced?
  - How will information be recorded?

Managing Change Decisions

- How will changes be instituted?
- Who will have change approval authority?
- How will plan changes be documented and evaluated?

Relationship Decisions

- What department or organizations will the team need to interact with during the project?
- What are the roles and responsibilities of each organization (reviewer, approver, creator, user)?
- How will all involved parties be kept informed of deliverables, schedule dates, expectations, etc.?
- How will the team members communicate among themselves?
- What information will and won't be exchanged?

Checklists like these are only a guide; items should be added or deleted as needed. Many of these procedures will have already been established by precedent and will only have to be briefly reviewed. For example, *Microsoft Project* or *Primavera* may be the standard software tool for planning and tracking. Likewise, a specific firm is likely to have an established format for reporting status information. How to deal with other issues will have to be determined by the project team. When appropriate, the project manager should actively solicit input from the project team members and draw upon their experience and preferred work habits. This process also contributes to their buying into the operational decisions. Decisions should be recorded and circulated to all members.

Establishing Team Norms

During the course of establishing these operational procedures, the project manager, through word and deed, should begin working with members to establish the norms for team interaction. Below are examples of some of the norms researchers have found associated with high-performance teams.[3]

- Confidentiality is maintained; no information is shared outside the team unless all agree to it.
- It is acceptable to be in trouble, but it is not acceptable to surprise others. Tell others immediately when deadlines or milestones will not be reached.
- There is zero tolerance for bulling a way through a problem or an issue.

[3] See J. R. Katzenbach and D. K. Smith, *The Wisdom of Teams* (Boston: Harvard Business School Press, 1993); L. G. Bolman and T. E. Deal, "What Makes Teams Work," *Organizational Dynamics,* vol. 21, no. 2, pp. 34–45; R. Katz, "How a Team at Digital Equipment Designed the 'Alpha' Chips," *The Human Side of Managing Technological Innovation,* R. Katz, ed. (New York: Oxford Press, 1997), pp. 137–148.

members see that they are not working alone. They are part of a larger project team, and project success depends on the collective efforts of all the team members. Timely gatherings of all the project participants help define team membership and reinforce a collective identity.

- *Co-location of team members.* The most obvious way to make the project team tangible is to have members work together in a common space. This is not always possible in matrix environments where involvement is part time and members are working on other projects and activities. A worthwhile substitute for co-location is the creation of a project office, sometimes referred to as the project war room or clubhouse. Such rooms are the common meeting place and contain the most significant project documentation. Frequently, their walls are covered with Gantt charts, cost graphs, and other output associated with project planning and control. These rooms serve as a tangible sign of project effort.

- *Creation of project team name.* The development of a team name such as the "A-Team" or "Casey's Crusaders" is a common device for making a team more tangible. Frequently an associated team logo is also created. Again the project manager should rely on the collective ingenuity of the team to come up with the appropriate name and logo. Such symbols then can be affixed to stationery, T-shirts, coffee mugs, etc., to help signify team membership.

- *Get the team to build or do something together early on.* Nothing reinforces a sense of a team more than working on something together. In the case of one international project, the manager simply hosted a potluck dinner where each member brought a dish his or her country was famous for.

- *Team rituals.* Just as corporate rituals help establish the unique identity of a firm, similar symbolic actions at the project level can contribute to a unique team subculture. For example, on one project members were given ties with stripes that corresponded to the number of milestones on the project. After reaching each milestone, members would gather and cut the next stripe off their ties to signify progress.[4] Ralph Katz (2004) reports it was common practice for Digital Equipment's alpha chip design team to recognize people who found a bug in the design by giving them a phosphorescent toy roach. The bigger the bug that was discovered, the bigger the toy roach received. Such rituals help set project work apart from mainstream operations and reinforce a special status.

Creating a Shared Vision

Unlike project scope statements, which include specific cost, completion dates, and performance requirements, a **project vision** involves the less tangible aspects of project performance. It refers to an image a project team holds in common about how the project will look upon completion, how they will work together, and/or how customers will accept the project. At its simplest level, a shared vision is the answer to the question, "What do we want to create?" Not everyone will have the same vision, but the images should be similar. Visions come in a variety of shapes and forms; they can be captured in a slogan or a symbol or can be written as a formal vision statement.

What a vision is, is not as important as what it does. A vision inspires members to give their best effort. (See Snapshot from Practice 11.4: A Good Man in a Storm.) Moreover, a shared vision unites professionals with different backgrounds and agendas to a common aspiration. It helps motivate members to subordinate their individual agendas and do what is best for the project. As psychologist Robert Fritz puts it,

[4] This anecdote was provided by Dr. Frances Hartman, University of Calgary, Alberta.

SNAPSHOT FROM PRACTICE 11.4 A Good Man in a Storm*

Once upon a time, back in 1976, Data General Corporation needed to come up quickly with a fast, reasonably priced 32-bit mini-computer to compete with Digital Equipment Corporation's VAX. Data General CEO Edson de Castro launched the Fountainhead Project and gave it the best people and ample resources to complete the 32-bit initiative. As a back-up to the Fountainhead project, Data General created the Eagle project within the Eclipse group under the leadership of Tom West. Work on both projects began in 1978.

In 1980 Data General announced its new computer, featuring simplicity, power, and low cost. This computer was not the Fountainhead from the well-funded "best" DG group but the Eagle from Tom West's underfunded Eclipse team. Tracy Kidder saw all this happen and told the story in *The Soul of a New Machine,* which won a Pulitzer Prize in 1982. This book, which Kidder thought might be of interest to a handful of computer scientists, has become a project management classic.

In the beginning of his book, Kidder introduces the readers to the book's protagonist Tom West by telling the story of him sailing a yacht across rough seas off the coast of New England. Kidder's title for the prologue was "A Good Man in a Storm."

Twenty years after Kidder's book was published Tom West was interviewed by Lawrence Peters for the *Academy of Management Executive.* Below are some excerpts that capture Tom's views on managing innovative projects:

On selecting team members:

> You explain to a guy what the challenge was, and then see if his eyes light up.

On motivating team members:

> Challenge was everything. People, especially creative technical people who really want to make a difference, will do whatever is possible or whatever is necessary. I've done this more than once, and I've repeated it over and over. It seems to work.

On the importance of having a vision:

> You've got to find a rallying cry. You need to have something that can be described very simply and has that sort of ring of truth to an engineer that says "yes that's the thing to be doing right now." Otherwise you're going to be rolling rocks up hill all the time.

On the role of being a project manager:

> You have to act as a cheerleader. You have to act as the instructor. You have to constantly bring to mind what the purpose is and what's moving the ball towards the goal post, and what's running sideways, and you have to take up a lot of battles for them. I mean you really don't want your design engineer arguing with the guy in the drafting shop about why he ought to do it the designer's way. I can do that, and I can pull rank too, and sometimes I did just that.

* Tracy Kidder, *The Soul of a New Machine* (New York: Avon Books, 1981); Lawrence H. Peters, "'A Good Man in a Storm': An Interview with Tom West," *Academy of Management Executive,* vol. 16, no. 4 (2002), pp. 42–43.

"In the presence of greatness, pettiness disappears."[5] Visions also provide focus and help communicate less tangible priorities, helping members make appropriate judgment calls. Finally, a shared vision for a project fosters commitment to the long term and discourages expedient responses that collectively dilute the quality of the project.

Visions can be surprisingly simple. For example, the vision for a new car could be expressed as a "pocket rocket." Compare this vision with the more traditional product description—"a sports car in the midprice range." The "pocket rocket" vision provides a much clearer picture of what the final product should be. Design engineers would immediately understand that the car will be both small and fast and that the car should be quick at the getaway, nimble in the turns, and very fast in the straightaways (Bowen et al., 1994). Alternatively, visions can be more concrete:

"The Helpdesk Automated Site (HASS) Version 4.5 will address the top 10 customer complaints across the university without any negative impact on average performance, reliability or response time across the system."[6]

[5] Quoted in P. Senge, *The Fifth Discipline* (New York, Doubleday,1990) p. 209.

[6] S. Berkun, *The Art of Project Management* (Sebastopol. CA: O'Reilly, 2005), p. 79.

FIGURE 11.4
Requirements for an Effective Project Vision

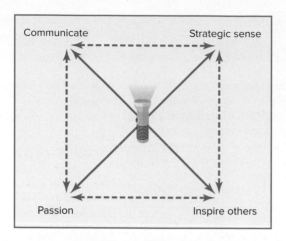

There appear to be four essential qualities of an effective vision (see Figure 11.4). First, its essential qualities must be able to be communicated. A vision is worthless if it only resides in someone's head. Here, the use of concrete, image-based language is considered critical, e.g., "pocket rocket" (Murphy and Clark 2016). Second, visions have to be challenging but also realistic. For example, a task force directed at overhauling the curriculum at the college of business at a state university is likely to roll its collective eyes if the dean announces that their vision is to compete against the Harvard Business School. Conversely, developing the best undergraduate business program in that state may be a realistic vision for that task force. Third, the project manager has to believe in the vision. Passion for the vision is an essential element of an effective vision. Finally, it should be a source of inspiration to others.

Once a project manager accepts the importance of building a shared vision, the next question is how to get a vision for a particular project. First, project managers don't get visions. They act as catalysts and midwives for the formation of a shared vision of a project team (Smith, 1994). In many cases visions are inherent in the scope and objectives of the project. People get naturally excited about being the first ones to bring a new technology to the market or solving a problem that is threatening their organization. Even with mundane projects, there are often ample opportunities for establishing a compelling vision. One way is to talk to various people involved in the project and find out early on what gets them excited about the project. For some it may be doing a better job than on the last project or the satisfaction in the eyes of the customers when the project is over. Many visions evolve reactively in response to competition: for example, Samsung engineers trying to develop a next generation smartphone that critics will proclaim superior to the iPhone.

Some experts advocate engaging in formal vision-building meetings. These meetings generally involve several steps, beginning with members identifying different aspects of the project and generating ideal scenarios for each aspect. For example, on a construction project the scenarios may include "no accidents," "no lawsuits," "winning a prize," or "how we are going to spend our bonus for completing the project ahead of schedule." The group reviews and chooses the scenarios that are most appealing and translates them into vision statements for the project. The next step is to identify strategies for achieving the vision statements. For example, if one of the vision statements is that there will be no lawsuits, members will identify how they will have to work with the owner and subcontractors to avoid litigation. Next, members volunteer to be the keeper of the flame for each statement. The vision, strategies, and the name of the responsible team member are published and distributed to relevant stakeholders.

In more cases than not, shared visions emerge informally. Project managers collect information about what excites participants about the project. They test bits of their working vision in their conversations with team members to gauge the level of excitement the early ideas elicit in others. To some extent they engage in basic market research. They seize opportunities to galvanize the team, such as a disparaging remark by an executive that the project will never get done on time or the threat of a competing firm launching a similar project. Consensus in the beginning is not essential. What is essential is a core group of at least one-third of the project team that is genuinely committed to the vision. They will provide the critical mass to draw others aboard. Once the language has been formulated to communicate the vision, then the statement needs to be a staple part of every working agenda, and the project manager should be prepared to deliver a "stump" speech at a moment's notice. When problems or disagreements emerge, all responses should be consistent with the vision.

Much has been written about visions and leadership. Critics argue that vision is a glorified substitute for shared goals. Others argue that it is one of the things that separate leaders from managers. The key is discovering what excites people about a project, being able to articulate this source of excitement in an appealing manner, and finally protecting and nurturing this source of excitement throughout the duration of the project.

Managing Project Reward Systems

Project managers are responsible for managing the reward system that encourages team performance and extra effort. One advantage they have is that often project work is inherently satisfying, whether it is manifested in an inspiring vision or simple sense of accomplishment. Projects provide participants with a change in scenery, a chance to learn new skills, and an opportunity to break out of their departmental cocoon. Another inherent reward is what was referred to in Tracy Kidder, *The Soul of a New Machine,* as "pinball"—project success typically gives team members an option to play another exciting game.[7]

Still, many projects are underappreciated, boring, interfere with other more significant priorities, and are considered an extra burden. In some of these cases, the biggest reward is finishing the project so that team members can go back to what they really enjoy doing and what will yield the biggest personal payoffs. Unfortunately, when this attitude is the primary incentive, project quality is likely to suffer. In these circumstances, external rewards play a more important role in motivating team performance.

Most project managers we talk to advocate the use of group rewards. Because most project work is a collaborative effort, it only makes sense that the reward system would encourage teamwork. Recognizing individual members regardless of their accomplishments can distract from team unity. Project work is highly interdependent, so it can become problematic to distinguish who truly deserves additional credit. Cash bonuses and incentives need to be linked to project priorities. It makes no sense to reward a team for completing their work early if controlling cost was the number one priority.

One of the limitations of lump-sum cash bonuses is that all too often they are consumed by the household budget to pay the dentist or mechanic. To have more value, rewards need to have lasting significance (Smith and Reinertsen, 1997). Many companies convert cash into vacation rewards, sometimes with corresponding time off. For example, there is one firm that rewarded a project team for getting the job done ahead of schedule with a four-day, all-expenses-paid trip to Walt Disney World for the members' entire families. That vacation not only will be remembered for

---

[7] T. Kidder, *The Soul of a New Machine* (New York: Avon Books, 1981), pp. 221–22.

years, but it also recognizes spouses and children who, in a sense, also contributed to the project's success. Similarly, other firms have been known to give members home computers and entertainment centers. Wise project managers negotiate a discretionary budget so that they can reward teams' surpassing milestones with gift certificates to popular restaurants or tickets to sporting events. Impromptu pizza parties and barbecues are also used to celebrate key accomplishments.

Sometimes project managers have to use negative reinforcement to motivate project performance. For example, Ritti and Levy (2009) recount the story of one project manager who was in charge of the construction of a new, state-of-the-art manufacturing plant. His project team was working with a number of different contracting firms. The project was slipping behind schedule, mostly because of a lack of cooperation among the different players. The project manager did not have direct authority over many key people, especially the contractors from the other companies. He did, however, have the freedom to convene meetings at his convenience. So the project manager instituted daily "coordination meetings," which were required of all the principals involved, at 6:00 a.m. The meetings continued for about two weeks until the project got back on schedule. At that time the project manager announced that the next meeting was canceled, and no further sunrise meetings were ever scheduled.[8]

While project managers tend to focus on group rewards, there are times when they need to reward individual performance. This is done not only to compensate extraordinary effort but also to signal to the others what exemplary behavior is. Examples of this kind of rewards include:

- **Letters of commendation.** While project managers may not have responsibility for their team members' performance appraisals, they can write letters commending their project performance. These letters can be sent to the workers' supervisors to be placed in their personnel files.
- **Public recognition for outstanding work.** Superlative workers should be publicly recognized for their efforts. Some project managers begin each status review meeting with a brief mention of project workers who have exceeded their project goals.
- **Job assignments.** Good project managers recognize that, while they may not have much budgetary authority, they do have substantial control over who does what, with whom, when, and where. Good work should be rewarded with desirable job assignments. Managers should be aware of member preferences and, when appropriate, accommodate them.
- **Flexibility.** Being willing to make exceptions to rules, if done judiciously, can be a powerful reward. Allowing members to work at home when a child is sick or excusing a minor indiscretion can engender long-lasting loyalty.

Individual rewards should be used judiciously, and under extraordinary circumstances. Nothing undermines the cohesiveness of a team more than members beginning to feel that others are getting special treatment or that they are being treated unfairly. Camaraderie and collaboration can quickly vanish only to be replaced by bickering and obsessive preoccupation with group politics. Such distractions can absorb energy that otherwise would be directed toward completing the project. Individual rewards typically should be used only when everyone in the team recognizes that a member is deserving of special recognition.

[8] R. R. Ritti and S. L. Levy, *The Ropes to Skip and Ropes to Know: Studies in Organizational Theory and Behavior* (New York: Wiley, 2009) pp. 93–94.

Orchestrating the Decision-Making Process

Most decisions on a project do not require a formal meeting to discuss alternatives and determine solutions. Instead decisions are made in real time as part of the daily interactions between project managers, stakeholders, and team members. For example, as a result of a routine "how's it going?" question, a project manager discovers that a mechanical engineer is stuck trying to meet the performance criteria for a prototype he is responsible for building. The project manager and engineer go down the hallway to talk to the designers, explain the problem, and ask what, if anything, can be done. The designers distinguish which criteria are essential and which ones they think can be compromised. The project manager then checks with the marketing group to make sure the modifications are acceptable. They agree with all but two of the modifications. The project manager goes back to the mechanical engineer and asks whether the proposed changes would help solve the problem. The engineer agrees. Before authorizing the changes he calls the project sponsor, reviews the events, and gets the sponsor to sign off on the changes. This is an example of how, by practicing MBWA (management by wandering around), project managers consult team members, solicit ideas, determine optimum solutions, and create a sense of involvement that builds trust and commitment to decisions.

Still, projects encounter problems and decisions that require the collective wisdom of team members as well as relevant stakeholders. Group decision making should be used when it will improve the quality of important decisions (Vroom and Jago, 1988). This is often the case with complex problems that require the input of a variety of different specialists. Group decision making should also be used when strong commitment to the decision is needed and there is a low probability of acceptance if only one person makes the decision. Participation is used to reduce resistance and secure support for the decision. Guidelines for managing group decision making are provided below.

Facilitating Group Decision Making

Project managers play a pivotal role in guiding the group decision-making process. They must remind themselves that their job is not to make a decision but to facilitate the discussion within the group so that the team reaches a consensus on the best possible solution. Consensus within this context does not mean that everyone supports the decision 100 percent, but that they all agree what the best solution is under the circumstances. Facilitating group decision making essentially involves four major steps. Each step is briefly described next with suggestions for how to manage the process.[9]

1. **Problem identification.** The project manager needs to be careful not to state the problem in terms of choices (e.g., should we do X or Y?). Rather the project manager should identify the underlying problem to which these alternatives and probably others are potential solutions. This allows group members to generate alternatives, not just choose among them. One useful way of defining problems is to consider the gap between where a project is (i.e., the present state) and where it should be (desired state). For example, the project may be four days behind schedule or the prototype weighs two pounds more than the specifications. Whether the gap is small or large, the purpose is to eliminate it. The group must find one or more courses of action that will change the existing state into the desired one.

   If one detects defensive posturing during the problem identification discussion, then it may be wise to postpone the problem-solving step if possible. This allows for emotions to subside and members to gain a fresh perspective on the issues involved.

---

[9] This discussion is based on the classic work of N. R. F. Maier, *Problem-Solving Discussion and Conferences* (New York: McGraw-Hill, 1963); and *Problem Solving and Creativity in Individuals and Groups* (Belmont, CA: Brooks-Cole, 1970).

2. **Generating alternatives.** Once there is general agreement as to the nature of the problem(s), then the next step is to generate alternative solutions. If the problem requires creativity, then **brainstorming** is commonly recommended. Here the team generates a list of possible solutions on a flipchart or blackboard. During that time the project manager establishes a moratorium on criticizing or evaluating ideas. Members are encouraged to "piggyback" on others' ideas by extending them or combining ideas into a new idea. The object is to create as many alternatives as possible no matter how outlandish they may appear to be. Some project managers report that for really tough problems they have found it beneficial to conduct such sessions away from the normal work environment; the change in scenery stimulates creativity.

3. **Reaching a decision.** The next step is to evaluate and assess the merits of alternative solutions. During this phase it is useful to have a set of criteria for evaluating the merits of different solutions. In many cases the project manager can draw upon the priorities for the project and have the group assess each alternative in terms of its impact on cost, schedule, and performance as well as reducing the problem gap. For example, if time is critical, then the solution that solves the problem as quickly as possible would be chosen.

   During the course of the discussion the project manager attempts to build consensus among the group. This can be a complicated process. Project managers need to provide periodic summaries to help the group keep track of its progress. They must protect those members who represent the minority view and ensure that such views get a fair hearing. They need to guarantee that everyone has an opportunity to share opinions and no one individual or group dominates the conversation. It may be useful to bring a two-minute timer to regulate the use of air time. When conflicts occur, managers need to apply some of the ideas and techniques discussed in the next section.

   Project managers need to engage in consensus testing to determine what points the group agrees on and what are still sources of contention. They are careful not to interpret silence as agreement; they confirm agreement by asking questions. Ultimately, through thoughtful interaction, the team reaches a "meeting of the minds" as to what solution is best for the project.

4. **Follow-up.** Once the decision has been made and implemented, it is important for the team to find the time to evaluate the effectiveness of the decision. If the decision failed to provide the anticipated solution, then the reasons should be explored and the lessons learned added to the collective memory bank of the project team.

Managing Conflict within the Project

LO 11-5

Distinguish functional conflict from dysfunctional conflict and describe strategies for encouraging functional conflict and discouraging dysfunctional conflict.

Disagreements and conflicts naturally emerge within a project team during the life of the project. Participants will disagree over priorities, allocation of resources, the quality of specific work, solutions to discovered problems, and so forth. Some conflicts support the goals of the group and improve project performance. For example, two members may be locked in a debate over a design trade-off decision involving different features of a product. They argue that their preferred feature is what the primary customer truly wants. This disagreement may force them to talk to or get more information from the customer, with the result that they realize neither feature is highly valued, but instead the customer wants something else. On the other hand, conflicts can also hinder group performance. Initial disagreements can escalate into heated arguments with both parties storming out of the room and refusing to work together.

SNAPSHOT FROM PRACTICE 11.5   Managing Low-Priority Projects

So far the discussion of team building has been directed primarily to significant projects that command the attention and involvement of assigned members. But what about projects that have low priority for team members: the perfunctory task forces that members begrudgingly join? the committee work people get assigned to do? the part-time projects that pull members away from the critical work they would rather be doing? projects that cause members to privately question why they are doing this?

There is no magic wand available that transforms mildly interested, part-time project teams into high-performance teams. We interviewed several project managers about such project scenarios. They all agreed that these can be very difficult and frustrating assignments and that there are limits to what is possible. Still, they offered tips and advice for making the best of the situation. Most of these tips focus on building commitment to the project when it does not naturally exist.

One project manager advocated orchestrating a large "time" investment upfront on such projects—either in the form of a lengthy meeting or a significant early assignment. He viewed this as a form of down payment that members would forfeit if they didn't carry the project to completion.

Others emphasize interjecting as much fun into activities as possible. Here rituals discussed under building team identity come into play. People become committed because they enjoy working together on the project. One project manager even confided that the perfect attendance at her project meetings was due primarily to the quality of the doughnuts she provided.

Another strategy is to make the benefits of the project as real to the team members as possible. One project manager escalated commitment to a mandated accidents prevention task force by bringing accident victims to a project meeting. Another project manager brought the high-ranking project sponsor to recharge the team by reinforcing the importance of the project to the company.

Most project managers emphasized the importance of building a strong personal relationship with each of the team members. When this connection occurs, members work hard not so much because they really care about the project but because they don't want to let the project manager down. Although not couched in influence currency terms, these managers talked about getting to know each member, sharing contacts, offering encouragement, and extending a helping hand when needed.

Finally, all project managers cautioned that nothing should be taken for granted on low-priority projects. They recommend reminding people about meetings and bringing extra copies of materials to meetings for those who have forgotten them or can't find them. Project managers should remain in frequent contact with team members and remind them of their assignments. One manager summed it up best when he said, "Sometimes it all boils down to just being a good nag."

Sources of conflict are likely to change as projects progress along the project life cycle (Thamhain and Wilemon, 1975; Posner, 1986; Adams and Brandt, 1988). Figure 11.5 summarizes the major sources of conflict in each phase.

FIGURE 11.5
Sources of Conflict over the Project Life Cycle

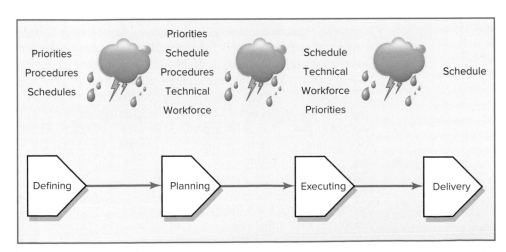

During project definition, the most significant sources of conflict are priorities, administrative procedures, and schedule. Disputes occur over the relative importance of the project compared with other activities, which project management structure to use (especially how much control the project manager should have), the personnel to be assigned, and the scheduling of the project into existing workloads.

During the planning phase, the chief source of conflict remains priorities, followed by schedules, procedures, and technical requirements. This is the phase where the project moves from a general concept to a detailed set of plans. The relative importance of the project is still trying to be established as well as project priorities (time, cost, scope). Disagreements often emerge over the final schedule, the assignment of resources, communication and decision making procedures, and technical requirements for the project.

During the execution phase, friction arises over schedule slippage, technical problems, and staff issues. Milestones become more difficult to meet because of accumulating schedule slippages. This leads to tension within the team as delays prevent others from starting or completing their work. Managing the trade-offs between time, cost, and performance becomes paramount. Project managers must decide between letting the schedule slip, investing additional funds to get back on track, or scaling back the scope of the project in order to save time. Technical problems involve finding solutions to unexpected problems and integrating the contributions of different people. The strain of the project may be expressed in interpersonal conflicts as well as pressures to use resources more effectively.

During the delivery phase, the level of conflict tends to subside. On troubled projects schedules continue to be the biggest source of conflict as schedule slippages make it more difficult to meet target completion dates. Pressures to meet objectives coupled with growing anxiety over future assignments increase interpersonal tensions. Technical problems are rare since most of them have been worked out during the earlier phases.

Encouraging Functional Conflict

The demarcation between **functional** and **dysfunctional conflict** is neither clear nor precise. In one team, members may exchange a diatribe of four-letter expletives and eventually resolve their differences. Yet in another project team, such behavior would create irreconcilable divisions and would prohibit the parties from ever working together productively again. The distinguishing criterion is how the conflict affects project performance, not how individuals feel. Members can be upset and dissatisfied with the interchange, but as long as the disagreement furthers the objectives of the project, then the conflict is functional. Project managers should recognize that conflict is an inevitable and even a desirable part of project work; the key is to encourage functional conflict and manage dysfunctional conflict.

A shared vision can transcend the incongruities of a project and establish a common purpose to channel debate in a constructive manner. Without shared goals there is no common ground for working out differences. In the previous example involving the design trade-off decision, when both parties agreed that the primary goal was to satisfy the customer, there was a basis for more objectively resolving the dispute. Therefore, agreeing in advance which priority is most important—cost, schedule, or scope—can help a project team decide what response is most appropriate.

Sometimes it's not the presence of conflict, but the absence of conflict that is the problem. Oftentimes as a result of compressed time pressures, self-doubt, and the desire to preserve team harmony, members are reluctant to voice objections. This hesitation robs the team of useful information that might lead to better solutions and the avoidance of critical mistakes. Project managers need to encourage healthy dissent in order to improve problem solving and innovation. They can demonstrate this process by asking tough questions and challenging the rationale behind recommendations. They can also orchestrate healthy conflict by bringing in people with different points of view to critical meetings.

Project managers can legitimize dissent within the team by designating someone to play the role of devil's advocate or by asking the group to take 15 minutes to come up with all the reasons the team should not pursue a course of action. Functional conflict plays a critical role in obtaining a deeper understanding of the issues and coming up with the best decisions possible.

One of the most important things project managers can do is model an appropriate response when someone disagrees or challenges their ideas. They need to avoid acting defensively and instead encourage critical debate. They should exhibit effective listening skills and summarize the key issues before responding. They should check to see if others agree with the opposing point of view. Finally, project managers should value and protect dissenters. Organizations have a tendency to create too many yes-men, and the emperor needs to be told when he doesn't have any clothes on.

Managing Dysfunctional Conflict

Managing dysfunctional conflict is a much more challenging task than encouraging functional conflict. First, dysfunctional conflict is hard to identify. A manager might have two highly talented professionals who hate each other's guts, but in the heat of competition they produce meritorious results. Is this a pleasant situation? No. Is it functional? Yes, as long as it contributes to project performance. Conversely, sometimes functional conflict degenerates into dysfunctional conflict. This change occurs when technical disagreements evolve into irrational personality clashes or when failure to resolve an issue causes unnecessary delays in critical project work.

The second major difficulty managers face is that there is often no easy solution to dysfunctional conflict. Project managers have to decide among a number of different strategies to manage it; here are five possibilities:

1. **Mediate the conflict.** The manager intervenes and tries to negotiate a resolution by using reasoning and persuasion, suggesting alternatives and the like. One of the keys is trying to find common ground. In some cases the project manager can make the argument that the win/lose interchange has escalated to the point that it has become lose/lose for everyone and now is the time to make concessions.

2. **Arbitrate the conflict.** The manager imposes a solution to the conflict after listening to each party. The goal is not to decide who wins but to have the project win. In doing so, it is important to seek a solution that allows each party to save face; otherwise the decision may provide only momentary relief. One project manager admits that she has had great success using a King Solomon approach to resolving conflict. She confides she announces a solution that neither party will like and gives the opponents two hours to come up with a better solution they can both agree on.

3. **Control the conflict.** Reducing the intensity of the conflict by smoothing over differences or interjecting humor is an effective strategy. If feelings are escalating, the manager can adjourn the interaction and hope cooler heads prevail the next day. If the conflict continues to escalate, project assignments may need to be rearranged if possible so that two parties don't have to work together.

4. **Accept it.** In some cases the conflict will outlive the life of the project and, though a distraction, it is one the manager has to live with.

5. **Eliminate the conflict.** Sometimes the conflict has escalated to the point that it is no longer tolerable. If there is a clear villain then only he or she should be removed. If, as is often the case, both parties are at fault, then it would be wise if possible to eliminate both individuals. Their removal would give a clear signal to the others on the team that this kind of behavior is unacceptable.

In summary, project managers establish the foundation for functional conflict by establishing clear roles and responsibilities, developing common goals or a shared vision, and using group incentives that reward collaboration. Project managers have to be adroit at reading body language to identify unspoken disagreement. They also have to keep in touch with what is going on in a project to identify small problems that might escalate into big conflicts. Well-timed humor and redirecting the focus to what is best for the project can alleviate the interpersonal tensions that are likely to flare up on a project team.

Rejuvenating the Project Team

Over the course of a long project, a team sometimes drifts off course and loses momentum. The project manager needs to swing into action to realign the team with the project objectives and step on the pedal. There are both formal and informal ways of doing this. Informally, the project manager can institute new rituals like the "toy roaches" to reenergize a team. On one project that was experiencing rough going, the project manager stopped work and took the team bowling to relieve frustrations. On another project, a manager showed her team the movie *The Shawshank Redemption* to rekindle hope and commitment to success.

Another option is to have the project sponsor give a pep talk to the "troops." In other cases, a friendly challenge can reinvigorate a team. For example, one project sponsor offered to cook a five-course meal if the project got back on track and hit the next milestone.

Sometimes more formal action needs to be taken. The project manager may recognize the need for a team-building session devoted to improving the work processes of the team. This meeting is particularly appropriate if she senses that the team is approaching a transition point in its development. The goal of such a session is to improve the project team's effectiveness through better management of project demands and group processes. It is an inward look by the team at its own performance, behavior, and culture for the purpose of eliminating dysfunctional behaviors and strengthening functional ones. The project team critiques its performance, analyzes its way of doing things, and attempts to develop strategies to improve its operation.

Oftentimes an external consultant is hired, or an internal staff specialist is assigned to facilitate the session. This process brings a more objective, outside perspective to the table, frees the project manager to be part of the process, and provides a specialist trained in group dynamics. Furthermore, if preliminary information is to be collected, team members may be more candid and open to an outsider.

One caveat about using outside consultants is that too often managers resort to this as a method for dealing with a problem that they have been unable or unwilling to deal with. The marching order to the consultant is "fix my team for me." What the managers fail to recognize is that one of the keys to fixing the team is improving the working relationship between themselves and the remainder of the team. For such sessions to be effective, project managers have to be willing to have their own role scrutinized and be receptive to changing their own behavior and work habits based on the comments and suggestions of the project team.

Consultants use a wide variety of **team-building** techniques to elevate team performance. Here is a brief description of one of the more common approaches. The first step is to gather information and make a preliminary diagnosis of team performance. Whether through individual interviews or in a group forum, the consultant asks general questions about the project team performance, that is, what obstacles are getting in the way of the team being able to perform better? This information is summarized in terms of themes. When everyone has understood the themes, the group ranks them in terms of both their importance and the extent the team has ownership over them. This last dimension is critical. *Ownership* refers to whether the team has direct influence over the issue. For example, a team probably has little influence over delivery of contracted supplies, but team members do control how quickly they inform each other of sudden changes in plans.

If the group becomes preoccupied with issues outside its control, the meeting can quickly evolve into a demoralizing gripe session. Therefore, the most important issues they have direct control over become the subjects of the agenda. During the course of the meeting, much interpersonal and group process information will be generated, and that is examined too. Thus, the group works on two sets of items: the agenda items and the items that emerge from the interaction of the participants. This is where the expertise of the external facilitator becomes critical for identifying interaction patterns and their implications for team performance.

As important problems are discussed, alternatives for action are developed. The team-building session concludes by deciding on specific action steps for remedying problems and setting target dates for who will do what, when. These assignments can be reviewed at project status meetings or at a special follow-up session.

It has become fashionable to link team-building activities with outdoor experiences. The outdoor experience—whether it is whitewater rafting down the Rogue River in Oregon or rock climbing in Colorado—places group members in a variety of physically challenging situations that must be mastered through teamwork, not individual effort. By having to work together to overcome difficult obstacles, team members are supposed to experience increased self-confidence, more respect for another's capabilities, and a greater commitment to teamwork. No empirical data are available to support such exotic endeavors other than the enthusiastic support of the participants. Such activities are likely to provide an intense common experience that may accelerate the social development of the team. Such an investment of time and money communicates the importance of teamwork and is considered by some a perk for being on the project. At the same time, unless the lessons from these experiences can be immediately transferred to actual project work, their significance is likely to vanish.

11.4 Managing Virtual Project Teams

 LO 11-6

Understand the challenges of managing virtual project teams.

Building a high-performance project team among a mixture of part-time and full-time members is a challenging task. Consider how much more challenging it is to build a team when members cannot engage in face-to-face interactions. Such would be the case for a **virtual project team** in which the team members are geographically situated so that they may seldom, if ever, meet face-to-face as a team. For example, Hewlett-Packard's integrated circuit business headquarters and a portion of the R&D facilities are located in Palo Alto, California; the two wafer fabrication operations are located in Corvallis, Oregon, and Fort Collins, Colorado; and the packaging assembly process is primarily in Singapore and Korea. It is not uncommon for professionals at each of these locations to be involved in the same project. When team members are

SNAPSHOT FROM PRACTICE 11.6   Managing Virtual Global Teams*

Carl A. Singer, a senior program manager at IBM Global Services, described how global time zones were used to complete a time intensive project. The project required subject matter experts (SMEs) to document existing best practices in maintenance domain and to port these into a knowledge management tool. The most proficient SMEs available were on opposite sides of the globe—Australia and Scotland. Review and control of the project was from the United States.

Management realized that just working harder and smarter was not going to meet the time and quality targets. For this project they used the dimension of time to their benefit. Applying sound management principles as well as taking advantage of electronic communication systems, the team was able to create a virtual 24-hour workday for quick responses and accelerated reviews.

Each team consisted of veteran professionals familiar with the rigors of time-pressured consulting projects. A local point person was identified for each team and mutually agreed-upon targets, terminology, and processes were established.

An all-hands kick-off meeting was organized in which participants were able to socialize, understand local and projectwide constraints, and finalize an agreed-upon plan. The meeting was held at a corporate hotel with dining accommodations. The facility was considered an "assisted living community for IBM consultants." This hastened recovery from jet lag and provided an interruption-free work environment.

Upon returning to their home bases, each team created the majority of their deliverables independently with periodic three-way conference calls to maintain coordination. A project control book was established electronically so that all participants had access to the latest project documents.

The final phase of the project required intense interfacing and reviews between the teams. These reviews necessitated changes to deal with concerns, differences among subprojects, and other issues. It was here that the worldwide nature of the project was leveraged. Using a "dry cleaning approach" (in by 5 p.m. out by 9 a.m.) team members in Australia and Scotland were able to address issues generated during the U.S.-based external reviews and provide concrete responses by the beginning of the next business day. Conference calls at 6:00 a.m. (U.S. EST) were used to coordinate responses and resolve issues. Conference calls at the end of the U.S. workday were used to finalize issues and assignments. Figure 11.6 depicts the 24-hour clock used to align communication schedules.

Telephone conferencing was used instead of videoconferencing due to the setup lead time and because it would force participants to leave their offices. E-mail was used extensively for general communication. An electronic repository of project work was used to coordinate global involvement. In practice, a participant could draft a document and deposit it electronically only to wake up the next day to find the document annotated with suggested revisions. Likewise, one could start the day by checking an in-basket populated with documents to review and issues to address. Over time, "G'day" and "Cheers" crept into the U.S. speech—a clear indicator of team cohesion.

Singer identified a number of lessons learned from the project. These included:

- The all-hands kick-off meeting was critical for establishing goals and procedures as well as "rules of courtesy."
- Loosen the reins—establish clear deliverables and then step out of the way and let the professionals do their work.
- Establish and enforce agreed-upon quality standards and deliverable templates.
- Maintain a regular schedule of conference calls, even if only to say "Hello, we have nothing to talk about today." Conference calls should be guided by pre-established agendas, note-taking procedures, and reviews.

* Carl A. Singer, "Leveraging a Worldwide Project Team," *PM Network*, April 2001, pp. 36–40.

spread across different time zones and continents, the opportunity for direct communication is severely limited. Electronic communication such as the Internet, e-mail, and teleconferencing takes on much more importance in virtual projects because this is the primary means of communication. See Snapshot from Practice 11.6: Managing Virtual Global Teams for an example of how this works.

FIGURE 11.6 24-Hour Global Clock

United States (East Coast)	Australia	Scotland	Comments
12 midnight	2 PM	5 AM	
1 AM	3 PM	6 AM	
2 AM	4 PM	7 AM	
3 AM	5 PM	8 AM	
4 AM	6 PM	9 AM	Australia handoff for off-shift review
5 AM	7 PM	10 AM	
6 AM	8 PM	11 AM	3-way conferencing window (primary)
7 AM	9 PM	12 noon	3-way conferencing window (primary)
8 AM	10 PM	1 PM	3-way conferencing window (primary)
9 AM	11 PM	2 PM	
10 AM	12 midnight	3 PM	
11AM	1 AM	4 PM	
12 noon	2 AM	5 PM	Scotland handoff for off-shift review
1 PM	3 AM	6 PM	
2 PM	4 AM	7 PM	
3 PM	5 AM	8 PM	
4 PM	6 AM	9 PM	3-way conferencing window (secondary)
5 PM	7 AM	10 PM	3-way conferencing window (secondary)
6 PM	8 AM	11 PM	U.S. handoff for off-shift review
7 PM	9 AM	12 midnight	
8 PM	10 AM	1 AM	
9 PM	11 AM	2 AM	
10 PM	12 noon	3 AM	
11 PM	1 PM	4 AM	
12 midnight	2PM	5 AM	

☐ Prime time   ☐ Secondary time   ☐ Downtime

Two of the biggest challenges involved in managing a virtual project team are developing trust and effective patterns of communication (Lipsinger and DeRosa, 2010). Trust is difficult to establish in virtual project management. Unlike working as a traditional team, where members can see whether someone has done what they say they have done, virtual team members depend on the word of distant members. At the

Ericksen, J., and L. Dyer, "Right from the Start: Exploring the Effects of Early Team Events on Subsequent Project Team Performance," *Administrative Science Quarterly*, vol. 49, no. 3 (2004), pp. 438–71.

Frame, J. D., *Managing Projects in Organizations* (San Francisco: Jossey-Bass, 1995).

Hackman, J. R., *Leading Teams: Setting the Stage for Great Performances* (Cambridge, MA: Harvard Business School Press, 2002).

Homans, G. C., *Social Behavior: Its Elementary Forms* (New York: Harcourt Brace Jovanovich, 1961).

Janis, I. L., *Groupthink* (Boston: Houghton Mifflin, 1982).

Johansen, R., D. Sibbett, S. Benson, A. Martin, R. Mittman, and P. Saffo, *Leading Business Teams: How Teams can use Technology and Group Process Tools to Enhance Performance* (Reading, MA: Addison-Wesley, 1991).

Katz, R., "How a Team at Digital Equipment Designed the 'Alpha' Chip," *The Human Side of Managing Technological Innovation,* 2nd ed., ed. Ralph Katz (New York: Oxford University Press, 2004), pp. 121–33.

Katzenbach, J. R., and D. K. Smith, *The Wisdom of Teams* (Boston: Harvard Business School Press, 1993).

Kidder, T., *The Soul of a New Machine* (New York: Avon Books, 1981).

Kirkman, B. L., B. Rosen, C. B. Gibson, P. E. Tesluk, and S. O. McPherson, "Five Challenges to Virtual Team Success: Lessons From Sabre, INC.," *Academy of Management Executive,* vol. 16, no. 2 (2002), pp. 67–79.

Kuruppuarachchi, P. "Virtual Team Concepts in Projects: A Case Study," *Project Management Journal*, June 2009, pp. 19–33.

Leavitt, H. J., and J. Lipman-Blumen, "Hot Groups," *Harvard Business Review,* vol. 73 (1995), pp. 109–16.

Likert, R., *New Patterns in Management,* (New York: McGraw-Hill, 1961).

Linetz, B. P., and K. P. Rea, *Project Management for the 21st Century* (San Diego: Academic Press, 2001).

Lipsinger, R., and D. DeRosa, *Virtual Team Success: A Practical Guide for Working and Leading from a Distance* (San Francisco: Jossey-Bass, 2010).

Maier, N. R. F., *Problem Solving and Creativity in Individuals and Groups* (Belmont, CA: Brooks-Cole, 1970).

Maier, N. R. F., *Problem-Solving Discussion and Conference* (New York: McGraw-Hill, 1963).

Malhotra, A., A. Majchrzak, and B. Rosen, "Leading Virtual Teams," *Academy of Management Perspectives*, vol. 21, no. 1 (2007), pp. 60–70.

Maznevski, M. L., and K. M. Chudoba, "Bridging Space over Time: Global Virtual Team Dynamics and Effectiveness," *Organization Science,* vol. 11. no. 5 (September–October 2000), pp. 473–92.

Murphy, C. and J. Clark, "Picture This: How the Language of Leaders Drives Performance," *Organizational Dynamics*, 45 (2), March, 2016, pp. 139–146.

Peters, T., *Thriving on Chaos: Handbook for a Management Revolution* (New York: Knopf, 1988).

Posner, B. Z., "What's All the Fighting About? Conflicts in Project Management," *IEEE Transactions in Engineering Management*, EM-33, 1986, pp. 207–211.

Ritti, R. R., and S. L. Levy, *The Ropes to Skip and the Ropes to Know: Studies in Organizational Theory and Behavior* (New York: Wiley, 2009).

Senge, P. M., *The Fifth Discipline* (New York: Doubleday, 1990).

Seta, J. J., P. B. Paulus, and J. Schkade, "Effects of Group Size and Proximity under Cooperative and Competitive Conditions," *Journal of Personality and Social Psychology,* vol. 98, no. 2 (1976), pp. 47–53.

Sherif, M., *Group Conflict and Cooperation: Their Social Psychology* (Chicago: Aldine, 1967).

Siebdrat, F., M. Hoegl, and H. Ernst, "How to Manage Virtual Teams," *MIT Sloan Management Review,* http://sloanreview.mit.edu/the-maazine/2009-summer/50412/how-to manage-virtual teams/2009.

Skilton, P. F., and K. J. Dooley, "The Effects of Repeat Collaboration on Creative Abrasion," *Academy of Management Review,* vol. 35, no. 1 (2010), pp. 118–34.

Smith, B. J., "Building Shared Visions: How to Begin," *The Fifth Discipline Fieldbook: Strategies and Tools for Building a Learning Organization,* ed. P. M. Senge, C. Roberts, R. B. Ross, B. J. Smith, and A. Kleiner (New York: Doubleday, 1994), pp. 312–327.

Smith, P. G., and D. G. Reinertsen, *Developing Products in Half the Time* (New York: Wiley, 1997, 2nd ed).

Thamhain, H. J., and D. L. Wilemon, "Conflict Management in Project Life Cycle," *Sloan Management Review,* vol. 16, no. 3 (1975), pp. 31–41.

Thoms, P., "Creating a Shared Vision with a Project Team," *PM Network,* January 1997, pp. 33–35.

3M, "Leading a Distributed Team," *www.3m.com/meetingnetwork/readingroom/meetingguide_distribteam.html.* Accessed June 6, 2006.

Tuchman, B. W., "Development Sequence of Small Groups," *Psychological Bulletin,* vol. 63 (1965), pp. 384–399.

Tuchman, B. W., and M. C. Jensen, "Stages of Small Group Development Revisited," *Group and Organizational Studies,* vol. 2 (1977), pp. 419–427.

Vroom, V. H., and A. G. Jago, *The New Leadership* (Englewood Cliffs, NJ: Prentice Hall, 1988).

Zander, A., *Making Groups Effective* (San Francisco: Jossey-Bass, 1994).

Kerzner Office Equipment

Amber Briggs looked nervously at her watch as she sat at the front of a large table in the cafeteria at Kerzner Office Equipment. It was now 10 minutes after 3:00 and only 10 of the 14 members had arrived for the first meeting of the Kerzner anniversary task force. Just then two more members hurriedly sat down and mumbled apologies for being late. Briggs cleared her throat and started the meeting.

KERZNER OFFICE EQUIPMENT

Kerzner Office Equipment is located in Charleston, South Carolina. It specializes in the manufacture and sales of high-end office furniture and equipment. Kerzner enjoyed steady growth during its first five years of existence with a high-water employment mark of more than 1,400 workers. Then a national recession struck, forcing Kerzner to lay off 25 percent of its employees. This was a traumatic period for the company. Justin Tubbs was brought in as the new CEO, and things began to slowly turn around. Tubbs was committed to employee participation and redesigned operations around the concept of self-managing teams. The company soon introduced an innovative line of ergonomic furniture designed to reduce back strain and carpal tunnel. This line of equipment proved to be a resounding success, and Kerzner became known as a leader in the industry. The company currently employs 1,100 workers and has just been selected for the second straight time by the *Charleston Post and Courier* as one of the 10 best local firms to work for in South Carolina.

AMBER BRIGGS

Amber Briggs is a 42-year-old human resource specialist who has worked for Kerzner for the past five years. During this time she has performed a variety of activities involving recruitment, training, compensation, and team building. David Brown, vice president of human resources, assigned Briggs the responsibility for organizing Kerzner's 10th anniversary celebration. She was excited about the project because she would report directly to top management.

CEO Tubbs briefed her as to the purpose and objectives of the celebration. Tubbs stressed that this should be a memorable event and that it was important to celebrate Kerzner's success since the dark days of the layoffs. Moreover, he confided that he had just read a book on corporate cultures and believed that such events were important for conveying the values at Kerzner. He went on to say that he wanted this to be an employee celebration—not a celebration conjured up by top management. As such, she would be assigned a task force of 14 employees from each of the major departments to organize and plan the event. Her team was to present a preliminary plan and budget for the event to top management within three months. When discussing budgets, Tubbs revealed that he felt the total cost should be somewhere in the $150,000 range. He concluded the meeting by offering to help Briggs in any way he could to make the event a success.

Soon thereafter Briggs received the list of the names of the task force members, and she contacted them either by phone or e-mail to arrange today's meeting. She had to scramble to find a meeting place. Her cubicle in human resources was too small to accommodate such a group, and all the meeting rooms at Kerzner were booked or being refurbished. She settled on the cafeteria because it was usually deserted in the late afternoon. Prior to the meeting she posted the agenda on a flip-chart (see Figure C11.1) adjacent to the table. Given everyone's busy schedules, the meeting was limited to just one hour.

THE FIRST MEETING

FIGURE C11.1
Celebration Task Force

Agenda

3:00	Introductions
3:15	Project overview
3:30	Ground rules
3:45	Meeting times
4:00	Adjourn

Briggs began the meeting by saying, "Greetings. For those who don't know me, I'm Amber Briggs from human resources and I've been assigned to manage the 10th anniversary celebration at Kerzner. Top management wants this to be a special event—at the same time they want it to be our event. This is why you are here. Each of you represents one of the major departments, and together our job is to plan and organize the celebration." She then reviewed the agenda and asked each member to introduce him/herself. The tall, red-haired woman to the right of Briggs broke the momentary silence by saying, "Hi, I'm Cara Miller from Plastics. I guess my boss picked me for this task force because I have a reputation for throwing great parties."

In turn each member followed suit. Below is a sampling of their introductions:

"Hi, I'm Mike Wales from maintenance. I'm not sure why I'm here. Things have been a little slow in our department, so my boss told me to come to this meeting."

"I'm Megan Plinski from domestic sales. I actually volunteered for this assignment. I think it will be a lot of fun to plan a big party."

"Yo, my name is Nick Psias from accounting. My boss said one of us had to join this task force, and I guess it was my turn."

"Hi, I'm Rick Fennah. I'm the only one from purchasing who has been here since the beginning. We've been through some rough times, and I think it is important to take time and celebrate what we've accomplished."

"Hi, I'm Ingrid Hedstrom from international sales. I think this is a great idea, but I should warn you that I will be out of the country for most of the next month."

"I'm Abby Bell from engineering. Sorry for being late, but things are a bit crazy in my department."

Briggs circled the names of the two people who were absent and circulated a roster so that everyone could check to see if their phone numbers and e-mail addresses were correct. She then summarized her meeting with Tubbs and told the group that he expected them to make a formal presentation to top management within 10 weeks. She acknowledged that they were all busy people and that it was her job to manage the project as efficiently as possible. At the same time, she reiterated the importance of the project and that this would be a very public event: "If we screw up, everyone will know about it."

Briggs went over the ground rules and emphasized that from now on meetings would start on time and that she expected to be notified in advance if someone was going to be absent. She summarized the first part of the project as centering on five key questions: when, where, what, who, and how much? She created a stir in the group when she responded to a question about cost by informing them that top management was willing to pay up to $150,000 for the event. Megan quipped, "This is going to be one hell of a party."

Briggs then turned the group's attention to identifying a common meeting time. After jousting for 15 minutes, she terminated the discussion by requesting that each member submit a schedule of free time over the next month by Friday. She would use this information and a new planning software to identify optimal times. She ended the meeting by thanking the members for coming and asking them to begin soliciting ideas from co-workers about how this event should be celebrated. She announced that she would meet individually with each of them to discuss their role on the project. The meeting was adjourned at 4:00 p.m.

1. Critique Briggs's management of the first meeting. What, if anything, should she have done differently?
2. What barriers is she likely to encounter in completing this project?
3. What can she do to overcome these barriers?
4. What should she do between now and the next meeting?

Case 11.2

Ajax Project

Tran was taking his dog Callie on her evening walk as the sun began to set over the coastal range. He looked forward to this time of the day. It was an opportunity to enjoy some peace and quiet. It was also a time to review events on the Ajax project and plot his next moves.

Ajax is the code name given by CEBEX for a high-tech security system project funded by the U.S. Department of Defense (DOD). Tran is the project manager and his core team consisted of 30 full-time hardware and software engineers.

Tran and his family fled Cambodia when he was four years old. He joined the U.S. Air Force when he was 18 and used the education stipend to attend Washington State University. He joined CEBEX upon graduating with a dual degree in mechanical and electrical engineering. After working on a variety of projects for 10 years Tran decided he wanted to enter management. He went to night school at the University of Washington to earn an MBA.

Tran became a project manager for the money. He also thought he was good at it. He enjoyed working with people and making the right things happen. This was his fifth project and up to now he was batting .500, with half of his projects coming ahead of schedule. Tran was proud that he could now afford to send his oldest child to Stanford University.

Ajax was one of many defense projects the CEBEX Corporation had under contract with DOD. CEBEX is a huge defense company with annual sales in excess of $30 billion and more than 120,000 employees worldwide. CEBEX's five major business areas are Aeronautics, Electronic Systems, Information & Technology Services, Integrated Systems & Solutions, and Space Systems. Ajax was one of several new projects sponsored by the Integrated Systems & Solutions division aimed at the homeland security business. CEBEX was confident that it could leverage its technical expertise and political connections to become a major player in this growing market. Ajax was one of several projects directed at designing, developing, and installing a security system at an important government installation.

Tran had two major concerns when he started the Ajax project. The first was the technical risks inherent in the project. In theory the design principles made sense and the project used proven technology. Still the technology had never been applied in the field in this matter. From past experience, Tran knew there was a big difference between the laboratory and the real world. He also knew that integrating the audio, optical, tactile, and laser subsystems would test the patience and ingenuity of his team.

The second concern involved his team. The team was pretty much split down the middle between hardware and electrical engineers. Not only did these engineers have different skill sets and tend to look at problems differently, but generational differences between the two groups were evident as well. The hardware engineers were almost all former military, family men with conservative attire and beliefs. The electrical engineers were a much motlier crew. They tended to be young, single, and at times very cocky. While the hardware engineers talked about the Seattle Mariners, raising teenagers, and going to Palm Desert to play golf, the software engineers talked about Vapor, the latest concert at the Gorge amphitheater, and going mountain biking in Peru.

To make matters worse, tension between these two groups within CEBEX festered around salary issues. Electrical engineers were at a premium, and the hardware engineers resented the new hires' salary packages, which were comparable to what they were earning after 20 years of working for CEBEX. Still the real money was to be made from the incentives associated with project performance. These were all contingent on meeting project milestones and the final completion date.

Before actual work started on the project, Tran arranged a two-day team-building retreat at a lodge on the Olympic peninsula for his entire team as well as key staff from the government installation. He used this time to go over the major objectives of the project and unveil the basic project plan. An internal consultant facilitated several team-building activities that made light of cross-generational issues. Tran felt a real sense of camaraderie within the team.

The good feelings generated from the retreat carried over to the beginning of the project. The entire team bought into the mission of the project and technical challenges it represented. Hardware and electrical engineers worked side by side to solve problems and build subsystems.

The project plan was built around a series of five tests, with each test being a more rigorous verification of total system performance. Passing each test represented a key milestone for the project. The team was excited about conducting the first Alpha test one week early—only to be disappointed by a series of minor technical glitches that took two weeks of problem solving to resolve. The team worked extra hard to make up for the lost time. Tran was proud of the team and how hard members had worked together.

The Alpha II test was conducted on schedule, but once again the system failed to perform. This time three weeks of debugging was needed before the team received the green light to move to the next phase of the project. By this time, team goodwill had been tested, and emotions were a bit frayed. A cloud of disappointment descended over the team as hopes of bonuses disappeared with the project falling further behind schedule. This was augmented by cynics who felt that the original schedule was unfair and the deadlines were impossible to begin with.

Tran responded by starting each day with a status meeting where the team reviewed what they accomplished the previous day and set new objectives for that day. He believed these meetings were helpful in establishing positive momentum and reinforcing a team identity among the engineers. He also went out of his way to spend more time with the "troops," helping them solve problems, offering encouragement, and a sincere pat on the back when one was deserved.

He was cautiously optimistic when the time came to conduct the Alpha III test. It was the end of the day when the switch was turned on, but nothing happened. Within minutes the entire team heard the news. Screams could be heard down the hallway. Perhaps the most telling moment was when Tran looked down at the company's parking lot and saw most of his project team walking by themselves to their cars.

As his dog Callie chased some wild bunnies, Tran pondered what he should do next.

1. How effective has Tran been as a project manager? Explain.
2. What problem(s) does Tran face?
3. How would you go about solving them? Why?

Case 11.3

Franklin Equipment, Ltd.*

Franklin Equipment, Ltd. (FEL), with headquarters and main fabrication facilities in Saint John, New Brunswick, was founded 75 years ago to fabricate custom-designed large machines for construction businesses in the Maritime Provinces. Over the years its product lines became strategically focused on creating rock-crushing equipment for dam and highway construction and for a few other markets that require the processing of aggregate. FEL now designs, fabricates, and assembles stationary and portable rock-crushing plants and services its own products and those of its competitors.

In the 1970s, FEL began to expand its market from the Maritime Provinces to the rest of Canada. FEL currently has several offices and fabrication facilities throughout the country. More recently, FEL has made a concerted effort to market its products internationally.

Last month, FEL signed a contract to design and fabricate a rock-crushing plant for a Middle East construction project, called Project Abu Dhabi. Charles Gatenby secured this contract and has been assigned as project manager. This project is viewed as a coup because FEL has wanted to open up markets in this area for a long time and has had difficulty getting prospective customers to realize that FEL is a Canadian firm and not from the United States. Somehow these customers view all North American vendors as the same and are reluctant to employ any of them because of international political considerations.

A project of this scope typically starts with the selection of a team of managers responsible for various aspects of the design, fabrication, delivery, and installation of the product. Manager selection is important because the product design and fabrication vary with the unique needs of each customer. For example, the terrain, rock characteristics, weather conditions, and logistical concerns create special problems for all phases of plant design and operations. In addition, environmental concerns and labor conditions vary from customer to customer and from region to region.

In addition to the project manager, all projects include a design engineer; an operations manager, who oversees fabrication and on-site assembly; and a cost accountant, who oversees all project financial and cost reporting matters. Each of these people must work closely together if a well-running plant is to be delivered on time and within cost constraints. Because international contracts often require FEL to employ host nationals for plant assembly and to train them for operations, a human resource manager is also assigned to the project team. In such cases, the human resource manager needs to understand the particulars of the plant specifications and then use this knowledge to design selection procedures and assess particular training needs. The human resource manager also needs to learn the relevant labor laws of the customer's country.

FEL assigns managers to project teams based on their expertise and their availability to work on a particular project given their other commitments. This typically means that managers without heavy current project commitments will be assigned to new projects. For instance, a manager finishing one project will likely be assigned a management position on a new project team. The project manager typically has little to say about who is assigned to his or her team.

* Courtesy of John A. Drexler Jr., Oregon State University.

Because he secured Project Abu Dhabi and has established positive working relationships with the Abu Dhabi customer, Gatenby was assigned to be project manager. Gatenby has successfully managed similar projects. The other managers assigned to Project Abu Dhabi are Bill Rankins, a brilliant design engineer, Rob Perry, operations manager with responsibility for fabrication and installation, Elaine Bruder, finance and cost accounting manager, and Sam Stonebreaker, human resource manager. Each of these managers has worked together on numerous past projects.

A few years ago, FEL began contracting for team facilitator services from several consulting firms to help new project teams operate effectively. Last month, FEL recruited Carl Jobe from one of these consulting firms to be a full-time internal consultant. A number of managers, including Gatenby, were so impressed with Jobe's skills that they convinced FEL top management of the need to hire a permanent internal facilitator; Jobe was the obvious choice.

Because Gatenby was instrumental in hiring Jobe at FEL, he was excited at the prospect of using Jobe to facilitate team building among Project Abu Dhabi team members. Gatenby was very proud of having secured this project and had expected to be appointed project manager. He knew that this project's success would be instrumental in advancing his own career.

Gatenby told Jobe, "This project is really important to FEL and to me personally. I really need for you to help us develop into a team that works well together to achieve the project's goals within budget. I've observed your success in developing teams on other projects, and I expect you'll do the same for Project Abu Dhabi. I'll take care of you if you help me make this work."

Jobe outlined for Gatenby how he would proceed. Jobe would begin by interviewing team members individually to learn their perceptions of each other and of the promises and pitfalls of being involved in this project. Meetings of the entire team would follow these interviews using the information he collected to help establish a team identity and a shared vision.

Jobe interviewed Bruder first. She expressed skepticism about whether the project could succeed. During the interview, Bruder appeared to be distant, and Jobe could not figure out why he had not established good rapport with her. Bruder intimated that she expected a lot of cost overruns and a lot of missed production deadlines. But not knowing Jobe well, Bruder was reluctant to identify any specific barriers to the project's success. While she would not directly say so, it was clear to Jobe that Bruder did not want to be a part of Project Abu Dhabi. Jobe left this interview confused and wondering what was going on.

Jobe's next interview was with Perry, the operations manager. Perry has worked at FEL for 15 years, and he immediately came to the point: "This project is not going to work. I cannot understand why upper management keeps assigning me to work on projects with Rankins. We simply cannot work together, and we don't get along. I've disliked him from day one. He keeps dropping the fact that he has earned all these advanced degrees from Purdue. And he keeps telling us how things are done there. I know he's better educated than I am, and he's really smart. But I'm smart too and am good at what I do. There's no need for Rankins to make me feel like an idiot because I don't have a degree. Jobe, I'll be honest with you. Rankins has only been here for five years, but I hold him personally responsible for my problem with alcohol, and for its resulting effect on my marriage. I got divorced last year, and it's Rankins's fault."

Jobe next talked with Rankins, who said, "I don't care what you do. Perry and I simply can't work closely together for the nine months it will take to get it done. One of us will kill the other. Ever since I arrived at FEL, Perry has hated my guts and does everything he can to sabotage my designs. We usually worry about customers creating change orders; here it's the fabrication and operations manager who is responsible for them. Perry second-guesses everything I do and makes design changes on his own, and these are always bad decisions. He is out of control. I swear he stays awake at nights thinking up ways to ruin my designs. I don't have this problem with any other manager."

Jobe left these interviews thoroughly discouraged and could not imagine what would come up in his interview with Stonebreaker. But Stonebreaker was quite positive: "I enjoy these international projects where I get to travel abroad and learn about different cultures. I can't wait to get started on this."

Jobe asked Stonebreaker about the ability of various team members to work together. Stonebreaker replied, "No problem! We've all worked together before and have had no problems. Sure, there have been ruffled feathers and hurt feelings between Rankins and Perry. Rankins can be arrogant and Perry stubborn, but it's never been anything that we can't work around. Besides, both of them are good at what they do—both professionals. They'll keep their heads on straight."

Jobe was even more bewildered. Gatenby says this project's success rides on Jobe's facilitation skills. The finance manager appears to want off this project team. The design engineer and operations manager admit they detest each other and cannot work together. And the human resources manager, having worked on projects with Perry and Rankins before, expects a rosy working relationship and anticipates no problems.

Jobe had a second meeting with Gatenby. Before discussing the design of the team-building sessions, he asked questions to learn what Gatenby thought about the ability of team members to work together. Gatenby admitted that there has been very bad blood between Perry and Rankins, but added, "That's why we hired you. It's your job to make sure that the history between those two doesn't interfere with Project Abu Dhabi's success. It's your job to get them to work well together. Get it done."

Their dialogue toward the end of this meeting progressed as follows:

Jobe: "Why do you expect Rankins and Perry to work well together, given their history? What incentives do they have to do so?"

Gatenby: "As you should know, FEL requires formal goal setting between project managers and functional managers at the beginning of each project. I've already done this with Bruder, Stonebreaker, Perry, and Rankins. Perry and Rankins have explicit goals stating they must work well together and cooperate with each other."

Jobe: "What happens if they do not meet these goals?"

Gatenby: "I've already discussed this with top management. If it appears to me after two months that things are not working out between Perry and Rankins, FEL will fire Rankins."

Jobe: "Does Perry know this?"

Gatenby: "Yes."

1. Evaluate the criteria FEL uses to assign managers to project teams. What efficiencies do these criteria create? What are the resulting problems?

2. Why is it even more important that project team members work well together on international projects such as Project Abu Dhabi?

3. Discuss the dilemma that Jobe now faces.

4. What should Jobe recommend to Gatenby?

12 Outsourcing: Managing Interorganizational Relations

LEARNING OBJECTIVES

After reading this chapter you should be able to:

12-1 Understand the advantages and disadvantages of outsourcing project work.

12-2 Describe the basic elements of a Request for Proposal (RFP).

12-3 Identify best practices for outsourcing project work.

12-4 Practice principled negotiation.

12-5 Describe the met-expectations model of customer satisfaction and its implications for working with customers on projects.

OUTLINE

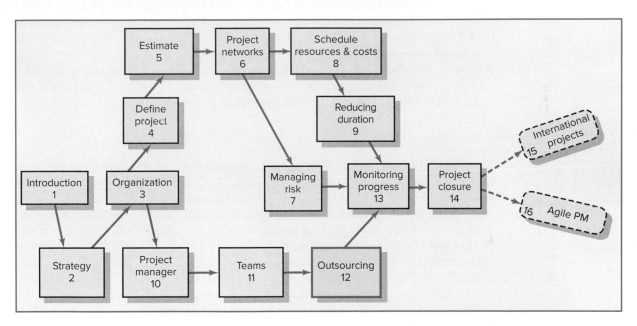

. . . being a good partner has become a key corporate asset. I call it a company's collaborative advantage. In the global economy, a well-developed ability to create and sustain fruitful collaborations gives companies a significant competitive leg up.

—Rosabeth Moss Kanter, Harvard Business School professor

It is rare in today's flat world to find important projects that are being completed totally in-house. Outsourcing or contracting significant segments of project work to other companies is commonplace. For example, nine states attempting to unify the accounting of all their state agencies did not have the internal resources to implement such a large project. Hence, project teams were formed consisting of personnel from software, hardware, and accounting firms to implement the projects. Small high-tech firms outsource research to determine what features customers value in new products they are developing. Even industry giants such as Microsoft and Intel commonly hire independent firms to test new products they are developing.

Contracting project work has long been the norm in the construction industry, where firms hire general contractors who, in turn, hire and manage cadres of subcontractors to create new buildings and structures. For example, the Chunnel project, which created a transportation tunnel between France and England, involved more than 250 organizations. Contracting is not limited to large projects. For example, an insurance company worked with an outside contractor to develop an answering service that directs customers to specific departments and employees. The trend for the future suggests that more and more projects will involve working with people from different organizations.

This chapter extends the previous two chapters' discussion of building and managing relations by focusing specifically on issues surrounding working with people from other organizations to complete a project. First, the advantages and disadvantages of outsourcing project work are introduced. This is followed by a discussion of Request for Proposals (RFPs) and the solicitation process. Best practices used by firms to outsource and collaborate with each other on are discussed next. The focus then shifts to the art of negotiating, which is at the heart of effective collaboration. Negotiating skills and techniques for resolving disagreements and reaching optimal solutions are then presented. The chapter closes with a brief, but important, note on managing customer relations. In addition, an appendix on contract management is included to augment our discussion of how organizations work together on projects.

12.1 Outsourcing Project Work

Understand the advantages and disadvantages of outsourcing project work.

The term **outsourcing** has traditionally been applied to the transferring of business functions or processes (e.g., customer support, IT, accounting) to other, often foreign companies. For example, when you call your Internet provider to solve a technical problem you are likely to talk to a technician in Bangalore, India, or Bucharest, Romania. Outsourcing is now being applied to contracting significant chunks of project work. For example, Apple and Motorola work closely with manufacturers in China to develop next-generation smartphones. Toyota and DaimlerChrysler collaborate with suppliers to develop new automobile platforms.

The shift toward outsourcing is readily apparent in the film industry. During the golden era of Hollywood, huge, vertically integrated corporations made movies. Studios such as MGM, Warner Brothers, and 20th Century–Fox owned large movie lots and employed thousands of full-time specialists—set designers, camera people, film editors, and directors. Star actors like Humphrey Bogart and Marilyn Monroe were signed to exclusive studio contracts for a set number of films (e.g., six films over three years). Today, most movies are made by a collection of individuals and small companies who come together to make films project-by-project. This structure allows each project to be staffed with the talent most suited to its demands rather than choosing from only those people the studio employs. This same approach is being applied to the creation of new products and services. For example, see Figure 12.1.

Figure 12.1 depicts a situation in which a zero-gravity reclining chair is being developed. The genesis for the chair comes from a mechanical engineer who developed the idea in her garage. The inventor negotiates a contract with a catalog firm to develop and manufacture the chair. The catalog company in turn creates a project team of manufacturers, suppliers, and marketing firms to create the new chair. Each participant adds requisite expertise to the project. The catalog firm brings its brand name and distribution channels to the project. Tool and die firms provide customized parts which are delivered to a manufacturing firm that will produce the chair. Marketing firms refine the design, develop packaging, and test market potential names. A project manager is assigned by the catalog firm to work with the inventor and the other parties to complete the project.

FIGURE 12.1
Reclining Chair Project

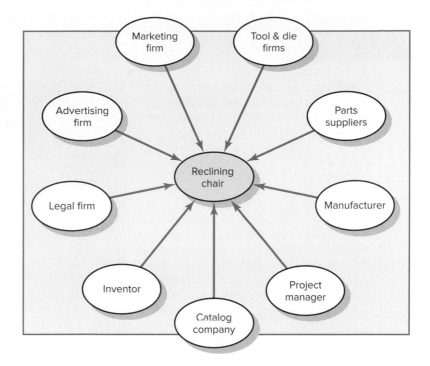

Many outsourced projects operate in a virtual environment in which people are linked by computers, faxes, computer-aided design systems, and video teleconferencing. They rarely, if ever, see one another face-to-face. On other projects, participants from different organizations work closely together, for example, at a construction site or in shared office space. In either case, people come and go as services are needed, much as in a matrix structure, but they are not formal members of one organization, just technical experts who form a temporary alliance with an organization, fulfill their contractual obligations, and then move on to the next project.

The advantages of outsourcing project work are many:

1. *Cost reduction.* Companies can secure competitive prices for contracted services, especially if the work can be outsourced offshore. Furthermore, overhead costs are dramatically cut since the company no longer has to internally maintain the contracted services.

2. *Faster project completion.* Not only can work be done more cheaply, but it can also be done faster. Competitive pricing means more resources for the dollar. For example, you can hire three Indian software engineers for the price of one American software engineer. Furthermore, outsourcing can provide access to equipment that can accelerate completion of project tasks. For example, by contracting a backhoe operater you are able to accomplish in four hours what it would take a landscaping crew four days to complete.

3. *High level of expertise.* A high level of expertise and technology can be brought to bear on the project. A company no longer has to keep up with technological advances. Instead, it can focus on developing its core competencies and hire firms with the know-how to work on relevant segments of the project.

4. *Flexibility.* Organizations are no longer constrained by their own resources but can pursue a wide range of projects by combining their resources with talents of other companies. Small companies can instantly go global by working with foreign partners.

SNAPSHOT FROM PRACTICE 12.1 The Boeing 787 Dreamliner*

BACKGROUND

In 2002 the basic design and plans for Boeing's 787 Dreamliner were accepted and given the charter to "Go." The Dreamliner boasts the latest design and revolutionary technology in the history of commercial air travel. But the project met bumpy weather. The first 787 aircraft, scheduled to be tested in July 2007, was delayed until December 2009. Orders for the advanced 787 grew quickly to over 800 planes. This rosy picture presented Boeing with a giant-sized headache. For various reasons (such as design, outsourcing, and labor issues) delivery dates slipped behind three years or more and costs ballooned to several billion dollars. Many analysts blame outsourcing work to foreign suppliers for a majority of the cost and schedule overruns.

KEY FACTORS INFLUENCING OUTSOURCING DECISION

The Dreamliner outsourcing decision that gave 70 percent of plane content to outside suppliers included 30 percent to foreign suppliers. These percentages are greater than any previous commercial plane built by Boeing. Boeing's outsourcing rationale was based on typical economic considerations of cost, sales, and risk. In Boeing's case this meant:

Cost. Establishing partnerships with suppliers to lower risks and development costs, along with gaining some valuable expertise and process innovation.

Sales. Farming out numerous designs and components to foreign countries (e.g., Sweden, Italy, South Korea, and China) with the expectation that these countries will buy planes from Boeing in the future.

© Kyodo/AP Photo

Risk. Recognizing the need to balance risk of outsourcing at the organizational and operational levels is crucial. The different levels are co-dependent. Taking gigantic steps away from successful outsourcing small amounts of past aircraft to foreign suppliers increases risk. The complexities in coordinating new technology and advance capabilities are daunting.

* http://seattletimes.nwsource.com/html/sundaybuzz /2014125414_sundaybuzz06.html; http://atwonline.com /aircraft-engines-components/news/boeing-commercial -airplanes-ceo-concedes-787-outsourcingbackfired. Accessed: 1/12/2013.

The disadvantages of outsourcing project work are less well documented:

1. *Coordination breakdowns.* Coordination of professionals from different organizations can be challenging, especially if the project work requires close collaboration and mutual adjustment. Breakdowns are exacerbated by physical separation with people working in different buildings, different cities, if not different countries.

2. *Loss of control.* There is potential loss of control over the project. The core team depends on other organizations that they have no direct authority over. While long-term survival of participating organizations depends on performance, a project may falter when one partner fails to deliver.

3. *Conflict.* Projects are more prone to interpersonal conflict since the different participants do not share the same values, priorities, and culture. Trust, which is essential to project success, can be difficult to forge when interactions are limited and people come from different organizations.

Clearly, the outsourcing decision ricocheted. Costs are over budget, some sales have been rescinded, customers are seeking compensation for delays, and potential ROI is reduced.

IMPACTS

Boeing's brand has been seriously tarnished by delays and mismanagement. The process to manage the logistics of outsourcing was not able to handle the volume of logistical problems and change management issues. Chronic delays of a few nonperforming partners induced Boeing to buy out or support partners and consumed cash. Wall Street estimates cost overruns range between 12 and 18 billion dollars over the original planned investment of $5 billion. Lessons learned from outsourcing of the 787 Dreamliner can point the way to bring back the shine to Boeing's reputation as the leader in design, technology, and integration.

LESSONS LEARNED

The lessons learned in the Dreamliner launch have been well documented. A few obvious relevant lessons are noted in suggestion form here:

- Identify and analyze all risks of outsourcing at organization *and* component levels. For example, assess the risks and implications of farming out large portions (30 percent) of the design and manufacture of crucial components to foreign suppliers. Outsourcing tends to work better in noncore areas.

- Thoroughly investigate partnership capabilities and resources. Due diligence reduces problems.

- Develop processes for quickly addressing issues and problems. Increase liaison and supervision of supply chain logistics with outsource partners.

- Reconsider seriously the implications of farming out key expertise. This runs the risk of becoming fully reliant on suppliers and transferring unique intellectual property. Partners get risk-free technical know-how, high margin markets for component parts over the life of the plane, and perhaps the future ability to become a future competitor.

- The risk of outsourcing complex, high technology components carries the burden of careful coordination and liaison.

Boeing executives have acknowledged the problems associated with outsourcing large portions of the 787 Dreamliner. For example, Boeing's Commercial Airplanes Chief, Jim Albaugh, expressed to students at Seattle University, "We spent a lot more money in trying to recover [the project] than we ever would have spent if we'd tried to keep the key technologies closer to home. The pendulum swung too far." He added that, in part, chasing the financial measure of return on assets led Boeing astray. Boeing CEO Jim McNerney noted that the 787 game plan may have been overly ambitious, incorporating too many firsts all at once.

THE FUTURE

Although Boeing's 787 outsourcing experience was very costly, outsourcing will continue and evolve. Lessons learned will prompt aircraft builders to reevaluate future outsourcing and move on. Expect to see emphasis on risk- and cost-sharing partnerships.

The major short-term challenge for Boeing is to ramp up production to satisfy the hundreds of waiting orders. Boeing can recoup by adjusting their integrative outsourcing and logistics model as a top priority.

4. *Security issues.* Depending on the nature of the project, trade and business secrets may be revealed. This can be problematic if the contractor also works for your competitor. Confidentiality is another concern and companies have to be very careful when outsourcing processes like payroll, medical transcriptions, and insurance information.

5. *Political hot potato.* Foreign outsourcing of work is perceived as a major cause of underemployment and U.S. companies are under increased pressure to keep jobs local. Furthermore, companies like Apple have been criticized for the oppressive labor practices of some of their suppliers in China.

Few people disagree that reducing costs is the primary motive behind outsourcing project work. However, there are limits to outsourcing (see Snapshot from Practice 12.1: Boeing 787 Dreamliner), and there appears to be a shift away from simply nailing the best low-cost deal to securing services from companies that provide the best value in terms of both cost and performance. Performance is not limited to simply the quality of specific work but also ability to collaborate and work together. Companies are doing their homework to determine "Can we work with these people?"

12.2 Request for Proposal (RFP)

LO 12-2

Describe the basic elements of a Request for Proposal (RFP).

Once an organization decides to outsource project work, the customer or project manager is frequently responsible for developing a **Request for Proposal (RFP)**.

The responsible project manager will require input from all stakeholders connected to the activities covered in the RFP. The RFP will be announced to external contractors/vendors with adequate experience to implement the project. For example, government projects frequently advertise with a "request for proposal" to outside contractors for roads, buildings, airports, military hardware, space vehicles. Similarly, businesses use RFPs to solicit bids for building a clean room, developing a new manufacturing process, delivering software for insurance billing, conducting a market survey. In all of these examples, requirements and features should be in enough detail that contractors have a clear description of the final deliverable that will meet the customer's needs.

RFPs are important. In practice, the most common error is to offer an RFP that lacks sufficient detail. This lack of detail typically results in conflict issues, misunderstandings, often legal claims between the contractor and owner, and, ultimately, a dissatisfied customer. All RFPs are different, but the outline in Figure 12.2 is a good starting point for the development of a detailed RFP. Each step is briefly described next.

1. **Summary of needs and request for action.** The background and a simple description of the final project deliverable are given first. For example, through simulated war games, the U.S. Navy has found their giant warships of the past are too vulnerable against today's technology (an example is the Silkworm antiship missiles). In addition, the Navy's mission has shifted to supporting ground forces and peace-keeping missions, which require getting closer to shore. As a result, the Navy is revamping ships for near-shore duty. The Navy will select three designs for further refinement from the responses to its RFP. In general, it is expected that the new ship will be capable of at least 55 knots, measure between 80 and 250 feet in length, and be fitted with radar absorbing panels to thwart guided missiles.

2. **Statement of work (SOW) detailing the scope and major deliverables.** For example, if the project involves a market research survey, the major deliverables could be design, data collection, data analysis, and providing recommendations by February 21, 2014, for a cost not to exceed $300,000.

3. **Deliverable specifications/requirements, features, and tasks.** This step should be very comprehensive so bid proposals from contractors can be validated and later

FIGURE 12.2
Request for Proposal

1. Summary of needs and request for action
2. Statement of work (SOW) detailing the scope and major deliverables
3. Deliverable specifications/requirements, features, and tasks
4. Responsibilities—vendor and customer
5. Project schedule
6. Costs and payment schedule
7. Type of contract
8. Experience and staffing
9. Evaluation criteria

used for control. Typical specifications cover physical features such as size, quantity, materials, speed, and color. For example, an IT project might specify requirements for hardware, software, and training in great detail. Tasks required to complete deliverables can be included if they are known.

4. **Responsibilities—vendor and customer.** Failing to spell out the responsibilities for both parties is notorious for leading to serious problems when the contractor implements the project. For example, who pays for what? (If the contractor is to be on site, will the contractor be required to pay for office space?) What are the limits and exclusions for the contractor? (For example, who will supply test equipment?) What communication plan will be used by the contractor and owner? If escalation of an issue becomes necessary, what process will be used? How will progress be evaluated? Well-defined responsibilities will avoid many unforeseen problems later.

5. **Project schedule.** This step is concerned with getting a "hard" schedule which can be used for control and evaluating progress. Owners are usually very demanding in meeting the project schedule. In today's business environment, time-to-market is a major "hot button" that influences market share, costs, and profits. The schedule should spell out what, who, and when.

6. **Costs and payment schedule.** The RFP needs to set out very clearly how, when, and the process for determining costs and conditions for progress payments.

7. **Type of contract.** Essentially there are two types of contracts—fixed-price and cost-plus. Fixed-price contracts agree on a price or lump sum in advance, and it remains as long as there are no changes to the scope provisions of the agreement. This type is preferred in projects that are well defined with predictable costs and minimal risks. The contractor must exercise care estimating cost because any underestimating of costs will cause the contractor's profit to be reduced. In cost-plus contracts the contractor is reimbursed for all or some of the expenses incurred during performance of the contract. This fee is negotiated in advance and usually involves a percent of total costs. "Time and materials" plus a profit factor are typical of cost-plus contracts. Both types of contracts can include incentive clauses for superior performance in time and cost, or in some cases, penalties—for example, missing the opening date of a new sports stadium. Appendix 12.1 elaborates further on contract management.

8. **Experience and staffing.** The ability of the contractor to implement the project may depend on specific skills; this necessary experience should be specified, along with assurance such staff will be available for this project.

9. **Evaluation criteria.** The criteria for evaluating and awarding the project contract should be specified. For example, selection criteria frequently include methodology, price, schedule, and experience; in some cases these criteria are weighted. Use of the outline in Figure 12.2 will help to ensure key items in the proposal are not omitted. A well-prepared RFP will provide contractors with sufficient guidelines to prepare a proposal that clearly meets the project and customer's needs.

Selection of Contractor from Bid Proposals

Interested contractors respond to project RFPs with a written bid proposal. It is likely that several contractors will submit bid proposals to the customer.

The final step in the RFP process is to select the contractor who best meets the requirements requested in the RFP. The selection criteria given in the RFP are used to evaluate which contractor is awarded the contract to implement the project. Losing contractors

FIGURE 12.3 **Contractor Evaluation Template**

Contractor Evaluation Template	Maximum Weight	Proposal 1	Proposal 2	Proposal 3	Proposal 4
Contractor qualifications	Weight = 10				
Technical skills available	Weight = 20				
Understanding of contract and conditions	Weight = 5				
Financial strength to implement project	Weight = 15				
Understanding of proposal specifications	Weight = 10				
Innovativeness and originality of proposal	Weight = 5				
Reputation for delivering on time and budget	Weight = 15				
Price	Weight = 20				
Total	**100**				

should be given an explanation of the key factors that led to the selection of the winning contractor/vendor; appreciation for their participation and effort should be acknowledged. See Figure 12.3, Contractor Evaluation Template, adapted from one used in practice.

12.3 Best Practices in Outsourcing Project Work

 12-3

Identify best practices for outsourcing project work.

This section describes some of the best practices we have observed being used by firms that excel in project management (see Figure 12.4). Although the list is by no means comprehensive, it reflects strategies used by organizations with extensive outsourcing experience. These practices reveal an underlying theme in how firms approach contracted work on projects. Instead of the traditional master–slave relationship between owner and provider or buyer and seller, all parties work together as partners sharing the ultimate goal of a successful project.

Differences between the traditional approach and the partnering approach to managing contracted relationships are summarized in Table 12.1.[1] Partnering requires more than a simple hand-shake. It typically entails a significant commitment of time and energy to forge and sustain collaborative relations among all parties. This commitment is reflected in the seven best practices which will be discussed next.

Well-Defined Requirements and Procedures

Convincing people from different professions, organizations, and cultures to work together is difficult. If expectations and requirements are fuzzy or open to debate, this is even harder. Successful firms are very careful in selecting the work to be outsourced. They often choose to contract only work with clearly defined deliverables with

FIGURE 12.4
Best Practices in Outsourcing Project Work

- Well-defined requirements and procedures.
- Extensive training and team-building activities.
- Well-established conflict management processes in place.
- Frequent review and status updates.
- Co-location when needed.
- Fair and incentive-laden contracts.
- Long-term outsourcing relationships.

[1] C. Cowan, C. F. Gray, and E. W. Larson, "Project Partnering," *Project Management Journal*, 12 (4) December 1992, pp. 5–15.

TABLE 12.1
Key Differences Between Partnering and Traditional Approaches to Managing Contracted Relationships

Partnering Approach	Traditional Approach
Mutual trust forms the basis for strong working relationships.	Suspicion and distrust; each party is wary of the motives for actions by the other.
Shared goals and objectives ensure common direction.	Each party's goals and objectives, while similar, are geared to what is best for them.
Joint project team exists with high level of interaction.	Independent project teams; teams are spatially separated with managed interactions.
Open communications avoid misdirection and bolster effective working relationships.	Communications are structured and guarded.
Long-term commitment provides the opportunity to attain continuous improvement.	Single project contracting is normal.
Objective critique is geared to candid assessment of performance.	Objectivity is limited due to fear of reprisal and lack of continuous improvement opportunity.
Access to each other's organization resources is available.	Access is limited with structured procedures and self-preservation taking priority over total optimization.
Total company involvement requires commitment from CEO to team members.	Involvement is normally limited to project-level personnel.
Integration of administrative systems equipment takes place.	Duplication and/or translation takes place with attendant costs and delays.
Risk is shared jointly among the partners, which encourages innovation and continuous improvement.	Risk is transferred to the other party.

measurable outcomes. For example, contractors hire electric firms to install heating and air-conditioning systems, electronic firms use design firms to fabricate enclosures for their products, and software development teams outsource the testing of versions of their programs. In all of these cases, the technical requirements are spelled out in detail. Even so, communicating requirements can be troublesome, especially with foreign providers (see the Snapshot from Practice 12.2: Four Strategies for Communicating with Outsourcers), and extra care has to be taken to ensure that expectations are understood.

Not only do requirements have to be spelled out, but the different firms' project management systems need to be integrated. Common procedures and terminology need to be established so that different parties can work together. This can be problematic when you have firms with more advanced project management systems working with less developed organizations. Surprisingly, this often is the case when U.S. firms outsource software work to India. We have heard reports that Indian providers are shocked at how unsystematic their U.S. counterparts are in their approach to managing software projects.

The best companies address this issue up front instead of waiting for problems to emerge. First they assess "fit" between providers' project management methods and their own project management system. This is a prime consideration in choosing vendors. Work requirements and deliverables are spelled out in detail in the procurement process. They invest significant time and energy to establishing project communication systems to support effective collaboration.

Finally, whenever you work with other organizations on projects, security is an important issue. Security extends beyond competitive secrets and technology to include access to information systems. Firms have to establish robust safeguards to prevent information access and the introduction of viruses due to less secure provider systems. Information technology security is an additional cost and risk that needs to be addressed up front before outsourcing project work.

SNAPSHOT FROM PRACTICE 12.2 — Four Strategies for Communicating with Outsourcers*

Dr. Adam Kolawa offers four strategies for overcoming poor communication with offshore project partners.

STRATEGY 1: RECOGNIZE CULTURAL DIFFERENCES

Realize that not everyone you communicate with shares your assumptions. What is obvious to you is not necessarily obvious to your partner. This is especially true with foreign outsourcers. As an American, you likely assume that laws are generally obeyed. Believe it or not, that's generally not true in most of the world, where laws are guidelines that are not necessarily followed. This can lead to major communication problems! You think if you write a contract, everybody is going to adhere to it. For many people, a contract is merely a suggestion.

STRATEGY 2: CHOOSE THE RIGHT WORDS

When you explain your requirements to an outsourcer, word choice is critical. For many outsourcers, English is still a foreign language—even in India, where both outsourcing and the English language are common. No matter how prevalent English has become, your outsourcer might have a basic understanding of each word you utter yet be not completely clear on the exact meaning of the message you're trying to convey. This is why you should speak in a direct manner using short sentences made of basic, simple words.

STRATEGY 3: CONFIRM YOUR REQUIREMENTS

You should take the following steps to confirm that the outsourcer thoroughly understands your requirements:

1. *Document your requirements.* Follow up your conversations in writing. Commit your requirements to paper for the outsourcer. Many people understand written language better than spoken language, probably because they have more time to process the message.

2. *Insist your outsourcer re-document your requirements.* Leave nothing to chance. Require outsourcers to write the requirements in their own words. If outsourcers cannot relay to you what you explained to them, then they didn't understand.

3. *Request a prototype.* After the requirements are written, ask the outsourcer to create a prototype for you. This is a safety net to ensure that your wants and needs are positively understood. Ask the provider to sketch what you want your final product to look like or build a quick, simple program that reflects how the final product will look.

STRATEGY 4: SET DEADLINES

Another important cultural difference relates to schedules and deadlines. To most Americans, a deadline is a set completion date. In many other cultures, a deadline is a suggestion that maybe something will be finished by that indicated date. To ensure that outsourced work is completed on time it is imperative to add a penalty clause to your contract or enforce late fees.

Although these strategies were directed toward working with foreign outsourcers, you would be surprised to find how many project managers use them when working with their American counterparts!

*Adam Kolawa, "Four Strategies for Communicating with Outsourcers," *Enterprise Systems Journal* at www.esj.com, accessed September 13, 2005.

Extensive Training and Team-Building Activities

Too often managers become preoccupied with the plans and technical challenges of the project and assume that people issues will work themselves out over time. Smart firms recognize that people issues are as important, if not more important, than technical issues. They train their personnel to work effectively with people from other organizations and countries. This training is pervasive. It is not limited to management but involves all the people, at all levels, who interact with and are dependent upon outsourcers. Whether in a general class on negotiation or a specific one on working with Chinese programmers, team members are provided with a theoretical understanding of the barriers to collaboration as well as the skills and procedures to be successful.

The training is augmented by interorganizational team-building sessions designed to forge healthy relationships before the project begins. Team-building workshops involve the key players from the different firms, for example, engineers, architects, lawyers, specialists, and other staff. In many cases, firms find it useful to hire an outside consultant to design and facilitate the sessions. Such a consultant is typically well-versed in interorganizational team building and can provide an impartial perspective to the workshop.

The length and design of the team-building sessions will depend on the experience, commitment, and skill level of the participants. For example, one project, in which the owner and the contractors were relatively inexperienced at working together, utilized a two-day workshop. The first day was devoted to ice-breaking activities and establishing the rationale behind partnering. The conceptual foundation was supported by exercises and minilectures on teamwork, synergy, win/win, and constructive feedback. The second day began by examining the problems and barriers that prevented collaboration in the past. Representatives from the different organizations were separated and each asked the following:

- What actions do the other groups engage in that create problems for us?
- What actions do we engage in that we think create problems for them?
- What recommendations would we make to improve the situation?

The groups shared their responses and asked questions on points needing clarification. Agreements and disparities in the lists were noted and specific problems were identified. Once problem areas were noted, each group was assigned the task of identifying its specific interests and goals for the project. Goals were shared across groups, and special attention was devoted to establishing what goals they had in common. Recognition of shared goals is critical for transforming the different groups into a cohesive team.

The team-building sessions often culminate with the creation of a **partnering charter** signed by all of the participants. This charter states their common goals for the project as well as the procedures that will be used to achieve these goals (see Figure 12.5 for an example of the first page of a project charter).

Well-Established Conflict Management Processes in Place

Conflict is inevitable on a project and, as pointed out in the previous chapter, disagreements handled effectively can elevate performance. Dysfunctional conflict, however, can catch fire and severely undermine project success. Outsourced projects are susceptible to conflicts since people are unaccustomed to working together and have different values and perspectives. Successful firms invest significant time and energy up front in establishing the "rules of engagement" so that disagreements are handled constructively.

Escalation is the primary control mechanism for dealing with and resolving problems. The basic principle is that problems should be resolved at the lowest level within a set time limit (say, 24 hours), or they are "escalated" to the next level of management. If so, the principals have the same time limit to resolve the problem, or it gets passed on to the next higher level. No action is not an option. Nor can one participant force concessions from the other by simply delaying the decision. There is no shame in pushing significant problems up the hierarchy; at the same time, managers should be quick to point out to subordinates those problems or questions that they should have been able to resolve on their own.

If possible, key personnel from the respective organizations are brought together to discuss potential problems and responses. This is usually part of a coordinated series of team-building activities discussed earlier. Particular attention is devoted to establishing the change management control system where problems often erupt. People who are dependent on each other try to identify potential problems that may occur and

FIGURE 12.5 Project Partnering Charter

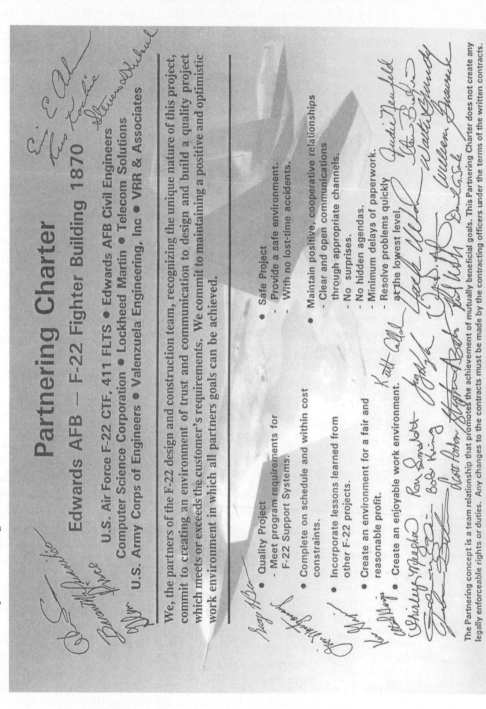

Partnering Charter

Edwards AFB — F-22 Fighter Building 1870

U.S. Air Force F-22 CTF, 411 FLTS ● **Edwards AFB Civil Engineers**
Computer Science Corporation ● **Lockheed Martin** ● **Telecom Solutions**
U.S. Army Corps of Engineers ● **Valenzuela Engineering, Inc** ● **VRR & Associates**

We, the partners of the F-22 design and construction team, recognizing the unique nature of this project, commit to creating an environment of trust and communication to design and build a quality project which meets or exceeds the customer's requirements. We commit to maintaining a positive and optimistic work environment in which all partners goals can be achieved.

- **Quality Project**
  - Meet program requirements for F-22 Support Systems.
- Complete on schedule and within cost constraints.
- Incorporate lessons learned from other F-22 projects.
- Create an environment for a fair and reasonable profit.
- Create an enjoyable work environment.

- **Safe Project**
  - Provide a safe environment.
  - With no lost-time accidents.
- Maintain positive, cooperative relationships
  - Clear and open communications through appropriate channels.
  - No surprises.
  - No hidden agendas.
  - Minimum delays of paperwork.
  - Resolve problems quickly at the lowest level.

The Partnering concept is a team relationship that promotes the achievement of mutually beneficial goals. This Partnering Charter does not create any legally enforceable rights or duties. Any changes to the contracts must be made by the contracting officers under the terms of the written contracts.

SNAPSHOT FROM PRACTICE 12.3

"Partnering" a Flu Shot for Projects*

Before starting a bond-financed school construction project, Ohio does what a theater company does before opening night—it holds a dress rehearsal. Led by Cleveland-based Project Management Consultants, state and local school officials, construction managers, and architects get together before building begins to figure out how to talk to each other and how to handle problems. Each party discusses problems that have occurred in the past and collectively they problem solve ways for preventing them from occurring on the current project. Consultants help participants develop a set of guidelines for working together.

Just as a theatrical dress rehearsal can allow a company to find and fix glitches before they ruin a show, preconstruction partnering can find early solutions to problems before they become lawsuits. For example, during the discussions it becomes apparent that different parties are interpreting a key requirement differently. Instead of waiting for this difference to escalate into a major problem, the parties reach a shared understanding before work begins.

"This works because traditionally everyone does their own work on a project, behind their own walls," said Jeffrey Applebaum, a construction lawyer and managing director of Project Management Consultants, a wholly owned subsidiary of the law firm of Thompson, Hine, & Flory. "We're taking down the walls. This is more efficient."

"We couldn't be more pleased with this process," said Randy Fischer, executive director of the Ohio School Facilities Commission, which distributes state money to school construction projects. "We are currently administering $3 billion of construction, and we don't have any major disputes."

Crystal Canan, chief of contract administration for the commission, offered a medical metaphor, comparing partnering to a "flu shot" that will prevent the debilitating effects of litigation, work stoppages, and communication breakdowns. "Every building construction project is a candidate for the flu," Canan said. "We see partnering as a vaccination."

* Mary Wisneiski, "Partnering Used to Curb Costs in Ohio School Construction," *Bond Buyer*, 11/22/2000, 334 (31023) 3/4p, 2bw.

agree in advance how they should be resolved. See the Snapshot from Practice 12.3: "Partnering" a Flu Shot for Projects for the benefits of doing this.

Finally, principled negotiation is the norm for resolving problems and reaching agreements. This approach, which emphasizes collaborative problem solving, is discussed in detail later in this chapter.

Frequent Review and Status Updates

Project managers and other key personnel from all involved organizations meet on a regular basis to review and assess project performance. Collaborating as partners is considered a legitimate project priority which is assessed along with time, cost, and performance. Teamwork, communication, and timely problem resolution are evaluated. This provides a forum for identifying problems not only with the project but also with working relationships so that they can be resolved quickly and appropriately.

More and more companies are using online surveys to collect data from all project participants about the quality of working relations (see Figure 12.6 for a partial example). With this data one can gauge the "pulse" of the project and identify issues that need to be addressed. Comparison of survey responses period by period permits tracking areas of improvement and potential problems. In some cases, follow-up team-building sessions are used to focus on specific problems and recharge collaboration.

Finally, when the time to celebrate a significant milestone arrives, no matter who is responsible, all parties gather if possible to celebrate the success. This reinforces a

FIGURE 12.6
Sample Online Survey

Evaluation of partnering process: attitudes, teamwork, process.
(Collected separately from owner and contractor participants, compared, and aggregated.)

1. Communications between the owner/contractor personnel are

1	2	3	4	5

Difficult,
guarded

Easy, open,
up front

2. Top management support of partnering process is

1	2	3	4	5

Not evident or
inconsistent

Obvious and
consistent

3. Problems, issues, or concerns are

1	2	3	4	5

Ignored

Attacked
promptly

4. Cooperation between owner and contractor personnel is

1	2	3	4	5

Cool, detached,
unresponsive,
removed

Genuine,
unreserved,
complete

5. Responses to problems, issues, or concerns frequently become

1	2	3	4	5

Personal issues

Treated as
project problems

common purpose and project identity. It also establishes positive momentum going into the next phase of the project.

Co-Location When Needed

One of the best ways to overcome interorganizational friction is to have people from each organization working side by side on the project. Smart companies rent or make available the necessary accommodations so that all key project personnel can work collectively together. This allows the high degree of face-to-face interaction needed to coordinate activities, solve difficult problems, and form a common bond. This is especially relevant for complex projects in which close collaboration from different parties is required to be successful. For example, the U.S government provides housing and common office space for all key contractors responsible for developing disaster response plans.

Our experience tells us that co-location is critical and well worth the added expense and inconvenience. When creating this is not practically possible, the travel budget for the project should contain ample funds to support timely travel to different organizations.

Co-location is less relevant for independent work that does not require ongoing coordination between professionals from different organizations. This would be the case if you are outsourcing discrete, independent deliverables like beta testing or a marketing campaign. Here normal channels of communication can handle the coordination issues.

Fair and Incentive-Laden Contracts

When negotiating contracts the goal is to reach a fair deal for all involved. Managers recognize that cohesion and cooperation is undermined if one party feels he or she is being unfairly treated by others. They also realize that negotiating the best deal in terms of price can come back to haunt them with shoddy work and change order gouging.

Performance-based contracts, in which significant incentives are established based on priorities of the project, are becoming increasingly popular. For example, if time is critical, then contractors accrue payoffs for beating deadlines; if scope is critical, then bonuses are issued for exceeding performance expectations. At the same time contractors are held accountable with penalty clauses for failure to perform up to standard, meet deadlines, and/or control costs. More specific information about different types of contracts is presented in this chapter's appendix on contract management.

Companies recognize that contracts can discourage continuous improvement and innovation. Instead of trying some new, promising technique that may reduce costs, contractors will avoid the risks and apply tried and true methods to meet contracted requirements. Companies that treat contractors as partners consider continuous improvement as a joint effort to eliminate waste and pursue opportunities for cost savings. Risks as well as benefits are typically shared 50/50 between the principals, with the owner adhering to a fast-track review of proposed changes.

How the U.S. Department of Defense reaps the benefits of continuous improvement through value engineering is highlighted in the Snapshot from Practice 12.4: Value Engineering Awards.

Long-Term Outsourcing Relationships

Many companies recognize that major benefits can be enjoyed when outsourcing arrangements extend across multiple projects and are long term. For example, Corning and Toyota are among the many firms that have forged a network of long-term strategic partnerships with their suppliers. The average large corporation is involved in around 30 alliances today versus fewer than 3 in the early 1990s. Among the many advantages for establishing a long-term partnership are the following:

- **Reduced administrative costs**—The costs associated with bidding and selecting a contractor are eliminated. Contract administration costs are reduced as partners become knowledgeable of their counterpart's legal concerns.
- **More efficient utilization of resources**—Contractors have a known forecast of work while owners are able to concentrate their workforce on core businesses and avoid the demanding swings of project support.
- **Improved communication**—As partners gain experience with each other, they develop a common language and perspective, which reduces misunderstanding and enhances collaboration.
- **Improved innovation**—The partners are able to discuss innovation and associated risks in a more open manner and share risks and rewards fairly.
- **Improved performance**—Over time partners become more familiar with each other's standards and expectations and are able to apply lessons learned from previous projects to current projects.

Working as partners is a conscious effort on the part of management to form collaborative relationships with personnel from different organizations to complete a project. For outsourcing to work, the individuals involved need to be effective

U.S. Department of Defense's Value Engineering Awards*

As part of an effort to cut costs the United States Department of Defense (DoD) issues annual Value Engineering Awards. Value engineering is a systematic process to analyze functions to identify actions to reduce cost, increase quality, and improve mission capabilities across the entire spectrum of DoD systems, processes, and organizations. The Value Engineering Awards Program is an acknowledgment of outstanding achievements and encourages additional projects to improve in-house and contractor productivity.

In 2015, 48 different individuals and project teams received recognition from the DoD, reporting over $5.5 billion in savings or cost reduction.

One team that received an award was AMRDEC Maintenance Engineering Division at Corpus Christ, Texas, which reported a savings of $66 million with 91 value engineering projects completed.

Kevin Rees leads a team of 62 employees responsible for the airworthiness of all helicopters that go through the depot in South Texas for maintenance.

"Each aircraft component has an overhaul manual that requires parts to be replaced at certain times. Those parts have to be thrown away," Rees said. "We worked to repair and reclass those parts so they wouldn't have to be thrown away. We used new technologies for welding repairs, composite repairs,

© Cultura Creative/Alamy RF

plating repairs, metal spray repairs and technology repairs. There are 20,000 to 25,000 engine parts, and we are working to reclaim those parts when they have to be replaced."

"Value engineering is so important to what we are doing, especially in these days with budgets coming down. It's nice to be able to save cost while also improving quality," Rees said. "But it goes beyond that for us as a team. We all have an intrinsic motivation. We want to do well for the taxpayer and the Soldier. We take a lot of pride in our work. Getting recognized isn't our motivator, but it does encourage us."

* K. Hawkins "AMCOM, Partners Take Home Big Wins for Value Engineering," www.army.mil, June 26, 2015.

negotiators capable of merging interests and discovering solutions to problems that contribute to the project. The next section addresses some of the key skills and techniques associated with effective negotiation.

12.4 The Art of Negotiating

LO 12-4

Practice principled negotiation.

Effective negotiating is critical to successful collaboration. All it takes is one key problem to explode to convert a sense of "we" into "us versus them." At the same time, negotiating is pervasive through all aspects of project management work. Project managers must negotiate support and funding from top management. They must negotiate staff and technical input from functional managers. They must coordinate with other project managers and negotiate project priorities and commitments. They must negotiate within their project team to determine assignments, deadlines, standards, and priorities. Project managers must negotiate prices and standards with vendors and suppliers. A firm understanding of the negotiating process, skills, and tactics is essential to project success.

Many people approach negotiating as if it is a competitive contest. Each negotiator is out to win as much as he or she can for his or her side. Success is measured by how

TABLE 12.2
Principled
Negotiation

> 1. Separate the people from the problem.
> 2. Focus on interests, not positions.
> 3. Invent options for mutual gain.
> 4. When possible, use objective criteria.

much is gained compared with the other party. While this may be applicable when negotiating the sale of a house, it is not true for project management. *Project management is not a contest!* First, the people working on the project, whether they represent different companies or departments within the same organization, are not enemies or competitors but rather allies or partners. They have formed a temporary alliance to complete a project. For this alliance to work requires a certain degree of trust, cooperation, and honesty. Second, if conflicts escalate to the point where negotiations break down and the project comes to a halt, then everyone loses. Third, unlike bartering with a street vendor, the people involved on project work have to continue to work together. Therefore, it behooves them to resolve disagreements in a way that contributes to healthy working relationships. Finally, as pointed out in the previous chapter, conflict on a project can be good. When dealt with effectively it can lead to innovation, better decisions, and more creative problem solving.

Project managers accept this noncompetitive view of negotiation and realize that negotiation is essentially a two-part process: The first part deals with reaching an agreement; the second part is the implementation of that agreement. It is the implementation phase, not the agreement itself, that determines the success of negotiations. All too often, managers reach an agreement with someone only to find out later that they failed to do what they agreed to do or that their actual response fell far short of expectations. Experienced project managers recognize that implementation is based on satisfaction not only with the outcome but also with the process by which the agreement was reached. If someone feels bullied or tricked into doing something, this feeling will invariably be reflected by half-hearted performance.

Veteran project managers do the best they can to merge individual interests with what is best for the project and come up with effective solutions to problems. Fisher and Ury from the Harvard Negotiation Project champion an approach to negotiating that embodies these goals.[2] It emphasizes developing win/win solutions while protecting yourself against those who would take advantage of your forthrightness. Their approach is called **principled negotiation** and is based on four key points listed in Table 12.2 and discussed in the following sections.

1. Separate the People from the Problem

Too often personal relations become entangled with the substantive issues under consideration. Instead of attacking the problem(s), people attack each other. Once people feel attacked or threatened their energy naturally goes to defending themselves, and not to solving the problem. The key, then, is to focus on the problem—not the other person—during the negotiation. Avoid personalizing the negotiation and framing the negotiation as a contest. Instead, try to keep the focus on the problem to be resolved. In Fisher and Ury's words: *Be hard on the problem, soft on the people.*

By keeping the focus on the issues and not the personalities, negotiators are better able to let the other person blow off steam. On important problems it is not uncommon for people to become upset, frustrated, and angry. However, one angry attack produces

---

[2] R. Fisher and W. Ury, *Getting to Yes: Negotiating Agreement without Giving In*, 2nd ed. (New York: Penguin Books, 1991).

an angry counterattack, and the discussion quickly escalates into a heated argument, an emotional chain reaction.

In some cases people use anger as a means of intimidating and forcing concessions because the other person wishes to preserve the relationship. When people become emotional, negotiators should keep a cool head and remember the old German proverb, "Let anger fly out the window."[3] In other words, in the face of an emotional outburst, imagine opening a window and letting the heat of the anger out the window. Avoid taking things personally, and redirect personal attacks back to the question at hand. Don't react to the emotional outburst, but try to find the issues that triggered it. Skilled negotiators keep their cool under stressful times and, at the same time, build a bond with others by empathizing and acknowledging common sources of frustration and anger.

While it is important to separate the people from the problem during actual negotiations, it is beneficial to have a friendly rapport with the other person prior to negotiating. Friendly rapport is consistent with the social network tenet introduced in Chapter 10 of building a relationship before you need it. If, in the past, the relationship has been marked by healthy give-and-take, in which both parties have demonstrated a willingness to accommodate the interests of the other, then neither individual is likely to adopt an immediate win/lose perspective. Furthermore, a positive relationship adds a common interest beyond the specific points of contention. Not only do both parties want to reach an agreement that suits their individual interests, but they also want to do so in a manner that preserves their relationship. Each is therefore more likely to seek solutions that are mutually beneficial.

2. Focus on Interests, Not Positions

Negotiations often stall when people focus on positions:

I'm willing to pay $10,000. No, it will cost $15,000.

I need it done by Monday. That's impossible, we can't have it ready until Wednesday.

While such interchanges are common during preliminary discussions, managers must prevent this initial posturing from becoming polarized. When such positions are stated, attacked, and then defended, each party figuratively begins to draw a line he or she will not cross. This line creates a win/lose scenario in which someone has to lose by crossing the line in order to reach an agreement. As such, the negotiations can become a war of wills, with concessions being seen as a loss of face.

The key is to focus on the interests behind your positions (what you are trying to achieve) and separate these goals from your ego as best you can. Not only should you be driven by your interests, but you should try to identify the interests of the other party. Ask why it will cost so much or why it can't be done by Monday. At the same time, make your own interests come alive. Don't just say that it is critical that it be done by Monday; explain what will happen if it isn't done by Monday.

Sometimes when the true interests of both parties are revealed, there is no basis for conflict. Take, for example, the Monday versus Wednesday argument. This argument could apply to a scenario involving a project manager and the production manager of a small, local firm that was contracted to produce prototypes of a new generation of computer mouse. The project manager needs the prototypes on Monday to demonstrate to a users' focus group. The production manager said it would be impossible. The project manager said this would be embarrassing because marketing had spent a

[3] Ibid.

lot of time and effort setting up this demonstration. The production manager again denied the request and added that he already had to schedule overtime to meet the Wednesday delivery date. However, when the project manager revealed that the purpose of the focus group was to gauge consumers' reactions to the color and shape of the new devices, not the finished product, the conflict disappeared. The production manager told the project manager that she could pick up the samples today if she wanted because production had an excess supply of shells.

When focusing on interests, it is important to practice the communication habit: *Seek first to understand, then to be understood.* This involves what Stephen Covey calls empathetic listening, which allows a person to fully understand another person's frame of reference—not only what that person is saying but also how he or she feels. Covey asserts that people have an inherent need to be understood. He goes on to observe that satisfied needs do not motivate human behavior, only unsatisfied needs do. People try to go to sleep when they are tired, not when they are rested. The key point is that until people believe they are being understood, they will repeat their points and reformulate their arguments.[4] If, on the other hand, you satisfy this need by seeking first to understand, then the other party is free to understand your interests and focus directly on the issues at hand. Seeking to understand requires discipline and compassion. Instead of responding to the other person by asserting your agenda, respond by summarizing both the facts and feelings behind what the other person has said and checking the accuracy of comprehension.

3. Invent Options for Mutual Gain

Once the individuals involved have identified their interests, then they can explore options for mutual gain. This is not easy. Stressful negotiations inhibit creativity and free exchange. What is required is collaborative brainstorming in which people work together to solve the problem in a way that will lead to a win/win scenario. The key to brainstorming is separating the inventing from the deciding. Begin by taking 15 minutes to generate as many options as possible. No matter how outlandish any option is, it should not be subject to criticism or immediate rejection. People should feed off the ideas of others to generate new ideas. When all the possible options are exhausted, then sort through the ideas that were generated to focus on those with the greatest possibilities.

Clarifying interests and exploring mutual options create the opportunity for dovetailing interests. Dovetailing means one person identifies options that are of low cost to them but of high interest to the other party. This is only possible if each party knows what the other's needs are. For example, in negotiating price with a parts supplier, a project manager learned from the discussion that the supplier was in a cash flow squeeze after purchasing a very expensive fabrication machine. Needed cash was the primary reason the supplier had taken such a rigid position on price. During the brainstorming session, one of the options presented was to prepay for the order instead of the usual payment on delivery arrangement. Both parties seized on this option and reached an amicable agreement in which the project manager would pay the supplier for the entire job in advance in exchange for a faster turnaround time and a significant price reduction. Such opportunities for win/win agreements are often overlooked because the negotiators become fixated on solving their problems and not on opportunities to solve the other person's problems.

---

[4] S. R. Covey, *The Seven Habits of Highly Effective People* (New York: Simon and Schuster, 1990).

4. When Possible, Use Objective Criteria

Most established industries and professions have developed standards and rules to help deal with common areas of dispute. Both buyers and sellers rely on the blue book to establish price parameters for a used car. The construction industry has building codes and fair practice policies to resolve proof of quality and safe work procedures. The legal profession uses precedents to adjudicate claims of wrongdoing.

Whenever possible, you should insist on using external, objective criteria to settle disagreements. For example, a disagreement arose between a regional airlines firm and the independent accounting team entrusted with preparing the annual financial statement. The airline firm had made a significant investment by leasing several used airplanes from a larger airline. The dispute involved whether this lease should be classified as an operating or capital lease. This was important to the airline because if the purchase was classified as an operating lease, then the associated debt would not have to be recorded in the financial statement. However, if the purchase was classified as a capital lease, then the debt would be factored into the financial statement and the debt/equity ratio would be much less attractive to stockholders and would-be investors. The two parties resolved this dispute by deferring to formulas established by the Financial Accounting Standards Board. As it turns out the accounting team was correct, but, by deferring to objective standards, they were able to deflect the disappointment of the airline managers away from the accounting team and preserve a professional relationship with that firm.

Dealing with Unreasonable People

Most people working on projects realize that in the long run it is beneficial to work toward mutually satisfying solutions. Still, occasionally you encounter someone who has a dominant win/lose attitude about life and will be difficult to deal with. Fisher and Ury recommend that you use negotiation jujitsu when dealing with such a person. That is, when the other person begins to push, don't push back. As in the martial arts, avoid pitting your strengths against another's directly; instead use your skill to step aside and turn that person's strength to your ends. When someone adamantly sets forth a position, neither reject it nor accept it. Treat it as a possible option and then look for the interests behind it. Instead of defending your ideas, invite criticism and advice. Ask why it's a bad idea and discover the other's underlying interest.

Those who use negotiation jujitsu rely on two primary weapons. They ask questions instead of making statements. Questions allow for interests to surface and do not provide the opponent with something to attack. The second weapon is silence. If the other person makes an unreasonable proposal or attacks you personally, just sit there and don't say a word. Wait for the other party to break the stalemate by answering your question or coming up with a new suggestion.

The best defense against unreasonable, win/lose negotiators is having what Fisher and Ury call a strong **BATNA (best alternative to a negotiated agreement).** They point out that people try to reach an agreement to produce something better than the result of not negotiating with that person. What those results would be is the true benchmark for determining whether you should accept an agreement. A strong BATNA gives you the power to walk away and say, "No deal unless we work toward a win/win scenario."

Your BATNA reflects how dependent you are on the other party. If you are negotiating price and delivery dates and can choose from a number of reputable suppliers, then you have a strong BATNA. If on the other hand there is only one vendor who can supply you with specific, critical material on time, then you have a weak BATNA.

Under these circumstances you may be forced to concede to the vendor's demands. At the same time, you should begin to explore ways of increasing your BATNA for future negotiations. This can be done by reducing your dependency on that supplier. Begin to find substitutable material or negotiate better lead times with other vendors.

Negotiating is an art. There are many intangibles involved. This section has reviewed some time-tested principles of effective negotiating based on the groundbreaking work of Fisher and Ury. Given the significance of negotiating, you are encouraged to read their book as well as others on negotiating. In addition, attending training workshops can provide an opportunity to practice these skills. You should also take advantage of day-to-day interactions to sharpen negotiating acumen.

12.5 A Note on Managing Customer Relations

LO 12-5

Describe the met-expectations model of customer satisfaction and its implications for working with customers on projects.

In Chapter 4 it was emphasized that ultimate success is not determined by whether the project was completed on time, within budget, or according to specifications, but whether the customer is satisfied with what has been accomplished. Customer satisfaction is the bottom line. Bad news travels faster and farther than good news. For every happy customer who shares his satisfaction regarding a particular product or service with another person, a dissatisfied customer is likely to share her dissatisfaction with eight other people. Project managers need to cultivate positive working relations with clients to preserve their reputations.

Customer satisfaction is a complex phenomenon. One simple but useful way of viewing customer satisfaction is in terms of **met expectations.** According to this model, customer satisfaction is a function of the extent to which perceived performance (or outcome) exceeds expectations. Mathematically, this relationship can be represented as the ratio between perceived performance and expected performance (see Figure 12.7). When performance falls short of expectations (ratio < 1), the customer is dissatisfied. If the performance matches expectations (ratio = 1), the customer is satisfied. If the performance exceeds expectations (ratio > 1), the customer is very satisfied or even delighted.

High customer satisfaction is the goal of most projects. However, profitability is another major concern. Exceeding expectations typically entails additional costs. For example, completing a construction project two weeks ahead of schedule may involve significant overtime expenses. Similarly, exceeding reliability requirements for a new electronic component may involve considerably more design and debugging effort. Under most circumstances, the most profitable arrangement occurs when the customer's expectations are only slightly exceeded. Returning to the mathematical model, with all other things being equal, one should strive for a satisfaction ratio of 1.05, not 1.5!

The met-expectations model of customer satisfaction highlights the point that whether a client is dissatisfied or delighted with a project is not based on hard facts and objective data but on perceptions and expectations. For example, a customer may be dissatisfied with a project that was completed ahead of schedule and under budget

FIGURE 12.7
The Met-Expectations Model of Customer Satisfaction

$$\underset{\text{Dissatisfied}}{0.90} = \frac{\text{Perceived performance}}{\text{Expected performance}} = \underset{\text{Very satisfied}}{1.10}$$

if he thought the work was poor quality and that his fears and concerns were not adequately addressed. Conversely, a customer may be very satisfied with a project that was over budget and behind schedule if she felt the project team protected her interests and did the best job possible under adverse circumstances.

Project managers must be skilled at managing customer expectations and perceptions. Too often they deal with these expectations after the fact when they try to alleviate a client's dissatisfaction by carefully explaining why the project cost more or took longer than planned. A more proactive approach is to begin to shape the proper expectations up front and accept that this is an ongoing process throughout the life of a project. Project managers need to direct their attention both to the customer's base expectations, the standard by which perceived performance will be evaluated, and to the customer's perceptions of actual performance. The ultimate goal is to educate clients so that they can make a valid judgment as to project performance.

Managing customer expectations begins during the preliminary project approval phase of negotiations. It is important to avoid the temptation to oversell the virtues of a project to win approval because this may create unrealistic expectations that may be too difficult, if not impossible, to achieve. At the same time, project proponents have been known to lower customer expectations by underselling projects. If the estimated completion time is 10 to 12 weeks, they will promise to have the project completed within 12 to 14 weeks, therefore increasing the chances of exceeding customer expectations by getting the project completed early.

Once the project is authorized, the project manager and team need to work closely with the client organization to develop a well-defined project scope statement that clearly states the objectives, parameters, and limits of the project work. The project scope statement is essential to establishing customer expectations regarding the project. It is critical that all parties are in agreement as to what is to be accomplished and that people are reading as best they can from the same page. It is also important to share significant risks that might disrupt project execution. Customers do not like surprises, and if they are aware in advance of potential problems they are much more likely to be accepting of the consequences.

Once the project is initiated it is important to keep customers abreast of project progress. The days when you would simply take orders from customers and tell them to return when the project is done are over. More and more organizations and their project managers are treating their customers as de facto members of the project team and are actively involving them in key aspects of project work. In the case of consulting assignments project managers sometimes *morph* into a member of the client organization (see Research Highlight 12.1: IT Project Managers).

Project managers need to keep customers informed of project developments so that customers can make adjustments in their own plans. When circumstances dictate changing the scope or priorities of the project, project managers need to be quick to spell out as best they can the implications of these changes to the customers so that they can make an informed choice. Active customer involvement allows customers to naturally adjust their expectations in accordance with the decisions and events that transpire on a project, while at the same time, the customer's presence keeps the project team focused on the customer's objectives for the project.

Active customer involvement also provides a firmer basis for assessing project performance. The customer not only sees the results of the project but also acquires glimpses of the effort and actions that produced those results. Naturally project managers want to make sure these glimpses reflect favorably on their project teams, so they

Webber and Torti studied the multiple roles project managers play on IT projects. Based on a comprehensive set of interviews with project managers and clients in three different information-technology service organizations, they identified five key roles critical to successfully implement IT projects in client organizations: entrepreneur, politician, friend, marketer, and coach. They are described in part in Table 12.3.

Webber and Torti observed that instead of maintaining a clearly defined relationship with the client, project managers become part of the client organization. They report that project managers attempt to "dress like the client, act like the client, and participate in the client organization's activities (i.e., social gatherings, blood drives, etc.)." They become such an integral part of their existence that many client employees, over the course of time, forget that the project manager is not an employee of the client organization. This helps establish a degree of trust essential to effective collaboration.

* S. S. Webber, and M. T. Torti, "Project Managers Doubling as Client Account Executives," *Academy of Management Executive*, vol. 18, no. 1 (2004), pp. 60–71.

TABLE 12.3 Project Roles, Challenges, and Strategies

Project Manager Roles	Challenges	Strategies
Entrepreneur	Navigate unfamiliar surroundings	Use persuasion to influence others
Politician	Understand two diverse cultures (parent and client organization)	Align with the powerful individuals
Friend	Determine the important relationships to build and sustain outside the team itself	Identify common interests and experiences to bridge a friendship with the client
Marketer	Understand the strategic objectives of the client organization	Align new ideas/proposals with the strategic objectives of the client organization
Coach	Motivate client team members without formal authority	Provide challenging tasks to build the skills of the team members

exercise extra care that customer interactions are handled in a competent and professional manner. In some respects, customer perceptions of performance are shaped more by how well the project team deals with adversity than by actual performance. Project managers can impress customers with how diligently they deal with unexpected problems and setbacks. Likewise, industry analysts have noted that customer dissatisfaction can be transformed into customer satisfaction by quickly correcting mistakes and being extremely responsive to customer concerns.

Managing customer relations on a project is a broad topic; we have only highlighted some of the central issues involved. This brief segment concludes with two words of advice passed on by veteran project managers:

Speak with one voice. Nothing erodes confidence in a project more than for a customer to receive conflicting messages from different project members. The project manager should remind team members of this fact and work with them to ensure that appropriate information is shared with customers.

Speak the language of the customer. Too often project members respond to customer inquiries with technical jargon that exceeds the customer's vocabulary. Project managers and members need to describe problems, trade-offs, and solutions in ways that the customer can understand.

Summary

Outsourcing has become an integral part of project management. More and more companies are collaborating with each other on projects to compete in today's business world. The advantages of outsourcing include cost reduction, quicker completion times, greater flexibility, and higher level of expertise. Disadvantages include coordination problems, loss of control, conflicts, security issues and political fallout.

A number of proactive best practices have emerged among firms that have mastered the outsourcing process. These practices include establishing well-defined requirements and procedures and utilizing fair and incentive-laden contracts. Team-building sessions are held before the project begins to forge relationships between personnel from different organizations. Escalation guidelines for resolving conflicts are established, as are provisions for process improvement and risk sharing. On highly critical work, arrangements are made so that key personnel work together, face to face. Joint assessments of how well people are collaborating is the norm during status report briefings. Finally, many companies are realizing the benefits of forming long-term alliances with each other on projects. The ultimate goal is to work together as partners.

Effective negotiating skills are essential to working on projects as partners. People need to resolve differences at the lowest level possible in order to keep the project on track. Veteran project managers realize that negotiating is not a competitive game and work toward collaborative solutions to problems. They accomplish this by separating people from the problem, focusing on interests and not positions, inventing options for mutual gain, and relying on objective criteria whenever possible to resolve disagreements. They also recognize the importance of developing a strong BATNA, which provides them with the leverage necessary to seek collaborative solutions.

Customer satisfaction is the litmus test for project success. Project managers need to take a proactive approach to managing customer expectations and perceptions. They need to actively involve customers in key decisions and keep them abreast of important developments. Active customer involvement keeps the project team focused on the objectives of the project and reduces misunderstandings and dissatisfaction.

Key Terms

Best alternative to a negotiated agreement (BATNA), *438*	Escalation, *429*	Partnering charter, *429*
	Met-expectations, *439*	Principled negotiation, *435*
	Outsourcing, *420*	

Review Questions

1. Why do firms outsource project work?
2. What are the best practices used by firms to outsource project work?
3. What does the term "escalate" refer to, and why is it essential to project success?
4. Why is the principled negotiation approach recommended for negotiating agreements on projects?
5. What does the acronym BATNA refer to, and why is it important to being a successful negotiator?
6. How can a project manager influence customer expectations and perceptions?

Exercises

1. Break into groups of four to five students. Assign half of the groups the role of Owner and the other half the role of Contractor.

   Owners: After saving for many years you are about to hire a contractor to build your "dream home." What are your objectives for this project? What concerns or issues do you have about working with a general contractor to build your home?

   Contractors: You specialize in building customized homes. You are about to meet with prospective owners to begin to negotiate a contract for building their "dream home." What are your objectives for this project? What concerns or issues do you have about working with the owners to build their home?

   Each Owner group meets with another Contractor group and shares their objectives, concerns, and issues.

   Identify what objectives, issues, and concerns you have in common and which ones are unique. Discuss how you could work together to realize your objectives. What would be the keys to working as partners on this project?

2. Enter "outsourcing" in an Internet search engine and browse different websites. Who appears to be interested in outsourcing? What are the advantages of outsourcing? What are the disadvantages? Does outsourcing mean the same thing to different people? What are future trends in outsourcing?

3. Break into four groups and review the instructions for "Get the most you can" exercise provided by your teacher. Complete the exercise. What was your initial strategy? Did it change? If so, why? What does this exercise tell you about our ability to collaborate with each other?

References

Covey, S. R., *The Seven Habits of Highly Effective People* (New York: Simon and Schuster, 1990).

Cowan, C., C. F. Gray, and E. W. Larson, "Project Partnering," *Project Management Journal,* vol. 12, no. 4 (December 1992), pp. 5–15.

DiDonato, L. S., "Contract Disputes: Alternatives for Dispute Resolution (Part 1)," *PM Network,* May 1993, pp. 19–23.

Drexler, J. A., and E. W. Larson, "Partnering: Why Project Owner-Contractor Relationships Change," *Journal of Construction Engineering and Management,* vol. 126, no. 4 (July/August 2000), pp. 293–397.

Dyer, S., *Partner Your Project* (Warwickshire, UK: Pendulum Pub., 1997).

Economy, P., *Business Negotiating Basics* (Burr Ridge, IL: Irwin Professional Publishing, 1994).

Fisher, R., and W. Ury, *Getting to Yes: Negotiating Agreement without Giving In,* 2nd ed. (New York: Penguin Books, 1991).

Hedberg, B., G. Dahlgren, J. Hansson, and N. Olve, *Virtual Organizations and Beyond* (New York: Wiley, 1997).

Hoang, H., and F. T. Rothaermel, "The Effect of General and Partner-Specific Alliance Experience on Joint R&D Project Performance," *Academy of Management Journal,* vol. 48, no. 2 (2005), pp. 332–345.

Kanter, R. M., "Collaborative Advantage: The Art of Alliances," *Harvard Business Review,* July–August 1994, pp. 92–113.

Kezsbom, D. S., D. L. Schilling, and K. A. Edward, *Dynamic Project Management* (New York: Wiley, 1989).

Larson, E. W., "Partnering on Construction Projects: A Study of the Relationship between Partnering Activities and Project Success," *IEEE Transactions in Engineering Management,* vol. 44, no. 2 (May 1997), pp. 188–195.

Larson, E. W., "Project Partnering: Results of a Study of 280 Construction Projects," *Journal of Management Engineering,* vol. 11, no. 2 (March/April 1995), pp. 30–35.

Larson, E. W., and J. A. Drexler, "Barriers to Project Partnering: Report from the Firing Line," *Project Management Journal,* vol. 28, no. 1 (March 1997), pp. 46–52.

Magenau, J. M., and J. K. Pinto, "Power, Influence, and Negotiation in Project Management," in *The Wiley Guide to Managing Projects*, P. W. G. Morris and J. K. Pinto, eds. (New York: Wiley, 2004), pp. 1033–60.

Maurer, I., "How to Build Trust in Inter-organizational Projects: The Impact of Project Staffing and Project Rewards on the Formation of Trust, Knowledge Acquisition, and Product Innovation," *International Journal of Project Management*, vol. 28, no. 7 (2010), pp. 629–37.

Nambisan, S., "Designing Virtual Customer Environments for New Product Development: Toward a Theory," *Academy of Management Review,* vol. 27, no. 3 (2002), pp. 392–413.

Nissen, M. E., "Procurement: Process Overview and Emerging Project Management Techniques," in *The Wiley Guide to Managing Projects*, P. W. G. Morris and J. K. Pinto, eds. (New York: Wiley, 2004), pp. 643–54.

Quinn, R. E., S. R. Faerman, M. P. Thompson, and M. R. McGrath, *Becoming a Master Manager: A Competency Framework* (New York: Wiley, 1990).

Schultzel, H. J., and V. P. Unruh, *Successful Partnering: Fundamentals for Project Owners and Contractors* (New York: Wiley, 1996).

Shell, G. R., *Bargaining for Advantage: Negotiation Strategies for Reasonable People* (New York: Penguin, 2000).

Case 12.1

Shell Case Fabricators

BACKGROUND

Shell Case Fabricators (SCF) designs and builds shell casings that enclose electronic products such as calculators, cell phones, modems. Typically the cases are plastic or plastic compounds. SCF has six different production lines that cover different types of product. For example, the largest high-volume production line for modems can produce three different colors and two models (vertical and flat). Air Connection Links (ACL) is the biggest customer that buys product from this line. This high-output line now runs at full capacity on an eight-hour shift. The other five lines run smaller quantities and tend to meet the needs of other specialty products manufactured by different smaller firms.

Ninety-five percent of SCF's product casings line is designed by the original hardware manufacturer. Getting a casing to the production stage requires a great deal of collaboration and interaction between the original hardware and case design manufacturer (e.g., ACL) and SCF's shell design engineers and production department. The latest new product of ACL is a modem designed to be used for monitoring water activity in bays, e.g., ship traffic, pollution, floating debris. Because of the product's high functionality and low cost, potential demand for the new product is out of sight. It seems every country with small bays used for shipping wants enough underwater modems to cover their respective bays.

THE UNDERWATER MODEM PROJECT

At SCF each new product is assigned a project manager to coordinate and manage the shell design, budgets, and manufacturing startup. Songsee is SCF's star project manager and is the project manager of the shell for the new short-range, underwater acoustical modem. The shell casing for the underwater modem required special design, materials, custom equipment, and a seal to withstand pressure to 50 meters. Air Connection Links, the product owner, needs sixty thousand modems in 91 days (next January 15) for the Estuary Control Institute meeting in Hong Kong.

CLIENT CHANGE REQUEST

Songsee has felt the project was moving along smoothly, with the exception of being two weeks behind schedule. She feels she can "lean on" the design department to put the project on top priority and make up the two weeks. Yesterday, ACL's project manager, Sabin, came in with a "*simple* change." Change the outer shell shape from rectangular to dome shape; it will improve performance 2 percent. Songsee couldn't believe Sabin. He knows better. He knows the engineering implications, and it is NOT simple! Yet Sabin tells Songsee, "It shouldn't cost much." Songsee imagined a sharp retort, but she counted to five and aborted. At this late stage of the game, changes and schedule compression cost big money! Songsee said she would get together with her team and start on a new time and cost estimate today. She told Sabin he would have to give her a written change request of the new requirements by tomorrow. Sabin appeared disappointed. "Why don't we just add €100,000 to the price and get on with it? We have been doing business with SCF for six years. With expected demand out of sight, SCF will break even quickly and have a great profit on the production side." Songsee sighed. "Let's proceed with the change order process. I will bring your request to the change order governance committee."

Songsee's meeting with her team about the change went about as expected. Every department moaned about changing at this late date. The guesstimate cost and time estimates were over triple Sabin's idea of €100,000. For example, designing a new seal for a dome style modem will require a new custom water sealing approach, possibly an untested different sealant, and new molds. Has ACL frozen the design of the new style modem? Songsee asked the team to come in with a more detailed estimate by tomorrow afternoon, before her meeting with the change order governance committee.

THE NEXT DAY (FRIDAY)

Sabin called from ACL at midmorning the next day. "Our senior management is upset that we have to be so formal for such a small change. They just want to get on with the project and meet the time to market launch date. €100,000 seems like a fair price. They believe you need to talk to your management. They want a response by Monday."

The team estimates came close to yesterday's guesstimate (€391,000). Not good news. Songsee knew the answer of the change committee would be to hold for the full amount. She was right. The change committee believed the costs are there and need to be covered to meet the launch date. The committee was also concerned that priorities and resource scheduling would have to change for SCF's design and production departments. In three hours she would meet with senior management to decide to accept the client's request at their price or come up with an alternate plan. Songsee realized she should have several options for senior management to consider, along with a recommendation.

1. Should SCF accept or reject ACL's request? Which option would you select? What risks are involved?
2. How should SCF negotiate with ACL? How can SCF and ACL develop a positive, long-range relationship? Give some specifics.

Case 12.2

The Accounting Software Installation Project

Sitting in her office, Karin Chung is reviewing the past four months of the large corporate accounting software installation project she has been managing. Everything seemed so well planned before the project started. Each company division had a task force that provided input into the proposed installation along with potential problems. All the different divisions had been trained and briefed on exactly how their division would interface and use the forthcoming accounting software. All six contractors, which included one of the Big Four consulting companies, assisted in developing the work breakdown structure—costs, specifications, time.

Karin hired a consultant to conduct a one-day "partnering" workshop attended by the major accounting heads, a member of each task force group, and key representatives from each of the contractors. During the workshop, several different team-building exercises were used to illustrate the importance of collaboration and effective communication. Everyone laughed when Karin fell into an imaginary acid pit during a human bridge-building exercise. The workshop ended on an upbeat note with everyone signing a partnering charter that expressed their commitment to working together as partners to complete the project.

TWO MONTHS LATER

One task force member came to Karin to complain that the contractor dealing with billing would not listen to his concerns about problems that could occur in the Virginia division when billings are consolidated. The contractor had told him, the task force member, he had bigger problems than consolidation of billing in the Virginia division. Karin replied, "You can settle the problem with the contractor. Go to him and explain how serious your problem is and that it will have to be settled before the project is completed."

Later in the week in the lunchroom she overheard one consulting contractor badmouthing the work of another—"never on time, interface coding not tested." In the hallway the same day an accounting department supervisor told her that tests showed the new software will never be compatible with the Georgia division's accounting practices.

While concerned, Karin considered these problems typical of the kind she had encountered on other smaller software projects.

FOUR MONTHS LATER

The project seemed to be falling apart. What happened to the positive attitude fostered at the team-building workshop? One contractor wrote a formal letter complaining that another contractor was sitting on a coding decision that was delaying their work. The letter went on: "We cannot be held responsible or liable for delays caused by others." The project was already two months behind, so problems were becoming very real and serious. Karin finally decided to call a meeting of all parties to the project and partnering agreement.

She began by asking for problems people were encountering while working on the project. Although participants were reluctant to be first for fear of being perceived as a complainer, it was not long before accusations and tempers flared out of control. It was always some group complaining about another group. Several participants complained that others were sitting on decisions that resulted in their work being held up. One consultant said, "It is impossible to tell who's in charge of what." Another participant complained that although the group met separately on small problems, it never met as a total group to assess new risk situations that developed.

Karin felt the meeting had degenerated into an unrecoverable situation. Commitment to the project and partnering appeared to be waning. She quickly decided to stop the meeting and cool things down. She spoke to the project stakeholders: "It is clear that we have some serious problems, and the project is in jeopardy. The project must get back on track, and the backbiting must stop. I want each of us to come to a meeting Friday morning with concrete suggestions of what it will take to get the project back on track and specific actions of how we can make it happen. We need to recognize our mutual interdependence and bring our relationships with each other back to a win/win environment. When we do get things back on track, we need to figure out how to stay on track."

1. Why does this attempt at project partnering appear to be failing?
2. If you were Karin, what would you do to get this project back on track?
3. What action would you take to keep the project on track?

Case 12.3

Buxton Hall

Chad Cromwell, head of university housing, gazed up at the tower at Buxton Hall and smiled as he walked toward the landmark building.

Buxton Hall was built in 1927 as a residential complex for over 350 students at Pacifica State University. At the time Buxton was the tallest building on campus, and its tower had a panoramic view of the athletic fields and coastal range. Buxton quickly became a focal point at Pacifica State. Students perched on the tower dominated the campus during the annual spring water fight with their huge slingshots and catapults. The first intranet on the Pacific coast was created at Buxton that linked students' computers and allowed them to share printers. Around the 1970s, some student artists began the tradition of painting their room doors. Whether a Rolling Stones logo or Bugs Bunny on a skateboard, these colorful doors were an artistic legacy that caught the attention of students and faculty.

Buxton Hall served as a residence hall for the university for many years, but time was not kind to the stately building. Leaks destroyed plaster in the interior. Wiring and plumbing became outdated and so dangerous that the building was deemed unsafe. Buxton Hall's doors were closed to students and windows boarded up at the end of the 1996 spring quarter. For 10 years Buxton sat silent and over time became a symbol of the general decline of Pacifica State. Now thanks to state bonds and generous contributions, Buxton Hall was about to be reopened after a $20 million renovation.

18 MONTHS AGO

Chad and key representatives from university facilities were engaged in the second of a two-day partnering workshop. Also in attendance were managers from Crawford Construction, the chief contractor for the Buxton renovation project, as well as several key subcontractors and architects from the firm of Legacy West. During the first day a consultant ran them through a series of team-building and communication exercises that accentuated the importance of open communication, principle negotiation, and win/win thinking. The second day began with the "project from hell" exercise, with each group describing the worst project they had ever worked on. Chad was surprised that the people from Crawford and Legacy West descriptions were very similar to his own. For example, each group talked about how frustrating it was when changes were made without proper consultation or costs were hidden until it was too late to do anything about them. This was followed by a discussion of the best project they had ever worked on. The consultant then asked the groups which of the two they wanted the Buxton project to be. A genuine sense of common purpose emerged, and everyone became actively engaged in spelling out in specific terms how they wanted to work together. The session concluded with all of the participants signing a partnering charter followed by a picnic and a friendly softball game.

12 MONTHS AGO

Chad was on his way, with Nick Bolas, to meet Dat Nguyen, the Crawford Project Manager, on the third floor at Buxton tower. Dat had contacted him to discuss a problem with the tile work in one of the communal bathrooms. Dat's people had completed the work, but Nick, who was a Pacifica facilities manager, refused to sign off on it claiming that it was not up to spec. After a 24-hour impasse, the Crawford foreman exercised the escalation clause in partnering agreement and passed the issue up to management's level to be resolved. Dat and Chad inspected the work. While both agreed that the job could have been prettier, it did meet specification and Chad told Nick to sign off on it.

Chad met Dat again later in the day at the weekly Buxton status report meeting. The meeting kicked off with a brief review of what had been accomplished during the past week.

Discussion centered on the removal of elm trees. Alternative strategies for dealing with the city inspector, who had a reputation of being a stickler for details, were considered. The project was two weeks behind schedule, which was an important issue since it was imperative that the building be ready for students to move in at the 2008 fall term. The project was also on a very tight budget, and the management reserve had to be carefully administered. Renovation of existing buildings was always a bit of a gamble, since you never knew what you would find once you began tearing down walls. Fortunately, only small amounts of asbestos were found, but rot was much more severe than anticipated.

The meeting included a partnering assessment. The results of a Web survey filled out by all the principals were distributed. The results revealed a dip in the ratings between the Crawford foremen and university officials regarding timely collaboration and effective problem solving. One of Chad's people said that the primary source of frustration was Crawford foremen failing to respond to e-mail and telephone messages. Dat asked for the names of his people and said he would talk to each of them. The Crawford foremen complained that the university officials were being too nit-picky. "We don't have the time or money to do A+ work on everything," argued a foreman. Chad told Dat and his people that he would talk to the facilities guys and ask them to focus on what was really important.

6 MONTHS AGO

The project status report meeting started on time. Crawford had been able to make up for lost time, and it now looked like the building would open on time. Chad was glad to see that the partnering assessment had been positive and steady over the past month. The big issue was the surge in costs consuming all but $50,000 of management reserve. With six months to go everyone knew that this would not cover all the change orders needed to have the building ready. After all, there was already $24,000 worth of change orders pending.

Chad looked across the table and saw nothing but grim faces. Then one of the Crawford foremen proposed postponing treating all of the exterior walls. "Instead of cleaning and preserving the entire brick building, let's only do the front entrance and the North and South walls that the public sees. We can just refurbish the interior court walls as well as the West side. This would be adequate for at least eight years, in which time money should be available to complete the job."

At first Chad didn't like this idea, but eventually he realized that this was the only way they could have the building ready for the students. Friendly arguments broke out over which exterior segments needed the full treatment and which ones didn't. The whole team ended up touring the outside of the building identifying what kind of work needed to be done. In the end, only 70 percent of exterior brick walls were reconditioned according to plan with a savings of over $250,000. While this boost to the reserve would still make things tight, everyone felt that they now had a fighting chance to complete the project on time.

TODAY

As Chad mingled with a glass of champagne, no one talked about the walls that still needed to be refurbished—tonight was a night to celebrate. All of the major participants and their spouses were at the party, and the university was hosting a five-course meal at the top of the tower. During the toasts, jokes were exchanged and stories told about the ghosts in the west wing and the discovery of a dead skunk in the south basement. Everyone talked about how proud they felt about bringing back to life the grand old building. More than one person mentioned that this was much more satisfying than tearing down an old relic and constructing a new building. The president of the university concluded the festivities by thanking everyone for their hard work and proclaiming that Buxton would become a bright, shining icon for Pacifica State.

1. How successful was this project?
2. What best practices were evident in the case? How did they contribute to project objectives?

Case 12.4

Goldrush Electronics Negotiation Exercise

OBJECTIVE

The purpose of this case is to provide you with an opportunity to practice negotiations.

PROCEDURE

STEP 1

The class is divided into four groups, each comprising the project management group for one of four projects at Goldrush Electronics.

STEP 2

Read the Goldrush Electronics "Background Information" section given below. Then read the instructions for the project you represent. Soon you will meet with the management of the other projects to exchange personnel. Plan how you want to conduct those meetings.

BACKGROUND INFORMATION

Goldrush Electronics (GE) produces a range of electronic products. GE has a strong commitment to project management. GE operates as a projectized organization with each project organized as a fully dedicated team. The compensation system is based on a 40 + 30 + 30 formula. Forty percent is based on your base salary, 30 percent on your project performance, and 30 percent on overall performance of the firm.

Four new product development projects have been authorized. They are code named: Alpha, Beta, Theta, and Zeta. The preliminary assignment of personnel is listed below. You are assigned to represent the management of one of these projects.

The policy at GE is that once preliminary assignments are made, project managers are free to exchange personnel as long as both parties agree to the transaction. You will have the opportunity to adjust your team by negotiating with other project managers.

Alpha Project		
Software Engineer	**Hardware Engineer**	**Design Engineer**
Jill	Cameron	Mitch
John	Chandra	Marsha

Beta Project		
Software Engineer	**Hardware Engineer**	**Design Engineer**
Jake	Casey	Mike
Jennifer	Craig	Maria

Theta Project		
Software Engineer	**Hardware Engineer**	**Design Engineer**
Jack	Chuck	Monika
Johan	Cheryl	Mark

Zeta Project		
Software Engineer	**Hardware Engineer**	**Design Engineer**
Jeff	Carlos	Max
Juwoo	Chad	Maile

Personnel may be traded for one or more other personnel.

STEP 3

Meet and negotiate with the other project managers.

STEP 4

Individual project scores are totaled and posted.

STEP 5

DISCUSSION QUESTIONS

1. What was your initial strategy before starting the actual negotiations? How did you view the other groups?
2. Did your initial strategy change once negotiations began? If so, how and why?
3. What could top management at GE have done to make it easier to reach agreement with the other groups?

Appendix 12.1

Contract Management

LEARNING OBJECTIVES

After reading this appendix you should be able to:

LO A12-1 Describe the procurement management process.

LO A12-2 Describe the differences between Fixed-Price and Cost-Plus Contracts and their advantages and disadvantages.

LO A12-1

Describe the procurement management process.

Since most outsourced work on projects is contractual in nature, this appendix discusses the different kinds of contracts that are used, their strengths and weaknesses, and how contracts shape the motives and expectations of different participants. Contract management is a key element of any project procurement management system. It is beyond the scope of this book to describe this system. However, the basic processes are listed here to put contract management and related topics like Request for Proposal (RFP) (see Appendix 12.1) in perspective. Six main steps comprise procurement management:

- **Planning purchases and acquisitions** involves determining what to procure, when, and how. This entails the classic build-versus-buy analysis as well as determination of the type of contract to use.
- **Planning contracting** involves describing the requirements for products or services desired from outsourcing and identifying potential suppliers or sellers. Outputs include procurement documents such as a RFP as well as selection criteria.
- **Requesting seller responses** involves obtaining information, quotes, bids, or proposals from sellers and providers. The main outputs of this process include a qualified sellers list and specific proposals.
- **Selecting sellers** involves choosing from potential suppliers through a process of evaluating potential providers and negotiating a contract.
- **Administering the contract** involves managing the relationship with the selected seller or provider.
- **Closing the contract** involves completion and settlement of the contract.

Most companies have purchasing departments that specialize in procurement. Often purchasing agents will be assigned to project teams and they work with other team members to come up with optimum solutions for the project. Even if project teams are not directly involved in contract negotiations and the decision to outsource project work, it is important that the team understand the procurement process and the nature of different kinds of contracts.

CONTRACTS

LO A12-2

Describe the differences between Fixed-Price and Cost-Plus Contracts and their advantages and disadvantages.

A contract is a formal agreement between two parties wherein one party (the contractor) obligates itself to perform a service and the other party (the client) obligates itself to do something in return, usually in the form of a payment to the contractor. For example, an insurance firm contracted with a consulting firm to reprogram segments of their information system to conform to Windows 10.

A contract is more than just an agreement between parties. A contract is a codification of the private law, which governs the relationship between the parties to it. It defines the responsibilities, spells out the conditions of its operations, defines the rights of the parties in relationship to each other, and grants remedies to a party if the other party breaches its obligations. A contract attempts to spell out in specific terms the transactional obligations of the parties involved as well as contingencies associated with the execution of the contract. An ambiguous or inconsistent contract is difficult to understand and enforce.

There are essentially two different kinds of contracts. The first is the "fixed-price" contract in which a price is agreed upon in advance and remains fixed as long as there are no changes to scope or provisions of the agreement. The second is a "cost-plus" contract in which the contractor is reimbursed for all or some of the expenses incurred during the performance of the contract. Unlike the fixed-price contract, the final price is not known until the project is completed. Within these two types of contracts, several variations exist.

FIXED-PRICE CONTRACTS

Under a fixed-price (FP) or lump-sum agreement, the contractor agrees to perform all work specified in the contract at a fixed price. Clients are able to get a minimum price by putting out the contract to competitive bid. Advertising an invitation for bid (IFB) that lists customer requirements usually results in low bids. Prospective contractors can obtain IFB notices through various channels. In the case of large business organizations and government agencies, potential contractors can request to be included on the bidder's list in the area of interest. In other cases, IFBs can be found by scanning appropriate industry media such as newspapers, trade journals, and websites. In many cases, the owner can put restrictions on potential bidders, such as requiring that they be ISO 9000 certified.

With fixed-price contract bids, the contractor has to be very careful in estimating target cost and completion schedule because once agreed upon, the price cannot be adjusted. If contractors overestimate the target cost in the bidding stage, they may lose the contract to a lower-priced competitor; if the estimate is too low, they may win the job but make little or no profit.

Fixed-price contracts are preferred by both owners and contractors when the scope of the project is well defined with predictable costs and low implementation risks. Such might be the case for producing parts or components to specifications, executing training programs, or orchestrating a banquet. With fixed-price contracts, clients do not have to be concerned with project costs and can focus on monitoring work progress and performance specifications. Likewise, contractors prefer fixed-price contracts because the client is less likely to request changes or additions to the contract. Fewer potential changes reduce project uncertainty and allow the contractors to more efficiently manage their resources across multiple projects.

The disadvantage of a fixed-price contract for owners is that it is more difficult and more costly to prepare. To be effective, design specifications need to be spelled out in sufficient detail to leave little doubt as to what is to be achieved. Because the contractor's profit is determined by the difference between the bid and the actual costs, there is some incentive for contractors to use cheaper quality materials, perform marginal workmanship, or extend the completion date to reduce costs. The client can counteract these by stipulating rigid end-item specifications and completion date and by supervising work. In many cases, the client will hire a consultant who is an expert in the field to oversee the contractor's work and protect the client's interest.

The primary disadvantage of a fixed-price contract for contractors is that they run the risk of underestimating. If the project gets into serious trouble, cost overruns may make the project unprofitable, and, in some cases, may lead to bankruptcy. To avoid this, contractors have to invest significant time and money to ensure that their estimates are accurate.

Contracts with long lead times such as construction and production projects may include escalation provisions that protect the contractor against external cost increases in materials, labor rates, or overhead expenses. For example, the price may be tied to an inflation index, so it can be adjusted to sudden increases in labor and material prices, or it may be redetermined as costs become known. A variety of redetermination contracts are used. Some establish a ceiling price for a contract and permit only downward adjustments, others permit upward and downward adjustments; some establish one readjustment period at the end of the project, others use more than one period. Redetermination contracts are appropriate where engineering and design efforts are difficult to estimate or when final price cannot be estimated for lack of accurate cost data.

While, in principle, redetermination contracts are used to make appropriate adjustments in cost uncertainties, they are prone to abuse. A contractor may win an initial low bid contract, initiate the contracted work, and then "discover" that the costs are much higher than expected. The contractor can take advantage of redetermination provisions and a client's ignorance to justify increasing the actual cost of the contract. The contract evolves into a cost-plus contract.

To alleviate some of the disadvantages of a fixed-price contract while maintaining some certainty as to final cost, many fixed-price contracts contain incentive clauses designed to motivate contractors to reduce costs and improve efficiency. For example, a contractor negotiates to perform the work for a target price based on a target cost and a target profit. A maximum price and maximum profit are also established. If the total cost ends up being less than the target cost, the contractor makes a higher profit up to the profit maximum. If there is a cost overrun, the contractor absorbs some of the overrun until a profit floor is reached.

Profit is determined according to a formula based on a cost-sharing ratio (CSR). A CSR of 75/25, for example, indicates that for every dollar spent above target costs, the client pays 75 cents and the contractor pays 25 cents. This provision motivates contractors to keep costs low since they pay 25 cents on every dollar spent above the expected cost and earn 25 cents more on every dollar saved below the expected cost. Fixed-price incentive contracts tend to be used for long-duration projects with fairly predictable cost estimates. The key is being able to negotiate a reasonable target cost estimate. Unscrupulous contractors have been known to take advantage of the ignorance of the client to negotiate an unrealistically high target cost and use performance incentives to achieve excessive profits.

COST-PLUS CONTRACTS

Under a cost-plus contract the contractor is reimbursed for all direct allowable costs (materials, labor, travel) plus an additional fee to cover overhead and profit. This fee is negotiated in advance and usually involves a percentage of the total costs. On small projects this kind of contract comes under the rubric "time and materials contract" in which the client agrees to reimburse the contractor for labor cost and materials. Labor costs are based on an hourly or daily rate, which includes direct and indirect costs as well as profit. The contractor is responsible for documenting labor and materials costs.

Unlike fixed-price contracts, cost-plus contracts put the burden of risk on the client. The contract does not indicate what the project is going to cost until the end of the project. Contractors are supposed to make the best effort to fulfill the specific technical requirements of the contract but cannot be held liable, in spite of their best efforts, if the work is not produced within the estimated cost and time frame. These contracts are often criticized because there is little formal incentive for the contractors to control costs or finish on time because they get paid regardless of the final cost. The major factor motivating contractors to control costs and schedule is the effect overruns have on their reputation and their ability to secure future business.

The inherent weakness of cost-plus contracts has been compensated for by a variety of incentive clauses directed at providing incentives to contractors to control costs, maintain performance, and avoid schedule overruns. Contractors are reimbursed for costs, but instead of the fee being fixed, it is based on an incentive formula and subject

FIGURE A12.1
Contract Type versus Risk

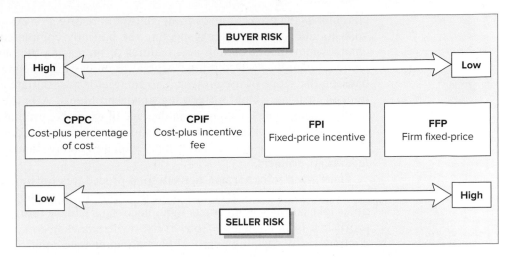

to additional provisions. This is very similar to fixed-price incentive contracts, but instead of being based on a target cost, the fee is based on actual cost, using a cost-sharing formula.

Most contracts are concerned with the negotiated cost of the project. However, given the importance of speed and timing in today's business world, more and more contracts involve clauses concerning completion dates. To some extent schedule incentives provide some cost-control measures because schedule slippage typically but not always involves cost overruns. Schedule incentives/penalties are stipulated depending on the significance of time to completion for the owner. For example, the contract involving the construction of a new baseball stadium is likely to contain stiff penalties if the stadium is not ready for opening day of the season. Conversely, time-constrained projects in which the number one priority is getting the project completed as soon as possible are likely to include attractive incentives for completing the project early.

A good example of this can be seen in Snapshot from Practice 9.2: Responding to the Northridge Earthquake in which the construction firm pulled out all the stops to restore the damaged highway system 74 days ahead of schedule. The firm received a $14.8 million bonus for these efforts!

Figure A12.1 summarizes the spectrum of risk to the buyer and supplier for different kinds of contracts. Buyers have the lowest risk with firm fixed-price contracts because they know exactly what they will need to pay the supplier. Buyers have the most risk with cost-plus percentage of cost contracts because they do not know in advance what the suppliers' costs will be and suppliers may be motivated to increase costs. From the suppliers' perspective, the cost-plus contract offers the least risk and the firm fixed-price contract entails the most risk.

CONTRACT CHANGE CONTROL SYSTEM

A contract change control system defines the process by which the contract may be modified. It includes the paperwork, tracking systems, dispute resolution procedures, and approval levels necessary for authorizing changes. There are a number of reasons a contract may need to be changed. Clients may wish to alter the original design or scope of the project once the project is initiated. This is quite common as the project moves from concept to reality. For example, an owner may wish to add windows after inspecting the partially completed homesite. Market changes may dictate adding new features or increasing the performance requirements of equipment. Declining financial resources may dictate that the owner cut back on the scope of the project. The contractor may initiate changes in the contract in response to unforeseen legitimate problems. A building contractor may need to renegotiate the contract in the face of excessive groundwater or the lack of availability of specified materials. In some cases, external forces may dictate contract changes, such as a need to comply with new safety standards mandated by the federal government.

There need to be formal, agreed-upon procedures for initiating changes in the original contract. Contract change orders are subject to abuse. Contractors sometimes take advantage of owners' ignorance to inflate the costs of changes to recoup profit lost from a low bid. Conversely, owners have been known to "get back" at contractors by delaying approval of contract changes, thus delaying project work and increasing the costs to the contractor. All parties need to agree upon the rules and procedures for initiating and making changes in the original terms of the contract in advance.

CONTRACT MANAGEMENT IN PERSPECTIVE

Contract management is not an exact science. For decades, the federal government has been trying to develop a more effective contract administration system. Despite their best efforts, abuses are repeatedly exposed in the news media. The situation is similar to trying to take a wrinkle out of an Oriental rug. Efforts to eliminate a wrinkle in one part of the rug invariably create a wrinkle in another part. Likewise, each new revision in government procurement procedures appears to generate a new loophole that can be exploited. There is no perfect contract management system. Given the inherent uncertainty involved in most project work, no contract can handle all the issues that emerge. Formal contracts cannot replace or eliminate the need to develop effective working relationships between the parties involved that are based on mutual goals, trust, and cooperation. For this reason, the earlier discussion of best practices in outsourcing and effective negotiating is very important.

APPENDIX REVIEW QUESTIONS

1. What are the fundamental differences between fixed-price and cost-plus contracts?
2. For what kinds of projects would you recommend that a fixed-price contract be used? For what kinds of projects would you recommend that a cost-plus contract be used?

APPENDIX REFERENCES

Angus, R. B., N. A. Gundersen, and T. P. Cullinane, *Planning, Performing, and Controlling Projects* (Upper Saddle River, NJ: Prentice Hall, 2003).

Cavendish, J., and M. Martin, *Negotiating and Contracting for Project Management* (Upper Darby, PA: Project Management Institute, 1982).

Fleming, Q. W., *Project Procurement Management: Contracting, Subcontracting, Teaming* (Tustin, CA: FMC Press, 2003).

Fraser, J., *Professional Project Proposals* (Aldershot, U.K.: Gower/Ashgate, 1995).

Lowe, D., "Contract Management" in *The Wiley Guide to Managing Projects,* P. W. G. Morris and J. K. Pinto, eds. (New York: Wiley, 2004), pp. 678–707.

Schwalbe, K., *Information Technology Project Management,* 4th ed. (Boston: Thomson Course Technology, 2006).

Worthington, M. M., and L. P. Goldsman, *Contracting with the Federal Government,* 4th ed. (New York: Wiley, 1998).

13 Progress and Performance Measurement and Evaluation

LEARNING OBJECTIVES

After reading this chapter you should be able to:

13-1 Identify the four steps for controlling a project.

13-2 Utilize a tracking Gantt to monitor time performance.

13-3 Understand and appreciate the significance of earned value.

13-4 Calculate and interpret cost and schedule variance.

13-5 Calculate and interpret performance and percent indexes.

13-6 Forecast final project cost.

13-7 Identify and manage scope creep.

OUTLINE

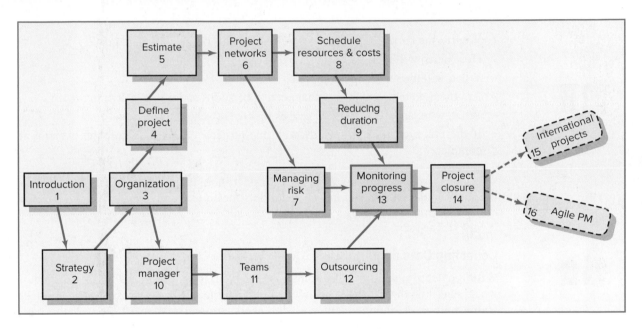

How does a project get one year late?

. . . One day at a time.

—*Frederick P. Brooks,* The Mythical Man Month, *p. 153*

Evaluation and control are part of every project manager's job. Control by "wandering around" and "involvement" can overcome most problems in small projects. But large projects need some form of formal control. Control holds people accountable, prevents small problems from mushrooming into large problems, and keeps focus. Except for accounting controls, project control is not performed well in most organizations. Control is one of the most neglected areas of project management. Unfortunately, it is not uncommon to find resistance to control processes. In essence, those who minimize the importance of control are passing up a great opportunity to be effective managers and, perhaps, allow the organization to gain a competitive edge. Neglecting control in organizations with multiple projects is even more serious. For effective control, the project manager needs a single information system to collect data and report progress on cost, schedule, and specifications. The general structure of such a system is discussed next.

13.1 Structure of a Project Monitoring Information System

A project monitoring system involves *determining what* data to collect; *how, when,* and *who* will collect the data; *analysis* of the data; and *reporting* current progress.

What Data Are Collected?

Data collected are determined by *which* metrics will be used for project control. Typical key data collected are actual activity duration times, resource usage and rates, and actual costs, which are compared against planned times, resources, and budgets. Since a major portion of the monitoring system focuses on cost/schedule concerns, it is crucial to provide the project manager and stakeholders with data to answer questions such as:

- What is the current status of the project in terms of schedule and cost?
- How much will it cost to complete the project?
- When will the project be completed?
- Are there potential problems that need to be addressed now?
- What, who, and where are the causes for cost or schedule overruns?
- If there is a cost overrun midway in the project, can we forecast the overrun at completion?

The performance metrics you need to collect should support answering these questions. Examples of specific metrics and tools for collecting data will be discussed in detail later in this chapter.

Collecting Data and Analysis

With the determination of what data are collected, the next step is to establish who, when, and how the data will be assembled. Will the data be collected by the project team, contractor, independent cost engineers, project manager? Or will the data be derived electronically from some form of surrogate data such as cash flow, machine hours, labor hours, or materials in place? Should the reporting period be one hour, one day, one week, or what? Is there a central repository for the data collected and is someone responsible for its dissemination?

Electronic means of collecting data have vastly improved data assembly, analysis, and dissemination. Numerous software vendors have programs and tools to analyze your customized collected data and present it in a form that facilitates monitoring the project, identifying sources of problems, and updating your plan.

Reports and Reporting

First, who gets the progress reports? We have already suggested that different stakeholders and levels of management need different kinds of project information. Senior management's major interests are usually, "Are we on time and within budget? If not, what corrective action is taking place?" Likewise, an IT manager working on the project is concerned primarily about her deliverable and specific work packages. The reports should be designed for the right audience.

Typically, project progress reports are designed and communicated in written or oral form. A common topic format for progress reports follows:

- Progress since last report
- Current status of project
  1. Schedule
  2. Cost
  3. Scope
- Cumulative trends
- Problems and issues since last report
  1. Actions and resolution of earlier problems
  2. New variances and problems identified
- Corrective action planned

Given the structure of your information system and the nature of its outputs, we can use the system to interface and facilitate the project control process. These interfaces need to be relevant and seamless if control is to be effective.

13.2 The Project Control Process

 13-1

Identify the four steps for controlling a project.

Control is the process of comparing actual performance against plan to identify deviations, evaluate possible alternative courses of actions, and take appropriate corrective action. The project control steps for measuring and evaluating project performance are presented below.

1. Setting a baseline plan.
2. Measuring progress and performance.
3. Comparing plan against actual.
4. Taking action.

Each of the control steps is described in the following paragraphs.

Step 1: Setting a Baseline Plan

The baseline plan provides us with the elements for measuring performance. The baseline is derived from the cost and duration information found in the work breakdown structure (WBS) database and time-sequence data from the network and resource scheduling decisions. From the WBS the project resource schedule is used to time-phase all work, resources, and budgets into a baseline plan. See Chapter 8.

Step 2: Measuring Progress and Performance

Time and budgets are quantitative measures of performance that readily fit into the integrated information system. Qualitative measures such as meeting customer technical specifications and product function are most frequently determined by on-site inspection or actual use. This chapter is limited to quantitative measures of time and budget. Measurement of time performance is relatively easy and obvious. That is, is the critical path early, on schedule, or late; is the slack of near-critical paths decreasing to cause new critical activities? Measuring performance against budget (e.g., money, units in place, labor hours) is more difficult and is *not* simply a case of comparing actual versus budget. Earned value is necessary to provide a realistic estimate of performance against a time-phased budget. **Earned value** (EV) is defined as the budgeted cost of the work performed.

Step 3: Comparing Plan against Actual

Because plans seldom materialize as expected, it becomes imperative to measure deviations from plan to determine if action is necessary. Periodic monitoring and measuring the status of the project allow for comparisons of actual versus expected plans. It is crucial that the timing of status reports be frequent enough to allow for early detection of variations from plan and early correction of causes. Usually status reports should take place every one to four weeks to be useful and allow for proactive correction.

Step 4: Taking Action

If deviations from plans are significant, corrective action will be needed to bring the project back in line with the original or revised plan. In some cases, conditions or scope can change, which, in turn, will require a change in the baseline plan to recognize new information.

The remainder of this chapter describes and illustrates monitoring systems, tools, and components to support managing and controlling projects. Several of the tools you developed in the planning and scheduling chapters now serve as input to your information system for monitoring performance. Monitoring time performance is discussed first, followed by cost performance.

13.3 Monitoring Time Performance

A major goal of progress reporting is to catch any negative variances from plan as early as possible to determine if corrective action is necessary. Fortunately, monitoring schedule performance is relatively easy. The project network schedule, derived from the WBS/OBS, serves as the baseline to compare against actual performance.

Gantt charts (bar charts), control charts, and milestone schedules are the typical tools used for communicating project schedule status. As suggested in Chapter 6, the Gantt chart is the most favored, used, and understandable. This kind of chart is commonly referred to as a tracking Gantt chart. Adding actual and revised time estimates to the Gantt chart gives a quick overview of project status on the report date.

Tracking Gantt Chart

LO 13-2

Utilize a tracking Gantt to monitor time performance.

Figure 13.1 presents a baseline Gantt chart and a **tracking Gantt** chart for a project at the end of period 6. The solid bar below the original schedule bar represents the actual start and finish times for completed activities or any portion of an activity completed (see activities A, B, C, D, and E). For example, the actual start time for activity C is period 2; the actual finish time is period 5; the actual duration is three time units, rather than four scheduled time periods. Activities in process show the actual start time; the extended bar represents the expected remaining duration (see activities D and E). The remaining duration for activities D and E are shown with the hatched bar. Activity F, which has not started, shows a revised estimated actual start (9) and finish time (13).

Note how activities can have durations that differ from the original schedule, as in activities C, D, and E. Either the activity is complete and the actual is known, or new information suggests the estimate of time be revised and reflected in the status report.

FIGURE 13.1
Baseline and Tracking Gantt Charts

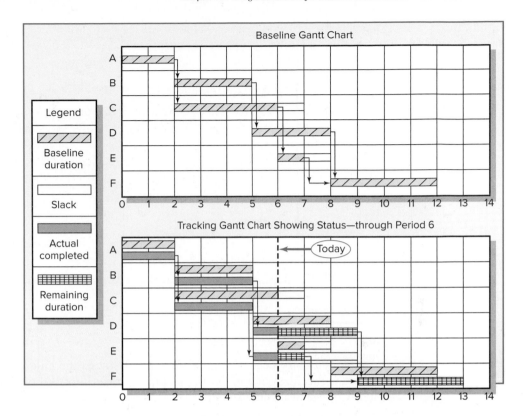

Activity D's revised duration results in an expected delay in the start of activity F. The project is now estimated to be completed one period later than planned. Although sometimes the Gantt chart does not show dependencies, when it is used with a network, the dependencies are easily identified if tracing is needed.

Control Chart

This chart is another tool used to monitor past project schedule performance and current performance and to estimate future schedule trends. Figure 13.2 depicts a project **control chart**. The chart is used to plot the difference between the scheduled time on the critical path at the report date with the actual point on the critical path. Although Figure 13.2 shows the project was behind early in the project, the plot suggests corrective action brought the project back on track. If the trend is sustained, the project will come in ahead of schedule. Because the activity scheduled times represent average durations, four observations trending in one direction indicate there is a very high probability that there is an identifiable cause. The cause should be located and action taken if necessary. Control chart trends are very useful for giving warning of potential problems so appropriate action can be taken if necessary.

Milestone Schedules

Milestone schedules are often used to keep more distal stakeholders informed on the progress of a project. Such stakeholders, whether it is senior management, the owner, or regulatory agencies often neither need or desire a detailed accounting of project progress. Instead, their interests can be satisfied by reporting progress towards major project milestones. Remember from Chapter 4, milestones are significant project

FIGURE 13.2
Project Schedule Control Chart

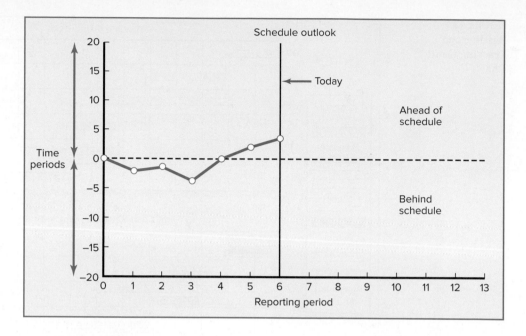

events that mark major accomplishments. Below is the milestone schedule used to keep the president of a university and her cabinet informed on the construction of a new College of Business building.

- Programming: June–August 31, 2014
- Schematic Design: September–January 15, 2012
- Design Development: January–August 31, 2012
- Historic Review: June–October 31, 2012
- Construction Documents: Sept. 2012–January 15, 2013
- 1% For Art Selection: November 2012–May 31, 2013
- Bid and Permit: January–March 31, 2013
- Construction: April 2013–August 31, 2014
- Furnishing Selections: September–November 30, 2013
- Occupancy: September 7, 2014

Project managers recognize the need to use a more macro schedule of significant deliverables to keep external stakeholders informed and a more detailed milestone driven schedule to manage and motivate the project team to achieve those deliverables. For more on the latter, see the Snapshot from Practice 13.1 Guidelines for Setting Milestones.

13.4 Development of an Earned Value Cost/Schedule System

LO 13-3

Understand and appreciate the significance of earned value.

Earned value is not new; the original earned value cost/schedule system was pioneered by the U.S. Department of Defense (DoD) in the 1960s. It is probably safe to say project managers in every major country are using some form of the system. The system is being used on internal projects in the manufacturing, pharmaceutical, and high-tech industries. For example, organizations such as EDS, NCR, Levi Strauss, Tektronics, and Disney have used earned value systems to track projects. The basic framework of the earned value system is withstanding the test of time. Most project management

SNAPSHOT FROM PRACTICE 13.1   Guidelines for Setting Milestones

In medieval times mounds of stones were used to mark distance traveled along a path or road. Travelers would use these rock formations to gauge their progress and adjust their plans. In modern times, milestones are distinct events along the project timeline that are used to gauge progress and adjust plans. Milestones are building blocks for the project's schedule and often create positive momentum to propel the project along to completion. To be effective milestones need to be concrete, specific, measurable events.

Here are some guidelines for setting milestones gleaned from conversations with veteran project managers:

© Erik Larson

Avoid the temptation to overuse milestones as a motivational tool by labeling every task a milestone. Only important deliverables or achievements should be used as milestones.

Timing of milestones is important. Milestones that are placed too far apart will not generate momentum. Conversely, milestones placed too close together quickly lose their distinctiveness. As a rule of thumb, space milestones at intervals no longer than every two weeks for projects of several months in duration.

Critical merge and burst activities are often useful milestones since they indicate significant work has

been or is about to be accomplished. Here it is important to remember that milestones are events not tasks, and the start of a merge activity (i.e., patent application submitted) or the completion of a burst activity (i.e., building permit approved) should be used.

Rates of completion can be used on projects involving repetition and not sequential advancement. For example, on a training project, milestones could be set as percentages of employees fully trained and certified, e.g., 25%, 50%, 75%, and 100%.

Completing a high anxiety, high risk task is always worthy of milestone consideration.

software includes the original framework; many systems have added industry-specific variations to more precisely track progress and costs. This chapter presents the "generic" core of an integrated cost/schedule information system.[1]

The earned value system starts with the time-phased costs that provide the project budget *baseline,* which is called the planned budgeted value of the work scheduled (PV). Given this time-phased baseline, comparisons are made with actual and planned schedule and costs using earned value. The earned value approach provides the missing links not found in conventional cost-budget systems. At any point in time, a status report can be developed for the project.

The earned value cost/schedule system uses several acronyms and equations for analysis. Table 13.1 presents a glossary of these acronyms. You will need this glossary as a reference. In recent years acronyms have been shortened to be more phonetically friendly. This movement is reflected in material from the Project Management Institute, in project management software, and by most practitioners. This text edition follows the recent trend. The acronyms found in brackets represent the older acronyms, which are often found in software programs. To the uninitiated, the terms used in practice appear horrendous and intimidating. However, once a few basic terms are understood, the intimidation index will evaporate.

---

[1] See Fleming and Koppelman (2010) for a more complete earned value description.

TABLE 13.1
Glossary of Terms

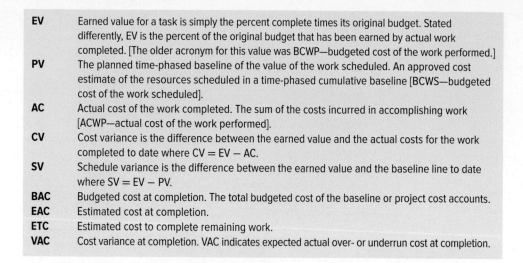

EV	Earned value for a task is simply the percent complete times its original budget. Stated differently, EV is the percent of the original budget that has been earned by actual work completed. [The older acronym for this value was BCWP—budgeted cost of the work performed.]
PV	The planned time-phased baseline of the value of the work scheduled. An approved cost estimate of the resources scheduled in a time-phased cumulative baseline [BCWS—budgeted cost of the work scheduled].
AC	Actual cost of the work completed. The sum of the costs incurred in accomplishing work [ACWP—actual cost of the work performed].
CV	Cost variance is the difference between the earned value and the actual costs for the work completed to date where CV = EV − AC.
SV	Schedule variance is the difference between the earned value and the baseline line to date where SV = EV − PV.
BAC	Budgeted cost at completion. The total budgeted cost of the baseline or project cost accounts.
EAC	Estimated cost at completion.
ETC	Estimated cost to complete remaining work.
VAC	Cost variance at completion. VAC indicates expected actual over- or underrun cost at completion.

Following five careful steps ensures that the cost/schedule system is integrated. These steps are outlined here. Steps 1, 2, and 3 are accomplished in the planning stage. Steps 4 and 5 are sequentially accomplished during the execution stage of the project.

1. Define the work using a WBS. This step involves developing documents that include the following information (see Chapters 4 and 5):
   a. Scope.
   b. Work packages.
   c. Deliverables.
   d. Organization units.
   e. Resources.
   f. Budgets for each work package.
2. Develop work and resource schedule.
   a. Schedule resources to activities (see Chapter 8).
   b. Time-phase work packages into a network.
3. Develop a time-phase budget using work packages included in an activity. The cumulative values of these budgets will become the baseline and will be called the planned budgeted cost of the work scheduled (PV). The sum should equal the budgeted amounts for all the work packages in the cost accounts (see Chapter 8).
4. At the work package level, collect the actual costs for the work performed. These costs will be called the actual cost of the work completed (AC). Collect percent complete and multiply this times the original budget amount for the value of the work actually completed. These values will be called earned value (EV).
5. Compute the **schedule variance** (SV = EV − PV) and **cost variance** (CV = EV − AC). Prepare hierarchical status reports for each level of management—from work package manager to customer or project manager. The reports should also include project rollups by organization unit and deliverables. In addition, actual time performance should be checked against the project network schedule.

Figure 13.3 presents a schematic overview of the integrated information system, which includes the techniques and systems presented in earlier chapters. Those who have tenaciously labored through the early chapters can smile! Steps 1 and 2 are

FIGURE 13.3
Project Management Information System Overview

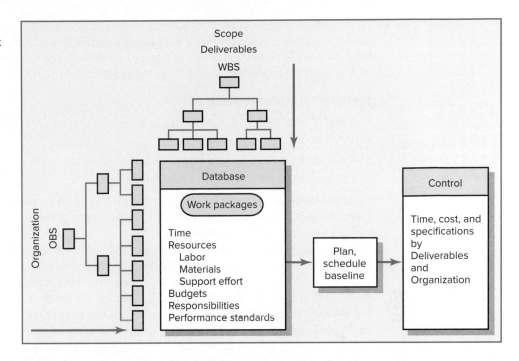

already carefully developed. Observe that control data can be traced backward to specific deliverables and organization unit responsible.

The major reasons for creating a baseline are to monitor and report progress and to estimate cash flow. Therefore, it is crucial to integrate the baseline with the performance measurement system. Costs are placed (time-phased) in the baseline exactly as managers expect them to be "earned." This approach facilitates tracking costs to their point of origin. In practice, the integration is accomplished by using the same rules in assigning costs to the baseline as those used to measure progress using earned value. You may find several rules in practice, but percent complete is the workhorse most commonly used. Someone familiar with each task estimates what percent of the task has been completed or how much of the task remains.

Percent Complete Rule

This rule is the heart of any earned value system. The best method for assigning costs to the baseline under this rule is to establish frequent checkpoints over the duration of the work package and assign completion percentages in dollar terms. For example, units completed could be used to assign baseline costs and later to measure progress. Units might be lines of code, hours, drawings completed, cubic yards of concrete in place, workdays, prototypes complete, etc. This approach to percent complete adds "objectivity" to the subjective observation approaches often used. When measuring percent complete in the monitoring phase of the project, it is common to limit the amount earned to 80 or 90 percent until the work package is 100 percent complete.

What Costs Are Included in Baselines?

The baseline (PV) is the sum of the cost accounts, and each cost account is the sum of the work packages in the cost account. Three direct costs are typically included in baselines—labor, equipment, and materials. The reason: these are direct costs the project manager can control. Overhead costs and profit are typically added later by accounting processes. Most work packages should be discrete, of short time span, and have measurable outputs. If materials and/or equipment are a significant portion of the cost of work packages, they can be budgeted in separate work packages and cost accounts.

Methods of Variance Analysis

LO 13-4

Calculate and interpret cost and schedule variance.

Generally the method for measuring accomplishments centers on two key computations:

1. Comparing earned value with the expected schedule value.
2. Comparing earned value with the actual costs.

These comparisons can be made at the project level or down to the cost account level. Project status can be determined for the latest period, all periods to date, and estimated to the end of the project.

Assessing the current status of a project using the earned value cost/schedule system requires three data elements—planned cost of the work scheduled (PV), budgeted cost of the work completed (EV), and actual cost of the work completed (AC). From these data the schedule variance (SV) and cost variance (CV) are computed each reporting period. *A positive variance indicates a desirable condition, while a negative variance suggests problems or changes that have taken place.*

Cost variance tells us if the work accomplished costs more or less than was planned at any point over the life of the project. If labor and materials have not been separated, cost variance should be reviewed carefully to isolate the cause to either labor or materials—or to both.

Schedule variance presents an overall assessment of *all* work packages in the project scheduled to date. It is important to note schedule variance contains *no* critical path information. Critical and non-critical activities are combined in the calculation. Schedule variance measures progress in dollars rather than time units. Therefore, it is unlikely that any translation of dollars to time will yield accurate information telling if any milestone or critical path is early, on time, or late (even if the project occurs exactly as planned). *The only accurate method for determining the true time progress of the project is to compare the project network schedule against the actual network schedule to measure if the project is on time* (refer to Figure 13.1). However, SV is very useful in assessing the direction all the work in the project is taking—after 20 or more percent of the project has been completed.

Figure 13.4 presents a sample cost/schedule graph with variances identified for a project at the current status report date. Note the graph also focuses on what remains to be accomplished and any favorable or unfavorable trends. The "today" label marks the report date (time period 25) of where the project has been and where it is going. Because our system is hierarchical, graphs of the same form can be developed for different levels of management. In Figure 13.4 the top line represents the actual costs (AC) incurred for the project work to date. The middle line is the baseline (PV) and ends at the scheduled project duration (45). The bottom line is the budgeted value of the work actually completed to date (EV) or the earned value. The dotted line extending the actual costs from the report date to the new estimated completion date represents revised estimates of *expected* actual costs; that is, additional information suggests the costs at completion of the project will differ from what was planned. Note that the project duration has been extended and the **variance at completion (VAC)** is negative (BAC − EAC).

Another interpretation of the graph uses percentages. At the end of period 25, 75 percent of the work was scheduled to be accomplished. At the end of period 25, the

FIGURE 13.4
Cost/Schedule Graph

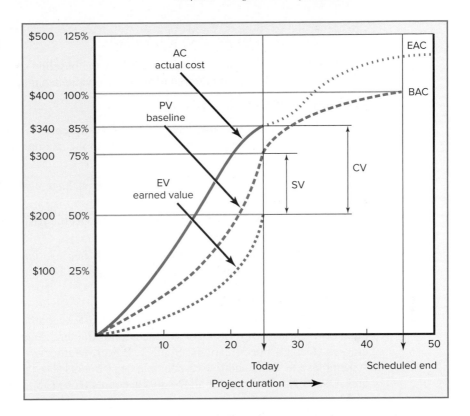

value of the work accomplished is 50 percent. The actual cost of the work completed to date is $340, or 85 percent of the total project budget. The graph suggests the project will have about an 18 percent cost overrun and be five time units late. The current status of the project shows the cost variance (CV) to be over budget by $140 (EV − AC = 200 − 340 = −140). The schedule variance (SV) is negative $100 (EV − PV = 200 − 300 = −100), which suggests the project is behind schedule. Before moving to an example, consult Figure 13.5 to practice interpreting the outcomes of cost/schedule graphs. Remember, PV is your baseline and anchor point.

FIGURE 13.5
Earned-Value Review Exercise

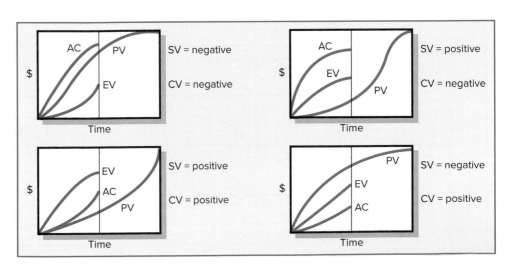

13.5 Developing a Status Report: A Hypothetical Example

Working through an example demonstrates how the baseline serves as the anchor from which the project can be monitored using earned value techniques.

Assumptions

Because the process becomes geometrically complex with the addition of project detail, some simplifying assumptions are made in the example to more easily demonstrate the process:

1. Assume each cost account has only one work package, and each cost account will be represented as an activity on the network.
2. The project network early start times will serve as the basis for assigning the baseline values.
3. From the moment work on an activity task begins, some actual costs will be incurred each period until the activity is completed.

Baseline Development

Figure 13.6 (Work Breakdown Structure with Cost Accounts) depicts a simple work breakdown structure (WBS/OBS) for the Digital Camera example. There are six deliverables (Design Specifications, Shell & Power, Memory/Software, Zoom System, Assemble, and Test), and five responsible departments (Design, Shell, Storage, Zoom, and Assembly). The total for all the cost accounts (CA) is $320,000, which represents

FIGURE 13.6 **Work Breakdown Structure with Cost Accounts**

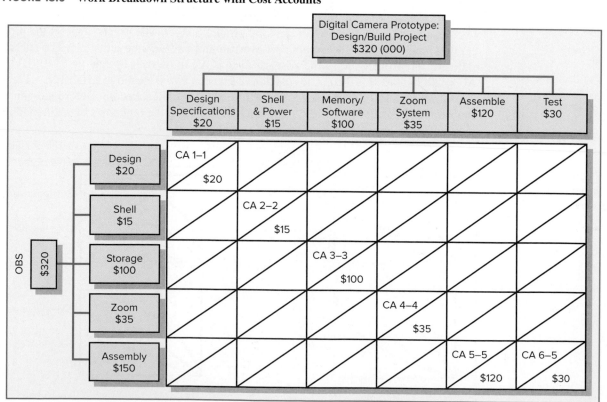

the total project cost. Figure 13.7, derived from the WBS, presents a planning Gantt chart for the Digital Camera project. The planned project duration is 11 time units. This project information is used to time-phase the project budget baseline. Figure 13.8 (Project Baseline Budget) presents a worksheet with an early start baseline developed with costs assigned. They are assigned "exactly" as managers plan to monitor and measure schedule and cost performance.

Development of the Status Report

A status report is analogous to a camera snapshot of a project at a specific point in time. The status report uses earned value to measure schedule and cost performance. Measuring earned value begins at the work package level. Work packages are in one of three conditions on a report date:

1. Not yet started.
2. Finished.
3. In-process or partially complete.

Earned values for the first two conditions present no difficulties. Work packages that are not yet started earn zero percent of the PV (budget). Packages that are completed earn 100 percent of their PV. In-process packages apply the percent complete rule to the PV baseline to measure earned value (EV). In our camera example we will only use the percent complete rule to measure progress.

Table 13.2 presents the completed, separate status reports of the Digital Camera Prototype project for periods 1 through 7. Each period percent complete and actual

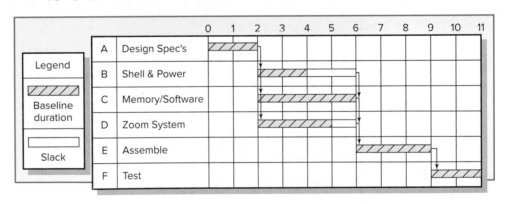

FIGURE 13.7
Digital Camera Prototype Project Baseline Gantt Chart

FIGURE 13.8
Digital Camera Prototype Project Baseline Budget ($000)

ACT/ WP	DUR	ES	LF	SL	Total PV	0	1	2	3	4	5	6	7	8	9	10	11
		Schedule information							Baseline budget needs								
									Time period								
A	2	0	2	0	20	10	10										
B	2	2	6	2	15			5	10								
C	4	2	6	0	100			20	30	30	20						
D	3	2	6	1	35			15	10	10							
E	3	6	9	0	120								30	40	50		
F	2	9	11	0	30											10	20
Total PV by period						10	10	40	50	40	20	30	40	50	10	20	
Cumulative PV by period						10	20	60	110	150	170	200	240	290	300	320	

TABLE 13.2
Digital Camera Prototype Status Reports: Periods 1–7

Cost Variance		$CV = EV - AC$				
Schedule Variance		$SV = EV - PV$				

Status Report: Ending Period 1

Task	%Complete	EV	AC	PV	CV	SV
A	50%	10	10	10	0	0
Cumulative Totals		**10**	**10**	**10**	**0**	**0**

Status Report: Ending Period 2

Task	%Complete	EV	AC	PV	CV	SV
A	Finished	20	30	20	−10	0
Cumulative Totals		**20**	**30**	**20**	**−10**	**0**

Status Report: Ending Period 3

Task	%Complete	EV	AC	PV	CV	SV
A	Finished	20	30	20	−10	0
B	33%	5	10	5	−5	0
C	20%	20	30	20	−10	0
D	60%	21	20	15	+1	+6
Cumulative Totals		**66**	**90**	**60**	**−24**	**+6**

Status Report: Ending Period 4

Task	%Complete	EV	AC	PV	CV	SV
A	Finished	20	30	20	−10	0
B	Finished	15	20	15	−5	0
C	50%	50	70	50	−20	0
D	80%	28	30	25	−2	+3
Comulative Totals		**113**	**150**	**110**	**−37**	**+3**

Status Report: Ending Period 5

Task	%Complete	EV	AC	PV	CV	SV
A	Finished	20	30	20	−10	0
B	Finished	15	20	15	−5	0
C	60%	60	100	80	−40	−20
D	80%	28	50	35	−22	−7
Cumulative Totals		**123**	**200**	**150**	**−77**	**−27**

Status Report: Ending Period 6

Task	%Complete	EV	AC	PV	CV	SV
A	Finished	20	30	20	−10	0
B	Finished	15	20	15	−5	0
C	80%	80	110	100	−30	−20
D	Finished	35	60	35	−25	0
Cumulative Totals		**150**	**220**	**170**	**−70**	**−20**

Status Report: Ending Period 7

Task	%Complete	EV	AC	PV	CV	SV
A	Finished	20	30	20	−10	0
B	Finished	15	20	15	−5	0
C	90%	90	120	100	−30	−10
D	Finished	35	60	35	−25	0
E	0%	0	0	30	0	−30
F	0%	0	0	0	0	0
Cumulative Totals		**160**	**230**	**200**	**−70**	**−40**

cost were gathered for each task from staff in the field. The schedule and cost variance are computed for each task and the project to date. For example, the status in period 1 shows only Task A (Design Specifications) is in process and it is 50 percent complete and actual cost for the task is 10. The planned value at the end of period 1 for Task A is 10 (see Figure 13.8). The cost and schedule variance are both zero, which indicates the project is on budget and schedule. By the end of period 3, Task A is finished. Task B (Shell & Power) is 33 percent complete and AC is 10; Task C is 20 percent complete and AC is 30; and D is 60 percent complete and AC is 20. Again, from Figure 13.8 *at the end of period 3,* we can see that the PV for Task A is 20 (10 + 10 = 20), for Task B is 5, for Task C is 20, and for Task D is 15. At the end of period 3 it is becoming clear the actual cost (AC) is exceeding the value of the work completed (EV). The cost variance (see Table 13.2) for the project at the end of period 3 is negative 24. Schedule variance is positive 6, which suggests the project may be ahead of schedule.

It is important to note that since earned values are computed from costs (or sometimes labor hours or other metrics), the relationship of costs to time is not one-for-one. For example, it is possible to have a negative SV variance when the project is actually ahead on the critical path. This would occur when delays in noncritical activities outweigh progress on the critical path. Therefore, it is important to remember, SV is in dollars and is not an accurate measure of time; however, it is a fairly good indicator of the status of the whole project in terms of being ahead or behind schedule after the project is over 20 percent complete. Only the project network, or tracking Gantt chart, and actual work completed can give an accurate assessment of schedule performance down to the work package level.

By studying the separate status reports for periods 5 through 7, you can see the project will be over budget and behind schedule. By period 7 Tasks A, B, and D are finished, but all are over budget—negative 10, 5, and 25. Task C (Memory/Software) is 90 percent complete. Task E is late and hasn't started because Task C is not yet completed. The result is that, at the end of period 7, the digital camera project is over budget $70,000, with a schedule budget over $40,000.

Figure 13.9 shows the graphed results of all the status reports through period 7. This graph represents the data from Table 13.2. The cumulative actual costs (AC) to

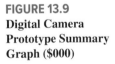

FIGURE 13.9
Digital Camera Prototype Summary Graph ($000)

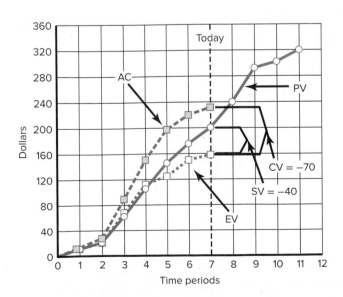

date and the earned value budgeted costs to date (EV) are plotted against the original project baseline (PV). The cumulative AC to date is $230; the cumulative EV to date is $160. Given these cumulative values, the cost variance (CV = EV − AC) is negative $70 (160 − 230 = −70). The schedule variance (SV = EV − PV) is negative $40 (160 − 200 = −40). Again, recall that only the project network or tracking Gantt chart can give an accurate assessment of schedule performance down to the work package level.

A tracking Gantt bar chart for the Digital Camera Prototype is shown in Figure 13.10. From this figure you can see Task C (Memory/Software), which had an original duration of 4 time units, now is expected to require 6 time units. This delay of 2 time units for Task C will also delay Tasks E and F two time units and result in the project being late 2 time periods.

Figure 13.11 shows an oversimplified project rollup at the end of period 7. The rollup is by deliverables and organization units. For example, the Memory/Software deliverable has an SV of $ −10 and a CV of −30. The responsible "Storage" department should have an explanation for these variances. Similarly, the assembly department, which is responsible for the Assemble and Test deliverables, has an SV of $ −30 due to the delay of Task C (see Figure 13.10). Most deliverables look unfavorable on schedule and cost variance.

In more complex projects, the crosstabs of cost accounts by deliverables and organization units can be very revealing and more profound. This example contains the basics for developing a status report, baseline development, and measuring schedule and cost variance. In our example, performance analysis had only one level above the cost account level. Because all data are derived from the detailed database, it is relatively easy to determine progress status at all levels of the work and organization breakdown structures. Fortunately, this same current database can provide additional views of the current status of the project and forecast costs at the completion of the project. Approaches for deriving additional information from the database are presented next.

To the uninitiated, a caveat is in order. In practice budgets may not be expressed in total dollars for an activity. Frequently, budgets are time-phased for materials and labor separately for more effective control over costs. Another common approach used in practice is to use labor hours in place of dollars in the earned value system. Later,

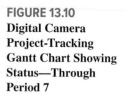

FIGURE 13.10
Digital Camera Project-Tracking Gantt Chart Showing Status—Through Period 7

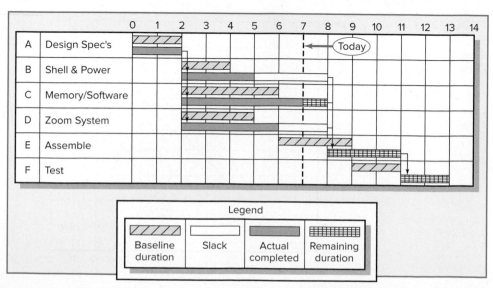

FIGURE 13.11 Project Rollup End Period 7 ($000)

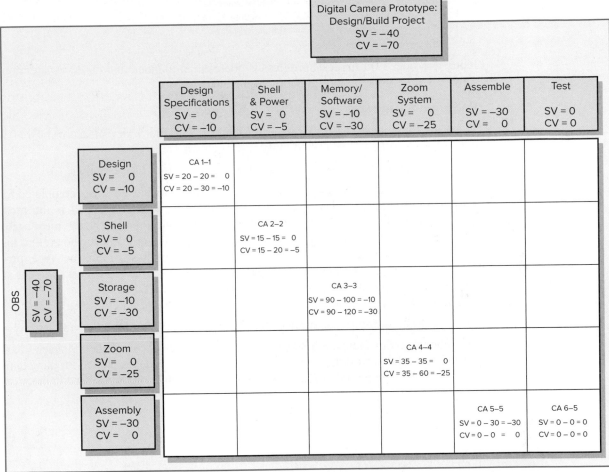

labor hours are converted to dollars. The use of labor hours in the earned value system is the *modus operandi* for most construction work. Labor hours are easy to understand and are often the way many time and cost estimates are developed. Most earned value software easily accommodates the use of labor hours for development of cost estimates.

13.6 Indexes to Monitor Progress

LO 13-5

Calculate and interpret performance and percent indexes.

Practitioners sometimes prefer to use schedule and cost indexes over the absolute values of SV and CV, because indexes can be considered efficiency ratios. Graphed indexes over the project life cycle can be very illuminating and useful. The trends are easily identified for deliverables and the whole project.

Indexes are typically used at the cost account level and above. In practice, the database is also used to develop indexes that allow the project manager and customer to view progress from several angles. An index of 1.00 (100 percent) indicates progress is as planned. An index greater than 1.00 shows progress is better than expected. An

TABLE 13.3
Interpretation of Indexes

Index	Cost (CPI)	Schedule (SPI)
>1.00	Under cost	Ahead of schedule
=1.00	On cost	On schedule
<1.00	Over cost	Behind schedule

index less than 1.00 suggests progress is poorer than planned and deserves attention. Table 13.3 presents the interpretation of the indexes.

Performance Indexes

There are two indexes of performance efficiency. The first index measures *cost* efficiency of the work accomplished to date: (Data from Table 13.2)

$$\text{Cost performance index (CPI)} = EV/AC = 160/230 = .696 \text{ or } .70$$

The CPI of .696 shows that $.70 worth of work planned to date has been completed for each $1.00 actually spent—an unfavorable situation indeed. The CPI is the most accepted and used index. It has been tested over time and found to be the most accurate, reliable, and stable. For example, U.S. government studies have shown that the CPI is stable from the 20 percent completion point regardless of contract type, program, or service. The CPI can provide an "early warning signal" as to cost overruns so that adjustments can be made to the budget or scope of a project.[2]

The second index is a measure of scheduling efficiency to date:

$$\text{Scheduling performance index (SPI)} = EV/PV = 160/200 = .80$$

The schedule index indicates $.80 worth of work has been accomplished for each $1.00 worth of scheduled work to date. Figure 13.12 shows the indexes plotted for our example project through period 7. This figure is another example of graphs used in practice.

FIGURE 13.12
Indexes Periods 1–7

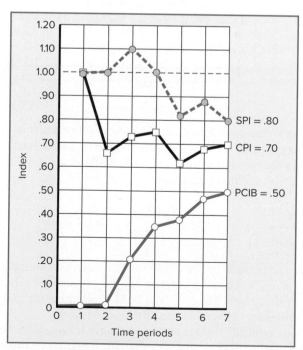

[2] Cited by Q. W. Fleming and J. M. Koppleman, *Earned Value Project Management* (Newton Square, PA: Project Management Institute, 2010), pp. 39–42.

Project Percent Complete Indexes

Two project percent complete indexes are used, depending on your judgment of which one is most representative of your project. The first index assumes the original budget of work complete is the most reliable information to measure project percent complete. The second index assumes the actual costs-to-date and expected cost at completion are the most reliable for measuring project percent complete. These indexes compare the to-date progress to the end of the project. The implications underlying use of these indexes are that conditions will not change, no improvement or action will be taken, and the information in the database is accurate. The first index looks at percent complete in terms of *budget* amounts:

Percent complete index budgeted costs

$$\text{PCIB} = \text{EV/BAC} = 160/320 = .50 \ (50\%)$$

This PCIB indicates the work accomplished represents 50 percent of the total budgeted (BAC) dollars to date. Observe that this calculation does not include actual costs incurred. Because actual dollars spent do not guarantee project progress, this index is favored by many project managers when there is a high level of confidence in the original budget estimates.

The second index views percent complete in terms of *actual* dollars spent to accomplish the work to date and the actual expected dollars for the completed project (EAC). For example, at the end of period 7 the staff re-estimates that the EAC will be 575 instead of 320. The application of this view is written as

Percent complete index actual costs

$$\text{PCIC} = \text{AC/EAC} = 230/575 = .40 \ (40\%)$$

Some managers favor this index because it contains actual and revised estimates that include newer, more complete information.

These two views of percent complete present alternative views of the "real" percent complete. These percents may be quite different as shown above. (Note: The PCIC index was not plotted in Figure 13.12. The new figures for EAC would be derived each period by estimators in the field.)

A third percent index that is popular in the construction industry reflects the amount of Management Reserve that has been absorbed by cost over-runs. Remember Management Reserve are funds set aside to cover unforeseen events (see Chapter 7). Let's assume that $40 was reserved for Digital Camera Project:

Management Reserve index MRI $= \text{CV/MR} = $ The percentage of $140/40 = 3.50$ (350%!)

Clearly this project is in trouble when it comes to cost and changes in either the scope and/or budget are required. Many managers assess cost overruns in terms of Management Reserve rather than simply cost variance since it reflects how much one can afford to spend on the project.

Software for Project Cost/Schedule Systems

Software developers have created sophisticated schedule/cost systems for projects that track and report budget, actual, earned, committed, and index values. These values can be labor hours, materials, and/or dollars. This information supports cost and schedule progress, performance measurements, and cash flow management. Recall from Chapter 5 that budget, actual, and committed dollars usually run in different time frames (see Figure 5.6). A typical computer-generated status report includes the following information outputs:

1. Schedule variance (EV − PV) by cost account and WBS and OBS.
2. Cost variance (EV − AC) by cost account and WBS and OBS.
3. Indexes—total percent complete and performance index.
4. Cumulative actual total cost to date (AC).
5. Expected costs at completion (EAC).
6. Paid and unpaid commitments.

The variety of software packages, with their features and constant updating, is too extensive for inclusion in this text. Software developers and vendors have done a superb job of providing software to meet the information needs of most project managers. Differences among software in the last decade have centered on improving "friendliness" and output that is clear and easy to understand. Anyone who understands the concepts and tools presented in Chapters 4, 5, 6, 8, and 13 should have little trouble understanding the output of any of the popular project management software packages. Appendix 13.2 details how to obtain earned value information from Microsoft Project software.

Additional Earned Value Rules

Although the percent complete rule is the most-used method of assigning budgets to baselines and for cost control, there are additional rules that are very useful for reducing the overhead costs of collecting detailed data on percent complete of individual work packages. (An additional advantage of these rules, of course, is that they remove the often subjective judgments of the contractors or estimators as to how much work has actually been completed.) The first two rules are typically used for short-duration activities and/or small-cost activities. The third rule uses gates before the total budgeted value of an activity can be claimed.

- **0/100 rule.** This rule assumes credit is earned for having performed the work once it is completed. Hence, 100 percent of the budget is earned when the work package is completed. This rule is used for work packages having very short durations.

- **50/50 rule.** This approach allows 50 percent of the value of the work package budget to be earned when it is started and 50 percent to be earned when the package is completed. This rule is popular for work packages of short duration and small total costs.

- **Percent complete with weighted monitoring gates.** This more recent rule uses subjective estimated percent complete in combination with hard, tangible monitoring points. This method works well on long-duration activities that can be broken into short, discrete work packages of no more than one or two report periods. These discrete packages limit the subjective estimated values. For example, assume a long-duration activity with a total budget of $500. The activity is cut into three sequentially discrete packages with monitoring gates representing 30, 50, and 100 percent of the total budget. The earned amount at each monitoring gate cannot exceed $150, $250, and $500. These hard monitoring points serve as a check on overly optimistic estimates.

Notice the only information needed for the first two rules is that the work package has started and the package has been completed. For those who wish to explore the application of these two rules, or who are studying for certification, Appendix 13.1 presents two exercises that apply these rules along with the percent complete rule.

The third rule is frequently used to authorize progress payments to contractors. This rule supports careful tracking and control of payments; it discourages payment to contractors for work not yet completed.

13.7 Forecasting Final Project Cost

LO 13-6

Forecast final project cost.

There are basically two methods used to revise estimates of future project costs. In many cases both methods are used on specific segments of the project. The result is confusion of terms in texts, in software, and among practitioners in the field. We have chosen to note the differences between the methods.

The first method allows experts in the field to change original baseline durations and costs because new information tells them the original estimates are not accurate. We have used EAC_{re} to represent revisions made by experts and practitioners associated with the project. The revisions from project experts are almost always used on smaller projects.

The equation for calculating revised estimated cost at completion (EAC_{re}) is as follows:

$$EAC_{re} = AC + ETC_{re}$$

where EAC_{re} = **revised estimated cost at completion.**

         AC = cumulative actual cost of work completed to date.

         ETC_{re} = revised estimated cost to complete remaining work.

A second method is used in large projects where the original budget is reliable. This method uses the actual costs to date plus an efficiency index (CPI = EV/AC) applied to the remaining project work. When the estimate for completion uses the CPI as the basis for forecasting cost at completion, we use the acronym EAC_f. The equation is presented here.

The equation for this forecasting model (EAC_f) is as follows:

$$EAC_f = ETC + AC$$

$$ETC = \frac{\text{Work remaining}}{CPI} = \frac{BAC - EV}{EV/AC}$$

where EAC_f = **forecasted total cost at completion.**

         ETC = estimated cost to complete remaining work.

         AC = cumulative actual cost of work completed to date.

         CPI = cumulative cost index to date.

         BAC = total budget of the baseline.

         EV = cumulative budgeted cost of work completed to date.

The following information is available from our earlier example; the estimate cost at completion (EAC_f) is computed as follows:

Total baseline budget (BAC) for the project	$320
Cumulative earned value (EV) to date	$160
Cumulative actual cost (AC) to date	$230

$$EAC_f = \frac{320 - 160}{160/230} + 230 = \frac{160}{.7} + 230 = 229 + 230$$

$$EAC_f = 459$$

The final project projected cost forecast is $459,000 versus $320,000 originally planned.

Another popular index is the **To Complete Performance Index** (TCPI), which is useful as a supplement to the estimate at complete (EAC_f) computation. This ratio measures the amount of value each *remaining* dollar in the budget must earn to stay within the budget. The index is computed for the Digital Camera project at the end of period 7.

$$TCPI = \frac{BAC - EV}{BAC - AC} = \frac{320 - 160}{320 - 230} = \frac{160}{90} = 1.78$$

The index of 1.78 indicates that each remaining dollar in the budget must earn $1.78 in value. There is more work to be done than there is budget left. Clearly, it would be tough to increase productivity that much to make budget. The work to be done will have to be reduced or you will have to accept running over budget. If the TCPI is less than 1.00, you should be able to complete the project without using all of the remaining budget. A ratio of less than 1.00 opens the possibility of other opportunities such as improving quality, increasing profit, or expanding scope.

Research data indicate that on large projects that are more than 15 percent complete, the model performs well with an error of less than 10 percent (Fleming and Koppleman, 2010; Christensen, 1998). This model can also be used for WBS and OBS cost accounts that have been used to forecast remaining and total costs. It is important to note that this model assumes conditions will not change, the cost database is reliable, EV and AC are cumulative, and past project progress is representative of future progress. This objective forecast represents a good starting point or benchmark that management can use to compare other forecasts that include other conditions and subjective judgments.

Exhibit 13.1 presents an abridged monthly status report similar to one used by a project organization. The form is used for all projects in their project portfolio. (Note that the schedule variance of −$22,176 does not translate directly to days. The 25 days were derived from the network schedule.)

Another summary report is shown in the Snapshot from Practice 13.2: Trojan Decommissioning Project. Compare the differences in format.

SNAPSHOT FROM PRACTICE 13.2   Trojan Decommissioning Project

Portland General Electric Company has been charged with decommissioning the Trojan Nuclear Plant. This is a long and complex project extending over two decades. The first segment of the project of moving the used reactors to a storage location is complete and was awarded the Project of the Year, 2000, by the Project Management Institute (PMI). The remainder of the project—decontamination of the remaining structures and waste—is ongoing.

Exhibit 13.2 shows their earned value status report. This report measures schedule and cost performance for monitoring the project. The report also serves as a basis for funding for rate filings with the Public Utilities Commission.

© Don Ryan/AP Photo

EXHIBIT 13.1
Monthly Status Report

Project number: 163   **Project manager:** Connor Gage

Project priority now: 4

Status as of: April 1

Earned value figures:

PV	EV	AC	SV	CV	BAC
588,240	566,064	596,800	−22,176	−30,736	1,051,200
EAC	**VAC**	**EAC$_f$**	**CPI**	**PCIB**	**PCIC**
1,090,640	−39,440	1,107,469	.95	.538	.547

Project description: A computer-controlled conveyor belt that will move and position items on the belt with accuracy of less than one millimeter.

Status summary: The project is approximately 25 days behind schedule. The project has a cost variance of ($30,736).

Explanations: The schedule variance has moved from noncritical activities to those on the critical path. Integration first phase, scheduled to start 3/26, is now expected to start 4/19, which means it is approximately 25 days behind schedule. This delay is traced to the loss of the second design team which made it impossible to start utilities documentation on 2/27 as planned. This loss illustrates the effect of losing valuable resources on the project. The cost variance to date is largely due to a design change that cost $21,000.

Major changes since last report: The major change was loss of one design team to the project.

Total cost of approved design changes: $21,000. Most of this amount is attributed to the improved design of the serial I/O drivers.

Projected cost at completion: EAC$_f$ is estimated to be $1,107,469. This represents an overrun of $56,269, given a CPI of .95. The CPI of .95 causes the forecast to be greater than the VAC −$39,440.

Risk watch: Nothing suggests the risk level of any segments has changed.

13.8 Other Control Issues

Technical Performance Measurement

LO 13-7

Identify and manage scope creep.

Measuring technical performance is as important as measuring schedule and cost performance. Although technical performance is often assumed, the opposite can be true. The ramifications of poor technical performance frequently are more profound—something works or it doesn't if technical specifications are not adhered to.

Assessing technical performance of a system, facility, or product is often accomplished by examining the documents found in the scope statement and/or work package documentation. These documents should specify criteria and tolerance limits against which performance can be measured. For example, the technical performance of a software project suffered because the feature of "drag and drop" was deleted in the final product. Conversely, the prototype of an experimental car exceeded the miles per gallon technical specification and, thus, its technical performance. Frequently tests are conducted on different performance dimensions. These tests become an integral part of the project schedule.

It is very difficult to specify how to measure technical performance because it depends on the nature of the project. Suffice it to say, measuring technical performance must be done. Technical performance is frequently where quality control processes are needed and used. Project managers must be creative in finding ways to control this very important area.

EXHIBIT 13.2

Cost/Budget Performance

Portland General Electric Co.-Trojan Nuclear Plant

			Decommissioning Cumulative Costs				Nominal Year Dollars			
			Report Run: 23-Jan-01			Report Number: DECT005			Page:	1 of 1
				Year-to-Date			YTD		CPI	SPI
Description	PV	EV	AC	PV	EV	AC	Variance EV-AC	PV	EV/AC	EV/PV
ISFSI	193,014	182,573	162,579	3,655,677	3,586,411	3,263,995	322,416	3,655,677	1.10	0.98
RVAIR	0	0	0	0	0	399	(399)	0	0.00	0.00
Equip removal—AB/FB	79,083	79,649	73,899	497,197	504,975	308,461	196,514	497,197	1.64	1.02
Equip removal—other	0	0	0	0	(36,822)	519	(37,341)	0	0.00	0.00
Embed piping—AB/FB	3,884	0	2,118	532,275	540,232	515,235	24,997	532,275	1.05	1.01
Embed piping—other	0	0	3,439	175,401	210,875	79,235	131,640	175,401	2.66	1.20
Surface decon—AB/FB	29,935	23,274	21,456	1,266,685	1,293,315	1,171,712	121,603	1,266,665	1.10	1.02
Surface decon—other	2,875	2	11,005	308,085	199,853	251,265	(51,412)	308,085	0.80	0.65
Surface decon—containment	680,502	435,657	474,427	5,271,889	4,950,528	4,823,338	127,190	5,271,889	1.03	0.94
Radwaste disposal	884,873	453,032	(28,675)	10,680,118	8,276,616	10,807,916	(2,531,300)	10,880,118	0.77	0.77
Final survey	58,238	57,985	27,091	780,990	780,990	700,942	80,048	780,990	1.11	1.00
Nonradiological areas	92,837	91,956	58,538	2,471,281	2,376,123	834,643	1,541,480	2,471,281	2.85	0.96
Staffing	714,806	714,509	468,858	9,947,775	9,947,775	8,241,383	1,706,392	9,947,775	1.21	1.00
ISFSI—Long-term ops	85,026	85,028	19,173	2,004,398	2,004,398	337,206	1,667,192	2,004,398	5.94	1.00
Labor loadings	258,289	258,289	240,229	3,216,194	3,216,194	2,755,604	460,590	3,216,194	1.17	1.00
Material loadings	17,910	17,910	(95,128)	211,454	211,454	136,973	74,481	211,454	1.54	1.00
Corporate governance	153,689	228,499	228,521	1,814,523	1,814,523	1,814,520	3	1,814,523	1.00	1.00
Undistributable costs	431,840	401,720	242,724	5,541,679	5,575,879	4,007,732	1,567,947	5,541,679	1.39	1.01
Total decommissioning	3,688,481	3,008,081	1,905,084	48,375,399	45,453,119	40,051,079	5,402,040	48,375,399	1.13	0.94
Total (less ISFSI and RVAIR)	3,493,467	2,845,508	1,743,485	44,719,720	41,886,710	36,788,680	5,080,024	44,719,720	1.14	0.94

The SPI (0.94) suggests the project schedule is falling behind. Resolving issues with a major vendor and solutions for technical problems should solve these delay problems. The CPI (1.14) for the project is positive. Some of this good cost performance is attributed to partnering and incentive arrangements with vendors and labor unions.

Interview with Michael B. Lackey, general manager, Trojan, PGE.

Scope Creep

Large changes in scope are easily identified. It is the "minor refinements" that eventually build to be major scope changes that can cause problems. These small refinements are known in the field as **scope creep.** For example, the customer of a software developer requested small changes in the development of a custom accounting software package. After several minor refinements, it became apparent the changes represented a significant enlargement of the original project scope. The result was an unhappy customer and a development firm that lost money and reputation.

Although scope changes are usually viewed negatively, there are situations when scope changes result in positive rewards. Scope changes can represent significant opportunities.[3] In product development environments, adding a small feature to a product can result in a huge competitive advantage. A small change in the production process may get the product to market one month early or reduce product cost.

Scope creep is common early in projects—especially in new-product development projects. Customer requirements for additional features, new technology, poor design assumptions, etc., all manifest pressures for scope changes. Frequently these changes are small and go unnoticed until time delays or cost overruns are observed. Scope creep affects the organization, project team, and project suppliers. Scope changes alter the organization's cash flow requirements in the form of fewer or additional resources, which may also affect other projects. Frequent changes eventually wear down team motivation and cohesiveness. Clear team goals are altered, become less focused, and cease being the focal point for team action. Starting over again is annoying and demoralizing to the project team because it disrupts project rhythm and lowers productivity. Project suppliers resent frequent changes because they represent higher costs and have the same effect on their team as on the project team.

The key to managing scope creep is change management. One project manager of an architectural firm related that scope creep was the biggest risk his firm faced in projects. The best defense against scope creep is a well-defined scope statement. Poor scope statements are one of the major causes of scope creep.

A second defense against scope creep is stating what the project is not, which can avoid misinterpretations later. (Chapter 7 discusses the process. See Figure 7.9 to review key variables to document in project changes.) First, the original baseline must be well defined and agreed upon with the project customer. Before the project begins, it is imperative that clear procedures be in place for authorizing and documenting scope changes by the customer or project team. If a scope change is necessary, the impact on the baseline should be clearly documented—for example, cost, time, dependencies, specifications, responsibilities, etc. Finally, the scope change must be quickly added to the original baseline to reflect the change in budget and schedule; these changes and their impacts need to be communicated to all project stakeholders.

Baseline Changes

Changes during the life cycle of projects are inevitable and will occur. Some changes can be very beneficial to project outcomes; changes having a negative impact are the ones we wish to avoid. Careful project definition can minimize the need for changes. The price for poor project definition can be changes that result in cost overruns, late schedules, low morale, and loss of control. Change comes from external sources or from within. Externally, for example, the customer may request changes that were not

---

[3] See S. Keifer, "Scope Creep ... Not Necessarily a Bad Thing," *PM Network,* vol. 10, no. 5 (1996), pp. 33–35.

included in the original scope statement and that will require significant changes to the project and thus to the baseline. Or the government may render requirements that were not a part of the original plan and that require a revision of the project scope. Internally, stakeholders may identify unforeseen problems or improvements that change the scope of the project. In rare cases scope changes can come from several sources. For example, the Denver International Airport automatic baggage handling system was an afterthought supported by several project stakeholders that included the Denver city government, consultants, and at least one airline customer. The additional $2 billion in costs were staggering, and the airport opening was delayed 16 months. If this automatic baggage scope change had been in the original plan, costs would have been only a fraction of the overrun costs, and delays would have been reduced significantly. Any changes in scope or the baseline should be recorded by the change management system that was set in place during risk control planning. (See Chapter 7.)

Generally, project managers monitor scope changes very carefully. They should allow scope changes only if it is clear that the project will fail without the change, the project will be improved significantly with the change, or the customer wants it and will pay for it. This statement is an exaggeration, but it sets the tone for approaching baseline changes. The effect of the change on the scope and baseline should be accepted and signed off by the project customer. Figure 13.13 depicts the cost impact of a scope change on the baseline at a point in time—"today." Line A represents a scope change that results in an increase in cost. Line B represents a scope change that decreases cost. Quickly recording scope changes to the baseline keeps the computed earned values valid. Failure to do so results in misleading cost and schedule variances.

Care should be taken to not use baseline changes to disguise poor performance on past or current work. A common signal of this type of baseline change is a constantly revised baseline that seems to match results. Practitioners call this a "rubber baseline" because it stretches to match results. Most changes will not result in serious scope changes and should be absorbed as positive or negative variances. Retroactive changes for work already accomplished should not be allowed. Transfer of money among cost

FIGURE 13.13
Scope Changes to a Baseline

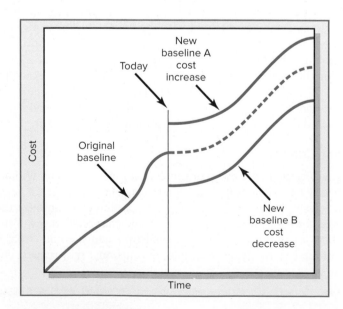

SNAPSHOT FROM PRACTICE 13.3

A Pseudo-Earned Value Percent Complete Approach

A consultant for the U.S. Forest Service suggested the use of earned value to monitor the 50-plus timber sale projects taking place concurrently in the district. As projects were completed, new ones were started. Earned value was tried for approximately nine months. After a nine-month trial, the process was to be reviewed by a task force. The task force concluded the earned value system provided good information for monitoring and forecasting project progress; however, the costs and problems of collecting timely percent complete data were unacceptable because there were no funds available to collect such data.

The level of detail dilemma was discussed, but no suggestions satisfied the problem. The discussion recognized that too little data fail to offer good control, while excessive reporting requires paperwork and people, which are costly. The task force concluded progress and performance could be measured using a

pseudo-version of percent complete while not giving up much accuracy for the total project. This modified approach to percent complete required that very large work packages (about 3 to 5 percent of all work packages in a project) be divided into smaller work packages for closer control and identification of problems sooner. It was decided work packages of about a week's duration would be ideal. The pseudo-version required only a telephone call and "yes/no" answers to one of the following questions to assign percent complete:

Has work on the work package started?	No = 0%
Working on the package?	Yes = 50%
Is the work package completed?	Yes = 100%

Data for the pseudo-earned value percent complete system was collected for all 50-plus projects by an intern working fewer than eight hours each week.

accounts should not be allowed after the work is complete. Unforeseen changes can be handled through the contingency reserve. The project manager typically makes this decision. In some large projects, a partnering "change review team," made up of members of the project and customer teams, makes all decisions on project changes.

The Costs and Problems of Data Acquisition

Data acquisition is time consuming and costly. The Snapshot from Practice 13.3: A Pseudo-Earned Value Percent Complete Approach captures some of the frequent issues surrounding resistance to data collection of percent complete for earned value systems. Similar pseudo-percent complete systems have been used by others. Such pseudo-percent complete approaches appear to work well in multiproject environments that include several small and medium-sized projects. Assuming a one-week reporting period, care needs to be taken to develop work packages with a duration of about one week long so problems are identified quickly. For large projects, there is no substitute for using a percent complete system that depends on data collected through observation at clearly defined monitoring points.

In some cases data exist but are not sent to the stakeholders who need information relating to project progress. Clearly, if the information does not reach the right people in a timely manner, you can expect serious problems. Your communication plan developed in the project planning stage can greatly mitigate this problem by mapping out the flow of information and keeping stakeholders informed on all aspects of project progress and issues. See Figure 13.14 for an internal communication plan for a WiFi Project. The information developed in this chapter contributes significant data to support your communication plan and ensures correct dissemination of the data.

FIGURE 13.14
Conference Center
WiFi Project
Communication Plan

What Information	When?	Mode?	Responsible?	Recipient?
Milestone report	Bimonthly	E-mail	Project office	Senior management
Time/cost report	Weekly	E-mail	Project office	Staff and customer
Risk report	Weekly	E-mail	Project office	Staff and customer
Issues	Weekly	E-mail	Anyone	Staff and customer
Team meeting times	Weekly	Meeting	Project manager	Staff and customer
Outsourcing performance	Bimonthly	Meeting	Project manager	Project office, staff, and customer
Change requests	Anytime	Document	Project manager, customer, design	Project office, staff, and customer
Stage gate decisions	Monthly	Meeting	Project office	Senior management

Summary

The best information system does not result in good control. Control requires the project manager to *use* information to steer the project through rough waters. Control and Gantt charts are useful vehicles for monitoring time performance. The cost/schedule system allows the manager to have a positive influence on cost and schedule in a timely manner. The ability to influence cost decreases with time; therefore, timely reports identifying adverse cost trends can greatly assist the project manager in getting back on budget and schedule. The integrated cost/schedule model provides the project manager and other stakeholders with a snapshot of the current and future status of the project. The benefits of the cost/schedule model are as follows:

1. Measures accomplishments against plan and deliverables.
2. Provides a method for tracking directly to a problem work package and organization unit responsible.
3. Alerts all stakeholders to early identification of problems, and allows for quick, proactive corrective action.
4. Improves communication because all stakeholders are using the same database.
5. Keeps customer informed of progress, and encourages customer confidence that the money spent is resulting in the expected progress.
6. Provides for accountability over individual portions of the overall budget for each organizational unit.

With your information system in place, you need to use your communication plan to keep stakeholders informed so timely decisions can be made to ensure the project is managed effectively.

Key Terms

Control chart, *463*
Cost performance index (CPI), *476*
Cost variance (CV), *466*
Earned value (EV), *462*

Forecasted total cost at completion (EAC$_f$), *479*
Management Reserve Index (MRI), *477*

Percent complete index actual costs (PCIC), *477*
Percent complete index budgeted costs (PCIB), *477*

Revised estimated
cost at completion
(EAC$_{re}$), *479*
Schedule variance
(SV), *466*

Scheduling performance
index (SPI), *476*
Scope creep, *483*
To complete performance
index (TCPI), *480*

Tracking Gantt, *462*
Variance at completion
(VAC), *468*

Review Questions

1. How does a tracking Gantt chart help communicate project progress?
2. How does earned value give a clearer picture of project schedule and cost status than a simple plan versus actual system?
3. Schedule variance (SV) is in dollars and does not directly represent time. Why is it still useful?
4. How would a project manager use the CPI?
5. What are the differences between BAC and EAC?
6. Why is it important for project managers to resist changes to the project baseline? Under what conditions would a project manager make changes to a baseline? When would a project manager not allow changes to a baseline?

Exercises

1. In month 9 the following project information is available: actual cost is $2,000, earned value is $2,100, and planned cost is $2,400. Compute the SV and CV for the project.
2. On day 51 a project has an earned value of $600, an actual cost of $650, and a planned cost of $560. Compute the SV, CV, and CPI for the project. What is your assessment of the project on day 51?
3. Given the project network and baseline information below, complete the form to develop a status report for the project at the end of period 4 and the end of period 8. From the data you have collected and computed for periods 4 and 8, what information are you prepared to tell the customer about the status of the project at the end of period 8?

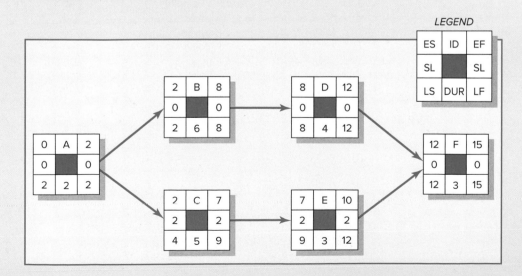

Task	DUR	ES	LF	SL	Budget (PV)	Project baseline (PV) (in $)															
						0	1	2	3	4	5	6	7	8	9	10	11	12	13	14	15
A	2	0	2	0	400	200	200														
B	6	2	8	0	2400			200	600	200	600	200	600								
C	5	2	9	2	1500			200	400	500	100	300									
D	4	8	12	0	1600										400	400	400	400			
E	3	7	12	2	900									300	400	200					
F	3	12	15	0	600														200	100	300
Period PV total						200	200	400	1000	700	700	500	900	800	600	400	400	200	100	300	
Cumulative PV total						200	400	800	1800	2500	3200	3700	4600	5400	6000	6400	6800	7000	7100	7400	

End of Period 4

Task	Actual % Complete	EV	AC	PV	CV	SV
A	Finished	—	300	400	—	—
B	50%	—	1000	800	—	—
C	33%	—	500	600	—	—
D	0%	—	0	—	—	—
E	0%	—	—	—	—	—
Cumulative Totals		—	—	—	—	—

End of Period 8

Task	Actual % Complete	EV	AC	PV	CV	SV
A	Finished	—	300	400	—	—
B	Finished	—	2200	2400	—	—
C	Finished	—	1500	1500	—	—
D	25%	—	300	0	—	—
E	33%	—	300	—	—	—
F	0%	—	0	—	—	—
Cumulative Totals		—	—	—	—	—

4. Given the following project network, baseline, and status information, develop status reports for periods 2, 4, 6, 8 and complete the performance indexes table. Calculate the EAC_f and the VAC_f. Based on your data, what is your assessment of the current status of the project? At completion?

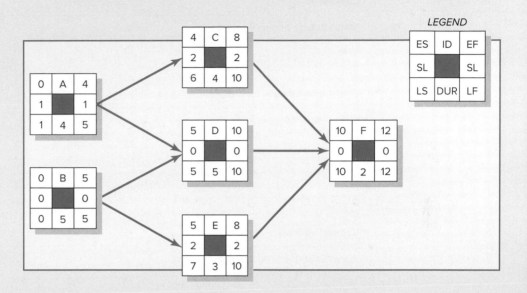

ID	Budget ($000)	0	1	2	3	4	5	6	7	8	9	10	11	12
A	40	10	10	10	10									
B	32	8	4	8	4	8								
C	48					12	12	12	12					
D	18						6	2	2	2	6			
E	28						8	8	12					
F	40												20	20
Total	206	18	14	18	14	20	26	22	26	2	6		20	20
Cumulative		18	32	50	64	84	110	132	158	160	166	186	206	

Status Report: Ending Period 2 ($000)

Task	% Complete	EV	AC	PV	CV	SV
A	75%	—	25	—	—	—
B	50%	—	12	—	—	—
Cumulative Totals		—	**37**	—	—	—

Status Report: Ending Period 4 ($000)

Task	% Complete	EV	AC	PV	CV	SV
A	100%	—	35	—	—	—
B	100%	—	24	—	—	—
Cumulative Totals		—	**59**	—	—	—

Status Report: Ending Period 6 ($000)

Task	% Complete	EV	AC	PV	CV	SV
A	100%	—	35	—	—	—
B	100%	—	24	—	—	—
C	75%	—	24	—	—	—
D	0%	—	0	—	—	—
E	50%	—	10	—	—	—
Cumulative Totals		—	**93**	—	—	—

Status Report: Ending Period 8 ($000)

Task	% Complete	EV	AC	PV	CV	SV
A	100%	—	35	—	—	—
B	100%	—	24	—	—	—
C	100%	—	32	—	—	—
D	33%	—	20	—	—	—
E	100%	—	20	—	—	—
Cumulative Totals		—	**131**	—	—	—

Performance Indexes Summary

Period	EV	AC	PV	SPI	CPI	PCI-B
2	—	—	—	—	—	—
4	—	—	—	—	—	—
6	—	—	—	—	—	—
8	—	—	—	—	—	—

$EAC_f =$ _____ $VAC_f =$ _____

5. Given the following project network, baseline, and status information, develop status reports for periods 1–4 and complete the project summary graph (or a similar one). Report the final SV, CV, CPI, and PCIB. Based on your data, what is your assessment of the current status of the project? At completion?

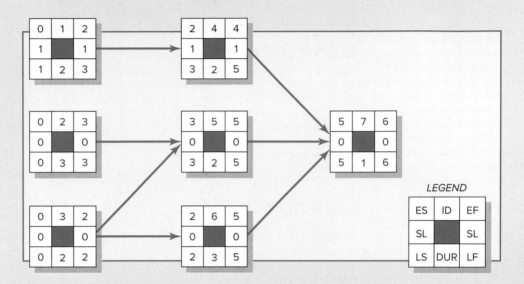

	Schedule information					Baseline budget needs ($ 000)						
ACT/ WP	DUR	ES	LF	SL	Total PV	Time period						
						0	1	2	3	4	5	6
1	2	0	3	1	12	4	8					
2	3	0	3	0	15	3	7	5				
3	2	0	2	0	8	4	4					
4	2	2	5	1	6			3	3			
5	2	3	5	0	10				6	4		
6	3	2	5	0	9			3	3	3		
7	1	5	6	0	5							5
Total PV by period						11	19	11	12	7	5	
Cumulative PV by period						11	30	41	53	60	65	

Status Report: Ending Period 1   ($000)

Task	%Complete	EV	AC	PV	CV	SV
1	50%	—	6	4	—	—
2	40%	—	8	3	—	—
3	25%	—	3	—	—	—
Cumulative Totals		—	**17**	—	—	—

Status Report: Ending Period 2   ($000)

Task	%Complete	EV	AC	PV	CV	SV
1	Finished	—	13	—	—	—
2	80%	—	14	—	—	—
3	75%	—	8	—	—	—
Cumulative Totals		—	**35**	—	—	—

Status Report: Ending Period 3   ($000)

Task	%Complete	EV	AC	PV	CV	SV
1	Finished	12	13	—	—	—
2	80%	—	15	—	—	—
3	Finished	—	10	—	—	—
4	50%	—	4	—	—	—
5	0%	—	0	—	—	—
6	33.3%	—	4	—	—	—
Cumulative Totals		—	—	—	—	—

Status Report: Ending Period 4   ($000)

Task	%Complete	EV	AC	PV	CV	SV
1	Finished	12	13	—	—	—
2	Finished	15	18	—	—	—
3	Finished	—	10	—	—	—
4	Finished	—	8	—	—	—
5	30%	—	3	—	—	—
6	66.7%	—	8	—	—	—
7	0%	—	0	—	—	—
Cumulative Totals		—	—	—	—	—

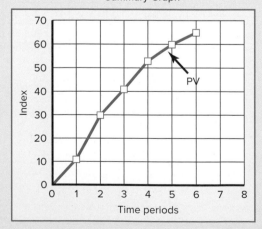

Summary Graph

6. The following labor hours data have been collected for a nanotechnology project for periods 1 through 6. Compute the SV, CV, SPI, and CPI for each period. Plot the EV and the AC on the summary graph provided (or a similar one). Plot the SPI, CPI, and PCIB on the index graph provided (or a similar one). What is your assessment of the project at the end of period 6?

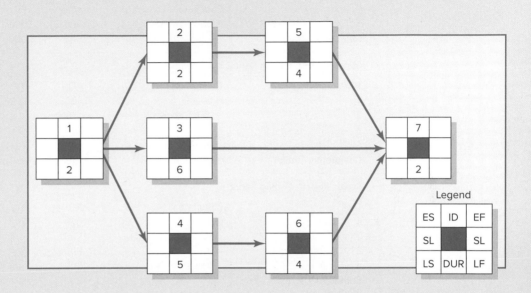

	Schedule information					Baseline budget needs—labor hours (00)														
												Time period								
ACT/ WP	DUR	ES	LF	SL	Total PV	0	1	2	3	4	5	6	7	8	9	10	11	12	13	14
1	2	0	2	0	20	10	10													
2	2	2	7	3	24			16	8											
3	6	2	11	3	30			5	5	10	3	2	5							
4	5	2	7	0	25			10	10	2	2	1								
5	4	4	11	3	16					4	4	4	4							
6	4	7	11	0	20								5	5	6	4				
7	2	11	13	0	10													5	5	
Total PV by period						10	10	31	23	16	9	7	14	5	6	4	5	5		
Cumulative PV by period						10	20	51	74	90	99	106	120	125	131	135	140	145		

Status Report: Ending Period 1

Task	%Complete	EV	AC	PV	CV	SV
1	50%	—	500	1000	—	—
Cumulative Totals		—	**500**	**1000**	—	—

Status Report: Ending Period 2

Task	%Complete	EV	AC	PV	CV	SV
1	Finished	—	1500	2000	—	—
Cumulative Totals		—	**1500**	**2000**	—	—

Status Report: Ending Period 3

Task	%Complete	EV	AC	PV	CV	SV
1	Finished	2000	1500	2000	—	—
2	0%	—	0	—	—	—
3	10%	—	200	—	—	—
4	20%	—	500	—	—	—
Cumulative Totals		—	**2200**	—	—	—

Status Report: Ending Period 4

Task	%Complete	EV	AC	PV	CV	SV
1	Finished	2000	1500	2000	—	—
2	50%	—	1000	—	—	—
3	30%	—	800	—	—	—
4	40%	—	1500	—	—	—
Cumulative Totals		—	**4800**	—	—	—

Status Report: Ending Period 5

Task	%Complete	EV	AC	PV	CV	SV
1	Finished	2000	1500	2000	—	—
2	Finished	—	2000	—	—	—
3	50%	—	800	—	—	—
4	60%	—	1500	—	—	—
5	25%	—	400	—	—	—
Cumulative Totals		—	**6200**	—	—	—

Status Report: Ending Period 6

Task	%Complete	EV	AC	PV	CV	SV
1	Finished	2000	1500	2000	—	—
2	Finished	—	2000	—	—	—
3	80%	—	2100	—	—	—
4	80%	—	1800	—	—	—
5	50%	—	600	—	—	—
Cumulative Totals		—	**8000**	—	—	—

Period	SPI	CPI	PCIB
1	—	—	—
2	—	—	—
3	—	—	—
4	—	—	—
5	—	—	—
6	—	—	—

SPI = EV/PV
CPI = EV/AC
PCIB = EV/BAC

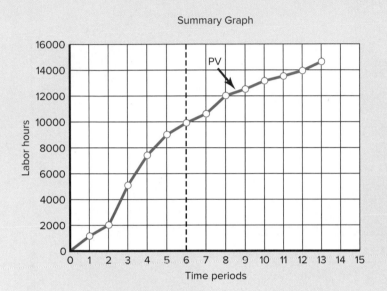

Summary Graph

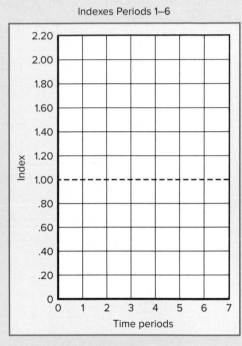

Indexes Periods 1–6

7. The following data have been collected for a British health care IT project for two-week reporting periods 2 through 12. Compute the SV, CV, SPI, and CPI for each period. Plot the EV and the AC on the summary graph provided. Plot the SPI, CPI, and PCIB on the index graph provided. (You may use your own graphs.) What is your assessment of the project at the end of period 12?

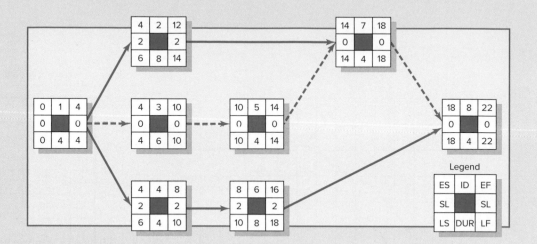

					Baseline (PV) ($00)											
Task	DUR	ES	LF	SL	PV ($00)	0	2	4	6	8	10	12	14	16	18	20	22
1	4	0	4	0	8	4	4										
2	8	4	14	2	40			10	10	10	10						
3	6	4	10	0	30			10	15	5							
4	4	4	10	2	20			10	10								
5	4	10	14	0	40						20	20					
6	8	8	18	2	60					20	20	10	10				
7	4	14	18	0	20								10	10			
8	4	18	22	0	30											20	10
Period PV total						4	4	30	35	35	50	30	20	10	20	10
Cumulative PV total						4	8	38	73	108	158	188	208	218	238	248

Status Report: Ending Period 2 ($00)

Task	%Complete	EV	AC	PV	CV	SV
1	50%	—	4	—	—	—
Cumulative Totals		—	**4**	—	—	—

Status Report: Ending Period 4 ($00)

Task	%Complete	EV	AC	PV	CV	SV
1	Finished	—	10	—	—	—
Cumulative Totals		—	**10**	—	—	—

Status Report: Ending Period 6 ($00)

Task	%Complete	EV	AC	PV	CV	SV
1	Finished	—	10	—	—	—
2	25%	—	15	—	—	—
3	33%	—	12	—	—	—
4	0%	—	0	—	—	—
Cumulative Totals		—	**37**	—	—	—

Status Report: Ending Period 8 ($00)

Task	%Complete	EV	AC	PV	CV	SV
1	Finished	—	10	—	—	—
2	30%	—	20	—	—	—
3	60%	—	25	—	—	—
4	0%	—	0	—	—	—
Cumulative Totals		—	**55**	—	—	—

Status Report: Ending Period 10 ($00)

Task	%Complete	EV	AC	PV	CV	SV
1	Finished	—	10	—	—	—
2	60%	—	30	—	—	—
3	Finished	—	40	—	—	—
4	50%	—	20	—	—	—
5	0%	—	0	—	—	—
6	30%	—	24	—	—	—
Cumulative Totals		—	**124**	—	—	—

Status Report: Ending Period 12 ($00)

Task	%Complete	EV	AC	PV	CV	SV
1	Finished	—	10	—	—	—
2	Finished	—	50	—	—	—
3	Finished	—	40	—	—	—
4	Finished	—	40	—	—	—
5	50%	—	30	—	—	—
6	50%	—	40	—	—	—
Cumulative Totals		—	**210**	—	—	—

Period	SPI	CPI	PCIB
2	—	—	—
4	—	—	—
6	—	—	—
8	—	—	—
10	—	—	—
12	—	—	—

SPI = EV/PV
CPI = EV/AC
PCIB = EV/BAC

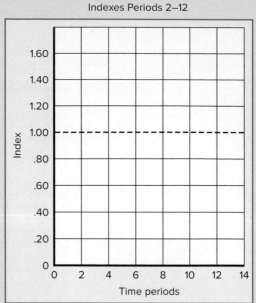

8. *Part A. You are in charge of the Aurora Project. Given the following project network, baseline, and status information, develop status reports for periods 1–8 and complete the performance indexes table. Calculate the EAC_f and VAC_f. Based on your data, what is the current status of the project? At completion?

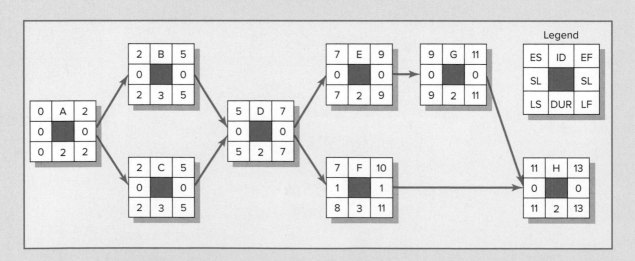

ID	Budget ($000)	0	1	2	3	4	5	6	7	8	9	10	11	12	13
A	100	50	50												
B	250			100	50	100									
C	450			150	150	150									
D	200						100	100							
E	300								200	100					
F	300								100	50	150				
G	200										150	50			
H	200												100	100	
Total	2000	50	50	250	200	250	100	100	300	150	300	50	100	100	
Cumulative		50	100	350	550	800	900	1000	1300	1450	1750	1800	1900	2000	

Status Report: Ending Period 1 ($000)

Task	% Complete	EV	AC	PV	CV	SV
A	25%	—	50	—	—	—
Cumulative Totals		—	**50**	—	—	—

Status Report: Ending Period 2 ($000)

Task	% Complete	EV	AC	PV	CV	SV
A	50%	—	100	—	—	—
Cumulative Totals		—	—	—	—	—

Status Report: Ending Period 3 ($000)

Task	% Complete	EV	AC	PV	CV	SV
A	100%	—	200	—	—	—
B	0%	—	0	—	—	—
C	0%	—	0	—	—	—
Cumulative Totals		—	—	—	—	—

Status Report: Ending Period 4 ($000)

Task	% Complete	EV	AC	PV	CV	SV
A	100%	—	200	—	—	—
B	60%	—	100	—	—	—
C	50%	—	200	—	—	—
Cumulative Totals		—	**500**	—	—	—

Status Report: Ending Period 5 ($000)

Task	% Complete	EV	AC	PV	CV	SV
A	100%	—	200	—	—	—
B	100%	—	200	—	—	—
C	100%	—	400	—	—	—
Cumulative Totals		—	**800**	—	—	—

Status Report: Ending Period 6 ($000)

Task	% Complete	EV	AC	PV	CV	SV
A	100%	—	200	—	—	—
B	100%	—	200	—	—	—
C	100%	—	400	—	—	—
D	75%	—	100	—	—	—
Cumulative Totals		—	**900**	—	—	—

Status Report: Ending Period 7 ($000)

Task	% Complete	EV	AC	PV	CV	SV
A	100%	—	200	—	—	—
B	100%	—	200	—	—	—
C	100%	—	400	—	—	—
D	100%	—	150	—	—	—
E	20%	—	100	—	—	—
F	5%	—	50	—	—	—
Cumulative Totals		—	**1100**	—	—	—

Status Report: Ending Period 8 ($000)

Task	% Complete	EV	AC	PV	CV	SV
A	100%	—	200	—	—	—
B	100%	—	200	—	—	—
C	100%	—	400	—	—	—
D	100%	—	150	—	—	—
E	100%	—	350	—	—	—
F	10%	—	100	—	—	—
Cumulative Totals		—	**1400**	—	—	—

Performance Indexes Summary

Period	EV	AC	PV	SPI	CPI	PCI-B
1	—	—	—	—	—	—
2	—	—	—	—	—	—
3	—	—	—	—	—	—
4	—	—	—	—	—	—
5	—	—	—	—	—	—
6	—	—	—	—	—	—
7	—	—	—	—	—	—
8	—	—	—	—	—	—

$EAC_f =$ _____ $VAC_f =$ _____

Part B. You have met with your Aurora project team and they have provided you with the following revised estimates for the remainder of the project:

- Activity F will be completed at the end of period 12 at a total cost of 500.
- Activity G will be completed at the end of period 10 at a total cost of 150.
- Activity H will be completed at the end of period 14 at a total cost of 200.

Calculate the EAC_{re} and VAC_{re}. Based on the revised estimates, what is the expected status of the project in terms of cost and schedule? Between the VAC_f and the VAC_{re}, which one would you have the greatest confidence in?

EAC_{re} = _____ VAC_{re} = _____

References

Abramovici, A., "Controlling Scope Creep," *PM Network,* vol. 14, no. 1 (January 2000), pp. 44–48.

Anbari, F. T., "Earned Value Project Management Method and Extensions," *Project Management Journal,* vol. 34, no. 4 (December 2003), pp. 12–22.

Bowles, M. "Keeping Score," *PMNetwork,* May 2011, pp. 50–59.

Brandon, D. M., Jr., "Implementing Earned Value Easily and Effectively," *Project Management Journal,* vol. 29, no. 3 (June 1998), pp. 11–17.

Christensen, D. S., "The Cost and Benefits of the Earned Value Management Process," *Acquisition Review Quarterly,* vol. 5 (1998), pp. 373–86.

Christensen, D. S., and S. Heise, "Cost Performance Index Stability," *National Contract Management Association Journal,* vol. 25 (1993), pp. 7–15.

Fleming, Q., and Joel M. Koppelman, *Earned Value Project Management,* 4th ed. (Newton Square, PA: Project Management Institute, 2010).

Kerzner, H., "Strategic Planning for a Project Office," *Project Management Journal,* vol. 34, no. 2 (June 2003), pp. 13–25.

Kim, E. H., W. G. Wells, and M. R. Duffey, "A Model for Effective Implementation of Earned Value Methodology," *International Journal of Project Management,* vol. 21, no. 5 (2003), pp. 375–82.

Naeni, L., S. Shadrokh, and A. Salehipour, "A Fuzzy Approach to the Earned Value Management," *International Journal of Project Management,* vol. 9, no. 6 (2011), pp. 764–72.

Webb, A., *Using Earned Value: A Project Manager's Guide* (Aldershot, UK: Gower Publishing Co., 2003).

Case 13.1

Tree Trimming Project

Wil Fence is a large timber and Christmas tree farmer who is attending a project management class in the spring, his off season. When the class topic came to earned value, he was perplexed. Isn't he using EV?

Each summer Wil hires crews to shear fields of Christmas trees for the coming Holiday season. Shearing entails having a worker use a large machete to shear the branches of the tree into a nice, cone-shaped tree.

Wil describes his business as follows:

A. I count the number of Douglas Fir Christmas trees in the field (24,000).
B. Next, I agree on a contract lump sum for shearing with a crew boss for the whole field ($30,000).
C. When partial payment for work completed arrives (5 days later), I count or estimate the actual number sheared (6,000 trees). I take the actual as a percent of the total to be sheared, multiply the percent complete by total contract amount for the partial payment [(6,000/$30,000 = 25%), (.25 × $30,000 = $7500)].

1. Is Wil over, on, or below cost and schedule? Is Wil using earned value?
2. How can Wil set up a scheduling variance?

Case 13.2

Shoreline Stadium Status Report Case

You are an assistant to Percival Young, president of G&L Construction. He has asked you to prepare a brief report on the status of the Shoreline Stadium project.

Shoreline stadium is a 47,000-seat professional baseball stadium. Construction started on April 3, 2018, and the stadium is schedule to be completed on March 25, 2020. The project is estimated to cost $310,000,000. There is a $35 million management reserve to deal with unexpected problems and delays.

The stadium must be ready for the 2020 major league season. G&L would accrue a $250,000 per day penalty for not meeting the April 3, 2020 deadline.

G&L expects to make more than $3 million on the project. The stadium is one of several major projects G&L has under way in North America, including a professional soccer stadium and another baseball stadium, which broke ground last month.

It is 8/8/2019 the day after the key milestone "Start Installing Seats" was to occur.

Tables C13.1 and C13.2 contain information submitted by your counterpart at the Shoreline site from which you are to prepare your report. Use the appropriate indexes/information to prepare a report informing Mr. Young on the overall status of the Shoreline project in terms of costs and schedule. Note: Mr. Young is not interested in specifics, but just how well the overall project is doing and if there is a need to take corrective action.

TABLE C13.1 Shoreline Project Earned Value Table as of 8/7/2019

	PV	EV	AC	CV	SV
Baseball Stadium	209,000,000	200,600,000	210,500,000	−9,900,000	−8,400,000
Clear stadium site	10,000,000	10,000,000	9,000,000	1,000,000	0
Demolish building	2,000,000	2,000,000	2,000,000	0	0
Set up construction site	2,000,000	2,000,000	1,500,000	500,000	0
Drive support piling	40,000,000	40,000,000	41,000,000	−1,000,000	0
Pour lower concrete bowl	50,000,000	50,000,000	55,000,000	−5,000,000	0
Pour main concourse	15,000,000	15,000,000	18,000,000	−3,000,000	0
Install playing field	5,000,000	5,000,000	5,000,000	0	0
Construct upper steel bowl	60,000,000	51,600,000	55,000,000	−3,400,000	−8,400,000
Install seats	10,000,000				
Build luxury boxes	25,000,000				
Install jumbotron	2,000,000				
Stadium infrastructure	22,000,000				
Construct steel canopy	20,000,000				
Light installation	5,000,000				
Build roof supports	10,000,000	10,000,000	10,000,000	0	0
Construct roof	15,000,000	15,000,000	14,000,000	1,000,000	0
Install roof tracks	10,000,000				
Install roof	5,000,000				
Inspection	2,000,000				

	BAC	EACf	VAC
Shoreline Stadium	310,000,000	325,299,103	−15,299,103

TABLE C13.2 Variance Table for Shoreline Project as of 8/7/2019

Task Name	Start	Finish	Baseline Start	Baseline Finish	Start Var.	Finish Var.
Greendale Stadium Project	**Mon 7/3/17**	**Thu 4/8/21**	**Mon 7/3/17**	**Thu 3/25/21**	**0 days**	**10 days**
Clear Stadium Site	Mon 7/3/17	Tue 10/10/17	Mon 7/3/17	Tue 10/10/17	0 days	0 days
Demolish Building	Wed 10/11/17	Tue 11/21/17	Wed 10/11/17	Tue 11/21/17	0 days	0 days
Set up Construction Site	Wed 11/22/17	Fri 2/23/18	Wed 11/22/17	Tue 3/6/18	0 days	−7 days
Drive Support Pilings	Mon 2/26/18	Wed 8/22/18	Wed 3/7/18	Thu 8/23/18	−7 days	−1 day
Pour Lower Concrete Bowl	Thu 8/23/18	Thu 2/21/19	Fri 8/24/18	Fri 2/15/19	−1 day	4 days
Pour Main Concourse	Fri 2/22/19	Fri 8/2/19	Mon 2/18/19	Tue 8/6/19	4 days	−2 days
Install Playing Field	Fri 2/22/19	Fri 6/28/19	Mon 2/18/19	Mon 6/24/19	4 days	4 days
Construct Upper Steel Bowl	Fri 2/22/19	Tue 8/20/19	Mon 2/18/19	Tue 8/6/19	4 days	10 days
Install Seats	Wed 8/21/19	Wed 3/11/20	Wed 8/7/19	Wed 2/26/20	10 days	10 days
Build Luxury Boxes	Wed 8/21/19	Mon 12/30/19	Wed 8/7/19	Thu 12/12/19	10 days	10 days
Install Jumbotron	Wed 8/21/19	Wed 10/2/19	Wed 8/7/19	Wed 9/18/19	10 days	10 days
Stadium Infrastructure	Wed 8/21/19	Wed 2/12/20	Wed 8/7/19	Wed 1/29/20	10 days	10 days
Construct Steel Canopy	Thu 3/12/20	Thu 6/25/20	Thu 2/27/20	Thu 6/11/20	10 days	10 days
Light Installation	Thu 3/12/20	Wed 4/22/20	Thu 2/27/20	Wed 4/8/20	10 days	10 days
Build Roof Supports	Mon 2/26/18	Mon 7/2/18	Wed 3/7/18	Thu 7/12/18	−7 days	−7 days
Construct Roof	Tue 7/3/18	Tue 4/14/20	Fri 7/13/18	Thu 4/23/20	−7 days	−7 days
Install Roof Tracks	Fri 6/26/20	Mon 11/2/20	Fri 6/12/20	Mon 10/19/20	10 days	10 days
Install Roof	Tue 11/3/20	Thu 3/11/21	Tue 10/20/20	Thu 2/25/21	10 days	10 days
Inspection	Fri 3/12/21	Thu 4/8/21	Fri 2/26/21	Thu 3/25/21	10 days	10 days

Case 13.3

Scanner Project

You have been serving as Electroscan's project manager and are now well along in the project. Develop a narrative status report for the board of directors of the chain store that discusses the status of the project to date (see Table C13.3) and at completion. Be as specific as you can using numbers given and those you might develop. Remember, your audience is not familiar with the jargon used by project managers and computer software personnel; therefore, some explanation may be necessary. Your report will be evaluated on your detailed use of the data, your total perspective of the current status and future status of the project, and your recommended changes (if any).

TABLE C13.3

Electroscan, Inc. 555 Acorn Street, Suite 5 Boston, Massachusetts			29 In-store Scanner Project (thousands of dollars) Actual Progress as of January 1					
Name	PV	EV	AC	SV	CV	BAC	EAC_f	
Scanner project	420	395	476	−25	−81	915	1103	
H 1.0 Hardware	92	88	72	−4	16	260	213	
H 1.1 Hardware specifications (DS)	20	20	15	0	5	20	15	
H 1.2 Hardware design (DS)	30	30	25	0	5	30	25	
H 1.3 Hardware documentation (DOC)	10	6	5	−4	1	10	8	
H 1.4 Prototypes (PD)	2	2	2	0	0	40	40	
H 1.5 Test prototypes (T)	0	0	0	0	0	30	30	
H 1.6 Order circuit boards (PD)	30	30	25	0	5	30	25	
H 1.7 Preproduction models (PD)	0	0	0	0	0	100	100	
OP 1.0 Operating system	195	150	196	−45	−46	330	431	
OP 1.1 Kernel specifications (DS)	20	20	15	0	5	20	15	
OP 1.2 Drivers	45	55	76	10	−21	70	97	
OP 1.2.1 Disk drivers (DEV)	25	30	45	5	−15	40	60	
OP 1.2.2 I/O drivers (DEV)	20	25	31	5	−6	30	37	
OP 1.3 Code software	130	75	105	−55	−30	240	336	
OP 1.3.1 Code software (C)	30	20	40	−10	−20	100	200	
OP 1.3.2 Document software (DOC)	45	30	25	−15	5	50	42	
OP 1.3.3 Code interfaces (C)	55	25	40	−30	−15	60	96	
OP 1.3.4 Beta test software (T)	0	0	0	0	0	30	30	
U 1.0 Utilities	87	108	148	21	−40	200	274	
U 1.1 Utilities specifications (DS)	20	20	15	0	5	20	15	
U 1.2 Routine utilities (DEV)	20	20	35	0	−15	20	35	
U 1.3 Complex utilities (DEV)	30	60	90	30	−30	100	150	
U 1.4 Utilities documentation (DOC)	17	8	8	−9	0	20	20	
U 1.5 Beta test utilities (T)	0	0	0	0	0	40	40	
S 1.0 System integration	46	49	60	3	−11	125	153	
S 1.1 Architecture decisions (DS)	9	9	7	0	2	10	8	
S 1.2 Integration hard/soft (DEV)	25	30	45	5	−15	50	75	
S 1.3 System hard/software test (T)	0	0	0	0	0	20	20	
S 1.4 Project documentation (DOC)	12	10	8	−2	2	15	12	
S 1.5 Integration acceptance testing (T)	0	0	0	0	0	30	30	

Appendix 13.1

The Application of Additional Earned Value Rules

LEARNING OBJECTIVES

After reading this appendix you should be able to:

LO A13.1-1 Apply pseudo earned value rules to measure progress on a project.

LO A13.1-1

Apply pseudo earned value rules to measure progress on a project.

The following example and exercises are designed to provide practice in applying the following three earned value rules:

- Percent complete rule
- 50/50 rule
- 0/100 rule

See the chapter for an explanation of each of these rules.

Simplifying Assumptions

The same simplifying assumptions used for the chapter example and exercises will also be used here.

1. Assume each cost account has only one work package, and each cost account will be represented as an activity on the network.
2. The project network early start times will serve as the basis for assigning the baseline values.
3. Except when the 0/100 rule or 50/50 rule is used, baseline values will be assigned linearly, unless stated differently. (Note: In practice estimated costs should be applied "exactly" as they are expected to occur so measures of schedule and cost performance are useful and reliable.)
4. For purposes of demonstrating the examples, from the moment work on an activity begins, some actual costs will be incurred each period until the activity is completed.
5. When the 0/100 rule is used, the total cost for the activity is placed in the baseline on the early finish date.
6. When the 50/50 rule is used, 50 percent of the total cost is placed in the baseline on the early start date and 50 percent on the early finish date.

Appendix Exercises

1. Given the information provided for development of a product warranty project for periods 1 through 7, compute the SV, CV, SPI, and CPI for each period. Plot the EV and the AC on the PV graph provided. Explain to the owner your assessment of the project at the end of period 7 and the future expected status of the project at completion. Figure A13.1A presents the project network. Figure A13.1B presents the project baseline noting those activities using the 0/100 (rule 3) and 50/50 (rule 2) rules. For example, activity 1 uses rule 3, the 0/100 rule. Although the early start

time is period 0, the budget is not placed in the time-phased baseline until period 2 when the activity is planned to be finished (EF). This same procedure has been used to assign costs for activities 2 and 7. Activities 2 and 7 use the 50/50 rule. Thus, 50 percent of the budget for each activity is assigned on its respective early start date (time period 2 for activity 2 and period 11 for activity 7) and 50 percent for their respective finish dates. Remember, when assigning earned value as the project is being implemented, if an activity actually starts early or late, the earned values must shift with the actual times. For example, if activity 7 actually starts in period 12 rather than 11, the 50 percent is not earned until period 12.

FIGURE A13.1-1A

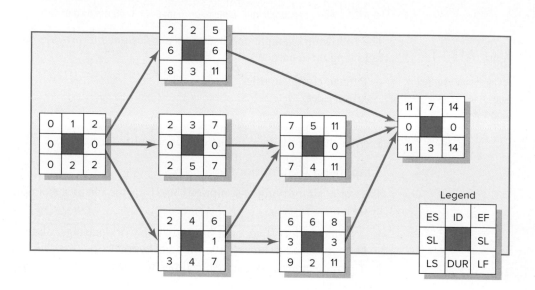

FIGURE A13.1-1B

Schedule information							Baseline budget needs															
EV Rule	ACT/ WP	DUR	ES	LF	SL	Total PV	Time period															
							0	1	2	3	4	5	6	7	8	9	10	11	12	13	14
③	1	2	0	2	0	6		6														
②	2	3	2	11	6	20			10		10											
①	3	5	2	7	0	30			9	6	6	6	3									
①	4	4	2	7	1	20			8	2	5	5										
①	5	4	7	11	0	16								4	4	4	4					
①	6	2	6	11	3	18								9	9							
②	7	3	11	14	0	8													4			4
Total PV by period							0	6	27	8	21	11	12	13	4	4	4	4	0	4		
Cumulative PV by period							0	6	33	41	62	73	85	98	102	106	110	114	114	118		

Rule
1 = %complete
2 = 50/50
3 = 0/100

Status Report: Ending Period 1

Task	%Complete	EV	AC	PV	CV	SV
1	0%	—	3	0	—	——
Cumulative Totals		—	**3**	**0**	—	—

Status Report: Ending Period 2

Task	%Complete	EV	AC	PV	CV	SV
1	Finished	6	5	——	——	——
Cumulative Totals		**6**	**5**	—	—	—

Status Report: Ending Period 3

Task	%Complete	EV	AC	PV	CV	SV
1	Finished	6	5	—	—	—
2	0%	—	5	—	—	—
3	30%	—	7	—	—	—
4	25%	—	5	—	—	—
Cumulative Totals		—	**22**	—	—	—

Status Report: Ending Period 4

Task	%Complete	EV	AC	PV	CV	SV
1	Finished	6	5	—	—	—
2	0%	—	7	—	—	—
3	50%	—	10	—	—	—
4	50%	—	8	—	—	—
Cumulative Totals		—	**30**	—	—	—

Status Report: Ending Period 5

Task	%Complete	EV	AC	PV	CV	SV
1	Finished	6	5	—	—	—
2	50%	—	8	—	—	—
3	60%	—	12	—	—	—
4	70%	—	10	—	—	—
Cumulative Totals		—	**35**	—	—	—

Status Report: Ending Period 6

Task	%Complete	EV	AC	PV	CV	SV
1	Finished	6	5	—	—	—
2	50%	—	10	—	—	—
3	80%	—	16	—	—	—
4	Finished	—	15	—	—	—
Cumulative Totals		—	**46**	—	—	—

Status Report: Ending Period 7

Task	%Complete	EV	AC	PV	CV	SV
1	Finished	6	5	—	—	—
2	Finished	—	14	—	—	—
3	Finished	—	20	—	—	—
4	Finished	—	15	—	—	—
5	0%	—	0	—	—	—
6	50%	—	9	—	—	—
Cumulative Totals		—	**63**	—	—	—

Period	SPI	CPI	PCIB
1	—	—	—
2	—	—	—
3	—	—	—
4	—	—	—
5	—	—	—
6	—	—	—
7	—	—	—

SPI = EV/PV
CPI = EV/AC
PCIB = EV/BAC

FIGURE A13.1-2C

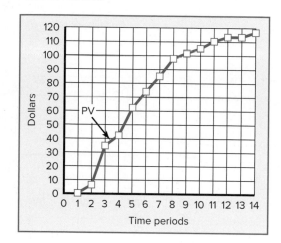

FIGURE A13.1-2D

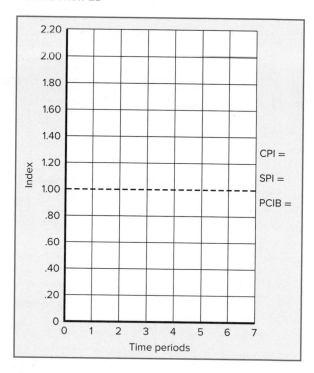

CPI =

SPI =

PCIB =

2. Given the information provided for development of a catalog product return process for periods 1 through 5, assign the PV values (using the rules) to develop a baseline for the project. Compute the SV, CV, SPI, and CPI for each period. Explain to the owner your assessment of the project at the end of period 5 and the future expected status of the project at the completion.

FIGURE A13.1-2A

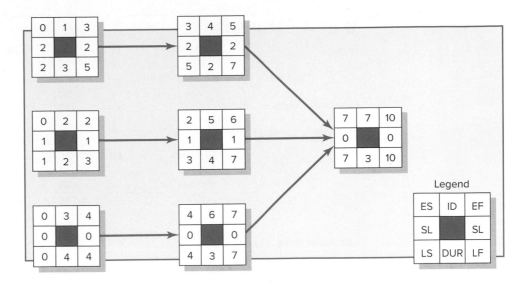

FIGURE A13.1-2B

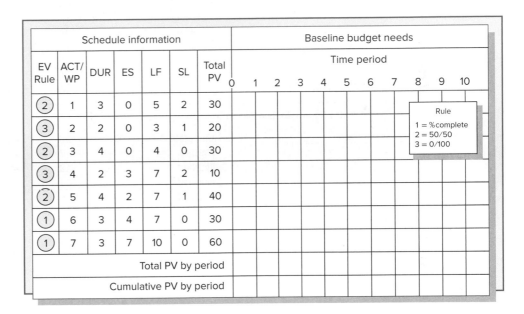

Status Report: Ending Period 1

Task	%Complete	EV	AC	PV	CV	SV
1	40%	—	8	—	—	—
2	0%	—	12	—	—	—
3	30%	—	10	—	—	—
Cumulative Totals		—	**30**	—	—	—

Status Report: Ending Period 2

Task	%Complete	EV	AC	PV	CV	SV
1	80%	—	20	—	—	—
2	Finished	—	18	—	—	—
3	50%	—	12	—	—	—
Cumulative Totals		—	**50**	—	—	—

Status Report: Ending Period 3

Task	%Complete	EV	AC	PV	CV	SV
1	Finished	—	27	—	—	—
2	Finished	—	18	—	—	—
3	70%	—	15	—	—	—
4	0%	—	5	—	—	—
5	30%	—	8	—	—	—
Cumulative Totals		—	**73**	—	—	—

Status Report: Ending Period 4

Task	%Complete	EV	AC	PV	CV	SV
1	Finished	—	27	—	—	—
2	Finished	—	18	—	—	—
3	Finished	—	22	—	—	—
4	0%	—	7	—	—	—
5	60%	—	22	—	—	—
Cumulative Totals		—	**96**	—	—	—

Status Report: Ending Period 5

Task	%Complete	EV	AC	PV	CV	SV
1	Finished	—	27	—	—	—
2	Finished	—	18	—	—	—
3	Finished	—	22	—	—	—
4	Finished	—	8	—	—	—
5	70%	—	24	—	—	—
6	30%	—	10	—	—	—
Cumulative Totals		—	**109**	—	—	—

FIGURE A13.1-2C

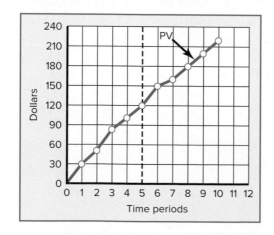

Period	SPI	CPI	PCIB
1	—	—	—
2	—	—	—
3	—	—	—
4	—	—	—
5	—	—	—

SPI = EV/AC
CPI = EV/AC
PCIB = EV/BAC

Appendix 13.2

Obtaining Project Performance Information from MS Project 2010 or 2015

LEARNING OBJECTIVES

After reading this appendix you should be able to:

LO A13.2-1 Obtain project performance information from MS Project 2010 or 2015.

LO A13.2-1

Obtain project performance information from MS Project 2010 or 2015.

The objective of this appendix is to illustrate how one can obtain the performance information discussed in Chapter 13 from MS Project 2010 or 2015. One of the great strengths of MS Project is its flexibility. The software provides numerous options for entering, calculating, and presenting project information. Flexibility is also the software's greatest weakness in that there are so many options that working with the software can be frustrating and confusing. The intent here is to keep it simple and present basic steps for obtaining performance information. Students with more ambitious agendas are advised to work with the software tutorial or consult one of many instructional books on the market.

For purposes of this exercise we will use the Digital Camera project, which was introduced in Chapter 13. In this scenario the project started as planned on March 1 and today's date is March 7. We have received the following information on the work completed to date:

Design Specs took 2 days to complete at a total cost of $20.

Shell & Power took 3 days to complete at a total cost of $25.

Memory/Software is in progress with 4 days completed and two days remaining.

Cost to date is $100.

Zoom System took 2 days to complete at a cost of $25.

All tasks started on time.

STEP 1 ENTERING PROGRESS INFORMATION

We enter this progress information in the TRACKING TABLE from the GANTT CHART VIEW ▸ VIEW ▸ TABLES ▸ TRACKING:

TABLE A13.2-1A Tracking Table

ID	Task Name	Act. Start	Act. Finish	% Comp.	Act. Dur.	Rem. Dur.	Act. Cost	Act. Work
1	**Digital Camera Prototype**	**3/1**	**NA**	**61%**	**6.72 days**	**4.28 days**	**$170.00**	**272 hrs**
2	Design Spec.s	3/1	3/2	100%	2 days	0 days	$20.00	32 hrs
3	Shell & Power	3/3	3/7	100%	3 days	0 days	$25.00	40 hrs
4	Memory/Software	3/3	NA	67%	4 days	2 days	$100.00	160 hrs
5	Zoom System	3/3	3/4	100%	2 days	0 days	$25.00	40 hrs
6	Assemble	NA	NA	0%	0 days	3 days	$0.00	0 hrs
7	Test	NA	NA	0%	0 days	2 days	$0.00	0 hrs

Note that the software automatically calculates the percent complete and actual finish, cost, and work. In some cases you will have to override these calculations if they are inconsistent with what actually happened. **Be sure to check** to make sure the information in this table is displayed the way you want it to be.

The final step is to enter the current status date (March 7). You do so by clicking PROJECT ▸ PROJECT INFORMATION and inserting the date into the status date window.

STEP 2 ACCESSING PROGRESS INFORMATION

MS Project provides a number of different options for obtaining progress information. The most basic information can be obtained from PROJECT ▸ REPORTS ▸ COSTS ▸ EARNED VALUE. You can also obtain this information from GANTT CHART view. Click VIEW ▸ TABLE ▸ MORE TABLES ▸ EARNED VALUE.

TABLE A13.2-1B Earned Value Table

ID	Task Name	PV	EV	AC	SV	CV	EAC	BAC	VAC
2	Design Spec.s	$20.00	$20.00	$20.00	$0.00	$0.00	$20.00	$20.00	$0.00
3	Shell & Power	$15.00	$15.00	$25.00	$0.00	($10.00)	$25.00	$15.00	($10.00)
4	Memory/Software	$100.00	$70.00	$100.00	($30.00)	($30.00)	$153.85	$100.00	($53.85)
5	Zoom System	$35.00	$35.00	$25.00	$0.00	$10.00	$25.00	$35.00	$10.00
6	Assemble	$0.00	$0.00	$0.00	$0.00	$0.00	$120.00	$120.00	$0.00
7	Test	$0.00	$0.00	$0.00	$0.00	$0.00	$30.00	$30.00	$0.00
		$170.00	$140.00	$170.00	($30.00)	($30.00)	$373.85	$320.00	($53.85)

When you scale this table to 80 percent you can obtain all the basic CV, SV and VAC information on one convenient page.

Note: Some versions of MS Project use the old acronyms:

BCWS = PV

BCWP = EV

ACWP = AC

and the EAC is calculated using the CPI and is what the text refers to as EAC_f.

STEP 3 ACCESSING CPI INFORMATION

To obtain additional cost information such as CPI and TCPI from the GANTT CHART view, click VIEW ▶ TABLE ▶ MORE TABLES ▶ EARNED VALUE COST INDICATORS, which will display the following information:

TABLE A13.2-1C   Earned Value Cost Indicators Table

ID	Task Name	PV	EV	CV	CV%	CPI	BAC	EAC	VAC	TCPI
1	**Digital Camera Prototype**	**$170.00**	**$140.00**	**($30.00)**	**−21%**	**0.82**	**$320.00**	**$373.85**	**($53.85)**	**1.2**
2	Design Spec.s	$20.00	$20.00	$0.00	0%	1	$20.00	$20.00	$0.00	
3	Shell & Power	$15.00	$15.00	($10.00)	−66%	0.6	$15.00	$25.00	($10.00)	
4	Memory/Software	$100.00	$70.00	($30.00)	−42%	0.7	$100.00	$153.85	($53.85)	
5	Zoom System	$35.00	$35.00	$10.00	28%	1.4	$35.00	$25.00	$10.00	
6	Assemble	$0.00	$0.00	$0.00	0%	0	$120.00	$120.00	$0.00	
7	Test	$0.00	$0.00	$0.00	0%	0	$30.00	$30.00	$0.00	

Note: For MS Project 2007 users the instructions are very similar except you can access the Tables option directly from Gantt View.

STEP 4 ACCESSING SPI INFORMATION

To obtain additional schedule information such as SPI from the GANTT CHART view, click VIEW ▶ TABLE ▶ MORE TABLES ▶ EARNED VALUE SCHEDULE INDICATORS, which will display the following information:

TABLE A13.2-1D Earned Value Schedule Indicators Table

ID	Task Name	PV	EV	SV	SV%	SPI
1	**Digital Camera Prototype**	**$170.00**	**$140.00**	**($30.00)**	**−18%**	**0.82**
2	Design Spec.s	$20.00	$20.00	$0.00	0%	1
3	Shell & Power	$15.00	$15.00	$0.00	0%	1
4	Memory/Software	$100.00	$70.00	($30.00)	−30%	0.7
5	Zoom System	$35.00	$35.00	$0.00	0%	1
6	Assemble	$0.00	$0.00	$0.00	0%	0
7	Test	$0.00	$0.00	$0.00	0%	0

STEP 5 CREATING A TRACKING GANTT CHART

You can create a tracking Gantt chart like the one presented in Figure 13.1 by simply clicking TASK ▶ GANTT CHART (upper left hand corner) ▶ TRACKING GANTT ▶ TRACKING GANTT.

FIGURE A13.2-1   Tracking Gantt Chart

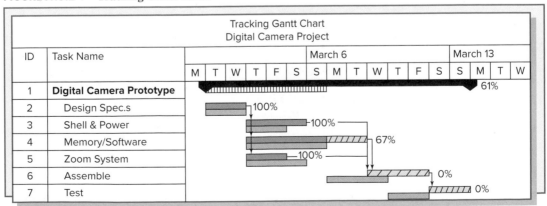

14 Project Closure

LEARNING OBJECTIVES

After reading this chapter you should be able to:

14-1 Identify different types of project closure.

14-2 Understand the challenges of closing out a project.

14-3 Explain the importance of a project audit.

14-4 Know how to use project retrospectives to obtain lessons learned.

14-5 Assess level of project management maturity.

14-6 Provide useful advice for conducting team performance reviews.

14-7 Provide useful advice for conducting performance reviews of project members.

OUTLINE

14.1 Types of Project Closure

14.2 Wrap-up Closure Activities

14.3 Project Audits

14.4 Post-Implementation Evaluation

Summary

Appendix 14.1: Project Closeout Checklist

Appendix 14.2: Euro Conversion

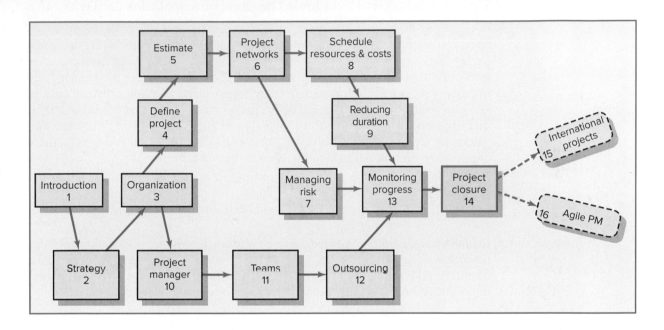

Those who cannot remember the past are condemned to relive it.

—*George Santayana, 1863–1952*

Every project comes to an end eventually. But how many project participants get excited about closing out a project? The deliverables are complete. Ownership is ready to be transferred. Everyone's focus is what's next—hopefully a new, exciting project. Carefully managing the closure phase is as important as any other phase of the project. Observation tells us that organizations that manage closure and review well prosper. Those who don't tend to have projects that drag on forever and repeat the same mistakes over and over.

Closing out a project includes a daunting number of tasks. In the past and on small projects the project manager was responsible for seeing all tasks and loose ends were completed and signed off. This is no longer true. In today's project-driven organizations that have many projects occurring simultaneously, the responsibility for completing closure tasks has been parsed among the project manager, project teams, project office, an oversight "review committee," and an independent retrospective facilitator. Many tasks overlap, occur simultaneously, and require coordination and cooperation among these stakeholders.

FIGURE 14.1
**Project Closure and
Review Deliverables**

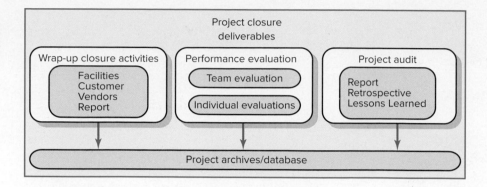

The three major deliverables for **project closure** are described below (see Figure 14.1):

1. *Wrapping up the project.* The major wrap-up task is to ensure the project is approved and accepted by the customer. Other wrap-up activities include closing accounts, paying bills, reassigning equipment and personnel, finding new opportunities for project staff, closing facilities, and the final report. Checklists are used extensively to ensure tasks are not overlooked. In many organizations, the lion's share of closure tasks is largely done by the project office in coordination with the project manager. The final report writing is usually assigned to one project office staff member, who assembles input from all stakeholders. In smaller organizations and projects, these closure activities are left to the project manager and team.

2. *Project audit.* Audits are post-project reviews of how successful the project was. They include causal analysis and thorough retrospectives which identify lessons learned. These post-project reviews should be held with the team and key stakeholders to catch any missing issues or gaps.

3. *Evaluation of performance and management of the project.* Evaluation includes team, individual team members, and project manager performance. Vendors and the customer may provide external input. Evaluation of the major players provides important information for the future.

This chapter begins with the recognition that projects are shut down for many reasons. Not all projects end with a clear "Finished" and are turned over to a customer. Regardless of the conditions for ending a project, the general process of closure is similar, though the endings may differ significantly. Wrap-up closure tasks are noted first. These tasks represent all the tasks that must be "cleaned up" before the project is terminated. Project audits are examined next. Finally, evaluation of individual and team performance is examined.

14.1 Types of Project Closure

LO 14-1

Identify different types of project closure.

On some projects the end may not be as clear as would be hoped. Although the scope statement may define a clear ending for a project, the actual ending may or may not correspond. Fortunately, a majority of projects are blessed with a well-defined ending. Regular project reviews will identify projects having endings different from plans. The different types of closure are identified here:

Normal   The most common circumstance for project closure is simply a completed project. For many development projects, the end involves handing off the final design to production and the creation of a new product or service line. For other internal IT projects, such as system upgrades or creation of new inventory control systems, the end occurs when the output is incorporated into ongoing operations. Some modifications in scope, cost, and schedule probably occurred during implementation.

Premature For a few projects, the project may be completed early with some parts of the project eliminated. For example, in a new product development project, a marketing manager may insist on production models before testing:

> Give the new product to me now, the way it is. Early entry into the market will mean big profits! I know we can sell a bazillion of these. If we don't do it now, the opportunity is lost!

The pressure is on to finish the project and send it to production. Before succumbing to this form of pressure, the implications and risks associated with this decision should be carefully reviewed and assessed by senior management and all stakeholders. Too frequently, the benefits are illusory, dangerous, and carry large risks.

Perpetual Some projects never seem to end. The major characteristic of this kind of project is constant "add-ons," suggesting a poorly conceived project scope. At some point the review group should recommend methods for bringing final closure to this type of project or the initiation of another project. For example, adding a new feature to an old project could replace a segment of a project that appears to be perpetual.

Failed Project Failed projects are usually easy to identify and easy for a review group to close down. However, every effort should be made to communicate the technical (or other) reasons for termination of the project; in any event project participants should not be left with an embarrassing stigma of working on a project that failed. Many projects will fail because of circumstances beyond the control of the project team. See Snapshot from Practice 14.1: The Wake, for a novel response to a canceled project.

SNAPSHOT FROM PRACTICE 14.1 The Wake[1]

Sally worked as a project manager for a high-tech electronics firm in the late eighties. The company had patented the use of "bubble ink" technology for color printing. She was in charge of a team tasked with cutting the prohibitive cost of printers in half. If successful significant bonuses would be earned and several team members would be given key positions when the product went into production. The team had overcome several difficult technical challenges and was well on its way to accomplishing their objective when the project was canceled. Top management discovered at a trade show that several competitors were about to introduce ink jet printers at a cost one-fifth the price of the printers Sally's team was developing.

What could Sally say to her team? Sally knew they would be devastated. She knew she had to do something to help them deal with this bitter disappointment. So she decided to hold a traditional Irish "wake" for the project. She persuaded management to hire a backhoe to dig a grave in the back yard of their office and purchase an actual coffin. After she and other members gave a brief eulogy about the project, each member dropped something from the project into the coffin. For some members it was a piece of a printer prototype, for others it was a memo or a plan. One by one each member put something personal in the coffin. After the coffin was buried, the team retreated to a local brew pub to imbibe and share fond memories of the work they had accomplished. The "wake" became part of the company's folklore and team members still laugh about the experience.

[1]A wake is a party in honor of deceased that usually involves the consumption of alcohol.

Changed Priority   Organizations' priorities often change and strategy shifts directions. For example, during the 2008–10 financial crisis organizations shifted their focus from money-making projects to cost savings projects. The oversight group continually revises project selection priorities to reflect changes in organizational direction. Projects in process may need to be altered or canceled. Thus, a project may start with a high priority but see its rank erode or crash during its project life cycle as conditions change. When priorities change, projects in process may need to be altered or canceled.

Different types of project termination present unique issues. Some adjustments to generic closure processes may be necessary to accommodate the type of project termination you face.

14.2 Wrap-up Closure Activities

LO 14-2

Understand the challenges of closing out a project.

The major challenges for the project manager and team members are over. Getting the project manager and project participants to wrap up the odds and ends necessary to fully complete a project is often difficult. It's like the party is over—now who wants to help clean up? Much of the work is mundane and tedious. Motivation can be the chief challenge. For example, accounting for equipment and completing final reports are perceived as dull administrative tasks by project professionals who are action-oriented individuals. The project manager's challenge is to keep the project team focused on the remaining project activities and delivery to the customer until the project is complete. Communicating a closure and review plan and schedule early allows the project team to (1) accept the psychological fact the project will end and (2) prepare to move on. The ideal scenario is to have the team member's next assignment ready when project completion is announced. Project managers need to be careful to maintain their enthusiasm for completing the project and hold people accountable to deadlines, which are prone to slip during the waning stages of the project.

Implementing the closure process includes several wrap-up activities. Many organizations develop lengthy lists for closing projects as they gain experience. These are very helpful and ensure nothing is overlooked. Implementing closedown includes the following six major activities:

1. Getting delivery acceptance from the customer.
2. Shutting down resources and releasing to new uses.
3. Reassigning project team members.
4. Closing accounts and seeing all bills are paid.
5. Delivering the project to the customer.
6. Creating a final report.

Administering the details of closing out a project can be intimidating. Some organizations have checklists of over 100 wrap-up tasks! These checklists deal with closure details such as facilities, teams, staff, customer, vendors, and the project itself. A partial administrative closure checklist is shown in Table 14.1.

Getting delivery acceptance by the customer is a major and critical closure activity. Delivery of some projects to the customer is straightforward. Others are more complex and difficult. Ideally there should be no surprises. This requires a well-defined scope and an effective change management system with active customer involvement. User involvement is critical to acceptance (see Snapshot from Practice 14.2: New Ball Goes Flat in the NBA).

TABLE 14.1
Wrap-up Closure
Checklist

	Task	Completed? Yes/No
	Team	
1	Has a schedule for reducing project staff been developed and accepted?	
2	Has staff been released or notified of new assignments?	
3	Have performance reviews for team members been conducted?	
4	Has staff been offered outplacement services and career counseling activities?	
	Vendors/contractors	
5	Have performance reviews for all vendors been conducted?	
6	Have project accounts been finalized and all billing closed?	
	Customer/Users	
7	Has the customer signed-off on the delivered product?	
8	Has an in-depth project review and evaluation interview with the customer been conducted?	
9	Have the users been interviewed to assess their satisfaction with the deliverables? With the project team? With vendors? With training? With support? With maintenance?	
	Equipment and facilities	
10	Have project resources been transferred to other projects?	
11	Have rental or lease equipment agreements been closed out?	
12	Has the date for the closure review been set and stakeholders notified?	
	Attach comments or links on any tasks you feel need explanation.	

The conditions for completing and transferring the project should be set before the project begins. A completed software program is a good example of the need to work out the details in advance. If the user has problems using the software, will the customer withhold final payments? Who is responsible for supporting and training the user? If these conditions are not clearly defined up front, getting delivery acceptance can be troublesome.

Another delivery tactic (briefly mentioned in Chapter 7) for a project that has been outsourced is known as build, own, operate, and transfer (BOOT). In this type of project the contractor builds, owns, and operates the project deliverable for a set period of time. For example, Haliburton will operate a hydro-electric plant for six months before turning over operations to their Indian counterparts. During this time all the bugs are worked out and conditions for delivery are satisfied. Again, note the delivery conditions need to be carefully set up before the project begins; if not, wrap-up activities can develop a life of their own.

Releasing the project team typically occurs gradually during the closure phase. For some people, termination of their responsible activities ends before the project is delivered to the customer or user. Reassignment for these participants needs to take place well before the final finish date. For the remaining team members (full or part time), termination may result in a new project or returning to their functional job. Sometimes, on product development efforts, team members will be assigned to operations positions and play an active role in the production of the new product. For contract people it may mean the end of their assignment to this project; in some cases there may be follow-up work or user support possibilities. A small number of part-time participants may be recommended to the user organization to train or operate new equipment or systems.

SNAPSHOT FROM PRACTICE 14.2 New Ball Goes Flat in the NBA*

On October 31, 2006, the National Basketball Association (NBA) opened its 57th season with new official game balls. The new ball, manufactured by Spalding, featured a new design and a new material that together were believed to offer better grip, feel, and consistency than the previous leather ball. The material is microfiber composite with moisture management that provides superior grip and feel throughout the course of a game. Additionally, the new composite material eliminates the need for a break-in period, which is necessary for the current leather ball, and achieves consistency from ball to ball.

The NBA and Spalding subjected the ball to a rigorous evaluation process that included laboratory and on-court testing process. Every NBA team received the new ball and had the opportunity to use it in practice. The ball was also tested in the NBA summer development league.

At the press conference announcing the shift from leather to microfiber balls, NBA commissioner David Stern pronounced, "The advancement that Spalding has made to the new game ball ensures that the best basketball players in the world will be playing with the best basketball in the world."

Animal rights advocates applauded the shift from leather to microfiber. Such was not the case for the players who would actually use the new ball. Grumblings emerged immediately when training camps opened in October. Washington Wizards guard Gilbert Arenas said the new basketball "gets slippery" when it comes in contact even with small amounts of sweat. Then Miami Heat center Shaquille O'Neil said, "It feels like one of those cheap balls that you buy at a toy store."

Some players, including league MVP Steve Nash, began complaining that the new ball was producing small cuts on their hands. "It's awful [the friction burns], its like an irritant . . . sometimes I even have to tape my fingers in practice." Perhaps LeBron James from the Cleveland Cavaliers best summed up the players' attitudes toward the NBA's introduction of the new ball when he said, "You

© Ingram Publishing/Alamy

can change the dress code, you can make our shorts shorter, but when you take our basketball away from us, that's not a transition we can handle."

On December 1, 2006, four weeks into the season, the NBA players union filed an unfair labor practice suit because the league management switched to the new ball without consulting the players. Ten days later, the NBA announced that they would revert back to the old leather ball beginning January 1, 2007. In a terse statement, Commissioner David Stern said, "Our players' response to this particular composite ball has been overwhelmingly negative and we are acting accordingly."

The failure to check with the players (the end-users) and get buy-in for the new basketball was loudly criticized by the press. "How they could actually even get it that far and not have run it by the players is just an amazing, amazing exercise in ineptitude," Rob Frankel, a Los Angeles–based branding expert told *Bloomberg News*.

* "NBA Introduces New Game Ball," www.nba.com/news, posted 6-28-2006; Howard Bloom, "The NBA--Uneventful 2006 II," *Sports Business News*, www.sportsbixnews .blogspot.com, 12-30-2006.

Since many work invoices are not submitted until after the project is officially over, closing out contracts is often messy and filled with untied ends. For example, it is improbable all invoices have been finalized, billed, and paid. Further, when contractors are used, there is a need to verify that all the contracted work has been done. Keeping contract records, such as progress reports, invoices, change records, and payment records, is important should a compliance or lawsuit occur. Too often in the haste to meet deadlines, paperwork and record keeping gets short-changed, only to create major headaches when it comes time for final documentation.

There are many more wrap-up activities; it is important to complete all of them. Experience has proved time and again that not doing all the little cleanup tasks well will create problems later. Two other examples of closure checklists are shown in this chapter: Appendix 14.1 presents an example used by the state of Virginia; and Appendix 14.2 presents an abridged closure checklist for the Euro Conversion project.

A final wrap-up activity is some form of celebration. For successful projects, an upbeat, festive celebration brings closure to the enjoyable experiences everyone has had and the need to say good-bye. Celebration is an opportunity to recognize the effort project stakeholders contributed. Even if the project did not reach its objectives, recognize the effort involved and goals that were achieved. If the project was a success, invite everyone who in some way contributed to project success. Thank the team and each one individually. The spirit of the celebration should be one in which the stakeholders are thanked for a job well done and leave with a good feeling of accomplishment.

14.3 Project Audits

LO 14-3

Explain the importance of a project audit.

Project audits are more than the status reports suggested in Chapter 13, which report on project performance. Project audits do use performance measures and forecast data. But project audits are more inclusive. Project audits not only examine project success but also review why the project was selected. Project audits include a reassessment of the project's role in the organization's priorities. Project audits include a check on the organizational culture to ensure it facilitates the type of project being implemented. Project audits assess if the project team is functioning well and is appropriately staffed. Audits of projects in process should include a check on external factors that might change where the project is heading or its importance—for example, technology, government laws, competitive products. Project audits include a review of all factors relevant to the project and to managing future projects.

Project audits can be performed while a project is in process and after a project is completed. There are only a few minor differences between these audits.

- **In-process project audits.** Project audits early in projects allow for corrective changes, if they are needed, on the audited project or others in progress. In-process project audits concentrate on project progress and performance and check if conditions have changed. For example, have priorities changed? Is the project mission still relevant? In rare cases, the audit report may recommend closure of a project that is in process.
- **Postproject audits.** These audits tend to include more detail and depth than in-process project audits. Project audits of completed projects emphasize improving the management of future projects. These audits are more long-term oriented than in-process audits. Postproject audits do check on project performance, but the audit represents a broader view of the project's role in the organization; for example, were the strategic benefits claimed actually delivered?

The depth and detail of the project audit depend on many factors. Some are listed in Table 14.1. Because audits cost time and money, they should include no more time or resources than are necessary and sufficient. Early in-process project audits tend to be perfunctory unless serious problems or concerns are identified. Then, of course, the audit would be carried out in more detail. Because in-process project audits can be worrisome and destructive to the project team, care needs to be taken to protect project team morale. The audit should be carried out quickly, and the report should be as positive and constructive as possible. Postproject audits are more detailed and inclusive and contain more project team input.

In summary, plan the audit, and limit the time for the audit. For example, in postproject audits, for all but very large projects, a one-week limit is a good benchmark. Beyond this time, the marginal return of additional information diminishes quickly. Small projects may require only one or two days and one or two people to conduct an audit.

The priority team functions well in selecting projects and monitoring performance—cost and time. However, reviewing and evaluating projects and the process of managing projects is usually delegated to independent audit groups. Each audit group is charged with evaluating and reviewing *all* factors relevant to the project and to managing future projects. The outcome of the project audit is a report.

The Project Audit Process

Below are guidelines that should be noted before you conduct a project audit. The guidelines below will improve your chances for a successful audit.

Guidelines for Conducting a Project Audit

1. First and foremost, the philosophy must be that the project audit is not a witch hunt.
2. Comments about individuals or groups participating in the project should be minimized. Keep to project issues, not what happened or by whom.
3. Audit activities should be intensely sensitive to human emotions and reactions. The inherent threat to those being evaluated should be reduced as much as possible.
4. Accuracy of data should be verifiable or noted as subjective, judgmental, or hearsay.
5. Senior management should announce support for the project audit and see that the audit group has access to all information, project participants, and (in most cases) project customers.
6. The attitude toward a project audit and its aftermath depends on the modus operandi of the audit leadership and group. The objective is not to prosecute. The objective is to learn and conserve valuable organization resources where mistakes have been made. Friendliness, empathy, and objectivity encourage cooperation and reduce anxiety.
7. The audit should be completed as quickly as is reasonable.

With these guidelines in mind, the process of the project audit is conveniently divided into three steps: initiation and staffing, data collection and analysis, and reporting. Each step is briefly discussed next.

Step 1: Initiation and Staffing

Initiation of the audit process depends primarily on organization size and project size along with other factors. In small organizations and projects where face-to-face contact at all levels is prevalent, an audit may be informal and only represent another staff meeting. But even in these environments the content of a formal project audit should be examined and covered with notes made of the lessons learned. In medium-sized organizations with few projects the audit is likely to be conducted by someone from management with project management experience. In large companies or organizations with many projects the audit is under the purview of the project office (see Snapshot from Practice 14.3: The Project Office).

SNAPSHOT FROM PRACTICE 14.3   The Project Office*

As more and more companies embrace project management as a critical vehicle for realizing corporate objectives, they are creating centralized project offices (POs) to oversee and improve the management of projects. PO functions vary widely by organization and need. In some cases, they serve as a simple clearinghouse for project management information. In other cases, they recruit, train, and assign managers to specific projects. As POs mature and evolve over time, they become full-service providers of project management expertise within a firm. The different services POs may provide include the following:

© Xavier Arnau/Getty Images

- Creating and maintaining the internal project management information system.
- Recruiting and selecting project managers both within and outside the organization.
- Establishing standardized project planning and reporting methodologies.
- Training personnel in project management techniques and tools.
- Auditing ongoing and recently completed projects.
- Developing comprehensive risk management programs.
- Providing in-house project management consulting and mentoring services.
- Maintaining an internal project management library containing critical documents, including project plans, funding papers, test plans, audit reports, and so forth.
- Establishing and benchmarking best practices in project management.
- Maintaining and tracking the portfolio of projects within an organization.

A good example of how project offices evolve is the global project office (GPO) at Citibank's Global Corporate Bank. GPO originated at the grassroots level within the small world of Operations and Technology for Global Cash Management. Committed to bringing order to the chaos of managing projects, GPO instituted training programs and professional project management practices on a very small scale. Soon the success of GPO-supported projects caught the eye of upper management. Within three years the department was expanded to offer a full range of PO services across Citibank's entire banking operation. GPO's mission is to establish project management as a core competency throughout the entire Citibank organization.

*T. R. Block and J. D. Frame, "Today's Project Office: Gauging Attitudes," *PM Network,* August 2001; W. Gradante and D. Gardner, "Managing Projects from the Future, Not from the Past," *Proceedings of the 29th Annual Project Management Institute 1998 Seminars and Symposium* (Newtown Square, PA: Project Management Institute, 1998), pp. 289–94.

A major tenet of the project audit is that the outcome must represent an independent, outside view of the project. Maintaining independence and an objective view is difficult, given that audits are frequently viewed as negative by project stakeholders. Careers and reputations can be tarnished even in organizations that tolerate mistakes. In less forgiving organizations, mistakes can lead to termination or exile to less significant regions of an organization. Of course, if the result of an audit is favorable, careers and reputations can be enhanced. Given that project audits are susceptible to internal politics, some organizations rely on outside consulting firms to conduct the audits.

Step 2: Data Collection and Analysis

Each organization and project is unique. Therefore, the specific kinds of information that will be collected will depend upon the industry, project size, newness of technology, and project experience. These factors can influence the nature of the audit. However, information and data are gathered to answer questions similar to those suggested next.

Organization View

1. Was the organizational culture supportive and correct for this type of project? Why? Why not?
2. Was senior management's support adequate?
3. Did the project accomplish its intended purpose?
4. Were the risks for the project appropriately identified and assessed? Were contingency plans used? Were they realistic? Have risk events occurred that have an impact greater than anticipated?
5. Were the right people and talents assigned to this project?
6. What does evaluation from outside contractors suggest?
7. Were the project start-up and hand-off successful? Why? Is the customer satisfied?

Project Team View

1. Were the project planning and control systems appropriate for this type of project? Should all similar size and type of projects use these systems? Why/why not?
2. Did the project conform to plan? Is the project over or under budget and schedule? Why?
3. Were interfaces and communications with project stakeholders adequate and effective?
4. Did the team have adequate access to organizational resources—people, budget, support groups, equipment? Were there resource conflicts with other ongoing projects?
5. Was the team managed well? Were problems confronted not avoided?

The audit group should not be limited to these questions. The audit group should include other questions related to their organization and project type—e.g., research and development, marketing, information systems, construction, facilities. The generic questions above, although overlapping, represent a good starting point and will go a long way toward identifying project problem and success patterns.

Step 3: Reporting

The major goal of the audit report is to improve the way future projects are managed. Succinctly, the report attempts to capture needed changes and lessons learned from a current or finished project. The report serves as a training instrument for project managers of future projects.

Audit reports need to be tailored to the specific project and organizational environment. Nevertheless, a generic format for all audits facilitates development of an audit database and a common outline for those who prepare audit reports and the managers who read and act on their content. A very general outline common to those found in practice is as follows:

1. Classification   The classification of projects by characteristics allows prospective readers and project managers to be selective in the use of the report content. Typical classification categories include the following:

- Project type—e.g., development, marketing, systems, construction.
- Size—monetary.
- Number of staff.
- Technology level—low, medium, high, new.
- Strategic or support.

Other classifications relevant to the organization should be included.

2. Analysis   The analysis section includes succinct, factual review statements of the project. For example,

- Project mission and objectives.
- Procedures and systems used.
- Organization resources used.
- **Outcomes achieved**

3. Recommendations   Usually audit recommendations represent major corrective actions that should take place. See, for example, Snapshot from Practice 14.4: Lessons Learned from Katrina. Audit recommendations are often technical in nature and focus on solutions to problems that surfaced. For example, to avoid rework, the report of a construction project recommended shifting to a more resilient building material. In other cases, recommendations may include terminating or sustaining vendor or contractor relationships.

4. Lessons Learned   These do not have to be in the form of recommendations. **Lessons learned** serve as reminders of mistakes easily avoided and actions easily taken to ensure success. In practice, new project teams reviewing audits of past projects similar to the one they are about to start have found audit reports very useful. Team members will frequently remark later, "The recommendations were good, but the 'lessons learned' section really helped us avoid many pitfalls and made our project implementation smoother." It is precisely this reason that lessons learned in the form of project retrospectives have taken on greater prominence and warrant further discussion. See Snapshot from Practice 14.5: Operation Eagle Claw.

5. Appendix   The appendix may include backup data or details of analysis that would allow others to follow up if they wish. It should not be a dumping ground used for filler; only critical pertinent information should be attached.

Project Retrospectives

LO 14-4

Know how to use project retrospectives to obtain lessons learned.

The term *retrospective* has emerged in recent years to denote specific efforts at identifying lessons learned on projects. Proponents believe that the traditional audit process focuses too much on project success and evaluation which interferes with the surfacing and transferal of important lessons learned. They advocate a separate effort toward capturing lessons learned. In many ways this effort mirrors the auditing process. Typically, an independent, trained facilitator acts as a guide who leads the project team through an analysis of project activities that went well, what needs improvements, and development of follow-up action plan with goals and accountability. This

SNAPSHOT FROM PRACTICE 14.4 — Lessons Learned from Katrina*

On August 25, 2005, winds of 145 miles per hour and rains covered 80 percent of New Orleans with some areas under 20 feet of water. Hurricane Katrina dispersed havoc on every corner of New Orleans. In its trail it left over 1,300 people dead in Louisiana and Mississippi. Katrina will long be remembered as the costliest and most deadly hurricane ever recorded in the United States.

Response came from many different groups within the country and from other countries. Katrina also drew the largest response of The National Guard to a national emergency in history. Governors from every state sent National Guard troops to support and assist the state of Mississippi. By September 8, 51,000 troops were responding to the emergency. Many other nonprofit groups offered help in a variety of ways—food, shelter, financial, health care, and transportation. Groups that contributed support have reviewed their efforts to see what lessons learned can be used to improve future emergency efforts. The results of the review of The National Guard efforts follow here:

Three of the key lessons from The National Guard retrospective are described.

- *Lack of equipment was one of the biggest problems—especially communication equipment. Ability to communicate among the many different support groups (e.g., civilian and military) was thwarted by incompatible systems or simple lack of availability.*
  Action Item: $1.3 billion has been authorized for new equipment that is compatible across major emergency groups.

- *Lack of protocols and standardization of reports, graphics, and communication caused delays and poor coordination among the many support groups.*
  Action Item: A single standard protocol for all states is now being applied.

- *The National Guard is under state control. Guard troops integrated quickly into the host-state command structures and cooperation ensued.*
  Action Item: Maintain status quo.

Because Guard soldiers are controlled by the states, they were empowered to enforce civil laws, something federal troops are prohibited from doing, except under the provisions of the insurrection laws. Fortunately, coordination and cooperation among state and federal troop command work reasonably well. However, the federal agencies (e.g., Homeland Security) need to incorporate the Guard into planning and preparation for the federal response to catastrophic disasters.

Lessons learned from the Katrina disaster are not limited to the military. Almost every agency and support group, such as individuals, communities, churches, and other groups, has developed lessons learned from their project response experience. For example, the Red Cross and state guard have better plans for handling thousands of people problems involving shelter, evacuation, and medical assistance. These lessons learned from Katrina are ready to go and should be enormously helpful in future hurricane situations.

*Les A. Melnyk, "Katrina Lessons Learned," *Soldiers Magazine,* June 20, 2006 and "Lessons Learned from Katrina: Preparing Your Institution for a Catastrophic Event." Federal Deposit Insurance Corporation is the source of this information. 1/20/08

facilitator may come from the project office or be an external consultant. Wherever this individual comes from, it is critical that she or he be perceived as being independent and unbiased.

In retrospecitive methodology, the facilitator uses several questionnaires to conduct post-project audits. These surveys focus not only on project operations, but also on how the organization's culture impacted project success and failures. Table 14.2 provides a sampling of the former while Table 14.3 provides a sample of the latter.

With survey information in hand, the facilitator visits one-on-one with project team members, project manager, and other stakeholders to dive deeper into cause-effect impacts. For example, the facilitator may discover that one of the primary reasons for lack of timely decision making and poor coordination between groups was that team members were bombarded with too much information and had a difficult time sorting through what was critical and what could be ignored.

SNAPSHOT FROM PRACTICE 14.5   Operation Eagle Claw*

On November 4, 1979, a mob in Iran stormed the U.S. Embassy and took 52 Americans hostage. After six months of failed negotiation, the green light was given to execute Operation Eagle Claw, a joint military effort to free the hostages.

The plan called for eight Navy RH-53D helicopters to fly 600 miles to a remote site in Iran, code named Desert One. Under the cover of darkness, the helicopters would be refueled by KC-130 tankers. The helicopters would then fly the assault force to a spot near the outskirts of Teheran where they would meet up with special agents already in the country. The agents would lead them to a safe house to await the assault on the embassy the next night. Upon rescuing the hostages, the assault team would escort them to a nearby airfield that had already been secured by a second assault team where they would be flown to safety.

What actually happened was far different from what was planned.

The helicopter pilots were ordered to fly at or below 200 feet to avoid radar. This caused them to run into "haboobs" or dust storms. Two helicopters malfunctioned and turned back. The remainder battled the dust storms and arrived at Desert One one hour late. The rescue attempt was dealt its final blow when it was discovered that a third helicopter had a hydraulic leak and was inoperable. Only five aircraft were serviceable and six were needed, so the mission had to be aborted. Things got worse when one of the helicopters moved into position to refuel and collided with a KC-130 plane. Both aircraft burst into flames. All told, eight soldiers died and dozens were injured. The Iranians scattered the hostages around the country afterward, making any further rescue attempts impossible.

Given the gravity of the situation, a special six-member commission was appointed by the Joint Chiefs of Staff to conduct a review of the project. They identified a number of issues that contributed to the failure. One

© Michael OchsArschives/Stringer/Getty

issue was the selection of the air crews. Given the significance of the mission, each military service wanted to be involved. Navy and Marine pilots with little experience in long-range overland navigation or refueling were chosen though more than one hundred experienced Air Force pilots were available. Another issue was the lack of a comprehensive mission rehearsal program. From the beginning, training was not conducted in a truly joint manner; it was compartmentalized by service and held in different locations across the United States. The limited rehearsals that were conducted assessed only segments of the total mission.

The commission concluded that 10 and perhaps 12 helicopters should have been launched to guarantee the minimum six required for mission completion. Finally, the hopscotch method for ground refueling was criticized. If planners had chosen en-route fueling, the entire Desert One scenario could have been avoided. The final report contained several important lessons learned that have contributed to successful subsequent missions, including the one against Osama bin Laden in 2011.

* D. M. Giangreco and T. A. Griswold, *Delta: America's Elite Counter-terrorist Force* (New York: Motorbooks International, 1992).

Armed with the information gleaned from one-on-one sessions and other sources, the facilitator leads a team retrospective session. The session first reviews the facilitator's report and attempts to add key information. So with regard to the information overload problem, team members not only identify failure to flag critical information, but also a tendency to "cc" everyone just in case. The facilitator works with the team to develop a system that not only prioritizes information, but also does it according to who needs to receive it.

TABLE 14.2
Project Process
Review Questionnaire

	Item	Comments
1.	Were the project objectives and strategic intent of the project clearly and explicitly communicated?	
2.	Were the objectives and strategy in alignment?	
3.	Were the stakeholders identified and included in the planning?	
4.	Were project resources adequate for this project?	
5.	Were people with the right skill sets assigned to this project?	
6.	Were time estimates reasonable and achievable?	
7.	Were the risks for the project appropriately identified and assessed before the project started?	
8.	Were the processes and practices appropriate for this type of project? Should projects of similar size and type use these systems? Why/why not?	
9.	Did outside contractors perform as expected? Explain.	
10.	Were communication methods appropriate and adequate among all stakeholders? Explain.	
11.	Is the customer satisfied with the project product?	
12.	Are the customers using the project deliverables as intended? Are they satisfied?	
13.	Were the project objectives met?	
14.	Are the stakeholders satisfied their strategic intents have been met?	
15.	Has the customer or sponsor accepted a formal statement that the terms of the project charter and scope have been met?	
16.	Were schedule, budget, and scope standards met?	
17.	Is there any one important area that needs to be reviewed and improved upon? Can you identify the cause?	

TABLE 14.3
Organizational
Culture Review
Questionnaire

	Item	Comments
1.	Was the organizational culture supportive for this type of project?	
2.	Was senior management support adequate?	
3.	Were people with the right skills assigned to this project?	
4.	Did the project office help or hinder management of the project? Explain.	
5.	Did the team have access to organizational resources (people, funds, equipment)?	
6.	Was training for this project adequate? Explain.	
7.	Were lessons learned from earlier projects useful? Why? Where?	
8.	Did the project have a clear link to organizational objectives? Explain.	
9.	Was project staff properly reassigned?	
10.	Was the Human Resources Office helpful in finding new assignments? Comment.	

Each lesson is assigned an owner, typically a team member who is very interested and familiar with the lesson. This team member/owner will serve as a contact point for anyone needing information (expertise, contacts, templates, etc.) relating to the lesson. This person often reports lessons learned to larger audiences within their organization that would benefit from the collective wisdom.

Not only is there a contact person, but lessons learned need to be documented and archived in a manner that makes them accessible and usable by others. Here the facilitator works with the Project Office to create repository that uses a sophisticated search engine that permits others to quickly sort through and access lessons specific to their needs. Failure to do so will produce a system that is undervalued and underutilized.

Project Audits: The Bigger Picture

LO 14-5

Assess level of project management maturity.

Individual audits or postproject retrospectives can yield valuable lessons and recommendations that team members can apply to future project work. When done on a consistent basis, they can lead to significant improvements in the processes and techniques that organizations use to complete projects. A more encompassing look from an organizationwide point of view is to use a project maturity model. The purposes of all maturity models (and there are many available) are to enable organizations to assess their progress in implementing the best practices in their industry and move to improvement. It is important to understand that the model does not ensure success; it only serves as a measuring stick and an indicator of progress.

The term *maturity model* was coined in the late 1980s from a research study by the United States government and the Software Engineering Institute (SEI) at Carnegie-Mellon University. The government wanted a tool to predict successful software development by contractors. The outcome of this research was the Capability Maturity Model (CMM). The model focuses on guiding and assessing organizations in implementing concrete best practices of managing software development projects. Since its development, the model is now used across all industries. Currently, over 2,400 organizations around the world report their maturity progress to the Software Engineering Institute. (See website at http://www.sei.cmu.edu/activities/sema/profile.html.)

One newer model has received a great deal of publicity. In January 2004, after eight years of development, the Project Management Institute rolled out its second version of the "Organizational Project Maturity Model." The latest version is called *OPM3*™. (See www.pmi.org/opm3.) Typically, these models are divided into a continuum of growth levels: Initial, Repeatable, Defined, Managed, and Optimized. Figure 14.2 presents our version, which borrows liberally from other models. What we have tried to do is focus less on a process and more on the state an organization has evolved to in managing projects.

Level 1: Ad Hoc Project Management   No consistent project management process is in place. How a project is managed depends upon the individuals involved. Characteristics of this level include

- No formal project selection system exists—projects are done because people decide to do them or because a high-ranking manager orders it done.
- How any one project is managed varies by individual—unpredictability.
- No investment in project management training is made.
- Working on projects is a struggle because it goes against the grain of established policies and procedures.

FIGURE 14.2
Project Management Maturity Model

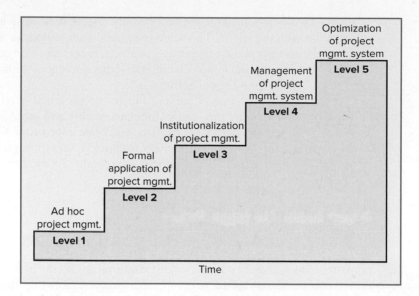

Level 2: Formal Application of Project Management The organization applies established project management procedures and techniques. This level is often marked by tension between project managers and line managers, who need to redefine their roles. Features of this level include

- Standard approaches to managing projects including scope statements, WBS, activity lists are used.
- Quality emphasis is on the product or outcome of the project and is inspected instead of built in.
- The organization is moving in the direction of stronger matrix with project managers and line managers working out their respective roles.
- Growing recognition of need for cost control, not just scope and time management, exists.
- There is no formal project priority system established.
- Limited training in project management is provided.

Level 3: Institutionalization of Project Management An organizationwide project management system, tailored to specific needs of the organization with the flexibility to adapt the process to unique characteristics of the project, is established. Characteristics of this level include

- An established process for managing projects is evident by planning templates, status report systems, and checklists for each stage of project life cycle.
- Formal criteria are used to select projects.
- Project management is integrated with quality management and concurrent engineering.
- Project teams try to build in quality not simply inspect it.
- The organization is moving toward a team-based reward system to recognize project execution.
- Risk assessment derived from WBS and technical analyses and customer input is in place.
- The organization offers expanded training in project management.

- Time-phased budgets are used to measure and monitor performance based on earned value analysis.
- A specific change control system for requirements, cost, and schedule is developed for each project, and a work authorization system is in place.
- Project audits tend to be performed only when a project fails.

Level 4: Management of Project Management System   The organization develops a system for managing multiple projects that are aligned with strategic goals of the organization. Characteristics of this level include

- Portfolio project management is practiced; projects are selected based on resource capacity and contribution to strategic goals.
- A project priority system is established.
- Project work is integrated with ongoing operations.
- Quality improvement initiatives are designed to improve both the quality of the project management process and the quality of specific products and services.
- Benchmarking is used to identify opportunities for improvement.
- The organization has established a Project Management Office or Center for Excellence.
- Project audits are performed on all significant projects; lessons learned are recorded and used on subsequent projects.
- An integrative information system is established for tracking resource usage and performance of all significant projects.

Level 5: Optimization of Project Management System   The focus is on continuous improvement through incremental advancements of existing practices and by innovations using new technologies and methods. Features include

- A project management information system is fine-tuned; specific and aggregate information is provided to different stakeholders.
- An informal culture that values improvement drives the organization, not policies and procedures.
- There is greater flexibility in adapting the project management process to demands of a specific project.

A major theme of this book is that the culture of the organization has a profound impact on how project management methodology operates. Audits and performance evaluation require informed judgment. Good decision making depends not only on the accuracy of the information, but also on the right information. For example, imagine how much different your response might be if you made an honest mistake but did not trust management and felt insecure versus if you had confidence and trust in management. Or think how different the quality of information that would surface from a team would be where trust was divided versus a team that works in a Level 5 environment.

Progress from one level to the next will not occur overnight. The Software Engineering Institute estimates the following median times for movement:

Maturity level 1 to 2 is 22 months.
Maturity level 2 to 3 is 19 months.
Maturity level 3 to 4 is 25 months.
Maturity level 4 to 5 is 13 months.

SNAPSHOT FROM PRACTICE 14.6

2015 PMO of the Year: Navy Federal Credit Union*

Like many financial institutions, the Navy Federal Credit Union struggled with adapting IT technologies to better serve their over 5 million members. Navy Federal had no clear method of prioritizing projects. Project execution processes were ad hoc. Delivery metrics weren't being tracked. Doomed projects lingered, with no one willing to hit the kill button.

In 2010 things began to change. Navy Federal began developing a team of project professionals who could advocate a standardized project delivery system as well as strategic alignment practices. In 2014 the IT department opened its project management office (PMO). The office was not greeted with open arms. The team had to work hard to avoid the perception that it was a document engine or needless bureaucracy.

"Throughout our journey, we've certainly faced challenges in terms of buy-in and acceptance of project management," says Kristin Earley, PMP, assistant vice president of the PMO. "We started with small wins. We had to highlight the demonstrated value that we brought in terms of consistent, repeatable delivery of projects."

The impact has been significant. The percentages of projects that closed according to plan jumped from 55 percent in 2014 to 88 percent in 2015. The PMO is now considered an integral part of how Navy Federal does business and was recognized by the Project Management Institute as 2015 PMO of the year.

While the initial push was to standardize project management processes, the PMO realized that not all projects are alike and some may benefit from less traditional methods.

"The PMO started with a one-size-fits-all approach to project delivery. We realized this really wasn't the most effective way to work with our business partners to deliver value frequently throughout the project life cycle," Ms. Earley says. "We've tailored our delivery practices to introduce both agile and incremental delivery practices, and that's helped us improve our delivery within the portfolio."

*Gantz, J., "Mission Accomplished," *PM Network* 29 (12) (December 2015), pp. 30–37.

Why does it take so long? One reason is simply organizational inertia. It is difficult for complex social organizations to institute significant changes while at the same time maintaining business efficacy. "How do we find time to change when we are so busy just keeping our heads above water?"

A second significant reason is that one cannot leapfrog past any one level. Just as a child cannot avoid the trials and tribulations of being a teenager by adopting all the lessons learned by his or her parents, people within the organization have to work through the unique challenges and problems of each level to get to the next level. Learning of this magnitude naturally takes time and cannot be avoided by using quick fixes or simple remedies. See Snapshot from Practice 14.6: 2015 PMO of the Year: Navy Federal Credit Union for how a PMO improved the maturity of project management operations at a large credit union.

14.4 Post-Implementation Evaluation

LO 14-6

Provide useful advice for conducting team performance reviews.

The purpose of **project evaluation** is to assess how well the project team, team members, and project manager performed.

Team Evaluation

Evaluation of performance is essential to encourage changes in behavior and to support individual career development and continuous improvement through organizational learning. Evaluation implies measurement against specific criteria. Experience corroborates that before commencement of a project, the stage must be set so

If team evaluation is not done well in practice, how bad is it? Joseph Fusco surveyed 1,667 project managers representing 134 different projects. Fifty-two percent of the respondents indicated their team received no collective evaluation of their team performance. Of the 22 percent who indicated their team was evaluated, further probing found their evaluation was informal, lasting little more than 20 minutes. This apparent lack of team evaluation practices may be sending the wrong signal.

Individual team members can slough off poor team performance by relying on the old saying, "I did my job." Strong team evaluation practices need to emphasize team members are "in this together," while minimizing individual performance. Nearly every company in Fusco's survey lacked an effective project management reward system.

* Joseph Fusco, "Better Policies Provide the Key to Implementing Project Management," *Project Management Journal,* Vol. 28, No. 3, September 1997, p. 38.

expectations, standards, supportive organizational culture, and constraints are in place; if not, the effectiveness of the evaluation process will suffer.

In a macro sense, the evidence today suggests that performance evaluation is not done well. See Research Highlight 14.1: Measures of Team Performance. The major reasons cited by practitioners are twofold:

1. Evaluations of individuals are still left to supervisors of the team member's home department.
2. Typical measures of team performance center on time, cost, and specifications.

Most organizations do not go beyond these measures, although they are important and critical. Organizations should consider evaluating the team-building process, effectiveness of group decision and problem-solving processes, group cohesion, trust among team members, and quality of information exchanged. Measurement of customer and user satisfaction with project deliverables (i.e., the project results) is often missed completely. Yet, project success depends significantly on satisfying these two very important groups. The quality of the deliverables is the responsibility of the team.

Before an evaluation of the project team can be effective and useful, a minimum core of conditions needs to be in place before the project begins (see Chapter 11). Some typical conditions are listed here in the form of questions:

1. Do standards for measuring performance exist? (You can't manage what you can't measure.) Are the goals clear for the team and individuals? Challenging? Attainable? Lead to positive consequences?
2. Are individual and team responsibilities and performance standards known by all team members?
3. Are team rewards adequate? Do they send a clear signal that senior management believes that the synergy of teams is important?
4. Is a clear career path for successful project managers in place?
5. Is the team empowered to manage short-term difficulties?
6. Is there a relatively high level of trust emanating from the organizational culture?
7. Team evaluation should go beyond time, cost, and specifications. Are there criteria beyond the constraint criteria? Creation of project deliverables would be a good place to start. The "characteristics of highly effective teams" from Chapter 11 can easily be adapted as measurements of team performance.

The "in-place conditions" will support any evaluation approach for teams and their members.

TABLE 14.4
Sample Team Evaluation and Feedback Survey

	Disagree				Agree
Using the scale below, assess each statement.					
1. The team shared a sense of common purpose, and each member was willing to work toward achieving project objectives.	1	2	3	4	5
2. Respect was shown for other points of view. Differences of opinion were encouraged and freely expressed.	1	2	3	4	5
3. All interaction among team members occurred in a comfortable, supportive atmosphere.	1	2	3	4	5

In practice, the actual team evaluation process takes many forms—especially when evaluation goes beyond time, budget, and specifications. The typical mechanism for evaluation of teams is a survey administered by a consultant, a staff member from the human resources department, or through computer e-mail. The survey is normally restricted to team members, but in some cases, other project stakeholders interacting with the team may be included in the survey. An example of a partial survey is found in Table 14.4. After the results are tabulated, the team meets with the facilitator and/or senior management, and the results are reviewed.

This session is comparable to the team-building sessions described in Chapter 11, except that the focus is on using the survey results to assess the development of the team, its strengths and weaknesses, and the lessons that can be applied to future project work. The results of team evaluation surveys are helpful in changing behavior to better support team communication, the team approach, and continuous improvement of team performance.

Individual, Team Member, and Project Manager Performance Reviews

LO 14-7

Provide useful advice for conducting performance reviews of project members.

Organizations vary in the extent to which their project managers are actively involved in the appraisal process of team members. In organizations where projects are managed within a functional organization, the team member's area manager, not the project manager, is responsible for assessing performance. The area manager may solicit the project manager's opinion of the individual's performance on a specific project; this will be factored into the individual's overall performance. In a balanced matrix, the project manager and the area manager jointly evaluate an individual's performance. In project matrix and project organizations in which the lion's share of the individual's work is project related, the project manager is responsible for appraising individual performance. One process that appears to be gaining wider acceptance is the multi-rater appraisal or "360-degree feedback," which involves soliciting feedback concerning team members' performance from all the people their work affects. This would include not only project and area managers, but also peers, subordinates, and even customers. See Snapshot from Practice 14.7: The 360-Degree Feedback.

Performance appraisals generally fulfill two important functions. The first is developmental in nature: the focus is on identifying individual strengths and weaknesses and developing action plans for improving performance. The second is evaluative and involves assessing how well the person has performed in order to determine salary or merit adjustments. These two functions are not compatible. Employees, in their eagerness to find out how much pay they will receive, tend to tune out constructive feedback on how they can improve their performance. Likewise, managers tend to be more concerned with justifying their decision than engaging in a meaningful discussion on how

SNAPSHOT FROM PRACTICE 14.7   The 360-Degree Feedback*

More and more companies are discarding the traditional superior-subordinate performance feedback process and replacing it with 360-degree feedback systems. The 360-degree feedback approach gathers behavioral observations from many sources within the organization and includes employee self-assessment. The individual completes the same structured evaluation process that superiors, project team members, peers and, in many cases, external customers use to evaluate a performance. Survey questionnaires, augmented by a few open-ended questions, are typically used to gather information.

Summary results are compared against organizational strategies, values, and business objectives. The feedback is communicated to the individual with the assistance of the company's human resource department or an outside consultant. The technique is used by a growing number of firms including General Electric, AT&T, Mobil Oil, Nabisco, Hewlett-Packard, and Warner-Lambert.

The objective of the 360-degree process is to identify areas for individual improvement. When anonymous feedback solicited from others is compared with the individual's self-evaluations, the individual may form a more realistic picture of her or his strengths and weaknesses. This may prompt behavioral change if the weaknesses identified were previously unknown to the individual. So, for example, a project manager who thinks he delegates work effectively finds out that subordinates disagree. This causes him to rethink how he delegates and to decide to delegate more and sooner.

Many firms obtain feedback from internal and external project customers. For example, a client may evaluate a project manager or member of the project team according to "How effectively does the individual get things done without creating unnecessary adversarial relationships?" Incorporating customer feedback in the evaluation process underscores collaboration and the importance of client expectations in determining project success.

* Brian O'Reilly, "360 Feedback Can Change Your Life," *Fortune,* October, 17, 1994, pp. 93–100; Robert Hoffman, "Ten Reasons You Should Be Using 360 Degree Feedback," *HR Magazine,* April 1995, pp. 82–85; Dick Cochran, "Finally, a Way to Completely Measure Project Manager Performance," *PM Network,* September 2000, pp. 75–80.

the employee can improve his or her performance. It is difficult to be both a coach and a judge. As a result, several experts on performance appraisal systems recommend that organizations separate **performance reviews**, which focus on individual improvement, and pay reviews, which allocate the distribution of rewards (cf., Romanoff, 1989; Latham and Wexley, 1993).

In some matrix organizations, project managers conduct the performance reviews, while area managers are responsible for pay reviews. In other cases, performance reviews are part of the project closure process, and pay reviews are the primary objective of the annual performance appraisal. Other organizations avoid this dilemma by allocating only group rewards for project work and providing annual awards for individual performance. The remaining discussion is directed at reviews designed to improve performance because pay reviews are often outside the jurisdiction of the project manager.

Individual Reviews

Organizations employ a wide range of methods to review individual performance on a project. In general, review methods of individual performance center on the technical and social skills brought to the project and team. Some organizations rely simply on an informal discussion between the project manager and the project member. Other organizations require project managers to submit written evaluations that describe and assess an individual's performance on a project. Many organizations use rating scales similar to the team evaluation survey in which the project manager rates the individual according to a certain scale (i.e., from 1 to 5) on a number of relevant performance dimensions (i.e., teamwork, customer relations). Some organizations augment these rating schemes with behaviorally anchored descriptions of what constitutes a 1 rating, a 2 rating, and so forth. Each method has its strengths and weaknesses, and, unfortunately, in many organizations the appraisal systems were designed to support mainstream operations and not unique project work. The bottom line is that project managers have to use as best they can the performance review system mandated by their organization.

Regardless of the method, the project manager needs to sit down with each team member and discuss his or her performance. Here are some general tips for conducting performance reviews:

- Always begin the process by asking the individual to evaluate his or her contributions to the project. First, this approach may yield valuable information that you were not aware of. Second, the approach may provide an early warning for situations in which there is disparity in assessments. Finally, this method reduces the judgmental nature of the discussion.

- Avoid, when possible, drawing comparisons with other team members; rather, assess the individual in terms of established standards and expectations. Comparisons tend to undermine cohesion and divert attention away from what the individual needs to do to improve performance.

- When you have to be critical, focus the criticism on specific examples of behavior rather than on the individual personally. Describe in specific terms how the behavior affected the project.

- Be consistent and fair in your treatment of all team members. Nothing breeds resentment more than if, through the grapevine, individuals feel they are being held to a different standard than are other project members.

- Treat the review as only one point in an ongoing process. Use it to reach an agreement as to how the individual can improve his or her performance.

Both managers and subordinates may dread a formal performance review. Neither side feels comfortable with the evaluative nature of the discussion and the potential for misunderstanding and hurt feelings. Much of this anxiety can be alleviated if the project manager is doing her job well. Project managers should be constantly giving team members feedback throughout the project so that individual team members can have a pretty good idea how well they have performed and how the manager feels before the formal meeting. Post-project angst can be avoided if pre-project expectations are discussed before the project and regularly reinforced during project performance.

While in many cases the same process that is applied to reviewing the performance of team members is applied to evaluating the project manager, many organizations augment this process, given the importance of the position to their organization. This is where conducting the **360-degree review** is becoming more popular. In project-driven organizations, the project office typically will be responsible for collecting information on a specific project manager from customers, vendors, team members, peers, and other managers. This approach has tremendous promise for developing more effective project managers (Cochran, 2000).

In addition to performance reviews, data are collected for project retrospectives, which can present situations that may influence performance. In these situations performance evaluations should recognize and note the unusual situation.

Summary

The goals of project closure are to complete the project and to improve performance of future projects. Implementing closure and review has three major closure deliverables: wrap-up, audit, and performance evaluation. Wrap-up activities put the project "to bed" and include completing the final project deliverable, closing accounts, finding new opportunities for project staff, closing facilities, and creating the final report. Project audits assess the overall success of the project. Retrospectives are used to identify lessons learned and improve future performance. Individual and team evaluations assess performance and opportunities for improvement. A project should not be considered closed until all three activities have been completed. The culture of the organization and the project team will play a major factor in the efficacy of these activities.

Key Terms

Lessons learned, *525*　　Project closure, *516*　　Retrospective, *525*
Performance review, *535*　　Project evaluation, *532*　　360-degree review, *536*

Review Questions

1. How does the project closure review differ from the performance measurement control system discussed in Chapter 13?
2. What major information would you expect to find in a project review?
3. Why is it difficult to perform a truly independent, objective review?
4. Comment on the following statement: "We cannot afford to terminate the project now. We have already spent more than 50 percent of the project budget."
5. Why should you separate performance reviews from pay reviews? How do you do this?
6. Advocates of retrospective methodology claim there are distinguishing characteristics that increase its value over past lessons learned methods. What are they? How does each characteristic enhance project closure and review?

Exercises

1. Consider a course that you recently completed. Perform a review of the course (the course represents a project and the course syllabus represents the project plan).
2. Imagine you are conducting a review of the International Space Station project. Research press coverage and the Internet to collect information on the current status of the project. What are the successes and failures to date? What forecasts would you make about the completion of the project, and why? What recommendations would you make to top management of the program, and why?
3. Interview a project manager who works for an organization that implements multiple projects. Ask the manager what kind of closure procedures are used to complete a project and whether lessons learned are used.
4. What are some of the lessons learned from a recent project in your organization? Was a retrospective done? What action plans were generated to improve processes as a result of the project?

References

Anonymous, "Annual Survey of Business Improvement Architects," Toronto, Canada, in *PM Network,* "Deliverables," vol. 21, no. 4 (April 2007), p. 18.

Cochran, D., "Finally, a Way to Completely Measure Project Manager Performance," *PM Network,* September 2000, pp. 75–80.

Cooke-Davies, T., "Project Management Closeout Management: More than Simply Saying Good Bye and Moving On," in J. Knutson (Ed.), *Project Management for Business Processionals* (Indianapolis, IN: John Wiley and Sons, 2001), pp. 200–14.

Fretty, P., "Why Do Projects Really Fail?" *PM Network,* March 2006, pp. 45–48.

Gobeli, D., and E. W. Larson, "Barriers Affecting Project Success," in *1986 Proceedings Project Management Institute: Measuring Success* (Upper Darby, PA: Project Management Institute, 1986), pp. 22–29.

Hoffman, R., "Ten Reasons You Should Be Using 360 Degree Feedback," *HR Magazine,* April 1995, pp. 82–85.

Jedd, Marcia, "Standing Guard," *PM Network,* vol. 21, no. 1 (January 2007), pp. 73–77.

Kendrick, Tom, *Identifying and Managing Project Risk,* 2nd ed. (New York: ANACOM, 2009).

Kerth, Norman L., *Project Retrospectives: A Handbook for Team Reviews* (New York: Dorset House, 2001).

Kwak, Y. H., and C. W. Ibbs, "Calculating Project Management's Return on Investment," *Project Management Journal,* vol. 31, no. 2 (March 2000), pp. 38–47.

Ladika, S., "By Focusing on Lessons Learned, Project Managers Can Avoid Repeating the Same Old Mistakes," *PM Network,* Vol. 22, No. 2 (February 2008), pp. 75–77.

Latham, G. P., and K. N. Wexley, *Increasing Productivity through Performance Appraisal,* 2nd ed. (Reading, MA: Addison-Wesley, 1993).

Lavell, Debra, and Russ Martinelli, "Program and Project Retrospectives: An Introduction," *PM World Today,* vol. 10, no. 1 (January 2008), p. 1.

Marlin, Mark, "Implementing an Effective Lessons Learned Process in a Global Project Environment," *PM World Today,* vol. 10, no. 11 (November 2008), pp. 1–6.

Nelson, Ryan R., "Project Retrospectives: Evaluating Project Success, Failure, and Everything in Between," *MIS Quarterly Executive,* vol. 4, no. 3 (September 2005), p. 372.

Pippett, D. D., and J. F. Peters, "Team Building and Project Management: How Are We Doing?" *Project Management Journal,* vol. 26, no. 4 (December 1995), pp. 29–37.

Romanoff, T. K., "The Ten Commandments of Performance Management," *Personnel,* vol. 66, no. 1 (1989), pp. 24–26.

Royer, I., "Why Bad Projects Are So Hard to Kill," *Harvard Business Review,* February 2003, pp. 49–56.

Senge, P., *The Fifth Discipline: The Art and Practice of the Learning Organization* (New York: Doubleday, 1990).

Sheperd, D. A., H. Patzelt, and M. Wolfe, "Moving Forward from Project Failure: Negative Emotions, Affective Commitment, and Learning from the Experience," *Academy of Management Journal,* vol. 54, no. 6 (2011), pp. 1229–60.

Staw, Berry M., and Jerry Ross, "Knowing When to Pull the Plug," *Harvard Business Review,* March-April 1987, pp. 68–74.

Wheatly, M., "Over the Bar," *PM Network,* vol. 17, no. 1 (January 2003), pp. 40–45.

Yates, J. K., and S. Aniftos, "ISO 9000 Series of Quality Standards and the E/C Industry," *Project Management Journal,* vol. 28, no. 2 (June 1997), pp. 21–31.

Zaitz, Les, "Rail Car Deal Snags Tri Met for Millions," *Oregonian,* December 14, 2008, p. 1, and January 7, 2009, p. D4.

Appendix 14.1

Project Closeout Checklist

Project Closeout Transition Checklist

Provide basic information about the project including: Project Title—The proper name used to identify this project; Project Working Title—The working name or acronym that will be used for the project; Proponent Secretary—The Secretary to whom the proponent agency is assigned or the Secretary that is sponsoring an enterprise project; Proponent Agency—The agency that will be responsible for the management of the project; Prepared by—The person(s) preparing this document; Date/Control Number—The date the checklist is finalized and the change or configuration item control number assigned.

Project Title: _____   *Project Working Title:* _____
Proponent Secretary: _____   *Proponent Agency:* _____
Prepared by: _____   *Date/Control Number:* _____

Complete the Status and Comments columns. In the Status column indicate: Yes, if the item has been addressed and completed; No, if the item has not been addressed, or is incomplete; N/A, if the item is not applicable to this project. Provide comments or describe the plan to resolve the item in the last column.

	Item	Status	Comments/Plan to Resolve
1	Have all the product or service deliverables been accepted by the customer?		
1.1	Are there contingencies or conditions related to the acceptance? If so, describe in the Comments.		
2	Has the project been evaluated against each performance goal established in the project performance plan?		
3	Has the actual cost of the project been tallied and compared to the approved cost baseline?		
3.1	Have all approved changes to the cost baseline been identified and their impact on the project documented?		

(Continued)

		Item	Status	Comments/Plan to Resolve
4		Have the actual milestone completion dates been compared to the approved schedule?		
4.1		Have all approved changes to the schedule baseline been identified and their impact on the project documented?		
5		Have all approved changes to the project scope been identified and their impact on the performance, cost, and schedule baselines documented?		
6		Has operations management formally accepted responsibility for operating and maintaining the product(s) or service(s) delivered by the project?		
6.1		Has the documentation relating to operation and maintenance of the product(s) or service(s) been delivered to, and accepted by, operations management?		
6.2		Has training and knowledge transfer of the operations organization been completed?		
6.3		Does the projected annual cost to operate and maintain the product(s) or service(s) differ from the estimate provided in the project proposal? If so, note and explain the difference in the Comments column.		
7		Have the resources used by the project been transferred to other units within the organization?		
8		Has the project documentation been archived or otherwise disposed of as described in the project plan?		
9		Have the lessons learned been documented in accordance with the Commonwealth Project Management guideline?		
10		Has the date for the post-implementation review been set?		
10.1		Has the person or unit responsible for conducting the post-implementation review been identified?		

Signatures

The signatures of the people below relay an understanding that the key elements within the Closeout Phase section are complete and the project has been formally closed.

Position/Title	Name	Date	Phone Number

Source: http://www.vita.virginia.gov/projects/cpm/cpmDocs/CPMG-SEC5-Final.pdf

Appendix 14.2

Euro Conversion—Project Closure Checklist

Project _____ *Euro Conversion* _____   Customer _____ *Finance Department* _____

Project manager _____ *Hans Kramer* _____   Completion date _____ *12 December XX* _____

	Due date	Person responsible	Notes
1. Document finance department acceptance	16/12	Hans	
2. Customer training in Euro software	28/12	Joan	Train all departments before conversion
3. Archive all			
Schedules/actuals	31/12	Maeyke	
Budgets/actual costs	31/12	Maeyke	
Changes	31/12	Maeyke	
4. Close out all accounts with vendors	31/12	Guido	
5. Close out all work orders	31/12	Mayo	
6. Close out partner accounts	31/12	Guido	
7. Reassign project staff	16/12	Sophie	
8. Evaluation of			
Vendors	31/12	Mayo	Use standard questionnaire for vendors
Staff members	31/12	Sophie	Have HR department develop and administer
9. Final report and lessons learned meeting	4/1	Hans	Send notice to all stakeholders
10. Lessons learned archive to database	10/1	Maeyke	Contact IS department
tribute awards		Sophie	Notify all stakeholders

Case A14.1

Maximum Megahertz Project

Olaf Gundersen, the CEO of Wireless Telecom Company, is in a quandary. Last year he accepted the Maximum Megahertz Project suggested by six up-and-coming young R&D corporate stars. Although Olaf did not truly understand the technical importance of the project, the creators of the project needed only $600,000, so it seemed like a good risk. Now the group is asking for $800,000 more and a six-month extension on a project that is already four months behind. However, the team feels confident they can turn things around. The project manager and project team feel that if they hang in there a little longer they will be able to overcome the roadblocks they are encountering—especially those that reduce power, increase speed, and use a new technology battery. Other managers familiar with the project hint that the power pack problem might be solved, but "the battery problem will never be solved." Olaf believes he is locked into this project; his gut feeling tells him the project will never materialize, and he should get out. John, his human resource manager, suggested bringing in a consultant to axe the project.

Olaf decided to call his friend Dawn O'Connor, the CEO of an accounting software company. He asked her, "What do you do when project costs and deadlines escalate drastically? How do you handle doubtful projects?" Her response was, "Let another project manager look at the project. Ask: 'If you took over this project tomorrow, could you achieve the required results, given the extended time and additional money?' If the answer is no, I call my top management team together and have them review the doubtful project in relation to other projects in our project portfolio." Olaf feels this is good advice.

Unfortunately, the Maximum Megahertz Project is not an isolated example. Over the last five years there have been three projects that were never completed. "We just seemed to pour more money into them, even though we had a pretty good idea the projects were dying. The cost of those projects was high; those resources could have been better used on other projects." Olaf wonders, "Do we ever learn from our mistakes? How can we develop a process that catches errant projects early? More importantly, how do we ease a project manager and team off an errant project without embarrassment?" Olaf certainly does not want to lose the six bright stars on the Maximum Megahertz Project.

Olaf is contemplating how his growing telecommunications company should deal with the problem of identifying projects that should be terminated early, how to allow good managers to make mistakes without public embarrassment, and how they all can learn from their mistakes.

Give Olaf a plan of action for the future that attacks the problem. Be specific and provide examples that relate to Wireless Telecom Company.

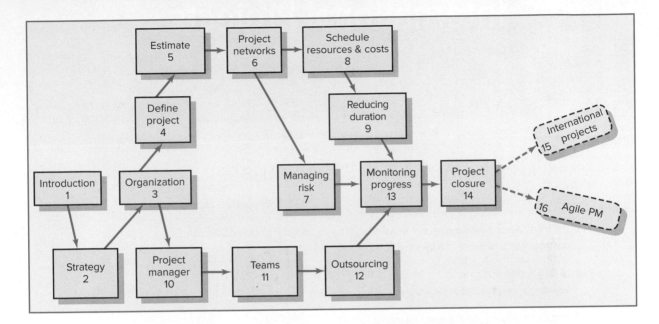

With Chapter 14 the project life cycle is complete. You have been exposed to the core elements of project management. We have consciously tried to incorporate a blend of sociocultural and process practices required to successfully manage any project. These best practices are transferable across industries. Your understanding of these chapters should enhance your ability to make a positive contribution in any project environment.

The supplemental chapters that follow expand on the core by covering international project management, and Agile methods.

- Chapter 15. Explores different international environments in which you may have to manage a project. In large high technology firms we estimate that 60–90 percent of their projects are virtual and across many cultures. If you find yourself new in this environment, the international chapter is an excellent primer on the types of conditions and issues you may encounter in an international project.

- Chapter 16. Agile methodology is used in complex projects (e.g., software and new innovation products) where the final design requirements are not known and evolve as the project is implemented. The methodology breaks requirements into small functional pieces that allow rapid response to change. Agile embraces flexibility, change, small teams, and owner involvement.

15 International Projects

LEARNING OBJECTIVES

After reading this chapter you should be able to:

15-1 Describe environmental factors that affect project management in different countries.

15-2 Identify factors that typically are considered in selecting a foreign location for a project.

15-3 Understand cross-cultural issues that impact working on international projects.

15-4 Describe culture shock and strategies for coping with it.

15-5 Understand how organizations select and prepare people to work on international projects.

OUTLINE

15.1 Environmental Factors

15.2 Project Site Selection

15.3 Cross-Cultural Considerations: A Closer Look

15.4 Selection and Training for International Projects

Summary

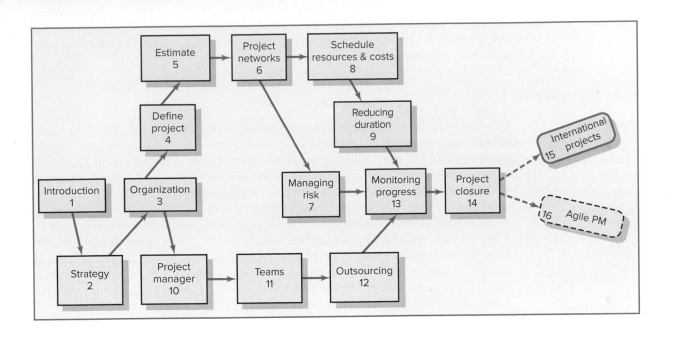

The principal benefit of living abroad is that it enables us to get glimpses of ourselves as others see us and to realize that others' views are more accurate than ours. Progress begins with grasping the truth about ourselves, however unpleasant it may be.

—*Russel Ackoff, The Wharton School, University of Pennsylvania*

Thanks to technology we live in a "flat world" in which more and more projects have an international element. It could be being sent to Zimbabwe for 9 months as a lead contractor on a bridge construction project or flying back and forth across the Atlantic to work on a joint product venture with German engineers. Or it could be relying on a Korean computer supplier on a business expansion project or Skyping with an Indian counterpart on a software project. This chapter targets the international project manager who must resettle in a foreign land to manage a project. The chapter also provides useful information for professionals whose project work requires interacting either directly or virtually with foreign counterparts from around the world.

There is no generally accepted framework or road map for project managers given international assignments. These project managers typically face a difficult set of problems—for example, absence from home, friends, and sometimes family; personal risks; missed career opportunities; foreign language, culture, and laws; adverse conditions. Of course there are positives—for example, increased income, increased responsibilities, career opportunities, foreign travel, new lifetime friends. How the international project manager adapts and approaches challenges encountered in the host country often determines the success or failure of a project.

This chapter focuses on four major issues surrounding the management of international projects. First, major environmental factors that impact project selection and implementation are briefly highlighted. Second, an example of how organizations decide where to expand globally is provided. Third, the challenge of working in a strange and foreign culture is addressed. Finally, how companies select and train professionals for international projects is discussed. Although by no means comprehensive, this chapter provides an understanding of the major issues and challenges confronting the international project manager.

15.1 Environmental Factors

LO 15-1

Describe environmental factors that affect project management in different countries.

The major challenge international project managers face is the reality that what works at home may not work in a foreign environment. Too often project managers impose practices, assumed to be superior, from their home country on host-country nationals without questioning their applicability to the new environment. Although there are similarities between domestic and international projects, it is a fact that good management practices vary across nations and cultures. It is these differences that can turn an international project into a nightmare. If potential international project managers have a keen awareness of differences in the host country's environment from their own domestic environment, dangers and obstacles of the global project can be reduced or avoided. There are several basic factors in the host country's environment that may alter how projects will be implemented: legal/political, security, geographical, economic, infrastructure, and culture (see Figure 15.1).

Legal/Political

Expatriate project managers should operate within the laws and regulations of the host country. Political stability and local laws strongly influence how projects will be

FIGURE 15.1
Environmental Factors Affecting International Projects

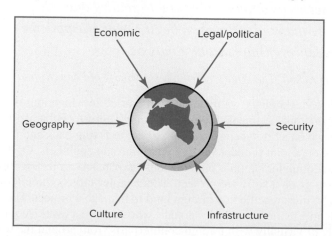

implemented. Typically, these laws favor protection of local workers, suppliers, and environment. For example, how much control will be imposed from government agencies? What is the attitude of federal and state bureaucracies toward regulations and approval policies that can cause project delays? How much government interference or support can one expect? For example, some governments interpret regulations arbitrarily, depending upon personal interests.

The constraints imposed by national and local laws need to be identified and adhered to. Are local ecological laws restrictive? Will manufacturing a new product in a computer chip plant require exporting toxic waste materials? What are the pollution standards? How will labor laws affect the use of indigenous workers to complete the project? Given that laws that affect business vary widely across countries, qualified legal assistance is essential.

Government corruption is a very real part of international business. In China various forms of obligatory "profit sharing" with city officials in the Hainan province have been reported. Employment of relatives, donations, and other "favors" are an expected cost of doing business in that region. Likewise, *Bloomberg BusinessWeek* reported that in Russia the threat of being targeted for abuse by government officials—sometimes operating in league with Russian businesses—is the primary reason that country has attracted less than one-fifth of the foreign investment in Brazil (Cahill, 2010).

Political stability is another key factor in deciding to implement a project in a foreign country. What are the chances that there will be a change in the party in power during the project? Are the tax provisions and government regulations stable or subject to change with the winds of political change? How are laws made, and what is the past record of fairness? How are labor unions treated in the political realm? Does labor unrest exist? Is there a chance for a coup d'état? Contingency plans need to be established to respond to emergencies.

Security

International terrorism is a fact of life in today's world. Tim Daniel, chief operating officer of International SOS Assistance, Inc., reported that the number of his firm's clients doubled after September 11th. SOS is a security firm that specializes in evacuating expatriates from dangerous situations around the world. The company cites PricewaterhouseCoopers, Nortel Networks Corp., and Citigroup among its clients (Scown, 1993).

While the 9/11 attacks magnified the fact that Americans are vulnerable to terrorism at home, they also heightened security concerns for working abroad. For example, after September 11th, several American firms canceled or scaled back projects in potential hotspots such as Somalia and the Philippines. Others reported increased pressures from expatriates who wanted to return home with their families. On May 7, 2009, the Nobel Peace Prize-winning relief agency *Médecins Sans Frontières* (Doctors Without Borders) reduced emergency projects in northwest Pakistan due to clashes between government forces and Taliban fighters.[1]

Crime is another factor. The growing presence of the Russian Mafia has discouraged many foreign firms from setting up operations in the former Soviet Union. Kidnapping of American professionals is also a very real threat in many parts of the world.

Security nationally involves the capacity of a country's military and police forces to prevent and respond to attacks. In many foreign countries, American firms will have to

[1] www.doctorswithoutborders.org/press/release, June 2009.

augment the countries' security system. For example, it is common practice to hire tribal bodyguards in such places as Angola and Uzbekistan.

Another real cost associated with international terrorism is the ease of commerce across borders. Heightened security measures have created border congestions that have expanded the time and cost of moving personnel, materials, and equipment across countries. These constraints need to be factored into the budget and schedule of projects.

Risk management is always a vital part of project management. It plays an even bigger role in managing projects overseas. For example, Strohl Systems Group, a global leader in recovery-planning software and services, includes the following among the questions it uses to evaluate vulnerability to terrorism: Have you included possible terrorist targets (facilities and personnel) in your hazard and vulnerability analysis? Have you conducted a counterterrorism exercise complete with law enforcement, fire, medical, and emergency management participation? What should your organization's policy be on negotiating with a person threatening a terrorist act?[2]

Managing projects in a dangerous world is a tough assignment. Security precautions are major cost considerations not only in dollars and cents, but also in the psychological well-being of personnel sent abroad. Effective risk management is critical.

Geography

One factor that is often underestimated until project personnel actually arrive at a foreign destination is the geography of the country. Imagine what it is like to deplane from a modern aircraft and encounter the 105-degree heat and 90 percent humidity of Jakarta, Indonesia, or three feet of fresh snow and −22 degree temperatures in Kokkla, Finland. Whether it is the wind, the rain, the heat, the jungle, or the desert, more than one project manager has asserted that the greatest challenge was overcoming the "elements." Mother Nature cannot be ignored.

The planning and implementation of a project must take into account the impact the country's geography will have on the project. For example, a salvage operation off the coast of Greenland can only be scheduled one month out of the year because the waterway is frozen over during the remainder of the year. Construction projects in Southeast Asia have to accommodate the monsoon season when rainfall can be as high as 50 inches per month.

Geography does not just affect outdoor projects. It can have an indirect effect on "indoor" projects. For example, one information systems specialist reported that his performance on a project in northern Sweden declined due to sleep deprivation. He attributed his problems to the 20 hours of daylight this part of the world experiences during summer months. Finally, extreme weather conditions can make extraordinary demands on equipment. Projects can grind to a halt because of equipment breakdown under the brunt of the wind and sand. Working under extreme conditions typically requires special equipment, which increases the costs and complexity of the project.

Before beginning a project in a foreign land, project planners and managers need to study carefully the unique characteristics of the geography of that country. They need to factor into project plans and schedules such items as climate, seasons, altitude, and natural geographical obstacles. See the Snapshot from Practice 15.1: The Filming of *Apocalypse Now* for an example of a poorly planned endeavor in the Philippines.

---

[2] Contingency Planning and Management.com, "Strohl Systems Offers Terrorism Readiness Questionnaire," September 24, 2001.

SNAPSHOT FROM PRACTICE 15.1   The Filming of *Apocalypse Now**

In February 1976, Francis Ford Coppola took his Hollywood film crew to the Philippines to shoot *Apocalypse Now,* a film adaptation of Joseph Conrad's *Heart of Darkness* within the context of the Vietnam conflict. The Philippines was chosen because the terrain was similar to Vietnam's, and the government was willing to rent out its helicopter force for the movie. At the time, the U.S. military was unwilling to cooperate on a film about Vietnam. An additional advantage was cheap labor. Coppola was able to hire more than 300 laborers at $1 to $3 per day to construct elaborate production sets, including an impressive Cambodian temple. *Apocalypse Now* was scheduled for 16 weeks of shooting at a budget of $12 to $14 million.

Months earlier, George Lucas, of *Star Wars* fame, warned Coppola against filming the movie in the Philippines. He said, "It's one thing to go over there for three weeks with five people and scrounge some footage with the Filipino Army, but if you go over there with a big Hollywood production, the longer you stay the more in danger you are of getting sucked into the swamp." His words turned out to be prophetic.

A civil war was going on between government forces and communist rebels. Shooting was repeatedly interrupted because the Philippine military ordered their helicopter pilots to leave the set and fly to the mountains to fight the rebels.

In May 1976, a typhoon struck the Philippine Islands, destroying most of the movie sets. The film team was forced to shut down production and returned to the United States for two months.

The lead character was played by Martin Sheen, who suffered a serious heart attack under the stress and heat of the filming and had to return to the United States. Coppola scrambled to film the scenes that did not require Sheen, but eventually production came to a standstill until Sheen's return nine weeks later.

The entire project proved to be a traumatic experience for Coppola, who had enjoyed Academy Award success with his previous *Godfather* movies. "There were times when I thought I was going to die, literally, from the inability to move the problems I had. I would go to bed at four in the morning in a cold sweat."

Film production ended in May 1977 after more than 200 days of shooting. The final cost was about $30 million.

* *Hearts of Darkness: A Filmmaker's Apocalypse* (Paramount Pictures, 1991).

Economic

Basic economic factors in foreign countries and regions influence choices of site selection and project success. The gross domestic product (GDP) of a country suggests the level of development of a country. A faltering economy may indicate fewer sources of capital funding. Changes in protectionist strategies of a host country, such as import quotas and tariffs, can quickly alter the viability of projects. Other factors such as balance of payments, taxation, labor laws, safety regulations, and market size can influence project choices and operations.

Skills, educational level, and labor supply prevalent in a host country can determine the choice of a project site. Is project selection driven by low wage levels or availability of technically skilled talent? For example, you can hire three computer programmers in Ukraine for the price of one programmer in the United States. Conversely, many high-tech companies are willing to endure the additional expense of setting up joint projects in Switzerland and Germany to take advantage of their engineering prowess.

Financial exposure is a significant risk for many international projects. Let's look first at the potential impact of currency fluctuations on project success. For example, a U.S. contractor agrees to build a customized product for a German client. The product will be built in the United States. The contractor estimates that the project will cost $925,000, and, in order to earn a nice profit, prices the project at $1,000,000. To accommodate the German buyer the price is converted to euros. Suppose at the time of the contract, the exchange rate is $1.15 per euro, and the price specified in the contract is €869,566.

Ten months later the project is completed as expected, with work costing the estimated $925,000 and the customer pays the agreed upon price of €869,566. However the exchange rate has changed; it is now $1.05 per Euro. That being the case, the payment equates to €869,566 × 1.05 = $913,044. Instead of reaping a nice profit the contractor suffers a $(913,044 − 925,000) = $−11,956 loss!

A company can protect against adverse currency fluctuations in a number of related ways. First, they can *hedge* against this risk by having all parties agree to finalize the deal and make payments at a specified future date. Finance people call this a *forward exchange* or *contract*. Second, they can stipulate in the contract certain conditions based on exchange rates to insure their profit margin. Finally, many multinational companies who do business in the client country avoid currency exchange and simply use local currency to manage operations in that country. Financiers refer to this as a *natural hedge* (Moffet et al., 2012).

Inflation is another significant risk. One of the greatest strengths of the U.S. economy is its relatively low inflation rate (below 3 percent from 1990–2012). Other countries, especially underdeveloped countries, do not enjoy such stability. Rapid inflation can strike at any time and have profound impact on project costs and profits. For example, a European contractor successfully wins the bid to build a bridge for the Tanzanian government in East Africa. Work started in 2010 and will be completed by the end of 2011. In 2010 the Tanzanian inflation ratio was less than 6 percent with an average inflation rate of 6.7 over the past decade. The contractor used what she considered a conservative inflation rate of 9 percent when estimating the costs of the project at 1,800,000 schillings (Tanzanian currency). In order to win the bid and enjoy a solid profit the agreed upon price is 2,000,000 schillings.

Early in 2011 Tanzania experiences a sporadic rainfall which, coupled with increased oil prices, causes the inflation rate to jump to over 20 percent! Suddenly costs of certain elements of the project increase dramatically and instead of garnering a nice profit the contractor barely breaks even. Companies can protect against inflation by tying costs to a strong currency such as the U.S. dollar, British pound, or euro and/or negotiating cost-plus contracts (see Chapter 12 Appendix) with the client.

Bartering is a form of compensation that is still used by some countries and organizations. For example, one project in Africa was paid in goat skins. The goat skins were eventually sold to an Italian manufacturer of gloves. Another project along the Caspian Sea was paid for in oil. There is a small group of firms that specialize in bartering for project contractors. These intermediaries charge a commission to sell the bartered goods (e.g., oil, diamonds, wheat) for the contractor. However, dealing with commodities can be a risky enterprise.

Infrastructure

Infrastructure refers to a country or community's ability to provide the services required for a project. Infrastructure needs for a project could be communication, transportation, power, technology, and education systems. Power outages are common in many parts of the world. For example, India's burgeoning economy came to a halt during the 2012 summer when over 670 million people were without power for more than two days. If reliable power is not sufficient, other alternatives need to be considered. For example, construction firms often rely on heavy diesel generators as backups on their projects. Software projects across borders are common today; however, they depend on reliable telecommunication networks. If the project depends on a high ratio of vendor suppliers, good roads, and other transportation modes such as air and seaports, a good infrastructure will be imperative.

An example of a project that failed to take into account the needs and infrastructure of the host nation involved a U.S. company that was awarded the contract for building a hospital in an African nation. The local African officials wanted a "low-tech" health care facility that would take local traditions into consideration. Because their relatives generally accompanied patients, space had to be provided for them, too. Electricity was not reliably supplied, and it was doubtful whether well-educated doctors would want to spend careers away from the city. Therefore, the locals wanted a hospital for basic care with minimum technology. The construction company doing the building, on the other hand, had a preconceived notion of what a hospital should be and was not going to be accused of building a second-rate facility. It built a modern hospital that could have stood in any U.S. city. The building was completed; however, even after several years it was not used because the electricity was not sufficient, the air-conditioning could not be used, and doctors refused to live in the rural area (Adler and Gunderson, 2007).

Organizations need to consider the needs of the families of personnel they send overseas. Will the facilities and living conditions for the expatriate families place an undue hardship on families? Will schooling for children be available? The welfare and comfort of expatriate families play an important role in retaining good project managers and promoting their peak performance.

Culture

Visiting project managers must respect the customs, values, philosophies, and social standards of their host country. Global managers recognize that if the customs and social cultural dimensions of the host country are not accommodated, projects will rarely succeed. Too many project audits and final reports of international projects reflect challenges and problems linked to cultural differences.

For most project managers, the biggest difference in managing an international project is operating in a national culture where things are done differently. For example, most developed nations use the same project management techniques (CPM, risk analysis, trade-off analysis). However, how activity work is performed can be very different in the host country. For example, a backhoe is used to dig a trench in France, while 20 laborers are used to dig a similar trench in Ethiopia.

Will English be the operating language, or will the project manager need to be fluent in the foreign language? Will translation services be available and sufficient? Communication problems—because of language differences—often become a major problem in carrying out even simple tasks. Although the use of translators can help tremendously, their use does not solve the communication problem completely because something is lost in translation. For example, consider the disastrous consequences of differences in interpretations and expectations between the Brazilians and Americans highlighted in Snapshot from Practice 15.2: River of Doubt.

Will religious factors influence the project? For example, religious factors touched the spouse of a Scandinavian project manager responsible for building a water desalination plant from sea water in a Middle East country. She was restricted to the living compound for families of foreign guest workers. Going outside the compound to a nearby city meant covering her head, arms, and legs and being accompanied by another woman or, preferably, a man. A physical altercation in the city concerning her clothing was traumatic for her. She left the country and returned home. Her husband requested a transfer back home three months later. The loss of the original project manager set the project back three months.

SNAPSHOT FROM PRACTICE 15.2 River of Doubt*

After his crushing election defeat in 1912 as a third-party candidate, former president Theodore ("Teddy") Roosevelt set his sights on a grand adventure, the first descent of an unmapped rapids-choked tributary of the Amazon aptly titled the "River of Doubt." Together with Brazil's most famous explorer, Candido Mariano da Silva Rondon, Roosevelt accomplished a feat that belongs in the annals of great expeditions.

Along the way, Roosevelt and his men faced an unbelievable series of hardships, losing their canoes and supplies to crushing whitewater rapids, and enduring starvation, Indian attacks, disease, drowning, and even murder within their ranks. Candice Millard brings alive these extraordinary events in her nonfiction thriller *The River of Doubt*. While her account details the ill-fated journey it also reveals insights into international project management as it describes the collaboration between the American and Brazilian cohorts. While each party ultimately earned the respect and admiration of the other, friction between the two parties simmered from the outset.

One source of consternation was the amount of supplies and luggage that the Americans required for the journey. Warned that the luggage requirements of the former president and his party would be extensive, the Brazilian commodore Rondon ordered 110 mules and 17 pack oxen to be used for the expedition's overland journey across the Brazilian highland to the great river. Surely, he felt, this would be more than necessary for such a trip.

The Brazilians were astounded by the sheer volume of baggage that was unloaded from Roosevelt's ship, the *Vandycks*. There were mountains of crates: guns and ammunition, chairs and tables, tents and cots, equipment for collecting and preserving specimens, surveying the river, and cooking meals. An exhausted stevedore elicited a roar of laughter from the onlooking crowd when he announced, "Nothing lacking but the piano!"

Rather than risk embarrassment by telling Roosevelt that they were not prepared to take so much luggage, Rondon scrambled to find additional animals. Extra oxen and mules were located, but they were far from tame. Loaded with supplies, the oxen would buck and throw off the packs. The expedition was delayed

© Fotomas/Topham/TheImageWorks

as gauchos (South American cowboys) endeavored to "break" the animals as quickly as possible.

Within days of finally setting off across the vast highlands, Roosevelt and his men began to experience the harsh realities that were to plague the expedition. After crossing a bone-strewn graveyard of oxen and mules that had starved to death or been eaten during previous expeditions, they were stunned by the sight of unopened supply crates, all clearly marked "Roosevelt South American Expedition." The pack animals, still making their weary away across the plateau ahead of the them, had begun bucking off their heavy loads!

As the officers rode slowly past the boxes, they wondered what they were leaving behind and how precious it might become in the months ahead. Little did they know how true those fears would be.

* Candice Millard, *The River of Doubt* (New York: Doubleday), 2005.

Not only do project managers have to adapt to the culture of the host country, but often overseas projects require working with people from other different countries. For example, on a light rail project in the Philippines, an American firm was hired to oversee the interests of local real estate companies who were funding the project. The American project manager had to work with Czech representatives who were providing the rail equipment, Japanese engineers responsible for building the rail, Australian bankers who were providing additional financing, an Indian firm that were the principal architects, as well as the native Filipinos.

Of all the factors, working within a multicultural environment is most often the greatest challenge for project managers. It will be dealt with in detail later in this chapter.

15.2 Project Site Selection

LO 15-2

Identify factors that typically are considered in selecting a foreign location for a project.

As the project manager studies the factors contributing to site selection, he will see that inherent in all of these factors is the risk level senior management and directors are willing to accept for the potential rewards of a successful international project. One approach for the project manager to digest, clarify, and understand the factors leading to the selection of a specific project is to use a risk matrix similar to those found in Chapter 7. The major difference lies in the selection of the risk factors for different project sites.

Figure 15.2 presents a truncated matrix for project site selection of the construction of a laser printer factory in Singapore, India, or Ireland. In this example, political stability, worker skill and supply, culture compatibility, infrastructure, government support, and product-to-market advantage were the major assessment factors. Each project site is compared against each factor. Figure 15.3 depicts a further breakdown of the infrastructure evaluation factor. In this example, transportation, educated workforce, utilities, telecommunications, and vendor suppliers are considered important to evaluating the infrastructure for each site. The scores given in Figure 15.3 are used to assign values to the infrastructure factor of the assessment matrix, Figure 15.2. In this project, Ireland was the choice. Clearly, Singapore and Ireland were very close in terms of infrastructure and several other factors. However, the major assessment factor of using Ireland to access the EEC (product-to-market advantage) turned the decision.

FIGURE 15.2
Assessment Matrix Project Site Selection

Score legend

5 = excellent
3 = acceptable
1 = poor

	Political stability	Worker skill, supply	Culture compatibility	Infrastructure	Government support	Product-to-market advantage
Singapore	5	4	4	4	4	3
India	3	4	3	3	3	3
Ireland	5	4	5	5	5	5

FIGURE 15.3
Evaluation Matrix Breakdown for Infrastructure

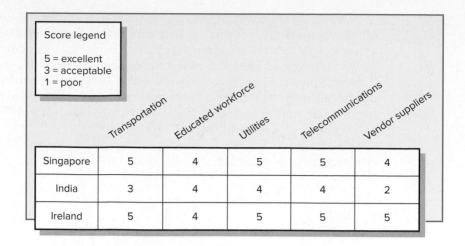

	Transportation	Educated workforce	Utilities	Telecommunications	Vendor suppliers
Singapore	5	4	5	5	4
India	3	4	4	4	2
Ireland	5	4	5	5	5

Score legend

5 = excellent
3 = acceptable
1 = poor

Given the macro economic factors, the firm's strategic posture toward global projects, and the major considerations for selecting this project, it is imperative the project manager quickly become sensitized to the foreign cultural factors that can spell project success or failure.

15.3 Cross-Cultural Considerations: A Closer Look

LO 15-3

Understand cross-cultural issues that impact working on international projects.

The concept of culture was introduced in Chapter 3 as referring to the unique personality of a particular firm. More specifically, culture was defined as a system of shared norms, beliefs, values, and customs that bind people together, creating shared meaning and a unique identity. *Culture* is a concept created for descriptive purposes and depends on the group that is the focus of attention. For example, within a global context culture can refer to certain regions (i.e., Europeans, Arabs), to specific nations (i.e., French, Thai), or to certain ethnic or religious groups (i.e., Kurds, African Americans). This chapter looks at national cultures; we freely recognize that many cultural characteristics are borderless and that there is considerable variation within any one country. Still, national cultures provide a useful anchor for understanding different habits, customs, and values around the world.

Right or wrong, Americans have a reputation for not being able to work effectively in foreign cultures. (When we use the term "American," we are referring to people from the United States; we apologize to our friends in Canada and Central and South America.) In the 1960s, the term "Ugly American" encapsulated the apparent indifference of Americans to native cultures when working or traveling abroad. Americans are often criticized for being parochial; that is, they view the world solely through their own eyes and perspectives. People with a parochial perspective do not recognize that other people have different ways of living and working effectively. American parochial attitudes probably reflect the huge domestic market of the United States, the geographic isolation of the United States, and the reality that English is becoming the international business language in many parts of the world.

It is important that Americans working on international projects anticipate cultural differences. Take, for example, a project manager from a large North American construction company who was given responsibility to select a site for the design and construction of a large fish-processing plant in a West African country. The manager assessed potential sites according to the availability of reliable power, closeness to transportation, nearness to the river for access of fishing boats from the Atlantic Ocean, proximity to main markets, and availability of housing and people for employment. After evaluating alternative sites, the project manager chose the optimum location. Just prior to requesting bids from local contractors for some of the site preparation, the manager discovered, in talking to the contractors, that the site was located on ground considered sacred by the local people, who believed this site was the place where their gods resided. None of the local people upon whom the project manager was depending for staff would ever consider working there! The project manager quickly revised his choice and relocated the site. In this case, he was lucky that the cultural gaffe was discovered prior to construction. Too often these errors are realized only after a project is completed.[3]

Some argue that Americans have become less parochial. International travel, immigration, movies, and the popularity of such international events as the Olympics have made more Americans sensitive to cultural differences. While Americans may be more worldly, there is still a tendency for them to believe that American cultural values and ways of doing things are superior to all others. This ethnocentric perspective is reflected in wanting to conduct business only on their terms and stereotyping other countries as lazy, corrupt, or inefficient. Americans need to make a serious effort to appreciate other ways of approaching work and problems in other countries.

Finally, American project managers have earned a reputation abroad for being very good at understanding technology but not good at understanding people. As one Indonesian engineer put it, "Americans are great at solving technical problems, but they tend to ignore the people factor." For example, Americans tend to underestimate the importance that relationship building plays in conducting business in other countries. Americans have a tendency to want to get down to work and let friendships evolve in the course of their work. In most other cultures just the opposite is true. Before a foreigner works with you, he wants to get to know you as a person. Trust is not established by credentials but rather evolves from personal interaction. Business deals often require a lengthy and elaborate courtship (Arms and Lucas, 1978; Chen and Miller, 2010). For example, it may take five to eight meetings before Arab managers are even willing to discuss business details.

Adjustments

Two of the biggest adjustments Americans typically have to make in working abroad are adapting to the general pace of life and the punctuality of people. In America "time is money," and a premium is placed on working quickly. Other cultures do not share Americans' sense of urgency and are accustomed to a much slower pace of life. They can't understand why Americans are always in such a hurry. Punctuality varies across cultures. For example, Americans will generally tolerate someone being 5 to 10 minutes late. In contrast, among Peruvians, the period before an apology or explanation for being late is expected might be 45 minutes to an hour!

While working on multicultural projects, managers sometimes encounter ethical dilemmas that are culturally bound. For example, the 1999 Olympic site selection scandal featured the sordid details of committee members peddling their votes for a wide range of gifts (i.e., university scholarships for their children, extravagant trips). In many societies such "bribes" or "tributes" are expected and the only way to conduct meaningful business. Moreover, many cultures will not grant a female project manager

[3] This incident was cited in H. W. Lane and J. J. DiStefano, *International Project Management,* 2nd ed. (Boston: PWS-Kent, 1992), p. 27.

the same respect they will a male project manager. Should U.S. management increase project risk or violate its own sex-discrimination policy?

These cultural differences are just the tip of the iceberg. There are numerous "How to Do Business in . . ." books written by people who have traveled and worked abroad. Although these books may lack rigor, they typically do a good job of identifying local customs and common mistakes made by outsiders. On the other hand, anthropologists have made significant contributions to our understanding of why and how the cultures of societies are different (see Research Highlights 15.1 and 15.2). Students of international project management are encouraged to study these works to gain a deeper understanding of the root causes of cultural diversity.

So what can be said to prepare people to work on international projects? The world is too diverse to do justice in one chapter to all the cultural variations managers are likely to encounter when working on international projects. Instead, a sample of some of these differences will be highlighted by discussing working on projects in four different countries: Mexico, France, Saudi Arabia, and China. We apologize to our readers outside the United States because briefings are presented from the viewpoint of a U.S. project manager working in these countries. Still, in an effort not to be too ethnocentric, we present a fifth scenario for foreign project managers assigned to working in the United States. Although by no means exhaustive, these briefings provide a taste of what it is like to work in and with people from these countries.

Working in Mexico

America developed historically in an environment where it was important for strangers to be able to get along, interact, and do business. On the American frontier almost everyone was a stranger, and people had to both cooperate and keep their distance. The New England Yankee sentiment that "Good fences make good neighbors" expresses this American cultural value well. Conversely, Mexico developed historically in an environment where the only people to trust were family and close friends—and by extension, people who were known to those whom you knew well. As a consequence, personal relationships dominate all aspects of Mexican business. While Americans are generally taught not to do business with friends, Mexicans and other Latin Americans are taught to do business with no one but friends.

The significance of personal relationships has created a *compadre* system in which Mexicans are obligated to give preference to relatives and friends when hiring, contracting, procuring, and sharing business opportunities. North Americans often complain that such practices contribute to inefficiency in Mexican firms. While this may or may not be the case, efficiency is prized by Americans, while Mexicans place a higher value on friendship.

Mexicans tend to perceive Americans as being "cold." They also believe that most Americans look down on them. Among the most effective things an American can do to prevent being seen as a typical *Gringo* is to take the time and effort in the beginning of a working relationship to really get to know Mexican counterparts. Because family is all-important to Mexicans, a good way for developing a personal relationship is exchanging information about each other's family. Mexicans will often gauge people's trustworthiness by the loyalty and attention they devote to their family.

The *mañana* syndrome reflects another cultural difference between Americans and Mexicans. Mexicans have a different concept of time than Americans do. Mexicans feel confined and pressured when given deadlines; they prefer open-ended schedules.

Anthropologists Kluckhohn and Strodtbeck assert that cultural variations reflect how different societies have responded to common issues or problems throughout time (see Figure 15.4). Five of the issues featured in their comparative framework are discussed here.

- *Relationship to nature*—This issue reflects how people relate to the natural world around them and to the supernatural. Should people dominate their environment, live in harmony with it, or be subjugated to it? North Americans generally strive to harness nature's forces and change them as they need. Other societies, as in India, strive to live in harmony with nature. Still other societies see themselves at the mercy of physical forces and/or subject to the will of a supreme being. Life in this context is viewed as predetermined, preordained, or an exercise in chance.

- *Time orientation*—Does the culture focus on the past, present, or future? For example, many European countries focus on the past and emphasize maintaining tradition. North Americans, on the other hand, are less concerned with tradition and tend to focus on the present and near future. Paradoxically, Japanese society, while rich with tradition, has a much longer time horizon.

- *Activity orientation*—This issue refers to a desirable focus of behavior. Some cultures emphasize "being" or living in the moment. This orientation stresses experiencing life and seeking immediate gratification. Other cultures emphasize "doing" and emphasize postponing immediate gratification for greater accomplishment. A third alternative is the "control" orientation, where people restrain their desires by detaching themselves from objects. The activity dimension affects how people approach work and leisure and the extent to which work-related concerns pervade their lives. It is reflected in the age-old question, "Do we live to work or work to live?"

- *Basic nature of people*—Does a culture view people as good, evil, or some mix of these two? In many Third World countries, people see themselves as basically honest and trustworthy. Conversely, some Mediterranean cultures have been characterized as taking a rather evil view of human nature. North Americans are somewhere in between. They see people as basically good but stay on guard so as not to be taken advantage of.

- *Relationships among people*—This issue concerns the responsibility one has for others. Americans, for instance, tend to be highly individualistic and believe everyone should take care of him- or herself. In contrast, many Asian societies emphasize concern for the group or community he or she is a member of. A third variation is hierarchical, which is similar to the group except that in these societies groups are hierarchically ranked, and membership is essentially stable over time. This is a characteristic of aristocratic societies and caste systems.

The Kluckhohn and Strodtbeck framework provides a basis for a deeper understanding of cultural differences. At the same time, they warn that not all members of a culture practice the same behavior all the time, and, as in the United States, there is likely to be considerable variation within a given culture.

* F. Kluckhohn and F. L. Strodtbeck, *Variations in Value Orientations* (Evanston, IL: Row, Peterson, 1961).

FIGURE 15.4
Kluckhohn-Strodtbeck's Cross-Cultural Framework

Note: The line indicates where the United States tends to fall along these issues.

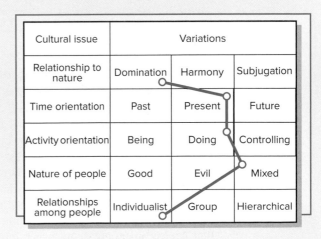

Cultural issue	Variations		
Relationship to nature	Domination	Harmony	Subjugation
Time orientation	Past	Present	Future
Activity orientation	Being	Doing	Controlling
Nature of people	Good	Evil	Mixed
Relationships among people	Individualist	Group	Hierarchical

The Hofstede framework grew from a study of 88,000 people working in IBM subsidiaries in 50 countries and 3 multicountry regions. Based on responses to a 32-item questionnaire, Dutch social scientist Geert Hofstede developed different dimensions for examining cultures:

1. Individualism versus collectivism. Identifies whether a culture holds individuals or the group responsible for each member's welfare.

2. Power distance. Describes the degree to which a culture accepts status and power differences among its members.

3. Uncertainty avoidance. Identifies a culture's willingness to accept uncertainty and ambiguity about the future.

4. Masculinity-femininity. Describes the degree to which the culture emphasizes competitive and achievement-oriented behavior or displays concerns for relationships.

Figure 15.5 shows how he ranked selected countries according to collectivism-individualism and power distance. Wealth appears to influence both factors. Power distance is correlated with income inequality in a country while individualism is correlated with national wealth (Per Capita Gross National Product). As a result high power distance and collectivism are often found together, as are low power distance and individualism. This can affect decision making on project teams. For example, while the high collectivism may lead a project team in Thailand to operate consensually, the high power distance may cause decisions to be heavily influenced by the desires of the project manager. Conversely, a similar team operating in a more individualistic and low power distance context such as Great Britain or America might make decisions with more open debate including challenging the preferences of the project manager.

* G. Hofstede, *Culture's Consequences: Comparing Values, Behaviors, Institutions and Organizations Across Nations,* 2nd Edition (Thousand Oaks, CA: Sage Publications, 2001). http://www.geerthofstede.nl

FIGURE 15.5

Sample Country Clusters on Hofstede's Dimensions of Individualism-Collectivism and Power Distance

Collectivism		Colombia, Peru, Thailand, Singapore, Mexico, Turkey, Indonesia
Individualism	Israel, Finland, Germany, Ireland, New Zealand, Canada, Great Britain, United States	Spain, South Africa, France, Italy, Belgium
	Low power distance	High power distance

They generally consider individuals to be more important than sticking to a schedule. If a friend drops in at work, most Mexicans will stop and talk, regardless of how long it takes, and even if chatting makes their work late. This sometimes contributes to the erroneous perception that Mexicans lack a work ethic. Quite the contrary; given a minimal incentive, Mexicans can be quite industrious and ambitious.

Finally, as in many other cultures, Mexicans do not share Americans' confidence that they control their own destiny. While Americans are taught, "When the going gets tough, the tough get going," Mexicans are taught, "Taking action without knowing what is expected or wanted can have dangerous consequences." Mexicans tend to be more cautious and want to spend more time discussing risks and potential problems that Americans might dismiss as improbable or irrelevant.

Other useful guidelines for working with Mexicans on projects include the following:

1. Americans tend to be impersonal and practical when making arguments; Mexicans can be very passionate and emotional when arguing. They enjoy a lively debate.

2. Where Americans tend to use meetings as the place to work things out publicly, Mexicans tend to see meetings as the place where persons with authority ratify what has been decided during informal private discussions.

3. While Mexicans can be emotional, they tend to shy away from any sort of direct confrontation or criticism. A long silence often indicates displeasure or disagreement.

4. Speech in Mexico is often indirect. People rarely say no directly but are more likely to respond by saying maybe *(quizas)*, or by saying "I will think about it" or changing the subject. Yes *(si)* is more likely to mean "I understand you" than "yes."

5. Titles are extremely important in Mexico and are always used when a person is introducing him- or herself or being introduced. Pay as much attention to remembering a person's title as to remembering his or her name.

Today, with NAFTA and increased international business activity in Mexico, old traditions are disappearing. American managers report that cultural differences are less evident in northern Mexico where many multinational firms operate. Here *hora americana* (American time) rather than *hora mexicana* tends to be used when dealing with foreigners. Project managers should devote up-front effort to understanding how much older mores of Mexican culture apply to their project.[4]

Working in France

Some Americans consider the French the most difficult to work with among Europeans. This feeling probably stems from a reflection of the French culture, which is quite different from that in the United States.

In France, one's social class is very important. Social interactions are constrained by class standing, and during their lifetimes most French people do not encounter much change in social status. Unlike an American, who through hard work and success can move from the lowest economic stratum to the highest, a successful French person might, at best, climb one or two rungs up the social ladder. Additionally, the French are very status conscious and like to provide signs of this status, such as knowledge of literature and arts; a well-designed, tastefully decorated house; and a high level of education.

The French tend to admire or be fascinated with people who disagree with them; in contrast, Americans are more attracted to those who agree with them. As a result, the French are accustomed to conflict and, during negotiations, accept the fact that some positions are irreconcilable and must be accepted as such. Americans, on the other hand, tend to believe that conflicts can be resolved if both parties make an extra effort and are willing to compromise. Also, the French often determine a person's trustworthiness based on their first-hand, personal evaluation of the individual's character. Americans, in contrast, tend to evaluate a person's trustworthiness on the basis of past achievements and other people's evaluations.

[4] Adapted from E. Kras, *Management in Two Cultures: Bridging the Gap between U.S. and Mexican Managers,* rev. ed. (Yarmouth, ME: Intercultural Press, 1995); L. W. Tuller, *An American's Guide to Doing Business in Latin America* (Avon, MA: Adams Business, 2008).

The French are often accused of lacking an intense work ethic. For example, many French workers frown on overtime and on average they have one of the longest vacations in the world (four to five weeks annually). On the other hand, the French enjoy a reputation for productive work, a result of the French tradition of craftsmanship. This tradition places a greater premium on quality than on getting things accomplished quickly.

Most French organizations tend to be highly centralized with rigid structures. As a result, it usually takes longer to carry out decisions. Because this arrangement is quite different from the more decentralized organizations in the United States, many U.S. project managers find the bureaucratic red tape a source of considerable frustration.

In countries like the United States, a great deal of motivation is derived from professional accomplishments. The French do not tend to share this same view of work. While they admire American industriousness, they believe that quality of life is what really matters. As a result they attach much greater importance to leisure time, and many are unwilling to sacrifice the enjoyment of life for a dedication to project work.

Cautions to remember with the French include these:

1. The French value punctuality. It is very important to be on time for meetings and social occasions.

2. Great importance is placed on neatness and taste. When interacting with French businesspeople, pay close attention to your own professional appearance and appear cultured and sophisticated.

3. The French can be very difficult to negotiate with. Often, they ignore facts, no matter how convincing they may be. They can be quite secretive about their position. It is difficult to obtain information from them, even in support for their position. Patience is essential for negotiating with them.

4. French managers tend to see their work as an intellectual exercise. They do not share the American view of management as an interpersonally demanding exercise, where plans have to be constantly "sold" upward and downward using personal skills.

5. The French generally consider managers to be experts. They expect managers to give precise answers to work-related questions. To preserve their reputation, some French managers act as if they know the answers to questions even when they don't.[5]

Working in Saudi Arabia

Project management has a long tradition in Saudi Arabia and other Arab countries. Financed by oil money, European and American firms have contributed greatly to the modernization of Arab countries. Despite this tradition, foreigners often find it very hard to work on projects in Saudi Arabia. A number of cultural differences can be cited for this difficulty.

One is the Arabian view of time. In North America, it is common to use the cliché, "The early bird gets the worm." In Saudi Arabia, a favorite expression is, "Bukra insha Allah," which means, "Tomorrow if God wills," an expression that reflects the Saudis' approach to time. Unlike Westerners, who believe they control their own time, Arabs believe that Allah controls time. As a result, when Saudis commit themselves to a date in the future and fail to show up, there is no guilt or concern on their part because they have

---

[5] Adapted from R. Hallowell, D. Bowen, and C. I. Knoop, "Four Seasons Goes to Paris," *Academy of Management Executive,* 16 (4) November 2002, pp. 7–24; J. Hooker, *Working across Cultures* (Stanford, CA: Stanford Business Books, 2003); T. Morrison and W. A. Conaway, *Kiss, Bow, or Shake Hands (The Bestselling Guide to Doing Business in More than 60 Countries),* 2nd ed. (New York: Adams Media, 2006).

no control over time in the first place. In planning future events with Arabs, it pays to hold lead time to a week or less, because other factors may intervene or take precedence.

An associated cultural belief is that destiny depends more on the will of a supreme being than on the behavior of individuals. A higher power dictates the outcome of important events, so individual action is of little consequence. As a result, progress or the lack of progress on a project is considered more a question of fate than effort. This leads Saudis to rely less on detailed plans and schedules to complete projects than Americans do.

Another important cultural contrast between Saudi Arabians and Americans is emotion and logic. Saudis often act on the basis of emotion; in contrast, those in an Anglo culture are taught to act on logic. During negotiations, it is important not only to share the facts but also to make emotional appeals that demonstrate your suggestion is the right thing to do.

Saudis also make use of elaborate and ritualized forms of greetings and leave-takings. A businessperson may wait far past the assigned meeting time before being admitted to a Saudi office. Once there, the individual may find a host of others present; one-on-one meetings are rare. Moreover, during the meeting there may be continuous interruptions. Visitors arrive and begin talking to the host, and messengers may come in and go out on a regular basis. The businessperson is expected to take all this activity as perfectly normal and to remain composed and ready to continue discussions as soon as the host is prepared to do so.

Initial meetings are typically used to get to know the other party. Business-related discussions may not occur until the third or fourth meeting. Business meetings typically conclude with an offer of coffee or tea. This is a sign that the meeting is over and that future meetings, if there are to be any, should now be arranged.

Saudis attach a great deal of importance to status and rank. When meeting with them, defer to the senior person. It is also important never to criticize or berate anyone publicly. This causes the individual to lose face; the same is true for the person who makes these comments. Mutual respect is expected at all times.

Other useful guidelines for working in an Arab culture such as Saudi Arabia include the following:

1. It is important never to display feelings of superiority because this makes the other party feel inferior. No matter how well someone does something, the individual should let the action speak for itself and not brag or draw attention to himself.

2. A lot of what gets done is a result of going through administrative channels in the country. It is often difficult to sidestep a lot of this red tape, and efforts to do so can be regarded as disrespect for legal and governmental institutions.

3. Connections are extremely important in conducting business. More important people get fast service from less important people. Close relatives take absolute priority; non-relatives are kept waiting.

4. Patience is critical to the success of business negotiations. Time for deliberations should be built into all negotiations to prevent a person from giving away too much in an effort to reach a quick settlement.

5. Important decisions are usually made in person and not by correspondence or telephone. While Saudis seek counsel from many people, the ultimate power to make a decision rests with the person at the top, and this individual relies heavily on personal impressions, trust, and rapport.[6]

[6] Adapted from R. T. Moran, P. R. Harris, and S. V. Moran, *Managing Cultural Differences,* 5th ed. (Houston, TX: Gulf Publishing, 2010); and J. Hooker, *Working across Cultures* (Stanford, CA: Stanford Business Books, 2003).

Working in China

In recent years the People's Republic of China (PRC, or China, for short) has moved away from isolation to encourage more business with the rest of the world. While China holds tremendous promise, many Western firms have found working on projects in China to be a long, grueling process that often results in failure. One of the primary reasons for problems is the failure to appreciate Chinese culture.

Chinese society, like those of Japan and Korea, is influenced by the teachings of Confucius (551–478 B.C.). Unlike America, which relies on legal institutions to regulate behavior, in Confucian societies the primary deterrent against improper or illegal behavior is shame or loss of face. Face is more than simply reputation. There is a Chinese saying: "Face is like the bark of a tree; without its bark, the tree dies." Loss of face not only brings shame to individuals but also to family members. A member's actions can cause shame for the entire family, hampering that family from working effectively in Chinese society.

In China, "whom you know is more important than what you know." The term *guanxi* refers to personal connections with appropriate authorities or individuals. China observers argue that *guanxi* is critical for working with the Chinese. Chinese are raised to distrust strangers, especially foreigners. Trust is transmitted via *guanxi*. That is, a trusted business associate of yours must pass you along to his trusted business associates. Many outsiders criticize *guanxi,* considering it to be like nepotism where decisions are made regarding contracts or problems based on family ties or connections instead of an objective assessment of ability.

Many believe that the quickest way to build *guanxi* relationships is through tendering favors. Gift-giving, entertainment at lavish banquets, questionable payments, and overseas trips are common. While Westerners see this as nothing short of bribery, the Chinese consider it essential for good business. Another common method for outsiders to acquire *guanxi* is by hiring local intermediaries, who use their connections to create contacts with Chinese officials and businesspeople.

In dealing with the Chinese, you must realize they are a collective society in which people pride themselves on being a member of a group. For this reason, you should never single out a Chinese for specific praise because this is likely to embarrass the individual in front of his peers. At the same time, you should avoid the use of "I" because it conveys that the speaker is drawing attention to himself or herself.

Chinese do not appreciate loud, boisterous behavior, and when speaking to each other they maintain a greater physical distance than is typical in America. Other cautions include the following:

1. Once the Chinese decide who and what is best, they tend to stick to their decisions. So while they may be slow in formulating a plan, once they get started they make good progress.

2. Reciprocity is important in negotiations. If Chinese give concessions, they expect some in return.

3. The Chinese tend to be less animated than Americans. They avoid open displays of affection and physical contact; they are more reticent and reserved than Americans.

4. The Chinese place less value on the significance of time and often get Americans to concede concessions by stalling.

5. In Confucian societies those in position of power and authority are obligated to assist the disadvantaged. In return they gain face and a good reputation.[7]

---

[7] Adapted from J. L. Graham and N. M. Lam, "The Chinese Negotiation," *Harvard Business Review,* October 1, 2003, pp. 82–91; I. Yeung and R. L. Tung, "Achieving Business Success in Confucian Societies: The Importance of Guanxi (Connections)," *Organizational Dynamics,* 25 (2) Autumn 1996, pp. 54–65; and Hooker, *Working across Cultures.*

SNAPSHOT FROM PRACTICE 15.3   Project Management X-Files

Americans tend to discount the significance of luck and believe that good fortune is generally a result of hard work. In other cultures, luck takes on greater significance and has supernatural ramifications. For example, in many Asian cultures certain numbers are considered lucky, while others are unlucky. In Hong Kong the numbers 7, 3, and especially 8 (which sounds like the word for prosperity) are considered lucky, while the number 4 is considered unlucky (because it is pronounced like the word "death"). Hong Kong businesspeople go to great lengths to avoid the number 4. For example, there is no fourth floor in office and hotel buildings. Business executives have been known to reject ideal sites in heavily congested Hong Kong because the address would contain the number 4. They pay premium prices for suitable sites containing addresses with the lucky numbers. Likewise, Hong Kong business managers avoid scheduling important events on the fourth day of each month and prefer to arrange critical meetings on the eighth day.

Hong Kong is also a place where the ancient art of *Feng shui* (literally "wind water") is practiced. This involves making sure a site and buildings are aligned in harmony with the earth's energy forces so that the location will be propitious. Feng shui practitioners are often called in on construction projects to make sure

© bikeriderlondon/Shutterstock

that the building is aligned correctly on the site. In some cases, the technical design of the building is changed to conform to the recommendations of such experts. Similarly, Feng shui experts have been known to be called in when projects are experiencing problems. Their recommendations may include repositioning the project manager's desk or hanging up mirrors to deflect the flow of unharmonious influences away from the building or site of the project.

In cultures where luck is believed to play a role in business, people who discount luck may not only insult the luck seekers, but risk being thought negligent in not paying enough attention to what is viewed as a legitimate business concern.

For more insights on Chinese culture see the Snapshot from Practice 15.3: Project Management X-Files.

Working in the United States

In the world of international projects, professionals from other countries will come to the United States to manage projects. To them, the United States is a foreign assignment. They will have to adapt their management style to the new environment they find in the States.

Immigration has made the United States a melting pot of diverse cultures. While many are quick to point out the differences between North and South, Silicon Valley and Wall Street, social anthropologists have identified certain cultural characteristics that shape how many Americans conduct business and manage projects.

Mainstream Americans are motivated by achievement and accomplishment. Their identity and, to a certain extent, their self-worth are measured by what they have achieved. Foreigners are often astounded by the material wealth accumulated by Americans and the modern conveniences most Americans enjoy. They are also quick to point out that Americans appear too busy to truly enjoy what they have achieved.

Americans tend to idolize the self-made person who rises from poverty and adversity to become rich and successful. Most Americans have a strong belief that they can influence and create their future, that with hard work and initiative, they can achieve whatever they set out to do. Self-determination and pragmatism dominate their approach to business.

Although Americans like to set precise objectives, they view planning as a means and not an end. They value flexibility and are willing to deviate from plans and improvise if they believe change will lead to accomplishment. Obstacles on a project are to be overcome, not worked around. Americans think they can accomplish just about anything, given time, money, and technology.

Americans fought a revolution and subsequent wars to preserve their concept of democracy, so they resent too much control or interference, especially by governments. While more an ideal than practice, there is deep-rooted belief in American management philosophy that those people who will be affected by decisions should be involved in making decisions. Many foreign businesspeople are surprised at the amount of autonomy and decision-making authority granted to subordinates. Foreign personnel have to learn to interact with American professionals below their rank in their own organizations.

Businesspeople from different African, Asian, and Latin American countries are amazed and often somewhat distressed at the rapid pace of America. "Getting things done" is an American characteristic. Americans are very time-conscious and efficient. They expect meetings to start on time. They tinker with gadgets and technological systems, always searching for easier, better, more efficient ways of accomplishing things. American professionals are often relentless in pursuing project objectives and expect that behavior of others also.

Americans in play or business generally are quite competitive, reflecting their desire to achieve and succeed. Although the American culture contains contradictory messages about the importance of success (i.e., "It's not whether you win or lose but how you play the game" versus "nice guys finish last"), winning and being number one are clearly valued in American society. Foreigners are often surprised at how aggressively Americans approach business with adversarial attitudes toward competitors and a desire to not just meet but to exceed project goals and objectives.

Other guidelines and cautions for working with Americans on projects include:

1. More than half of U.S. women work outside the home; females have considerable opportunity for personal and professional growth, guaranteed by law. It is not uncommon to find women in key project positions. Female professionals expect to be treated as equals. Behavior tolerated in other countries would be subject to harassment laws in the States.

2. In the United States, gifts are rarely brought by visitors in a business situation.

3. Americans tend to be quite friendly and open when first meeting someone. Foreigners often mistake this strong "come-on" for the beginning of a strong reciprocal friendship. This is in contrast to many other cultures where there is more initial reserve in interpersonal relations, especially with strangers. For many foreigners, the American comes on too strong, too soon, and then fails to follow up with the implicitly promised friendship.

4. Although in comparison to the rest of the world Americans tend to be informal in greeting and dress, they are a noncontact culture (e.g., they avoid embracing in public usually) and Americans maintain certain physical/psychological distance with others (e.g., about two feet) in conversations.

5. American decision making is results oriented. Decisions tend to be based on facts and expected outcomes, not social impact.[8]

---

[8] Adapted from Moran et al., *Managing Cultural Differences;* and D. Z. Milosevic, "Echoes of the Silent Language of Project Management," *Project Management Journal,* 30 (1) March 1999, pp. 27–39.

SNAPSHOT FROM PRACTICE 15.4   Dealing with Customs

Will corruption influence the project? Bribes are illegal in the United States, but in some countries they are the usual way to do business. For example, one American project manager in a foreign country requested that a shipment of critical project equipment be sent "overnight rush." Two days later, inquiries to the sender confirmed the materials had been delivered to the nearby airport. Further inquiries to the port found the shipment "waiting to pass customs." Locals quickly informed the American that money paid to the chief customs inspector would expedite clearance. The American project manager's response

was, "I will not be held hostage. Bribes are illegal!" Two more days of calling government officials did not move the shipment from customs. The manager related his problem to a friendly businessman of the host nation at a social affair. The local businessman said he would see if he could help. The shipment arrived the next morning at 10:00 A.M. The American called his local business friend and thanked him profusely. "I owe you one." "No," replied the local. "You owe me a $50 dinner when I visit you in the States." The use of an intermediary in such situations may be the only avenue available to a manager to reduce the stress and personal conflict with the U.S. value system.

Summary Comments about Working in Different Cultures

These briefings underscore the complexity of working on international projects. It is common practice to rely on intermediaries—often natives who are foreign educated—to bridge the gap between cultures. These intermediaries perform a variety of functions. They act as translators. They use their social connections to expedite transactions and protect the project against undue interference. They are used to sidestep the touchy bribery/gift dilemma (see Snapshot from Practice 15.4: Dealing with Customs). They serve as cultural guides, helping outsiders understand and interpret the foreign culture. In today's world, there are a growing number of consulting firms that perform these functions by helping foreign clients work on projects in their country.

The international briefings also highlight the importance of project managers doing their homework and becoming familiar with the customs and habits of the host country they are going to be working in. As far as possible, the project should be managed in such a way that local-country norms and customs are honored. However, there are limits to the extent to which you should accommodate foreign cultures. *Going native* is generally not an alternative. After all, it took a Russian his entire life to learn how to be a Russian. It would be foolish to think an outsider could learn to be one in six months, two years, or perhaps ever.

The remainder of this chapter focuses on the selection and training of project personnel for international projects. But before these issues are discussed, this section concludes with a discussion of the phenomenon of culture shock, which can have a profound effect on a foreigner's performance on a project in a strange culture.

Culture Shock

My first few weeks in Chiang Mai [Thailand] were filled with excitement. I was excited about the challenge of building a waste treatment plant in a foreign country. I was fascinated with Thai customs and traditions, the smells and sights of the night market. Soon I noticed a distinct change in my attitude and behavior. I started having problems sleeping and lacked energy. I became irritable at work, frustrated by how long things took to accomplish, and how I couldn't seem to get anything accomplished. I started staying up late at night drinking Thai whiskey and watching CNN in my hotel room.

FIGURE 15.6
Culture Shock Cycle

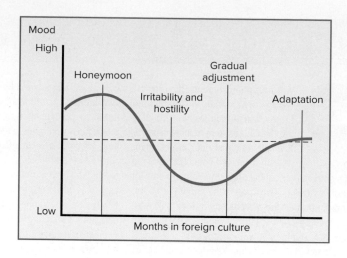

LO 15-4

Describe culture shock and strategies for coping with it.

This engineer is experiencing what many would call "culture shock." *Culture shock* is a natural psychological disorientation that most people suffer when they move into a culture different from their own. The culture shock cycle has four stages (see Figure 15.6):

1. *Honeymoon*—You start your overseas assignment with a sense of excitement. The new and the unusual are welcomed. At first it is amusing not to understand or be understood. Soon a sense of frustration begins to set in.

2. *Irritability and hostility*—Your initial enthusiasm is exhausted, and you begin to notice that differences are greater than you first imagined. You become frustrated by your inability to get things done as you are accustomed to. You begin to lose confidence in your abilities to communicate and work effectively in the different culture.

3. *Gradual adjustment*—You begin to overcome your sense of isolation and figure out how to get things done in the new culture. You acquire a new perspective of what is possible and regain confidence in your ability to work in the culture.

4. *Adaptation*—You recover from your sense of psychological disorientation and begin to function and communicate in the new culture.

Culture shock is not a disease but a natural response to immersing yourself in a new environment. Culture shock results from a breakdown in your selective perception and effective interpretation system. At a subliminal level, your senses are being bombarded by a wide variety of strange sounds, sights, and smells. At the same time, the normal assumptions you are accustomed to using in your home culture to interpret perceptions and to communicate intentions no longer apply. When this happens, whether in a business context or in normal attempts to socialize, confusion and frustration set in. The natives' behavior does not seem to make sense, and, even more importantly, your behavior does not produce expected results. Frustration occurs because you are used to being competent in such situations and now find you are unable to operate effectively.

Culture shock is generally considered a positive sign that the professional is becoming involved in the new culture instead of remaining isolated in an expatriate ghetto. The significant question is how best to manage culture shock, not how to avoid it. The key appears to be managing the stress associated with culture shock.

Stress-related culture shock takes many forms: disappointment, frustration, withdrawal, anxiety, and physiological responses such as fatigue, sleeplessness, and headaches. Stress is induced by the senses being overwhelmed by foreign stimuli and the inability to function effectively in a strange land. Stress is exacerbated when one encounters disturbing situations that, as a foreigner, are neither understood nor condoned. For example, many North Americans are appalled by the poverty and hunger in many underdeveloped countries.

Coping with Culture Shock

There are a wide range of stress management techniques for coping with culture shock. One method does not necessarily work any better than another; success depends on the particular individual and situation involved. Some people engage in regular physical exercise programs, some practice meditation and relaxation exercises, and others find it healthy to keep a journal.

Many effective international managers create "stability zones." They spend most of their time immersed in the foreign culture but then briefly retreat into an environment— a stability zone—that closely re-creates home. For example, when one of the authors was living in Kraków, Poland, with his family, they would routinely go to the Polish movie houses to see American movies with Polish subtitles. The two hours spent hearing English and seeing a familiar environment on the screen had a soothing effect on everyone.

On the project, managers can reduce the stress caused by culture shock by recognizing it and modifying their expectations and behavior accordingly. They can redefine priorities and develop more realistic expectations as to what is possible. They can focus their limited energy on only the most important tasks and relish small accomplishments.

After three to six months, depending on the individual and assignment, most people come up from their culture shock "low" and begin living a more normal life in the foreign country. They talk to acquaintances from the host country and experienced outsiders from their own culture to find out how to behave and what to expect. Little by little they learn how to make sense of the new environment. They figure out when "yes" means "yes" and when it means "maybe" and when it means "no." They begin to master the language so that they can make themselves understood in day-to-day conversations. See the Snapshot from Practice 15.5: Project X—Namibia, Africa, for further insights on coping with culture shock.

The vast majority of people eventually make the adjustment, although for some people it can take much longer than three to six months. A smaller number never recover, and their international experience turns into a nightmare. Some exhibit severe stress symptoms (e.g., alcoholism, drug abuse, nervous breakdown) and must return home before finishing their assignment.

Professionals can use project work as a bridge until they adjust to their new environment. Unfortunately, spouses who do not work do not have this advantage. When spouses are left to cope with the strange environment on their own, they often have a much more difficult time overcoming culture shock. The effect on spouses cannot be underestimated. The number one reason expatriate managers return home is that their spouses failed to adjust to the new environment (Tung, 1987).

Project professionals working overseas accept that they are in a difficult situation and that they will not act as effectively as they did at home, especially in the initial stages. They recognize the need for good stress management techniques, including stability zones. They also recognize that it is not an individual problem and invest extra time and energy to help their spouses and families manage the transition. At the same time, they appreciate that their colleagues are experiencing similar problems and are sensitive to their needs. They work together to manage the stress and pull out of a culture shock low as quickly as possible.

SNAPSHOT FROM PRACTICE 15.5   Project X—Namibia, Africa*

While U.S. reality TV shows focus on finding love, outwitting opponents, and garnering audience support, a Norwegian TV show shone a light on project management under extreme conditions. The plot was deceptively simple: send 10 Scandinavian volunteers 6,000 miles away from home to the dry sub-tropics of southern Africa and charge them with building a school for orphans and poor children in less than 30 days. Not only would they be forced to adjust to vastly different language, climate, and cuisines, but only one of the 10 had previous construction experience. The team's trials and tribulations were aired over Norwegian TV in 2009. The marketing blitz for the show, titled *Project X*, played up the drama with the tagline: "Can they achieve the mission?"

The team was enthusiastic at the outset, but discontent began as soon as they arrived at the small mining town of Tsumeb in Namibia. The team immediately experienced culture shock—all the while the TV crew followed them, sticking cameras in their faces and asking how they felt.

The sweltering heat, slumlike conditions, and limited cuisine immediately elicited complaints: "I can't sleep." "The food is awful." "Where are the toilets?"

One of the biggest mistakes the volunteers made was applying a Eurocentric sense of time and planning. "I brought my Danish mindset that 'On Friday we will do this and on Saturday we will do that,'" reported Merete Lange, one of the volunteers. "Then I came to understand African time, and that was the biggest surprise."

Hoping to secure local buy-in, Ms. Lange arranged for a local carpenter to build desks and tables. A few days before the furniture was needed, she discovered work hadn't even begun.

"I got pretty stressed and tried to be my best at being diplomatic," Ms. Lange recalls. "I asked, 'When do you think you will be ready with the furniture?'" The carpenter responded, "Time is unpredictable. I will call you."

Over time, Ms. Lange and her teammates were able to adapt to the elements and figure out ways to work with the locals to successfully build the school within 30 days. "The trick is reflecting upon 'where people were coming from, how to meet them there, and how to create a win-win situation that would satisfy both parties.'"

* B. G. Yovovich, "Worlds Apart," *PMNetwork,* October 2010, pp. 24–29.

It is somewhat ironic, but people who work on projects overseas experience culture shock twice. Many professionals experience the same kind of disorientation and stress when they return home, although it is usually less severe. For some, their current job has less responsibility and is boring compared with the challenge of their overseas assignment. For others, they have problems adjusting to changes made in the home organization while they were gone. This can be compounded by financial shock when the salary and fringe benefits they became accustomed to in the foreign assignment are now lost, and adjusting to a lower standard of living is difficult. It typically takes six months to a year before managers operate again at full effectiveness after a lengthy foreign assignment (Adler and Gunderson, 2007).

15.4 Selection and Training for International Projects

LO 15-5

Understand how organizations select and prepare people to work on international projects.

When professionals are selected for overseas projects and they do not work out, the overall costs can be staggering. Not only does the project experience a serious setback, but the reputation of the firm is damaged in the region. This is why many firms have developed formal screening procedures to help ensure the careful selection of personnel for international projects. Organizations examine a number of characteristics to determine whether an individual is suitable for overseas work. They may look for work experience with cultures other than one's own, previous overseas travel, good physical and emotional health, a knowledge of a host nation's language, and even recent immigration background or heritage. Prospective candidates and their family members are often interviewed by trained psychologists, who assess their ability to adapt and function in the new culture.

While there is growing appreciation for screening people for foreign assignments, the number one reason for selection is that the personnel assigned are the best people available for the technical challenges of the project (Mendenhall et al., 1987). Technical know-how takes precedence over cross-cultural sensitivity or experience. As a consequence, training is critical to fill in the cultural gaps and prepare individuals to work in a foreign land.

Training varies widely, depending on the individual, company, nature of the project, and cultures to work with. Project professionals assigned to foreign countries should have a minimal understanding of the following areas:

- Religion.
- Dress codes.
- Education system.
- Holidays—national and religious.
- Daily eating patterns.
- Family life.
- Business protocols.
- Social etiquette.
- Equal opportunity.

An example of a short-term training program is the one developed by Underwriter Laboratories, Inc., to train staff who travel to Japan to work with clients on projects. The program is designed around a series of mini-lectures that cover topics ranging from how to handle introductions to the proper way to exchange gifts to the correct way of interpreting Japanese social and business behavior. The two-day program consists of lectures, case studies, role plays, language practice, and a short test on cultural terminology; it concludes with a 90-minute question-and-answer period. At the end of the program, participants have a fundamental understanding of how to communicate with the Japanese. More importantly, they know the types of information they lack and how to go about learning more to become effective intercultural communicators.

Other training programs are more extensive. For example, Peace Corps volunteers undergo an intense two- to four-month training program in their country of service. The training includes classes on the history and traditions of the country, intensive language instruction, and cross-cultural training as well as home-stays with local families. Many companies outsource training to one of the many firms specializing in overseas and intercultural training.

Figure 15.7 attempts to link the length and type of training with the cultural fluency required to successfully complete the project. Three different learning approaches are highlighted (Mendenhall et al., 1987):

1. The "information-giving" approach—the learning of information or skills from a lecture-type orientation.
2. The "affective" approach—the learning of information/skills that raise the affective responses on the part of the trainee and result in cultural insights.
3. The "behavioral/experiential" approach—variant of the affective approach technique that provides the trainee with realistic simulations or scenarios.

FIGURE 15.7   **Relationship between Length and Rigor of Training and Cultural Fluency Required**

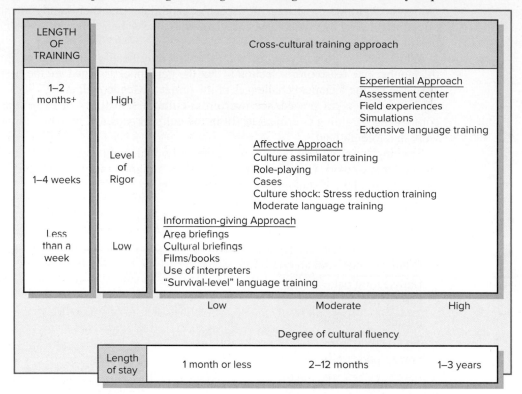

According to this framework, the length and level of training would depend on the degree of cultural fluency required to be successful. In general, the longer the person is expected to work in the foreign country, the more intensive the training should be. Length of stay should not be the only consideration; high levels of cultural fluency, and therefore more extensive training, may be required to perform short-term, intense projects. In addition, location is important. Working in Australia will likely require less cultural fluency than working on a project in Pakistan.

While English is rapidly becoming the international language for business in many parts of the world, you should not underestimate the value of being able to speak the language of the host country. At a minimum you should be able to exchange basic pleasantries in the native tongue. Most foreigners consider this a sign of respect, and even if you stumble they appreciate the effort.

In many situations translators are used to facilitate communication. While time-consuming, this is the only way to communicate with non-English-speaking personnel. Be careful in the selection of translators, and do not just assume they are competent. For example, one of the authors enlisted the help of a Polish translator to conduct a meeting with some Polish managers. After the meeting the translator, who taught English at a local university, asked if the author "had good time." I responded that I felt things went well. The translator repeated her question. Puzzled, I reaffirmed that I felt things went well. After the interchange was repeated several times, the translator finally grabbed my wrist, pointed at my watch, and asked again if I "had good time?" Doubts arose concerning the accuracy of the meeting translation!

Summary

The number of international projects continues to increase, and nothing on the horizon suggests things will change in the new millennium. More and more project managers will be needed to implement international projects. There are few guidelines for the fledgling international project manager. Preparing for international projects can be enhanced through training. As a general background, potential international project managers can benefit from a basic international business course that sensitizes them to the forces of change in the global economy and to cultural differences. Learning a foreign language is also strongly recommended.

Further training specific to the host country is a very useful preproject endeavor. The length and type of training usually depend on the duration of the project manager's assignment. Review Figure 15.7. Still, self-learning, on-the-job training, and experience are the best teachers for international project managers.

Preparing for a specific international project requires serious preproject homework. Understanding the motivation of the firm in selecting the project and its site provides important insights. What basic political, geographic, economic, and infrastructure factors were key considerations? How will they impact the implementation of the project?

Finally, preparation and understanding the cultural differences of the host country go a long way toward making positive first impressions with the nationals and managing the project. International projects have distinct personalities. All people are not the same. Differences within and among countries and cultures are numerous and complex. Project managers need to accept these differences and treat them as real—or live with the consequences. What works at home may not work in the foreign country. Americans are regarded as friendly by our neighbors in the global village, but Americans are also noted to be insensitive to differences in local cultures and customs and awkward in our use of languages other than English. Although most attention in foreign projects is focused on technical efforts and their cost, the project must be carried out within the environment of the country's social customs, work practices, government controls, and religious beliefs. In most cultures, sincerity and flexibility will pay off.

Key Terms

Cross-cultural orientations, *557*

Culture, *551*
Culture shock, *566*

Infrastructure, *550*

Review Questions

1. How do environmental factors affect project implementation?
2. What role do local intermediaries play in helping an outsider complete a project?
3. Why is it important to honor the customs and traditions of a country when working on an international project?
4. What is culture shock? What can you do to reduce the negative effects of culture shock?
5. How should you go about preparing yourself for an international project?

Exercises

1. Interview someone who has worked or lived in a foreign country for more than six months.
   a. What was his experience with culture shock?
   b. What did he learn about the culture of the country he lived in?
   c. What advice would he give to someone who would be working on a project in that country?

2. Try as best you can to apply the Kluckhohn-Strodtbeck cross-cultural framework to the four countries discussed in this chapter: Mexico, France, Saudi Arabia, and China. Where do you think these countries lie on each of the cultural issues?

3. Place in order the following countries in terms of what you would think would be the least to most corrupt:

> United States, Denmark, Saudi Arabia, Russia, Australia, Hong Kong, Nepal, China, Kenya, Indonesia, Botswana, Greece, Chile.

Use an Internet search engine to find the most recent International Corruptions Perceptions Index (CPI) released by the Berlin-based organization Transparency International.

a. Check your predictions with the Index.

b. How well did you do? What countries surprised you? Why?

4. Safety is a major concern when working on projects abroad. Select a country that you would consider dangerous to work in and look up the travel advisory provided for that country by the U.S. State Department (http://travel.state.gov/). How safe is it to work in that country?

References

Ackoff, R. L., *Ackoff's Fables: Irreverent Reflections on Business and Bureaucracy* (New York: Wiley, 1991), p. 221.

Adler, N., and A. Gunderson, *International Dimensions of Organizational Behavior,* 5th ed. (Mason, OH: Thomson Publishing, 2007).

Arms, P. B. and E. Lucas, "How do Foreign Clients Really See American Project Managers?" *Proceedings of the 1978 Annual Seminar/Symposium on Project Management* (Newtown, PA: Project Management Institute, 1978), pp. 11K 1–7.

Borsuk, R., "In Indonesia, a Twist on Spreading the Wealth: Decentralization of Power Multiplies Opportunities for Bribery, Corruption," *The Wall Street Journal,* January 29, 2003, p. A16.

Cahill, T., "Deadly Business in Moscow," *Bloomberg Businessweek,* March 1, 2010, pp. 22–23.

Chen, M., and D. Miller, "West Meets East: Toward an Ambicultural Approach to Management," *The Academy of Management Perspectives,* vol. 24, no. 4 (November 2010), pp. 17–24.

Contingency Planning and Management.com, "Strohl Systems Offers Terrorism Readiness Questionnaire," September 24, 2001.

Deneire, M., and M. Segalla, "Mr. Christian Pierret, Secretary of State for Industry (1997–2002), on French Perspectives on Organizational Leadership and Management," *Academy of Management Executive,* vol. 16, no. 4 (November 2002), pp. 25–30.

Doh, J. P., P. Rodriguez, K. Uhlenbruck, J. Collins, and L. Eden, "Coping with Corruption in Foreign Markets," *Academy of Management Executive,* vol. 17, no. 3 (August 2003), pp. 114–27.

Graham, J. L., and N. M. Lam, "The Chinese Negotiation," *Harvard Business Review,* October 1, 2003, pp. 82–91.

Hallowell, R., D. Bowen, and C. I. Knoop, "Four Seasons Goes to Paris," *Academy of Management Executive,* vol. 16, no. 4 (November 2002), pp. 7–24.

Hodgetts, R. M., and F. Luthans, *International Management: Culture, Strategy, and Behavior,* 5th ed. (Boston: McGraw-Hill/Irwin, 2003).

Hofstede, G., *Cultures Consequences: International Difference in Work-Related Values* (Beverly Hills, CA: Sage Publishing, 1980).

Hooker, J., *Working across Cultures* (Stanford, CA: Stanford Business Books, 2003).

Kluckhohn, F., and F. L. Strodtbeck, *Variations in Value Orientations* (Evanston, IL: Row, Peterson, 1961).

Krane, J., "Intelligence Companies Help Overseas Business Travelers," *The Cincinnati Enquirer,* April 2, 2002, website.

Kras, E., *Management in Two Cultures: Bridging the Gap between U.S. and Mexican Managers,* rev. ed. (Yarmouth, ME: Intercultural Press, 1995).

Lane, H. W., and J. J. DiStefano, *International Project Management,* 2nd ed. (Boston: PWS-Kent, 1992).

Lieberthal, K., and G. Lieberthal, "The Great Transition," *Harvard Business Review,* October 1, 2003, pp. 71–81.

Mendenhall, M. E., E. Dunbar, and G. R. Oddou, "Expatriate Selection, Training, and Career-Pathing: A Review and Critique," *Human Resource Management,* vol. 26, no. 3 (Fall 1987), pp. 331–45.

Meyer, E., *The Culture Map: Breaking through the Invisible Boundaries of Global Business,* (New York: Public Affair, 2014).

Milosevic, D. Z., "Echoes of the Silent Language of Project Management," *Project Management Journal,* vol. 30, no. 1 (March 1999), pp. 27–39.

Moffett, M. H., I. Stonehill, and D. K. Eiteman, *Fundamentals of Multinational Finance* (Boston: Pearson, 2012).

Moran, R. T., P. R. Harris, and S. V. Moran, *Managing Cultural Differences,* 5th ed. (Houston, TX: Gulf Publishing, 2010).

Morrison, T., and W. A. Conaway, *Kiss, Bow, or Shake Hands (The Bestselling Guide to Doing Business in More than 60 Countries),* 2nd ed. (New York: Adams Media, 2006).

Ricks, D. A., *Blunders in International Business* (London: Blackwell, 2000).

Saunders, C., C. Van Slyke, and D. R. Vogel, "My Time or Yours? Managing Time Visions in Global Virtual Teams," *Academy of Management Executive,* vol. 18, no. 1 (2004), pp. 19–31.

Scown, M. J., "Managers Journal: Barstool Advice for the Vietnam Investor," *Asian Wall Street Journal,* July 15, 1993.

Tung, R. L., "Expatriate Assignments: Enhancing Success and Minimizing Failure," *Academy of Management Executive,* vol. 1, no. 2 (1987), pp. 117–26.

Yeung, I., and R. L. Tung, "Achieving Business Success in Confucian Societies: The Importance of Guanxi (Connections)," *Organizational Dynamics,* vol. 25, no. 2 (Autumn 1996), pp. 54–65.

Case 15.1

AMEX, Hungary

Michael Thomas shouted, "Sasha, Tor-Tor, we've got to go! Our driver is waiting for us." Thomas's two daughters were fighting over who would get the last orange for lunch that day. Victoria ("Tor-Tor") prevailed as she grabbed the orange and ran out the door to the Mercedes Benz waiting for them. The fighting continued in the back seat as they drove toward the city of Budapest, Hungary. Thomas finally turned around and grabbed the orange and proclaimed that he would have it for lunch. The back seat became deadly silent as they made their way to the American International School of Budapest.

After dropping the girls off at the school, Thomas was driven to his office in the Belvéros area of Budapest. Thomas worked for AMEX Petroleum and had been sent to Budapest four months earlier to set up business operations in central Hungary. His job was to establish 10 to 14 gas stations in the region by purchasing existing stations, building new ones, or negotiating franchise arrangements with existing owners of stations. Thomas jumped at this project. He realized that his career at AMEX was going nowhere in the United States, and if he were going to realize his ambitions, it would be in the "wild, wild east" of the former Soviet empire. Besides, Thomas's mother was Hungarian, and he could speak the language. At least he thought he could until he arrived in Budapest and realized that he had greatly exaggerated his competence.

As he entered the partially refurbished offices of AMEX, he noticed that only three of his staff were present. No one knew where Miklos was, while Margit reported that she would not be at work today because she had to stay at home to take care of her sick mother. Thomas asked Béla why the workmen weren't present to work on finishing the office. Béla informed him that the work had to be halted until they received approval from the city historian. Budapest, anxious to preserve its historical heritage, required that all building renovations be approved by the city historian. When Thomas asked Béla how long it would take, Béla responded, "Who knows—days, weeks, maybe even months." Thomas muttered "great" to himself and turned his attention to the morning business. He was scheduled to interview prospective employees who would act as station managers and staff personnel.

The interview with Ferenc Erkel was typical of the many interviews he held that morning. Erkel was a neatly dressed, 42-year-old, unemployed professional who could speak limited English. He had a masters degree in international economics and had worked for 12 years in the state-owned Institute for Foreign Trade. Since being laid off two years ago, he had been working as a taxicab driver. When asked about his work at the Institute, Erkel smiled sheepishly and said that he pushed paper and spent most of the time playing cards with his colleagues.

To date Thomas had hired 16 employees. Four quit within three days on the job, and six were let go after a trial period for being absent from work, failing to perform duties, or showing a lack of initiative. Thomas thought that at this rate it would take him over a year just to hire his staff.

Thomas took a break from the interview schedule to scan the *Budapest Business Journal,* an English newspaper that covered business news in Hungary. Two items caught his eye. One article was on the growing threat of the Ukrainian Mafia in Hungary, which detailed extortion attempts in Budapest. The second story was that inflation had risen to 32 percent. This last item disturbed Thomas because at the time only one out of every five Hungarian families owned a car. AMEX's strategy in Hungary depended on a boom in first-time car owners.

Thomas collected his things and popped a few aspirin for the headache he was developing. He walked several blocks to the Kispipa restaurant where he had a supper meeting with Hungarian businessman Zoltán Kodaly. He had met Kodaly briefly at a reception sponsored by the U.S. consulate for American and Hungarian businesspeople. Kodaly reportedly owned three gas stations that Thomas was interested in.

Thomas waited, sipping bottled water for 25 minutes. Kodaly appeared with a young lady who could not have been older than 19. As it turned out Kodaly had brought his daughter Annia, who was a university student, to act as translator. While Thomas made an attempt to speak in Hungarian at first, Kodaly insisted that they use Annia to translate.

After ordering the house specialty, *szekelygulas,* Thomas immediately got down to business. He told Kodaly that AMEX was willing to make two offers to him. They would like to either purchase two of his stations at a price of $150,000 each, or they could work out a franchise agreement. Thomas said AMEX was not interested in the third station located near Klinikak because it would be too expensive to modernize the equipment. Annia translated, and as far as Thomas could tell she was doing a pretty good job. At first Kodaly did not respond and simply engaged in side conversations with Annia and exchanged pleasantries with people who came by. Thomas became frustrated and reiterated his offer. Eventually Kodaly asked what he meant by franchising, and Thomas tried to use the local McDonald's as an example of how it worked. He mentioned that Kodaly would still own the stations, but he would have to pay a franchisee fee, share profits with AMEX, and adhere to AMEX procedures and practices. In exchange, AMEX would provide petroleum and funds to renovate the stations to meet AMEX standards.

Toward the end of the meal Kodaly asked what would happen to the people who worked at the stations. Thomas asserted that according to his calculation the stations were over-staffed by 70 percent and that to make a profit, at least 15 workers would have to be let go. This statement was greeted with silence. Kodaly then turned the conversation to soccer and asked Thomas if it was true that in America girls play "football." Thomas said that both of his daughters played AYSO soccer in America and hoped to play in Hungary. Kodaly said girls don't play football in Hungary and that Annia was an accomplished volleyball player. Thomas pressed Kodaly for a response to his offer, but Kodaly rose and thanked Thomas for the meal. He said he would think about his offer and get back in touch with him.

Thomas left the Kispipa wondering if he would ever see Kodaly again. He returned to his office where an urgent message was waiting from Tibor. Tibor was responsible for retrofitting the first station Thomas had purchased for AMEX. The new tanks had not arrived from Vienna, and the construction crew had spent the day doing nothing. After several phone calls he found out that the tanks were being held at the border by customs. This irritated him because he had been assured by local officials that everything had been taken care of. He asked his secretary to schedule an appointment with the Hungarian trade office as soon as possible.

At the end of the day he checked his e-mail from the States. There was a message from headquarters asking about the status of the project. By this time he had hoped to have his office staffed and up and running and at least three stations secured. So far he had only one-third of his staff, his office was in shambles, and only one station was being retrofitted. Thomas decided to wait until tomorrow to respond to the e-mail.

Before returning home Thomas stopped off at the English Pub, a favorite hangout for expats in Budapest. There he met Jan Krovert, who worked for a Dutch company that was building a large discount retail store on the outskirts of Budapest. Thomas and Krovert often talked about being "strangers in a strange land" at the pub. Thomas talked about the interviews and how he could just see in their eyes that they didn't have the drive or initiative to be successful. Krovert responded that Hungary has high unemployment but a shortage of motivated workers. Krovert confided that he no longer interviewed anyone over the age of 30, claiming that what fire they had in their bellies was burned out after years of working in state-run companies.

1. What are the issues confronting Thomas in this case?
2. How well is Thomas dealing with these issues?
3. What suggestions would you have for Thomas in managing this project?

Case 15.2

Phuket A

On December 26, 2004, an earthquake reaching 9.1 on the Richter scale triggered a series of devastating tsunamis off the coast of Indonesia. They spread throughout the Indian Ocean, killing large numbers of people and inundating coastal communities across South and Southeast Asia, including parts of Indonesia, Sri Lanka, India, and Thailand. The 2004 Asian tsunami was one of the deadliest catastrophes in modern history, with more than 220,000 lives lost.

Nils Lofgrin, who had managed several construction projects in Australia and New Guinea, was sent by his construction firm to restore a five-star resort along the Andaman coast in southern Thailand that had been ravaged by this tsunami. Casualties at the resort included 12 staff and 37 guests. This was Nils's first assignment in Thailand.

Nils flew down and toured the site. His assessment of the damage was that it was not as severe as feared. The basic infrastructure was intact but debris needed to be cleared and the resort refurbished. He reported back to headquarters that with a bit of luck he should have the resort up and running in a matter of months. Little did he realize how soon he would regret making such a promise.

The problems began immediately when he was unable to recruit workers to help clean up the mess at the resort. Burmese migrant workers comprised a significant portion of the workforce in the region. The heavy government presence caused them to flee into the hills out of growing fears of being arrested and deported. Even when he offered double wages he was not able to recruit many Thais.

1. Why do you think Nils is unable to recruit Thai workers for his project?

16
An Introduction to Agile Project Management

LEARNING OBJECTIVES

After reading this chapter you should be able to:

16-1 Recognize the conditions in which traditional project management versus agile project management should be used.

16-2 Understand the value of incremental, iterative development for creating new products.

16-3 Identify core Agile principles.

16-4 Understand the basic methodology used in Scrum.

16-5 Recognize the limitations of Agile project management.

OUTLINE

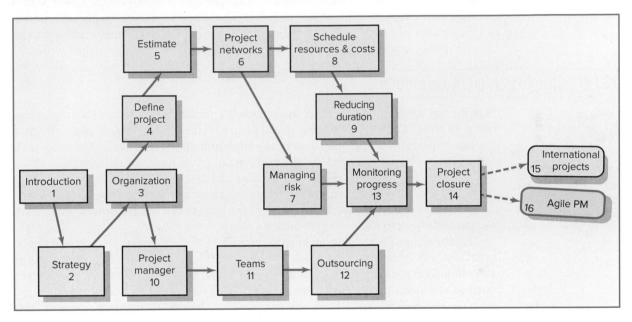

We know less about the project today than at any time in the future.

—Chet Hendrickson

As project management entered the new millennium, many professionals recognized that one-size fits all project management methods did not meet their needs. This was especially true for those working on software and product development projects in which the end product is not well defined and evolves over time. This project environment requires flexibility and the ability to manage changes as more information and learning take place. Enter **Agile Project Management** (Agile PM). Instead of attempting to plan the entire project up front, Agile PM relies on incremental, iterative development cycles to complete projects.

Ken Schwaber uses the analogy of building a house to explain the difference between **incremental, iterative development** and traditional project management.[1] The traditional approach would be that the buyers could not move into the house until the entire house is completed. The iterative approach would build the house room by room. The plumbing, electrical, and infrastructure would be built for the most important

[1] Schwaber, K., *Agile Project Management with Scrum* (Seattle: Microsoft, 2004) p. xviii.

room (i.e., kitchen) first and then extended to each room as it was constructed. Each time a room is completed, the builders and the buyers would assess progress and make adjustments. In some cases, the buyers would realize that they didn't need that extra room they felt they had to have. In other cases, they would add features they didn't realize they needed to have. Ultimately the house is built to fit the customer's wishes.

Agile PM is ideal for exploratory projects in which requirements need to be discovered and new technology tested. It focuses on active collaboration between the project team and customer representatives, breaking projects into small functional pieces, and adapting to changing requirements. While iterative development principles have been around for some time, it is only recently that agile methodologies have taken root within the project management profession.

In this chapter the core principles of Agile PM are discussed and compared with traditional project management methods. A specific agile methodology called Scrum is used to describe these principles in action. The chapter concludes with a discussion of limitations and concerns. The goal is not to provide a comprehensive account of all the methods associated with Agile PM but to provide a primer on how agile works.

16.1 Traditional versus Agile Methods

 16-1

Recognize the conditions in which traditional project management versus agile project management should be used.

Traditional approaches to project management concentrate firmly on thorough planning up front. The rationale is that if you plan, execute your plan, and take corrective action on deviations from plan, you have a high probability of success. Once the project scope has been firmly established, every detail of the project is defined through the WBS. Most problems and risks are identified and assessed before the project begins. Estimates are made, resources assigned, adjustments made, and ultimately a baseline schedule and budget are created. Control of the project is a comparison of plan versus actual and corrective action to get back on plan.

Traditional project management requires a fairly high degree of predictability to be effective. For plans to be useful managers have to have a firm idea on what is to be accomplished and how to do it. For example, when it comes to building a bridge across a river, engineers can draw upon proven technology and design principles to plan and execute the project. Not all projects enjoy such certainty. Figure 16.1 speaks to this issue and is often used to support the use of Agile PM.

Project uncertainty varies according to the extent the project scope is known and stable and the technology to be used is known and proven. Many projects, like the bridge example, as well as other construction projects, events, product extensions, marketing campaigns, and so forth have well-established scopes and use proven technology that provides a degree of predictability for effective planning. However, when the project scope and/or technology are not fully known, things become much less predictable and plan-driven methods suffer.

For example, before agile, software development projects relied on a "waterfall" approach to software development. The waterfall method features a series of logical phases in which progress flows from one phase to the next (see Figure 16.2). The key assumption is that essential requirements can be defined upfront so the software can be designed, built, and tested. Software projects typically involve many different customers with different needs. These needs frequently change and are often difficult to articulate. In many cases, customers only begin to understand what they actually desire when they are provided with someone's impression of what they want. Under these conditions it would be difficult if not futile to develop a detailed list of scope requirements at project launch. This is one of the major reasons why software projects utilizing the waterfall approach have a history of coming in late and/or being canceled.

FIGURE 16.1
Project Uncertainty

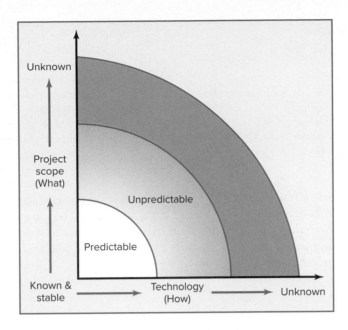

FIGURE 16.2
**The Waterfall
Approach to
Software
Development**

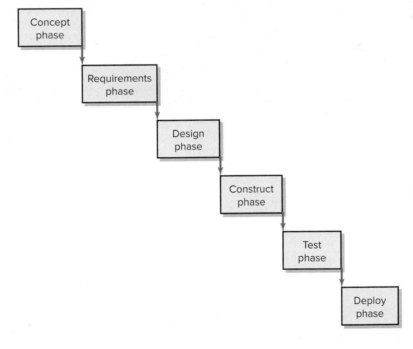

Technology can be another source of unpredictability. For example, a development team charged with designing the next generation electric car may know they are to build a car that seats four adults comfortably and travels over 200 miles before being charged, but they may not know if the battery technology exists to power such a vehicle. Again it would be very difficult to develop a reliable schedule when such questions exist.

The key point is that traditional PM techniques were developed to operate in the predictable zone where the scope of the project is fairly well defined and technology to be used is established. Projects also operate in a very different zone in which how or what has yet to be fully discovered. Agile lives in this unpredictable zone. Agile PM

TABLE 16.1
Traditional Project Management versus Agile Project Management

Traditional	Agile
Design up front	Continuous design
Fixed scope	Flexible scope
Deliverables	Features/requirements
Freeze design as early as possible	Freeze design as late as possible
Low uncertainty	High uncertainty
Avoid change	Embrace change
Low customer interaction	High customer interaction
Conventional project teams	Self-organized project teams

represents a fundamental shift away from the traditional plan-driven project management approach by adopting a more experimental and adaptive approach to managing projects. Projects evolve rather than are executed. Solutions are discovered not implemented. Some of the differences between Agile PM and traditional project management are displayed in Table 16.1.

16.2 Agile PM

LO 16-2

Understand the value of **incremental, iterative development** for creating new products.

Fundamentally, Agile PM is related to the rolling wave planning and scheduling project methodology (see Chapter 5). That is, the final project design is not known in great detail and is continuously developed through a series of incremental iterations over time. Iterations are short time frames ("time boxes") that typically last from one to four weeks. The goal of each iteration is to develop a workable product that satisfies one or more desired product features to demonstrate to the customer and other key stakeholders. At the end of each iteration, stakeholders and customers review progress and re-evaluate priorities to ensure alignment with customer needs and company goals. Adjustments are made and a different iterative cycle begins. Each new iteration subsumes the work of the previous iterations and adds new capabilities to the evolving product (see Figure 16.3) to produce a next, expanded version of the product. See Snapshot from Practice 16.1: IDEO for an example of iterative development in action.

FIGURE 16.3 Iterative, Incremental Product Development

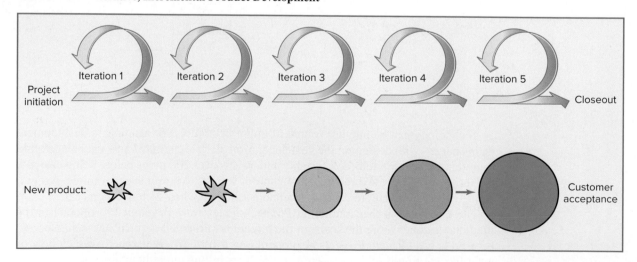

SNAPSHOT FROM PRACTICE 16.1   IDEO: Masters of Design*

IDEO, headquartered in Palo Alto, California, is one of the premier design firms in the world. They are responsible for a wide range of product innovations including the first Apple mouse, Head's Airflow Tennis Racket, Zyliss Salad Spinner, and Nokia N-Gage Smartphones. IDEO's many clients include Pepsi-Cola, 3M, Logitech, Nike, and HBO. IDEO has won more of the *Business-Week/IDSA Industrial Design Excellence Awards* than any other firm.

IDEO's approach to product design relies heavily on an iterative development process in which product prototypes are used to explore and further refine product ideas. CEO Tim Brown states that the goal of prototyping "is to learn about the strengths and weaknesses of the idea and identify new directions that the prototype might take."

For example, IDEO worked with Procter and Gamble to develop a new Crest toothpaste tube. The challenge was to improve the traditional screw-on cap, which always gets gunked up with toothpaste. IDEO's first solution was a pop-on, pop-off cap. However, when designers created rough prototypes and watched people use them, they quickly noticed that users kept trying to unscrew the cap even though they were told how it worked. The designers concluded that the action was a well-ingrained habit that would probably be impossible to break. So they came up with a hybrid: a twist-off cap that had a short thread but would still be easy to clean.

Focused prototyping resolves critical problems one by one. Brown recommends that prototypes should only take as much time and effort needed to generate useful feedback and evolve an idea.

© Cultura Creative/Alamy RF

For example, IDEO was working on a chair for Vecta, a high-end office furniture manufacturer. The project had evolved to the point where the height adjustment lever that tilted with the chair became critical. The team didn't build the whole chair or even the tilt mechanism. They just built the little lever and its interface with the tilt mechanism. It took only a couple of hours. When finished the prototype quickly demonstrated that the principle would work.

"It doesn't matter how clever you are, your first idea about something is never right," Brown says, "so the great value of prototyping—and prototyping quickly and inexpensively—is that you learn about the idea and make it better."

* J. M. Pethokoukis, "The Deans of Design: From the Computer Mouse to the Newest Swiffer, IDEO Is the Firm behind the Scenes," *U.S. News & World Report*, posted 9-24-2008; T. Brown, "Design Thinking," *Harvard Business Review*, June 2008, pp. 84–95.

Iterative development processes provide the following important advantages:

- Continuous integration, verification, and validation of the evolving product.
- Frequent demonstration of progress to increase the likelihood that the end product will satisfy customer needs.
- Early detection of defects and problems.

There is growing evidence that iterative and evolutionary development is superior to traditional plan-driven project management when it comes to creating new products. (See Research Highlight 16.1: Product Development Practices That Work.)

Alan MacCormack and his colleagues at Harvard Business School conducted a two-year in-depth study of 29 software projects to answer the question: "Does evolutionary development, rather than the waterfall model, result in better success?" The waterfall model is the name used in the software industry for the traditional approach to project management in which a process breakdown structure (PBS) is used to first define all the requirements up front and then initiate a design, build, test, deploy sequence. Conversely, evolutionary development is the term they use to describe an Agile approach in which customers test early versions of the software and requirements emerge and are refined after each demonstration.

The results of the study overwhelmingly favored the iterative, Agile approach to software development. Several key practices now associated with Agile Project Management were found to be statistically correlated with the most successful projects:

1. An iterative life cycle with early release of the evolving product to stakeholders for review and feedback.
2. Daily incorporation of new software and rapid feedback on design changes.
3. A flexible product architecture that is both modular and scaleable.

MacCormack asserts that uncertainty on software projects dictates short "microprojects"—down to level of features. This is not limited to just software projects but to any new product endeavor where uncertainty is high and the need for customer feedback and refinement is critical to success.

* A. MacCormack, "Product-Development Practices that Work: How Internet Companies Build Software," *MIT Sloan Management Review*, 42(2), 2001, pp. 75–84.

It should be noted that Agile PM is not one set method, but a family of methods designed to respond to the challenges of unpredictable projects. A few of the more popular ones are listed here:

Scrum	RUP (Rational Unified Process)
Extreme Programming (XP)	Crystal Clear
Agile Modeling	Dynamic Systems Development Method (DSDM)
Lean Development	Rapid Product Development (RPD)

LO 16-3

Identify core Agile principles.

While each of these methods has unique elements and applications, most are based on the following Agile principles:

- Focus on customer value—Employ business-driven prioritizations of requirements and features.
- Iterative and incremental delivery—Create a flow of value to customers by "chunking" project delivery into small, functioning increments.
- Experimentation and adaptation—Test assumptions early and build working prototypes to solicit customer feedback and refine product requirements.
- Self-organization—Team members decide among themselves what should be done and who should do it.
- Continuous improvement—Teams reflect, learn, and adapt to change; work informs the plan.

The Agile methodology known as "Scrum" will be used to illustrate how these core principles are put into action.

Soul Searching after 9/11*

Over 2,792 lives were lost in the collapse of the World Trade Center (WTC) on September 11, 2001. While rescuers labored night and day to recover the bodies, a small team of Michigan software engineers set about salvaging their identities.

New York City hired Gene Codes, the Ann Arbor, Michigan, bioinformatics company, to reinvent the science of DNA mass identification by creating software that would inventory and match the victims' remains and reunite them with their families. They were to do so as soon as possible with no errors. Experts predicted that the violence of the collapse and the intense heat of the fires meant that at best 25 percent of the victims would be identified.

Gene Codes hired William Wake, an independent software coach, to work with their team of eight software engineers on the project. Wake introduced the team to Agile PM. Under Wake's guidance an environment of intense interaction and communication was created within the programming team by scheduling frequent releases, tempered by constant testing, and feedback from its users. Testing was done before, during, and after the code was written to ensure the same bugs (errors) didn't surface twice.

At the end of each week's iteration, the staff held a retrospective. They listed things that worked well and what needed improvement on fluorescent pink, green, and yellow Post-It notes, transforming the entire wall

into a case of art imitating life. Under "Worked Well," a note said, "Figured out how to use debug form on a wrapped test class." One square under the "Needs Improvement" category merely read, "I'm tired."

Whether out of patriotism or professionalism, the team routinely arrived each day at 7:00 a.m. and worked till midnight. Engineers like Dave Relyea just wanted to help. "We thought about the victims, the families, and the people at the Office of the Chief Medical Examiner working around the clock. What they were going through made us feel like we could never work hard enough."

The product of their labor was the Mass Fatality Identification System (M-FISys) that contained more than 164,000 lines of code. M-FISys linked all the information in the identification project: 11,641 swab samples from 7,166 family members; 7,681 personal effects (i.e., toothbrushes, hair brushes) and the results of the three types of DNA tests; and nearly 20,000 human remains. The chance of false match was less than 1 in 3.58 million.

In the end, with the help of M-FISys, the New York Medical examiner was able to identify 1,521 of the 2,792 people who perished in the WTC disaster.

* Melissa Krause, "Soul Searching" *Bio-ITworld*. Accessed on 3/10/2008 at www.bio-itworld.com /archive/091103/soul.html.

16.3 Agile PM in Action: Scrum

LO 16-4

Understand the basic methodology used in Scrum.

Scrum can be traced back to the work of Hirotaka Takeuchi and Ikujiro Nonaka, who in 1986 described a new holistic approach in new commercial product development efforts. They compare this approach of a cross-functional team collaborating to develop a new product to rugby, where the whole team "tries to go the distance as a unit, passing the ball back and forth." The scrum metaphor has been expanded and refined into a fairly prescriptive framework that has enjoyed success on high-tech and software development projects (see Snapshot from Practice 16.2: Soul Searching).

Scrum, like other Agile methods, begins with a high-level scope definition and ballpark time and cost estimates for the project. The scope and cost estimates should be complete enough that management is comfortable with the estimates. The theory is that since requirements evolve over time, detailed up-front planning will be wasted. In place of a product WBS, Scrum uses product *features* as deliverables. *A* **feature** *is defined as a piece of a product that delivers some useful functionality to a customer*. In the case of a software project, a feature may be a bank customer being able to change her PIN. In the case of a high-tech product, it may be 3G wireless access. Features are

FIGURE 16.4 **Scrum Development Process**

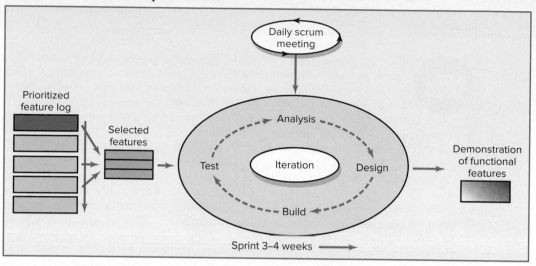

prioritized by their perceived highest value. The project team tackles the highest, feasible priority features first. Priorities are re-evaluated after each iteration. Iterations are called sprints and should last no longer than four weeks. The goal of each sprint is to produce fully functional features. This forces the team to tackle tough decisions early in order to create a workable demo.

Specific features are created according to four distinct phases: analysis, design, build, and test (see Figure 16.4). Each feature can be thought of as a mini-project. The first phase is analysis and review of functional requirements that will be needed to complete the feature. The team commits to meet these requirements. The second phase is the development of a design that meets the requirements of the feature. The third phase is to build the feature so that it is functional. Finally, the feature is tested and documented. At the end of each sprint, features are demonstrated. Within this sprint framework, Scrum relies on specific roles, meetings, and documents/logs to manage the project.

Roles and Responsibilities

There are three key roles to the scrum process: Product owner, development team, and scrum master.

Product Owner The **product owner** acts on behalf of customers/end users to represent their interests. For commercial development projects the product owner may be the product manager. For internal projects, the product owner could be the manager of the business group that will benefit from the software. In other cases, the product owner could be a representative of the client organization. They are responsible for ensuring that the development team focuses their efforts on developing a product that will fulfill the business objective of the project.

The product owner in consultation with others establishes the initial list of product requirements and prioritizes them in the product backlog. Owners often work with the development team to refine features through stories and end user cases (e.g., when the user clicks the F2 key an option drop-down window appears). The product owners negotiate sprint goals and backlog items with the development team. Owners have the option to change features and priorities at the end of each sprint if desired. *However, no changes should be made once a sprint has started.* Product owners are the final arbiter on requirements questions and are empowered to accept or reject each product increment. They ultimately decide whether the project is completed. Product owners are the keeper of the product vision and the watchdog on project cost.

Development Team   The team is responsible for delivering the product. A team is typically made up of five to nine people with cross-functional skill sets. There are no designated roles or titles; people take on different responsibilities depending on the nature of the work. The team is **self-organizing** in the sense they decide both who does the work and how the work is to be accomplished. Team members should be co-located so that intense face-to-face collaboration occurs. They are responsible for the achieving commitments they make at the sprint planning and sprint review meetings.

Scrum Master (aka Project Manager)   The **Scrum master** facilitates the scrum process and resolves impediments at the team and organization level. The Scrum master is not the leader of the team (the team leads itself!) but acts as a buffer between the team and outside interference. They have no formal authority. Instead, they are responsible for making sure that the scrum process is adhered to. They help the product owner with planning and try to keep the team energized. The Scrum master serves more as a coach than a manager.

Scrum Meetings

Scrum uses a series of coordinated meetings to manage the development process (see Figure 16.5).

Release Planning   The purpose of release planning is to establish the goals and general plan for the project. The product owner works with the team, Scrum master, and others to address the question of how the project can meet or exceed the desired customer expectations and return on investment. Outcomes of this meeting include establishing highest priority product backlog, the major risks, and the overall features and functionality that the released product will contain. The meeting also produces a probable delivery date and initial cost estimates if nothing changes. Management can then monitor progress and make changes to the release plan on a sprint-by-sprint basis.

Sprint Planning   At the start of each sprint, the product owner and development team negotiate which product backlog items the team will attempt this sprint. The product owner is responsible for identifying which features are most important, and the team is responsible for determining what is possible within the sprint. If it is impossible to

FIGURE 16.5   Scrum Meetings

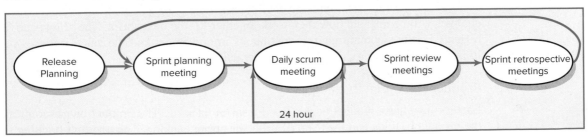

complete a certain key item within four weeks, the team works with the product owner to break the feature down into doable pieces. All committed items are recorded in a product backlog. The team uses this backlog to prioritize specific work to be done and assign initial responsibilities. These tasks are recorded in the sprint backlog. Once the meeting has adjourned, the goals for the sprint cannot be changed.

Daily Scrum The heartbeat of an Agile project is the daily meetings which are commonly referred to as the "Scrum." Each workday at the same time and place, team members stand in a circle and take turns answering the following key questions:

1. What have you done since the last Scrum?
2. What will you do between now and the next Scrum?
3. What is getting in the way of (blocks) your performing your work as effectively as possible?

The Scrum, which typically lasts 15 minutes, is held next to a whiteboard, after which time all tasks and blocks are recorded. The Scrum master erases blocks once they have been removed.

The meetings must start on time. A late fine (e.g., $1 to be collected and donated to charity by the Scrum master) is a popular rule. The meeting is limited to just those three core questions. Members stand to create a sense of urgency. Immediately afterward, specific members may meet to resolve issues that surfaced.

The value of the Scrum is that it creates a daily mechanism to quickly inform the team about the state of the project. It sustains a sense of team identity that encourages openness and resolution of problems in real time. Having everyone report what they plan to do for that day generates a social promise to the group, thereby building accountability.

Notice again that the team is self-managed. The Scrum master does not assign daily tasks to team members; the team decides among themselves. The Scrum master role is to see that the scrum is running correctly. They are not "master" of the team but rather "master" of the process.

Sprint Review At the end of each sprint, the team demonstrates the actual work product increments they have built to the product owner and other relevant stakeholders. Feedback is solicited from the product owner and other relevant stakeholders. The product owner declares which items are "done" and which items need further work and are returned to the product backlog. The team can take this opportunity to suggest improvements and new features for the product owner to accept or reject. The sprint review meeting is an opportunity to examine and adapt the product as it emerges and iteratively refine key requirements. Such refinements will be the subject of the next sprint planning meeting.

Sprint Retrospective The purpose of the retrospective meeting is to reflect on how well the previous sprint went and identify specific actions that can improve future sprints. The Scrum master typically facilitates this meeting and the team decides which changes will be made in how they work together for the next sprint. The retrospective reflects Scrum's commitment to continuous improvement and the value it places on improving not only products but team interactions.

Product and Sprint Backlogs

Each project has a product backlog and a sprint backlog. The product owner controls the product backlog and the team controls the sprint backlog. The **product backlog** is

FIGURE 16.6
Partial Product
Backlog

	A	B	C	D	E	F	G
1		**Phone-In Prescription Software Project**					
2		**Product Backlog**					
3							
4	**ID**	**Product**	**Priority**	**Status**	**Estimate Hours**	**Actual Hours**	
5							
6							
7	1	Customer Information	2	Complete	100	90	
8	2	Insurance Information	1	Complete	160	180	
9	3	Drug Information	3	Started	80		
10	4	Doctor Information	5	Not started	40		
11	5	Inventory status	4	Started	120		
12							

the customer's prioritized list of key features desired when the project is completed. The product backlog usually defines each feature and estimates of time, cost, and work remaining. See Figure 16.6 for a partial product backlog for a software project.

The **sprint backlog** is developed and controlled by the team. It represents the amount of work the team commits to complete during the next sprint. The sprint backlog lists the tasks (activities) that must be completed to deliver a functional feature or segment of a feature. The sprint backlog also serves as a status document by listing the person responsible for each task, remaining hours of work, and recording the task as *finished, in process*, or *not yet started*. See Figure 16.7 for a partial example of a sprint backlog.

Scrum does not use any of the conventional project management tools like Gantt charts or network diagrams. Instead it relies on the daily scrums and the active involvement of the product owner to manage work flow. Risk is mitigated by short developmental cycles and rigorous testing. For an alternative approach to tracking work see Snapshot from Practice 16.3: Kanban.

Sprint and Release Burndown Charts

Scrum uses "burndown" charts, which focus on the work remaining and are used to track progress. **Sprint burndown charts** are used to track progress on a daily basis (see Figure 16.8). The axis on the left shows the remaining effort required to complete the sprint backlog and the axis on the bottom contains the number of days until

FIGURE 16.7
Partial Sprint
Backlog

	A	B	C	D	E	F	G	H	I
1		**Phone-In Prescription Software Project**							
2		**Sprint Backlog**							
3									
4	**Sprint Description**	**Responsible**	**Actual Hours**	**Remaining Hours**	**Defined**	**In Progress**	**Tested**	**Accepted**	
5									
6									
7	Drug categories	RT	16	0	X	X	X	✓	
8	Generics	CG	32	0	X	X	X	✓	
9	Branded	AL	24	8	X	X	X		
10									
11									
12	Design drug inventory system	EL	40	0	X	X	X	✓	
13	Code inventory availability	CE		32					
14	Code manufacture order	MC		32					
15	Integrate all inventory systems	LE	4	16	X				
16									

SNAPSHOT FROM PRACTICE 16.3   Kanban

Kanban is a lean management methodology first developed by Toyota. It has been adapted by agile practitioners to help manage project work flow. In its simplest form, Kanban consists of a white board divided into three columns titled: Next, WIP (Work in Progress), and Done. The team identifies the distinct tasks, deliverables, or features associated with their projects. Each is labeled on post-it notes or special "Kanban" cards. The cards are prioritized in terms of what needs to be done first and a queue is created in the Next column. The team works on the top priority items. Once a task or feature has been completed the card is moved to the Done column and the next task is started. Like Scrum, the project team starts each day with a stand-up meeting to update the board, decide what needs to be done, and discuss impediments to progress.

Kanban is based on the idea of *pull*. A completed Kanban card signals when the team is ready for more work, which is pulled from the Next list. Work isn't pushed from start to finish. It's only when a task is completed that another task can be started. Limits are set based on the capability of the project team on the number of WIP tasks. For example, no more than three tasks can be in progress at any one time. This reduces the inefficiencies of multi-tasking and prevents

© anathomy/Shutterstock

lingering bottlenecks from emerging. Another strength of Kanban is that it helps the team visualize the work flow on the project and focus their attention on the most critical work. Finally, like Scrum, significant time is devoted to problem solving and developing better ways of accomplishing the work.

Depending upon the project more elaborate mapping schemes can be used. For example, Tarne (2011) described a system for an IT Helpdesk that consisted of six columns: Opened ticket, In Queue, Root Cause Analysis, Develop Fix, Test, and Deploy. More sophisticated Kaban tools can also be found online. For example, AGILEZEN (agilezen.com) provides a user-friendly, virtual Kanban board, customizable cards/tags and colors, and a performance metrics tracker.

the sprint is completed. The remaining effort is calculated by summing the time estimates for incomplete tasks recorded in the sprint backlog. These estimates are updated on a daily basis.

In Figure 16.8 the solid line shows the ideal scenario if the sprint progresses as predicted by the initial task estimates and the dotted line shows the actual performance. Ideally the dotted line should be very close to the solid line. When it is above the solid line the team is behind schedule and when it is below the solid line, the team is ahead of schedule. If the actual remaining line is above the ideal line for an extended period of time, then this signals that adjustments need to be made to the project. This could mean dropping a task, assigning additional resources, or working late. None of these are pleasant, but because of the burndown chart, the team can respond sooner than just before the sprint deadline.

The **release burndown chart** is used to monitor progress toward completion of the project (see Figure 16.8). This chart displays the amount of work remaining across time. Before the start of each sprint completion estimates are revised in the product backlog and totaled in the release burndown chart. Over time the chart becomes an excellent method for visualizing the relationship between amount of

FIGURE 16.8
Sprint Burndown
Chart

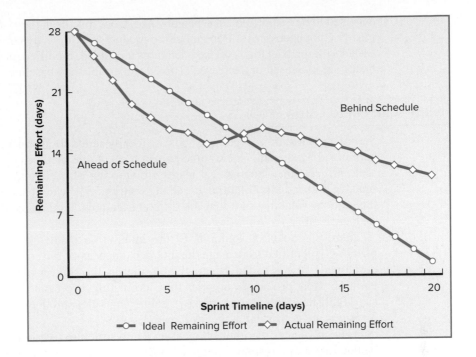

work remaining and the rate at which team is reducing this work. Also the intersection of the trend line for work remaining and the horizontal time line can be used to estimate probable completion date. The product owner and team use this information to "what if" the project by removing or adding functionality from the release to achieve a specific completion date or extend the date to include more functionality.

In Figure 16.9 work remaining is recorded for the first six sprints and a trend line is used to revise the expected completion date. Note that in this example the project is

FIGURE 16.9
Release Burndown
Chart after Six
Sprints

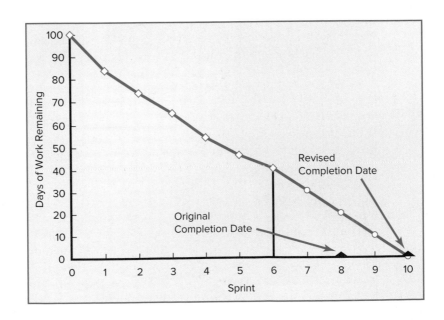

expected to be completed later than planned. Does this mean the team is underperforming? No, not necessarily! Remember the product backlog is dynamic and at the end of each sprint the backlog is revised. Features are added, modified, or deleted. Work estimates are increased or decreased. There is no established baseline in Agile PM.

16.4 Applying Agile PM to Large Projects

Scrum and most other Agile methods are ideally suited for distinct projects that can be completed by a small, five-to-nine-person team. Agile methods can be used on larger scale projects in which several teams are working on different features at the same time. In practice this condition is called "**scaling.**" The chief challenge with scaling is integration—making sure that the different features being created work in harmony with each other.

There are no easy solutions to the integration challenge. Significant up-front planning is required to manage the interdependences of different features that will be developed. This is called "staging" and often is the subject of the first development iteration. Here protocols and roles for coordinating efforts and assuring compatibility are established. This is supported by establishing a clear product vision so that trade-off decisions are consistent at the local team level.

Agile advocates recommend creating a hub structure (see Figure 16.10) with overlapping roles and responsibilities to manage large projects. There are several feature development teams. A separate integration and build team is formed consisting of part-time members of each feature team. This team tackles the sticky integration issue through testing and establishing requirements for the feature teams. To coordinate the multi-team structure a central project team is created consisting of a higher level project manager, a product manager (who represents the interests of the customer), and the

FIGURE 16.10
Hub Project Management Structure

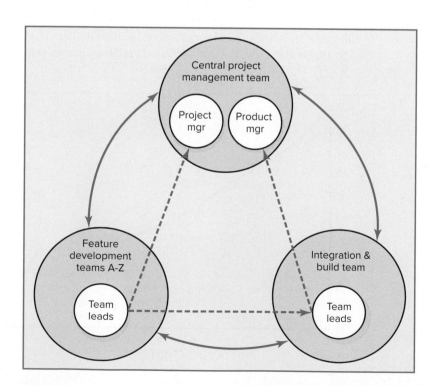

SNAPSHOT FROM PRACTICE 16.4   Agile Alliance

On February 11–13, 2001, at The Lodge at Snowbird ski resort in the Wasatch mountains of Utah, 17 representatives of various new software methodologies (such as Extreme Programming, Scrum, Adaptive Software Development, and Crystal Clear) met to discuss the need for lighter alternatives to the traditional, documentation-driven project management methodology. They were united by a desire to free themselves of Dilbert manifestations of make-work and arcane policies and spark a revolution in the software industry. By the end of two days they formed the Agile Alliance to champion change and published a manifesto that declared four core values:

We are uncovering better ways of developing software by doing it and helping others do it. Through this work we have come to value:

> Individuals and interactions over processes and tools
> Working software over comprehensive documentation
> Customer collaboration over contract negotiation
> Responding to change over following a plan

These four values were expanded upon by a set of 12 guiding principles:

1. Our highest priority is to satisfy the customer through early and continuous delivery of valuable software.

2. Welcome changing requirements, even late in development.

3. Deliver working software frequently, from a couple of weeks to a couple of months, with a preference to the shorter timescale.

4. Businesspeople and developers must work together daily throughout the project.

5. Build projects around motivated individuals. Give them the environment and support they need, and trust them to get the job done.

6. The most efficient and effective method of conveying information to and within a development team is face-to-face conversation.

7. Working software is the primary measure of progress.

8. Agile processes promote sustainable development.

9. Continuous attention to technical excellence and good design enhances agility.

10. Simplicity—the art of maximizing the amount of work not done—is essential.

11. The best architectures, requirements, and designs emerge from self-organizing teams.

12. At regular intervals, the team reflects on how to become more effective, then turns and adjusts its behavior accordingly.

To find a wealth of information on Agile PM, log onto the Agile Alliance website at: www.agilealliance.org/.

leads ("project managers") from the feature development teams. The project management team provides coordination and facilitates project decision making. Their role is to steer rather than command the other teams. Teams may be real, virtual, or a combination. The entire system requires a spirit of collaboration to work.

16.5 Limitations and Concerns

Agile methods in the software industry grew at a grass roots level. Many engineers saw traditional plan-driven project management as stifling effective development with too much emphasis on processes and documentation and not enough on creativity and experimentation. Early on there was a rebellious tone to the Agile movement, so much so that several of the key founders published an *Agile Manifesto* (see Snapshot from Practice 16.4: Agile Alliance). The manifesto affirmed a different set of values than those currently being applied by management to projects they were working on.

The revolutionary nature of Agile is reflected in the story one IT manager told the authors about her efforts several years ago at using Agile PM. She worked for a large, multinational high-tech firm that had spent five years institutionalizing a set of traditional project management policies and procedures. Despite their best efforts, her department consistently completed projects behind schedule with several cancellations. Out of desperation she started secretly using Agile methods to complete software projects. By using Agile PM her project teams were able to not only meet but beat project schedules—a rarity within her company. When top management confronted her for not conforming to procedure, she pointed to her recent success rate to defend being left alone. Ultimately management couldn't argue with success, and she was allowed to expand her efforts.

The repeated success and improvement in software development projects have led to key elements of Agile PM being incorporated in the Project Management Body of Knowledge (PMBOK). In 2011 the Project Management Institute began offering a certification in Agile PM along with the traditional Project Management Professional (PMP).

Agile PM does not satisfy top management's need for budget, scope, and schedule control. Remember the new house analogy. The buyers got exactly what they wanted but did not know how much it would cost. Nor did they know how long it would take or even what it would look like when it was done. While ballpark estimates are provided, Agile methods by their very nature do not provide the detailed estimates of time and costs that management likes. No matter how realistic "it depends" is, management as well as customers are accustomed to working with a greater level of certainty than Agile provides. In response to the financial concerns, many organizations establish "ceilings," which is the maximum budget that should not be exceeded in the development of a given product or service.

Even if management totally buys into the value of Agile PM, one cannot simply install it into an organization overnight; it needs to evolve over time. Many of the Agile principles, including self-organizing teams and intense collaboration, are incompatible with corporate cultures. For example, the principle of self-organizing teams, in which members decide who should do what, regardless of rank or title, contradicts command and control structures. Likewise, intense collaboration is not for everyone. One Agile manager confessed that she had to let several of her top engineers go because their lone-wolf personalities were not compatible with collaboration. Most companies report gradual introduction of Agile project management. For example, Siemens Medical Systems started with one Scrum team in 2004, then 10 Scrum teams in 2005, 70 teams in 2006, and over 97 teams in 2007.

A recent survey of over 3,900 respondents working in software/IT, financial and professional services provides a glimpse of the current state of Agile. Nine-four percent report their firm uses Agile approaches. Still only 53 percent report that their agile projects have been successful. The biggest reasons for failure were: (1) lack of experience with agile methods, (2) company culture at odds with core agile values, and (3) lack of management support (Schur, 2015).

As noted earlier, Agile methods appear to work best on small projects that require only five to nine dedicated team members to complete the work. Here face-to-face communication replaces time-consuming documentation and informal coordination supplants top-down control.

Although some companies have successfully applied Agile PM to large projects, others have struggled with the scaling challenge. Too often coordination requirements undermine the adaptability of small teams, which is a chief strength of Agile PM. This has led many companies to use hybrid models that combine Agile and waterfall methods. For example, IPC Media, a subsidiary of Time Inc., uses an iterative waterfall approach in which large projects are broken down into subprojects performed by different teams in parallel. Short sprints and additional check points are used within a structured planned process. A recent survey of more than 800 software engineers reported that 40 percent were using a hybrid approach on their projects.[2]

Companies that enjoy success on large projects tend to have had a strong history of using Agile on smaller projects, and Agile principles are part of their product development culture.

Agile requires active customer involvement. Involvement comes in different shapes and forms. Designating an internal person to act as a product owner to represent the interests of customers is relatively easy. Soliciting the active participation of external customers can be more problematic. Even though there is consistent evidence that customer participation enhances project success, not all customers want to be that actively involved. Many are simply too busy. Others believe that they hired the project team so they would not have to be involved. Securing the cooperation of customers to devote the requisite time to support Agile PM is a common source of frustration in the field.

Agile PM frameworks, like Scrum, are used exclusively to complete software development projects from beginning to end. Other companies are using Agile PM only during the early exploratory phase of a project. Agile PM is used to develop critical breakthrough technology or define essential features. Once the features and technology are known, then traditional project management is applied to complete the project.

Summary

Agile project management has emerged as a response to the challenges of managing projects with loosely defined scopes and high levels of uncertainty. Agile relies on an iterative development process in which the scope of the project evolves over time. Development teams create feature-driven working products at the end of each development cycle. Active customer involvement is used to guide this process. Here are some of the key advantages of Agile methods:

- Work is divided into smaller and smaller chunks that are more easily scheduled and controlled.

- Collaboration between the customer and designers is increased leading to solid change control.

- Methods demand that features be tested and functional when completed.

Agile PM is still evolving. While much of the attention in this chapter has been devoted to software development, Agile PM is being successfully applied to a wide range of unpredictable projects. New methods and approaches will continue to be developed and adapted to meet the specific needs of projects. Stay tuned.

---

[2] http://www.jamasoftware.com/media/documents/State_of_Requirements_Management_2011.pdf.

Key Terms

Agile Project Management, *579*

Feature, *585*

Iterative, incremental development (IID), *582*

Product backlog, *588*

Product owner, *586*

Release burndown chart, *590*

Scaling, *592*

Scrum master, *587*

Self-organizing team, *587*

Sprint backlog, *589*

Sprint burndown chart, *589*

Review Questions

1. Why is the traditional project management approach less effective when project scope and technology are not well known?

2. What is iterative incremental development? Why is it useful for developing new products?

3. What are the advantages of Agile PM? What are the disadvantages of Agile PM?

4. What similarities and differences exist between a traditional project manager and a Scrum master?

5. What are the differences between a self-organizing team and a conventional project team?

6. Why is it difficult to apply Agile PM to large-scale projects?

Exercises

1. Break into small groups and identify at least two real-life examples of projects in which:

   a. The scope and technology are well known.
   b. The scope is well known but the technology is less well known.
   c. The scope is not well known but the technology is known.
   d. Neither the scope nor the technology is well known.

2. Break into small groups and discuss the following question:

   What organizational, group, individual, and project factors do you think would promote the successful adoption of Agile PM methodologies like Scrum? Why?

3. Use a project you are currently working on to hold a Scrum meeting according to the steps outlined in Figure 16.5. Designate one member to act as the Scrum master and hold a standing meeting that lasts no longer than 15 minutes. Assess the value of such meetings.

4. Below are four mini-cases from practice. Break into small groups and (1) analyze the case and (2) provide five recommendations for the IT department.

Project A

You've just taken over a project from another project manager and have come back from a very uncomfortable meeting with your business sponsor. In the meeting, the sponsor told you how dissatisfied he is with the project's performance to date and that he's getting ready to pull the plug on the project entirely. Deadlines keep slipping, the application isn't complete, and the sponsor feels like he can't get in touch with anyone to give him an update on the project's status and progress.

From conversations with your project team, you learn that requirements still haven't been finalized, and the team is waiting for input before being able to proceed on several key parts of the application. Despite that, they've been able to push forward in other areas, and are quite proud of the work they've done. However, they haven't had a chance to show it to the sponsor.

To complicate matters further, your boss has made it clear that this project must be completed on schedule, because he needs the resources for another project.

What do you do? What impact do your decisions have on the project's cost, schedule, and performance?

Project B

Your project team has finished gathering the requirements and developing the solution design. Your team is broken into two main groups: The first group consists of the project manager, business analysts, and management and is located in the United States. The second group consists of the development and QA teams and they are located in India.

The WBS was developed based on estimates from the teams in India. The development team agreed to provide daily updates to you about progress against the WBS to make sure that the project's milestones are going to be met.

However, by the time the development team got close to the first milestone, it became obvious that they were behind even though their daily updates indicated that they are on track. In addition, the team adopted a different design approach than the one agreed upon at the beginning of the project.

The lack of meaningful updates from the development team along with a different design track has jeopardized the whole project by rendering the whole plan obsolete. Your team is now at risk of not delivering the project.

What do you do? What is the impact to cost, schedule, and performance?

Project C

You have just taken over as the program manager of a large program with multiple tracks and a go-live scheduled in three months. At the first meeting with the project sponsors and key stakeholders, you find out that the business requirements are not complete and in some cases not started, project scope is not realistic to meet the upcoming go-live, and overall the project teams are confused due to lack of communication and understanding of priorities.

What do you do? What impact do your decisions have on the project's schedule, and performance?

Project D

You've just been assigned to take over a new project from an outgoing project manager. The project is a high-visibility project that is using a development methodology that is new to you and to your company. In your transition meetings with the outgoing project manager, he assures you that development is complete, and all you have to do is shepherd the project through acceptance testing and release. As a result, several project team members were released as scheduled.

The acceptance testing does not go as smoothly as planned. The application has more defects than anticipated, and some core functionality is not able to be tested. The project team doesn't feel like they are getting the direction they need to continue moving forward, and the business sponsor has asked you when he can expect to test application functionality that wasn't a part of the original scope. In addition, your project's deadline is rapidly approaching, and interproject dependencies make it unlikely that you will be able to push your launch date.

What do you do? What impact do your decisions have on cost, schedule, and performance?

References

Boulter, M., *Smart Client Architecture and Design Guide* (Seattle: Microsoft Press, 2004).

Decarlo, D., *eXtreme Project Management* (Jossey-Bass, 2004).

Faris, R., and I. Abdelshafi, "Project Management and Agile: Perfect Fit," 2006 PMI Global Congress Proceedings, Seattle, Washington.

Gale, S. F., "The Evolution of Agile," *PM Network*, January 2012.

Griffiths, M., *Using Agile Principles Alongside: A Guide to the Project Management Body of Knowledge,* PMI Global Proceedings, Anaheim, California, 2004.

Highsmith, J., *Agile Project Management* (Boston: Addison Wesley, 2004).

Hildebrand, C., *Full Speed Ahead, PM Network,* vol. 21, no. 10 (October 2007), pp. 36–41.

Jackson, M. B., "Step by Step," *PM Network,* vol. 26, no. 6 (June 2012), pp. 57–61.

James, M., "Scrum," 2009 (downloaded PDF @ *http://refcardz.dzone.com/* on 5/18/2009).

Jonasson, Hans, *Determining Project Requirements* (Boca Raton, FL: Auerback Publications, 2008).

Kruchten, P., *The Rational Unified Process: An Introduction,* 3rd ed. (Upper Saddle River, NJ: Pearson Education, 2004).

Larman, C., *Agile & Iterative Development: A Manager's Guide* (Boston: Addison-Wesley, 2004).

McConnel, S., *Rapid Development: Taming Wild Software Schedules* (Redmond, WA: Microsoft Press, 1996).

Schur, M., "The State of Agile," *PM Network*, September 2015, pp. 16–17.

Schwaber, K., *Agile Project Management with Scrum* (Redmond, WA: Microsoft Press, 2004).

Takeuchi, H., and I. Nonaka, "The New Product Development Game," *Harvard Business Review,* January–February 1986.

Tarne, R., "Taking Off the Agile Training Wheels, Advance Agile Project Management using Kanban," *2011 PMI Global Proceedings*, Dallas, TX, 2011.

Vanderjack, B., "21 Methods to Engage and Retain Your Product Owner in an Agile Project," www.pmworldjournal.net, vol. 1, no. 4 (November 2012), pp. 1–6.

Worthen, B., "Try Software on Workers First, Fix It Later," *The Wall Street Journal,* September 25, 2007, pp. B1 and B4.

Case 16.1

Introducing Scrum at P2P

PART A

Kendra Hua had worked for six years as a software engineer in the IT department at Point 2 Point (P2P), a large freight moving company. She liked her job and the people she worked with. While she did some maintenance work, she worked primarily on projects, usually full time. Her work covered a wide range of projects including system upgrades, inventory control, GPS tracking, billing, and customer databases. These projects were typically able to meet project requirements but were consistently late. Within the IT department it was common practice for a betting pool to emerge regarding completion dates. The rule of thumb was to take the original schedule and multiply it by 1.5 and start guessing from then on.

Management decided to try to turn things around by changing the way P2P completed IT projects. Instead of the traditional waterfall approach in which all the requirements were defined upfront, the IT department was to start using Agile project management, and more specifically Scrum, to complete their projects.

Kendra had just been assigned to the Big Foot project, which involved developing a system for monitoring P2P's carbon footprint. To prepare for this project, Kendra and her entire team of software engineers would attend a two-day Scrum workshop.

Everyone was given a book on Scrum to prepare themselves for the workshop. At first Kendra was overwhelmed by terminology—Scrum master, sprints, product manager, sprint logs, and so forth. She questioned the rugby metaphor, since the only thing she knew about the sport was that one of her ex-boyfriends in college would come back to the dorm inebriated and bloodied after a match. And why was the project manager called a master? It seemed demeaning to her. Still, she had heard some good things about Scrum from a friend who was using it in another company. He claimed it gave programmers more freedom to do their work and work at a faster pace. So she approached the two-day workshop with an open mind.

The workshop was facilitated by a trainer who was well versed in the world of software development. Participants included her other five team members as well as Prem Gupta, a veteran project manager who would now assume the role of Scrum master, and Isaac Smith, who would act as the product manager representing the interests of the customers. At first everyone gave Prem a hard time, by bowing to him, pleading "master, master, master . . ." The facilitator quickly corrected them by saying he was not their master but rather master of the Scrum process. The facilitator went on to emphasize that they would work as a self-organizing team. Kendra wasn't exactly sure what that meant, but she felt it had something to do with the team managing itself, not Prem.

The workshop covered all the basic Scrum tools, concepts, and roles. Everyone got to practice the process by completing a simulated project involving the creation of a new board game. Kendra liked the idea of the standing Scrum meeting, since most of her meetings at P2P took way too long. She also liked having the product manager, who was the ultimate decider on features and when work was completed. Everyone laughed at the "only one neck to wring" analogy that the facilitator used to describe this role. Overall she thought the process had promise and she was excited about trying it out on the Big Foot project. The Big Foot project was estimated to be completed after five sprints with each sprint lasting four weeks.

THE FIRST SPRINT

The first sprint planning meeting went pretty much by the book. Isaac had done his homework and came to the meeting with a comprehensive list of features the software needed to provide. There was healthy discussion, and Isaac amended the list to include some features that the team felt was necessary. The afternoon session featured Isaac, the product owner, prioritizing the features in the product backlog with feedback from the team. The final segment was devoted to the team deciding among themselves which high priority features they would commit to build within the four-week sprint. Prem did a good job of reminding the team that they were expected to build a fully functional feature. This tempered the team's enthusiasm, and in the end a challenging but doable set of features was assigned to the sprint backlog for the first sprint.

The first couple of daily Scrum meetings were a bit awkward as members were careful not to step on each other's toes. One of the first impediments identified was not having a shared understanding of how a self-organizing team worked. Prem kept emphasizing that it was up to the team to decide who does what and when. Then one morning it just suddenly clicked and members came forward claiming work they felt needed to be done. After that the daily scrums took on a life of their own, interrupted only when a member had to do five push-ups for every minute late. The pace of work picked up, and there was a shared enthusiasm as tasks and ultimately functional features were completed in rapid fashion. Kendra worked side by side with the other software engineers to solve problems and share what they had learned. Occasionally Isaac would be called into the project room to answer questions about specific features and be shown work in progress.

By the time of the first sprint review meeting, the team was able to demonstrate all but one of the designated features to Isaac and even three more that were not on the initial hit list. The team got some useful feedback not only from Isaac but also from a couple of the end users he brought with him. Eighty percent of the features were proclaimed done by Isaac while the others needed only slight modifications. Everyone agreed that the next Sprint review would even be more successful.

The sprint retrospective meeting was refreshing as members spoke candidly about both the good and the bad. Everyone agreed that the team needed to do a better job at documentation. Issues regarding fairness and spreading both the fun work and the tough work among the entire team were brought to the surface. Kendra was impressed by how everyone focused on what was best for the project not just themselves.

THE SECOND SPRINT

The second sprint meeting went well. The features that needed rework after the first sprint review meeting were at the top of the backlog and Isaac made appropriate adjustments in priorities, and a couple of new features that were discovered during the sprint review meeting were added. The meeting convened with the team confident that they would be able to complete the work they had committed to.

Project work progressed quickly over the next week. Kendra felt pressure to accomplish what she said she would at the daily Scrum. At the same time, she felt a tremendous amount of satisfaction reporting work done. The entire team seemed energized. Then one day everything came to a standstill over a sticky integration problem. The team struggled over the next three days trying to solve the problem until, at the next Scrum, Prem stepped forward saying, "I think you should do this . . ." He then proceeded to outline a specific method for solving the problem, even assigning specific tasks to each team member. During the next two days Prem went back and forth between team members coordinating their work and solving problems. While there was some grumbling within the team, his solution worked, and Kendra was grateful to get back on track.

From then on Prem took a more active role in daily Scrum meetings, often having the final say as to the work agenda for that day. The meetings took on a different tone as members waited for Prem to speak first. Isaac was absent from the project room during this time as he was visiting sites that would be using the new software. Still, features were being completed and Kendra was happy with the progress. Then one day Isaac showed up at the morning Scrum meeting. He had just gotten back and had fresh information he wanted to introduce into the project. He had rewritten the product log and added several new, high priority features and eliminated a few of the features that the team had been working on. He wanted the team to shift their efforts and complete the new features by the end of the sprint.

The team was shocked because one of the principles they had been taught is that you don't change course midway through a sprint. Prem did his best to explain this to Isaac, but he was insistent. He kept saying that these changes had to be made, otherwise much of the sprint output would be a waste of time. He kept repeating that the team needed to be flexible. "After all, isn't that what the Agile approach is all about?" The meeting came to an impasse until Prem came forward with a compromise. The team would agree to do the new work, but the sprint needed to be extended by two weeks. Everyone agreed and Kendra went back to work.

Up till the end of the second sprint, Prem continued to direct project work. When it came for the sprint review meeting four of the five new features were completed as well as most of the original features. However, the feature demonstrations did not go well. Isaac and several of the end users that were present were critical of the user friendliness of several of the completed features. Kendra and other team members defended their work by saying, "Why didn't you tell us you wanted it to perform that way?" Prem did his best to keep the meeting under control, but the team had little to say when an important feature simply did not work. In the end, only half of the features were accepted as being done.

Kendra walked out of the sprint review discouraged. Tomorrow morning was the sprint retrospective meeting. She had a lot on her mind, but wasn't sure what she should say or how to say it at the meeting.

1. How well is Scrum working?
2. What are the issues confronting the Big Foot project?
3. Assume you are Kendra. What would you want to say at the retrospective? How would you say it?
4. What improvements or changes need to be made?

PART B

Prem opened the retrospective by saying he had gotten a call from his boss and she was not happy with the progress. Prem said that he and the team were under the gun to get back on track. The list of things that went well during the second sprint was short and when it came time to discuss improvements there was an awkward silence. Kendra spoke up and began by saying she had gone back and reviewed the Scrum book. She went on to say that she thought the whole idea behind Scrum was that the team was to work to solve their own problems and it wasn't Prem's role to play task master. A couple of other team members murmured agreement. Prem became defensive and said if he had not intervened it would have taken days for the team to solve the problem.

Another member said he thought it was a mistake allowing Isaac to change the sprint commitments. Prem agreed that in principle that was true, but said sometimes you have to bend the rules to do what is right. He admonished the team by saying that they had to practice being more agile. The retrospective ended with few specific recommendations other than that in order to get back on track, Prem felt he would have to get even more involved in the execution of the project.

The subsequent sprint 3 planning meeting was more of a formality. Isaac updated the product backlog with revised priorities and Prem signed off for the team as to what they would commit to. There was little interaction between the team and Isaac except seeking clarification on performance requirements for specific features.

The team met under Prem's leadership for their daily Scrums. Sometimes the Scrums went beyond the normal 15 minutes as Prem reviewed progress and described in detail what needed to be done that day. Isaac would occasionally show up, change priorities, review work and answer questions. Kendra worked hard on her assignments and often received praise from Prem for work well done.

One evening when the team got together for a few beers and sushi, one of the team members pulled out a spreadsheet and asked who wanted to make the first bet on when they thought the project would be done.

After several sprints, Isaac finally signed off on the last feature and declared the project completed. A collective "yahoo" sprang from the team. After the meeting Kendra went around collecting money from each of her teammates—she had predicted that the project would take 12 weeks longer than planned.

1. How would you assess P2P's effort at introducing Scrum?
2. What challenges does an organization face when adopting an Agile approach like Scrum?
3. What could P2P have done to enhance success?

Solutions to Selected Exercises

Chapter 2

2. $Payback = \dfrac{Investment}{Annual\ savings}$

   $Payback_{Project\ Alpha} = \dfrac{\$150,000}{\$40,000} = 3.75\ years$

   $Payback_{Project\ Beta} = \dfrac{\$200,000}{\$50,000} = 4.00\ years$

   A lower payback is better. Project Alpha has the lower payback and so has the better payback.

5. $Project\ NPV = I_0 + \sum_{t=1}^{n} \dfrac{F_t}{(1 + k)^t}$

   For Dust Devils Project using the NPV equation:

   $$NPV = -\$500,000 + \dfrac{\$50,000}{(1 + .20)^1} + \dfrac{\$250,000}{(1 + .20)^2} + \dfrac{\$350,000}{(1 + .20)^3}$$

   $$= -\$500,000 + \$41,667 + \$173,611 + \$202,546 = -\$82,176$$

   For Dust Devils Project using Excel:

	A	B	C	D	E	F
1	**Expected ROI**		20%			
2						
3	**Dust Devils**					
4						
5	**Year**	**Inflows**	**Outflows**	**New flows**	**NPV**	
6	0		$500,000	−$500,000	−$500,000	
7	1	$50,000		$50,000	$41,667	=D7/((1+$C$1)^A7
8	2	$250,000		$250,000	$173,611	
9	3	$350,000		$350,000	$202,546	
10					−$82,176	
11						
12					−$82,176	=D6+NPV($C$1,D7:D9)

The expected ROI is entered in cell C1 and that will be referenced in the worksheets for the next two projects. Cells E6 to E10 repeat the calculations shown in the previous equations, only using Excel. Cells E7 to E9 perform the three discounting calculations. The equation used is shown in cell F7. The dollar signs in "$C$1" keep that cell from changing when this formula is copied up or down. In Excel, this is called an absolute reference.

Cell E12 performs the NPV calculations as shown in the textbook. Excel gives the same answer either way. Cell F12 shows the formula for the direct NPV calculations.

For Osprey Project using the NPV equation:

$$NPV = -\$250{,}000 + \frac{\$75{,}000}{(1 + .20)^1} + \frac{\$75{,}000}{(1 + .20)^2} + \frac{\$75{,}000}{(1 + .20)^3} + \frac{\$50{,}000}{(1 + .20)^4}$$

$$= -\$250{,}000 + \$62{,}500 + \$52{,}083 + \$43{,}403 + \$24{,}113 = -\$67{,}901$$

For Osprey Project using Excel:

	A	B	C	D	E	F
15	**Osprey**					
16						
17	**Year**	**Inflows**	**Outflows**	**New flows**	**NPV**	
18	0		$250,000	−$250,000	−$250,000	
19	1	$75,000		$75,000	$62,500	=D19/((1+$C$1)^A19)
20	2	$75,000		$75,000	$52,083	
21	3	$75,000		$75,000	$43,403	
22	4	$50,000		$50,000	<u>$24,113</u>	
23					−$67,901	
24						
25					−$67,901	=D18+NPV($C$1,D19:D22)

For Voyagers Project using the NPV equation:

$$NPV = -\$75{,}000 + \frac{\$15{,}000}{(1 + .20)^1} + \frac{\$25{,}000}{(1 + .20)^2} + \frac{\$50{,}000}{(1 + .20)^3} + \frac{\$50{,}000}{(1 + .20)^4}$$

$$+ \frac{\$150{,}000}{(1 + .20)^5}$$

$$= -\$75{,}000 + \$12{,}500 + \$17{,}361 + \$28{,}935 + \$24{,}113 + \$60{,}282$$

$$= \$68{,}191$$

For Voyagers Project using Excel:

	A	B	C	D	E	F
28	**Voyagers**					
29						
30	**Year**	**Inflows**	**Outflows**	**New flows**	**NPV**	
31	0		$75,000	−$75,000	−$75,000	
32	1	$15,000		$15,000	$12,500	=D32/((1+$C$1)^A32)
33	2	$25,000		$25,000	$17,361	
34	3	$50,000		$50,000	$28,935	
35	4	$50,000		$50,000	$24,113	
36	5	$150,000		$150,000	$60,282	
37					$68,191	
38						
39					$68,191	=D31+NPV($C$1,D32:D36)

The only project SIMSOX should consider is Voyagers. Each of the other two projects would not satisfy the high rate of return SIMSOX expects from its projects.

Chapter 6

3.

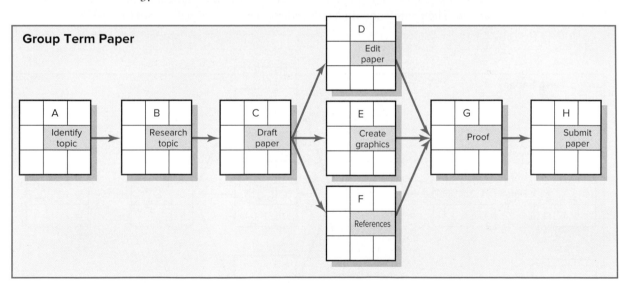

Activity C is a burst activity. Activity G is a merge activity.

11.

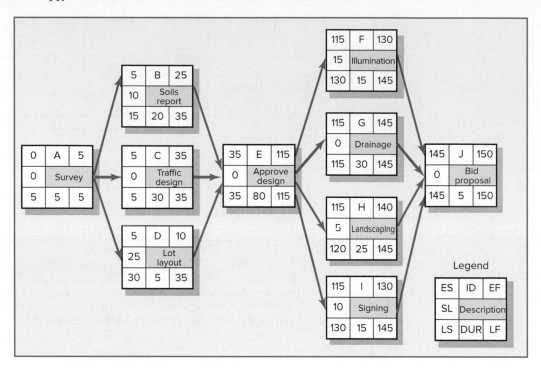

Early start, late start, early finish, late finish, and slack are shown on the diagram above. The completion time is 150 days. The critical path is A-C-E-G-J.

13.

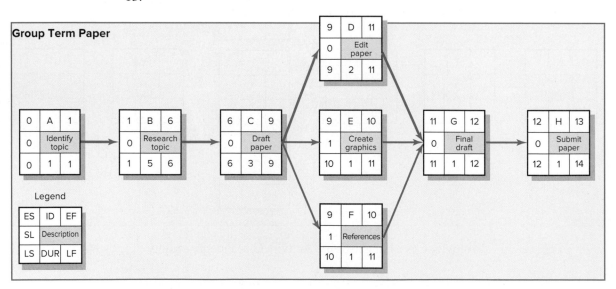

Early start, late start, early finish, late finish, and slack are shown on the diagram above. The Gantt chart is shown below.

21.

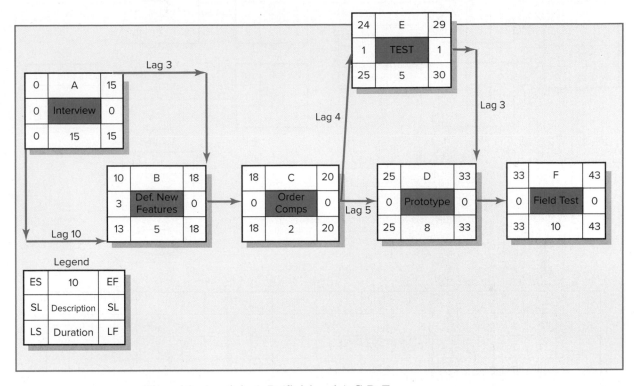

The critical path is A-B (finish only)-C-D-F.

Chapter 8

4. Log of Parallel Method of Scheduling: Exercise 8-4

Period	Activity	Changes
0–1	B	Schedule Activity B (first by minimum slack rule)
	A	Schedule Activity A
1–2	-	No changes
2–3	-	No changes
3–4	-	No changes
4–5	C	Delay ES of Activity C to 5. Reduce slack to 1
5–6	D	Schedule Activity D (minimum slack rule)
	C	Schedule Activity C
	E	Delay ES of Activity E to 6. Reduce slack to 1
6–7	E	Delay ES of Activity E to 7. Reduce slack to 0
7–8	E	Delay ES of Activity E to 8. Reduce slack to −1
	F	Delay ES of Activity F to 11. Reduce slack to −1
8–9	E	Delay ES of Activity E to 9. Reduce slack to −2
	F	Delay ES of Activity F to 12. Reduce slack to −2
9–10	E	Schedule Activity E
10–11	-	No changes
11–12	-	No changes
12–13	F	Schedule Activity F

7. You should not spend time planning how you are going to spend your bonus. The schedule will take 16 days.

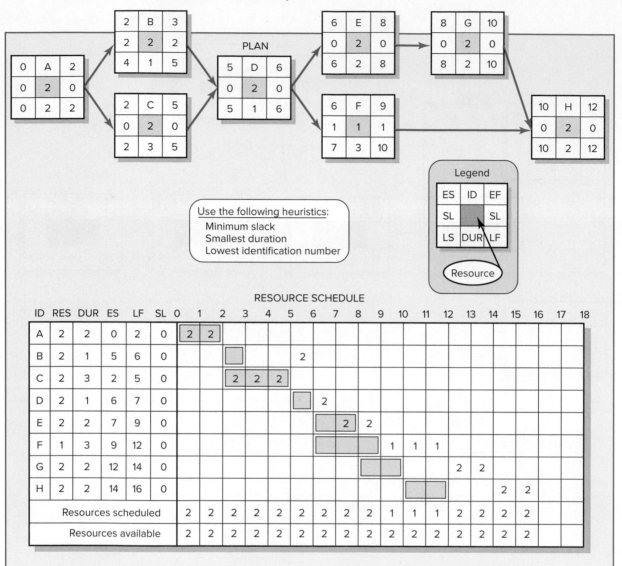

Use the following heuristics:
- Minimum slack
- Smallest duration
- Lowest identification number

Legend

ES	ID	EF
SL		SL
LS	DUR	LF

Resource

RESOURCE SCHEDULE

ID	RES	DUR	ES	LF	SL	0	1	2	3	4	5	6	7	8	9	10	11	12	13	14	15	16	17	18
A	2	2	0	2	0	2	2																	
B	2	1	5	6	0			2			2													
C	2	3	2	5	0			2	2	2														
D	2	1	6	7	0						2	2												
E	2	2	7	9	0							2	2	2										
F	1	3	9	12	0							2	2	2	1	1	1							
G	2	2	12	14	0									2	2			2	2					
H	2	2	14	16	0										2	2				2	2			
Resources scheduled						2	2	2	2	2	2	2	2	2	1	1	1	2	2	2	2			
Resources available						2	2	2	2	2	2	2	2	2	2	2	2	2	2	2	2			

10.

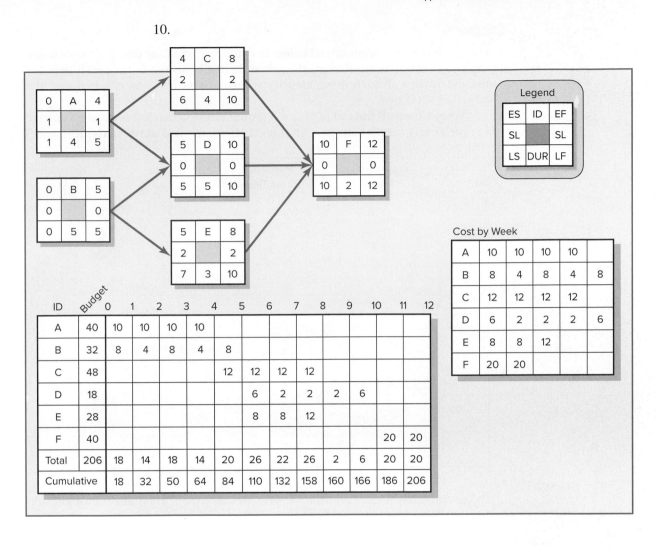

Legend

ES	ID	EF
SL		SL
LS	DUR	LF

Cost by Week

A	10	10	10	10	
B	8	4	8	4	8
C	12	12	12	12	
D	6	2	2	2	6
E	8	8	12		
F	20	20			

ID	Budget	0	1	2	3	4	5	6	7	8	9	10	11	12
A	40	10	10	10	10									
B	32	8	4	8	4	8								
C	48					12	12	12	12					
D	18							6	2	2	2	6		
E	28							8	8	12				
F	40												20	20
Total	206	18	14	18	14	20	26	22	26	2	6	20	20	
Cumulative		18	32	50	64	84	110	132	158	160	166	186	206	

Chapter 9

2. **Use the information contained below to compress one time unit per move using the least cost method. Reduce the schedule until you reach the crash point of the network. For each move identify what activity(ies) was crashed and the adjusted total cost.**

  Note: Choose B instead of C and E (equal costs) because it is usually smarter to crash early rather than late AND one activity instead of two activities.

Act.	Crash Cost (Slope)	Maximum Crash Time	Normal Time	Normal Cost
A	0		2	150
B	100	1	3	100
C	50	2	4	200
D	40	1	4	200
E	50	1	3	200
F	0		1	150

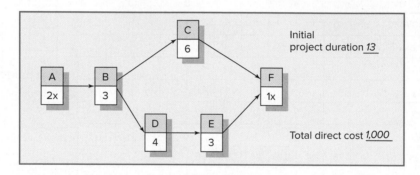

Initial project duration *13*

Total direct cost *1,000*

Project duration is reduced from 13 time periods to ten. Total direct cost goes up from 1,000 to 1,240. The steps are shown below:

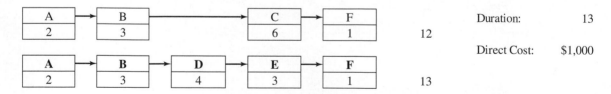

					Duration:	13
A	B	C	F	12		
2	3	6	1		Direct Cost:	$1,000
A	B	D	E	F	13	
2	3	4	3	1		

The project has two paths, A-B-C-F, which takes 12 time periods, and A-B-D-E-F, which takes 13 time periods. This gives the project a duration of 13 time periods. The total direct cost is $1,000.

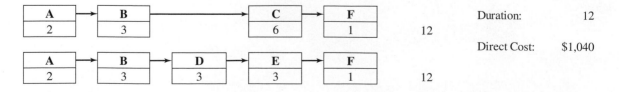

					Duration:	12
A	B	C	F	12		
2	3	6	1		Direct Cost:	$1,040
A	B	D	E	F	12	
2	3	3	3	1		

The cheapest activity to reduce is D at a cost of $40 for one time period. That makes both paths critical. That means that further reductions will require either reducing the same time from an activity on both paths or finding an activity shared by both paths and reducing that activity. Total direct cost goes up from $1,000 to $1,040.

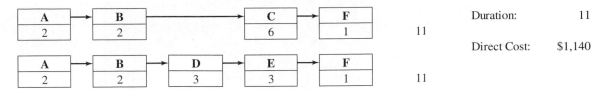

		Duration:	11
		Direct Cost:	$1,140

Activity B is on both paths and can be reduced by one time period at a cost of $100.[1] That lowers the completion time to 11 time periods and raises total direct cost to $1,140.

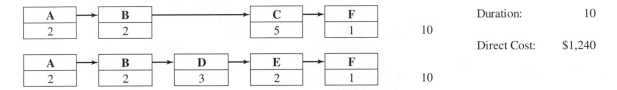

		Duration:	10
		Direct Cost:	$1,240

Finally, we can reduce C on the first path at a cost of $50 and E on the second path at a cost of $50. That reduces the completion time to 10 time units and raises total direct cost to $1,240. No further reductions are possible.

8.

Activity	Normal Time	Normal Cost	Maximum Crash Time	Crash Cost
A	3	150	0	0
B	4	200	1	100
C	3	250	1	60
D	4	200	1	40
E	2	250	0	0
F	3	200	2	30
G	2	250	1	20
H	4	300	2	60
I	2	200	1	200

[1]Activities C on the first path and E on the second path also have a combined cost of $100. We select B first since it is usually smarter to crash earlier activities first *and* it is usually smarter to crash one activity rather than two.

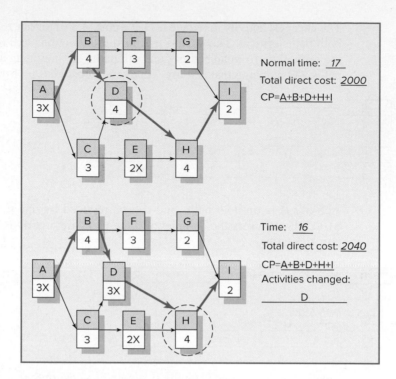

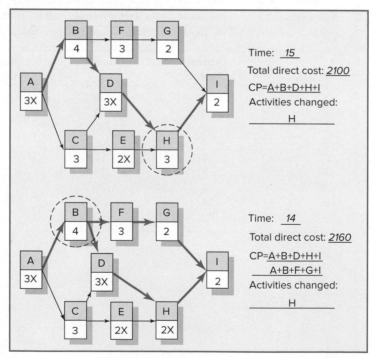

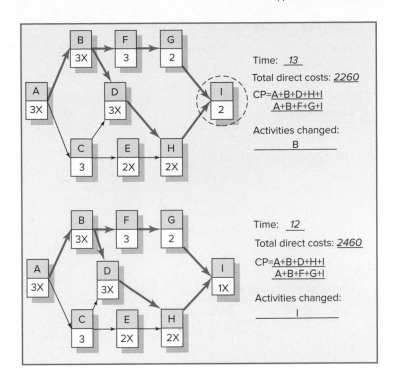

Duration	Direct Cost	Indirect Cost	Total Cost
17	2,000	1,500	3,500
16	2,040	1,450	3,490
15	2,100	1,400	3,500
14	2,160	1,350	3,560
13	2,260	1,300	3,660
12	2,460	1,250	3,860

The optimum time-cost schedule would be 16 weeks at a cost of $3,490.

Chapter 13

8.

Status Report: Ending Period 1 ($000)

Task	% Complete	EV	AC	PV	CV	SV
A	25%	25	50	50	−25	−25
Cumulative Totals		**25**	**50**	**50**	**−25**	**−25**

Status Report: Ending Period 2 ($000)

Task	% Complete	EV	AC	PV	CV	SV
A	50%	50	100	100	−50	−50
Cumulative Totals		**50**	**100**	**100**	**−50**	**−50**

Status Report: Ending Period 3 ($000)

Task	% Complete	EV	AC	PV	CV	SV
A	100%	100	200	100	−100	0
B	0%	0	0	100	0	−100
C	0%	0	0	150	0	−150
Cumulative Totals		**100**	**200**	**350**	**−100**	**−250**

Status Report: Ending Period 4 ($000)

Task	% Complete	EV	AC	PV	CV	SV
A	100%	100	200	100	−100	0
B	60%	150	100	150	50	0
C	50%	225	200	300	25	−75
Cumulative Totals		**475**	**500**	**550**	**−25**	**−75**

Status Report: Ending Period 5 ($000)

Task	% Complete	EV	AC	PV	CV	SV
A	100%	100	200	100	−100	0
B	100%	250	200	250	50	0
C	100%	450	400	450	50	0
Cumulative Totals		**800**	**800**	**800**	**0**	**0**

Status Report: Ending Period 6 ($000)

Task	% Complete	EV	AC	PV	CV	SV
A	100%	100	200	100	−100	0
B	100%	250	200	250	50	0
C	100%	450	400	450	50	0
D	75%	150	100	100	50	50
Cumulative Totals		**950**	**900**	**900**	**50**	**50**

Status Report: Ending Period 7 ($000)

Task	% Complete	EV	AC	PV	CV	SV
A	100%	100	200	100	−100	0
B	100%	250	200	250	50	0
C	100%	450	400	450	50	0
D	100%	200	150	200	50	0
E	20%	60	100	0	−40	60
F	5%	15	50	0	−35	15
Cumulative Totals		**1075**	**1100**	**1000**	**−25**	**75**

Status Report: Ending Period 8 ($000)

Task	% Complete	EV	AC	PV	CV	SV
A	100%	100	200	100	−100	0
B	100%	250	200	250	50	0
C	100%	450	400	450	50	0
D	100%	200	150	200	50	0
E	100%	300	350	200	−50	100
F	10%	30	100	100	−70	−70
Cumulative Totals		**1330**	**1400**	**1300**	**−70**	**30**

Performance Indexes Summary

Period	EV	AC	PV	SPI	CPI	PCIB
1	25	50	50	.50	.50	2%
2	50	100	100	.50	.50	3%
3	100	200	350	.29	.50	5%
4	475	500	550	.86	.95	24%
5	800	800	800	1.00	1.00	40%
6	950	900	900	1.06	1.06	48%
7	1075	1100	1000	1.08	.98	54%
8	1330	1400	1300	1.02	.95	67%

$$EAC_f = \frac{(BAC - EV)}{(EV/AC)} + AC = \frac{(2{,}000 - 1{,}300)}{(1{,}330/1{,}400)} + 1{,}400 = 2{,}105$$

$$VAC_f = BAC - EAC_f = 2{,}000 - 2{,}105 = -105$$

With two-thirds of the project completed the forecast is that the project will be $105,000 over budget at completion.

Computer Project Exercises

In developing the exercises, trade-offs had to be made to enrich the learning experience. One of the major problems students initially encounter is data and detail overload. This reduces their ability to identify project and data problems and to compare alternatives. Although the project found in the exercises is real, it has been reduced and detail has been eliminated many times to concentrate on applying project management principles and understanding linkages. In addition, other simplifying assumptions have been made so that students and instructors can trace problems and discuss outcomes. These assumptions detract from reality, but they keep the focus on the objectives of the exercises and reduce student frustration with software intricacies. Moving from these exercises to real projects is primarily one of increasing detail.

The POM+ Project*

Big Kola Company has been concerned that specialized fruit drinks have been eroding their cola market. The CEO mandates that "If you can't beat them, join them." Grape juice was the first product that was successful after an advertising blitz claiming the antitoxin benefits. Lately, competition is compressing grape juice margins and profits. Months of additional market surveys and focus groups have resulted in three potential high-margin drinks: cranberry, blueberry, and pomegranate. All these choices represent antitoxins. The decision is to produce the pomegranate drink that has many health claims. For example, the relative ability of these juices to eliminate harmful free radicals (antitoxins) is 71 percent for pomegranate, 33 percent for blueberry, and 20 percent for cranberry (Technion Institute of Technology). The market potential appears very attractive and should have a higher profit margin than the other potential juice products. Another appeal for pomegranate juice is its familiarity in the Middle East and Asia.

The Priority Matrix for the POM+ Project is:

	Time	Scope	Cost
Constrain			X
Enhance		X	
Accept	X		

* Cliff Gray, Erik Larson, & Pinyarat Sirisomboonsuk, doctoral candidate at Rawls College of Business, Texas Tech University.

Connor Gage, the project manager, has formed his project team and the members have come up with the following work breakdown structure.

1.0 POM+Project
1.1 R&D product development
    1.1.1 Need survey
    1.1.2 Set product specs
    1.1.3 Shelf life report
    1.1.4 Nutrition report
1.2 Secure fruit suppliers
1.3 Initial Production
    1.3.1 Equipment rehab
    1.3.2 Production trials
    1.3.3 Quality trials
    1.3.4 Quality metrics
    1.3.5 Quality training
1.4 Distribution
    1.4.1 Market testing
    1.4.2 Package design
    1.4.3 Select distributors
1.5 Legal
    1.5.1 Complete FDA certification
    1.5.2 Register trademark
1.6 Prepare product launch

Part 1

1. Develop the WBS outline using the software available (save your file).
2. Use this file and the information provided below to create a project schedule.
3. The following holidays are observed: January 1, Martin Luther King Day (third Monday in January), Memorial Day (last Monday in May), July 4th, Labor Day (first Monday in September), Thanksgiving Day (4th Thursday in November), December 25 and 26.
4. If a holiday falls on a Saturday then Friday will be given as an extra day off, and if it falls on a Sunday then Monday will be given off.
5. The project team works eight-hour days, Monday through Friday.
6. The project will begin on January 3, 2012.
7. Based on this schedule, submit a memo that answers the following questions:
    a. When is the project estimated to be completed? How many working days will it take?
    b. What is the critical path?
    c. Which activity has the most total slack?
    d. How sensitive is this network?
    e. Identify two sensible milestones and explain your choice.

Include the following (one page) printouts:

- A Gantt chart.
- A network diagram highlighting the critical path.
- A schedule table reporting ES, LS, EF, LF, and slack for each activity.

Hints: Change the timescale to months and weeks. The estimated duration of the project is 135 days.

Remember: Save your files for future exercises!

The following information has been derived from the WBS. *Note* that the activity number is what appears in the software with the complete WBS entered.

#*	Activity	Duration	Predecessor(s)
3	Need survey	20	None
4	Set product specs	15	3
5	Shelf life report	10	4
6	Nutrition report	5	4
7	Select fruit suppliers	20	5, 6
9	Equipment rehab	30	4
10	Production trials	15	7, 9
11	Quality trials	20	10
12	Quality metrics	5	11
13	Quality training	15	12
15	Market testing	30	5, 6
16	Package design	15	15
17	Select distributors	25	5, 6
19	Complete FDA certification	15	7, 15
20	Register trademark	5	7, 15
21	Prepare product launch	15	13, 16, 17, 19FS + 25 days, 20FS + 15 days

FS = Finish to Start lag

Part 2

Remember the old saying, "A project plan is not a schedule until resources are committed." This exercise illustrates this sometime subtle, but important point.

Using your files from Part 1, input resources and their costs if you have not already done so. All information is found in Tables A2.1 and A2.2.

Prepare a memo that addresses the following questions:

1. Which if any of the resources are overallocated?
2. Assume that the project is time constrained and try to resolve any overallocation problems by leveling within slack. What happens?
3. What is the impact of leveling within slack on the sensitivity of the network?

Include a Gantt chart with the schedule table after leveling within slack.

4. Assume the project is resource constrained and resolve any overallocation problems by leveling outside of slack. What happens?

TABLE A2.1
Resource
Assignments

Activity	Resources
Need survey	MRKT (500%)
Set product specs	R&D (400%), MRKT (200%)
Shelf life report	R&D (300%)
Nutrition report	R&D (300%)
Select fruit suppliers	PURCH (100%)
Equipment rehab	ENG (1,000%), PROD (2,000%)
Production trials	PROD (1,500%), PURCH (100%), ENG (1,000%)
Quality trials	QUAL (300%), PROD (500%)
Quality metrics	QUAL (300%), PROD (100%)
Quality training	QUAL (300%), PROD (1,500%)
Market testing	MRKT (500%)
Package design	DESIGN (300%), MRKT (100%)
Select distributors	MRKT (500%)
Complete FDA certification	LEGAL (300%)
Register trademark	LEGAL (300%)
Prepare product launch	QUAL (300%), PURCH (200%), PROD (1,500%), MRKT (500%), ENG (500%), R&D (100%)

TABLE A2.2
Resources
Availability and Pay
Rates

Resource	Abbrev	Available	Hourly rate
Marketing staff	MRKT	5	$ 80/hr
R&D	R&D	5	$ 80/hr
Engineering	ENG	10	$100/hr
Purchasing	PURCH	2	$ 60/hr
Quality engineers	QUAL	3	$ 80/hr
Designers	DESIGN	3	$ 60/hr
Legal staff	LEGAL	3	$120/hr
Production	PROD	20	$ 60/hr

Include a Gantt chart with the schedule table after leveling outside of slack.

Note: No splitting of activities is allowed.

Note: No partial assignments (e.g., 50 percent). All resources must be assigned 100 percent.

Part 3

Top management has accepted the July 19th completion schedule created at the end of Part 2. Prepare a brief memo that addresses the following questions:

1. How much will the project cost? What is the most expensive activity?
2. What does the cash flow statement tell you about how costs are distributed over the life span of the project?

Include a monthly cash flow for the project.

Once you are confident that you have the final schedule, save the file as a baseline. **Hint:** Save a backup file just in case without baseline!

TABLE A2.3
Status Report
March 31, 2012

Activity	Actual Start	Actual Finish	Actual Duration	Remaining Duration
Need survey	1/3/12	2/2/12	22	0
Set product specs	2/3/12	2/28/12	18	0
Shelf life report	2/29/12	3/13/12	10	0
Nutrition report	3/14/12	3/19/12	4	0
Equipment rehab	2/29/12		23	12

Part 4 A

Assume that today is March 31, 2012, and Table A2.3 contains the tracking information for the project up till now. Enter this information into your saved baseline file and prepare a status report for the first three months of the POM+ project.

Your status report should also address the following questions:

1. How is the project progressing in terms of cost and schedule?
2. What activities have gone well? What activities have not gone well?
3. What do the PCIB and PCIC indicate in terms of how much of the project has been accomplished to date?
4. What is the forecasted cost at completion (EAC_f)? What is the predicted VAC_f?
5. Report and interpret the TCPI for the project at this point in time.
6. What is the estimated date of completion?
7. How well is the project doing in terms of its priorities?

Try to present the above information in a form worthy of consideration by top management.

Include an Earned Value table and a Tracking Gantt Chart.

Note: Insert March 31, 2012, as the status date in the Project Information box.

Part 4 B

Assume that today is May 31, 2012, and Table A2.4 contains the tracking information for the project up till now. Enter this information into your saved baseline file and prepare a status report for the POM+ project.

Your status report should address the following questions:

1. How is the project progressing in terms of cost and schedule?
2. What activities have gone well? What activities have not gone well?
3. What do the PCIB and PCIC indicate in terms of how much of the project has been accomplished to date?
4. What is the forecasted cost at completion (EAC_f)? What is the predicted VAC_f?
5. Report and interpret the TCPI for the project at this point in time.
6. What is the estimated date of completion?
7. How well is the project doing in terms of its priorities?

Try to present the above information in a form worthy of consideration by top management.

Include an Earned Value table and a Tracking Gantt Chart.

Note: Insert May 31, 2012, as the status date in the Project Information box.

TABLE A2.4
Status Report
May 31, 2012

Activity	Actual Start	Actual Finish	Actual Duration	Remaining Duration
Need survey	1/3/12	2/2/12	22	0
Set product specs	2/3/12	2/28/12	18	0
Shelf life report	2/29/12	3/13/12	10	0
Nutrition report	3/14/12	3/19/12	4	0
Select fruit suppliers	4/3/12	4/30/12	20	0
Equipment rehab	2/29/12	4/11/12	31	0
Production trials	4/17/12	5/4/12	14	0
Quality trials	5/7/12	5/31/12	18	0
Market testing	4/4/12	5/9/12	26	0
Package design	5/10/12	5/25/12	12	0
Select distributors	5/28/12		4	18
Complete FDA certification	5/11/12	5/31/12	14	0

Red Zuma Project

The ARC Company specializes in developing and selling a wide range of high-quality scooters. Sales representatives report that there is a growing demand for racing scooters. ARC's president, Robin Lane, is excited about the possibilities and predicts that one day these kinds of razor scooters will be featured in X-Game events. ARC is a small company and uses a strong matrix to optimally utilize limited manpower.

The Project Priority Matrix for the Red Zuma Project is:

	Time	Scope	Cost
Constrain		X	
Enhance	X		
Accept			X

Part 1

You are a member of a project team assigned to develop the new razor scooter code named "Red Zuma." Table A2.5 contains the information necessary to create a project schedule. For the purpose of this case assume the following:

1. The project begins January 2, 2015.
2. The following holidays are observed: January 1, Martin Luther King Day (third Monday in January), Memorial Day (last Monday in May), July 4th, Labor Day (first Monday in September), Thanksgiving Day (4th Thursday in November), December 25.
3. If a holiday falls on a Saturday, then Friday will be given as an extra day off, and if it falls on a Sunday, then Monday will be given as a day off. If December 25th falls on a Friday then Monday will not be given a day off.
4. The project team works eight-hour days, Monday through Friday.

TABLE A2.5
Red Zuma:
Project Schedule

ID	Task Name	Duration	Predecessors
1	**1 Red Zuma Project**	260 days	
2	1.1 Market Analysis	25 days	
3	1.2 Product Design	30 days	2
4	1.3 Manufacturing Study	20 days	2
5	1.4 Product Design Selection	10 days	3, 4
6	1.5 Detailed Marketing Plan	15 days	5
7	1.6 Manufacturing Process	30 days	5
8	1.7 Detailed Product Design	45 days	5
9	1.8 Build Prototypes	25 days	8
10	1.9 Lab Test Prototypes	10 days	9
11	1.10 Field Test Prototypes	15 days	9
12	1.11 Finalized Product Design	20 days	7,10,11
13	1.12 Final Manufacturing Process	10 days	12
14	1.13 Order Components	7 days	12
15	1.14 Order Production Equipment	14 days	13
16	1.15 Install Production Equipment	35 days	14FS+20 days,15FS+30 days
17	1.16 Celebrate	1 days	6, 16

Note: FS refers to a Finish-to-Start lag.

Construct a network schedule for this project and prepare a memo that answers the following questions:

1. When is the project estimated to be completed? How long will the project take?
2. What is the critical path for the project?
3. Which activity has the greatest amount of slack?
4. How sensitive is this network?
5. Identify two sensible milestones and explain your choices.

Include the following printouts:

- A Gantt chart.
- A network diagram highlighting the critical path.
- A schedule table reporting ES, LS, EF, LF, and slack for each activity.

Part 2

The following personnel have been assigned full-time to the Red Zuma project team:

  4 marketing specialists
  4 design engineers
  4 development engineers
  4 industrial engineers
  4 test riders
  2 purchasing agents

Use the file from Part 1 and the information contained in Tables A2.6 and A2.7 to assign resources to the project schedule.

TABLE A2.6
Red Zuma Project
Resources

	$	Number available
Marketing specialist	$80,000/yr	4
Design engineer	$125,000/yr	4
Development engineer	$110,000/yr	4
Industrial engineer	$100,000/yr	4
Purchasing agent	$75,000/yr	2
Test rider	$70/hr	4

Note: MS Project considers resources in terms of percentages with one full-time worker being 100%.

TABLE A2.7   Red Zuma Resource Assignments

Task Name	Resource Names
Red Zuma Project	
Market Analysis	Marketing Specialist [400%]
Product Design	Marketing Specialist, Design Engineer [400%], Development Engineer [200%], Industrial Engineer, Purchasing Agent
Manufacturing Study	Industrial Engineer [400%], Development Engineer [200%]
Product Design Selection	Marketing Specialist [200%], Design Engineer [300%], Development Engineer [200%], Industrial Engineer [200%], Purchasing Agent [25%]
Detailed Marketing Plan	Marketing Specialist [400%]
Manufacturing Process	Design Engineer, Development Engineer [200%], Industrial Engineer [300%]
Detailed Product Design	Marketing Specialist [200%], Design Engineer [400%], Development Engineer [200%], Industrial Engineer [200%], Purchasing Agent [25%]
Build Prototypes	Design Engineer [200%], Development Engineer [200%], Industrial Engineer [400%]
Lab Test Prototypes	Design Engineer [200%], Development Engineer [200%], Test Rider
Field Tests	Marketing Specialist, Design Engineer [200%], Development Engineer, Industrial Engineer, Test Rider [300%]
Finalized Product Design	Marketing Specialist [200%], Design Engineer [300%], Development Engineer [300%], Industrial Engineer [200%], Purchasing Agent [25%]
Final Manufacturing Process	Industrial Engineer [300%], Design Engineer, Purchasing Agent [25%]
Order Components	Purchasing Agent
Order Production Equipment	Purchasing Agent
Install Production Equipment	Design Engineer, Development Engineer [300%], Industrial Engineer [400%]
Celebration	Design Engineer [400%], Development Engineer [400%], Industrial Engineer [400%], Marketing Specialist [400%], Purchasing Agent [200%]

Note: Resource assignments without brackets are 100%.

Part A

Prepare a memo that addresses the following questions:

1. Which if any of the resources are overallocated?
2. Assume that the project is time constrained and try to resolve any overallocation problems by leveling within slack. What happens?
3. What is the impact of leveling within slack on the sensitivity of the network?

Include a Gantt chart with the schedule table after leveling within slack.

4. Assume that the project is resource constrained and no additional personnel are available. How long will the project take given the resources assigned? (Hint: Undo leveling performed in Part A before answering this question.)

Note: No splitting of activities is allowed.

5. How does the new duration compare with the estimated completion date generated from Part 1? What does this tell you about the impact resources can have on a schedule?

Include a Gantt chart with a schedule table displaying free and total slack depicting the resource-constrained schedule.

Part B

Top management is not happy with the resource-constrained schedule. Robin Lane, the president, has promised retailers that ARC will begin production in time for the major trade show in Las Vegas on January 22, 2016, which means the project needs to be completed by January 17, 2016. She has authorized working the first available Saturday of each month to help the project get completed sooner. She realizes that this will only reduce the project duration by 12–13 days.

After talking to the engineers, everyone agrees that they do not have to wait for the Detailed Product Design to be 100% completed before starting to build the prototype. The consensus is that Building the Prototype can start 30 days after the start of the Detailed Product Design. Likewise the Final Manufacturing Process can start 15 days after the start of Finalized Product Design.

Dewey Martin, director of product development, is also willing to add personnel to the project. He is willing to make available at least one more Development, Design, and/or Industrial Engineer to the project as well as Marketing Specialist. Since there is an acute shortage of personnel at ARC he requests that you only use additional manpower that will help meet the deadline. Your objective is to develop a schedule which will satisfy the deadline with minimum additional resource usage.

Prepare a memo that addresses the following questions:

1. What was the impact of introducing Start-to-Start lags to the schedule and budget?
2. Which, if any additional personnel assignments, would you choose to complete the project before the January 17th deadline? Explain your choices as well as the reasons for not choosing other options.
3. How have these changes affected the sensitivity of the network and the critical path?

Include a Gantt chart with a schedule table displaying free and total slack for the new schedule.

Note: Do not assign new personnel to specific tasks, simply add them to the Resource Sheet. All new personnel are available full time (100%).

> At first glance—this appears to be a very complicated, difficult assignment, but if you enter the information correctly, the computer is able to generate the answers with a few simple clicks.

Part 3

Top management has accepted the schedule created at the end of Part 2. Prepare a brief memo that addresses the following questions:

1. How much will the project cost? What is the most expensive activity?
2. What does the cash flow statement tell you about how costs are distributed over the life span of the project?

Include a monthly cash flow for the project.

Once you are confident that you have the final schedule, save the file as a baseline. **Hint:** Save a backup file just in case without baseline!

Part 4

Part A

Today's date is July 8, 2015, the milestone date for the completion of the Prototype. You are charged with preparing a status report for top management. Table A2.8 summarizes progress on the Red Zuma project.

Submit a professional status report to Robin Lane that addresses the following questions:

1. How is the project progressing in terms of cost and schedule?
2. What activities have gone well? What activities have not gone well?
3. How much of the project has been accomplished (PCIB)?
4. What is the forecasted cost at completion (EAC$_f$)?
5. What is the estimated completion date?
6. How is the project doing in terms of priorities (see Part 1)?

Report and interpret relevant Earned Value metrics in your report.

Include a Tracking Gantt chart as well as an Earned Value Table with your memo.

TABLE A2.8   Red Zuma Project Update

	Task Name	Act. Start	Act. Finish	% Comp.	Phys. % Comp.	Act. Dur.	Rem. Dur.
1	**1 Red Zuma**	**Fri 1/9/15**	**NA**	**46%**	**0%**	**125.85 days**	**146.4 days**
2	1.1 Market Analysis	Fri 1/9/15	Thu 2/12/15	100%	0%	25 days	0 days
3	1.2 Product Design	Fri 2/13/15	Wed 4/1/15	100%	0%	35 days	0 days
4	1.3 Manufacturing Study	Fri 2/13/15	Fri 3/6/15	100%	0%	16 days	0 days
5	1.4 Product Design Selection	Thu 4/2/15	Fri 4/17/15	100%	0%	13 days	0 days
6	1.5 Detailed Marketing Plan	NA	NA	0%	0%	0 days	15 days
7	1.6 Manufacturing Process	NA	NA	0%	0%	0 days	30 days
8	1.7 Detailed Product Design	Mon 4/20/15	Wed 6/24/15	100%	0%	49 days	0 days
9	1.8 Build Prototypes	Wed 6/10/15	NA	39%	0%	9 days	14 days
10	1.9 Lab Test Prototypes	NA	NA	0%	0%	0 days	10 days
11	1.10 Field Test Prototypes	NA	NA	0%	0%	0 days	15 days
12	1.11 Finalized Product Design	NA	NA	0%	0%	0 days	20 days
13	1.12 Final Manufacturing Process	NA	NA	0%	0%	0 days	10 days
14	1.13 Order Components	NA	NA	0%	0%	0 days	7 days
15	1.14 Order Production Equipment	NA	NA	0%	0%	0 days	14 days
16	1.15 Install Production Equipment	NA	NA	0%	0%	0 days	35 days
17	1.16 Celebrate	NA	NA	0%	0%	0 days	1 days

Part B

You have told Robin Lane that based on what you know now you need to revise the estimates for some of the remaining activities. Detailed Product Design is expected to take 3 days longer than planned. Build Prototypes is expected to take 2 days less than planned and Finalized Product Design is expected to take 3 days longer than planned. Final Manufacturing Process is expected to take 2 days less than planned, while Install Production Equipment is now expected to take only 30 days. You also report that Detailed Marketing plan will be completed before the end of the New Year. She is insisting that the project be completed by January 17th in order to be ready for the Las Vegas show. She is willing to spend $50,000 from Management Reserves to expedite shipping if necessary. $25,000 would reduce the shipping of components by 5 days and/or $25,000 would reduce the shipping of manufacturing parts by 5 days (Hint: Adjust lag). Prepare a memo to Robin that addresses the following questions:

1. What is the impact of the revised estimates for Finalized Product Design and Install Production Equipment on the project schedule and cost?
2. Would you recommend authorizing the expenditure of $50,000? Explain.
3. What, if any other recommendations, would you make so that the project can achieve Robin's deadline? Justify your recommendations.

Include a Tracking Gantt chart with variance schedule that depicts your final recommendations and revised schedule.

Hint: After adjusting the Installation of Production Equipment and Finalized Product Design, level outside of slack to eliminate any resource over allocation problems.

Conveyor Belt Project

Part 1

Project Description

The new computer-controlled conveyor belt is an exciting project that moves and positions items on the conveyor belt within <1 millimeter. The project will produce a new system for future installations, and for replacement of those in the field, at a low cost. The computer-controlled conveyor belt has the potential to be a critical unit in 30 percent of the systems installed in factories. The new system is also easier to update with future technologies.

The Project Priority Matrix for the Conveyor Belt Project (CBP) is:

	Time	Scope	Cost
Constrain	X		
Enhance		X	
Accept			X

Table A2.9 has been developed for you to use in completing the project exercises.

Assignment

Develop the WBS outline using the software available to you.

Question

Does this information (WBS) allow you to define any milestones of the project? Why or why not? What are they?

Remember: Save your file for future exercises!

TABLE A2.9
Conveyor Belt
Project; WBS

Conveyor Belt Project	
Hardware	Hardware specifications
	Hardware design
	Hardware documentation
	Prototypes
	Order circuit boards
	Assemble preproduction models
Operating system	Kernel specifications
	Drivers
	Disk drivers
	Serial I/O drivers
	Memory management
	Operating system documentation
	Network interface
Utilities	Utilities specifications
	Routine utilities
	Complex utilities
	Utilities documentation
	Shell
System integration	Architectural decisions
	Integration first phase
	System hard/software test
	Project documentation
	Integration acceptance testing

Part 2

Use your file from Part 1 and the information provided below to complete this exercise. (See Table A2.10.)

1. Each work package will represent an activity.

2. The project begins January 4, 2010.

3. The following holidays are observed: January 1, Memorial Day (last Monday in May), July 4th, Labor Day (first Monday in September), Thanksgiving Day (4th Thursday in November), December 25 and 26.

4. If a holiday falls on a Saturday then Friday will be given as an extra day off, and if it falls on a Sunday, then Monday will be given as a day off.

5. The project teams work eight-hour days, Monday through Friday.

Warning: Experience has taught students to frequently make separate backup files for each exercise. The software is never as friendly as users expect!

Construct a network schedule for the conveyor belt project and prepare a memo that addresses the following questions:

1. When is the project estimated to be completed? How long will the project take?

2. What is the critical path(s) for the project?

3. Which activity has the greatest amount of slack?

4. How sensitive is this network?

5. Identify two sensible milestones and explain your choices.

6. Compare the advantages/disadvantages of displaying the schedule as a network versus a Gantt chart.

TABLE A2.10   **Conveyor Belt Project; Schedule**

Activity	Description	Resource	Duration (days)	Preceding Activity
1	Architectural decisions	Design	25	—
2	Hardware specifications	Development, design	50	1
3	Kernel specifications	Design	20	1
4	Utilities specifications	Development, design	15	1
5	Hardware design	Design, development	70	2
6	Disk drivers	Assembly, development	100	3
7	Memory management	Development	90	3
8	Operating system documentation	Design, documentation	25	3
9	Routine utilities	Development	60	4
10	Complex utilities	Development	80	4
11	Utilities documentation	Documentation, design	20	4
12	Hardware documentation	Documentation, design	30	5
13	Integration first phase	Assembly, development	50	6,7,8,9,10,11,12
14	Prototypes	Assembly, development	80	13
15	Serial I/O drivers	Development	130	13
16	System hard/software test	Assembly	25	14,15
17	Order circuit boards	Purchasing	5	16
18	Network interface	Development	90	16
19	Shell	Development	60	16
20	Project documentation	Documentation, development	50	16
21	Assemble preproduction models	Assembly, development	30	17F-S, lag 50 days
22	Integrated acceptance testing	Assembly, development	60	18,19,20,21

Note: F-S refers to a Finish-to-Start lag.

Include the following printouts:

- A Gantt chart.
- A network diagram highlighting the critical path.
- A schedule table reporting ES, LS, EF, LF, and slack for each activity.

Hint: the project should be completed in 530 days.
Remember: Save your file for future exercises!

Part 3

Remember the old saying, "A project plan is not a schedule until resources are committed." This exercise illustrates this subtle, but very important, difference.

Part A

Using your files from Part 2 input resources and their costs if you have not already done so. All information is found in Tables A2.10 and A2.11.

TABLE A2.11
Organization Resources

Name	Group	Cost ($/hr)
Design	R&D (2 teams)	$100
Development	R&D (2 teams)	70
Documentation	R&D (1 team)	60
Assembly/test	R&D (1 team)	70
Purchasing	Procurement (1 team)	40

Prepare a memo that addresses the following questions:

1. Which if any of the resources are overallocated?
2. Assume that the project is time constrained and try to resolve any overallocation problems by leveling within slack. What happens?
3. What is the impact of leveling within slack on the sensitivity of the network?

Include a Gantt chart with the schedule table after leveling within slack.

4. Assume the project is resource constrained and resolve any overallocation problems by leveling outside of slack. What happens? What are the managerial implications?
5. What options are available at this point in time?

Include a Gantt chart with the schedule table after leveling outside of slack.

Note: No splitting of activities is allowed.
Note: No partial assignments (e.g., 50 percent). All resources must be assigned 100 percent.

Part B

When you show the resource-constrained network to top management, they are visibly shaken. After some explanation and negotiation they make the following compromise with you:

- The project must be completed no later than February 2, 2012 (530 days).
- You may assign two additional development teams.
- If this does not suffice, you may hire other development teams from the outside. Hire as few external teams as possible because they cost $50 more per hour than your inside development people.

Internal Development

Add as many development units (teams) as needed to stay within the 530 days. If you need more than two internal development units, then hire as few external teams as necessary. Select the cheapest possibility! Change as few activities as possible. It is recommended you keep work packages which require cooperation of several organizational units inside your company. You decide how best to do this.

Hint: Undo leveling prior to adding new resources.

Once you have obtained a schedule that meets the time and resource constraints, prepare a memo that addresses the following questions:

1. What changes did you make and why?
2. How long will the project take?
3. How did these changes affect the sensitivity of the network?

Include a Gantt chart with a schedule table presenting the new schedule.

Part 4

Based on the file created at the end of Part 3, prepare a memo that addresses the following questions:

1. How much will the project cost?
2. What does the cash flow statement tell you about how costs are distributed over the life span of the project?

Include a monthly cash flow and a cost table for the project.

Once you are confident that you have the final schedule, save the file as a baseline.

Hint: Save a backup file just in case without baseline!

Part 5

Prepare status reports for each of the first four quarters of the project given the information provided here. This requires saving your resource schedule as a baseline and inserting the appropriate status report date in the program. Assume that no work has been completed on the day of the status report.

Your status report should include a table containing the PV, EV, AC, BAC, EAC, SV, CV, and CPI for each activity and the whole project. The report should also address the following questions:

1. How is the project progressing in terms of cost and schedule?
2. What activities have gone well? What activities have not gone well?
3. What do the PCIB and PCIC indicate in terms of how much of the project has been accomplished to date?
4. What is the forecasted cost at completion (EAC_f)? What is the predicted VAC_f?
5. Report and interpret the TCPI for the project at this point in time.
6. What is the estimated date of completion?
7. How well is the project doing in terms of its priorities?

Try to present the above information in a form worthy of consideration by top management.

Include a Tracking Gantt chart with each report.

First Quarter, April 1, 2010

Table A2.12 summarizes the information regarding activities accomplished to date.

Be sure to save your file after each quarterly report and use it to build the next report!

TABLE A2.12
April 1, 2010

Activity	Start Date	Finish Date	Actual Duration	Remaining Duration
Hardware specifications	2/9/10		37	8
Kernel specifications	2/8/10	3/12/10	25	0
Disk drivers	3/15/10		13	87
Memory management	3/15/10		13	77
Op. systems documentation	3/15/10		13	7
Utilities specifications	3/8/10	3/29/10	16	0
Complex utilities	3/30/10		2	85
Architectural decisions	1/4/10	2/5/10	25	0

TABLE A2.13
July 1, 2010

Activity	Start Date	Finish Date	Actual Duration	Remaining Duration
Hardware specifications	2/9/10	4/12/10	45	0
Hardware design	4/13/10		56	11
Kernel specifications	2/8/10	3/12/10	25	0
Disk drivers	3/15/10		77	33
Memory management	3/15/10		77	19
Op. systems documentation	3/15/10	4/16/10	25	0
Utilities specifications	3/8/10	3/29/10	16	0
Routine utilities*	4/26/10		47	18
Complex utilities	3/30/10		66	25
Utilities documentation	5/3/10	6/2/10	22	0
Architectural decisions	1/4/10	2/5/10	25	0

* The project manager for the external development team that was hired to perform routine utilities reported that due to commitments to other clients they would be able to start on that activity 4/26/10.

Second Quarter, July 1, 2010

Table A2.13 summarizes the information regarding activities accomplished since the last report.

Third Quarter, October 1, 2010

Table A2.14 summarizes the information regarding activities accomplished since the last report.

Fourth Quarter, January 1, 2011

Table A2.15 summarizes the information regarding activities accomplished since the last report.

Part 6

You have received revised estimates for the remaining activities at the end of the fourth quarter:

- Prototypes will be completed on 3/8/11.
- Serial I/O drivers will be completed on 6/30/11.

TABLE A2.14
October 1, 2010

Activity	Start Date	Finish Date	Actual Duration	Remaining Duration
Hardware specifications	2/9/10	4/12/10	45	0
Hardware design	4/13/10	7/16/10	67	0
Hardware documentation	7/19/10	8/24/10	27	0
Kernel specifications	2/8/10	3/12/10	25	0
Disk drivers	3/15/10	8/17/10	110	0
Memory management	3/15/10	7/30/10	98	0
Op. systems documentation	3/15/10	4/16/10	25	0
Utilities specifications	3/8/10	3/29/10	16	0
Routine utilities	4/26/10	7/27/10	65	0
Complex utilities	3/30/10	8/11/10	95	0
Utilities documentation	5/3/10	6/2/10	22	0
Architectural decisions	1/4/10	2/5/10	25	0
Integration 1st phase	8/25/10		26	24

TABLE A2.15
January 1, 2011

Activity	Start Date	Finish Date	Actual Duration	Remaining Duration
Hardware specifications	2/9/10	4/12/10	45	0
Hardware design	4/13/10	7/16/10	67	0
Hardware documentation	7/19/10	8/24/10	27	0
Prototypes	11/11/10		34	44
Kernel specifications	2/8/10	3/12/10	25	0
Disk drivers	3/15/10	8/17/10	110	0
Serial I/O drivers	11/11/10		34	119
Memory management	3/15/10	7/30/10	98	0
Op. systems documentation	3/15/10	4/16/10	25	0
Utilities specifications	3/8/10	3/29/10	16	0
Routine utilities	4/26/10	7/27/10	65	0
Complex utilities	3/30/10	8/11/10	95	0
Utilities documentation	5/3/10	6/2/10	22	0
Architectural decisions	1/4/10	2/5/10	25	0
Integration 1st phase	8/25/10	11/10/10	55	0

- System hardware/software test will start on 7/1/11 and take 25 days.
- Order circuit boards will start on 8/8/11 and take 5 days.
- Assemble preproduction model will begin on 10/14/11 and take 18 days.
- Project documentation is expected to start on 8/8/11 and will take 55 days.
- Network interface is expected to start on 8/8/11 and will take 99 days.
- Shell is expected to start on 8/8/11 and will take 55 days.
- Integrated acceptance testing is expected to start on 12/29/11 and will take 54 days.

Prepare a memo that addresses the following questions:

1. What is the new EAC for the project? How long should the project take given these revised estimates?
2. How happy will top management be with these forecasts given the priorities of the project?
3. What recommendations would you make?

Include a revised schedule, a Tracking Gantt chart, and cost table with your memo.

A

360-degree feedback   A multirater appraisal system based on performance information that is gathered from multiple sources (superiors, peers, subordinates, customers).

accept risk   When a conscious decision is made to accept the risk of an event occurring (i.e., if risk is too large, if chance of occurring is slim, or if the budget reserve can simply absorb the risk if it materializes).

activity   Task(s) of the project that consumes time while people/equipment either work or wait.

Agile Project Management (Agile PM)   A family of incremental, iterative development methods for completing projects.

AOA   Activity-on-arrow method for drawing project networks. The activity is shown as an arrow.

AON   Activity-on-node method for drawing project networks. The activity is on the node (rectangle).

apportionment method   Costs allocated to a specific segment of a project by using a percentage of planned total cost—for example, framing a house might use 25 percent of the total cost, or coding a teaching module 40 percent of total cost.

avoiding risk   Elimination of the risk cause before the project begins.

B

balanced matrix   A matrix structure in which the project manager and functional managers share roughly equal authority over the project. The project manager decides what needs to be done; functional managers are concerned with how it will be accomplished.

baseline   A concrete document and commitment; it represents the first real plan with cost, schedule, and resource allocation. The planned cost and schedule performance are used to measure actual cost and schedule performance. Serves as an anchor point for measuring performance.

BATNA   Best alternative to a negotiated agreement. Strong or weak BATNA indicates your power to negotiate with the other party.

bottom-up estimates   Detailed estimates of work packages usually made by those who are most familiar with the task (also called micro estimates).

brainstorming   Generating as many ideas/solutions as possible without critical judgment.

budget at completion (BAC)   Budgeted cost at completion. The total budgeted cost of the baseline or project cost accounts.

budget reserve   Reserve setup to cover identified risks that may occur and influence baseline tasks or costs. These reserves are typically controlled by the project manager and the project team. See management reserve.

burst activity   An activity that has more than one activity immediately following it.

C

change management systems   A defined process for authorizing and documenting changes in the scope of a project.

co-location   A situation in which project members including those from different organizations work together in the same location.

concurrent engineering   Cross-functional teamwork in new-product development projects that provides product design, quality engineering, and manufacturing process engineering all at the same time.

contingency plan   A plan that covers possible identified project risks that may materialize over the life of the project.

control chart   A chart used to monitor past project schedule performance and current performance as well as estimate future schedule trends.

cost account   A control point of one or more work packages used to plan, schedule, and control the project. The sum of all the project cost accounts represents the total cost of the project.

cost performance index (CPI)   The ratio of work performed to actual costs (EV/AC).

cost variance (CV)   The difference between EV and AC (CV = EV − AC). Tells if the work accomplished cost more or less than was planned at any point over the life of the project.

crash point   The most a project activity time can realistically be compressed with the resources available to the organization.

crash time   The shortest time an activity can be completed (assuming a reasonable level of resources).

crashing   Shortening an activity or project.

critical path   The longest activity path(s) through the network. The critical path can be distinguished by identifying the collection of activities that all have the same minimum slack.

cross-cultural orientations   A framework which describes and/or explains cultural differences.

culture   The totality of socially transmitted behavior patterns, beliefs, institutions, and all other products of human work and thought characteristic of a community or country.

culture shock   A natural psychological disorientation that most people suffer when they move to a culture different from their own.

D

dedicated project team   An organizational structure in which all of the resources needed to accomplish a project are assigned full time to the project.

Delphi technique   A group method to predict future events—e.g., time, cost.

direct costs   Costs that are clearly charged to a specific work package—usually labor, materials, or equipment.

dysfunctional conflict   Disagreement that does not improve project performance.

E

early time   The earliest an activity can start or finish based on network logic, the data date, and any schedule constraints.

earned value (EV)   The physical work accomplished plus the authorized budget for this work. Previously this was called the budgeted cost of work performed (BCWP).

emotional intelligence (EQ)   The ability or skill to perceive, assess, and manage the emotions of one's self and others.

escalation   A control mechanism for resolving problems in which people at the lowest appropriate level attempt to resolve a problem within a set time limit or the problem is "escalated" to the next level of management.

estimated cost at completion (EAC)   The sum of actual costs to date plus revised estimated costs for the work remaining in the WBS. The text uses EAC_{re} to represent revisions made by experts and practitioners associated with the project. A second method is used in large projects where the original budget is less reliable. This method uses the actual costs to date plus an efficiency index (CPI = EV/AC) applied to the remaining project work. When the estimate for completion uses the CPI as the basis for forecasting cost at completion, we use the acronym

EAC_f, where EAC_f = estimated costs at completion. Includes costs to date plus revised estimated costs for the work remaining. (Uses formula to compute EAC.)

F

fast-tracking   Accelerating project completion typically by rearranging the network schedule and using start-to-start lags.

feature   A piece of a product that delivers some useful functionality to a customer.

Forecasted total cost at completion (EAC_f).   The expected total cost of the project expressed as the sum of actual costs to date and forecasted estimate of the cost of remaining work based on the current CPI.

free slack   The maximum amount of time an activity can be delayed from its early start (ES) without affecting the early start (ES) of any activity immediately following it.

function points   Points derived from past software projects to estimate project time and cost, given specific features of the project.

functional conflict   Disagreement that contributes to the objectives of the project.

G

Gantt chart   See bar chart.

groupthink   A tendency of members in highly cohesive groups to lose their critical evaluative capabilities.

H

hammock activity   A special-purpose, aggregate activity that identifies the use of fixed resources or costs over a segment of the project—e.g., a consultant. Derives its duration from the time span between other activities.

heuristics   A rule of thumb used to make decisions. Frequently found in scheduling projects. For example, schedule critical activities first, then schedule activities with the shortest duration.

I

implementation gap   The lack of consensus between the goals set by top management and those independently set by lower levels of management. This lack of consensus leads to confusion and poor allocation of organization resources.

incremental, iterative development (IID)   A cyclical development process in which a project gradually evolves over time.

indirect costs   Costs that cannot be traced to a particular project or work package.

infrastructure   Basic services (i.e., communication, transportation, power) needed to support project completion.

inspiration-related currencies   Influence based on inspiration (opportunity to do good, be the best, etc.).

L

lag relationship   The relationship between the start and/or finish of a project activity and the start and/or finish of another activity. The most common lag relationships are (1) finish-to-start, (2) finish-to-finish, (3) start-to-start, and (4) start-to-finish.

late time   The latest an activity can start or finish without delaying the completion of the project.

law of reciprocity   People are obligated to grant a favor comparable to the one they received.

leading by example   Exhibiting the behaviors you want to see in others.

learning curve   A mathematical curve used to predict a pattern of time reduction as a task is performed over and over.

lessons learned   An analysis carried out during and shortly after the project life cycle; they attempt to capture positive and negative project learning.

leveling   Techniques used to examine a project for an unbalanced use of resources, and for resolving resource overallocations.

M

management by wandering around (MBWA)   A management style in which managers spend the majority of their time outside their offices interacting with key people.

management reserve   A percentage of the total project budget reserved for contingencies. The fund exists to cover unforeseen, new problems—not unnecessary overruns. The reserve is designed to reduce the risk of project delays. Management reserves are typically controlled by the project owner or project manager. See budget reserve.

management reserve index   The percentage of the management reserve that has been used to date.

matrix   Any organizational structure in which the project manager shares responsibility with the functional managers for assigning priorities and for directing the work of individuals assigned to the project.

mentor   Typically a more experienced manager who acts as a personal coach and champions a person's ambitions.

merge activity   An activity that has more than one activity immediately preceding it.

met expectations   Customer satisfaction is a function of the extent to which perceived performance exceeds expectations.

milestone   An event that represents significant, identifiable accomplishment toward the project's completion.

mitigating risk   Action taken to either reduce the likelihood that a risk will occur and/or the impact the risk will have on the project.

N

net present value (NPV)   A minimum desired rate of return discount (e.g., 15 percent) is used to compute present value of all future cash inflows and outflows.

nominal group technique (NGT)   A structured problem-solving process in which members privately rank-order preferred solutions.

O

opportunity   An event that can have a positive impact on project objectives.

organization breakdown structure (OBS)   A structure used to assign responsibility for work packages.

organizational culture   A system of shared norms, beliefs, values, and assumptions held by an organization's members.

organizational politics   Actions by individuals or groups of individuals to acquire, develop, and use power and other resources to obtain preferred outcomes when there is uncertainty or disagreement over choices.

outsourcing   Contracting for the use of external sources (skills) to assist in implementing a project.

overhead costs   Typically organization costs that are not directly linked to a specific project. These costs cover general expenses such as upper management, legal, market promotion, and accounting. Overhead costs are usually charged per unit of time or as a percentage of labor or material costs.

oversight   A set of principles and processes to guide and improve the management of projects. The intent is to ensure projects meet the needs of the organization through standards, procedures, accountability, efficient allocation of resources, and continuous improvement in the management of projects.

P

parallel activity   One or more activities that can be carried on concurrently or simultaneously.

partnering charter   A formal document that states common goals as well as cooperative procedures used to achieved these goals which is signed by all parties working on a project.

path   A sequence of connected activities.

payback method   The time it takes to pay back the project investment (investment/net annual savings). The method does not consider the time value of money or the life of the investment.

percent complete index actual costs   The amount of work accomplished based on actual costs and revised estimates (AC/EAC).

percent complete index budgeted costs   The amount of work accomplished based on project budget (EV/BAC).

percent complete index—actual costs (pcic)   The amount of work accomplished based on actual costs and revised estimates (AC/EAC).

performance review   In general, all review methods of individual performance center on the technical and social skills brought to the project and team. These reviews stress personal improvement and are frequently used for salary and promotion decisions.

personal integrity   Adherence to moral and ethical principles.

personal-related currencies   Influence based on enhancing another person's self-esteem.

phase estimating   This estimating method begins with a macro estimate for the project and then refines estimates for phases of the project as it is implemented.

phase gating   A structured process to review, evaluate, and document outcomes at each project phase and to provide management with information to guide resource deployment toward strategic goals.

planned value (PV)   The planned time-phased baseline of the value of the work scheduled. Previously this was called budgeted cost of work scheduled (BCWS).

portfolio management   Centralized selection and management of a portfolio of projects to ensure that

allocation of resources is directed and balanced toward the strategic focus of the organization.

position-related currencies   Influence based on the ability to enhance someone else's position within an organization.

positive synergy   A characteristic of high-performance teams in which group performance is greater than the sum of individual contributions.

principled negotiation   A process of negotiation that aims to achieve win/win results.

priority matrix   A matrix that is set up before the project begins that establishes which criterion among cost, time, and scope will be enhanced, constrained, or accepted.

priority system   The process used to select projects. The system uses selected criteria for evaluating and selecting projects that are strongly linked to higher-level strategies and objectives.

priority team   The group (sometimes the project office) responsible for selecting, overseeing, and updating project priority selection criteria.

proactive   Working within your sphere of influence to accomplish something.

process breakdown structure (PBS)   A phase-oriented grouping of project activities that defines the total scope of the project. Each descending level represents an increasingly detailed description of project work.

product backlog   A prioritized list of project requirements with estimated time to turn them into complete product functionality.

product owner   The person responsible for managing the product backlog in Scrum so as to maximize the value of the project. The product owner represents all stakeholders.

Program   A group of related projects designed to accomplish a common goal over an extended period of time.

project   A temporary endeavor undertaken to create a unique product, service, or result.

project charter   A document that authorizes the project manager to initiate and lead a project.

project closure   All of the activities of shutting down a project. The major activities are evaluation of project goals and performance, developing lessons learned, releasing resources, and preparing a final report.

project cost—duration graph   A graph that plots project cost against time; it includes direct, indirect, and total cost for a project over a relevant range of time.

project evaluation   The process of assessing, verifying, and documenting project results.

project facilitator   A guide who leads the project team through an analysis of project activities that went well, what needs improvement, and development of a follow-up action plan with goals and accountability.

project kick off meeting   Typically the first meeting of the project team.

project life cycle   The stages found in all projects— definition, planning, execution, and delivery.

Project Management Professional (PMP)   An individual who has met specific education and experience requirements set forth by the Project Management Institute, has agreed to adhere to a code of professional conduct, and has passed an examination designed to objectively assess and measure project management knowledge. In addition, a PMP must satisfy continuing certification requirements or lose the certification.

project office (po)   A centralized unit within an organization or department that oversees and improves the management of projects.

project portfolio   Group of projects that have been selected for implementation balanced by project type, risk, and ranking by selected criteria.

project sponsor   Typically a high-ranking manager who champions and supports a project.

project vision   An image of what the project will accomplish.

projectitis   A condition in which team members become strongly attached to their project and disconnected from the larger organization.

projectized organization   A multi-project organization in which project managers have full authority to assign priorities and direct the work of persons assigned to their project.

R

range estimating   An estimating technique in which multiple estimating points are given based on some logic (i.e., high vs. low or best case, worst case, and most likely case).

ratio (parametric) methods   Uses the ratio of past actual costs for similar work to estimate the cost for a potential project. This macro method of forecasting cost does not provide a sound basis for project cost control since it does not recognize differences among projects.

reference class forecasting   A sophisticated forecasting method in which you take an external view and forecast project costs based on actual outcomes of similar projects.

relationship-related currencies   Influence based on friendship.

release burndown chart   The trend of work remaining across time. In a release or product, the source of data is the product backlog with work remaining tracked on the vertical axis and number of sprints on the horizontal axis.

resource smoothing   A technique that uses slack to reduce peak resource demand to increase resource utilization.

resource-constrained project   A project that assumes resources are limited (fixed) and therefore time is variable.

responsibility matrix   A matrix whose intersection point shows the relationship between an activity (work package) and the person/group responsible for its completion.

retrospective   A methodology that analyzes a past project event to determine what worked and what didn't, develops lessons learned, and creates an action plan that ensures lessons learned are used to improve management of future projects.

Revised estimated cost at completion (EAC_{re}).   The expected total cost of the project expressed as the sum of actual costs to date and revised estimates of the cost of remaining work based on the judgment of those doing the work.

risk   The chance that an undesirable project event will occur and the consequences of all its possible outcomes.

risk breakdown structure (RBS)   A hierarchical depiction of the identified project risks arranged by risk category and subcategory that identifies the various areas and causes of potential risks.

risk profile   A list of questions that addresses traditional areas of uncertainty on a project.

risk register   A register detailing all identified risks, including descriptions, category, and probability of occurring, impact, responses, contingency plans, owners, and current status.

risk severity matrix   A tool used to assess the impact of risks on a project.

S

"sacred cow"   A project that is a favorite of a powerful management figure who is usually the champion for the project.

scaling   Adapting Agile PM to large, multi-team projects.

scenario analysis   Technique for analyzing risks where team members assess the significance of each risk event in terms of probability and impact of the event.

schedule performance index (SPI)   The ratio of work performed to work scheduled (EV/PV).

schedule variance (SV)   The difference between the planned dollar value of the work actually completed and the value of the work scheduled to be completed at a given point in time (SV = EV – PV). Schedule variance contains no critical path information.

scope creep   The tendency for the scope of a project to expand once it has started.

scope statement   A definition of the end result or mission of a project. Scope statements typically include project objectives, deliverables, milestones, specifications, and limits and exclusions.

Scrum master   The person responsible for the Scrum process and its correct application.

self-organizing team   A semi-autonomous team that manages itself.

sensitivity   A function of the number of critical or near-critical paths.

social network building   The process of identifying and building cooperative relationships with key people.

splitting   A scheduling technique in which work is interrupted on one activity and the resource is assigned to another activity for a period of time, then reassigned to work on the original activity.

sprint backlog   A list of tasks that defines a Scrum team's work for a sprint. Each task identifies those responsible for doing the work and the estimated amount of work remaining on the task on any given day during the sprint.

sprint burndown chart   The trend of work remaining across time in a sprint. The source of data is the sprint backlog with work remaining tracked on the vertical axis and days of a sprint on the horizontal axis.

stakeholders   Individuals and organizations that are actively involved in the project, or whose interests may be positively or negatively affected as a result of project execution or completion. They may also exert influence over the project and its results.

strategic management process   The process of assessing "what we are" and deciding and implementing "what we intend to be and how we are going to get there." Strategy describes how an organization intends to compete with the resources available in the existing and perceived future environment.

strong matrix   A matrix structure in which the project manager has primary control over project activities and functional managers support project work.

systems thinking   A holistic approach to viewing problems that emphasizes understanding the interactions among different problem factors.

T

task-related currencies   Influence based, helping someone else do their work.

team evaluation   Evaluating the performance of the project team using a minimum core of conditions in place before the project began. Evaluation practices should emphasize the team as a whole, while minimizing individual performance.

team rituals   Ceremonial actions that reinforce team identity and values.

team-building   A process designed to improve the performance of a team.

template method   Use of a prepared form to develop project networks, costs, and time estimates.

time and cost databases   Collection of actual versus estimated times and costs of work packages over many projects that are used for estimating new project tasks and their expected possible error.

time buffer   A contingency amount of time for an activity to cover uncertainty—for example, availability of a key resource or merge event.

time-constrained project   A project that assumes time is fixed and, if resources are needed, they will be added.

time-phased budget baseline   A cost baseline that is derived from the WBS and project schedule. The budgeted costs are distributed to mirror the project schedule.

to complete performance index (tcpi)   The calculated cost performance index that must be achieved on the remaining work in order to meet the project budget (BAC-EV)/(BAC-AC).

top-down estimates   Rough estimates that use surrogates to estimate project time and cost (also called macro estimates).

total slack (TS)   The amount of time an activity can be delayed and not affect the project duration (TS = LS – ES or LF – EF).

tracking Gantt   A Gantt chart that compares planned versus actual schedule information.

transferring risk   Shifting responsibility for a risk to another party.

V

variance at completion (VAC)   Indicates expected actual cost over- or underrun at completion (VAC = BAC – EAC).

virtual project team   Spatially separated project team whose members are unable to communicate face to face. Communication is usually by electronic means.

W

weak matrix   A matrix structure in which functional managers have primary control over project activities and the project manager coordinates project work.

white elephant   A burdensome possession which is not easily disposed of and whose cost (particulary upkeep) is out of proportion with its usefulness.

work breakdown dictionary   Provides detailed information about each element in the WBS. The dictionary typically includes the work package level (code), name, and functional description.

work breakdown structure (WBS)   A hierarchical method that successively subdivides the work of the project into smaller detail.

work package   A task at the lowest level of the WBS. Responsibility for the package should be assigned to one person and, if possible, limited to 80 hours of work.

AC	Actual cost of work completed	**IFB**	Invitation for bid
ACWP	Actual cost of work performed	**KISS**	Keep it simple, stupid
AOA	Activity-on-arrow	**LF**	Late finish
AON	Activity-on-node	**LS**	Late start
BAC	Budget at completion	**MRI**	Management reserve index
BATNA	Best alternative to a negotiated agreement	**MBWA**	Management by wandering around
BCWP	Budgeted cost of work performed	**NIH**	Not invented here
BCWS	Budgeted cost of work scheduled	**NPV**	Net present value
BOOT	Build-own-operate-transfer	**OBS**	Organization breakdown structure
CAPM	Certified Associate in Project Management	**PCI**	Percent complete index
		PCIB	Percent complete index—budget costs
CCPM	Critical-chain approach to project planning and management	**PCIC**	Percent complete index—actual costs
CPI	Cost performance index	**PDM**	Precedence diagramming method
CPM	Critical path method	**PERT**	Project evaluation review technique
CV	Cost variance	**PMP**	Project Management Professional
DUR	Duration	**PO**	Project office
EAC	Estimate at completion (with revised cost estimates)	**PV**	Planned value of work scheduled
		RBS	Risk breakdown structure
EF	Early finish	**RM**	Responsibility matrix
EQ	Emotional intelligence	**SL**	Slack
ES	Early start	**SPI**	Schedule performance index
ETC	Estimate to complete	**SV**	Schedule variance
EV	Earned value	**TCPI**	To complete performance index
FAC	Forecast at completion	**VAC**	Variance at completion
FF	Free float	**WBS**	Work breakdown structure

$$PCIB = \frac{EV}{BAC}$$

$$CV = EV - AC$$

$$CPI = \frac{EV}{AC}$$

$$EAC_f = \frac{(BAC - EV)}{\left(\dfrac{EV}{AC}\right)} + AC$$

$$EAC_{re} = AC + ETC_{re}$$

$$MRI = \frac{CV}{MR}$$

$$t_e = \frac{a + 4m + b}{6}$$

$$\sigma_{t_e} = \left(\frac{b - a}{6}\right)$$

$$TCPI = \frac{(BAC - EV)}{(BAC - AC)}$$

$$PCIC = \frac{AC}{EAC}$$

$$SV = EV - PV$$

$$SPI = \frac{EV}{PV}$$

$$VAC_f = BAC - EAC_f$$

$$VAC_{re} = BAC - EAC_{re}$$

$$\sigma_{T_E} = \sqrt{\Sigma \sigma_{t_e}^2}$$

$$Z = \frac{T_S - T_E}{\sqrt{\Sigma \sigma_{t_e}^2}}$$

Chapter 1　Modern Project Management

1.2 Project defined
1.7.1 Project manager
1.3 Project management defined
1.4 Projects and programs (.1)
1.7 Role of the project manager
2.4 The project life cycle (.1.2) (Fig 2.13)
4.1 Integration of project management processes [.2.3.4.5.6]

Chapter 2　Organization Strategy and Project Selection

1.4.1 Projects and programs (.2)
1.4.2 Managing the portfolio
1.4.3 Strategy and projects
13.1 Stakeholders (.2.3.4)(2.2.1) (A1.4.2) (A1.5.24)(A1.6.8)
12.1 RFP's and vendor selection (.3.4) (A1.6.7) (12.2)
11.2.2.6 SWOT analysis

Chapter 3　Organization: Structure and Culture

2.1.1 Organization cultures
2.1. Organization structures (.2.3.4.5)
9.1.2.1 Organization charts
1.4.4 Project offices

Chapter 4　Defining the Project

5.3.1.2 Project charter (A1.4.1)
5.2 Gather requirements
5.3 Defining scope (A1.5.2)
5.4 Creating a WBS
5.4.2 Tools and techniques
6.2 Define activities
9.1.2.1 Responsibility matrix
10.1 Communication planning (.2.3) (A1.7.8) (X3.4)

Chapter 5　Estimating Times and Costs

6.5 Activity duration estimates (.3.1)
6.5.2 Estimating tools (.1.2.3.4)
6.4 Identifying resources
6.4.2.4 Bottom-up estimates
7.2 Activity cost estimates (.1)
5.2.2.5 Delphi method (11.2.2.2) (6.5.2.5)

Chapter 6　Developing a Project Plan

4.2.2 Planning tools
6.3.2.1 Precidence diagramming
6.3 Sequence activities (.2) (Fig. 6-11) (Fig. 6-18)
6.6.3.2.1 Bar and milestone charts (8.1.2.3)
6.6.2.2 Critical path method
6.3.2.3 Lead and lag activities

Chapter 7　Managing Risk

11.1 Risk management process
11.2 Identifying risks
11.3.2.5 Impact matrix (11.3.2.2)
11.3.2.5 Risk assessment
11.5 Risk responses (.2–.1.2) (A1.5.22)
11.2.31 Risk register (11.5.12)
11.4.2.2 Contingency reserves
4.5.2.3 Change control management (A1.7.)

Chapter 8　Scheduling Resources and Cost

6.6.3.1 Setting a schedule baseline (7.2.1.4(6.5.1.4)
6.6.3.2 Setting a resource schedule
6.6.2.4 Resource leveling
7.3.3.1 Cost baseline development
6.6.2.3 Critical chain method
4.0 Change control (A1.7.2)

Chapter 9　Reducing Project Duration

6.6.2.7 Schedule compression

Chapter 10　Leadership

1.72 Leadership skills (A1.72) (X3.1) (X3.3)
13.0 Stakeholder management (13.1.2.3.)

Chapter 11　Teams

9.2 Building the team (.1.2.3) (A1.6.4) (X3.2)
9.4 Managing the team (A1.6.5)
9.3.2.3 Team building activities
9.2.4 Virtual teams
9.3.3.1 Team performance (9.4.2.2)
9.4.2.3 Conflict management
9.3.2.6 Recognition and awards

Chapter 12　Outsourcing

12.1 Procurement requirements (.3.2) (12.2.1.7)
12.1.3.3 Contract types
9.4.2.3 Conflict management (X3.8)
12.2.7 The art of negotiating
12.1.3.6 Change requests (12.2.4)

Chapter 13　Monitoring Progress

7.4.2.1 Cost/schedule system
6.0 Time performance
7.4.2.1 Earned value system
7.4.2.4 E.V., performance status report
7.4.2.2 E.V., forecasts
7.4.2. EV., to complete index (EAC)
7.4.2.1 Schedule and cost variance (Fig 7-12)

Chapter 14　Project Closure

10.2.2.5 Closure report (8.3.3.8) 8.2.2.)
4.5.1.5 Organization processes (12.1.1.9) (11.6.3.5)
4.6 Administrative tasks (A1.8.)
12.4.1.2 Lessons learned
9.4.2.2 Individual performance appraisals

Chapter 15　International Projects

4.1.1.4 Culture awareness

Chapter 16　Agile PM

1.5.22 Project management and governance
1.4.4 Project offices (PMO)(4.1) (4.5.2) (10.3.2.2) (2.2.2)
8.1.3.2 Continuous improvement
5.2 Requirements vs. actual (.1) (5.2.2) (5.2.3.1)
6.7 Schedule control
2.4.2.4 Adaptive life cycle
6.2.2.2 Rolling wave

A Socio-Technical Approach to Project Management

The Technical and Sociocultural Dimensions of the Project Management Process

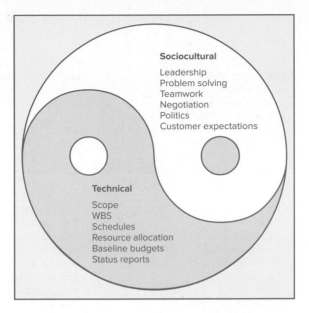

Sociocultural

Leadership
Problem solving
Teamwork
Negotiation
Politics
Customer expectations

Technical

Scope
WBS
Schedules
Resource allocation
Baseline budgets
Status reports

Project Life Cycle

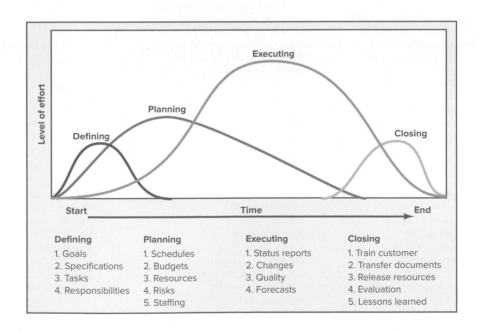

Defining	Planning	Executing	Closing
1. Goals	1. Schedules	1. Status reports	1. Train customer
2. Specifications	2. Budgets	2. Changes	2. Transfer documents
3. Tasks	3. Resources	3. Quality	3. Release resources
4. Responsibilities	4. Risks	4. Forecasts	4. Evaluation
	5. Staffing		5. Lessons learned

Index